MODERN MAN COMICS

by b. von alten

FEATURING:

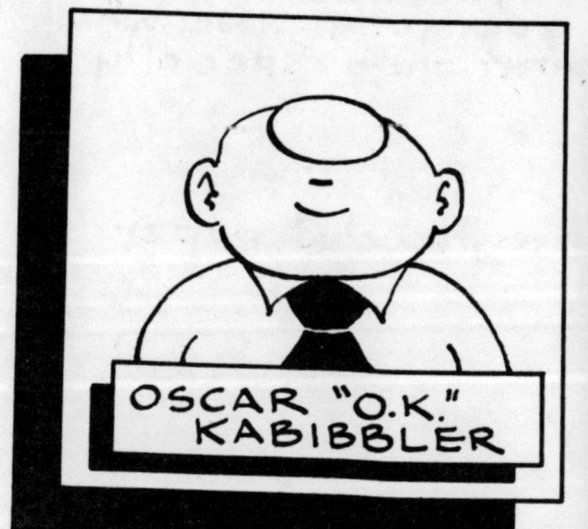

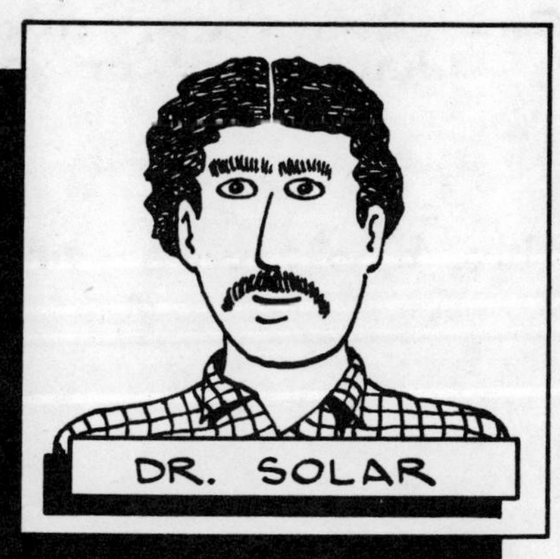

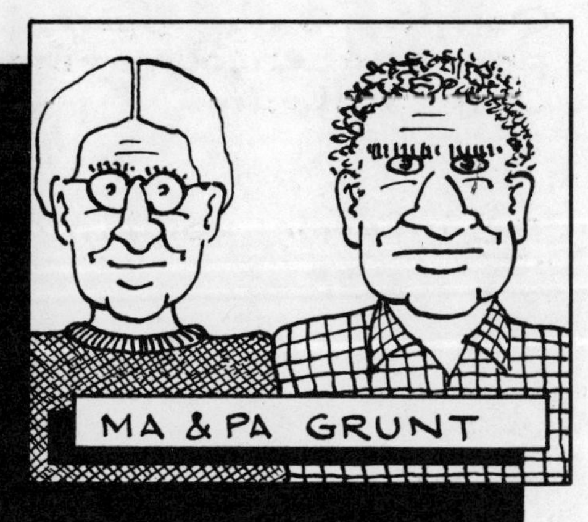

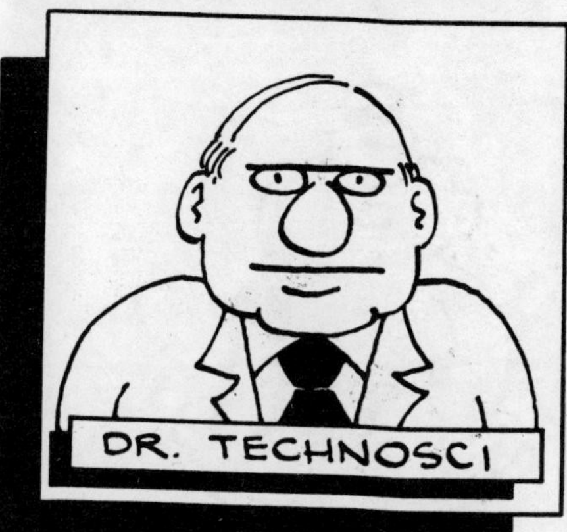

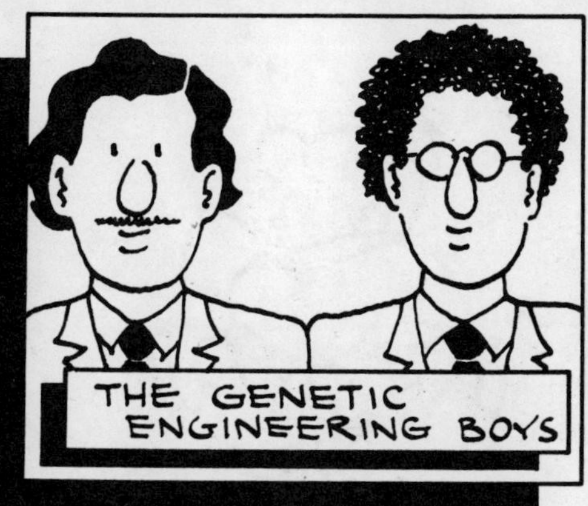

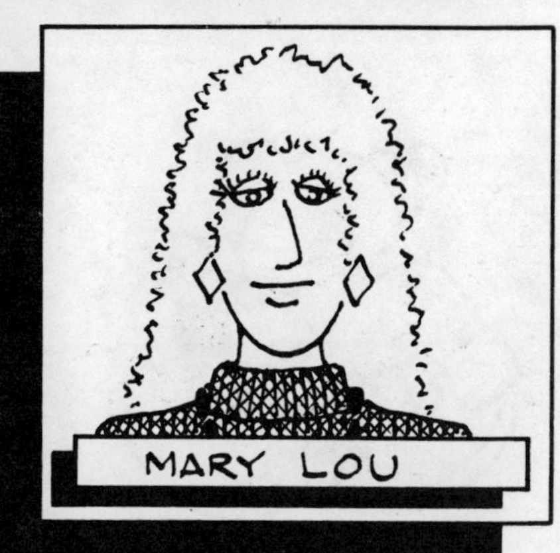

AND MANY MORE...

First printing September, 1989

Published by: O.K. Press
P.O. Box 521
Butte, MT 59703

Printed by: Mountain Moving Press
315 S. 4th St. East
Missoula, MT 59801

ISBN 0-9624218-0-4

Library of Congress Catalog Card Number: 89-92186

Thank you to Pat von Alten for story collaboration and moral support.

And thank you to the Walthers and Campbell families, Mindy Quivik, Sally Bowen, Ray Campeau, and everyone else who provided encouragement, advice, and/or inspiration. – especially Chip Sullivan.

The interior portion of this book was printed on recycled paper.

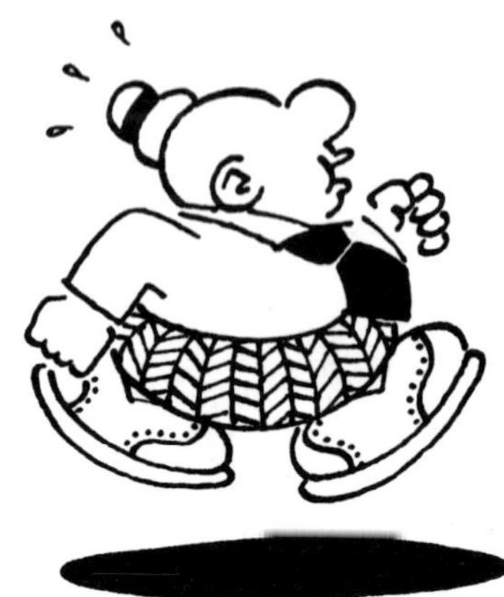
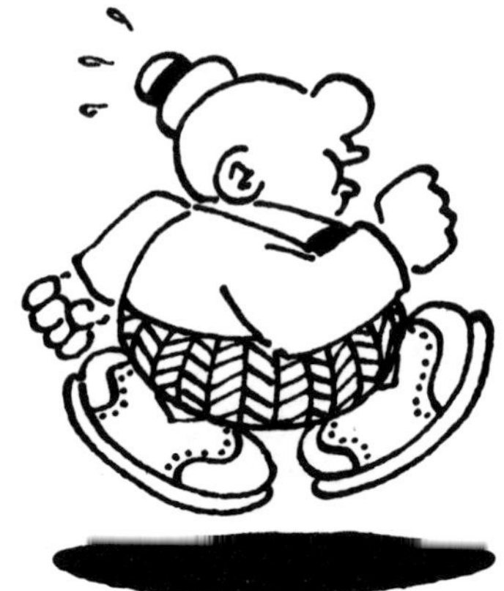
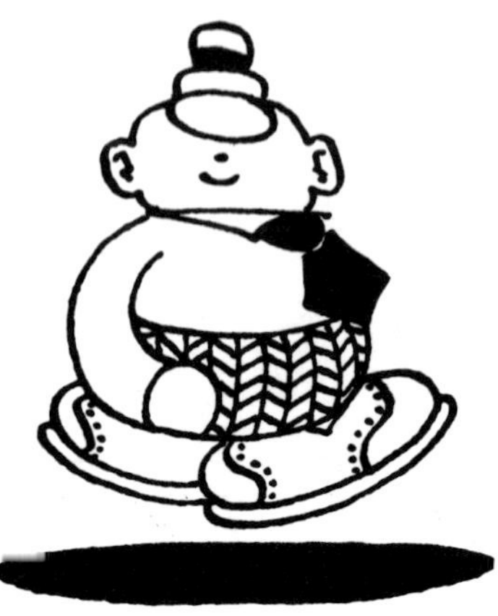

FOR P.

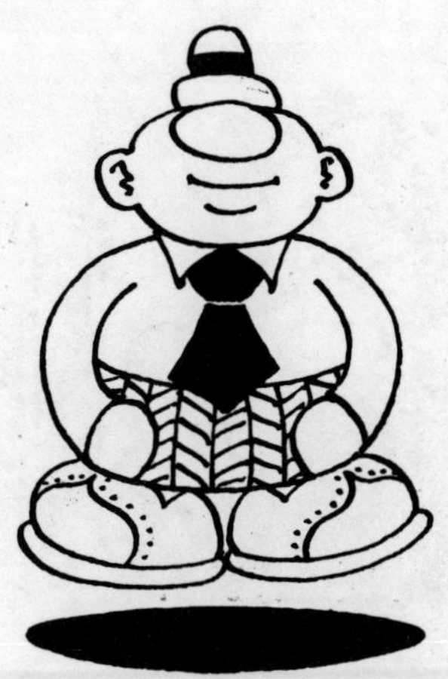

Sources of information on which some of the strips are based include: Earth First!, Earth Island Journal, Greenpeace, Environmental Action; Paul Dix; The Day We Bombed Utah, by John G. Fuller; Cadillac Desert, by Marc Reisner; This is a partial list. I apologize for omissions.

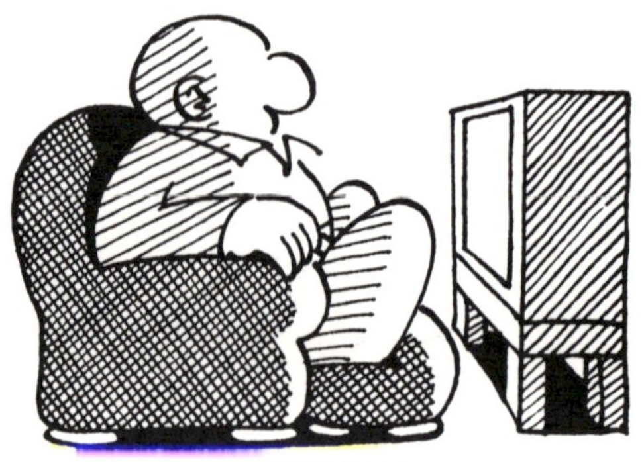

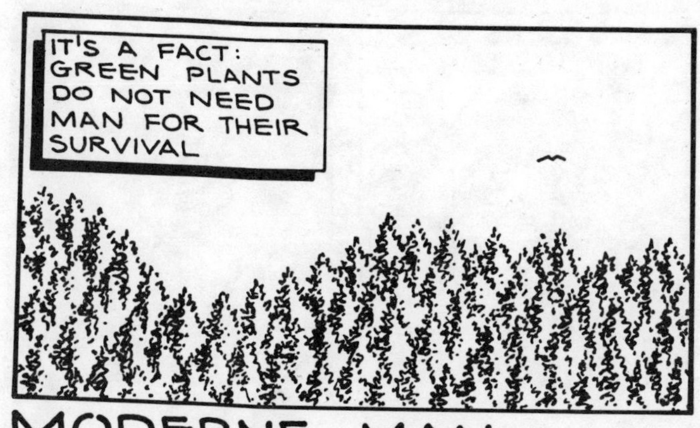
IT'S A FACT:
GREEN PLANTS DO NOT NEED MAN FOR THEIR SURVIVAL

BUT:
MAN DOES NEED GREEN PLANTS TO SURVIVE

BRRUP! BRRUP!

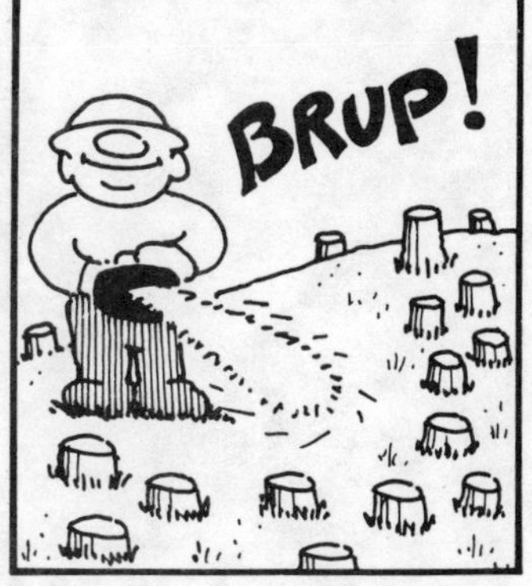
BRUP!

MODERNE MAN

b. von alten 1·13·84

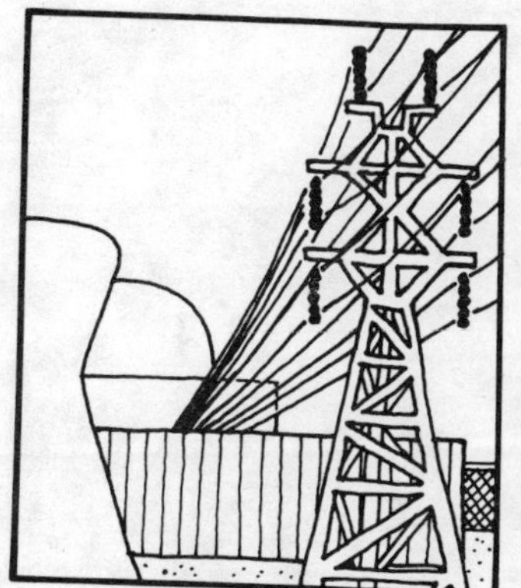

HUMMMMM

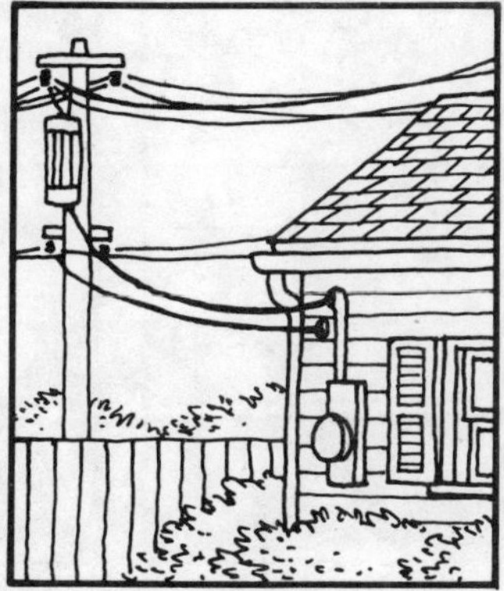

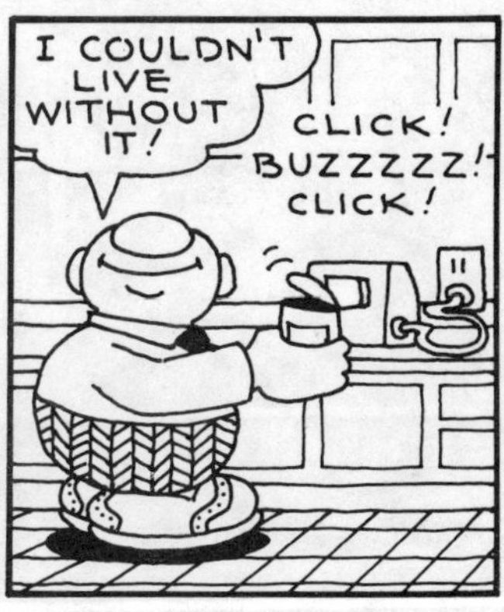
I COULDN'T LIVE WITHOUT IT!
CLICK! BUZZZZZ! CLICK!

MODERNE MAN

b. von alten 3·31·84

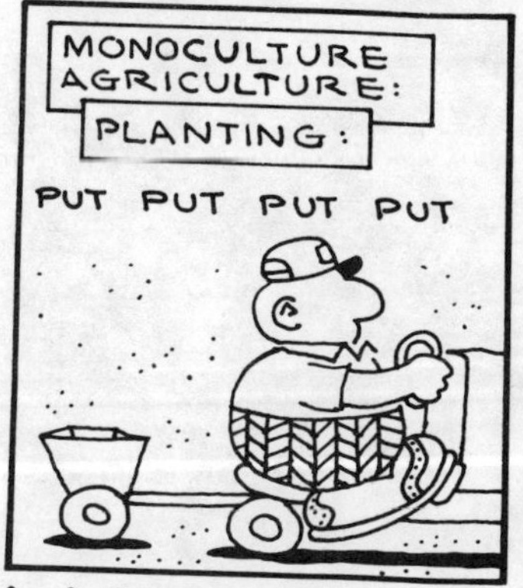
MONOCULTURE AGRICULTURE:
PLANTING:
PUT PUT PUT PUT

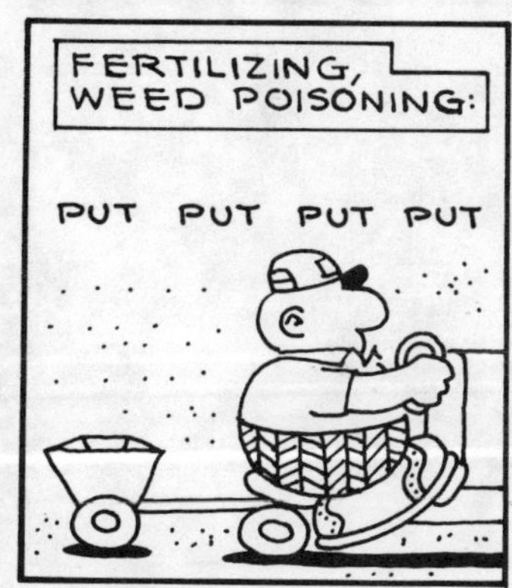
FERTILIZING, WEED POISONING:
PUT PUT PUT PUT

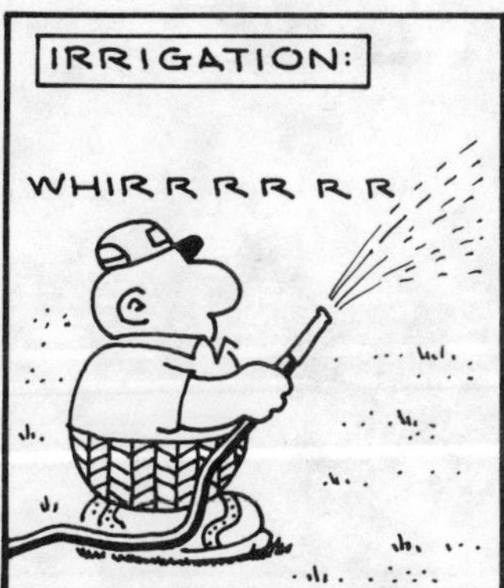
IRRIGATION:
WHIRRRRRRR

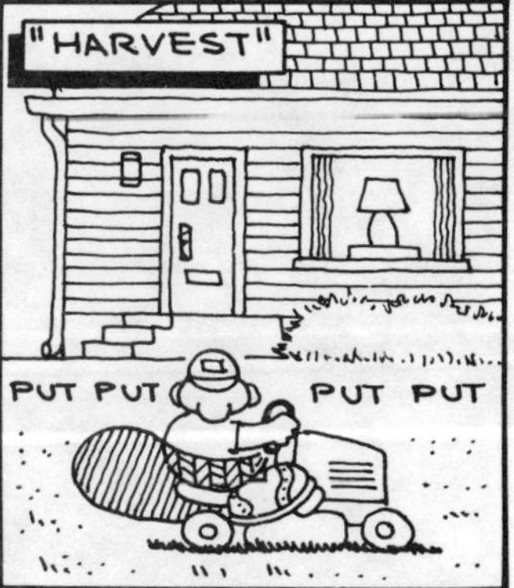
"HARVEST"
PUT PUT
PUT PUT

MODERNE MAN

b. von alten 2·22·84

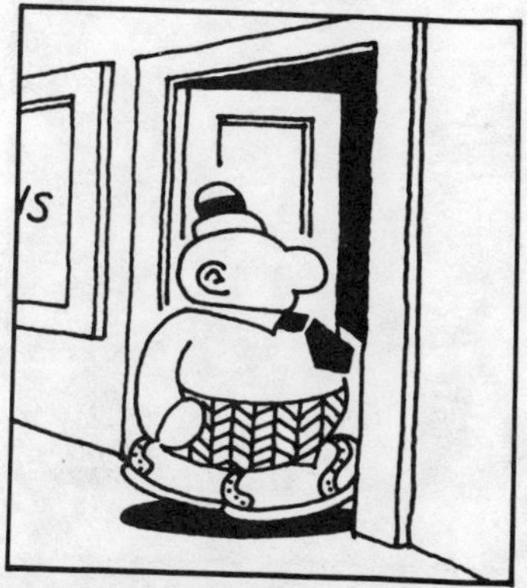

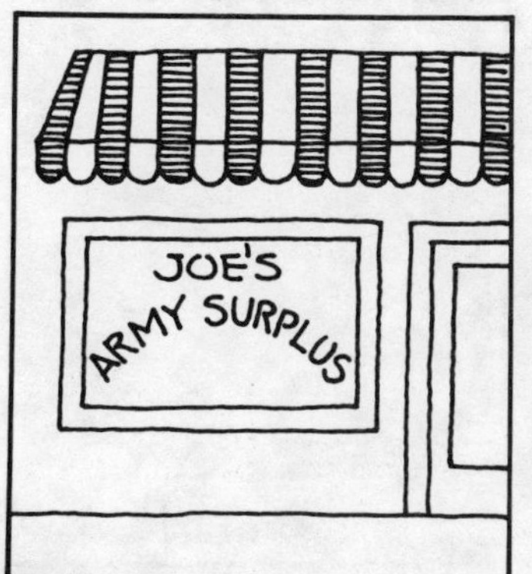
JOE'S ARMY SURPLUS

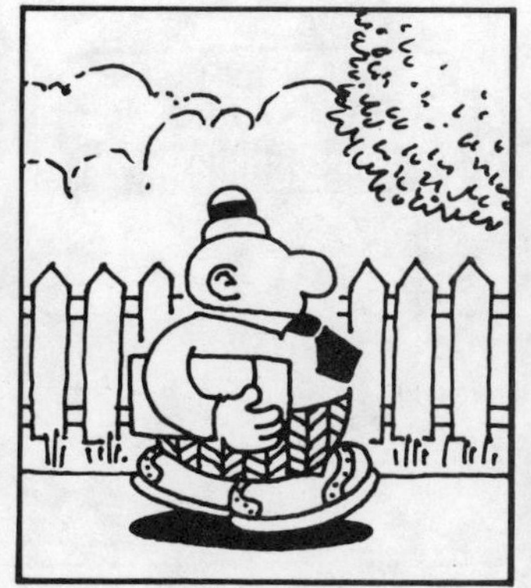

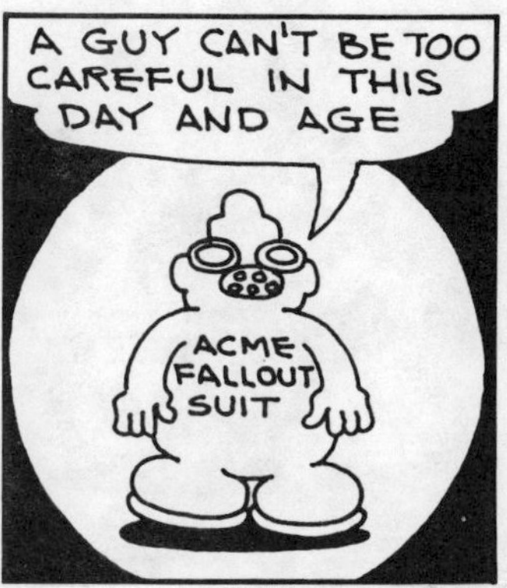
A GUY CAN'T BE TOO CAREFUL IN THIS DAY AND AGE
ACME FALLOUT SUIT

MODERNE MAN

b. von alten 3-16-84

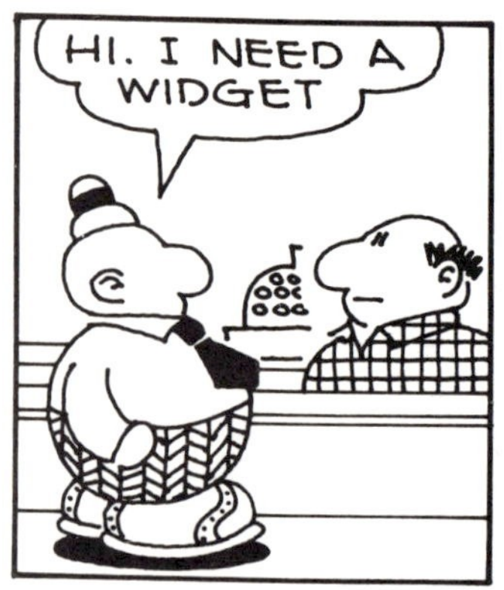
HI. I NEED A WIDGET

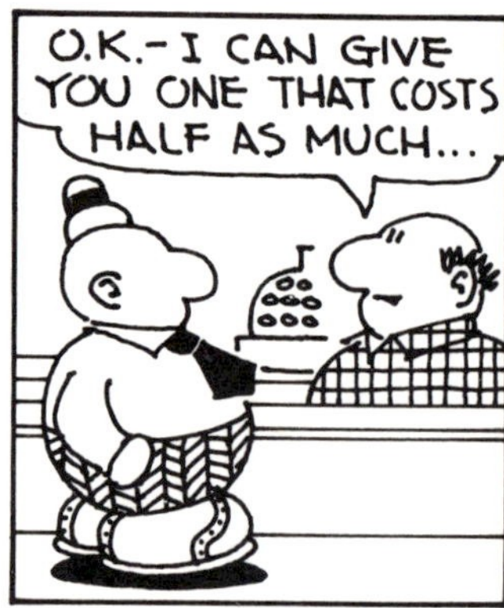
O.K.-I CAN GIVE YOU ONE THAT COSTS HALF AS MUCH...

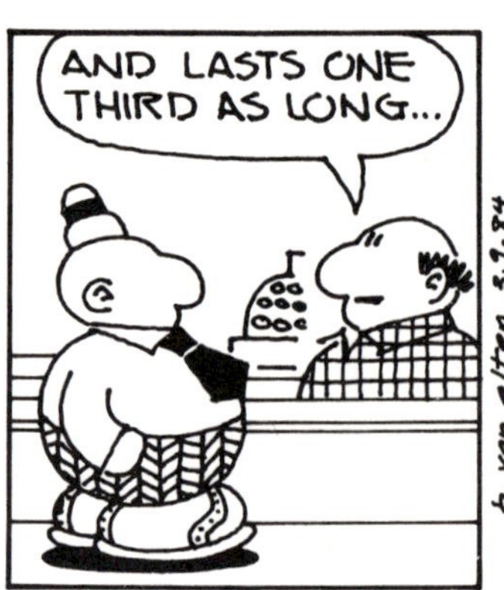
AND LASTS ONE THIRD AS LONG...
b. von alten 3.9.84

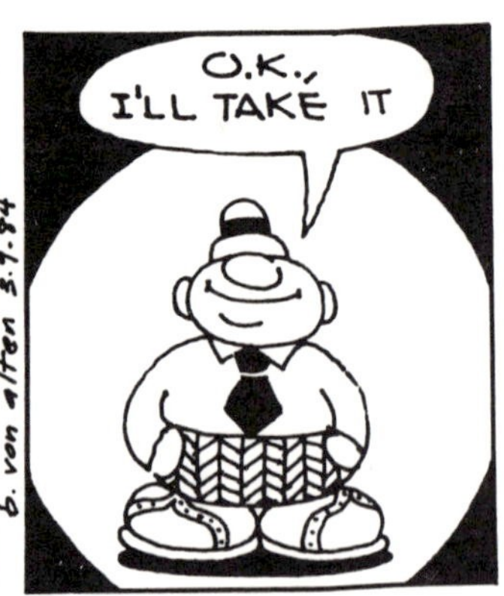
O.K., I'LL TAKE IT

MODERNE MAN

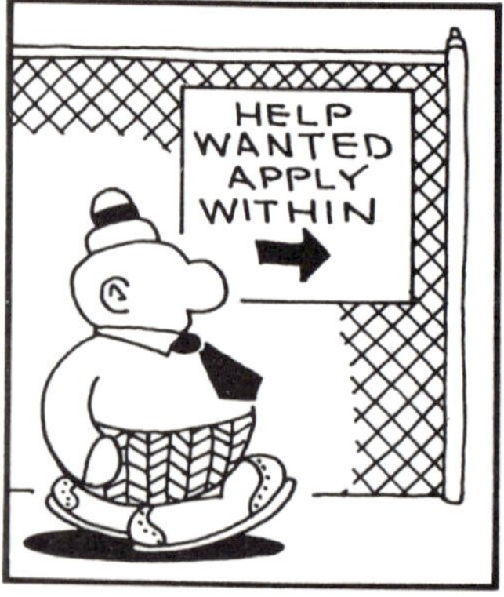
HELP WANTED APPLY WITHIN

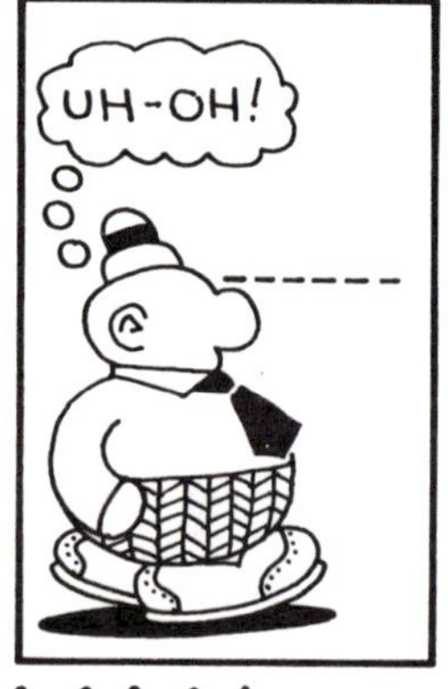
UH-OH!

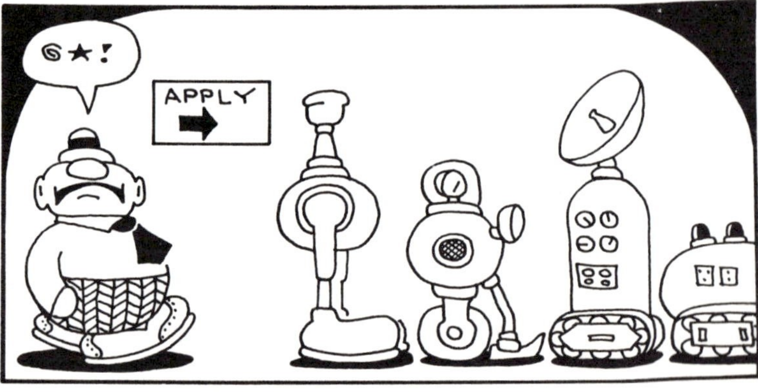
@★!
APPLY

MODERNE MAN

b. von alten

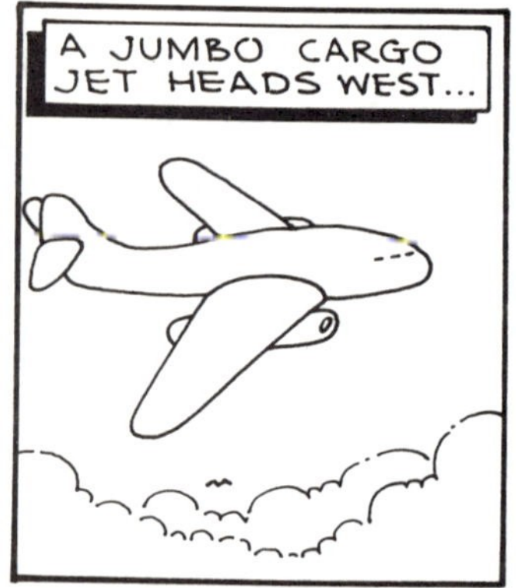
A JUMBO CARGO JET HEADS WEST...

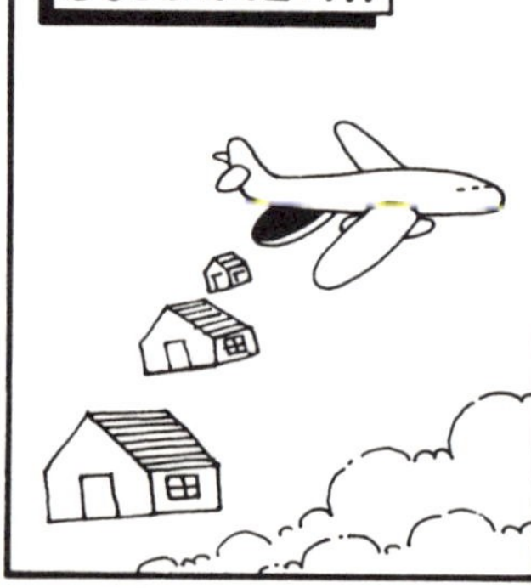
SUDDENLY...

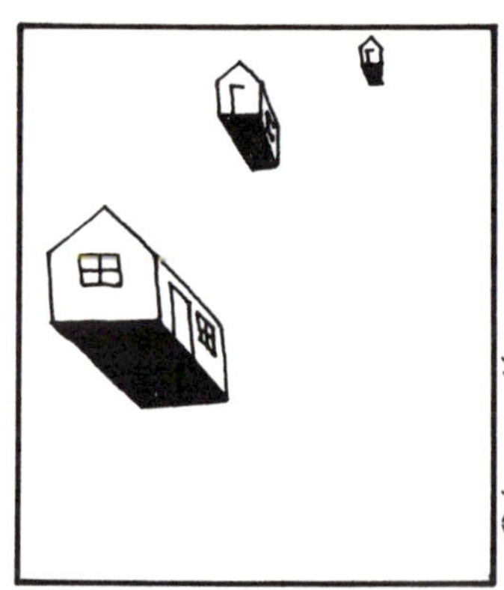
© b. von alten 1985

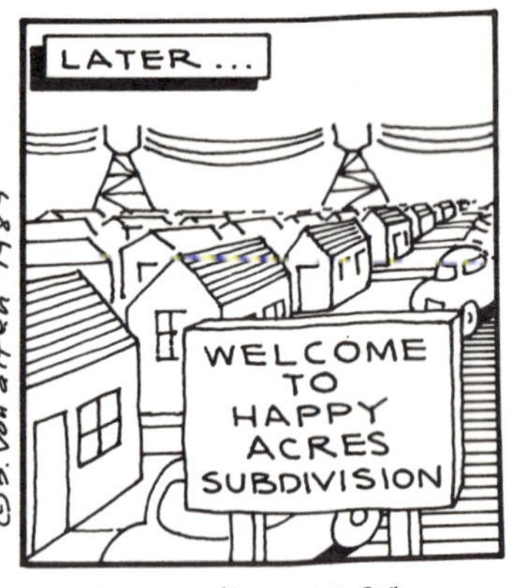
LATER...
WELCOME TO HAPPY ACRES SUBDIVISION

MODERNE MAN

b. von alten 1-14-84

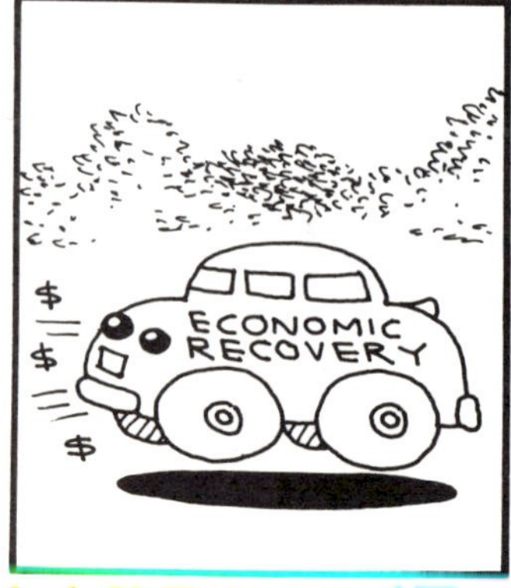
ECONOMIC RECOVERY

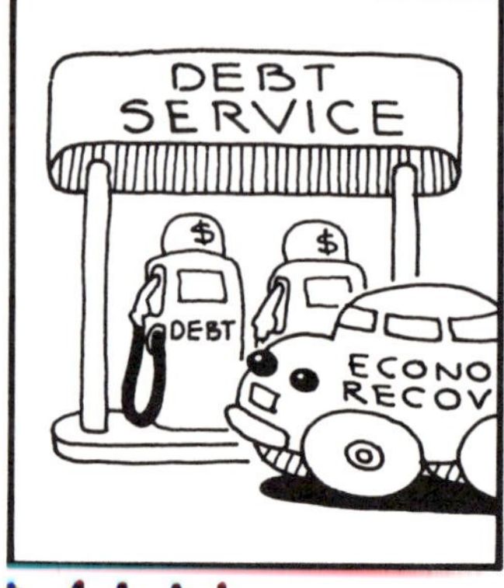
DEBT SERVICE
DEBT
ECONO RECOV

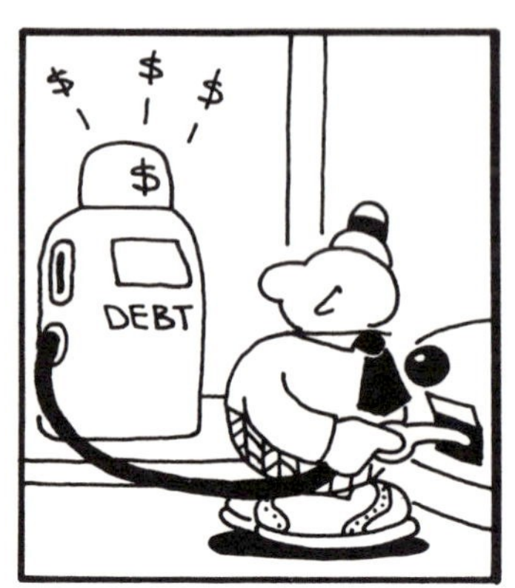
DEBT

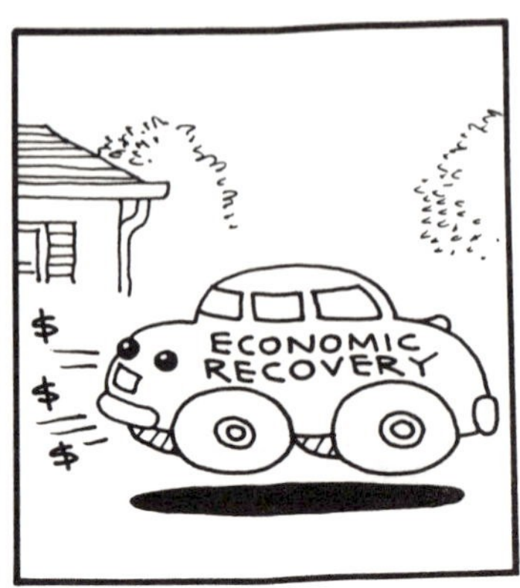
ECONOMIC RECOVERY

MODERNE MAN

b. von alten 7-7-84

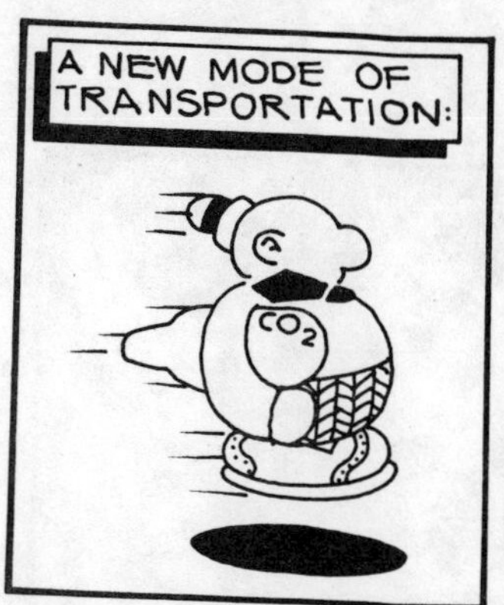
A NEW MODE OF
TRANSPORTATION:
CO_2

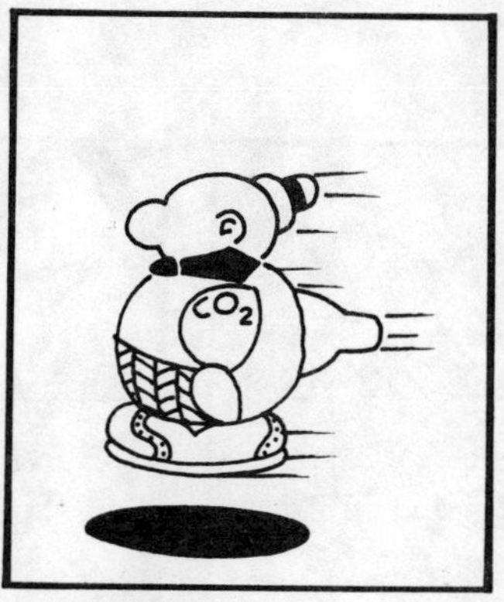
CO_2

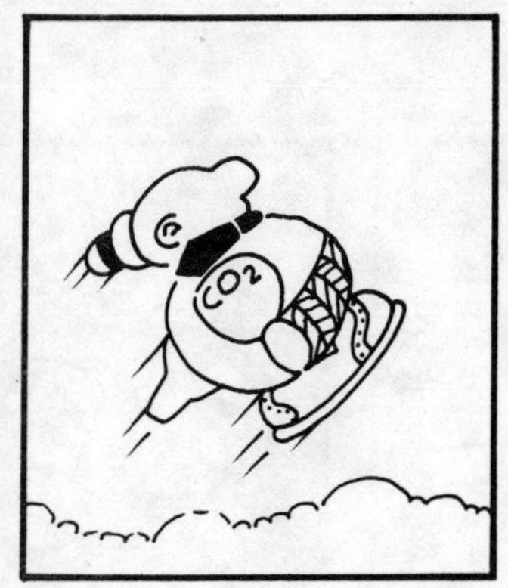
CO_2

MODERNE MAN

b. von alten 6·29·84

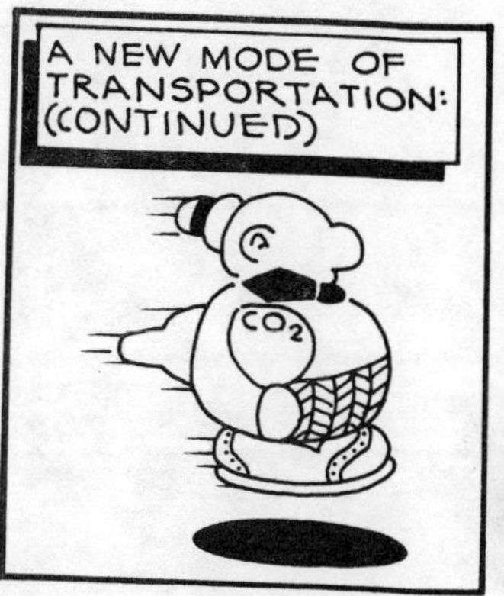
A NEW MODE OF
TRANSPORTATION:
(CONTINUED)
CO_2

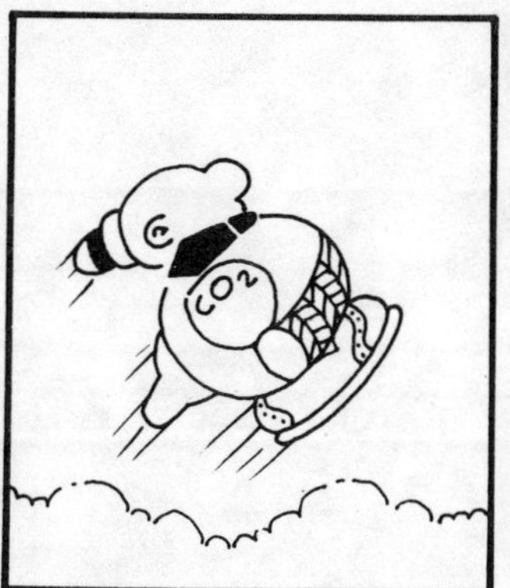
CO_2

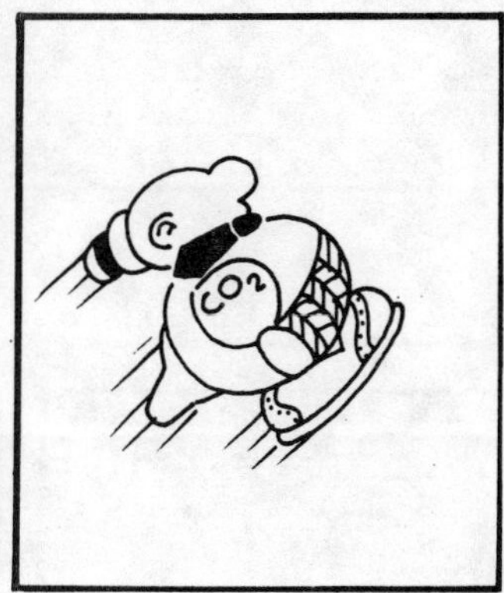
CO_2

MODERNE MAN

b. von alten & p. campbell 6·29·84

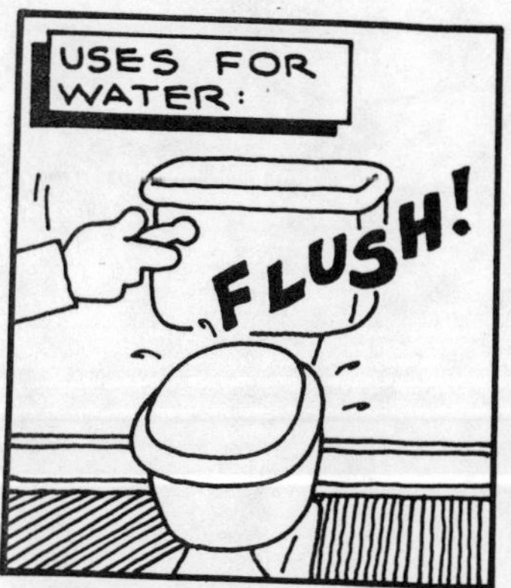
USES FOR
WATER:
FLUSH!

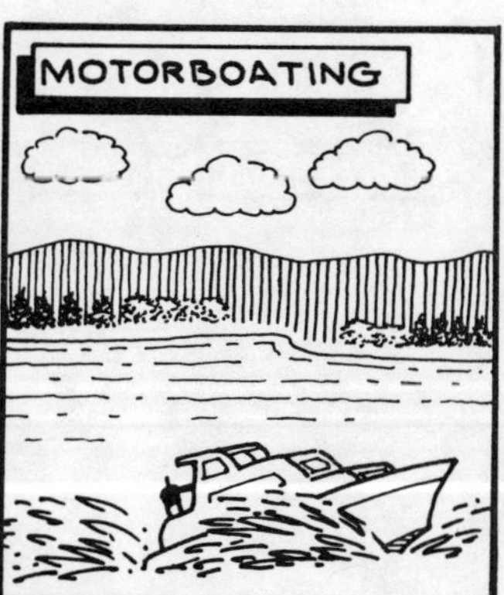
MOTORBOATING

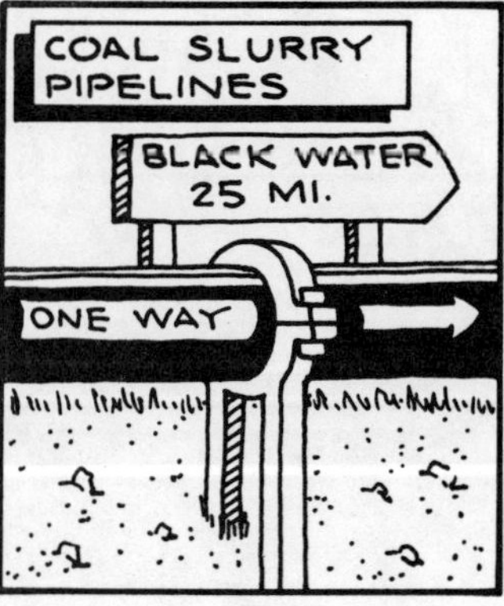
COAL SLURRY
PIPELINES
BLACK WATER
25 MI.
ONE WAY

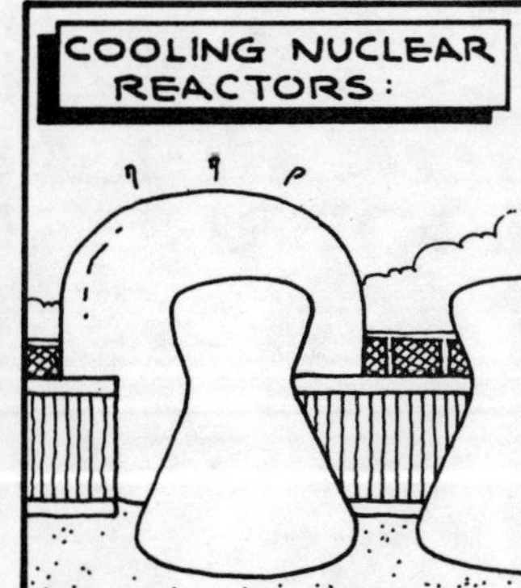
COOLING NUCLEAR
REACTORS:

MODERNE MAN

b. von alten 3·29·84

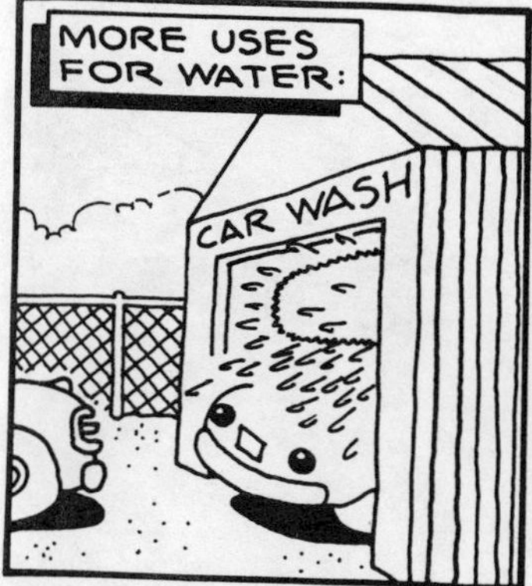
MORE USES
FOR WATER:
CAR WASH

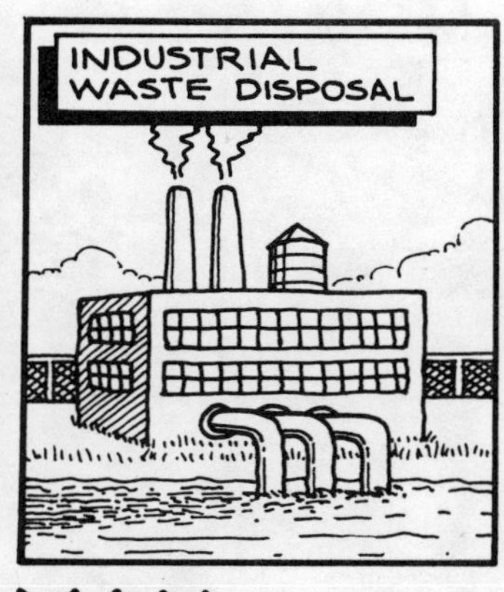
INDUSTRIAL
WASTE DISPOSAL

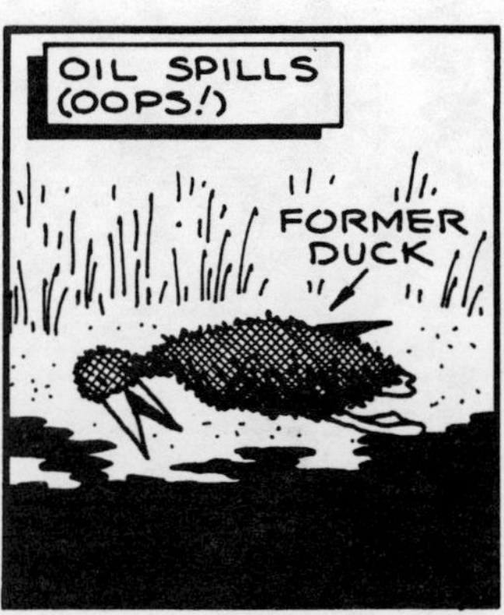
OIL SPILLS
(OOPS!)
FORMER
DUCK

NUCLEAR WASTE
DISPOSAL

MODERNE MAN

b. von alten 3·30·84

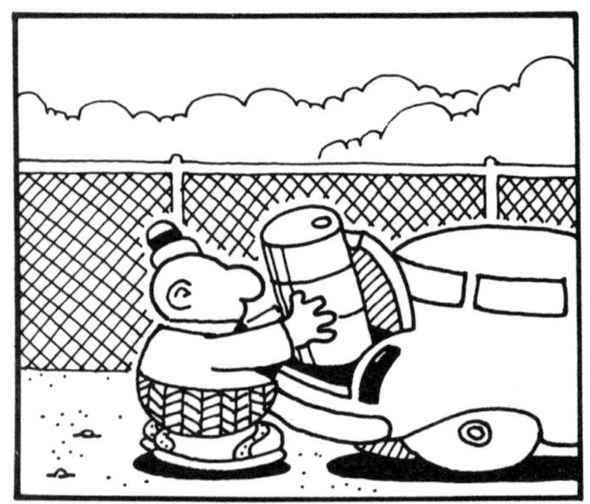

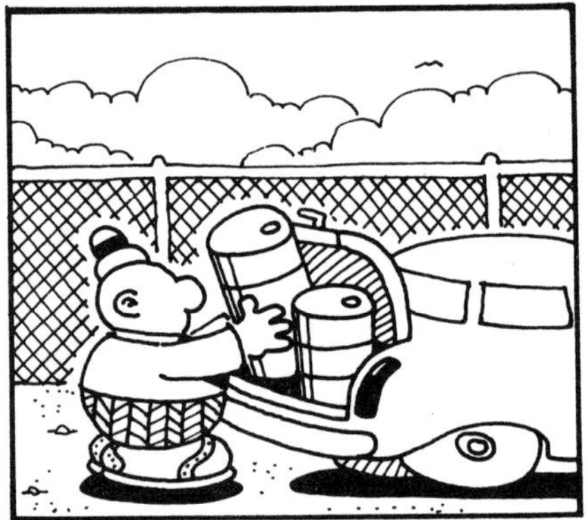

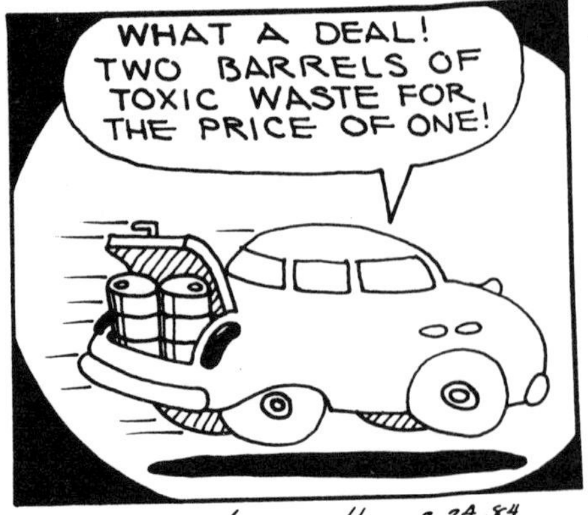
WHAT A DEAL! TWO BARRELS OF TOXIC WASTE FOR THE PRICE OF ONE!

MODERNE MAN

b. von alten 3.24.84

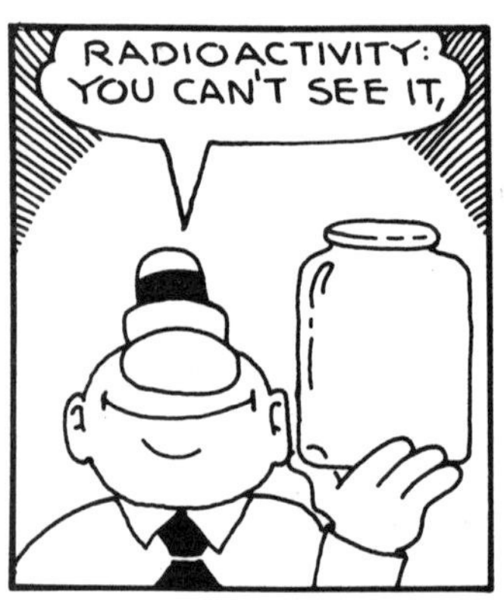
RADIOACTIVITY: YOU CAN'T SEE IT,

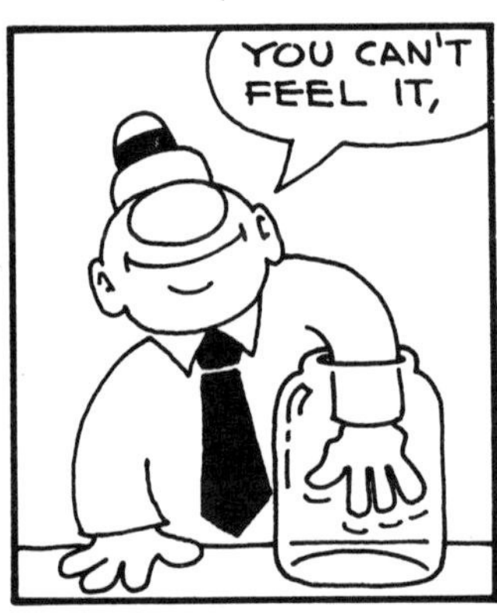
YOU CAN'T FEEL IT,

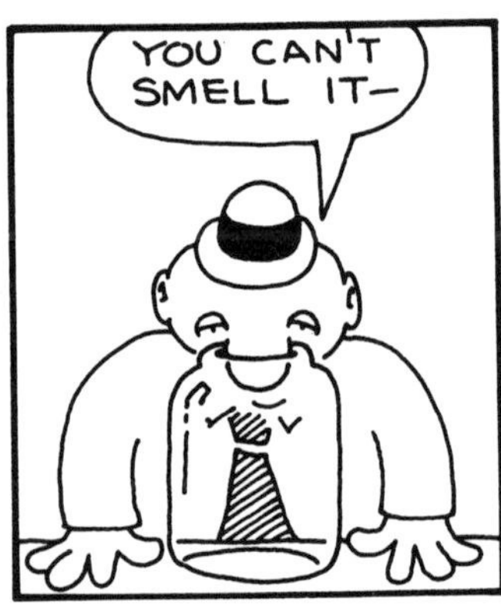
YOU CAN'T SMELL IT–

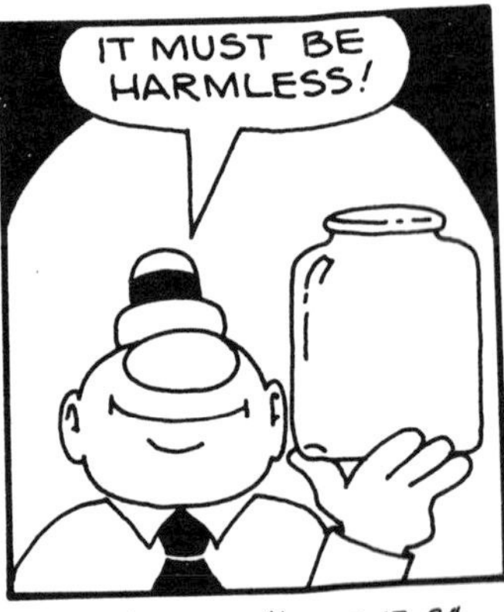
IT MUST BE HARMLESS!

MODERNE MAN

b. von alten 2.17.84

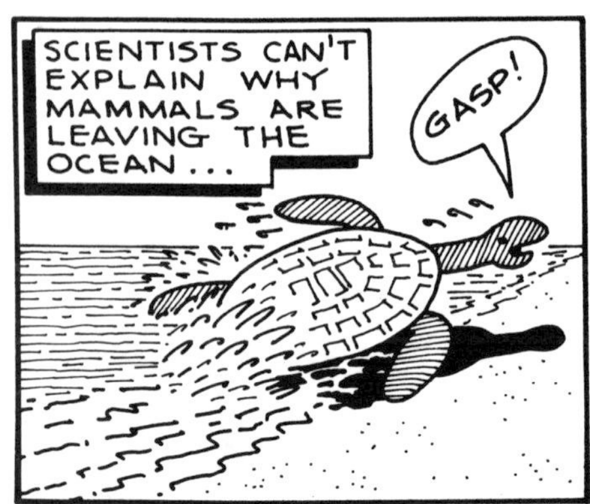
SCIENTISTS CAN'T EXPLAIN WHY MAMMALS ARE LEAVING THE OCEAN...
GASP!

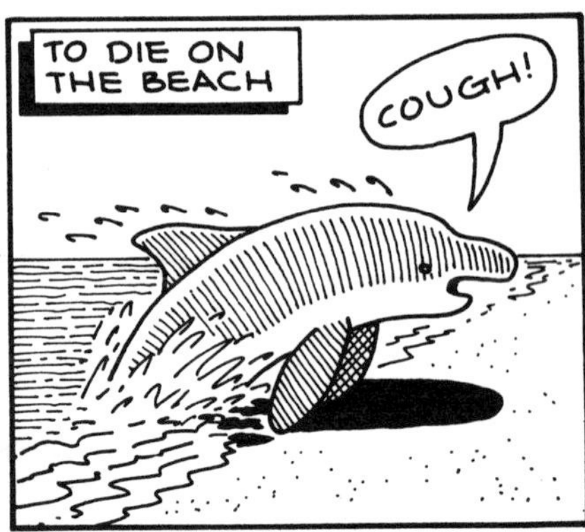
TO DIE ON THE BEACH
COUGH!

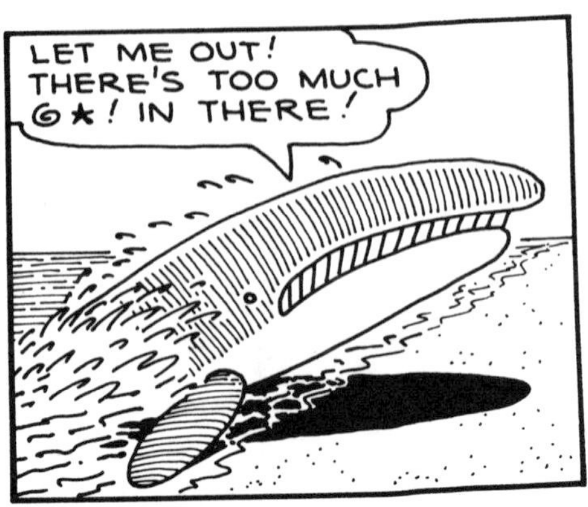
LET ME OUT! THERE'S TOO MUCH G★! IN THERE!

MODERNE MAN

b. von alten 2.17.84

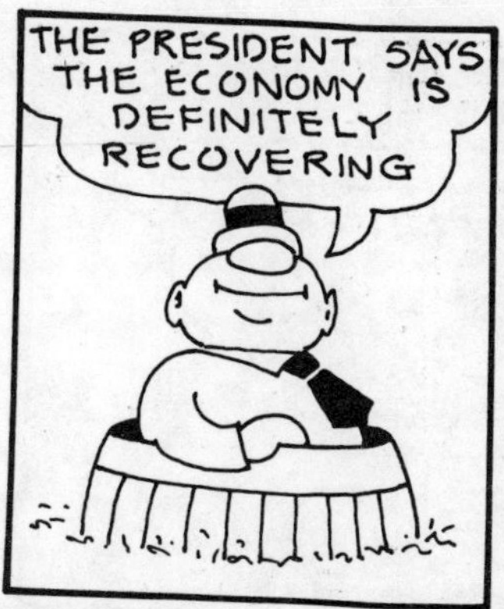
THE PRESIDENT SAYS THE ECONOMY IS DEFINITELY RECOVERING

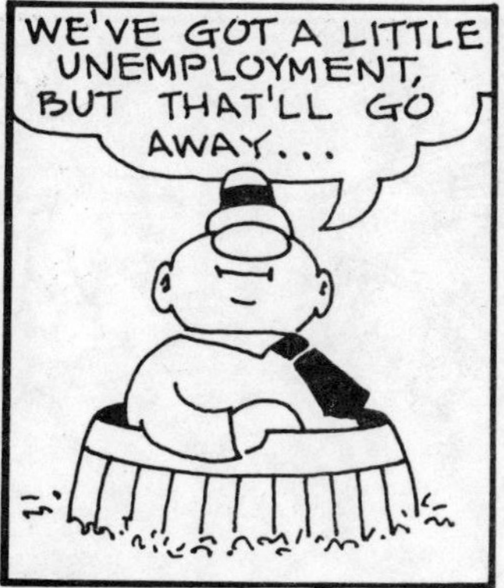
WE'VE GOT A LITTLE UNEMPLOYMENT, BUT THAT'LL GO AWAY...

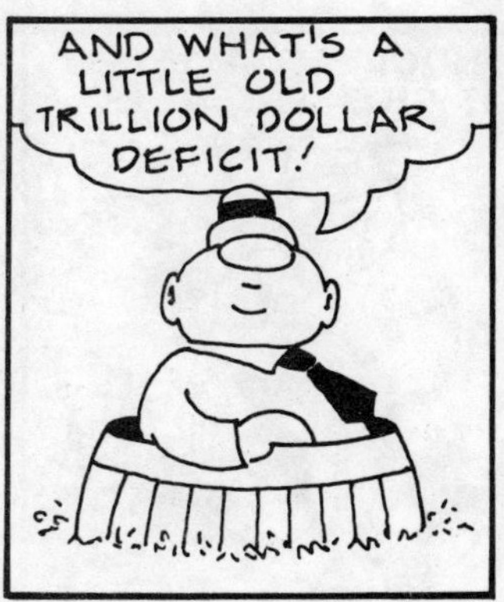
AND WHAT'S A LITTLE OLD TRILLION DOLLAR DEFICIT!

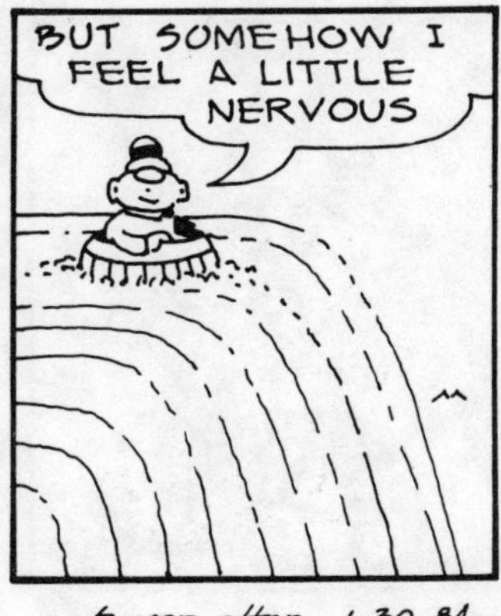
BUT SOMEHOW I FEEL A LITTLE NERVOUS

MODERNE MAN

b. von alten 1-30-84

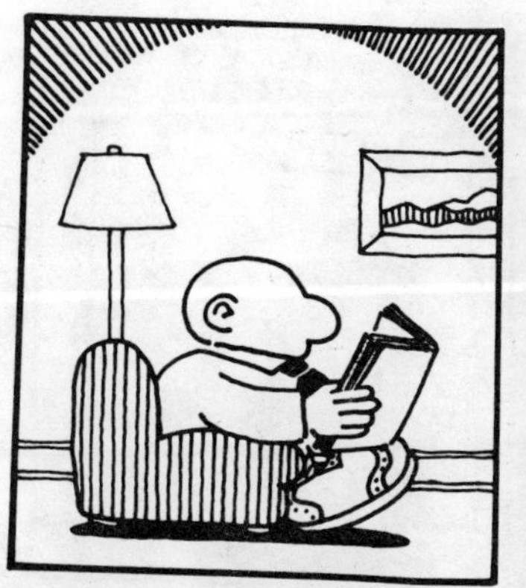

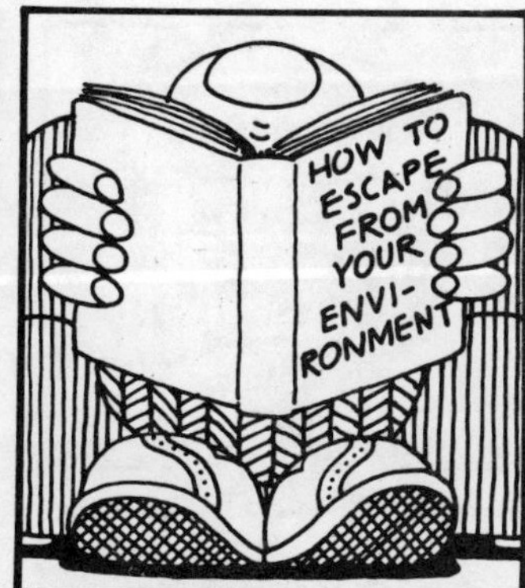
HOW TO ESCAPE FROM YOUR ENVIRONMENT

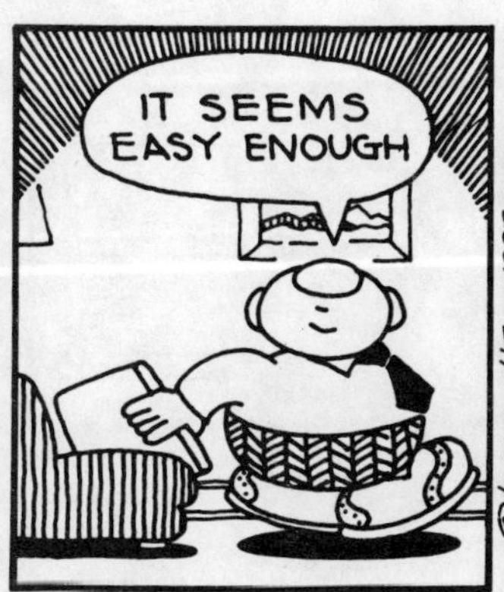
IT SEEMS EASY ENOUGH
©b. von alten 1984

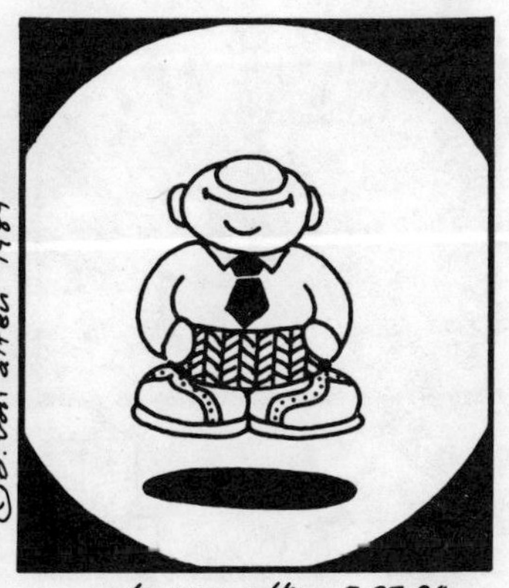

MODERNE MAN

b. von alten 3-27-84

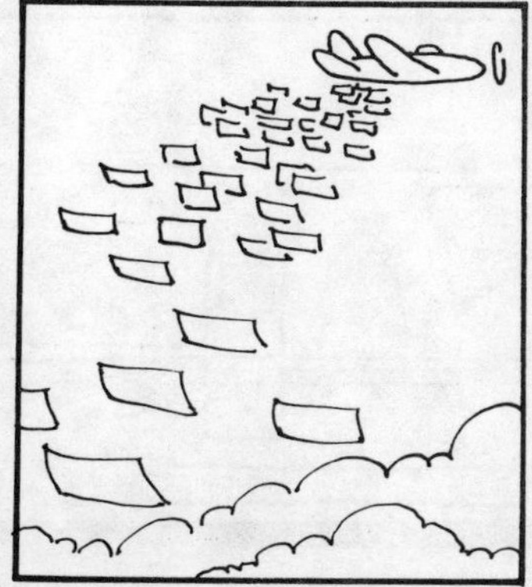

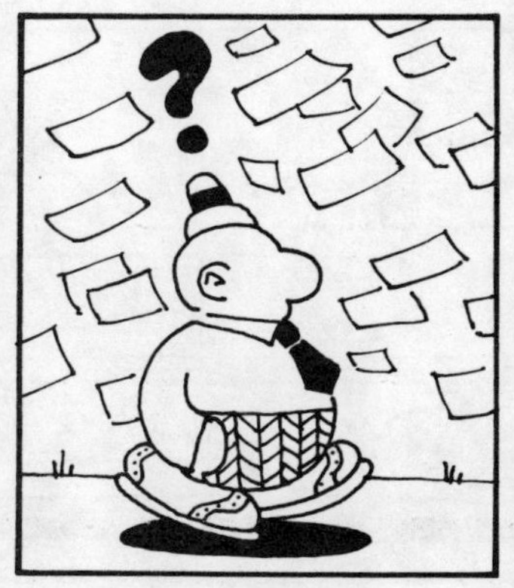
?

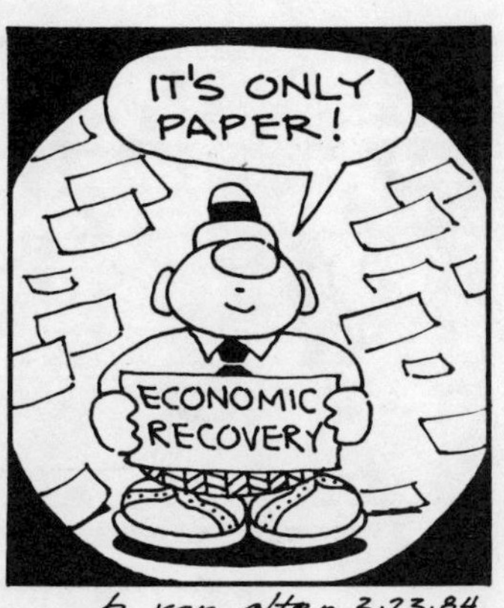
IT'S ONLY PAPER!
ECONOMIC RECOVERY

MODERNE MAN

b. von alten 3-23-84

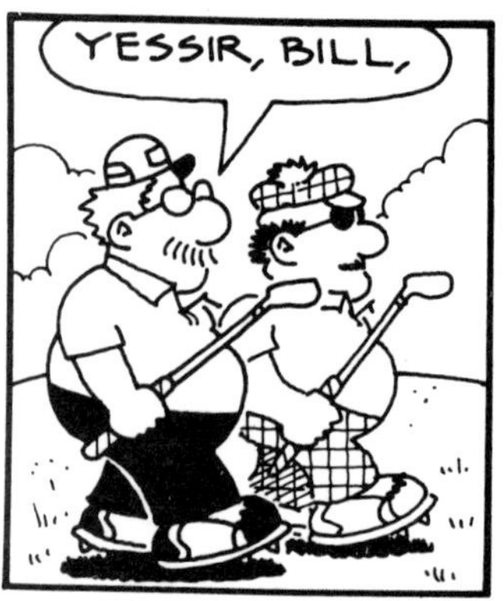
YESSIR, BILL,
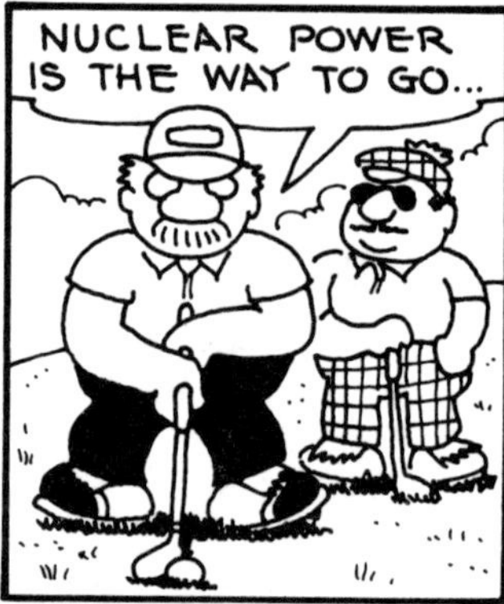
NUCLEAR POWER
IS THE WAY TO GO...
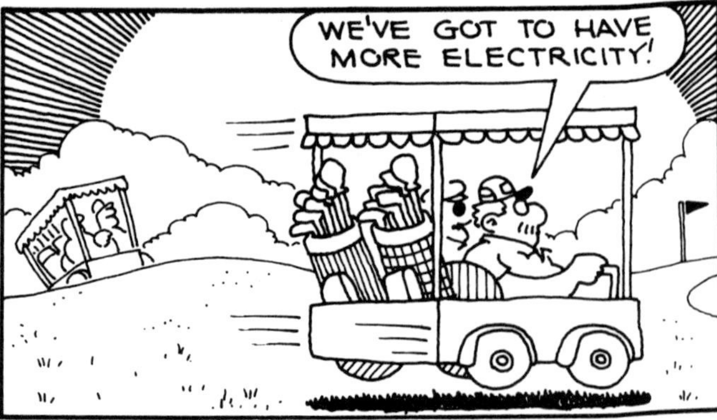
WE'VE GOT TO HAVE
MORE ELECTRICITY!

MODERNE MAN

b. von alten 3.28.84

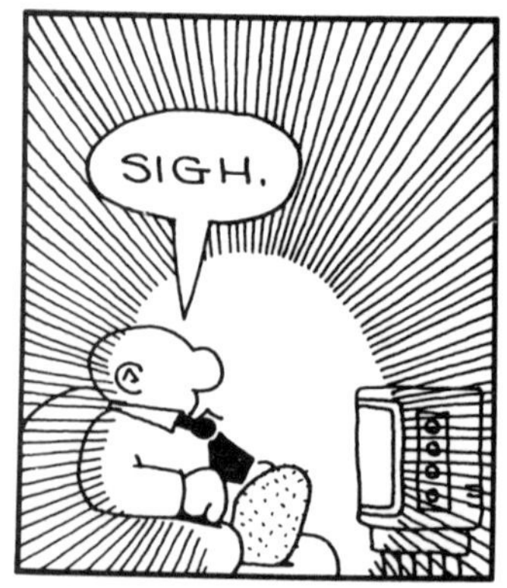
SIGH.
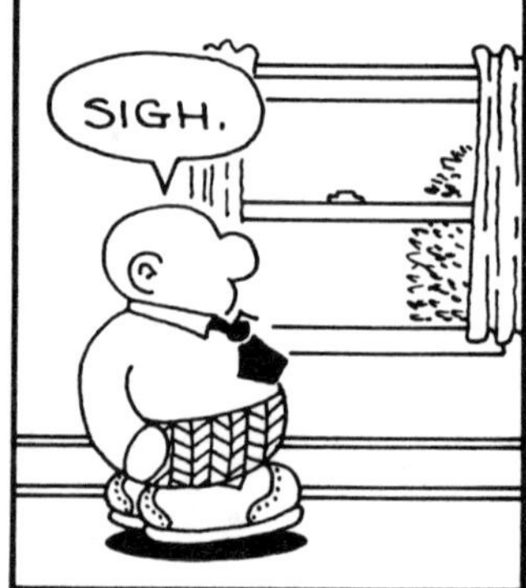
SIGH.
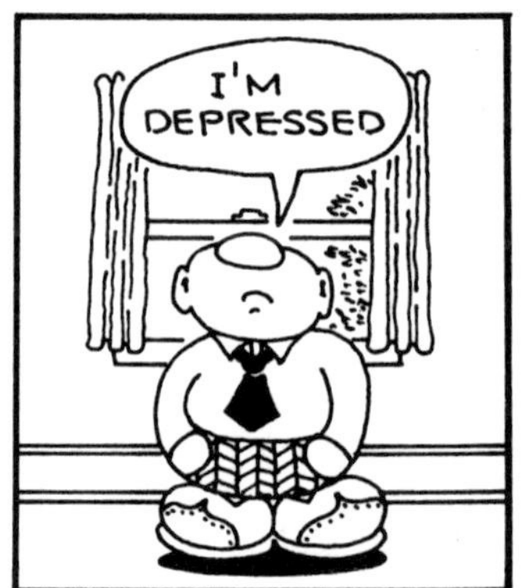
I'M
DEPRESSED
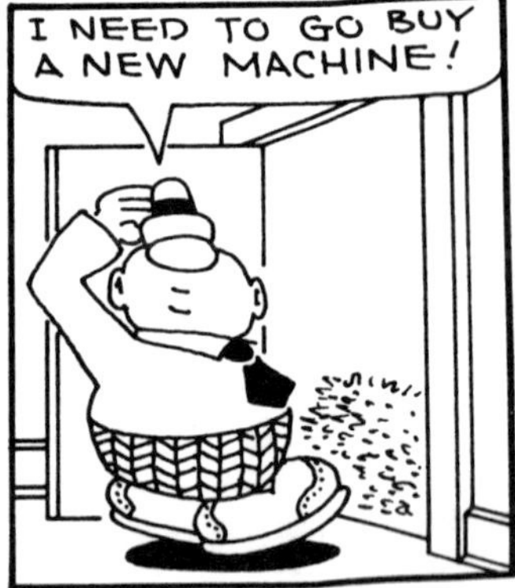
I NEED TO GO BUY
A NEW MACHINE!

MODERNE MAN

b. von alten

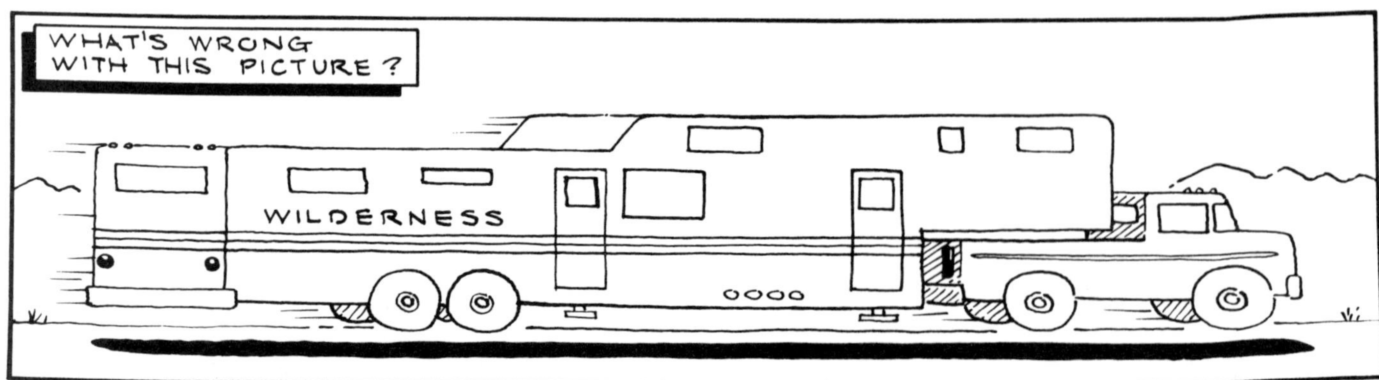
WHAT'S WRONG
WITH THIS PICTURE?
WILDERNESS

MODERNE MAN

b. von alten

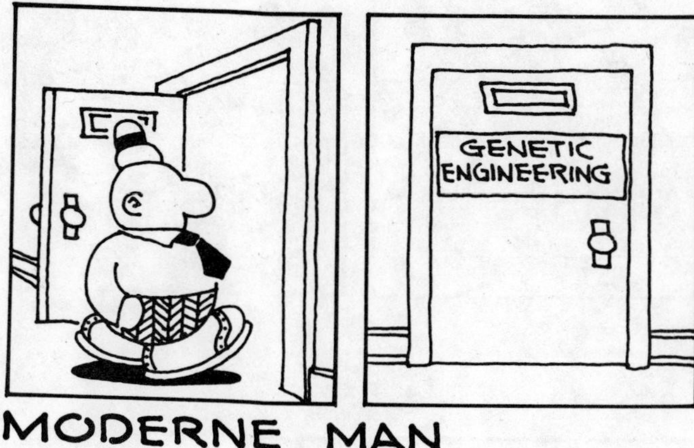
GENETIC
ENGINEERING
MODERNE MAN

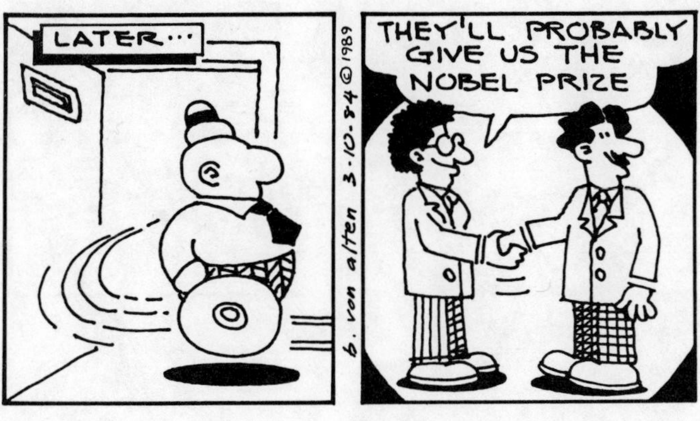
LATER...
b. von alten 3-10-84 ©1989
THEY'LL PROBABLY GIVE US THE NOBEL PRIZE

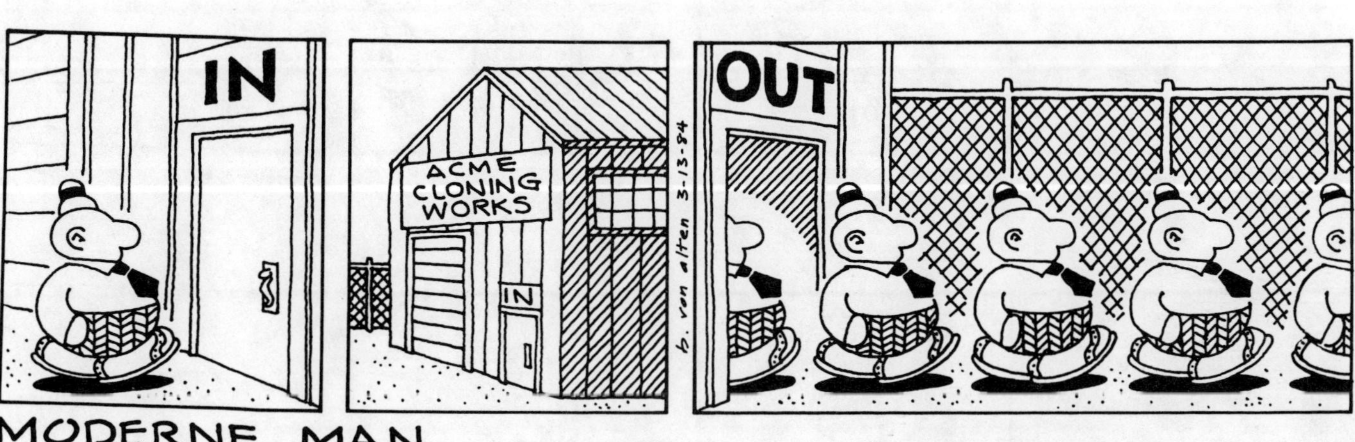
IN
ACME CLONING WORKS
IN
b. von alten 3-13-84
OUT
MODERNE MAN

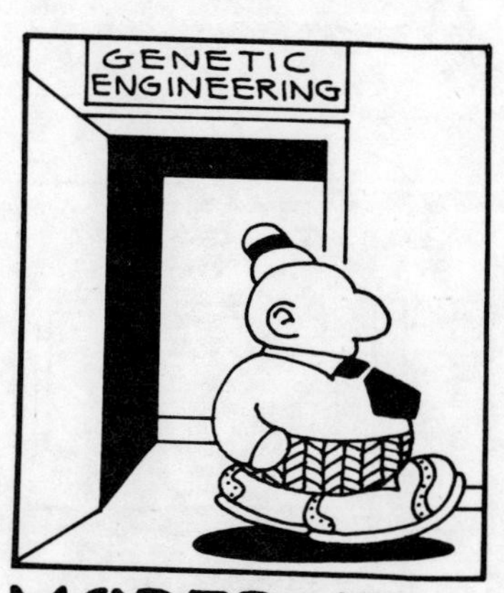
GENETIC
ENGINEERING

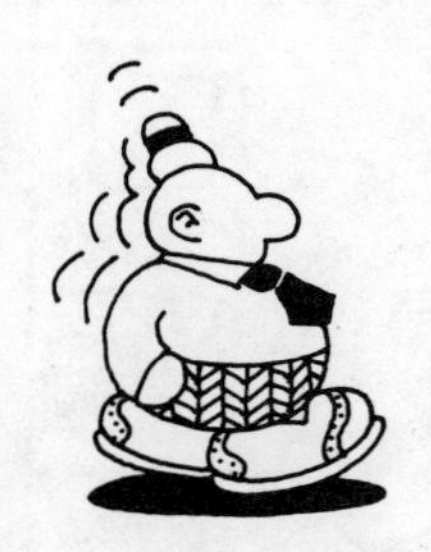

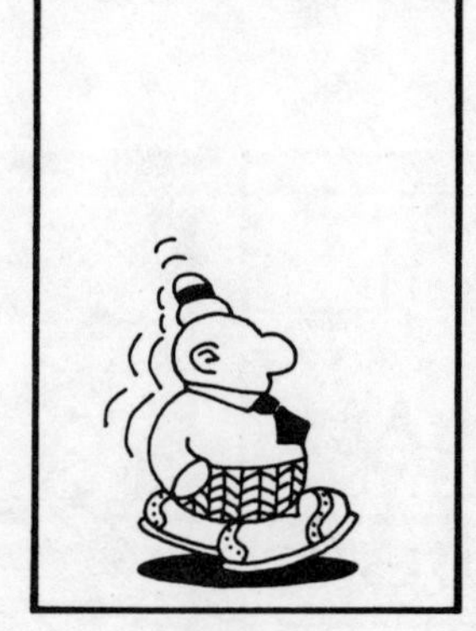

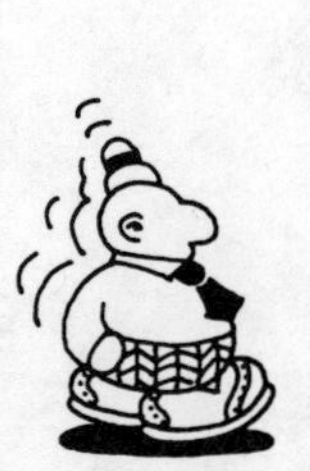

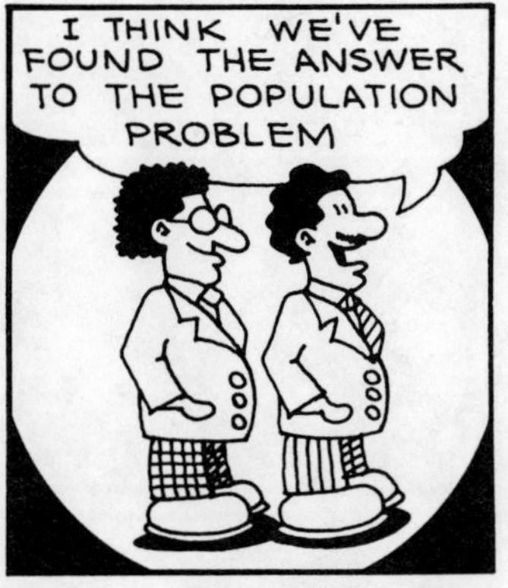
I THINK WE'VE FOUND THE ANSWER TO THE POPULATION PROBLEM

MODERNE MAN

b. von alten 5.14.84

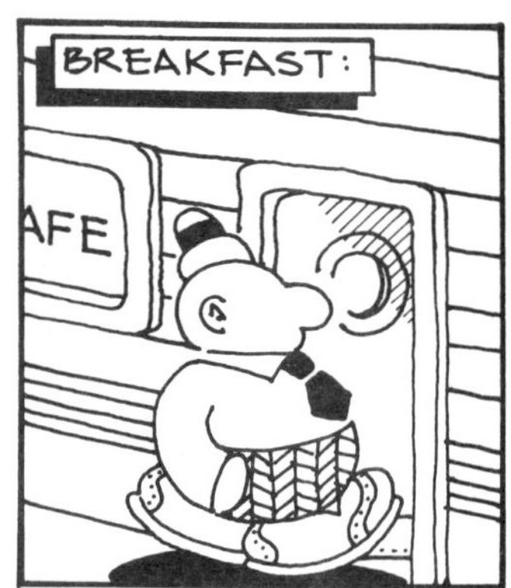
BREAKFAST:
AFE
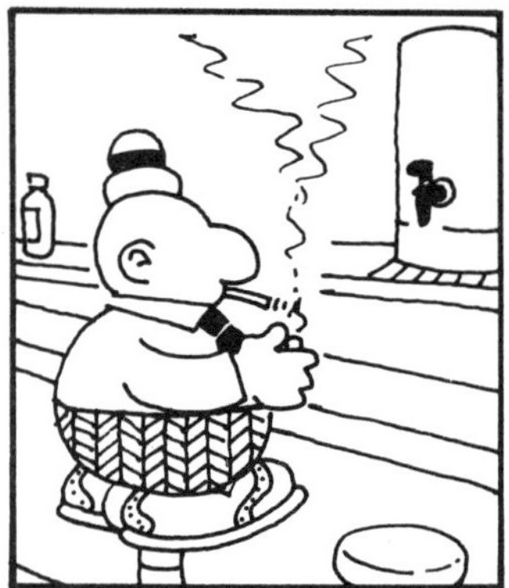
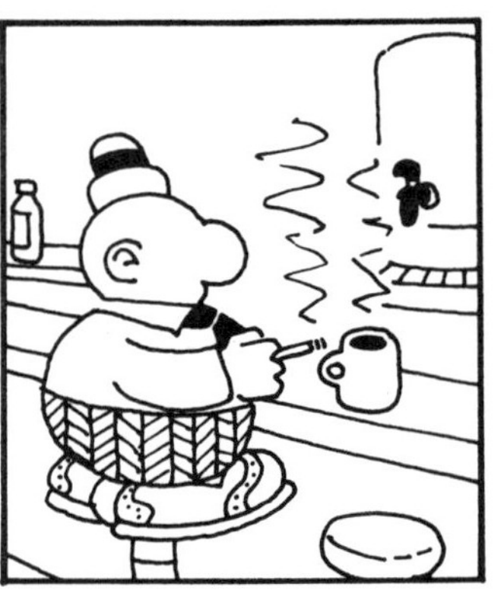
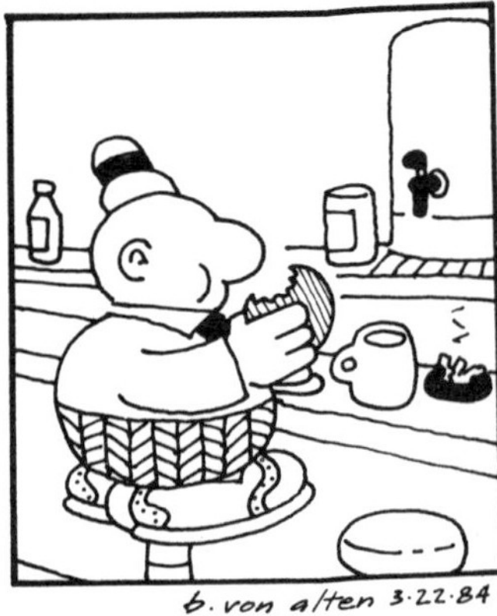

MODERNE MAN

b. von alten 3·22·84

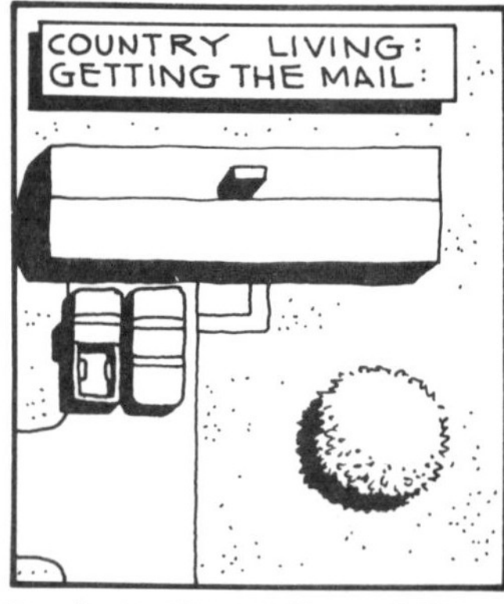
COUNTRY LIVING:
GETTING THE MAIL:
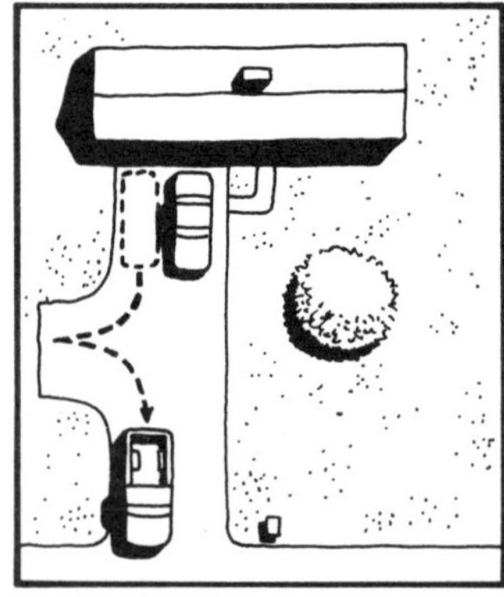
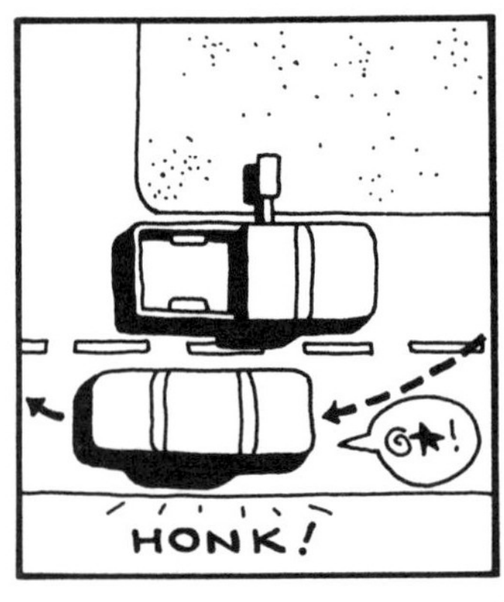
HONK!
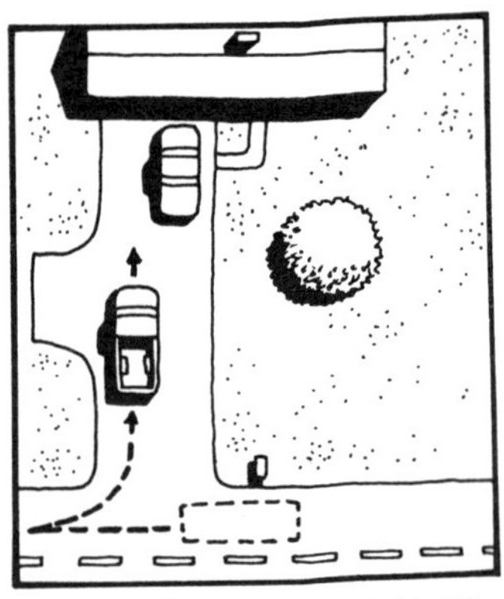

MODERNE MAN

p. campbell & b. von alten 6-12-84

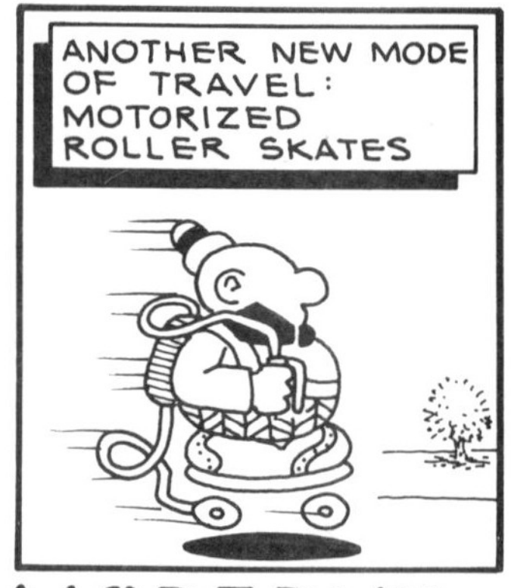
ANOTHER NEW MODE OF TRAVEL: MOTORIZED ROLLER SKATES
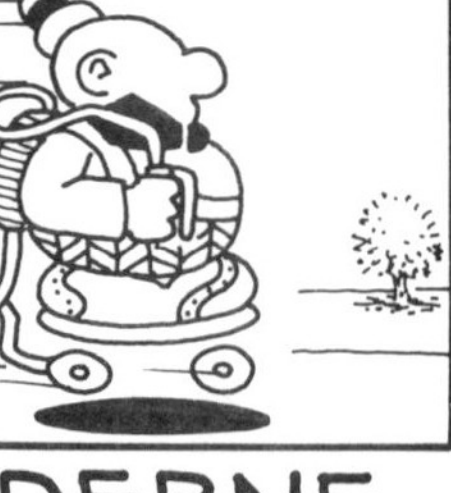
THEY GO PRETTY WELL...
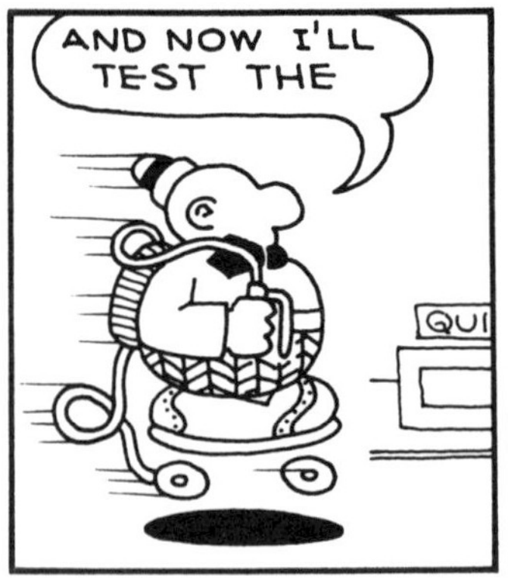
AND NOW I'LL TEST THE
QUI
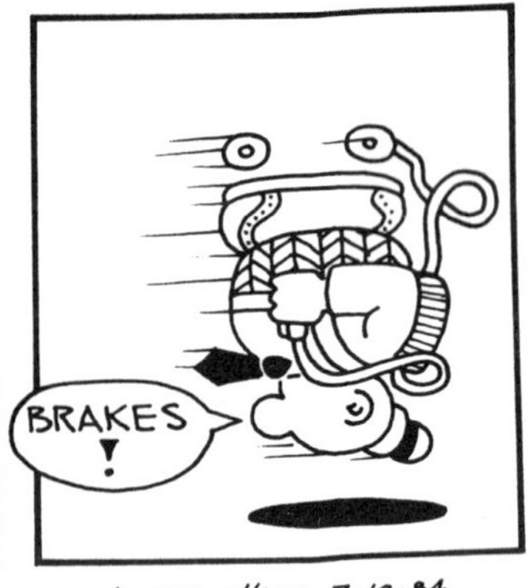
BRAKES!

MODERNE MAN

b. von alten 7-10-84

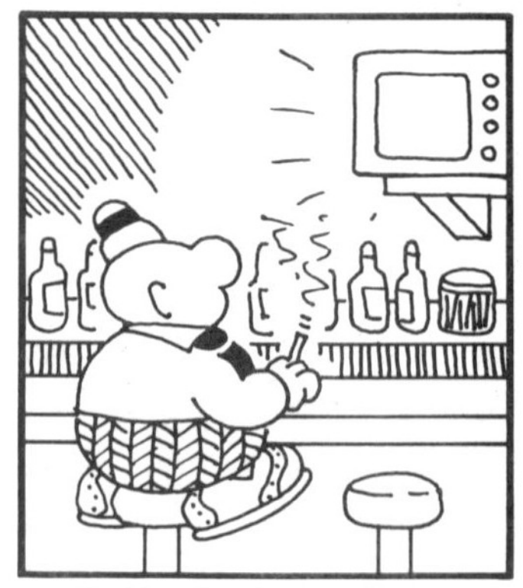
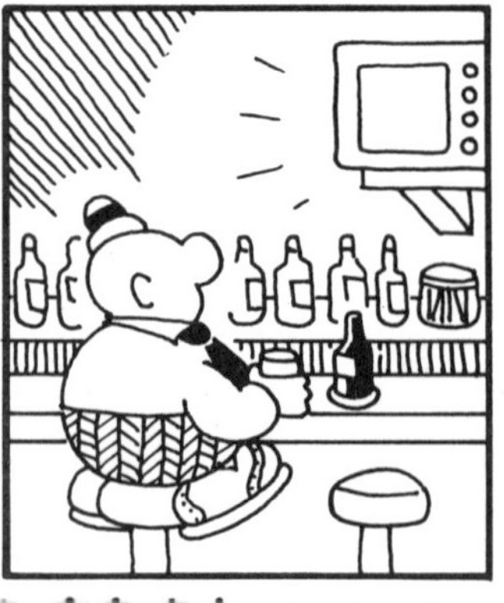
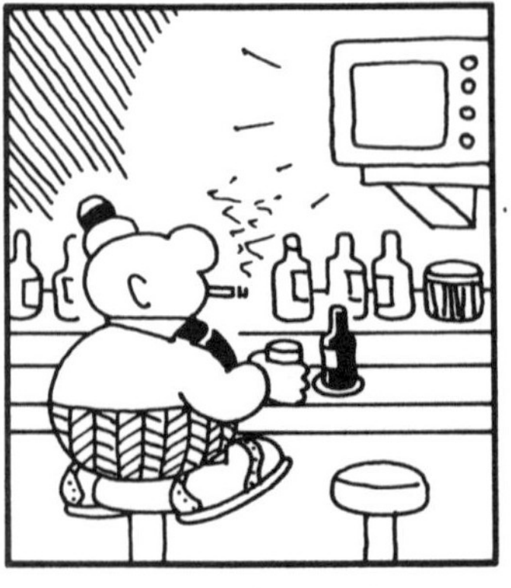
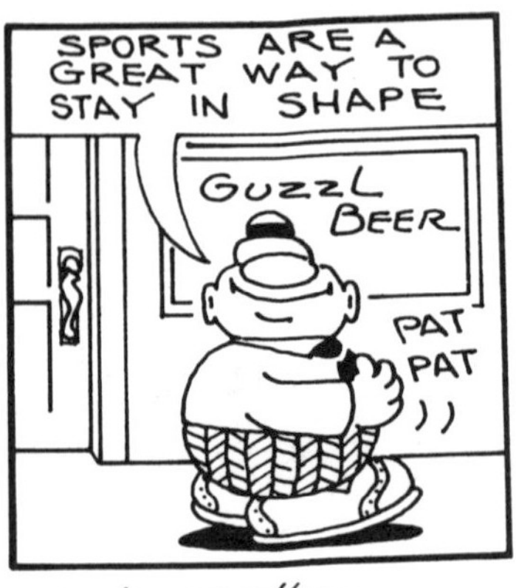
SPORTS ARE A GREAT WAY TO STAY IN SHAPE
GUZZL BEER
PAT PAT

MODERNE MAN

b. von alten

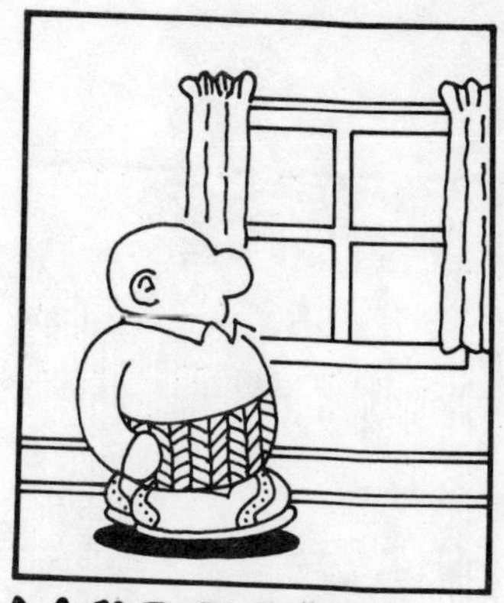

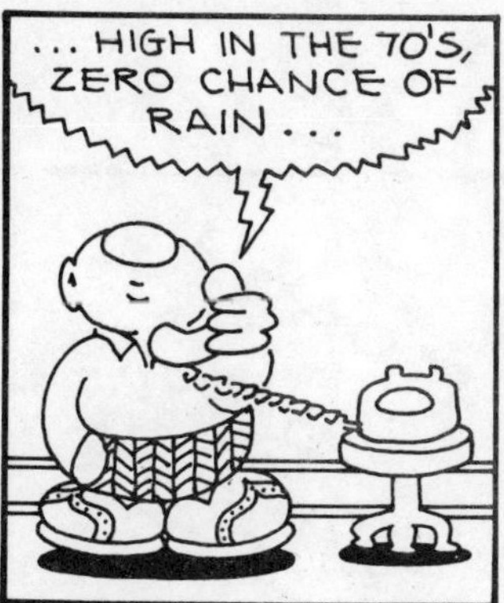
... HIGH IN THE 70'S, ZERO CHANCE OF RAIN ...

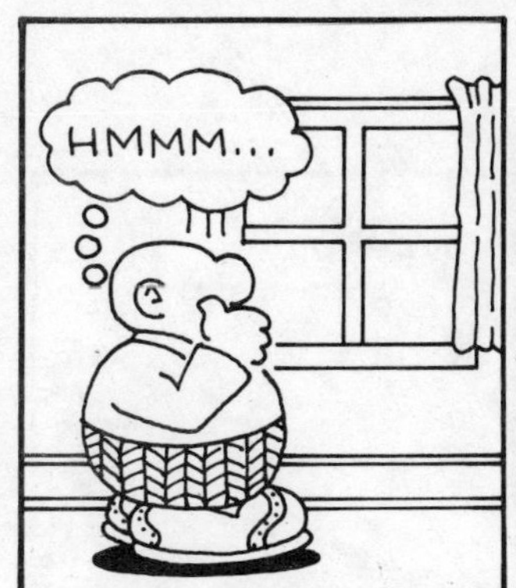
HMMM...

IT'S TOO NICE A DAY TO STAY INDOORS

MODERNE MAN

b. von alten 5.28.84

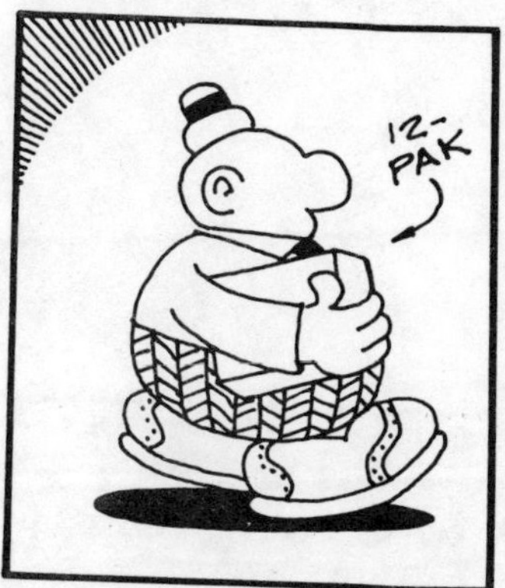
12-
PAK

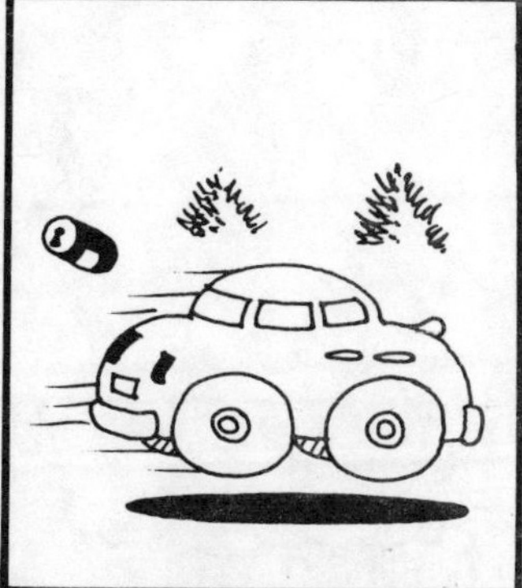

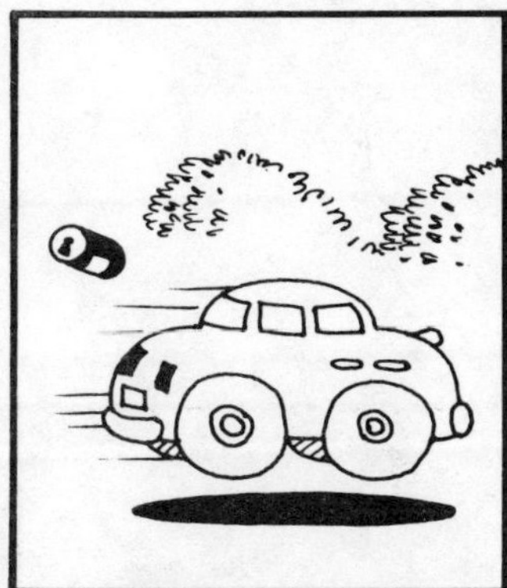

"PLEASE RECYCLE"

MODERNE MAN

b. von alten 8-1-84

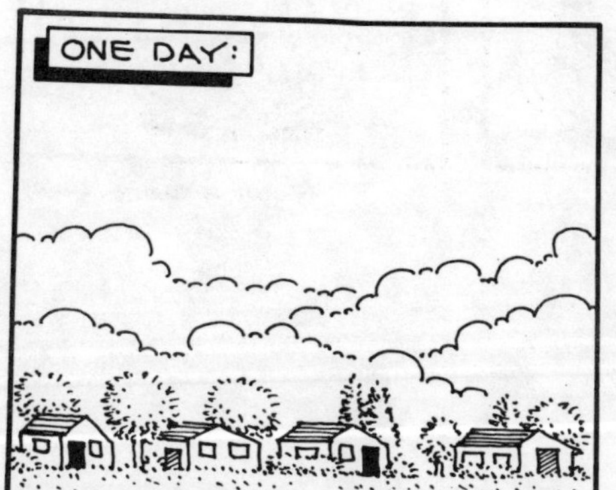
ONE DAY:

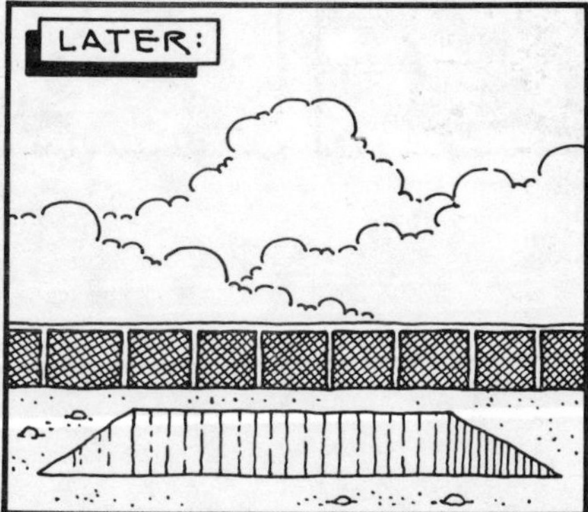
LATER:

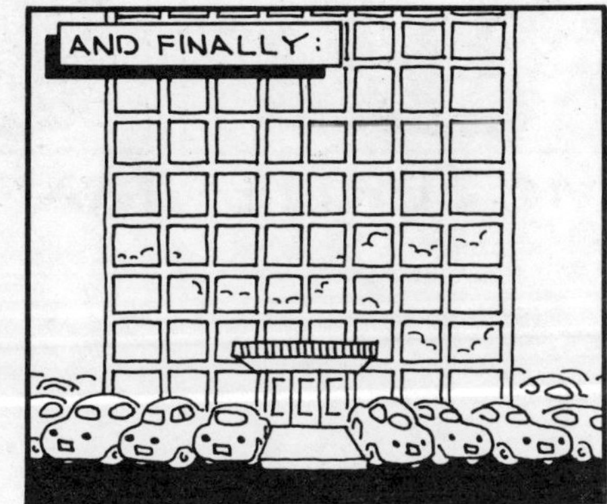
AND FINALLY:

MODERNE MAN

b. von alten

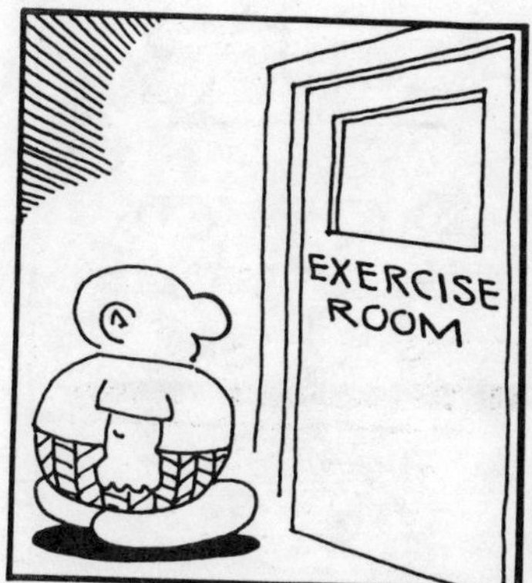
EXERCISE ROOM

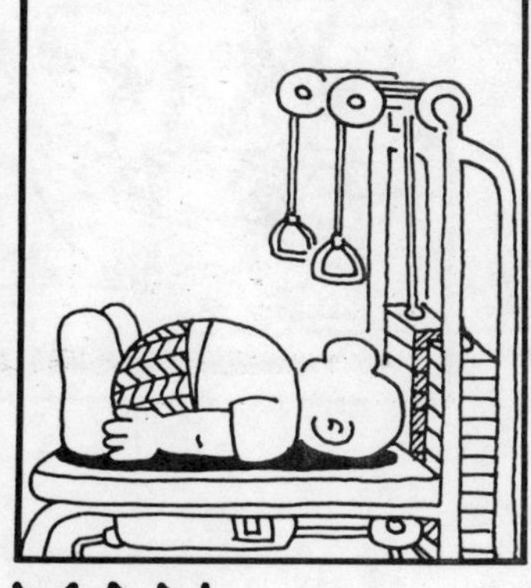

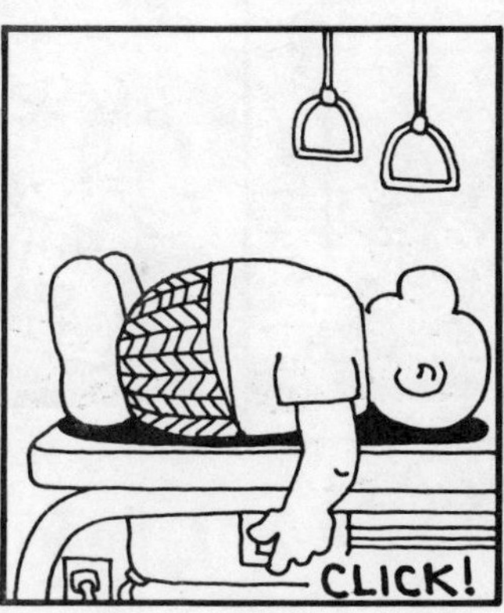
CLICK!

MOTORIZED! NO SWEAT!

M MMMMMMM!

MODERNE MAN

b. von alten 7·21·84

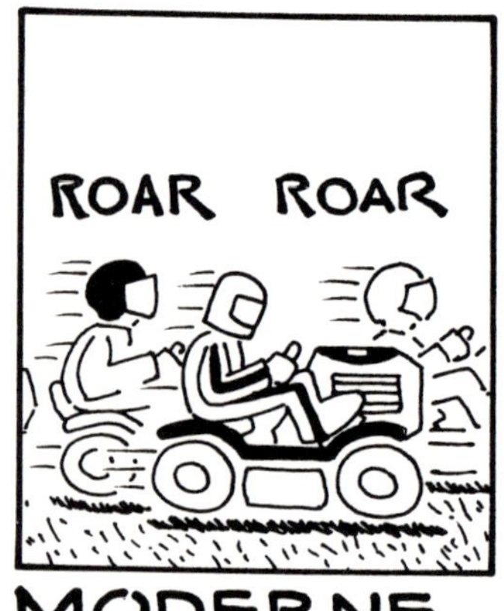
ROAR ROAR
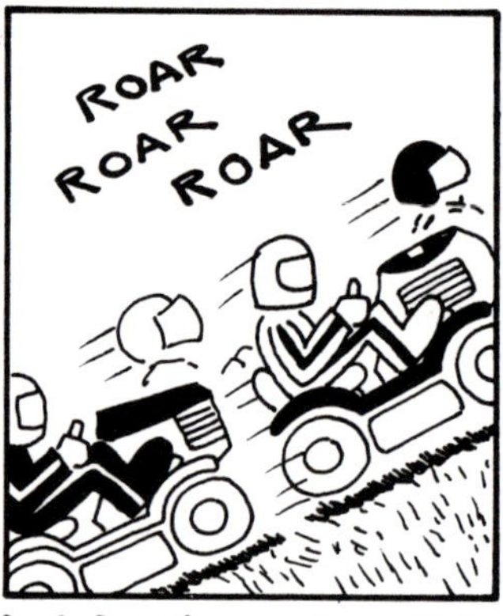
ROAR
ROAR ROAR
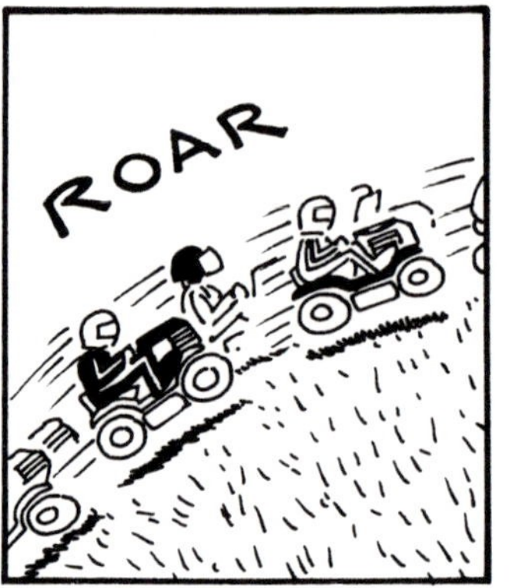
ROAR
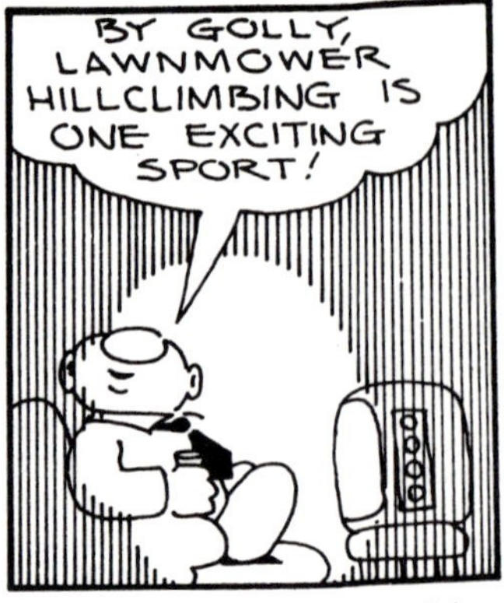
BY GOLLY, LAWNMOWER HILLCLIMBING IS ONE EXCITING SPORT!

MODERNE MAN

b. von alten 6-11-84

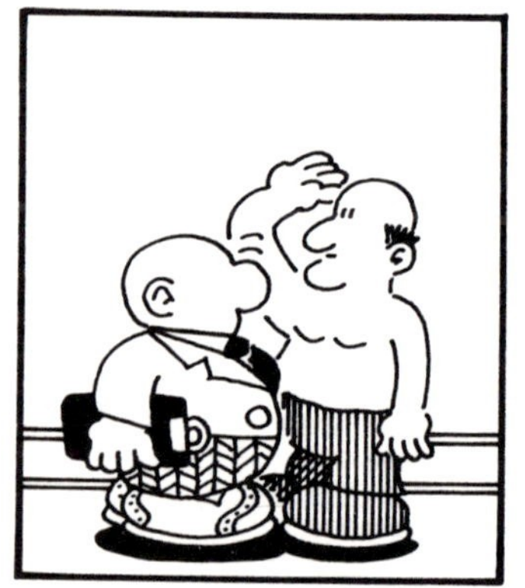
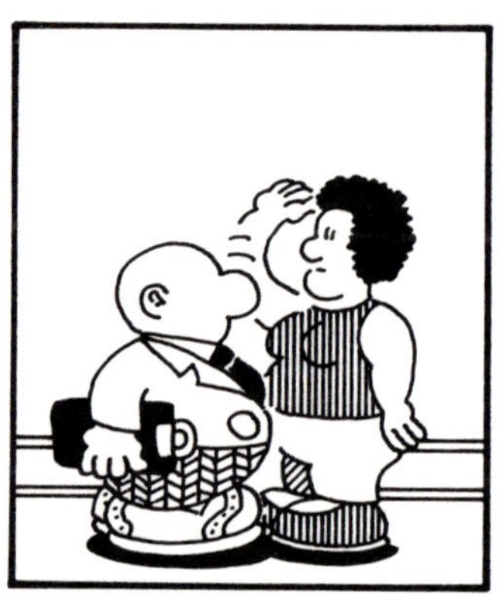
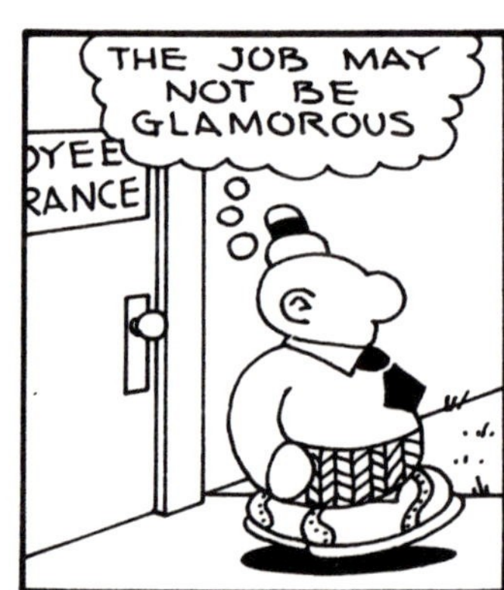
THE JOB MAY NOT BE GLAMOROUS
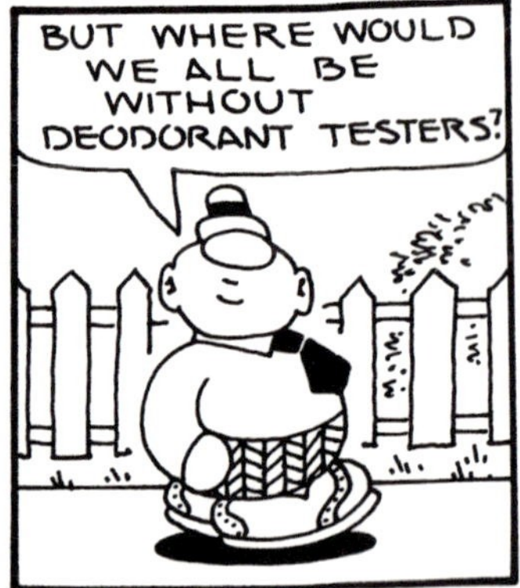
BUT WHERE WOULD WE ALL BE WITHOUT DEODORANT TESTERS?

MODERNE MAN

b. von alten 6-2-84

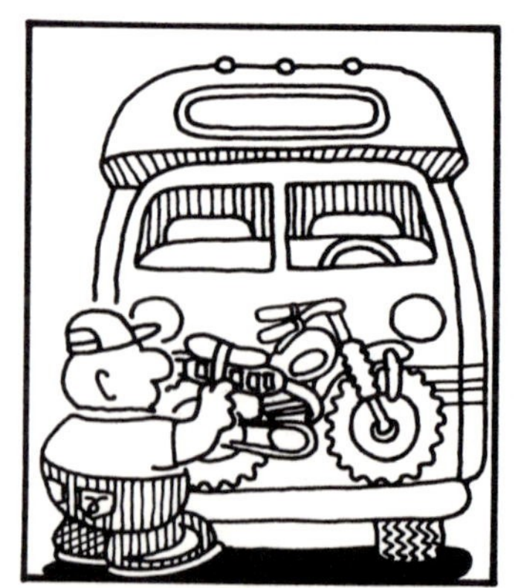
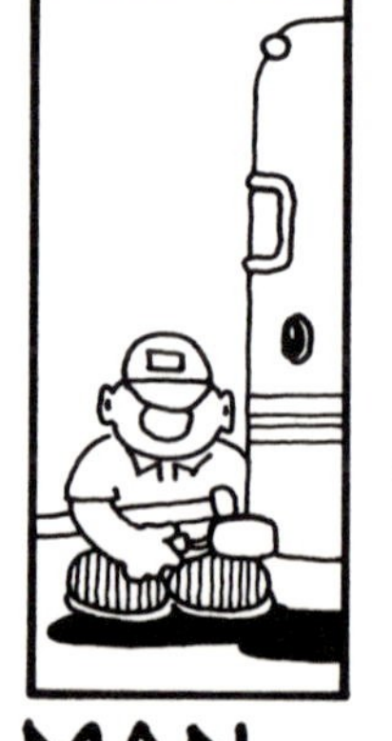
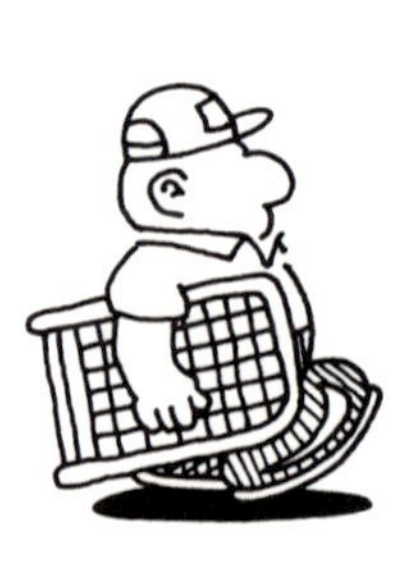
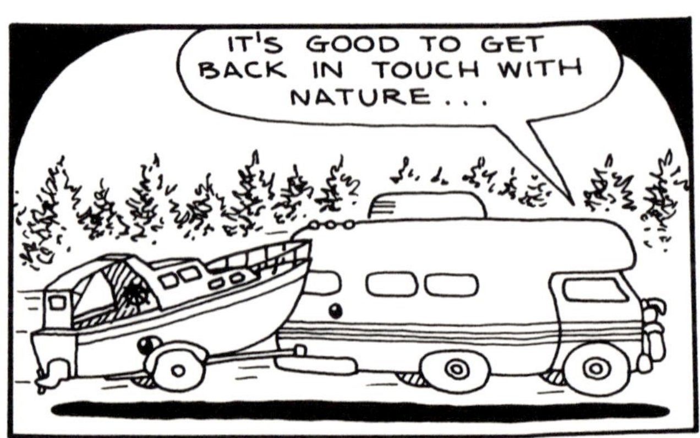
IT'S GOOD TO GET BACK IN TOUCH WITH NATURE...

MODERNE MAN

b. von alten 5-28-84

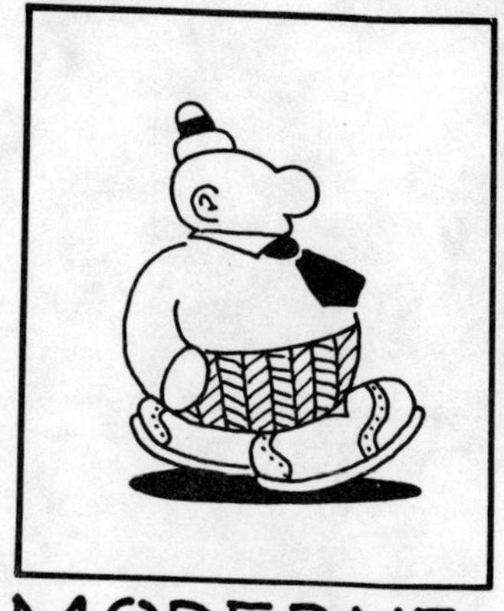

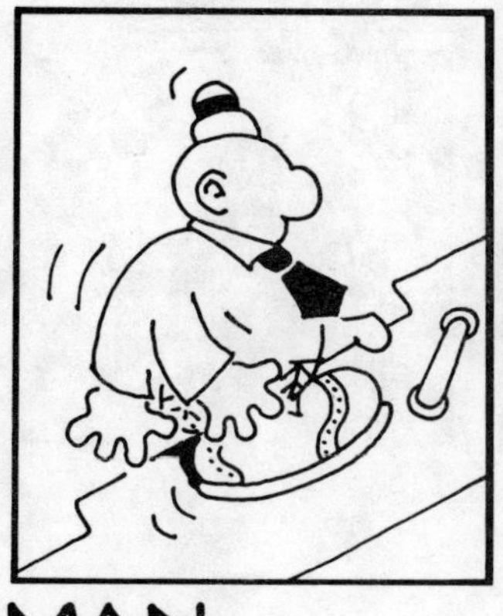

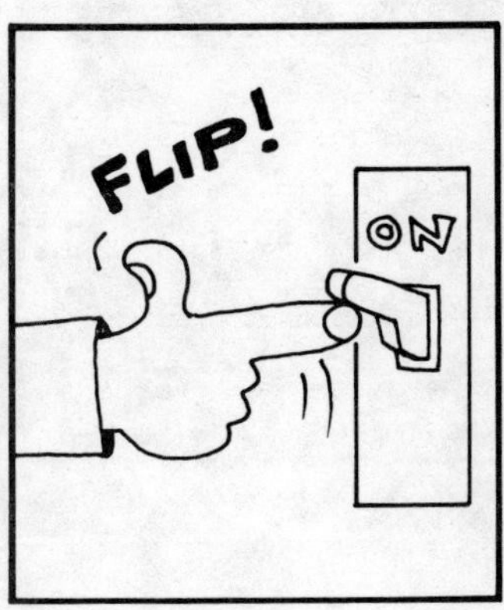

FLIP!
ON

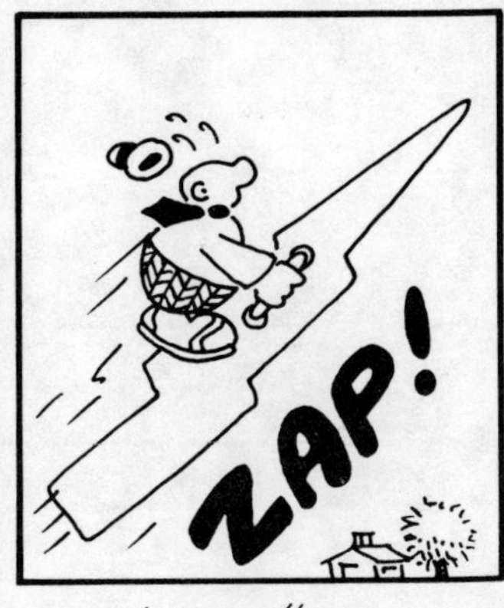

ZAP!

MODERNE MAN

b. von alten

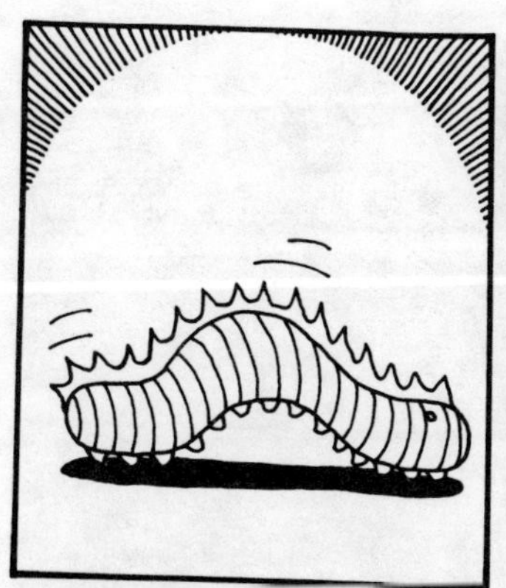

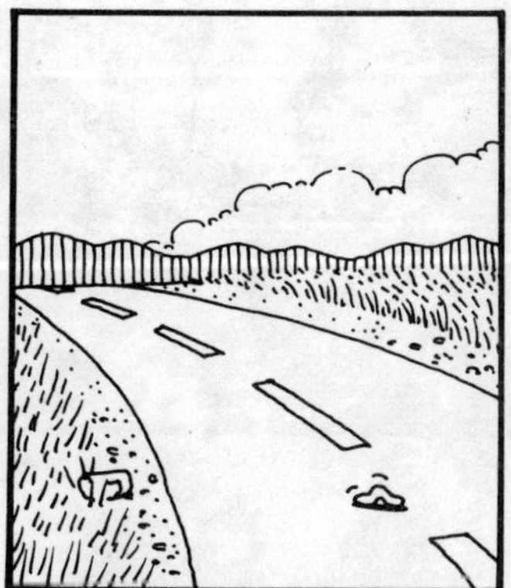

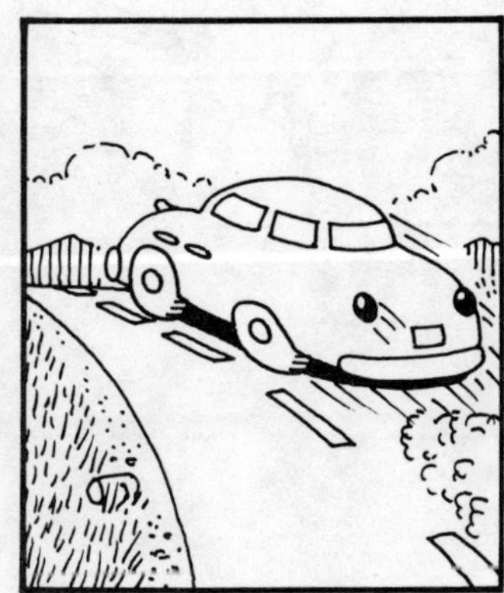

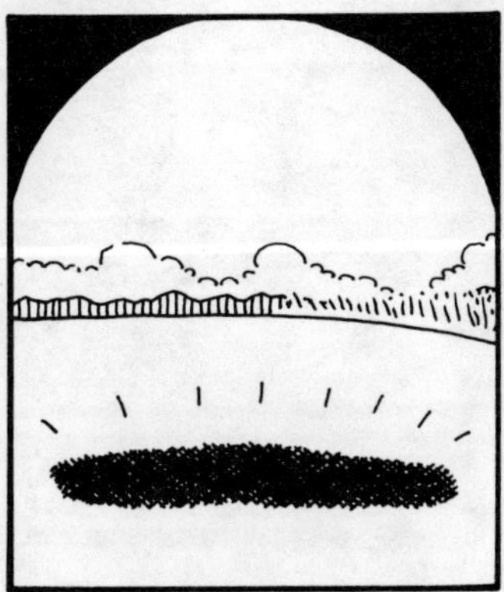

MODERNE MAN

b. von alten 6·4·84

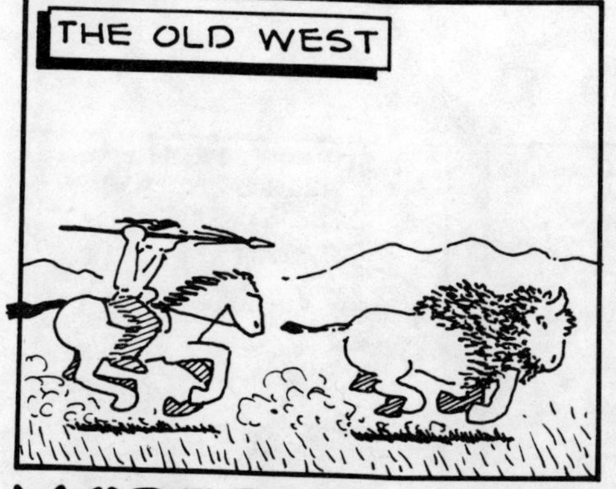

THE OLD WEST

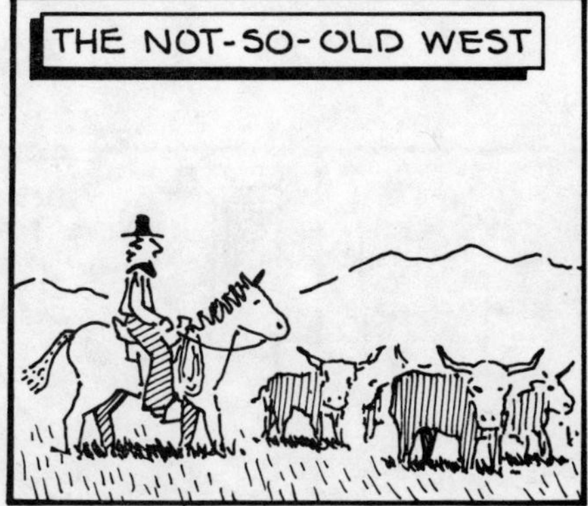

THE NOT-SO-OLD WEST

©b. von alten 1989

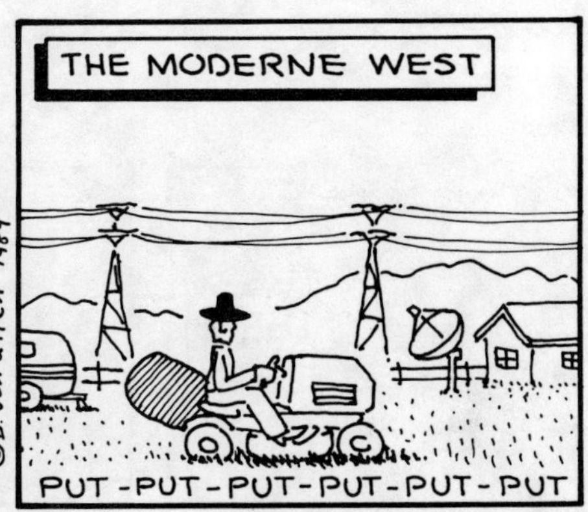

THE MODERNE WEST
PUT-PUT-PUT-PUT-PUT-PUT

MODERNE MAN

b. von alten 5-21-84

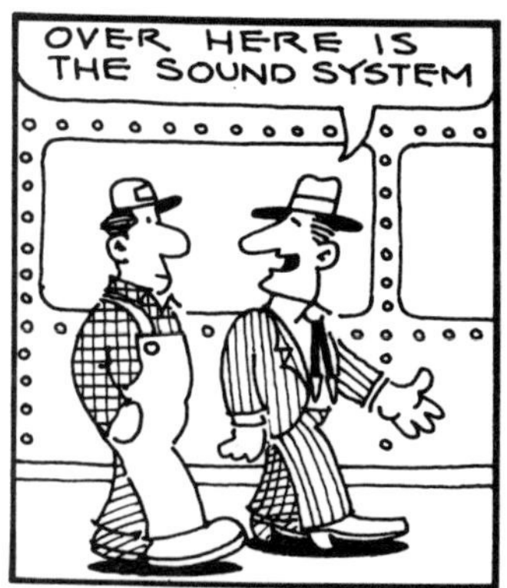
OVER HERE IS THE SOUND SYSTEM

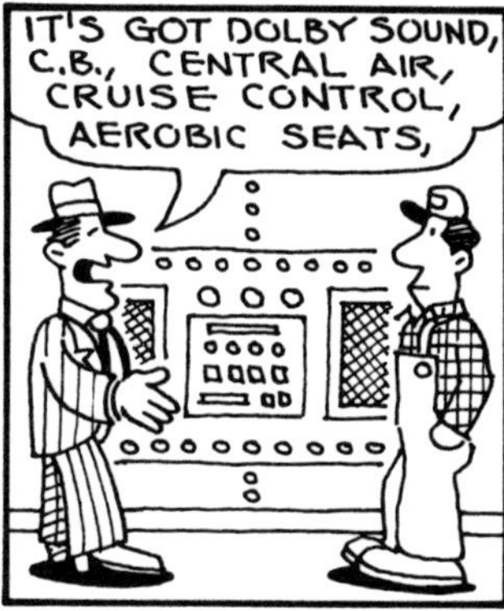
IT'S GOT DOLBY SOUND, C.B., CENTRAL AIR, CRUISE CONTROL, AEROBIC SEATS,

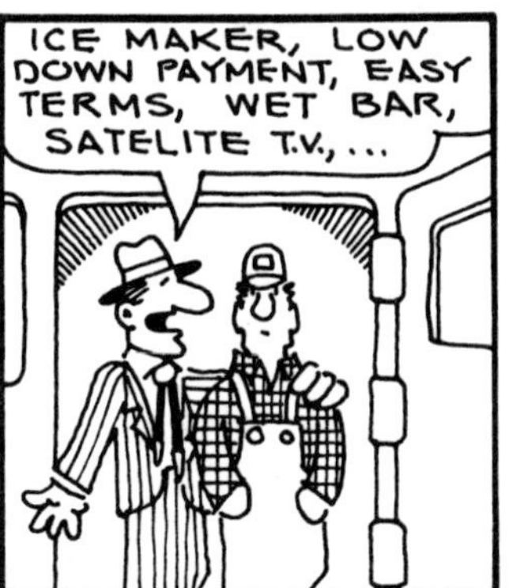
ICE MAKER, LOW DOWN PAYMENT, EASY TERMS, WET BAR, SATELITE T.V., ...

BOY, THEY SURE DON'T MAKE TRACTORS LIKE THEY USED TO...

MODERNE MAN

b. von alten

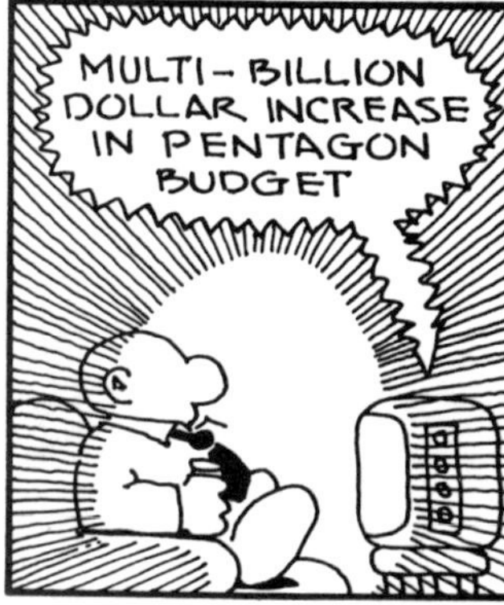
MULTI-BILLION DOLLAR INCREASE IN PENTAGON BUDGET

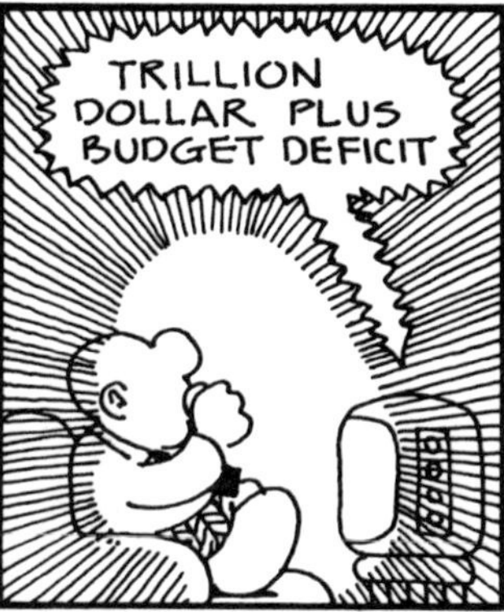
TRILLION DOLLAR PLUS BUDGET DEFICIT

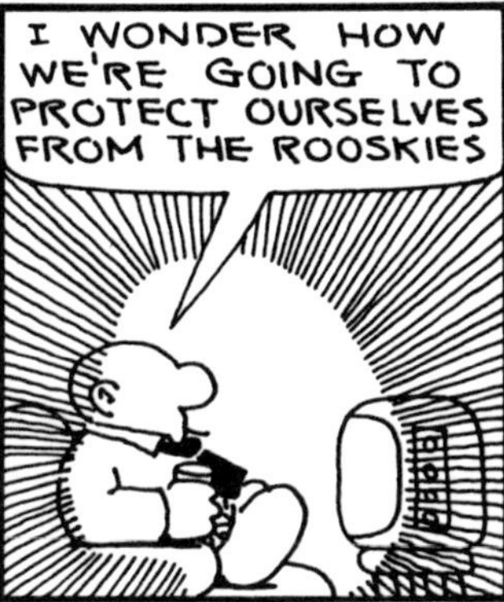
I WONDER HOW WE'RE GOING TO PROTECT OURSELVES FROM THE ROOSKIES

WHEN WE'RE BROKE?

MODERNE MAN

b. von alten · 84

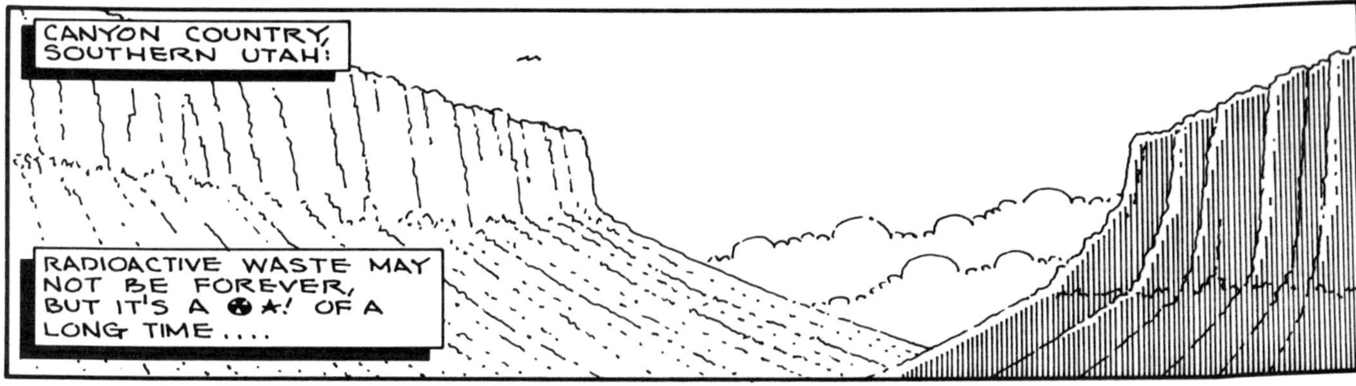
CANYON COUNTRY, SOUTHERN UTAH!
RADIOACTIVE WASTE MAY NOT BE FOREVER, BUT IT'S A ☢★! OF A LONG TIME....

MODERNE MAN

b. von alten 7-31-84

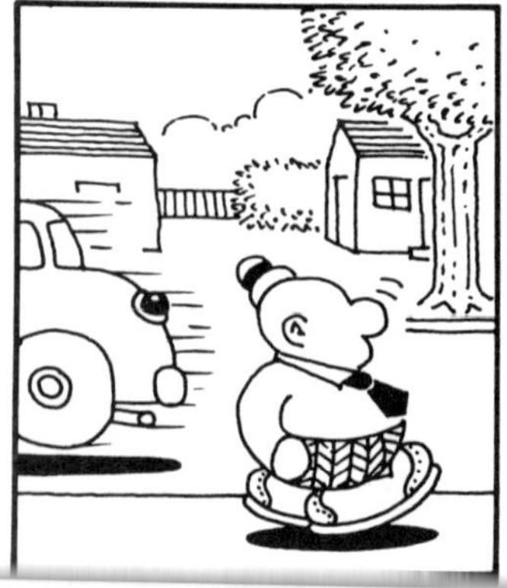

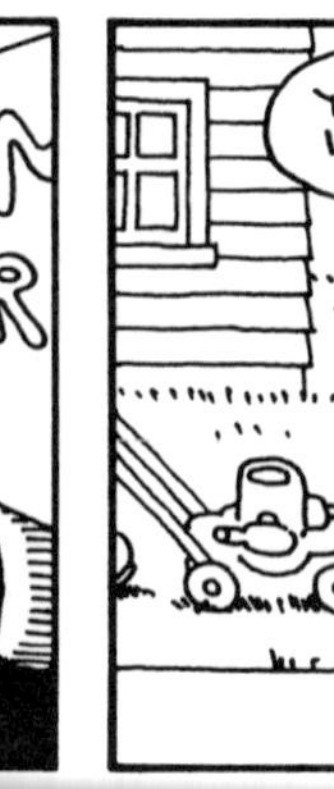
ACM
PR

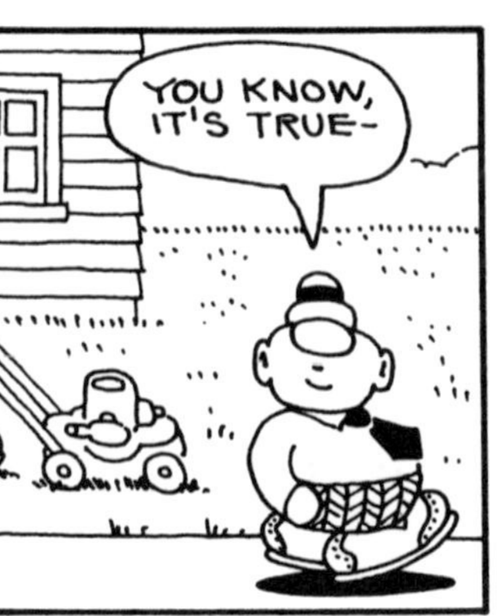
YOU KNOW, IT'S TRUE-

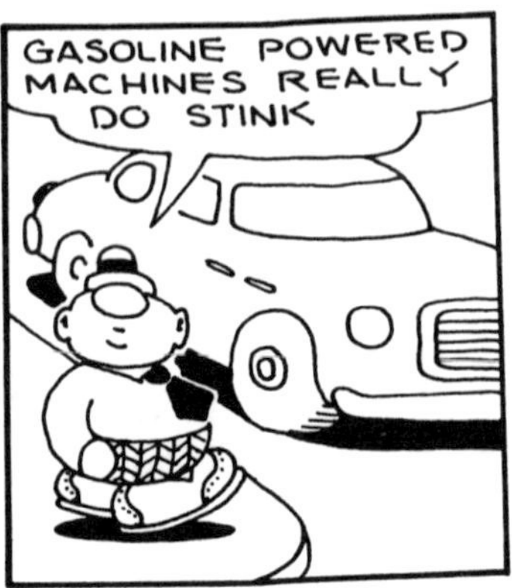
GASOLINE POWERED MACHINES REALLY DO STINK

MODERNE MAN

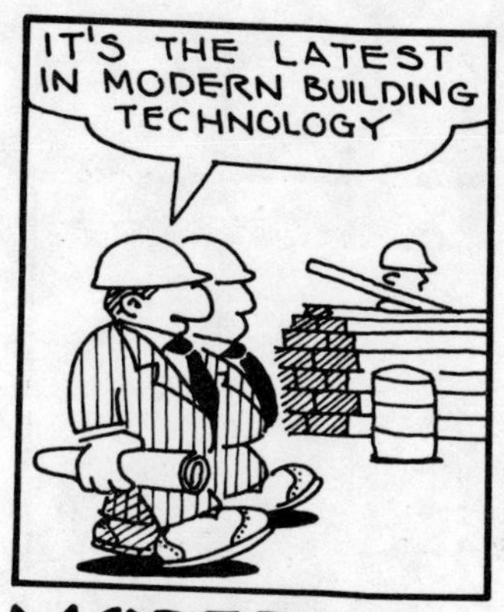
IT'S THE LATEST IN MODERN BUILDING TECHNOLOGY

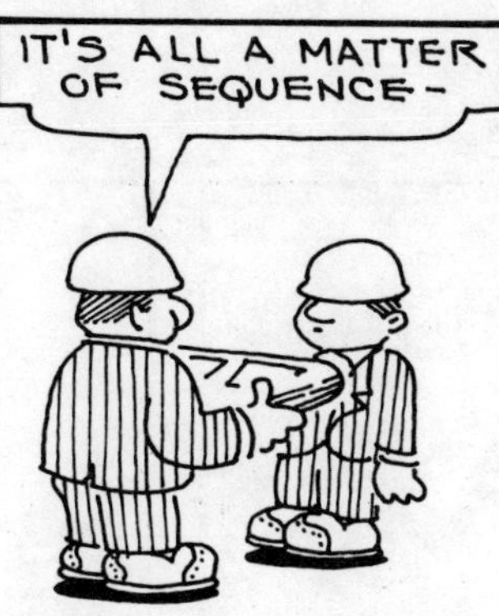
IT'S ALL A MATTER OF SEQUENCE-

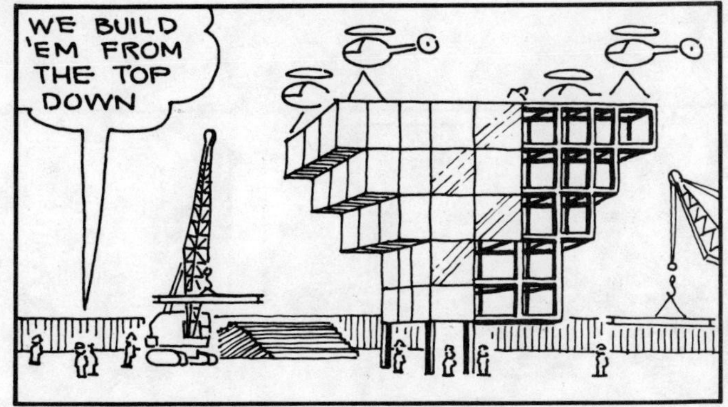
WE BUILD 'EM FROM THE TOP DOWN

MODERNE MAN

b. von alten

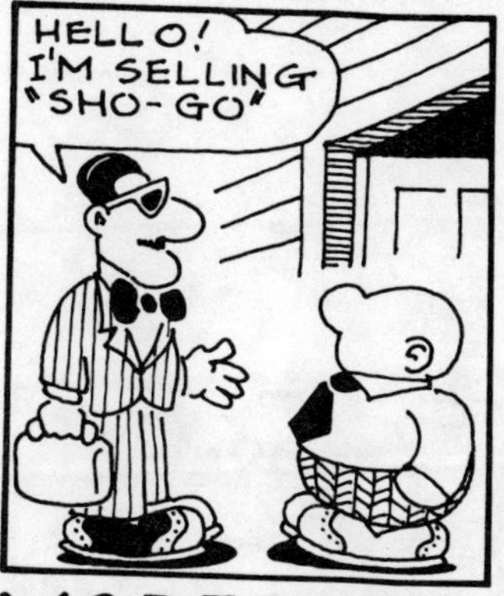
HELLO! I'M SELLING "SHO-GO"

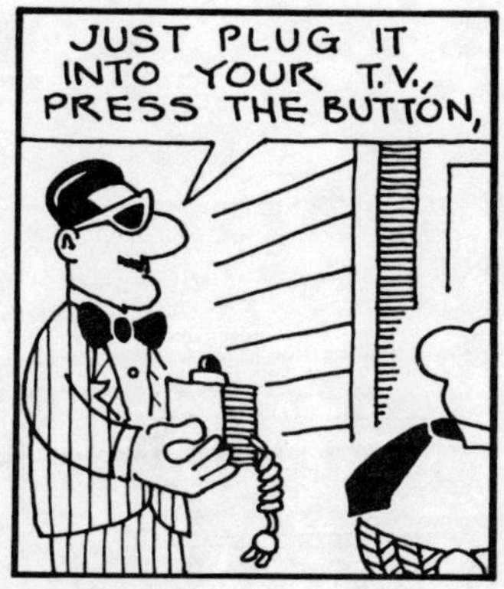
JUST PLUG IT INTO YOUR T.V., PRESS THE BUTTON,

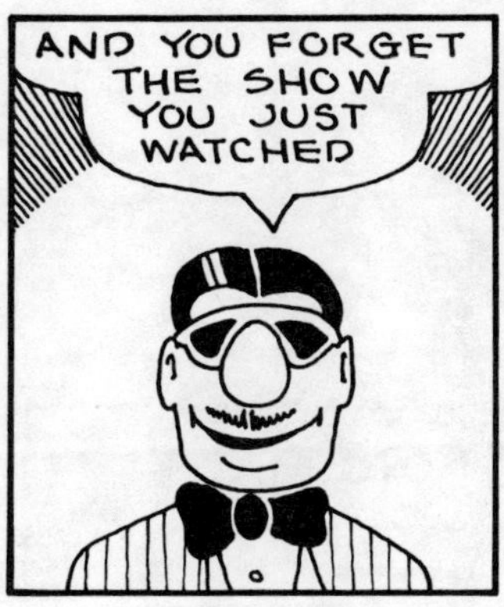
AND YOU FORGET THE SHOW YOU JUST WATCHED

GREAT! I'LL TAKE ONE!

MODERNE MAN

b. von alten

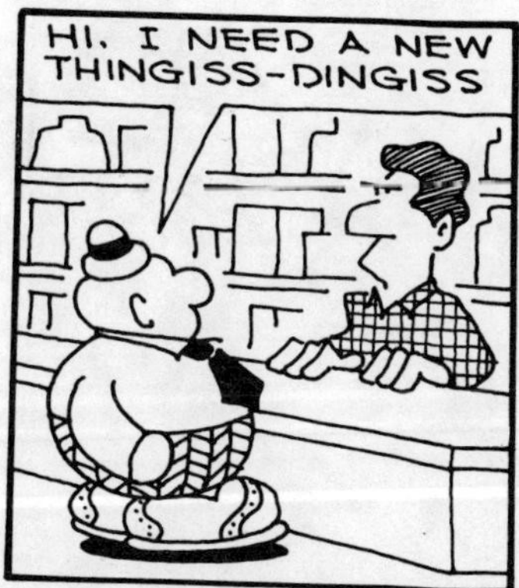
HI. I NEED A NEW THINGISS-DINGISS

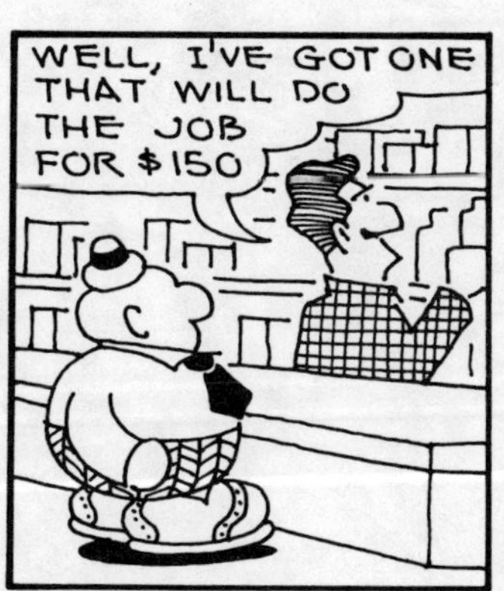
WELL, I'VE GOT ONE THAT WILL DO THE JOB FOR $150

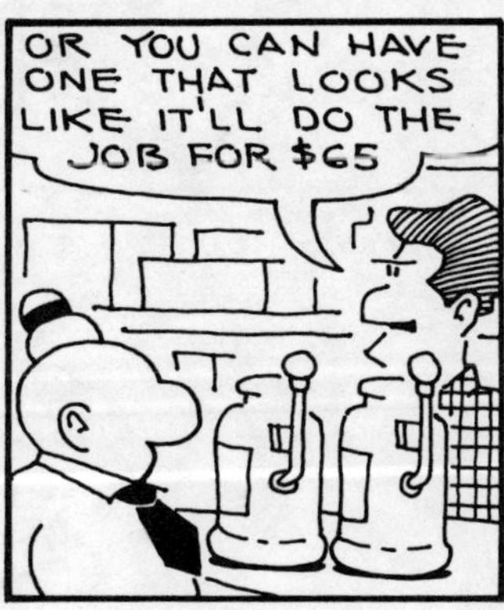
OR YOU CAN HAVE ONE THAT LOOKS LIKE IT'LL DO THE JOB FOR $65

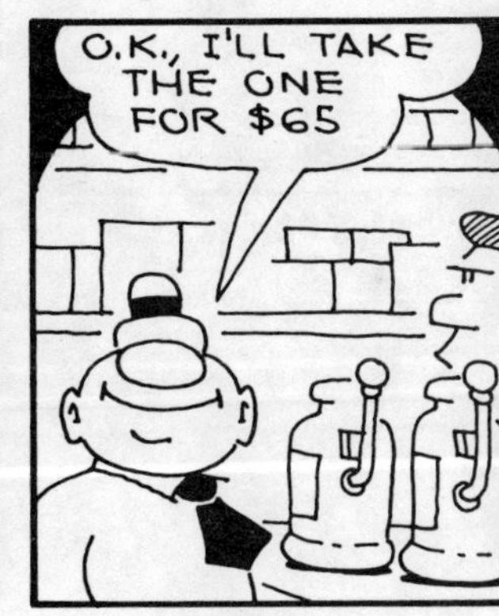
O.K., I'LL TAKE THE ONE FOR $65

MODERNE MAN

b. von alten

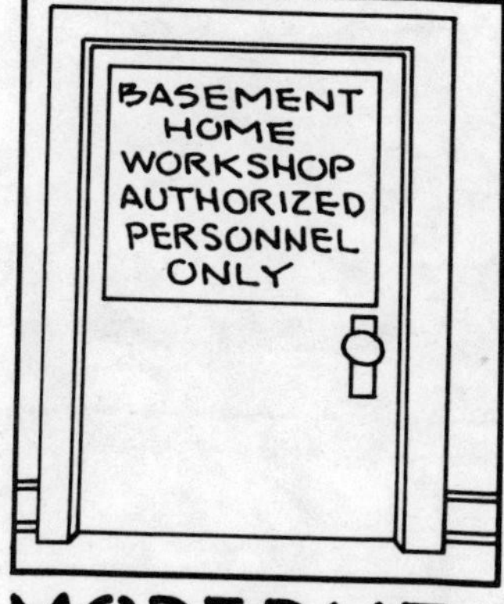
BASEMENT HOME WORKSHOP AUTHORIZED PERSONNEL ONLY

BANG! BANG! BANG! WHIRRR! WHIRRR! CLANK! CLANK! CLANK!

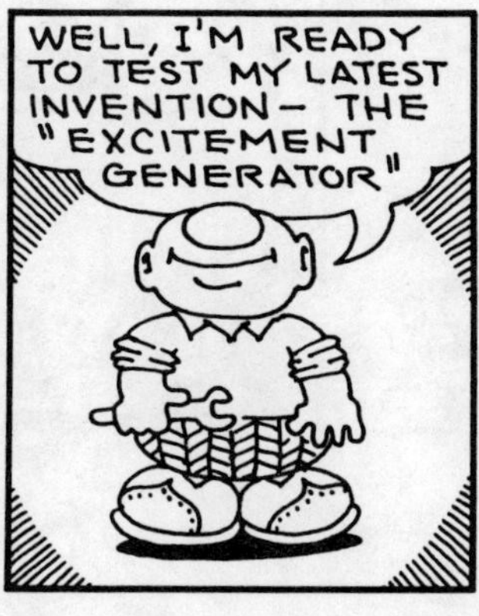
WELL, I'M READY TO TEST MY LATEST INVENTION— THE "EXCITEMENT GENERATOR"

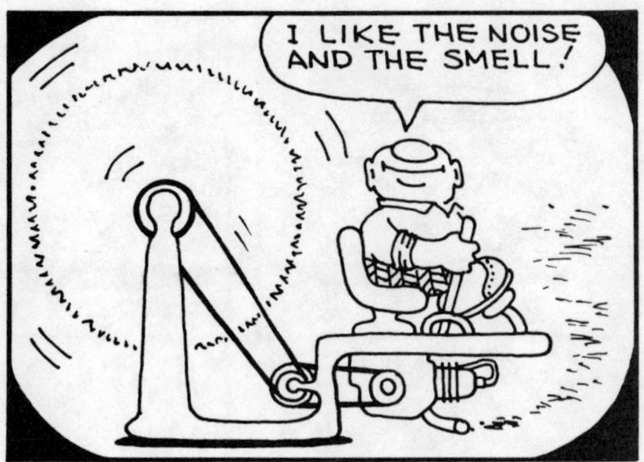
I LIKE THE NOISE AND THE SMELL!

MODERNE MAN

b. von alten

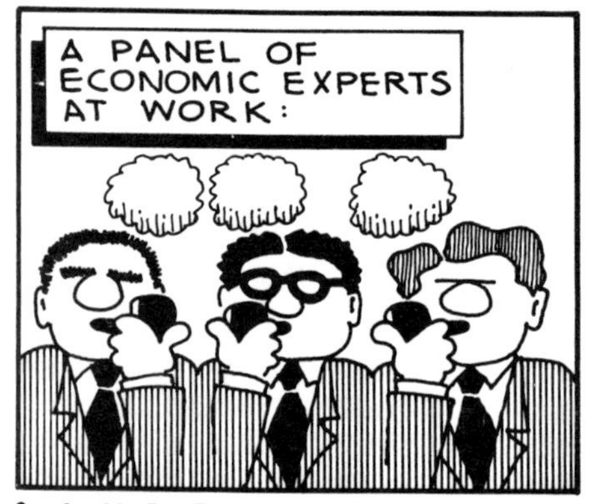
A PANEL OF ECONOMIC EXPERTS AT WORK:

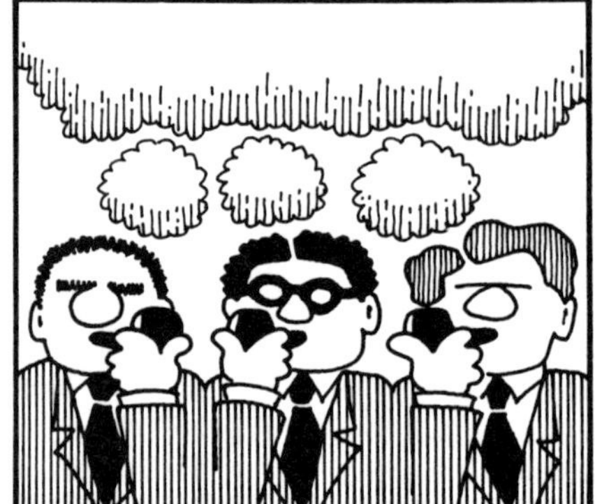

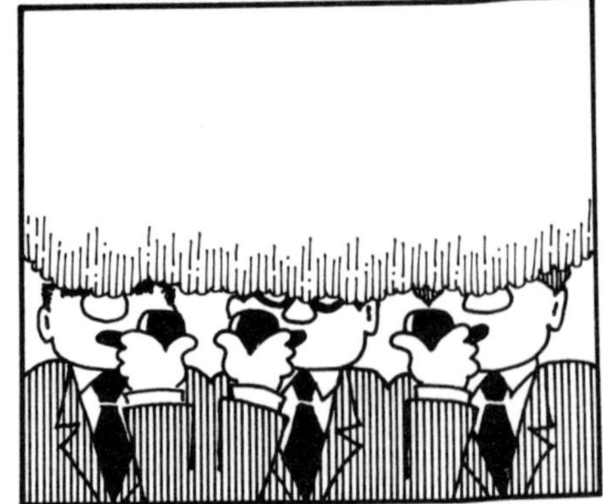

MODERNE MAN

b. von alten 7-10-84

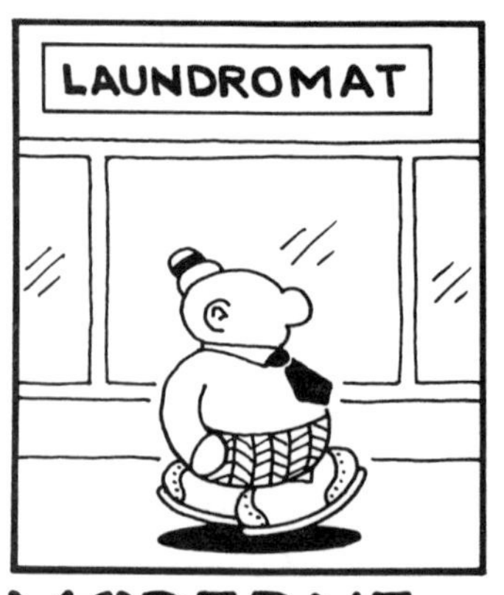
LAUNDROMAT

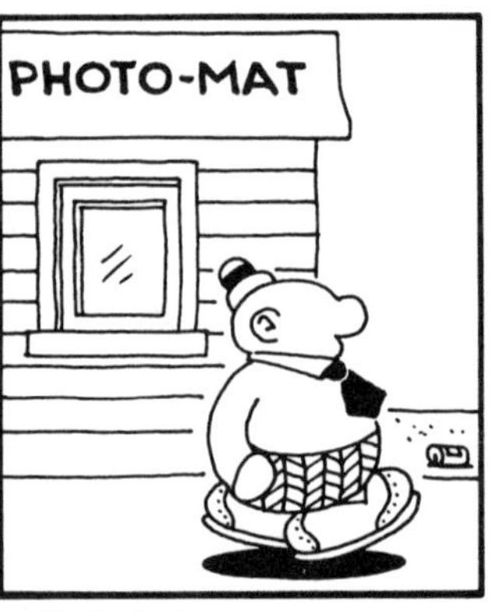
PHOTO-MAT

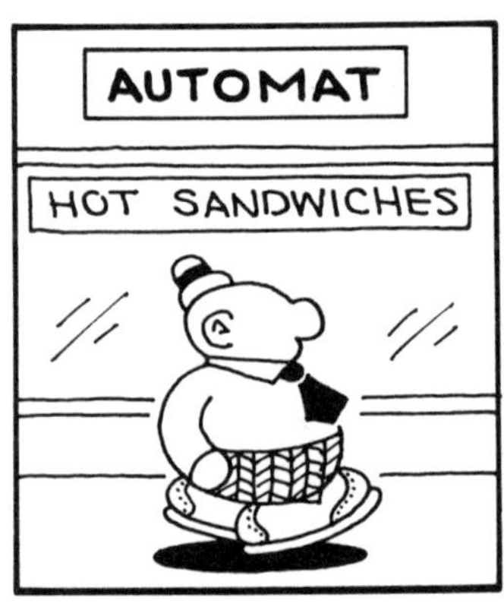
AUTOMAT
HOT SANDWICHES

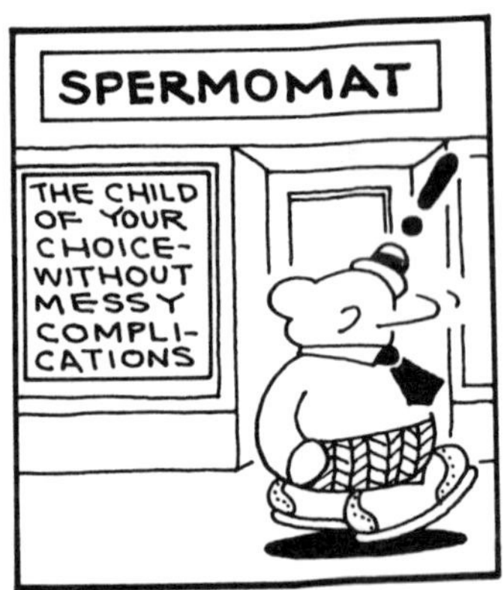
SPERMOMAT
THE CHILD OF YOUR CHOICE-WITHOUT MESSY COMPLI-CATIONS
!

MODERNE MAN

b. von alten

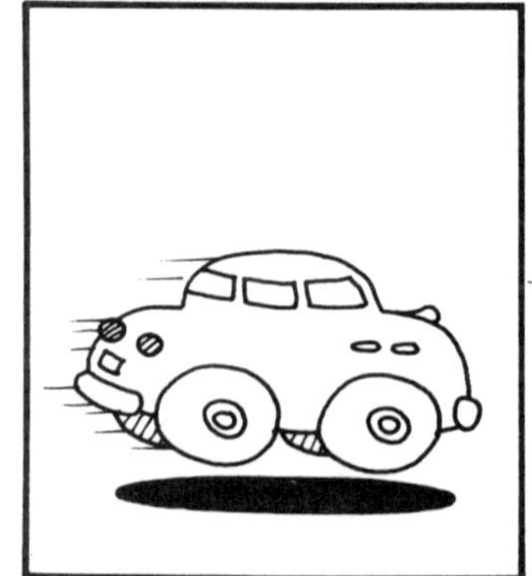

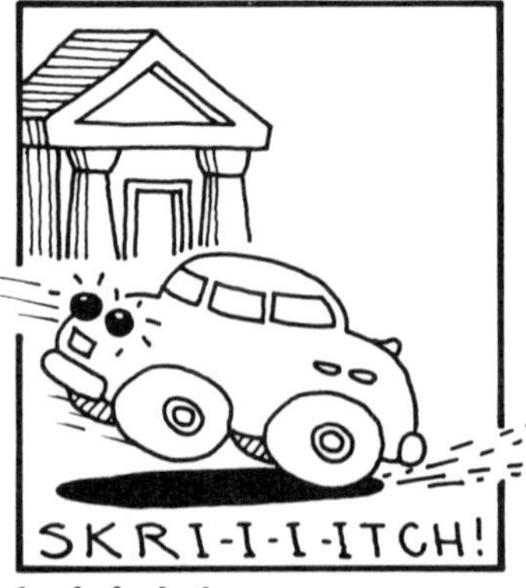
SKRI-I-I-ITCH!

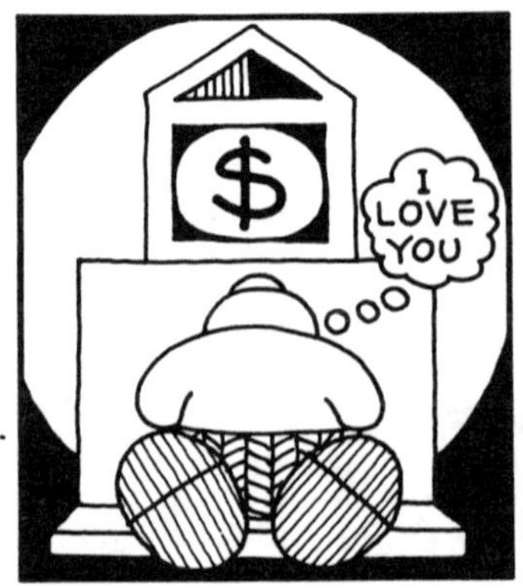
$
I LOVE YOU

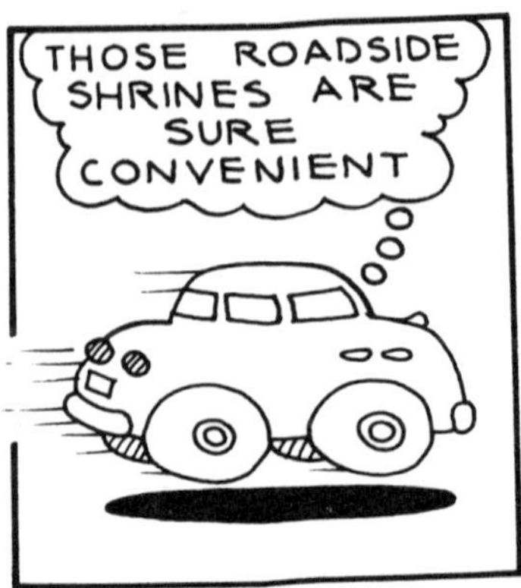
THOSE ROADSIDE SHRINES ARE SURE CONVENIENT

MODERNE MAN

b. von alten 7-10-84

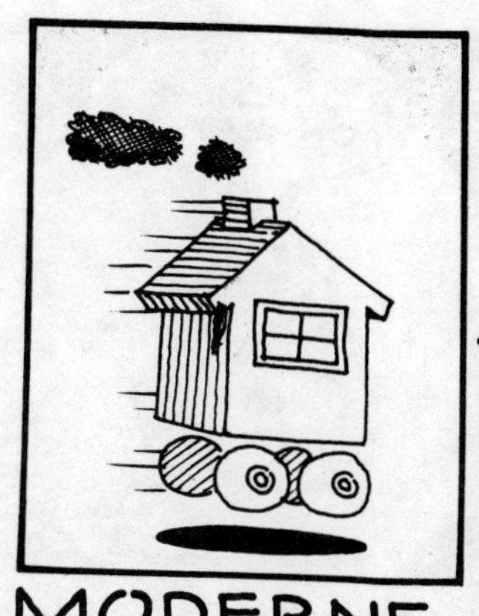

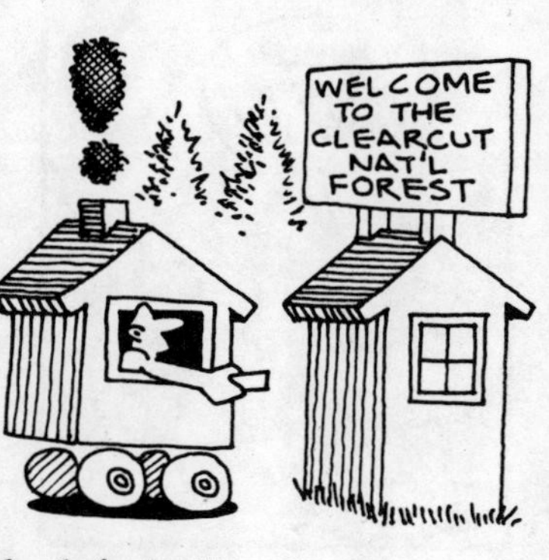
WELCOME TO THE CLEARCUT NAT'L FOREST

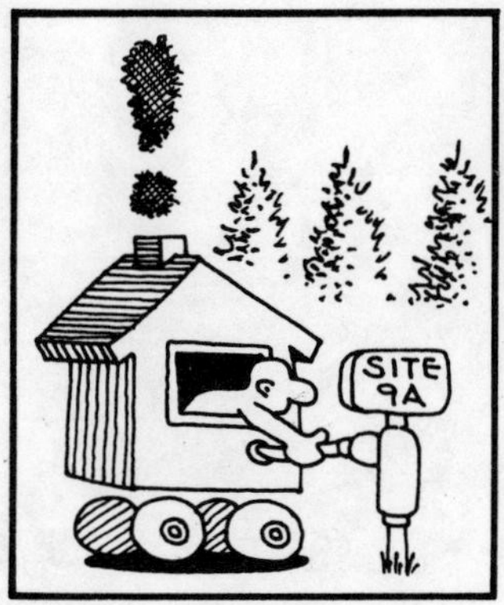
SITE 9A

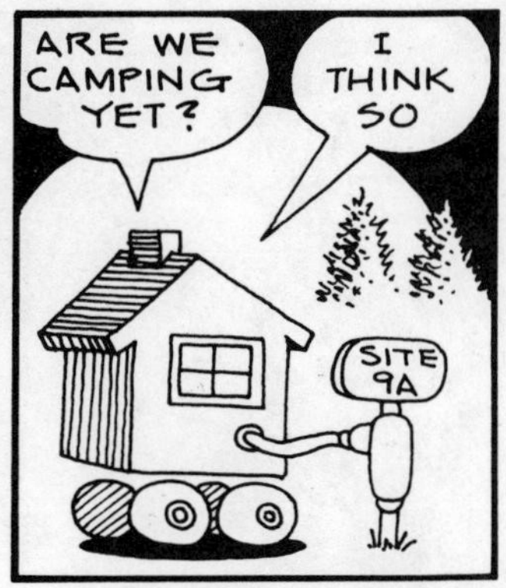
ARE WE CAMPING YET?
I THINK SO
SITE 9A

MODERNE MAN

b. von alten 7·20·84

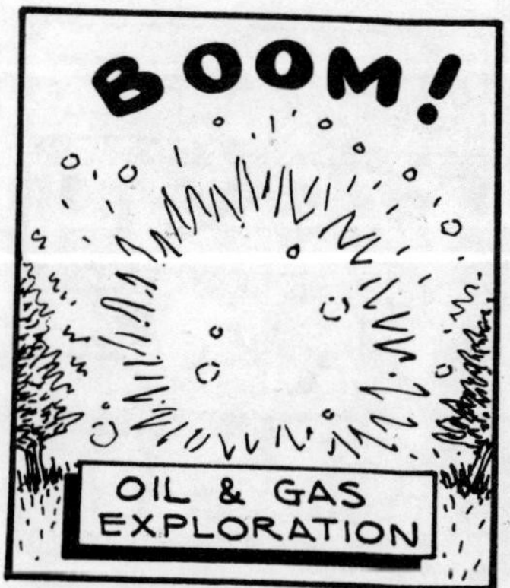
BOOM!
OIL & GAS EXPLORATION

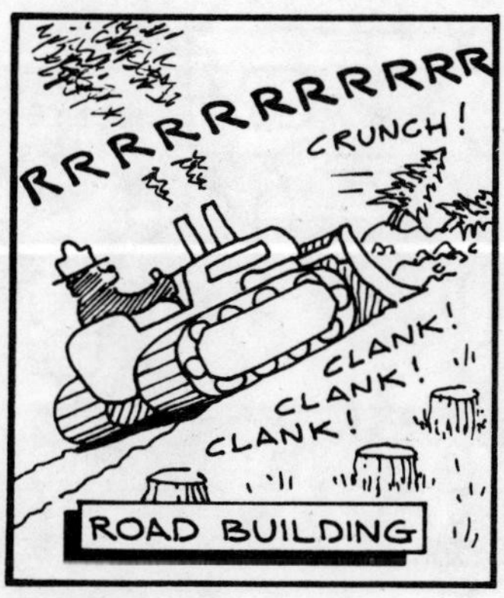
RRRRRRRRRRRRR
CRUNCH!
CLANK!
CLANK!
CLANK!
ROAD BUILDING

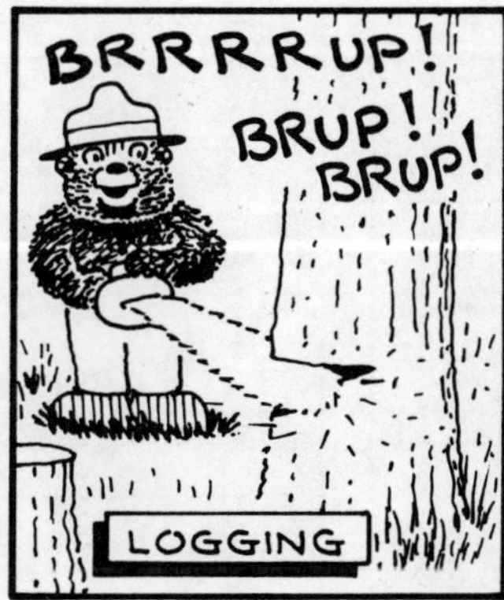
BRRRRRUP!
BRUP!
BRUP!
LOGGING

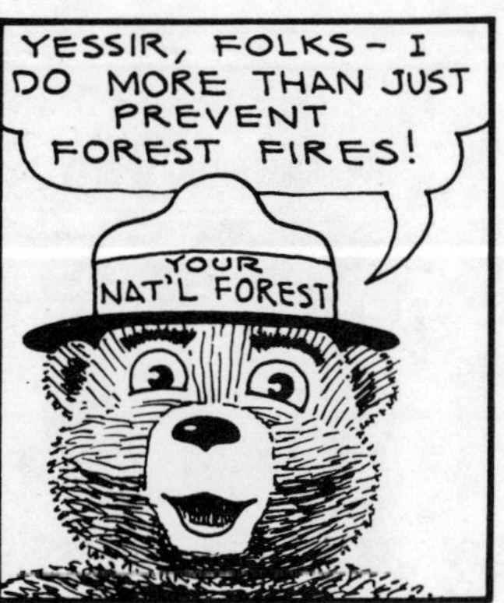
YESSIR, FOLKS - I DO MORE THAN JUST PREVENT FOREST FIRES!
YOUR NAT'L FOREST

MODERNE MAN

b. von alten 7·2·84

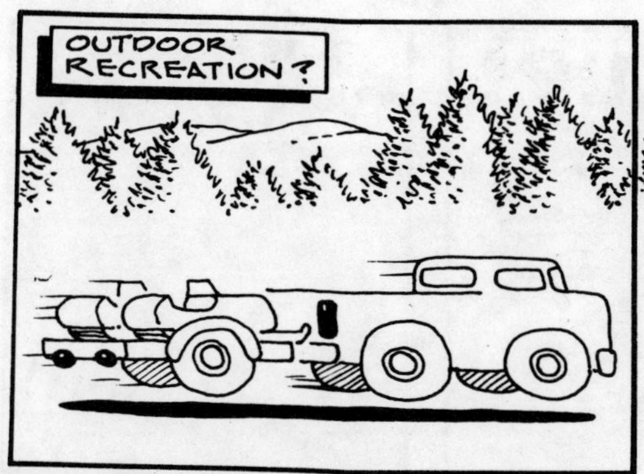
OUTDOOR RECREATION?

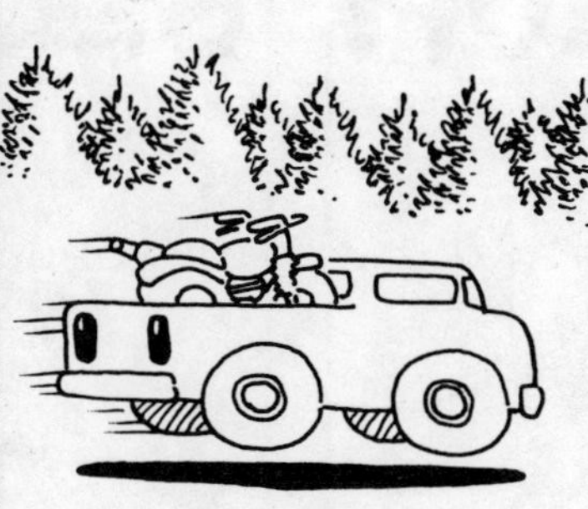

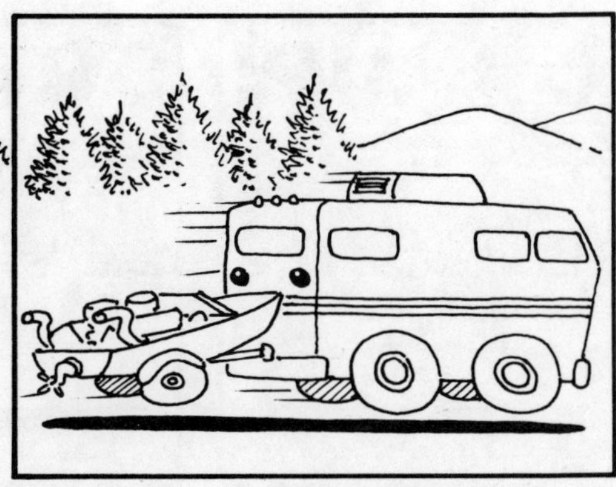

MODERNE MAN

b. von alten

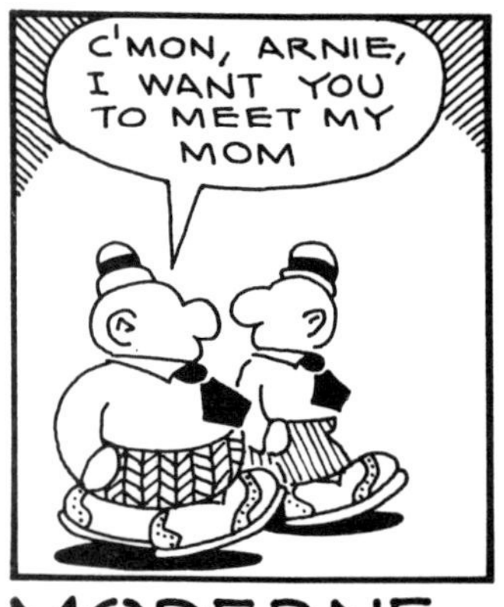
C'MON, ARNIE, I WANT YOU TO MEET MY MOM
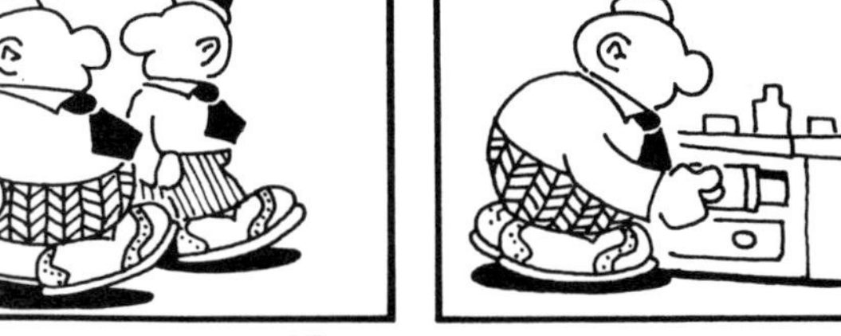
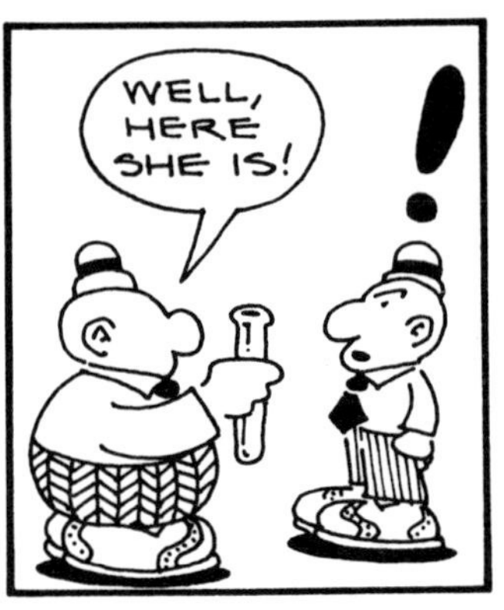
WELL, HERE SHE IS!
!
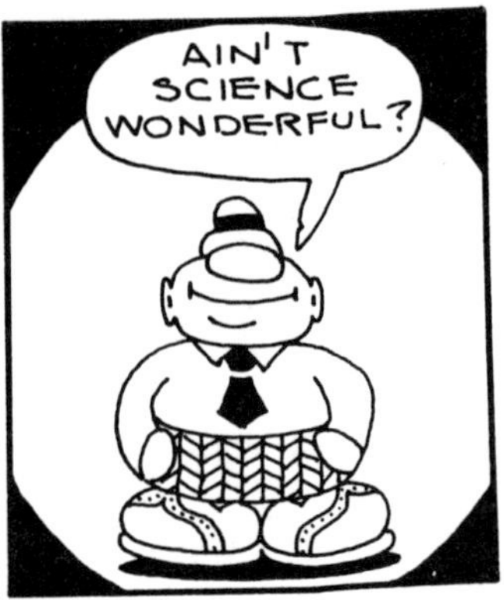
AIN'T SCIENCE WONDERFUL?

MODERNE MAN

b. von alten 7.20.84

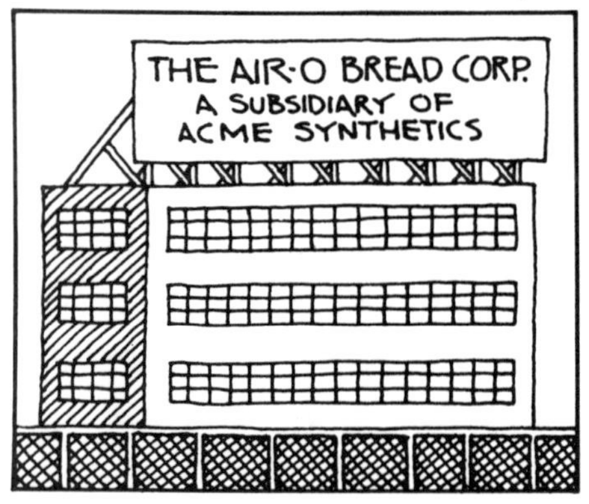
THE AIR-O BREAD CORP.
A SUBSIDIARY OF
ACME SYNTHETICS
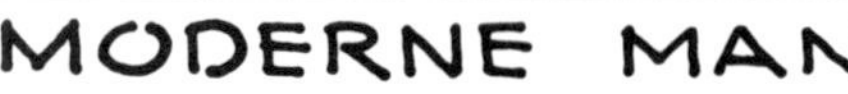
MODERNE MAN
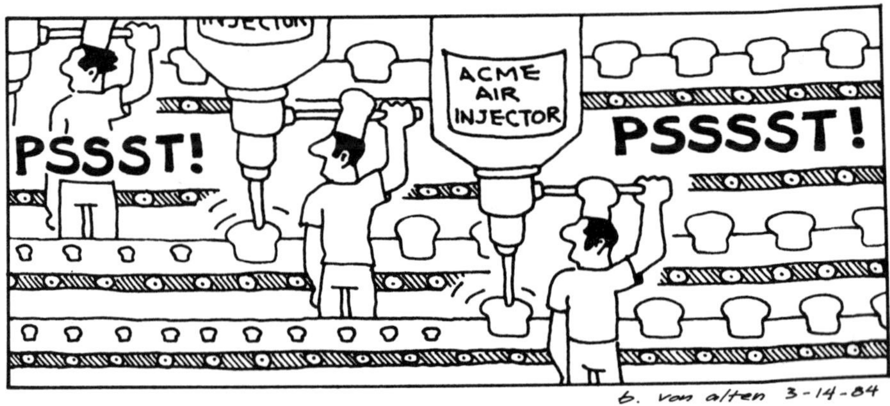
PSSST!
ACME AIR INJECTOR
PSSSST!

b. von alten 3-14-84

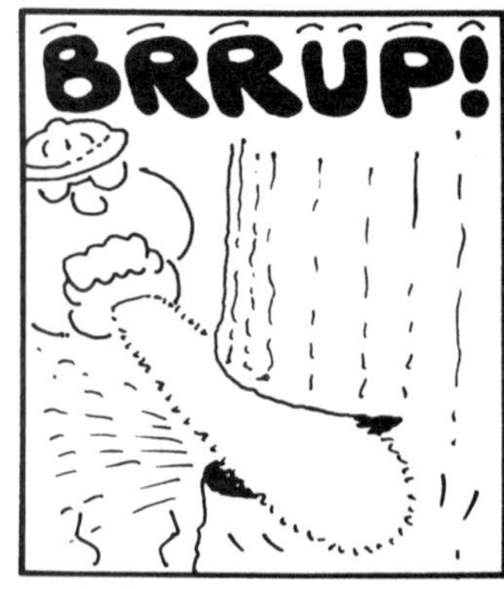
BRRUP!
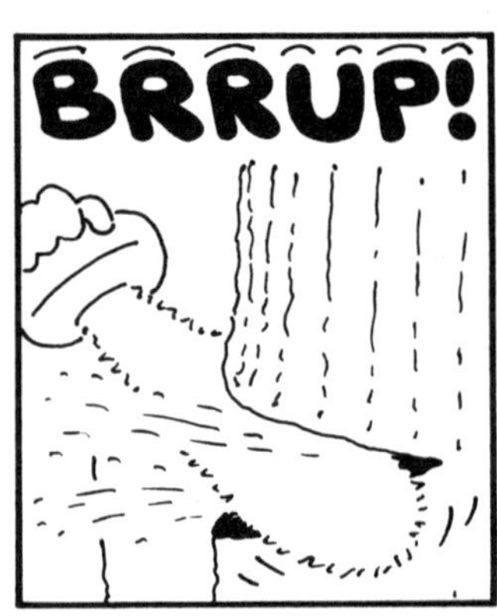
BRRUP!
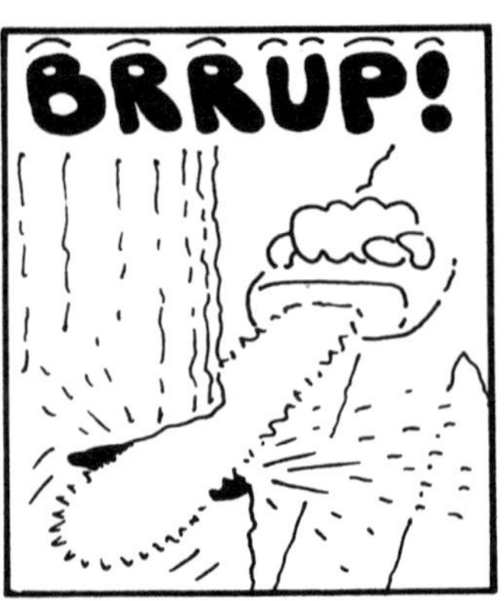
BRRUP!
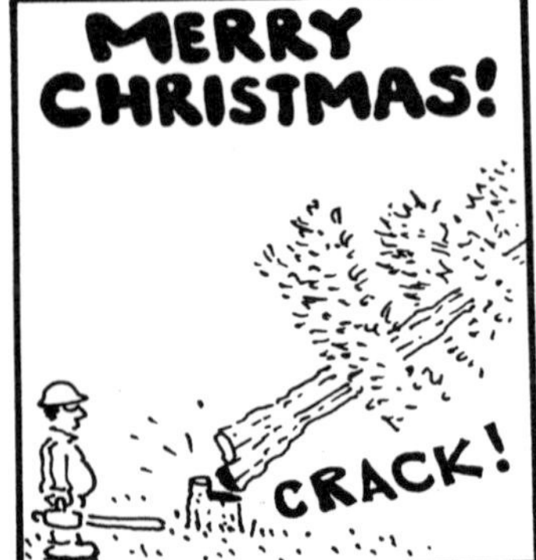
MERRY CHRISTMAS!
CRACK!

MODERNE MAN

b. von alten

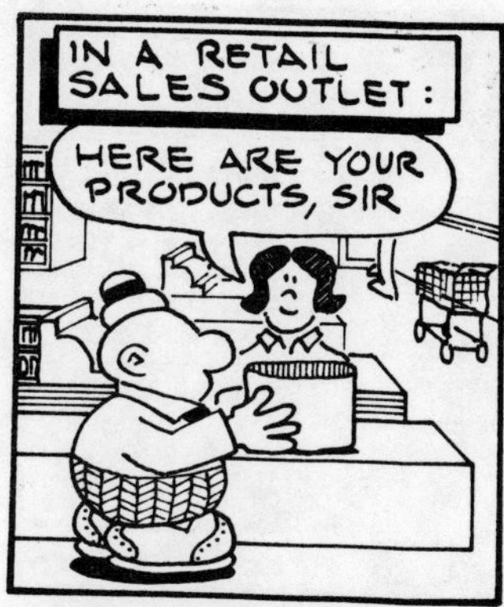
IN A RETAIL SALES OUTLET:
HERE ARE YOUR PRODUCTS, SIR

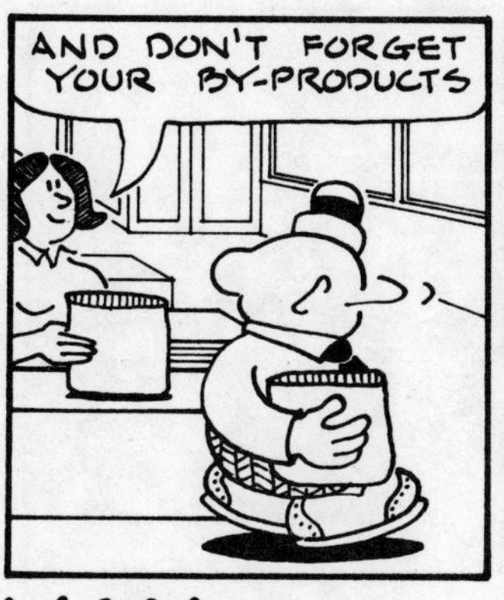
AND DON'T FORGET YOUR BY-PRODUCTS

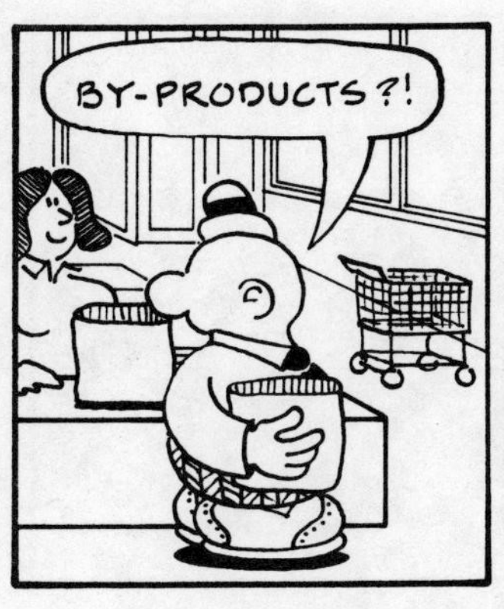
BY-PRODUCTS?!

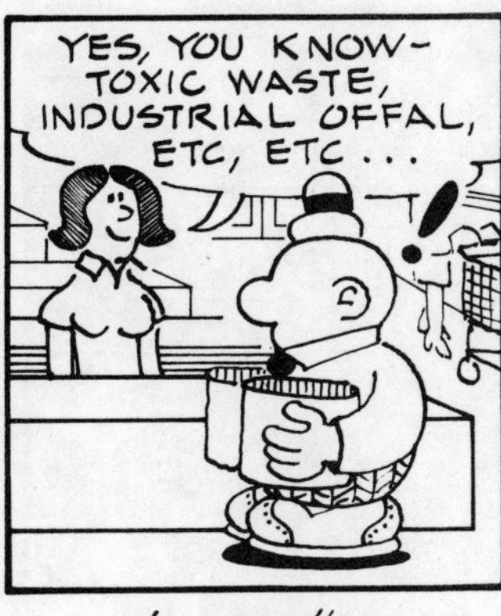
YES, YOU KNOW- TOXIC WASTE, INDUSTRIAL OFFAL, ETC, ETC...
!

MODERNE MAN

b. von alten

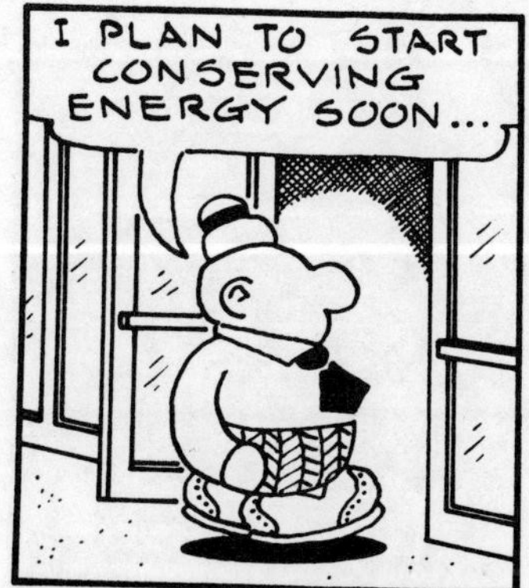
I PLAN TO START CONSERVING ENERGY SOON...

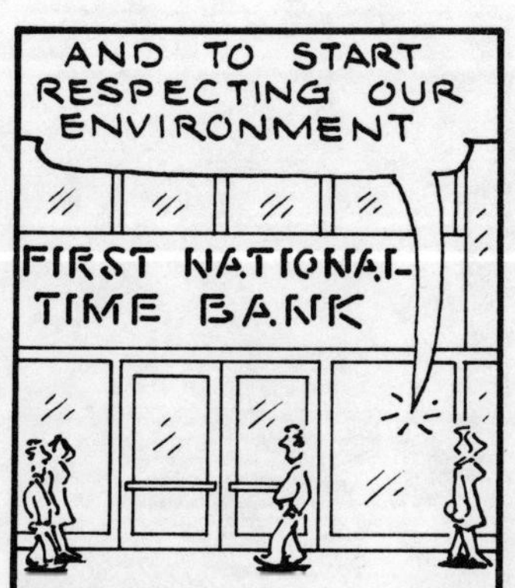
AND TO START RESPECTING OUR ENVIRONMENT
FIRST NATIONAL TIME BANK

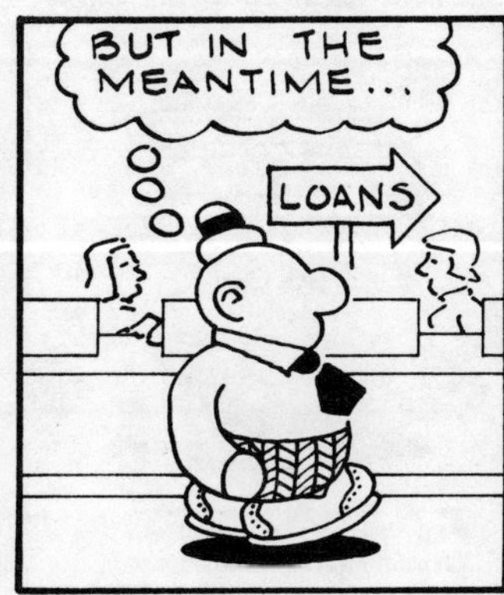
BUT IN THE MEANTIME...
LOANS

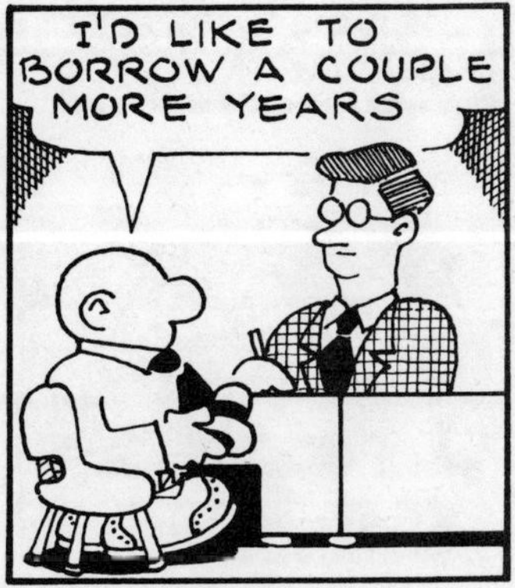
I'D LIKE TO BORROW A COUPLE MORE YEARS

MODERNE MAN

b. von alten

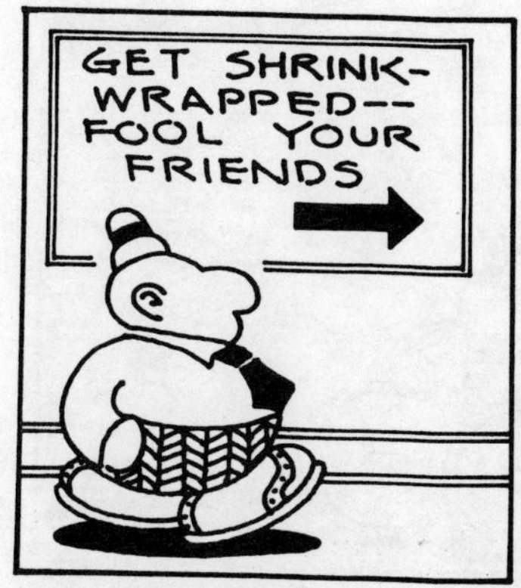
GET SHRINK-WRAPPED-- FOOL YOUR FRIENDS

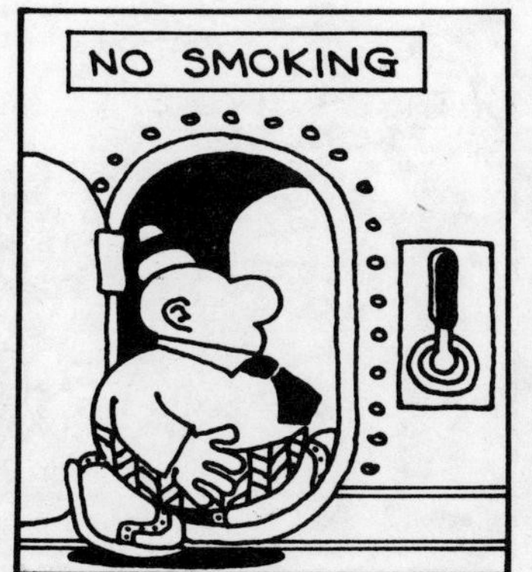
NO SMOKING

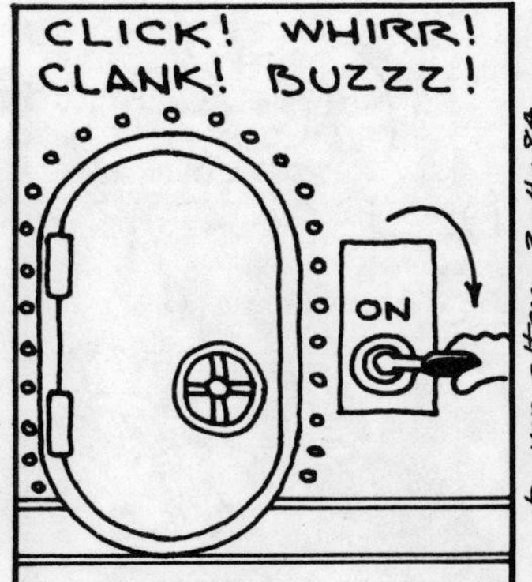
CLICK! WHIRR! CLANK! BUZZZ!
ON

b. von alten 3-4-84

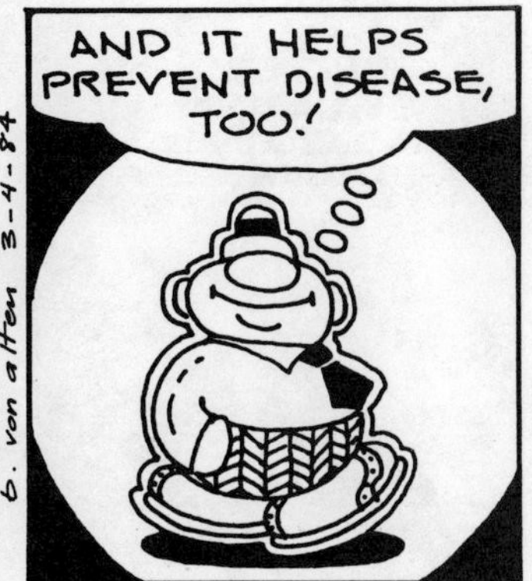
AND IT HELPS PREVENT DISEASE, TOO!

MODERNE MAN

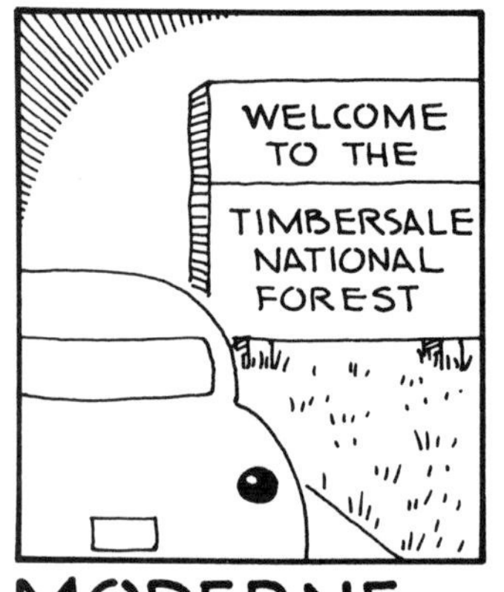
WELCOME TO THE
TIMBERSALE NATIONAL FOREST

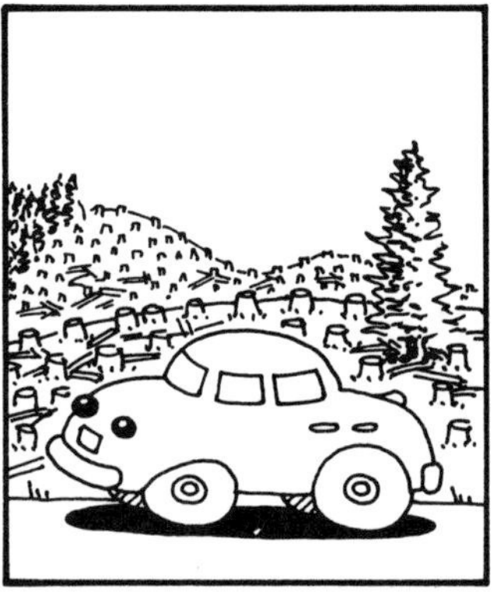

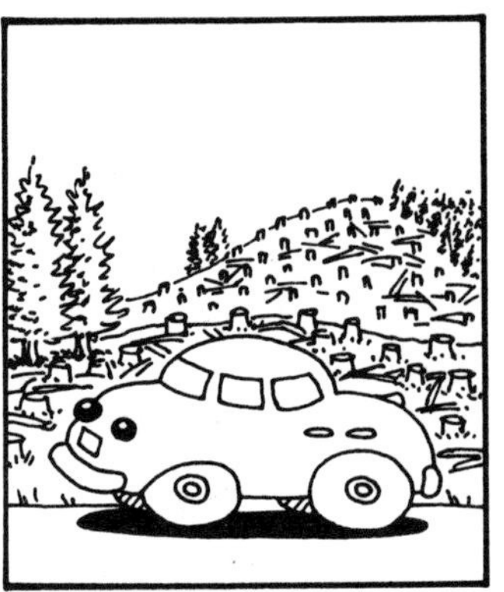

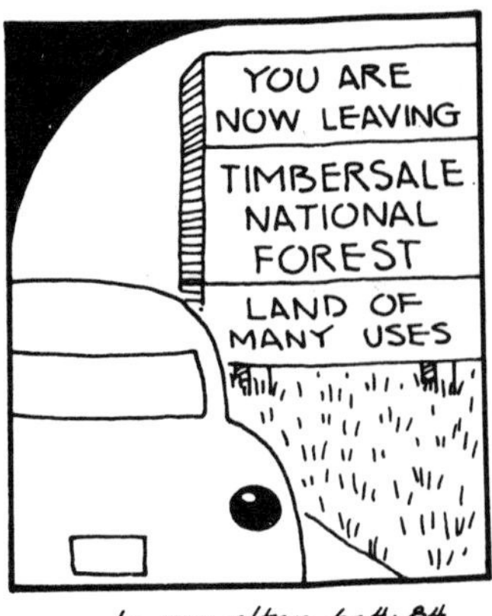
YOU ARE NOW LEAVING
TIMBERSALE NATIONAL FOREST
LAND OF MANY USES

MODERNE MAN

b. von alten 6-4-84

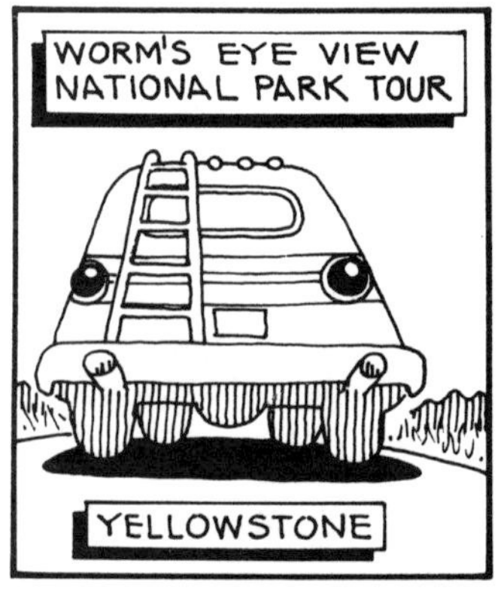
WORM'S EYE VIEW NATIONAL PARK TOUR
YELLOWSTONE

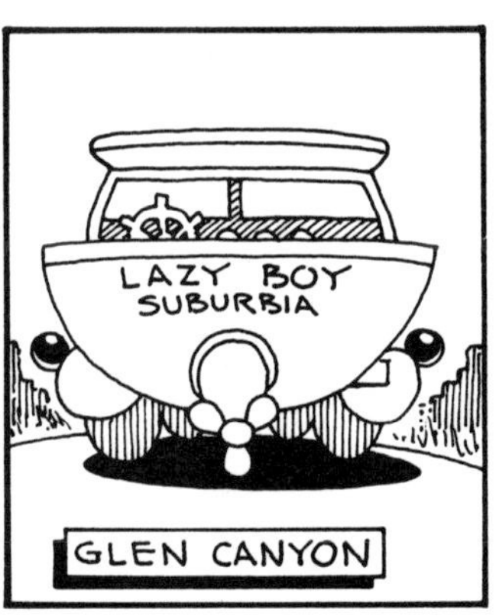
LAZY BOY SUBURBIA
GLEN CANYON

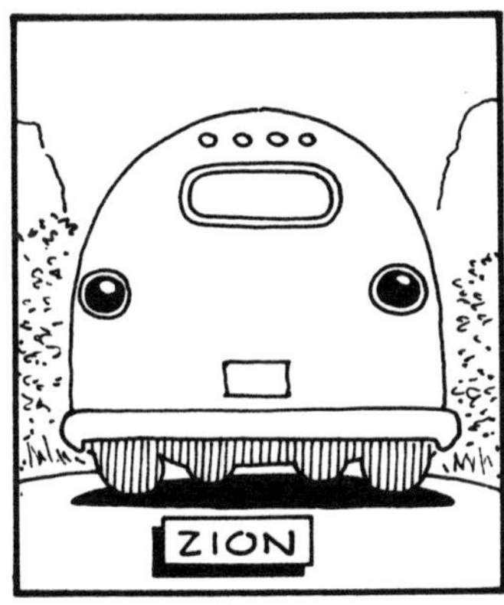
ZION

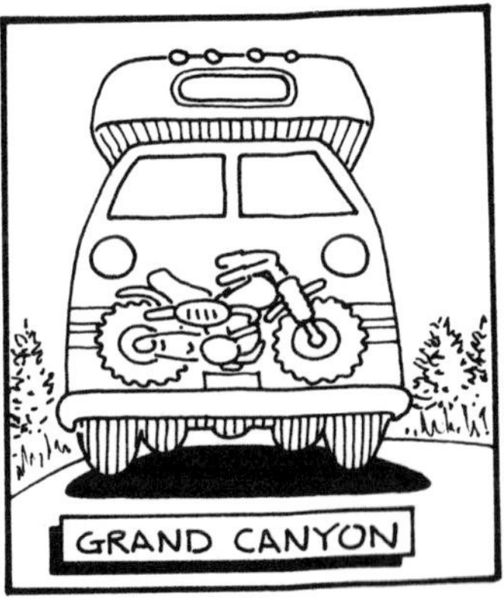
GRAND CANYON

MODERNE MAN

b. von alten 6-21-84

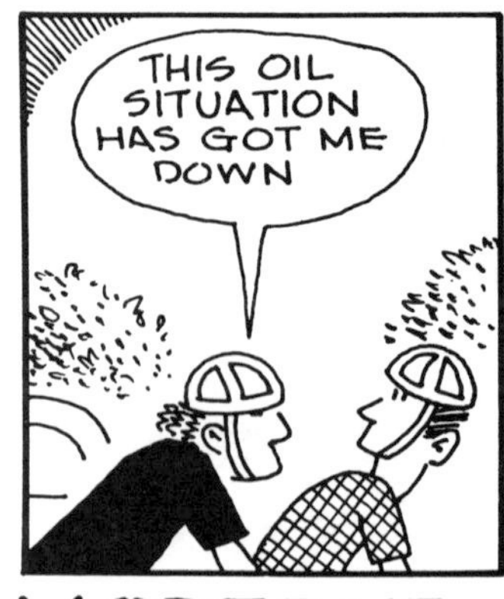
THIS OIL SITUATION HAS GOT ME DOWN

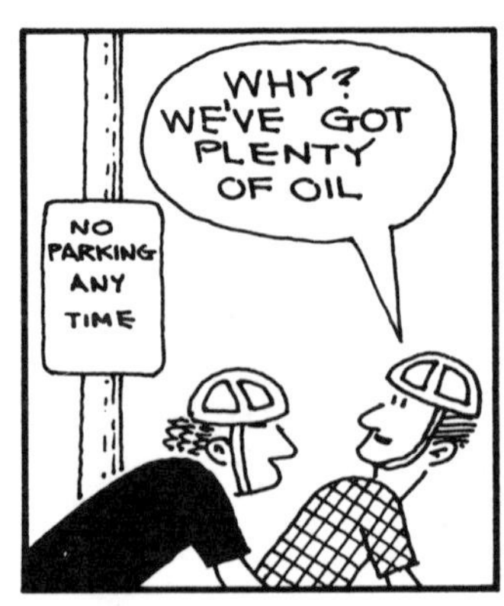
NO PARKING ANY TIME
WHY? WE'VE GOT PLENTY OF OIL

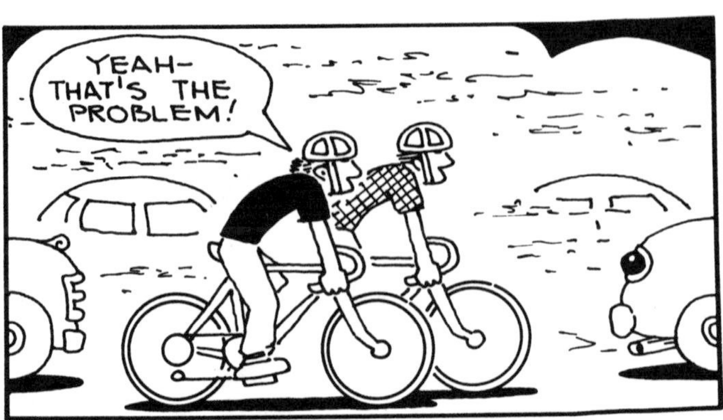
YEAH- THAT'S THE PROBLEM!

MODERNE MAN

b. von alten 7-30-84

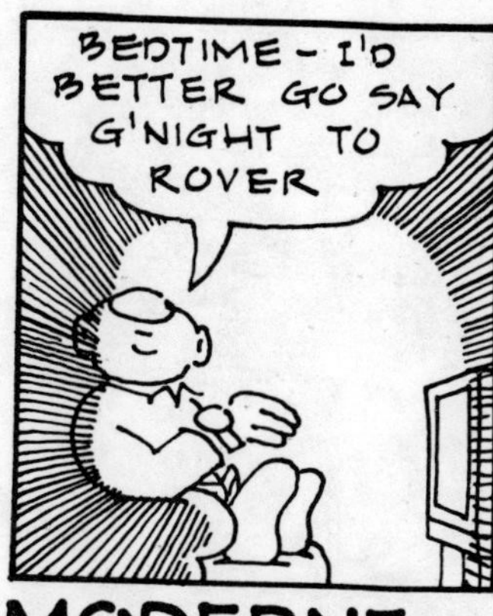
BEDTIME - I'D BETTER GO SAY G'NIGHT TO ROVER
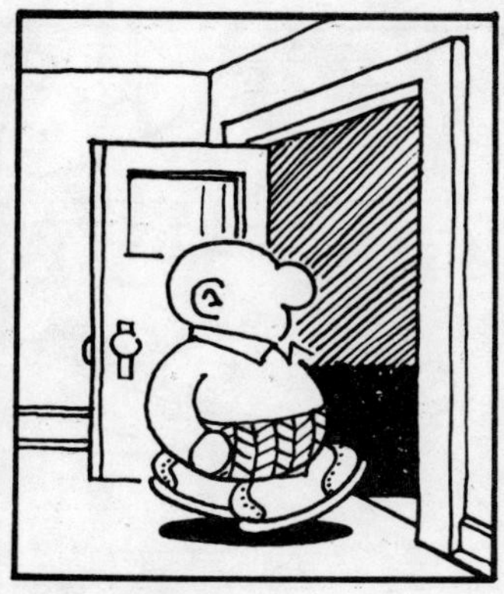
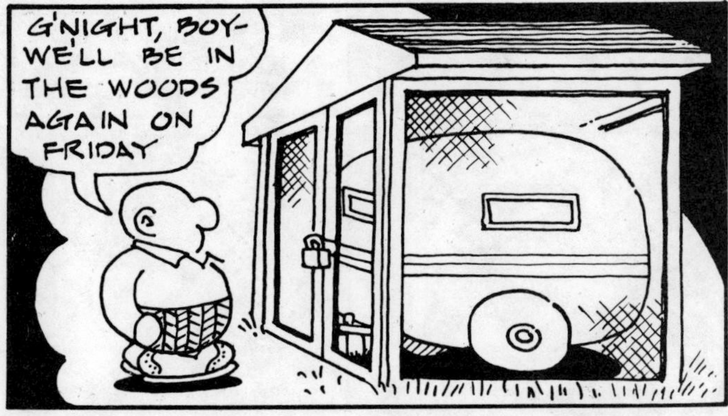
G'NIGHT, BOY- WE'LL BE IN THE WOODS AGAIN ON FRIDAY

MODERNE MAN

b. von alten

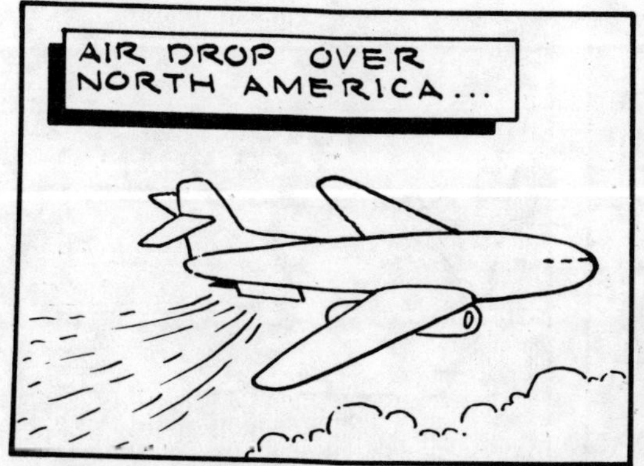
AIR DROP OVER NORTH AMERICA...
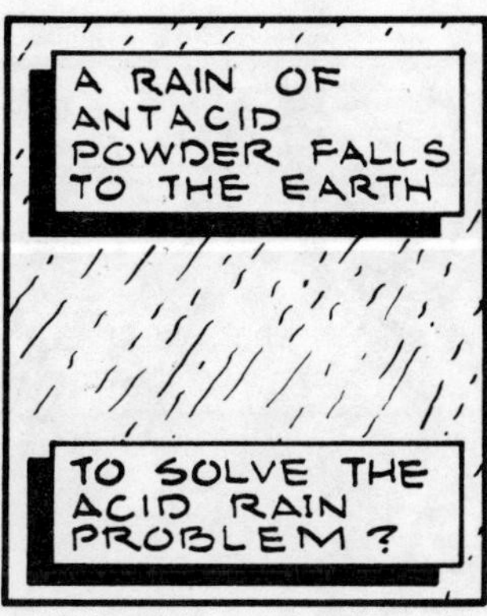
A RAIN OF ANTACID POWDER FALLS TO THE EARTH
TO SOLVE THE ACID RAIN PROBLEM?
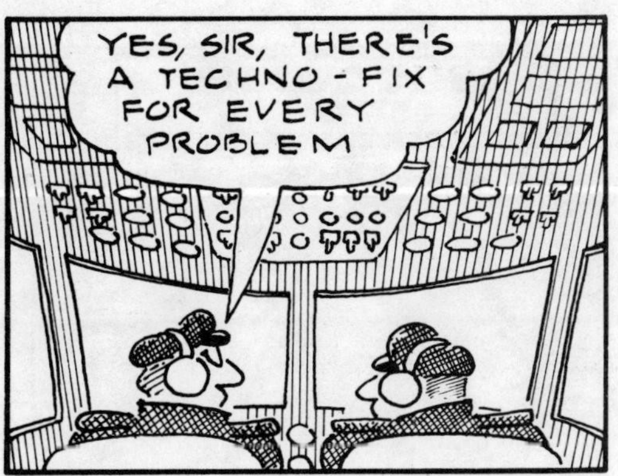
YES, SIR, THERE'S A TECHNO-FIX FOR EVERY PROBLEM

MODERNE MAN

b. von alten

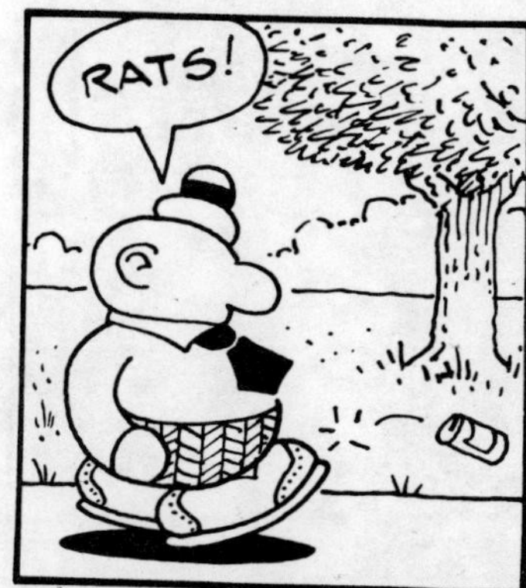
RATS!
LAID OFF FROM MY JOB
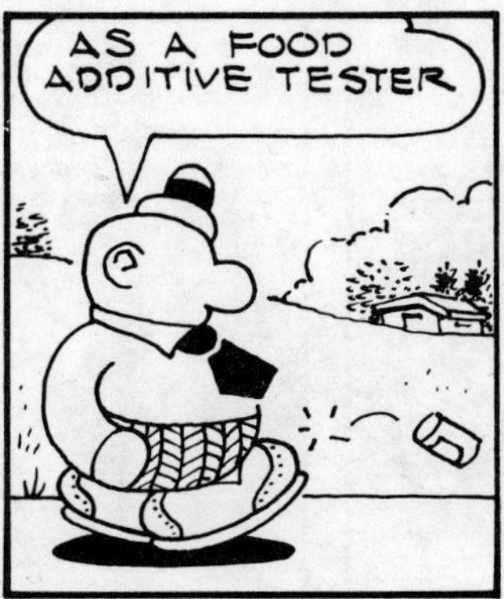
AS A FOOD ADDITIVE TESTER
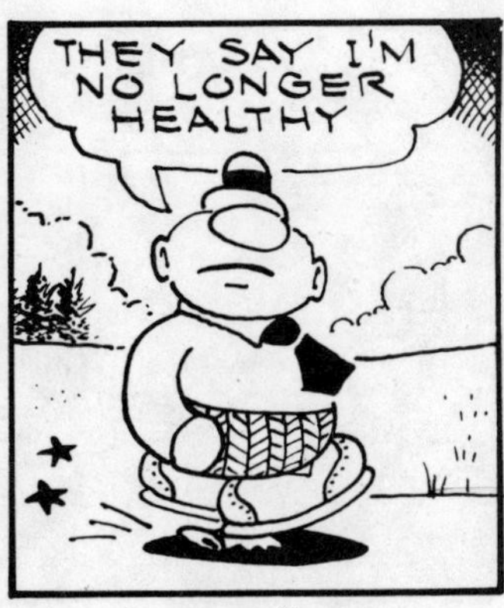
THEY SAY I'M NO LONGER HEALTHY

MODERNE MAN

b. von alten

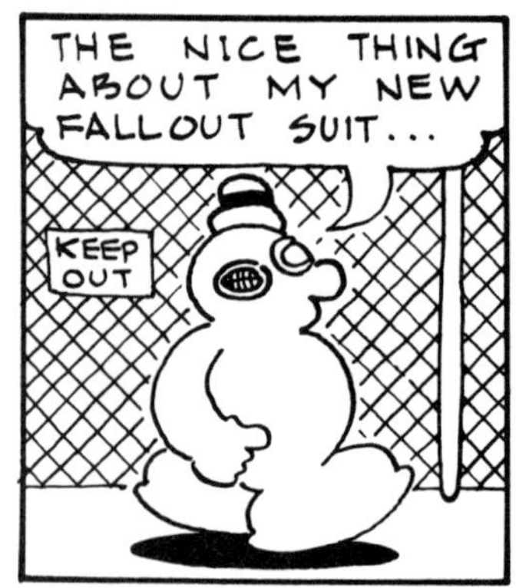
THE NICE THING ABOUT MY NEW FALLOUT SUIT...
KEEP OUT

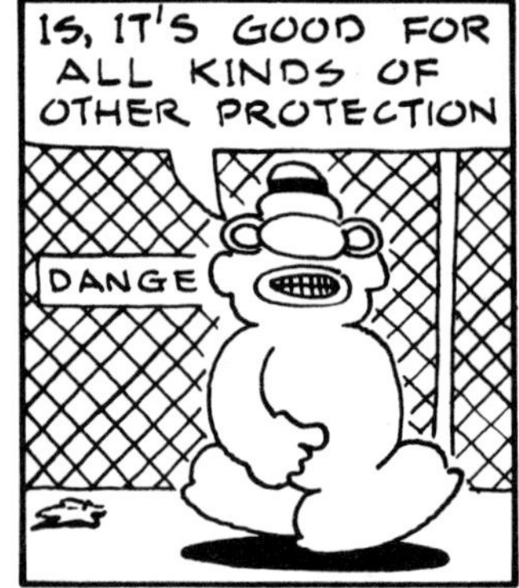
IS, IT'S GOOD FOR ALL KINDS OF OTHER PROTECTION
DANGE

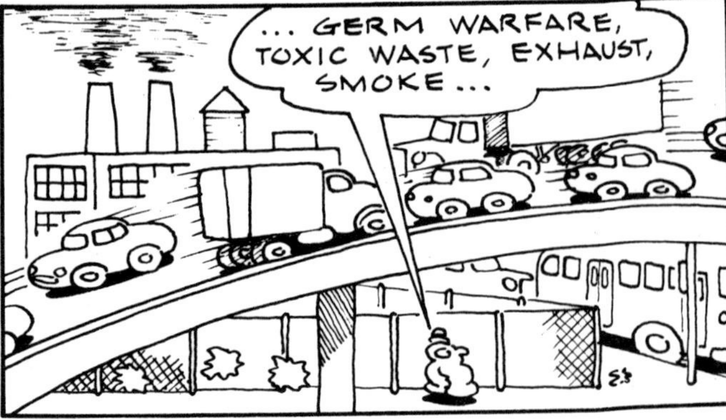
... GERM WARFARE, TOXIC WASTE, EXHAUST, SMOKE...

MODERNE MAN

b. von alten

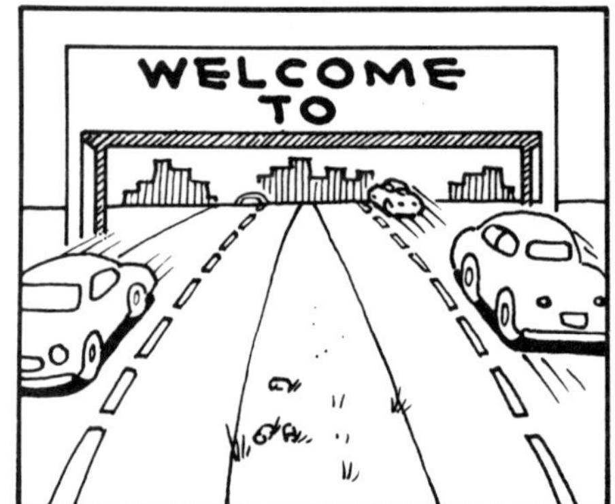
WELCOME TO

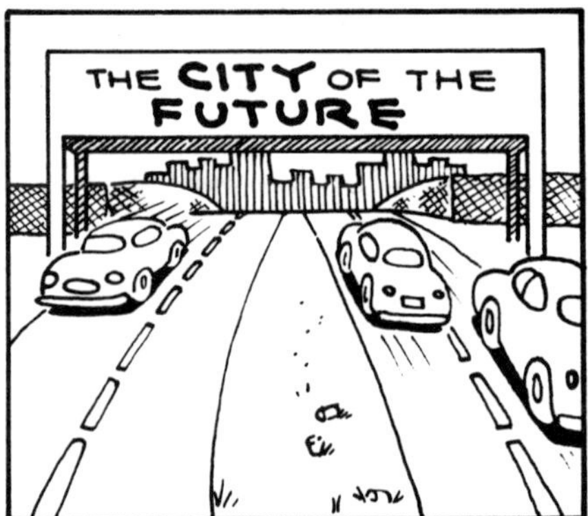
THE CITY OF THE FUTURE

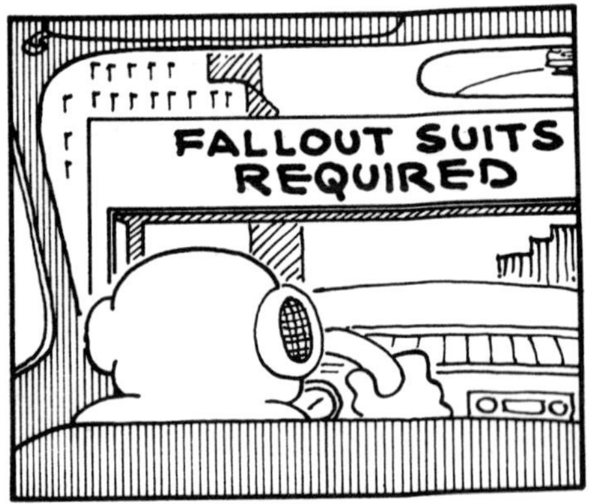
FALLOUT SUITS REQUIRED

MODERNE MAN

b. von alten

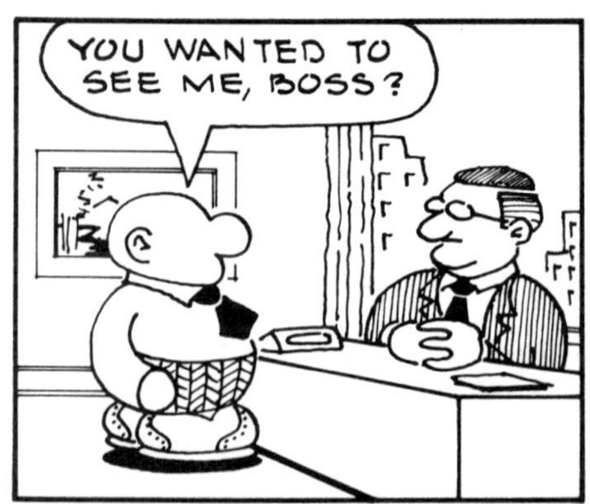
YOU WANTED TO SEE ME, BOSS?

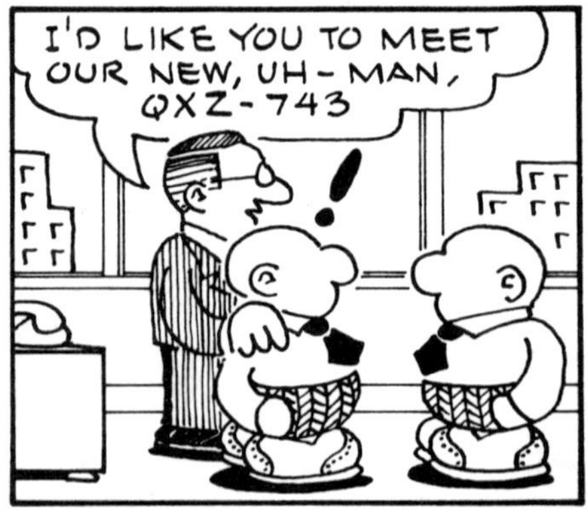
I'D LIKE YOU TO MEET OUR NEW, UH-MAN, QXZ-743
!

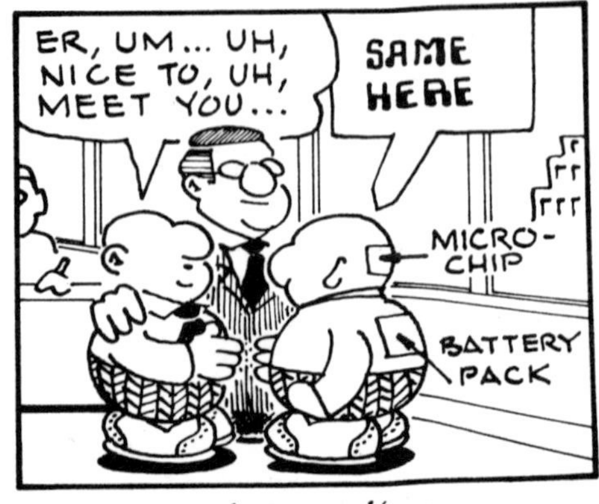
ER, UM... UH, NICE TO, UH, MEET YOU...
SAME HERE
MICRO-CHIP
BATTERY PACK

MODERNE MAN

b. von alten

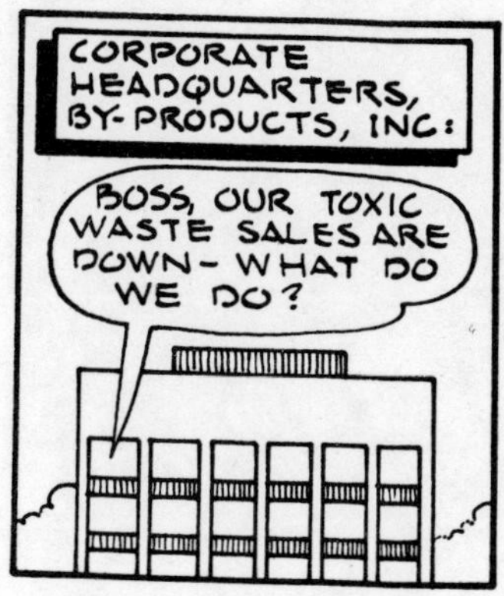
CORPORATE HEADQUARTERS, BY-PRODUCTS, INC:
BOSS, OUR TOXIC WASTE SALES ARE DOWN - WHAT DO WE DO?
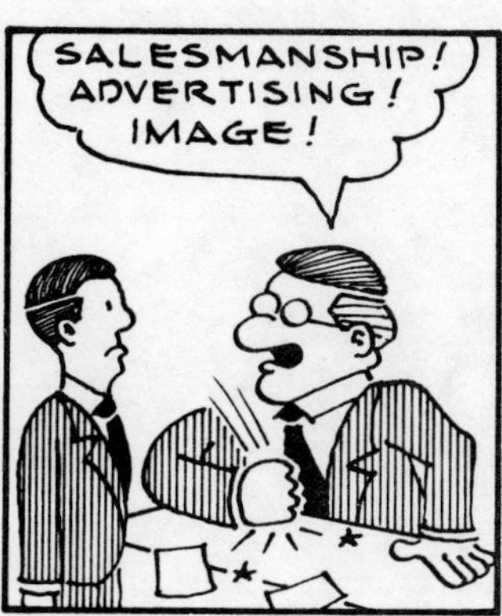
SALESMANSHIP! ADVERTISING! IMAGE!
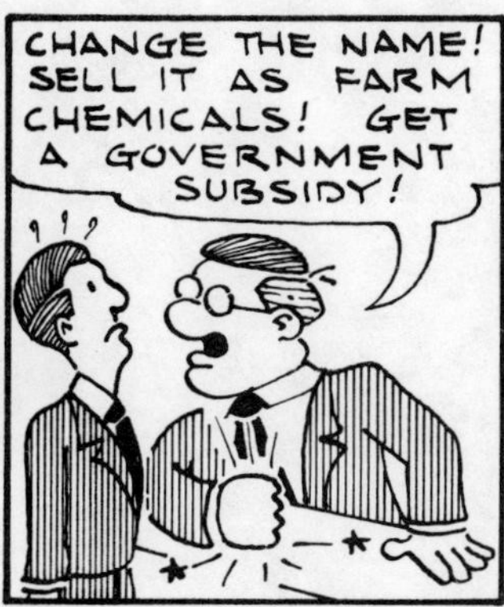
CHANGE THE NAME! SELL IT AS FARM CHEMICALS! GET A GOVERNMENT SUBSIDY!
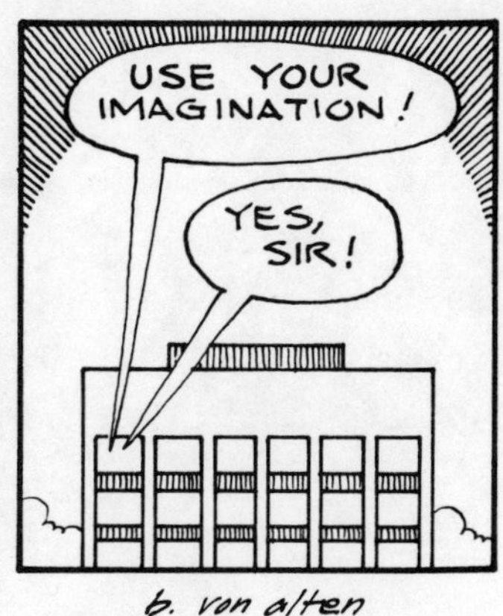
USE YOUR IMAGINATION!
YES, SIR!

b. von alten

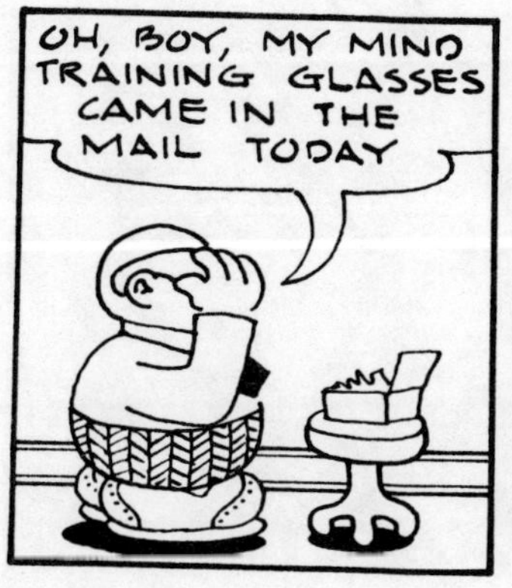
OH, BOY, MY MIND TRAINING GLASSES CAME IN THE MAIL TODAY
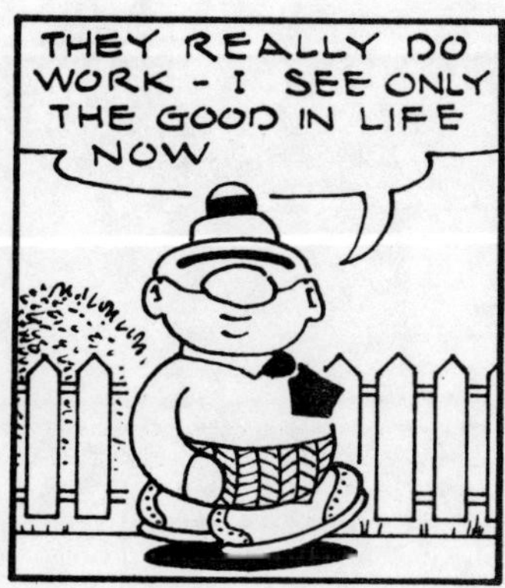
THEY REALLY DO WORK - I SEE ONLY THE GOOD IN LIFE NOW
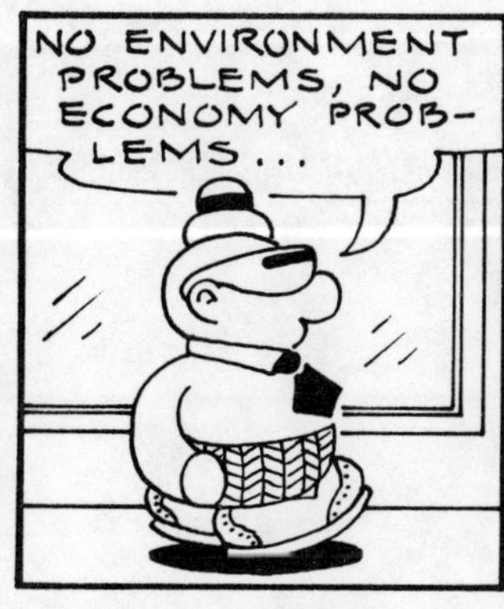
NO ENVIRONMENT PROBLEMS, NO ECONOMY PROB-LEMS...
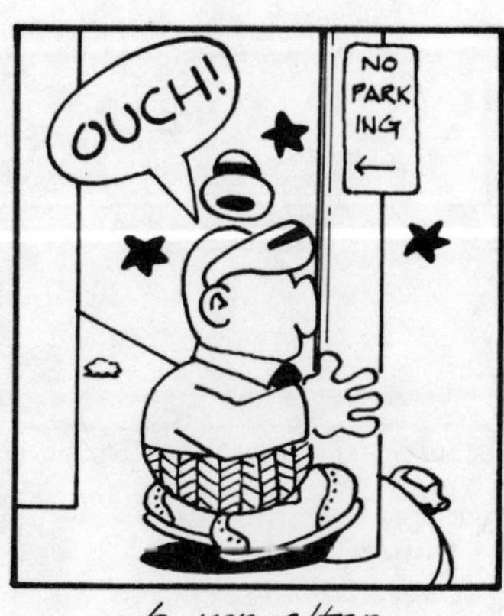
OUCH!
NO PARK ING ←

b. von alten

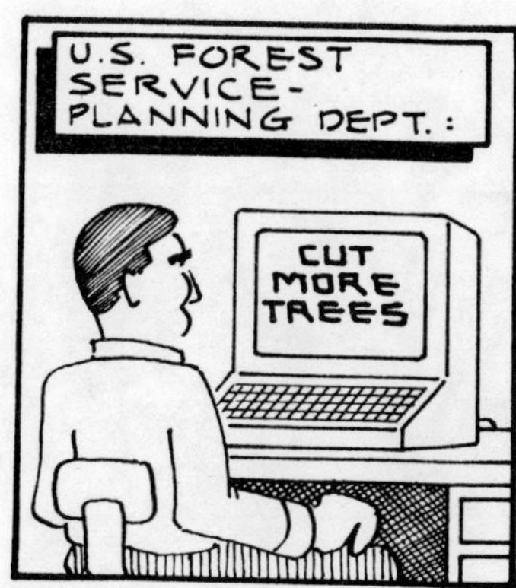
U.S. FOREST SERVICE-PLANNING DEPT.:
CUT MORE TREES
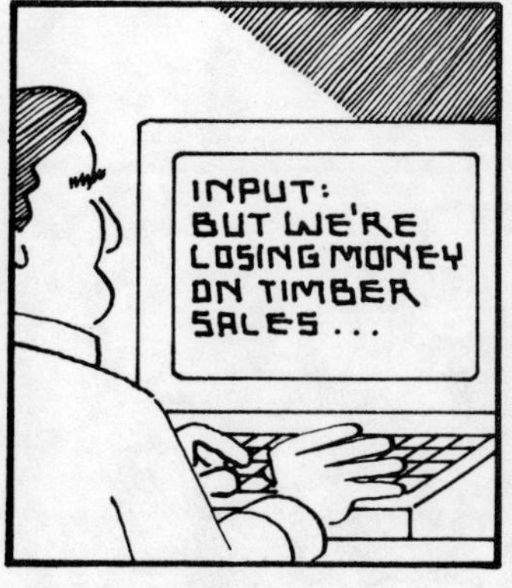
INPUT: BUT WE'RE LOSING MONEY ON TIMBER SALES...
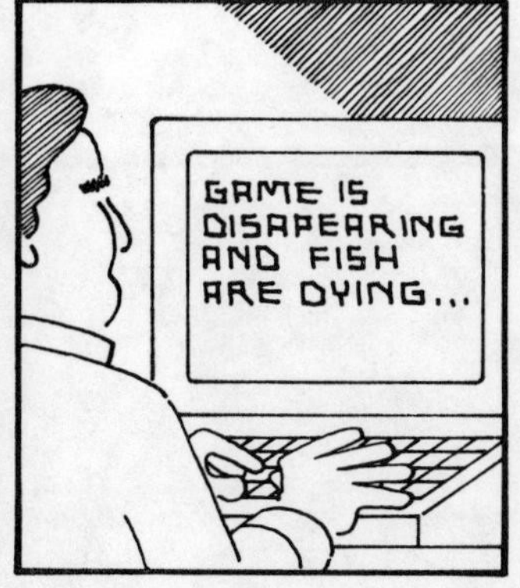
GAME IS DISAPEARING AND FISH ARE DYING...
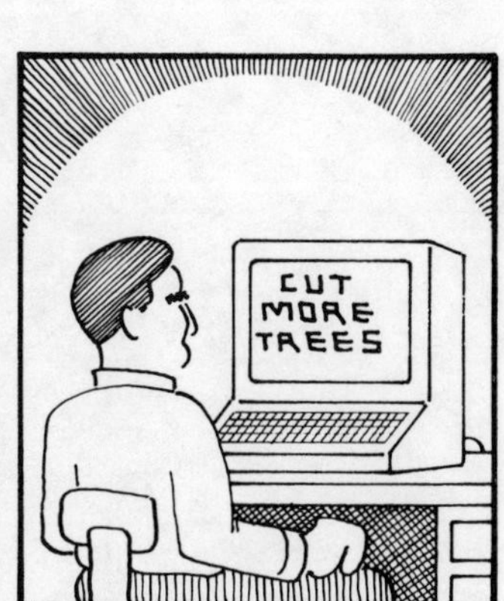
CUT MORE TREES

b. von alten

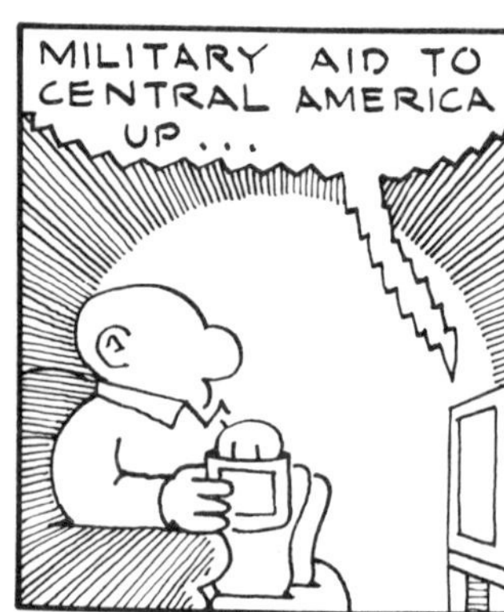
MILITARY AID TO CENTRAL AMERICA UP...
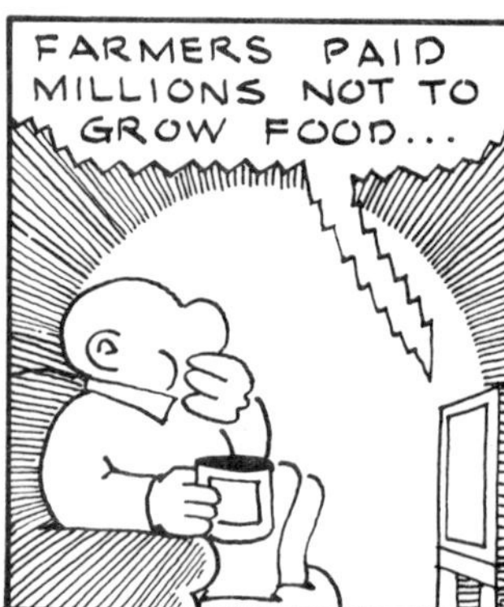
FARMERS PAID MILLIONS NOT TO GROW FOOD...
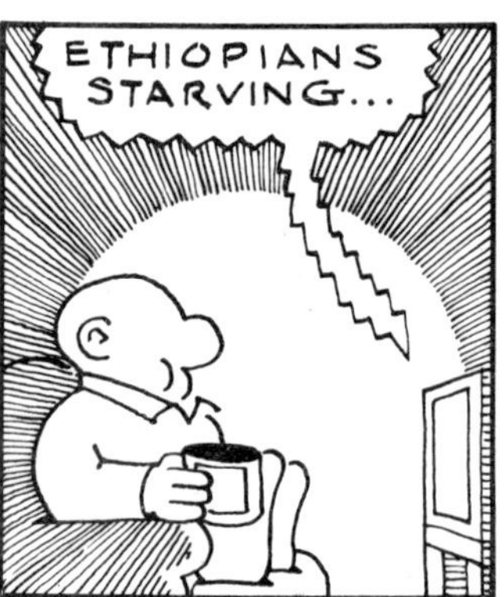
ETHIOPIANS STARVING...
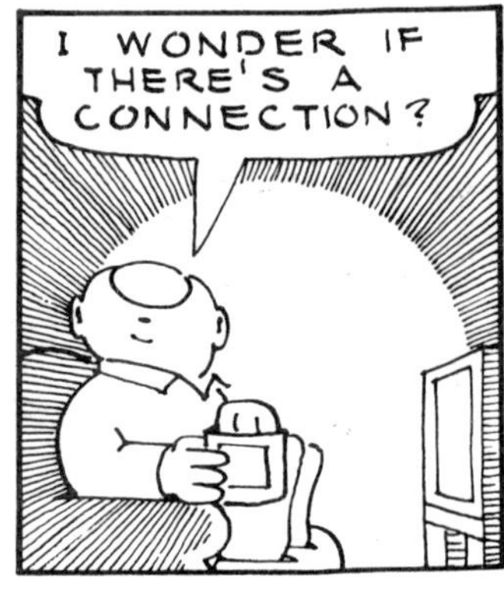
I WONDER IF THERE'S A CONNECTION?

b. von alten

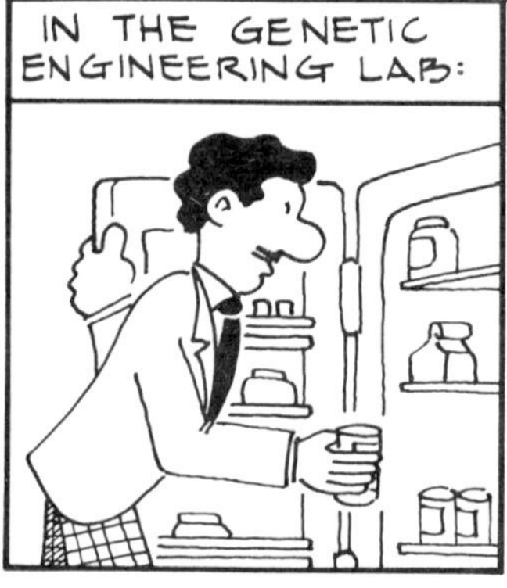
IN THE GENETIC ENGINEERING LAB:
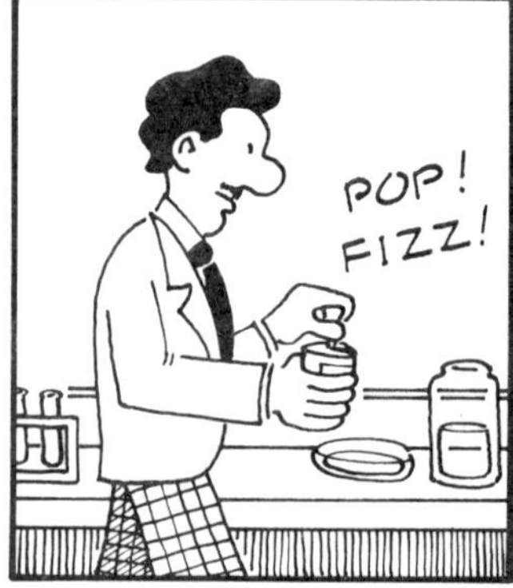
POP! FIZZ!
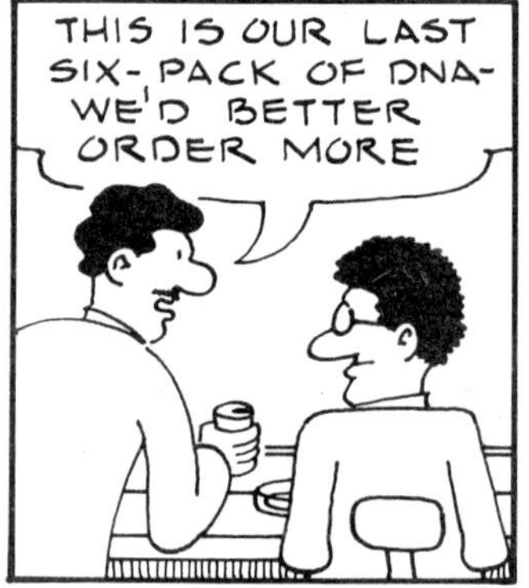
THIS IS OUR LAST SIX-PACK OF DNA-WE'D BETTER ORDER MORE
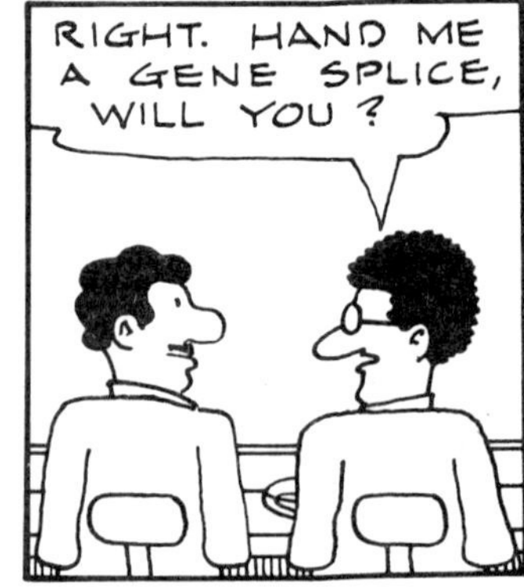
RIGHT. HAND ME A GENE SPLICE, WILL YOU?

b. von alten

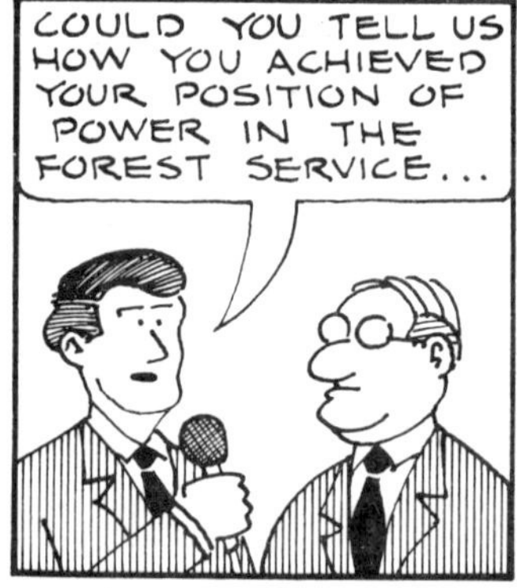
COULD YOU TELL US HOW YOU ACHIEVED YOUR POSITION OF POWER IN THE FOREST SERVICE...
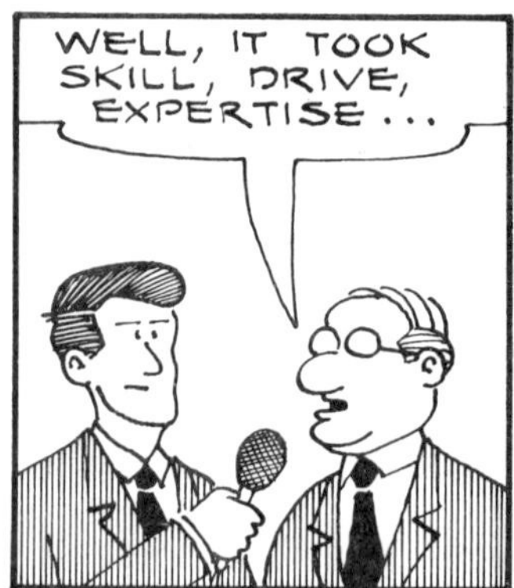
WELL, IT TOOK SKILL, DRIVE, EXPERTISE...
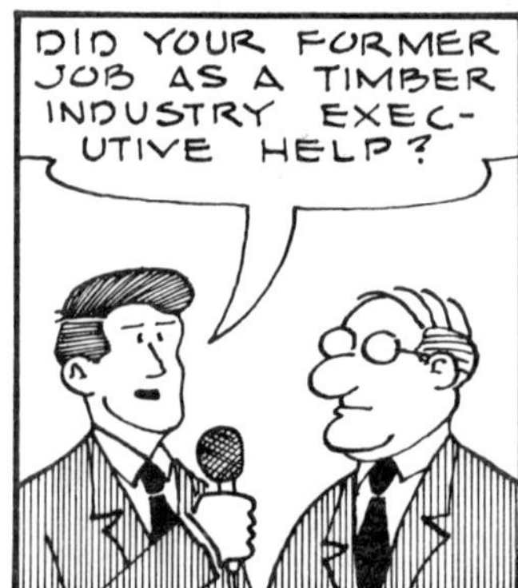
DID YOUR FORMER JOB AS A TIMBER INDUSTRY EXEC-UTIVE HELP?
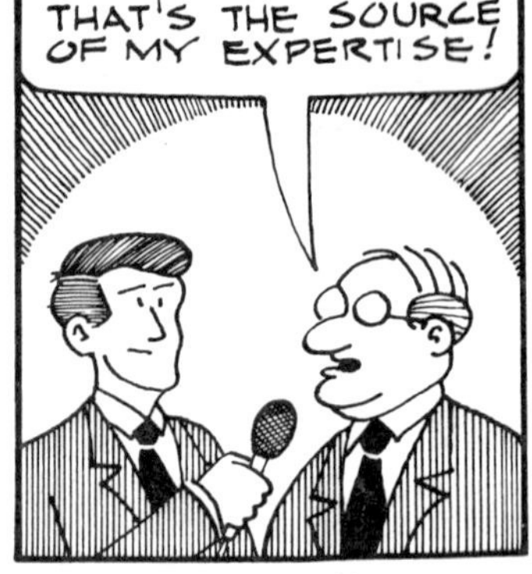
THAT'S THE SOURCE OF MY EXPERTISE!

b. von alten

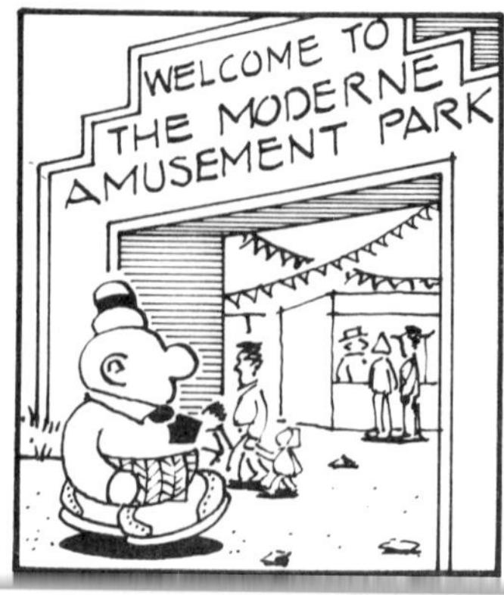
WELCOME TO THE MODERNE AMUSEMENT PARK
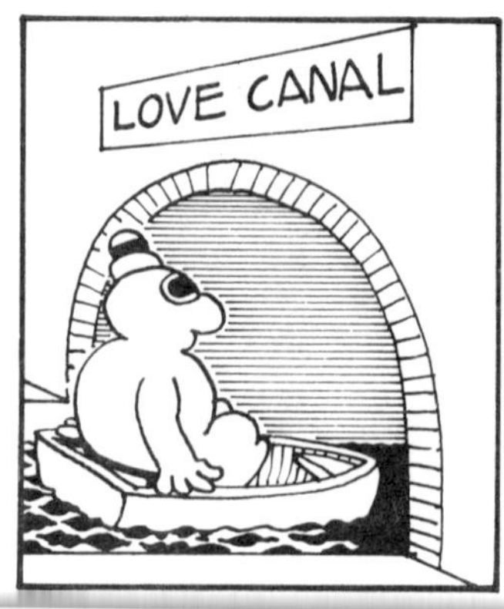
LOVE CANAL
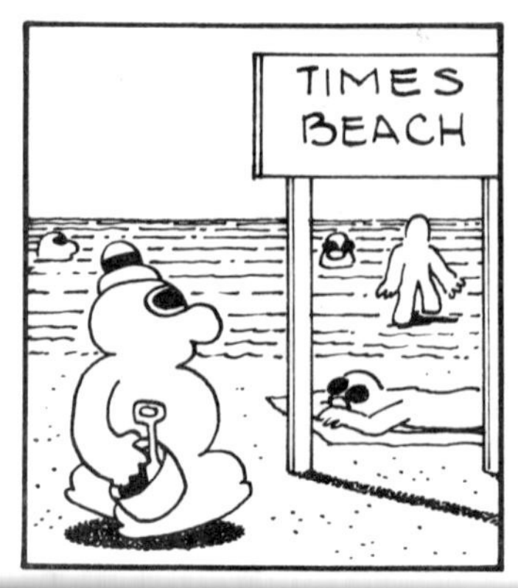
TIMES BEACH
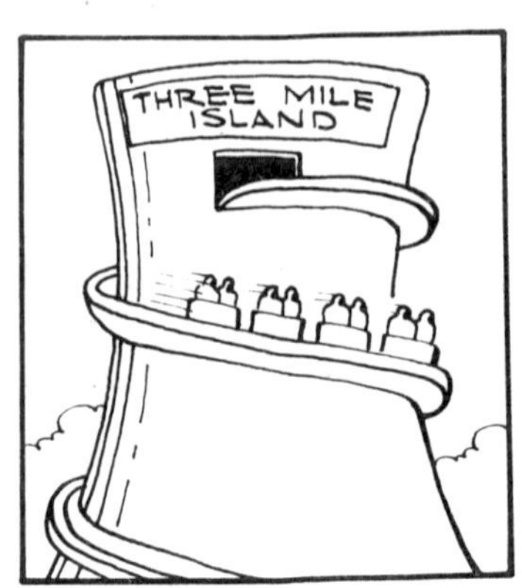
THREE MILE ISLAND

b. von alten

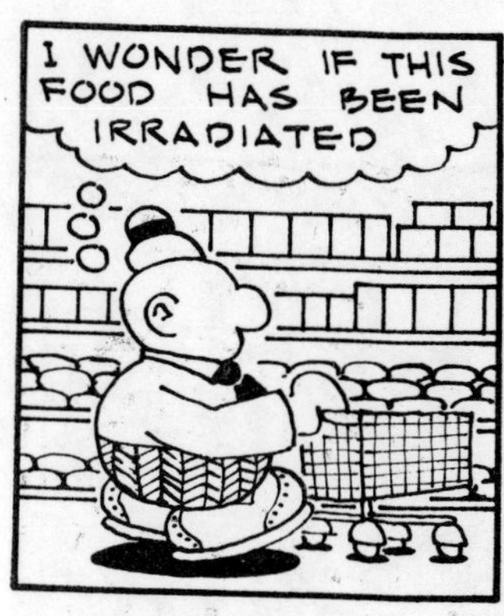
I WONDER IF THIS FOOD HAS BEEN IRRADIATED

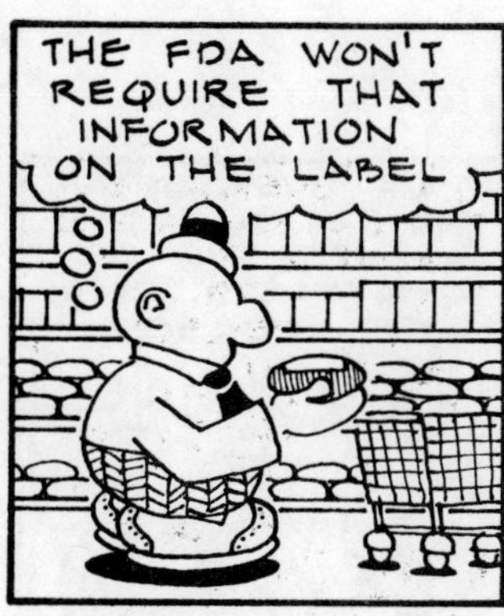
THE FDA WON'T REQUIRE THAT INFORMATION ON THE LABEL

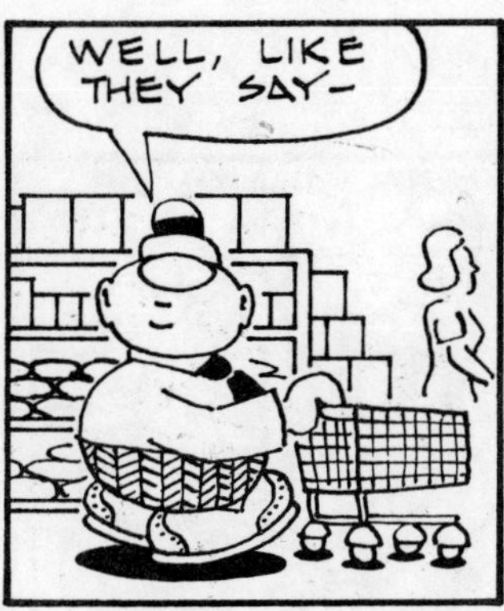
WELL, LIKE THEY SAY-

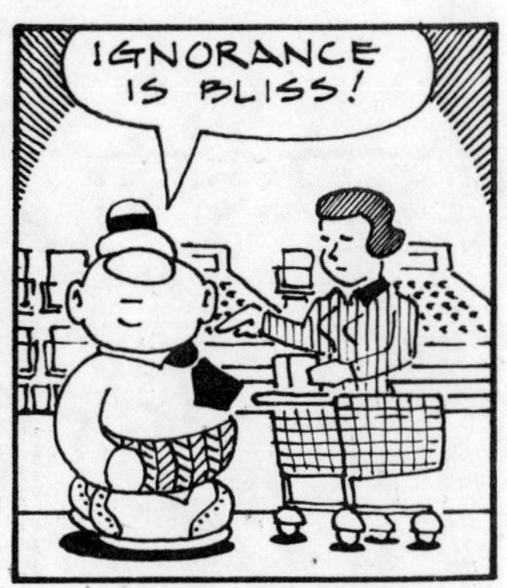
IGNORANCE IS BLISS!

b. von alten

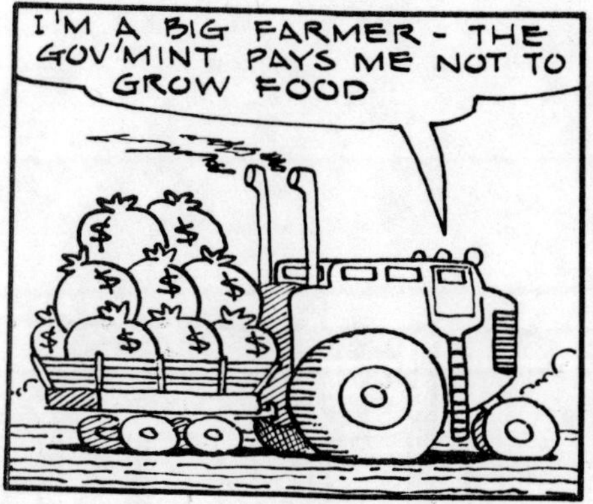
I'M A BIG FARMER - THE GOV'MINT PAYS ME NOT TO GROW FOOD

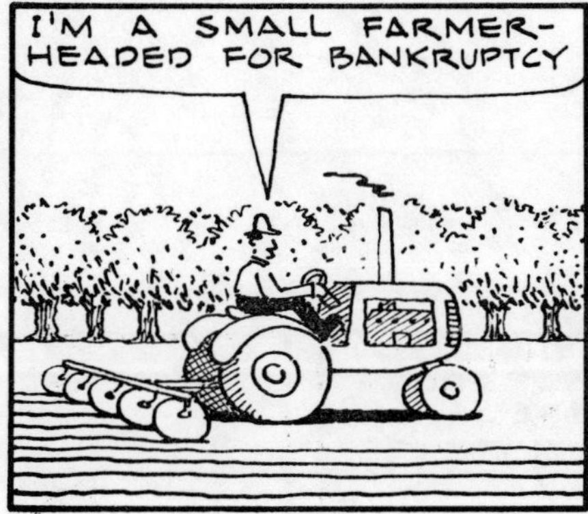
I'M A SMALL FARMER- HEADED FOR BANKRUPTCY

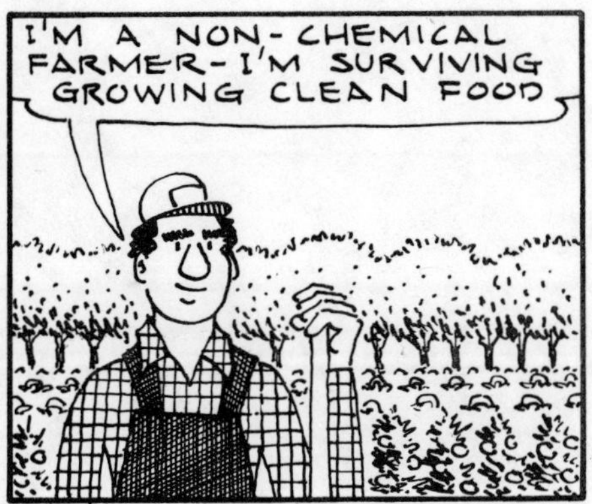
I'M A NON-CHEMICAL FARMER- I'M SURVIVING GROWING CLEAN FOOD

b. von alten

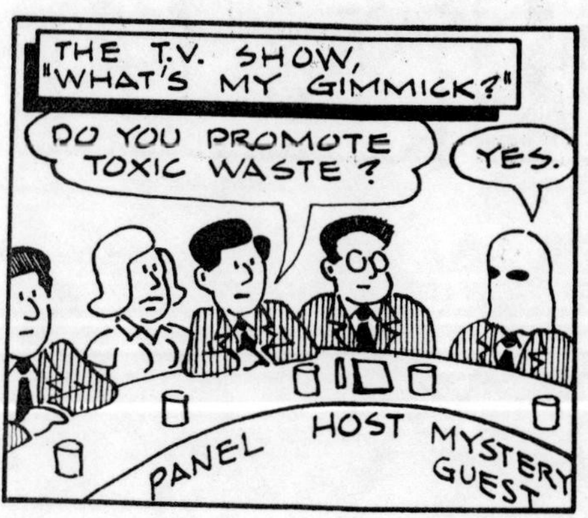
THE T.V. SHOW, "WHAT'S MY GIMMICK?"
DO YOU PROMOTE TOXIC WASTE?
YES.
PANEL
HOST
MYSTERY GUEST

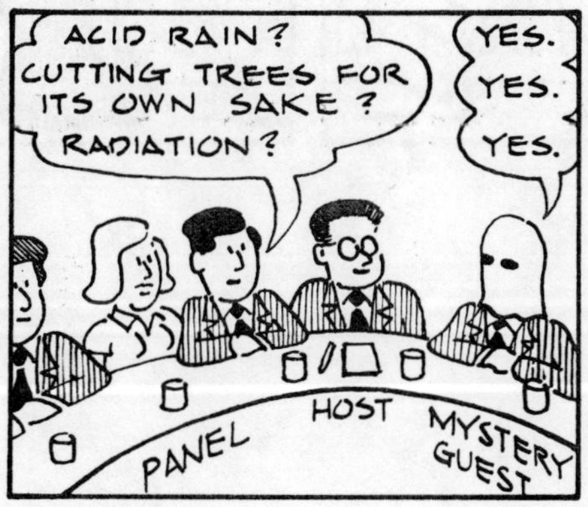
ACID RAIN?
YES.
CUTTING TREES FOR ITS OWN SAKE?
YES.
RADIATION?
YES.
PANEL
HOST
MYSTERY GUEST

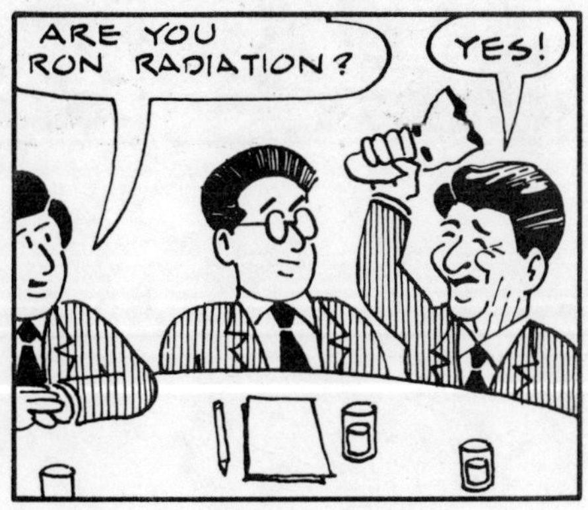
ARE YOU RON RADIATION?
YES!

b. von alten

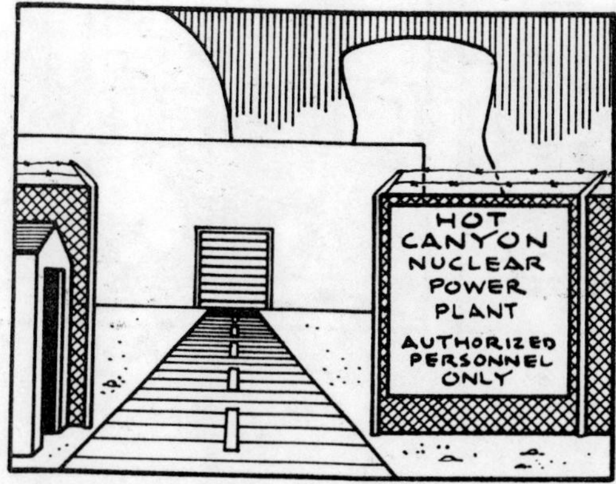
HOT CANYON NUCLEAR POWER PLANT
AUTHORIZED PERSONNEL ONLY

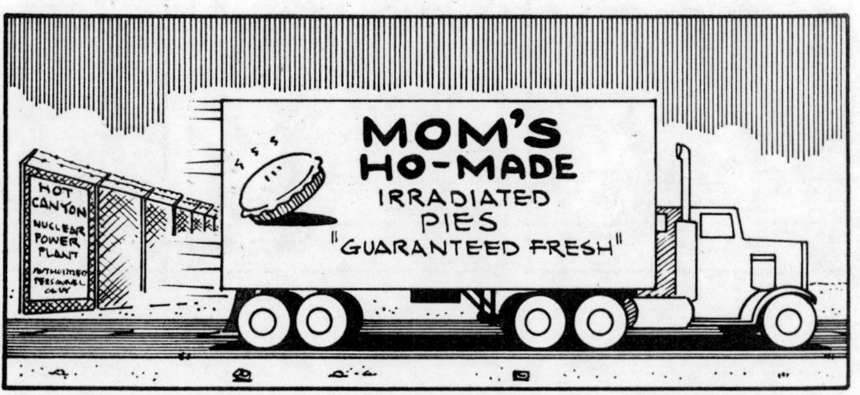
HOT CANYON NUCLEAR POWER PLANT
MOM'S HO-MADE IRRADIATED PIES "GUARANTEED FRESH"

b. von alten

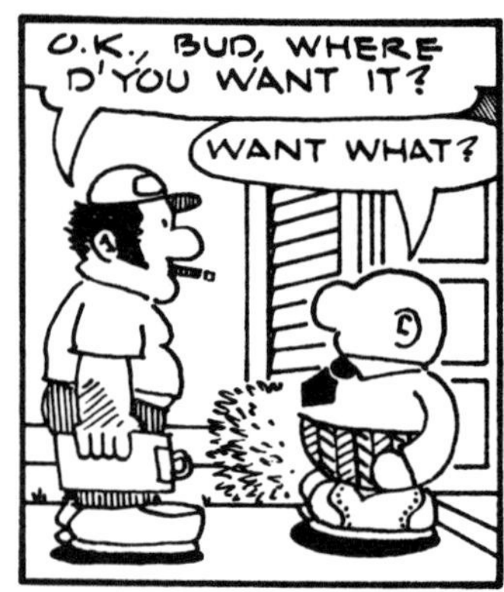
O.K., BUD, WHERE D'YOU WANT IT?
WANT WHAT?
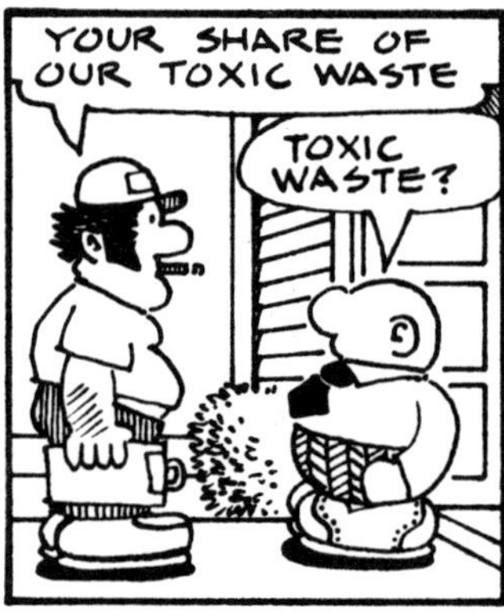
YOUR SHARE OF OUR TOXIC WASTE
TOXIC WASTE?
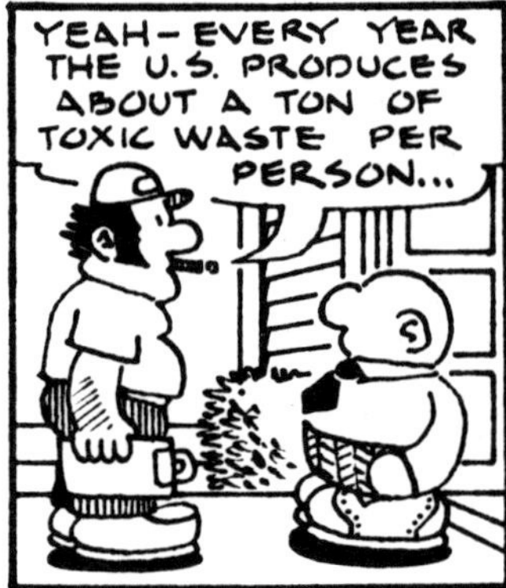
YEAH- EVERY YEAR THE U.S. PRODUCES ABOUT A TON OF TOXIC WASTE PER PERSON...
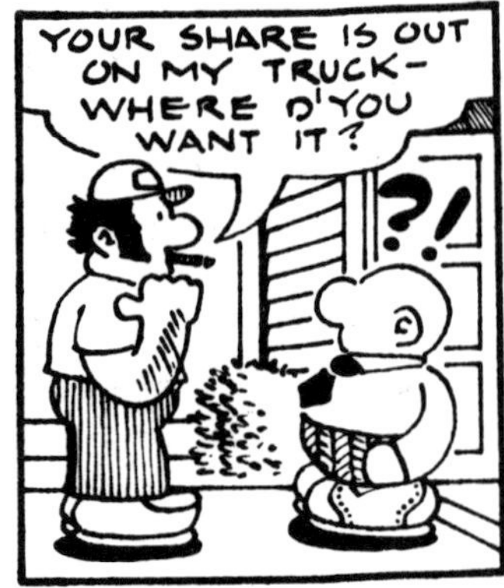
YOUR SHARE IS OUT ON MY TRUCK- WHERE D'YOU WANT IT?
?!

b. von alten

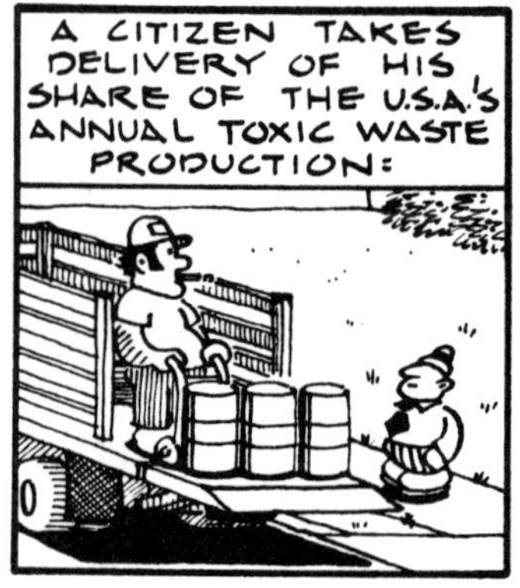
A CITIZEN TAKES DELIVERY OF HIS SHARE OF THE U.S.A.'S ANNUAL TOXIC WASTE PRODUCTION:
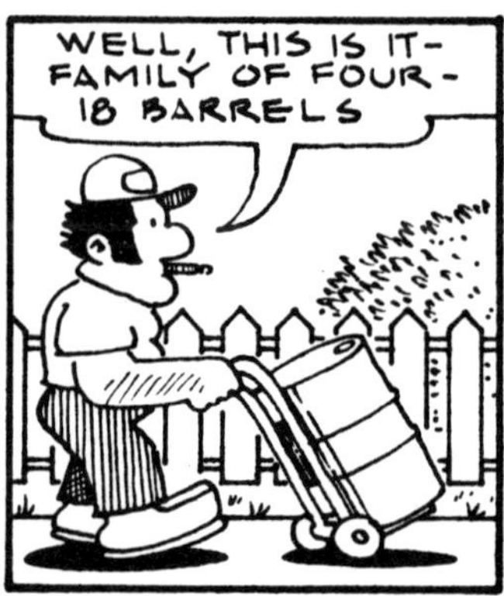
WELL, THIS IS IT- FAMILY OF FOUR- 18 BARRELS
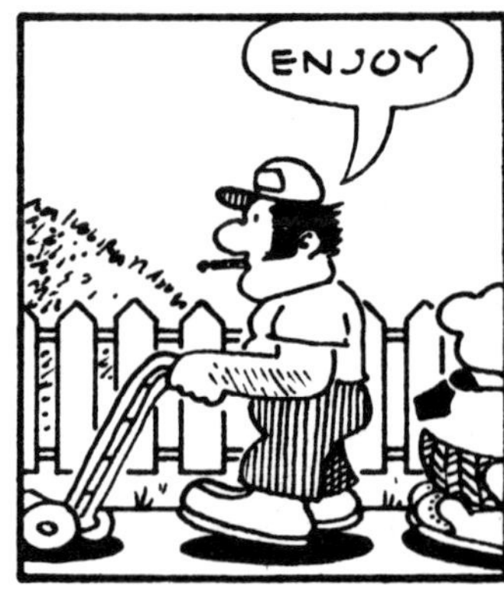
ENJOY
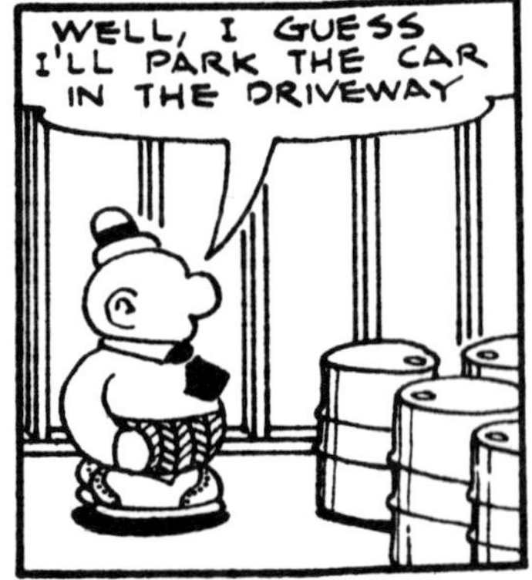
WELL, I GUESS I'LL PARK THE CAR IN THE DRIVEWAY

b. von alten

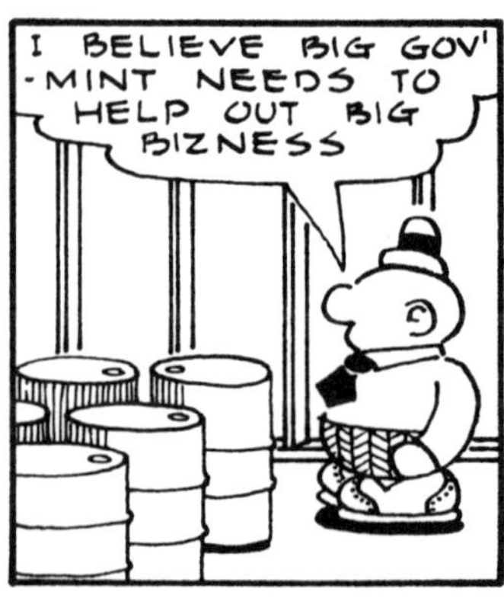
I BELIEVE BIG GOV' -MINT NEEDS TO HELP OUT BIG BIZNESS
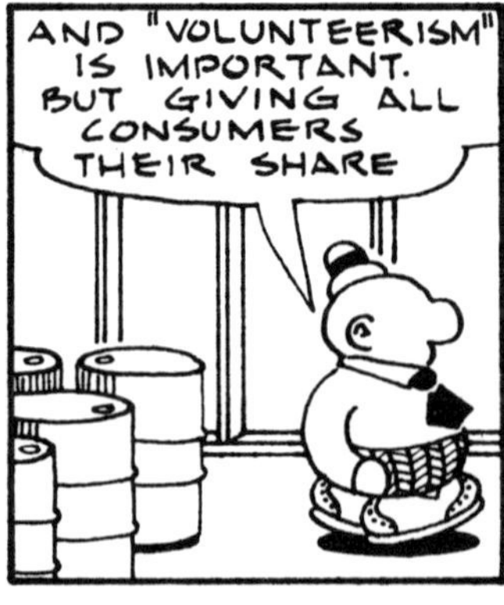
AND "VOLUNTEERISM" IS IMPORTANT. BUT GIVING ALL CONSUMERS THEIR SHARE
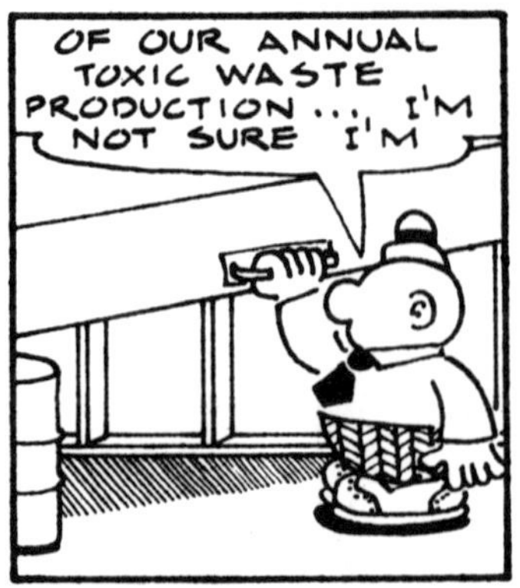
OF OUR ANNUAL TOXIC WASTE PRODUCTION... I'M NOT SURE I'M
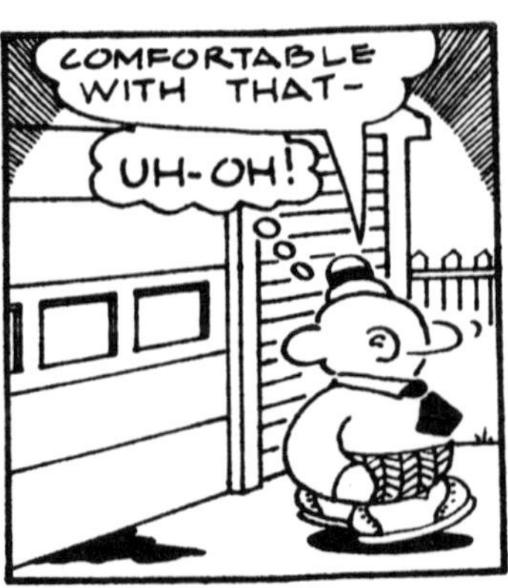
COMFORTABLE WITH THAT-
UH-OH!

b. von alten

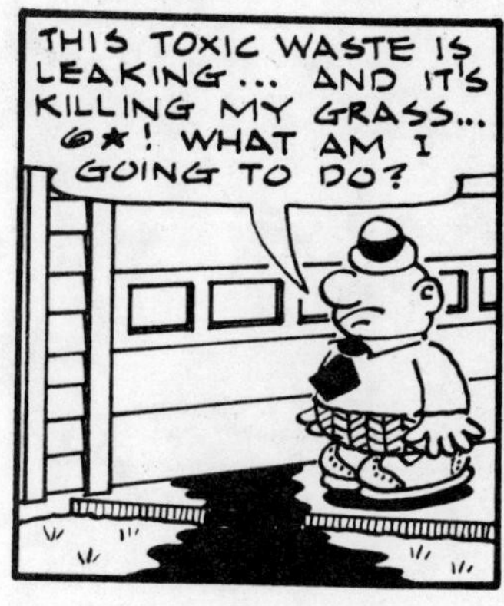
THIS TOXIC WASTE IS LEAKING... AND IT'S KILLING MY GRASS... @*! WHAT AM I GOING TO DO?

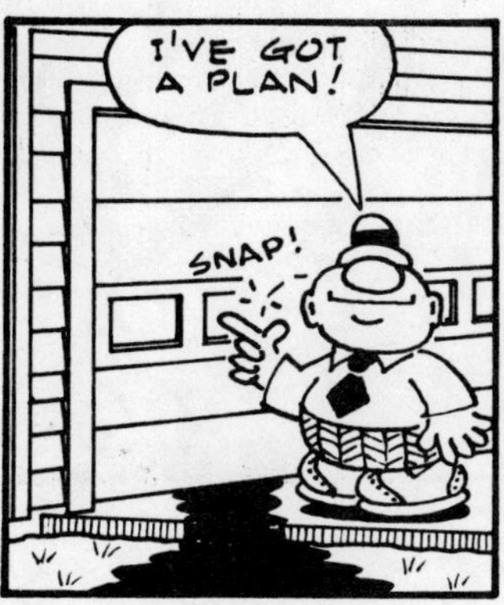
I'VE GOT A PLAN!
SNAP!

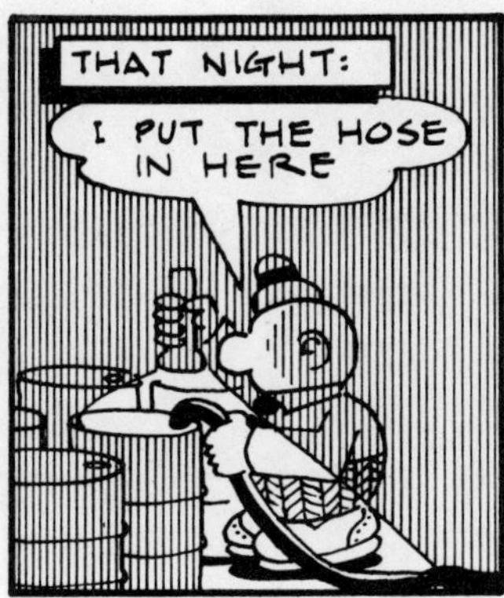
THAT NIGHT:
I PUT THE HOSE IN HERE

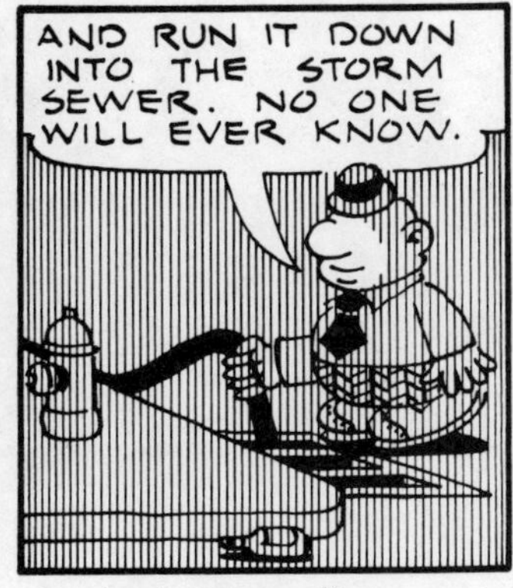
AND RUN IT DOWN INTO THE STORM SEWER. NO ONE WILL EVER KNOW.

b. von alten

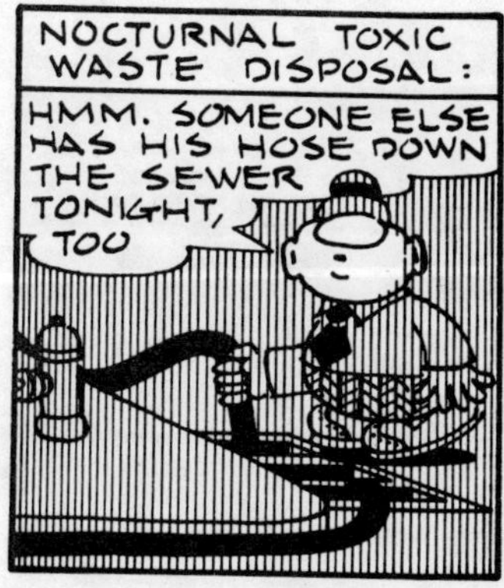
NOCTURNAL TOXIC WASTE DISPOSAL:
HMM. SOMEONE ELSE HAS HIS HOSE DOWN THE SEWER TONIGHT, TOO

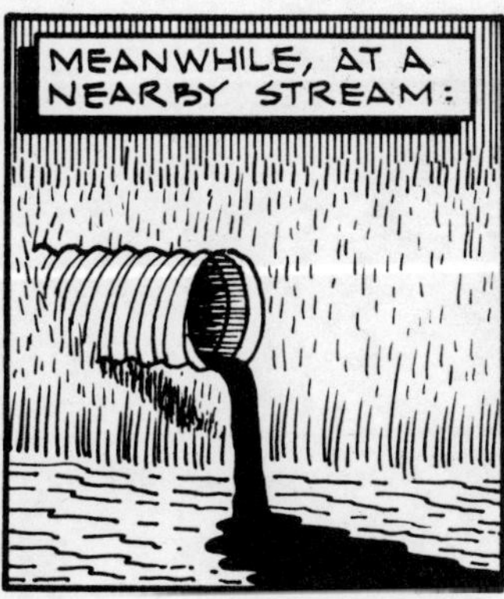
MEANWHILE, AT A NEARBY STREAM:

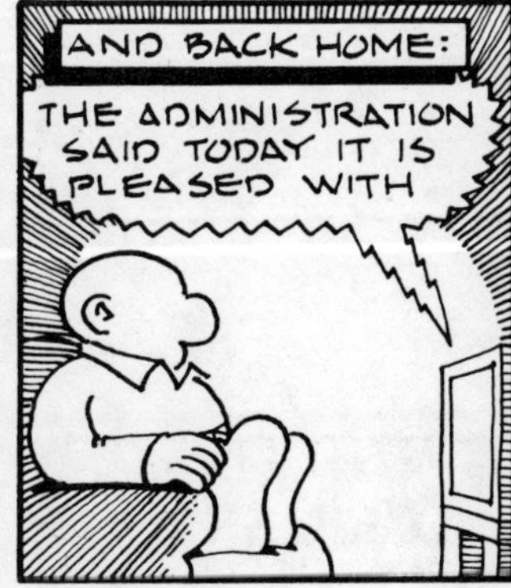
AND BACK HOME:
THE ADMINISTRATION SAID TODAY IT IS PLEASED WITH

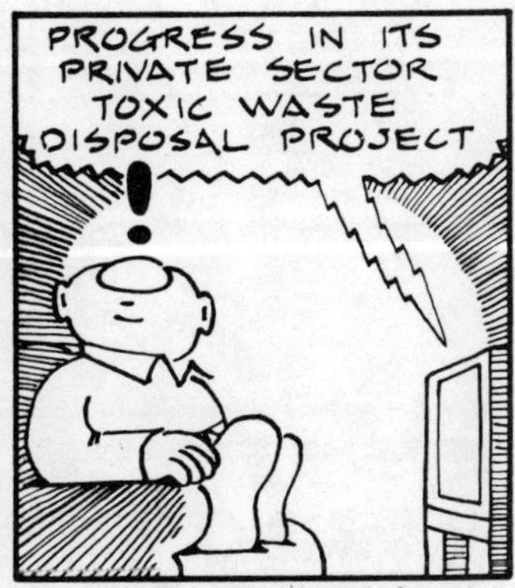
PROGRESS IN ITS PRIVATE SECTOR TOXIC WASTE DISPOSAL PROJECT
!

b. von alten

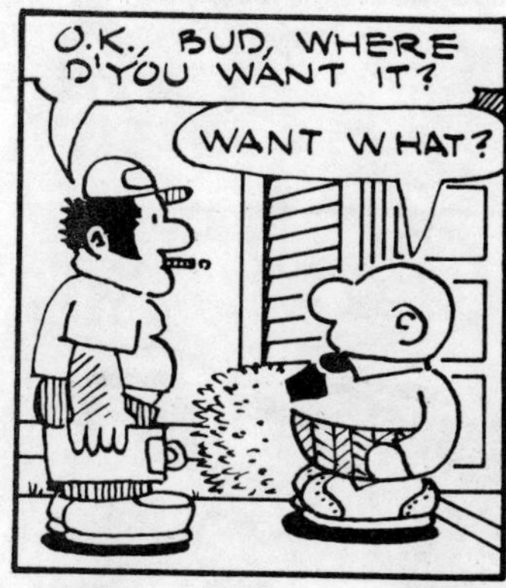
O.K., BUD, WHERE D'YOU WANT IT?
WANT WHAT?

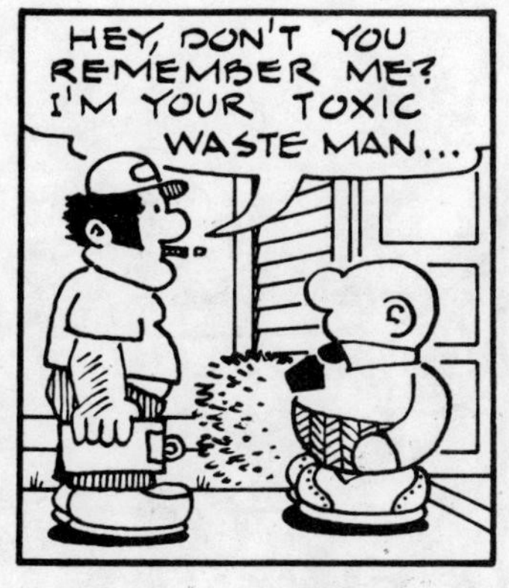
HEY, DON'T YOU REMEMBER ME? I'M YOUR TOXIC WASTE MAN...

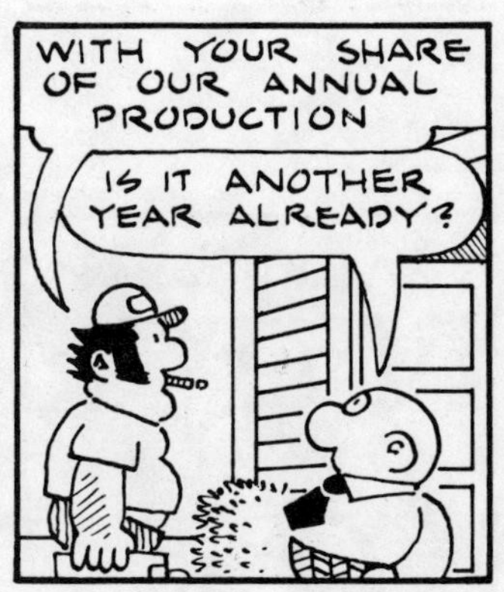
WITH YOUR SHARE OF OUR ANNUAL PRODUCTION
IS IT ANOTHER YEAR ALREADY?

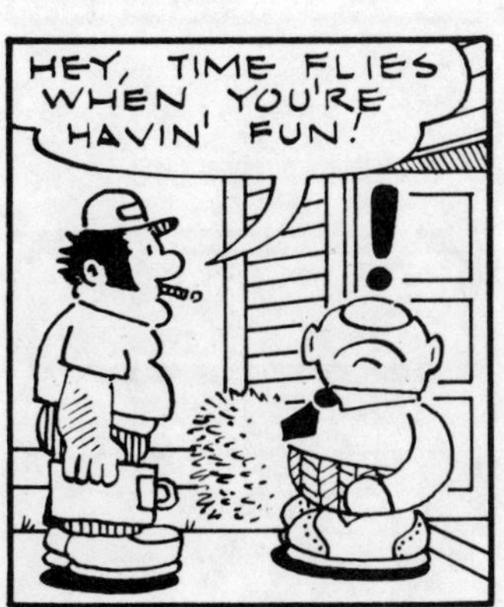
HEY, TIME FLIES WHEN YOU'RE HAVIN' FUN!
!

b. von alten

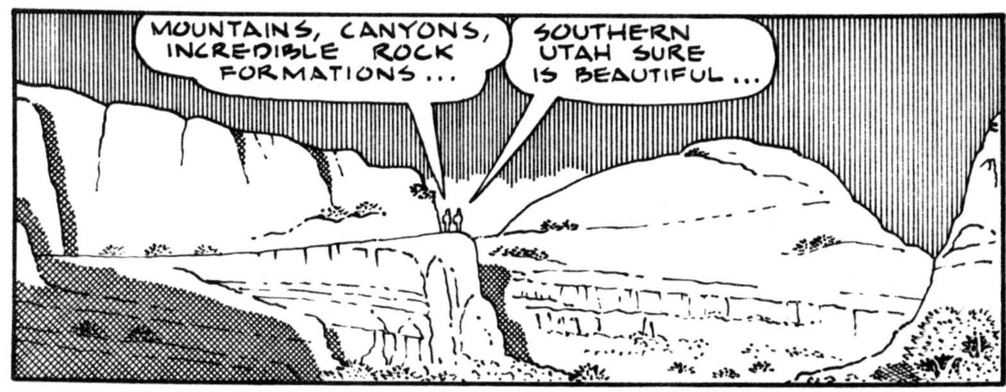
MOUNTAINS, CANYONS, INCREDIBLE ROCK FORMATIONS...
SOUTHERN UTAH SURE IS BEAUTIFUL...

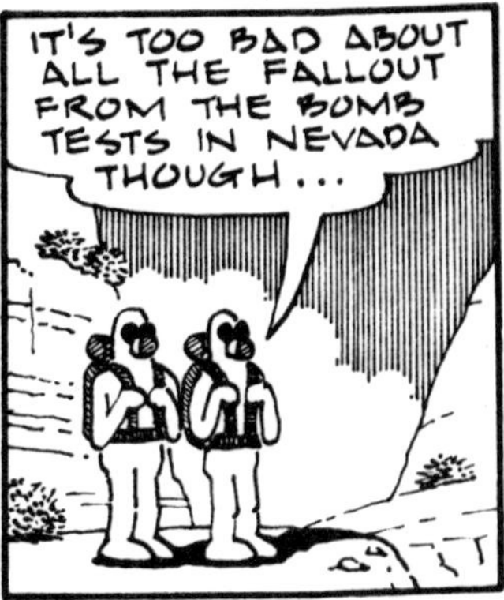
IT'S TOO BAD ABOUT ALL THE FALLOUT FROM THE BOMB TESTS IN NEVADA THOUGH...

b. von alten

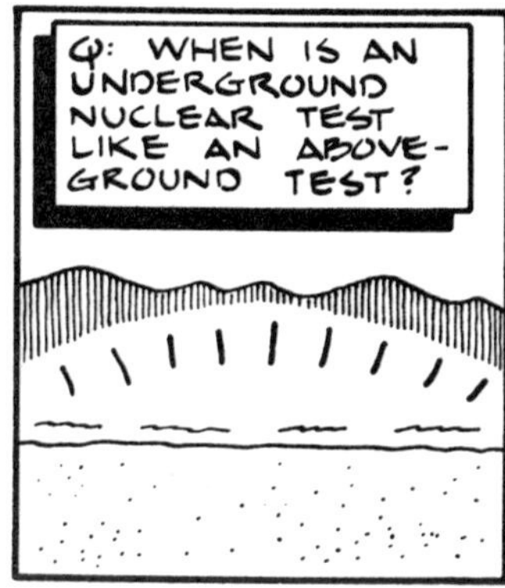
Q: WHEN IS AN UNDERGROUND NUCLEAR TEST LIKE AN ABOVE-GROUND TEST?

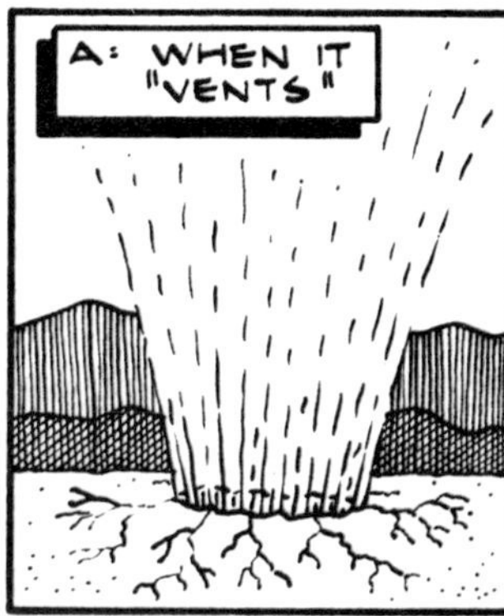
A: WHEN IT "VENTS"

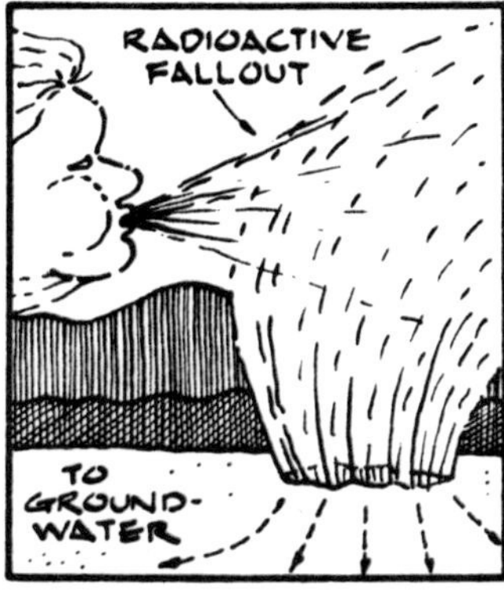
RADIOACTIVE FALLOUT
TO GROUND-WATER

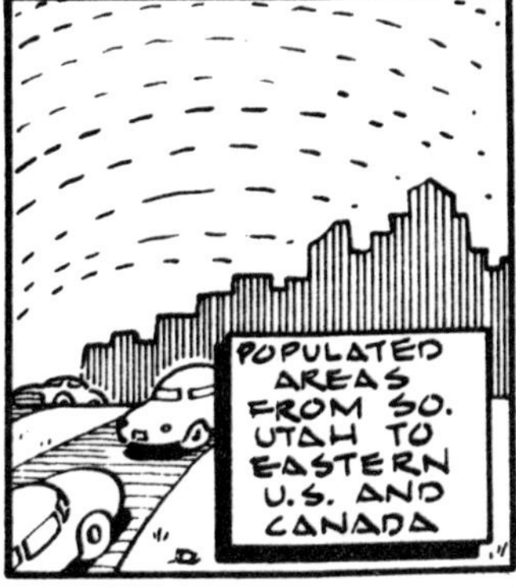
POPULATED AREAS FROM SO. UTAH TO EASTERN U.S. AND CANADA

b. von alten

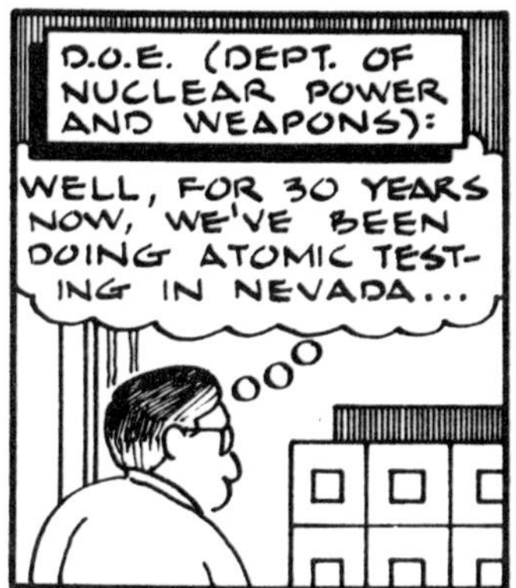
D.O.E. (DEPT. OF NUCLEAR POWER AND WEAPONS):
WELL, FOR 30 YEARS NOW, WE'VE BEEN DOING ATOMIC TESTING IN NEVADA...

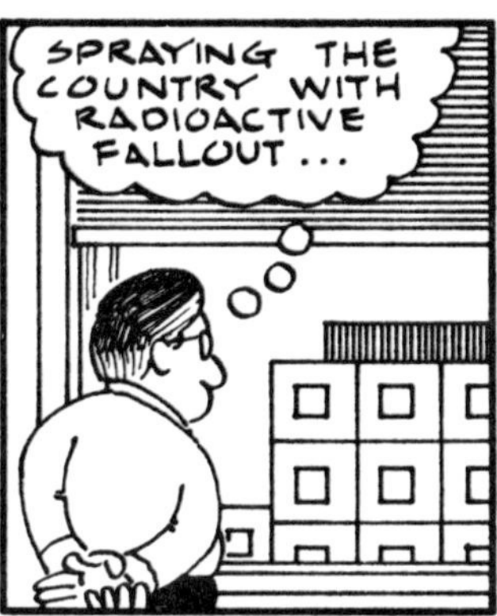
SPRAYING THE COUNTRY WITH RADIOACTIVE FALLOUT...

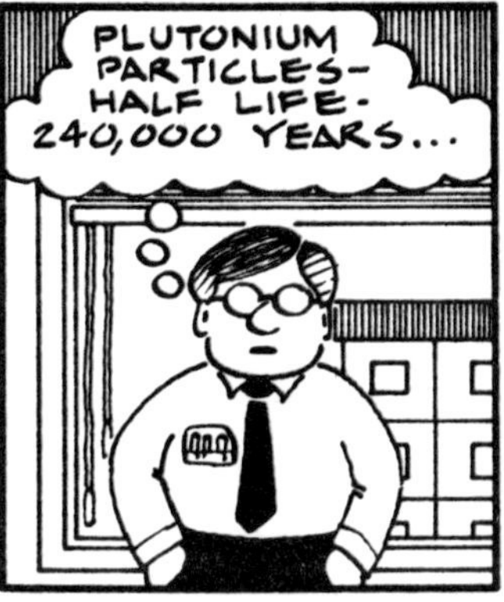
PLUTONIUM PARTICLES-HALF LIFE-240,000 YEARS...

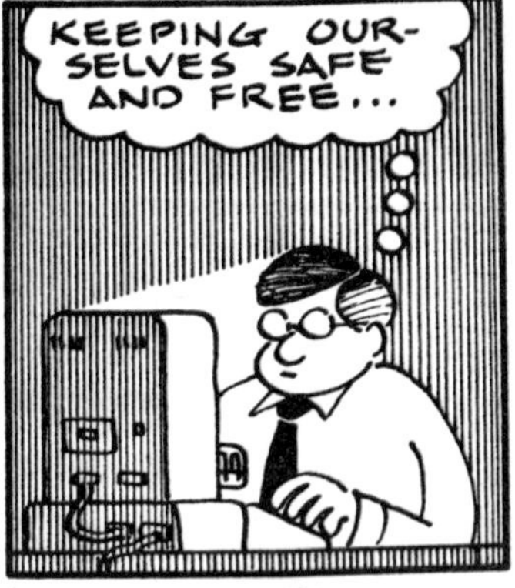
KEEPING OURSELVES SAFE AND FREE...

b. von alten

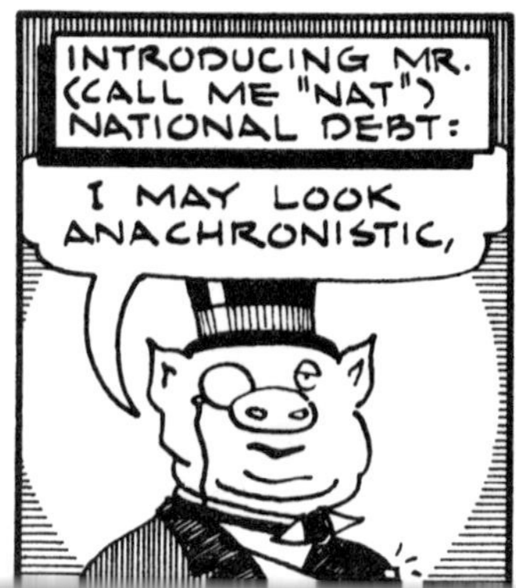
INTRODUCING MR. (CALL ME "NAT") NATIONAL DEBT:
I MAY LOOK ANACHRONISTIC,

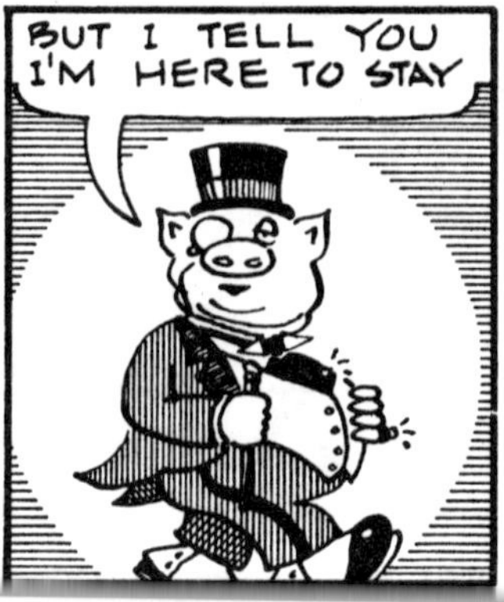
BUT I TELL YOU I'M HERE TO STAY

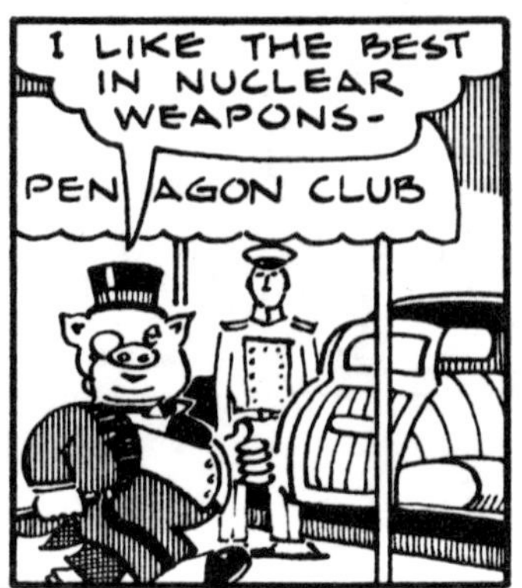
I LIKE THE BEST IN NUCLEAR WEAPONS-
PEN AGON CLUB

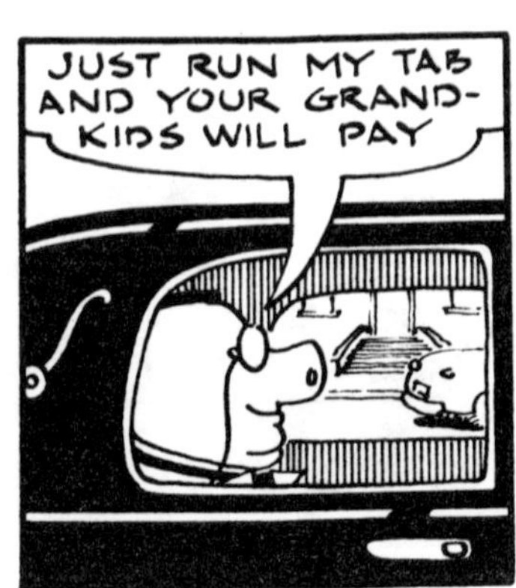
JUST RUN MY TAB AND YOUR GRAND-KIDS WILL PAY

b. von alten

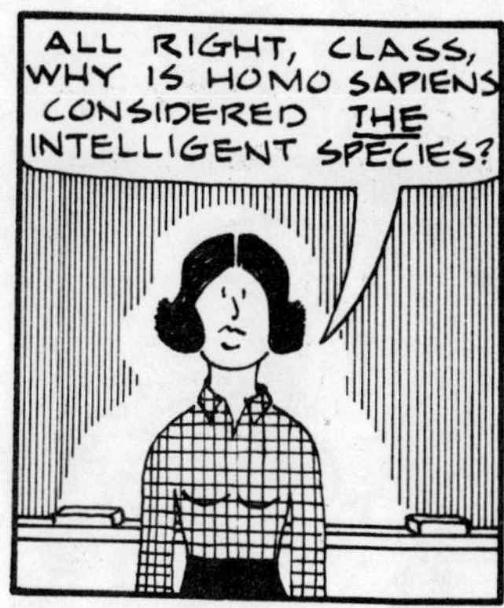
ALL RIGHT, CLASS, WHY IS HOMO SAPIENS CONSIDERED THE INTELLIGENT SPECIES?

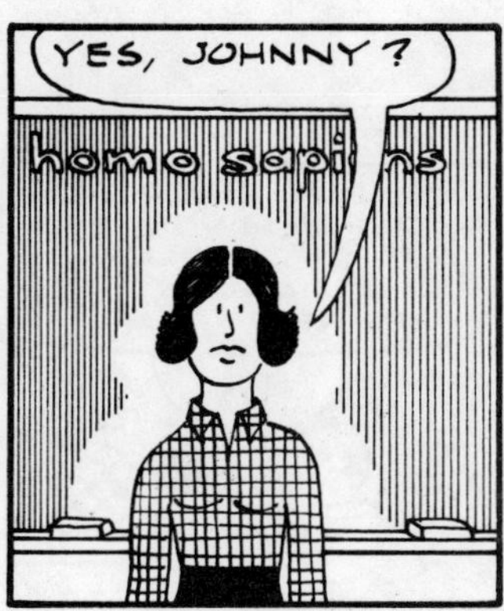
YES, JOHNNY?

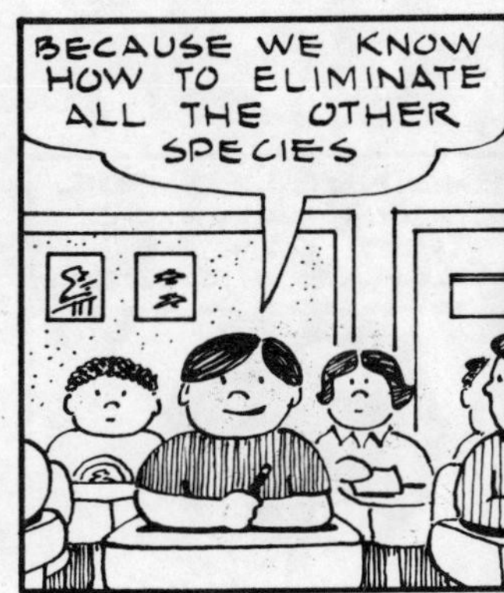
BECAUSE WE KNOW HOW TO ELIMINATE ALL THE OTHER SPECIES

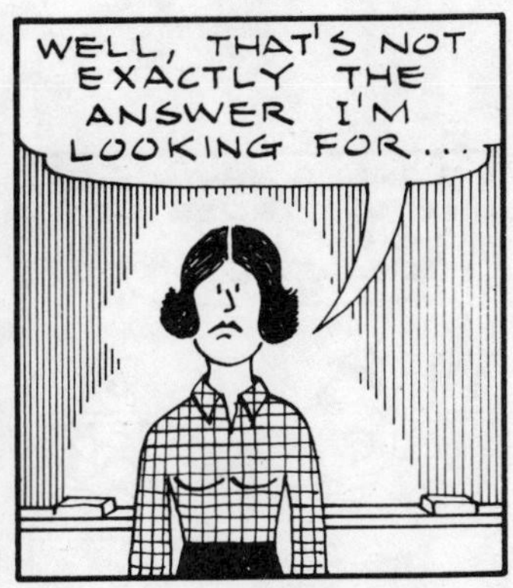
WELL, THAT'S NOT EXACTLY THE ANSWER I'M LOOKING FOR...

b. von alten

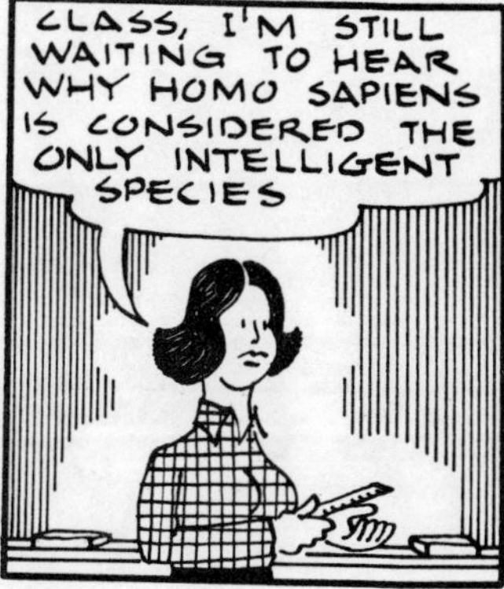
CLASS, I'M STILL WAITING TO HEAR WHY HOMO SAPIENS IS CONSIDERED THE ONLY INTELLIGENT SPECIES

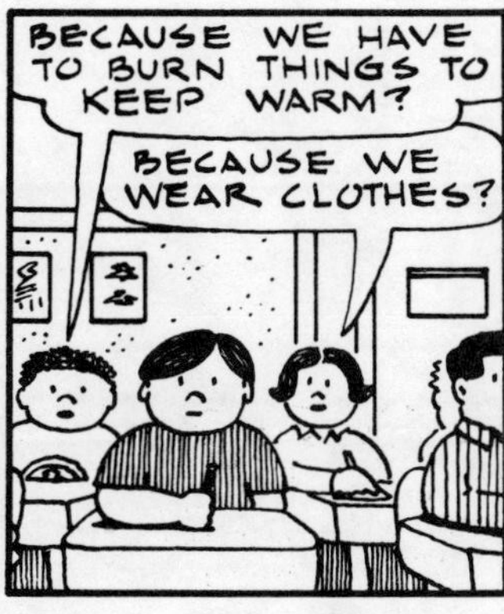
BECAUSE WE HAVE TO BURN THINGS TO KEEP WARM?
BECAUSE WE WEAR CLOTHES?

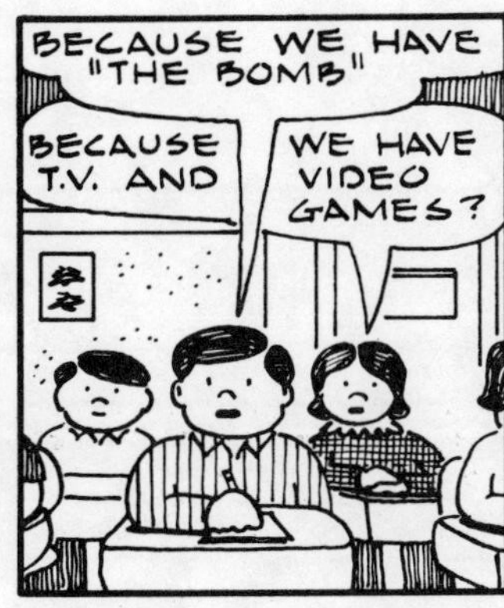
BECAUSE WE HAVE "THE BOMB"
BECAUSE T.V. AND
WE HAVE VIDEO GAMES?

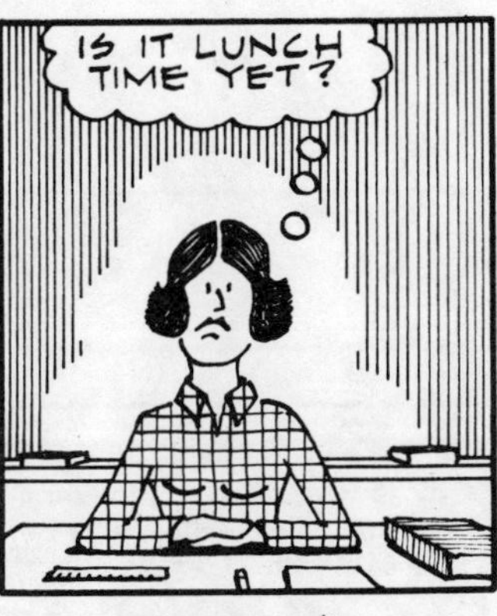
IS IT LUNCH TIME YET?

b. von alten

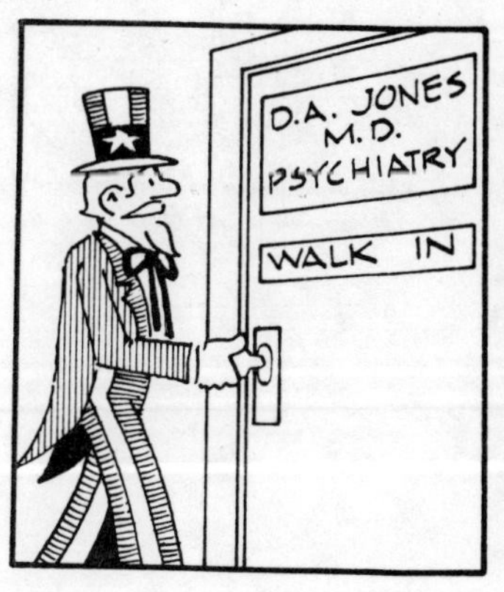
D.A. JONES
M.D.
PSYCHIATRY
WALK IN

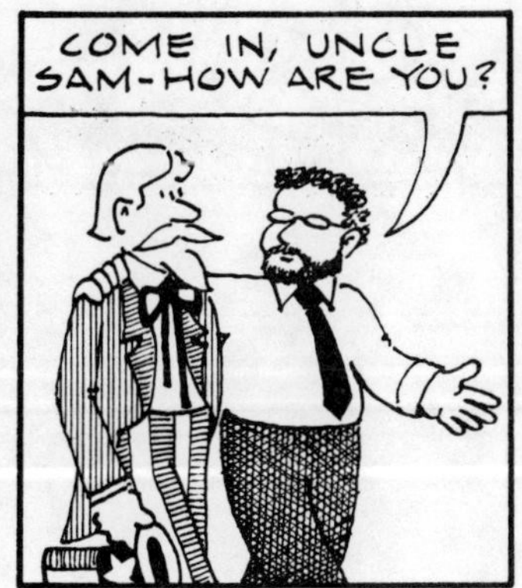
COME IN, UNCLE SAM-HOW ARE YOU?

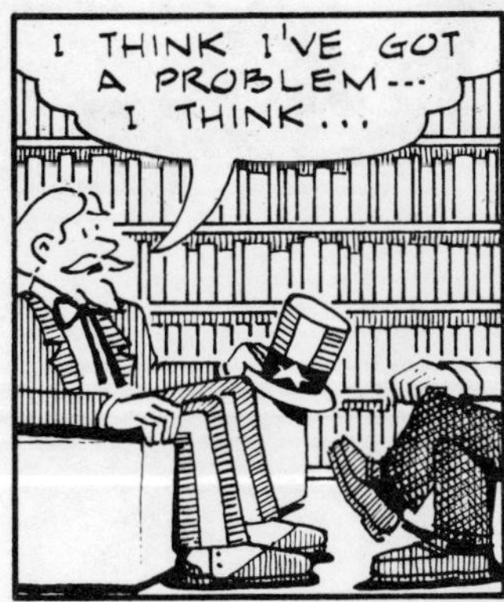
I THINK I'VE GOT A PROBLEM--- I THINK...

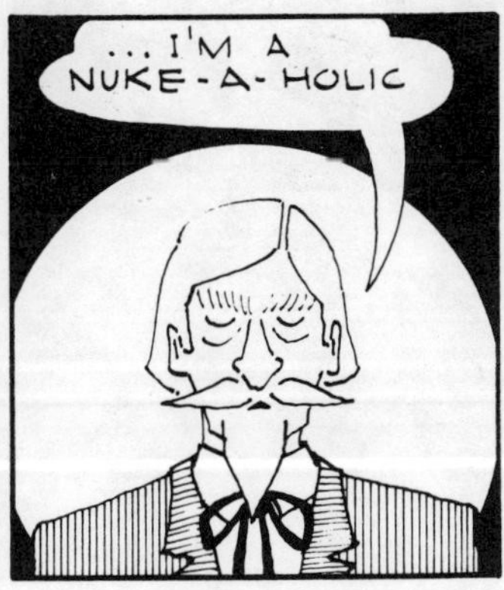
...I'M A NUKE-A-HOLIC

b. von alten

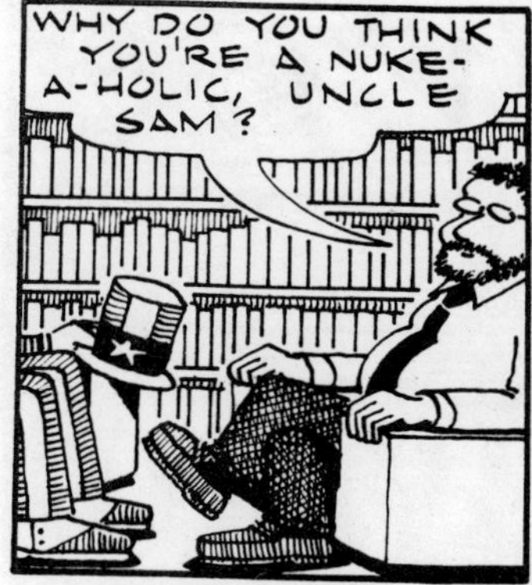
WHY DO YOU THINK YOU'RE A NUKE-A-HOLIC, UNCLE SAM?

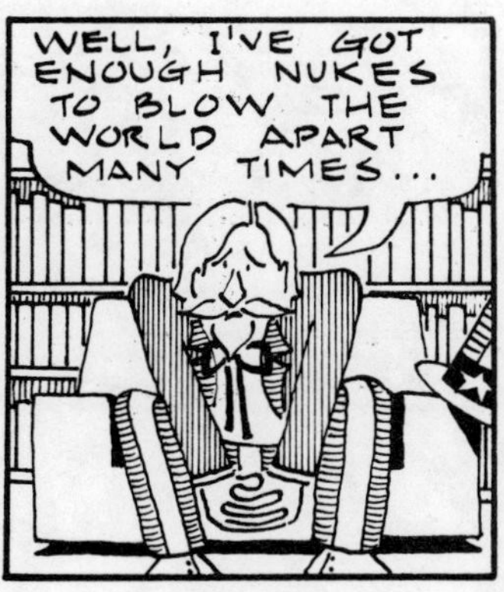
WELL, I'VE GOT ENOUGH NUKES TO BLOW THE WORLD APART MANY TIMES...

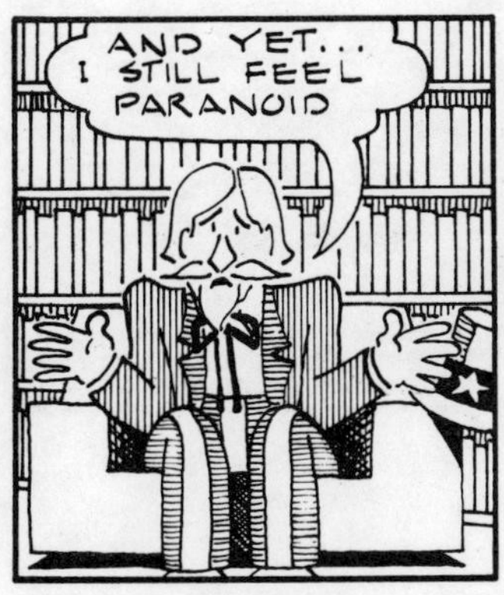
AND YET... I STILL FEEL PARANOID

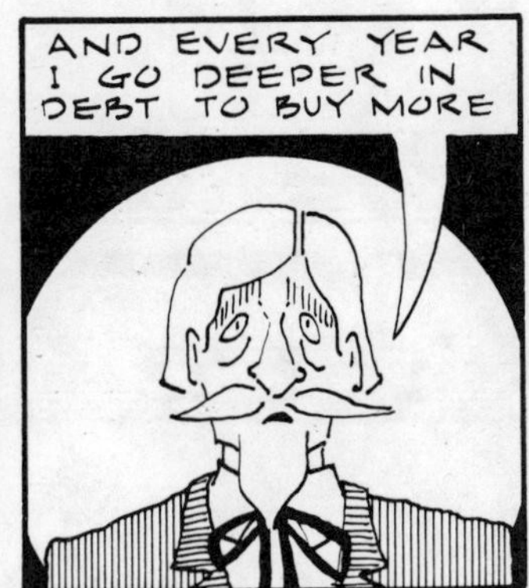
AND EVERY YEAR I GO DEEPER IN DEBT TO BUY MORE

b. von alten

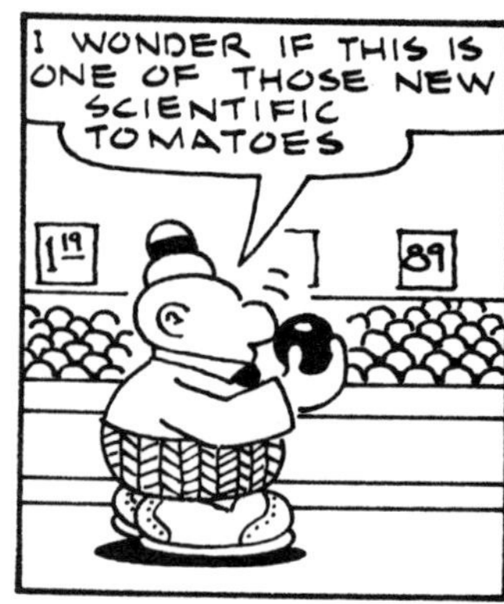
I WONDER IF THIS IS ONE OF THOSE NEW SCIENTIFIC TOMATOES
1.19
89

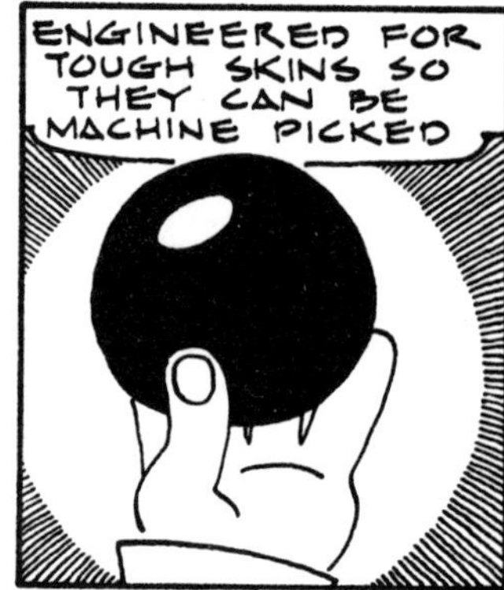
ENGINEERED FOR TOUGH SKINS SO THEY CAN BE MACHINE PICKED

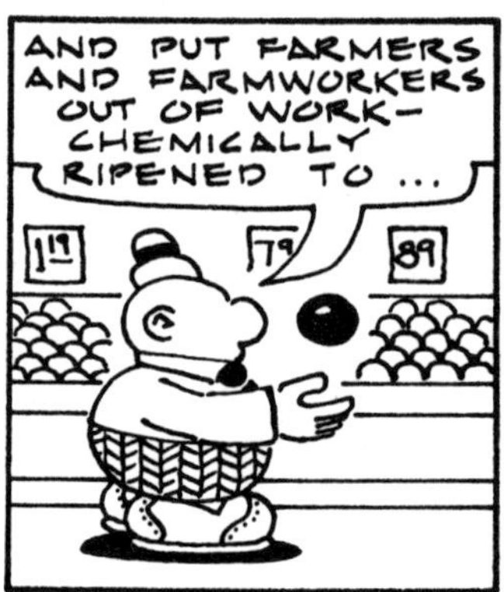
AND PUT FARMERS AND FARMWORKERS OUT OF WORK-CHEMICALLY RIPENED TO ...
1.19
79
89

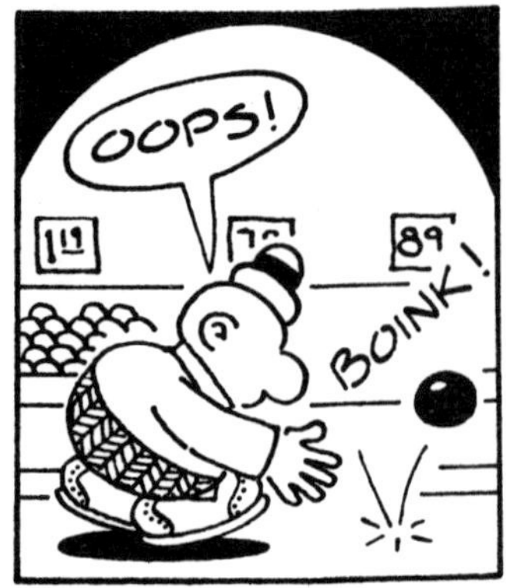
OOPS!
BOINK!
1.19
89

b. von alten

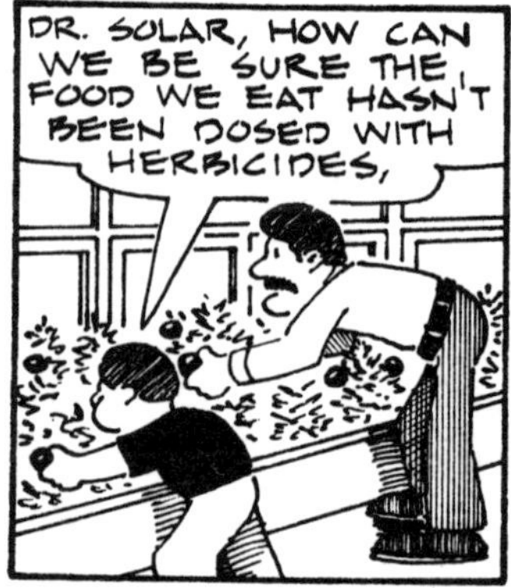
DR. SOLAR, HOW CAN WE BE SURE THE FOOD WE EAT HASN'T BEEN DOSED WITH HERBICIDES,

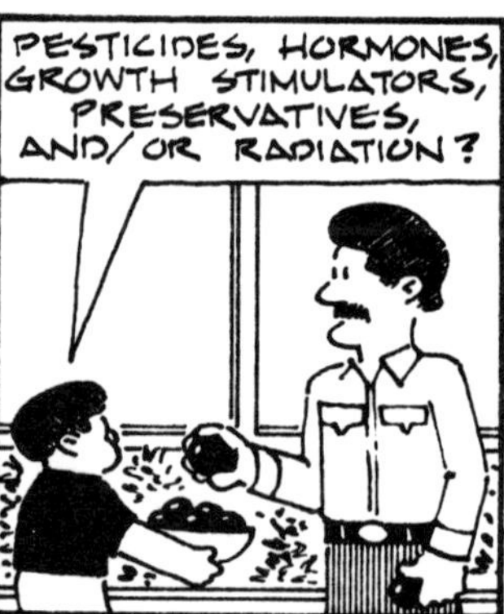
PESTICIDES, HORMONES, GROWTH STIMULATORS, PRESERVATIVES, AND/OR RADIATION?

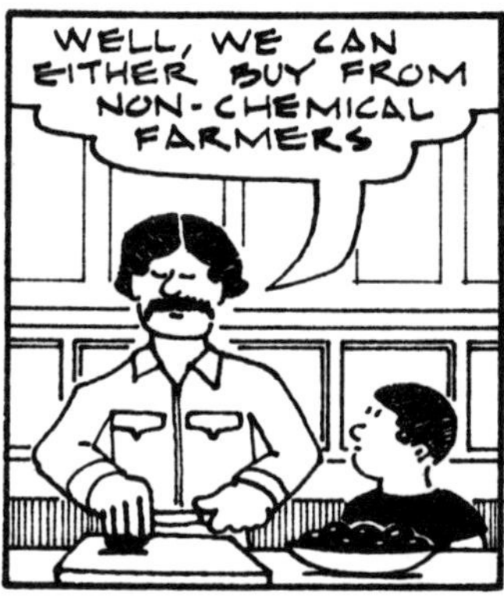
WELL, WE CAN EITHER BUY FROM NON-CHEMICAL FARMERS

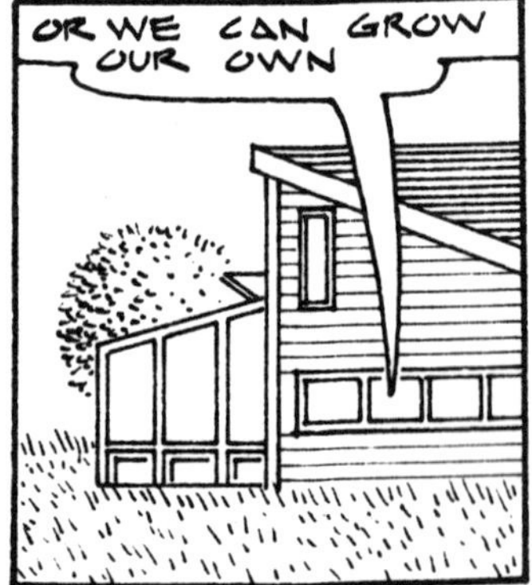
OR WE CAN GROW OUR OWN

b. von alten

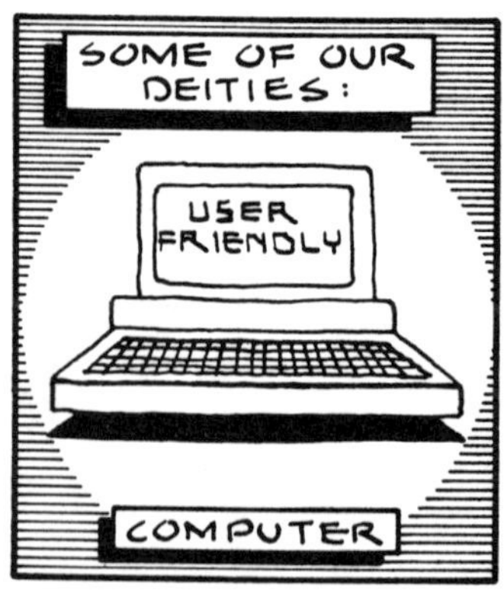
SOME OF OUR DEITIES:
USER FRIENDLY
COMPUTER

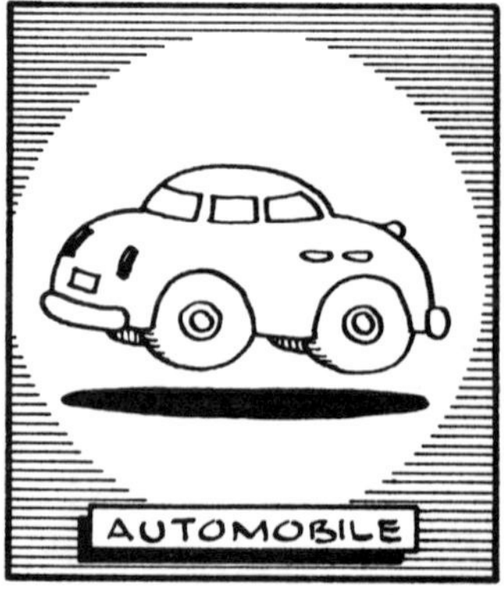
AUTOMOBILE

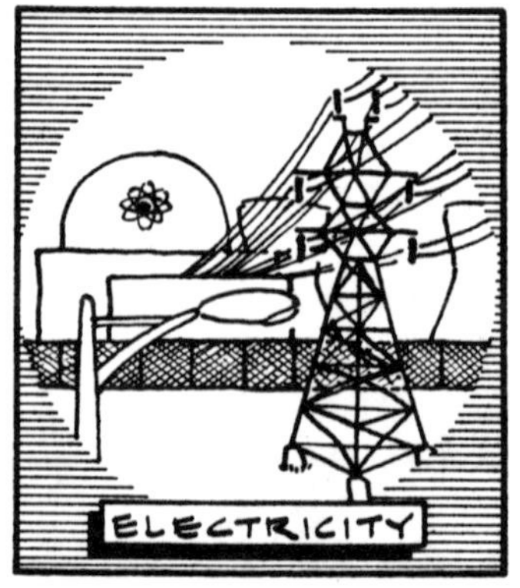
ELECTRICITY

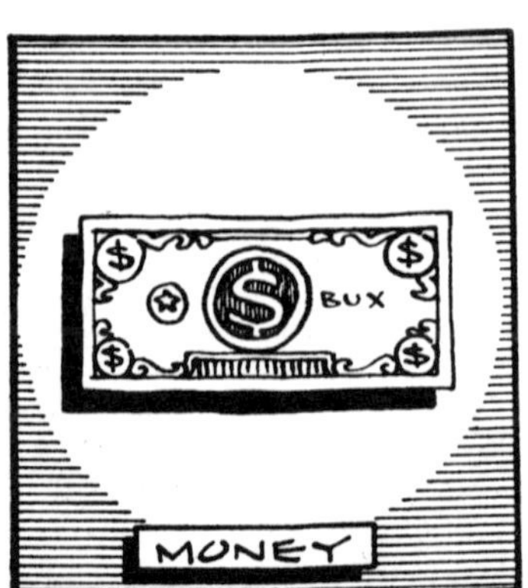
BUX
MONEY

b. von alten

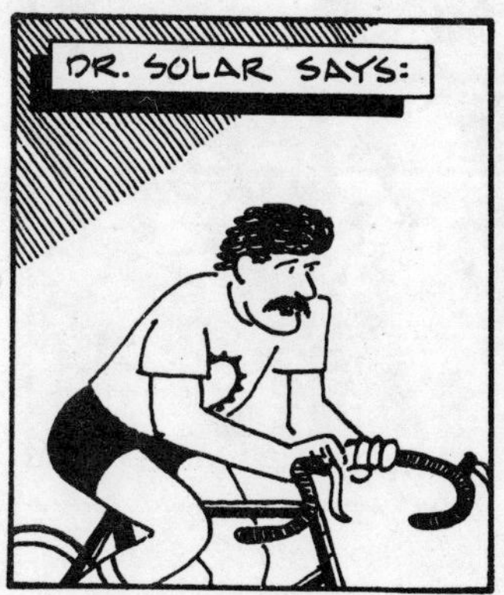
DR. SOLAR SAYS:

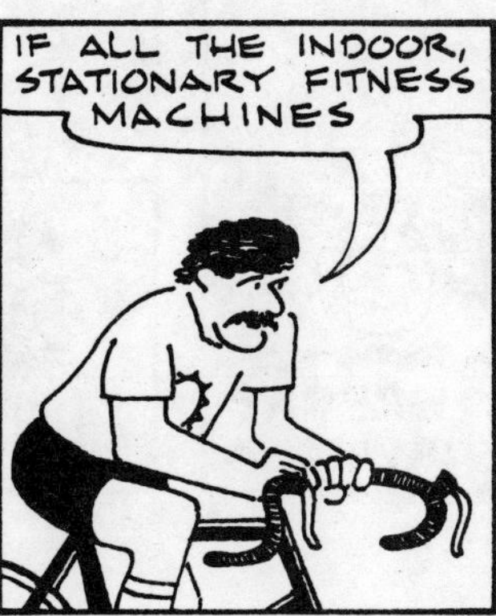
IF ALL THE INDOOR, STATIONARY FITNESS MACHINES

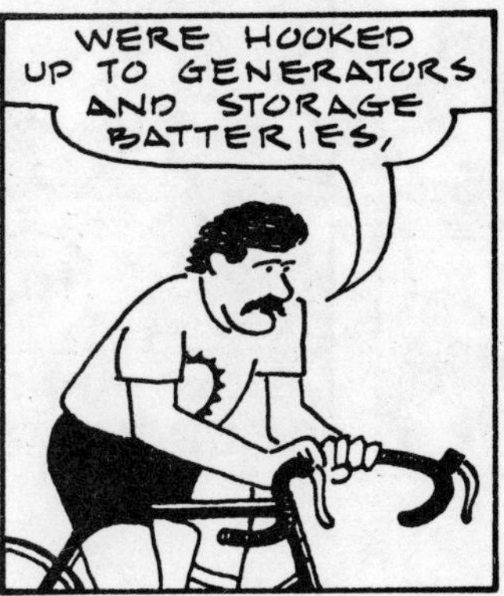
WERE HOOKED UP TO GENERATORS AND STORAGE BATTERIES,

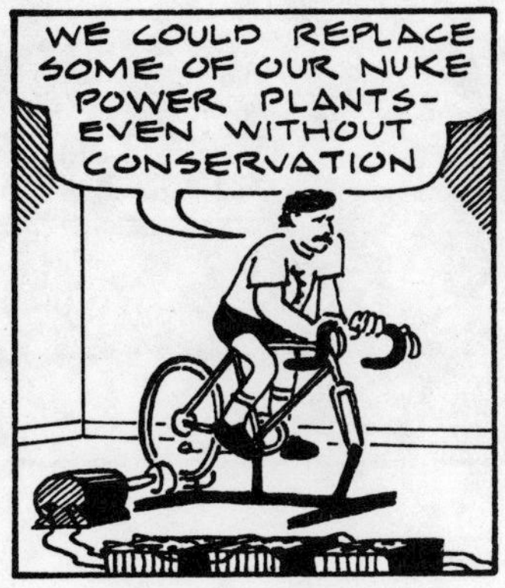
WE COULD REPLACE SOME OF OUR NUKE POWER PLANTS- EVEN WITHOUT CONSERVATION

b. von alten

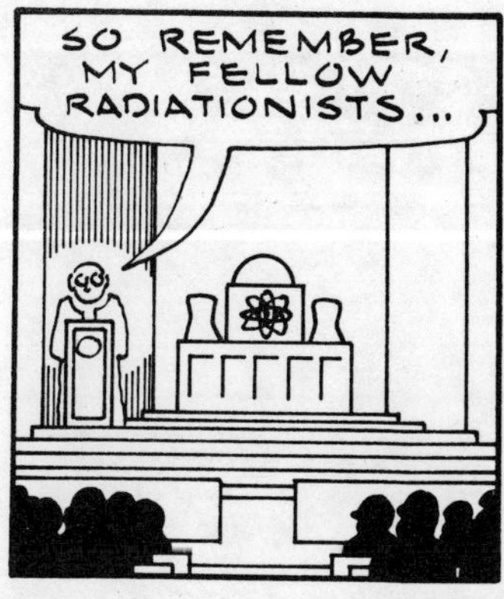
SO REMEMBER, MY FELLOW RADIATIONISTS...

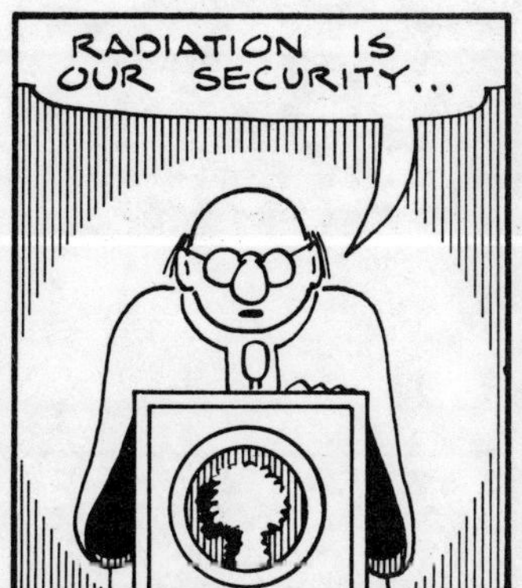
RADIATION IS OUR SECURITY...

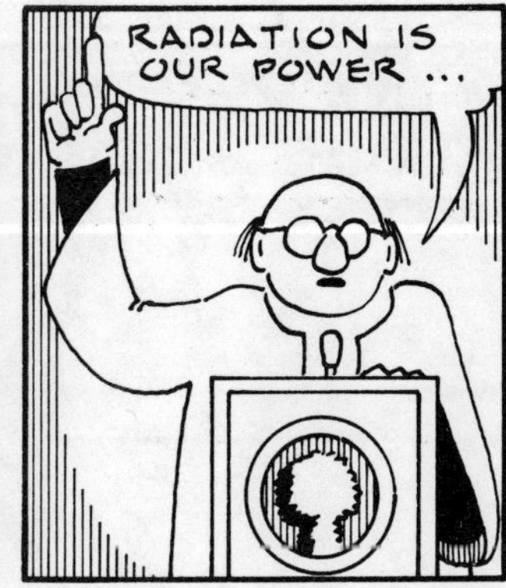
RADIATION IS OUR POWER ...

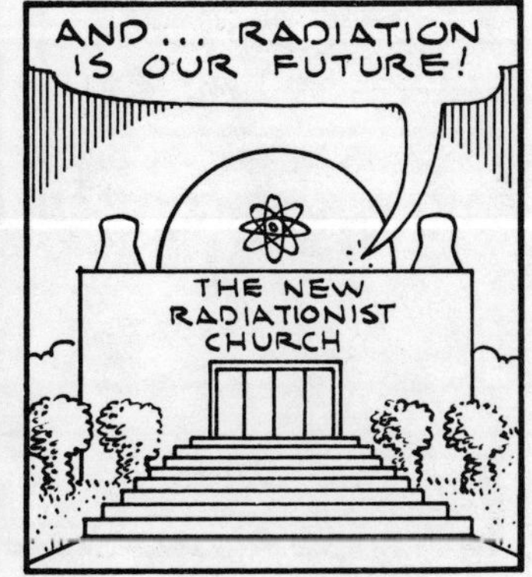
AND... RADIATION IS OUR FUTURE!
THE NEW RADIATIONIST CHURCH

b. von alten

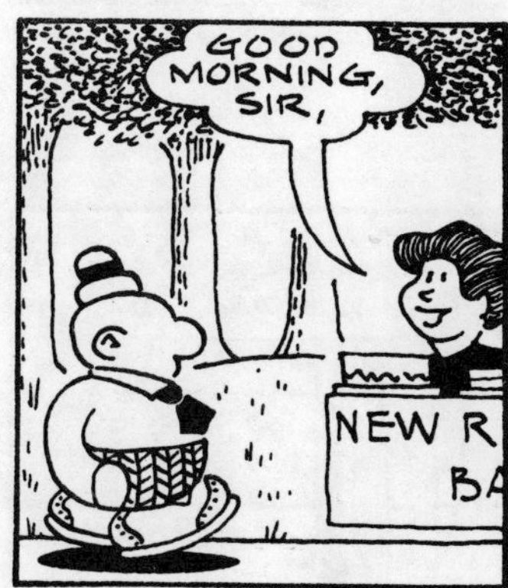
GOOD MORNING, SIR,
NEW R
BA

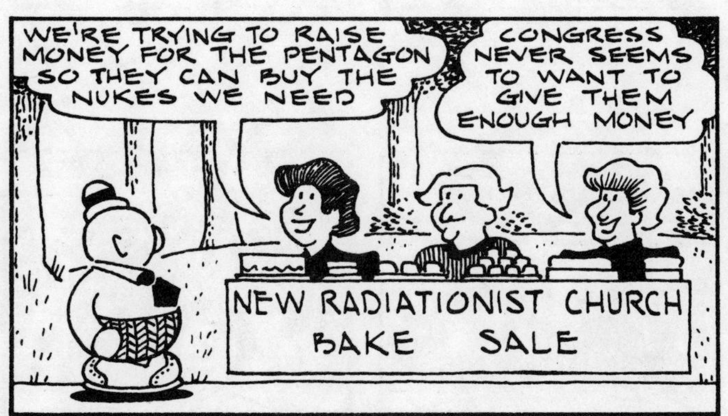
WE'RE TRYING TO RAISE MONEY FOR THE PENTAGON SO THEY CAN BUY THE NUKES WE NEED
CONGRESS NEVER SEEMS TO WANT TO GIVE THEM ENOUGH MONEY
NEW RADIATIONIST CHURCH
BAKE SALE

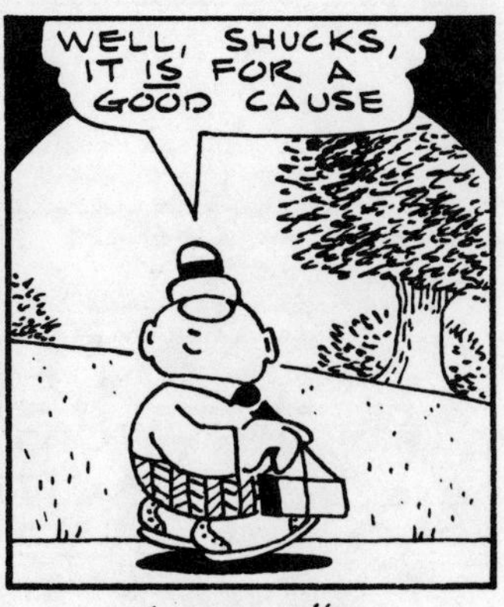
WELL, SHUCKS, IT IS FOR A GOOD CAUSE

b. von alten

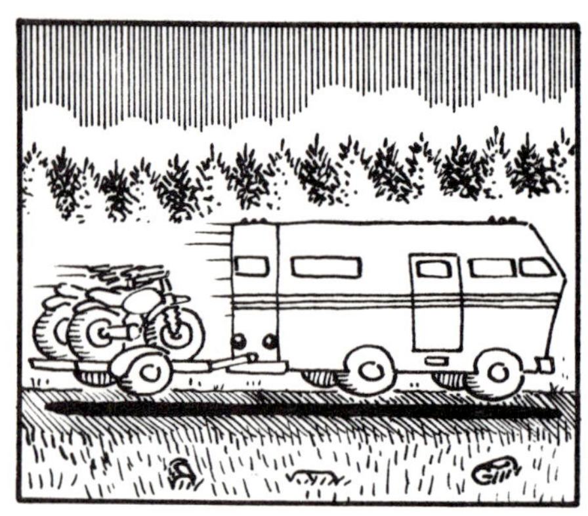
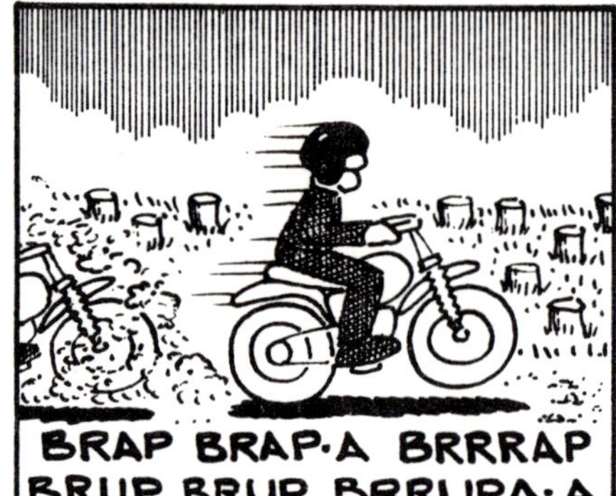
BRAP BRAP-A BRRRAP
BRUP BRUP BRRUPA-A
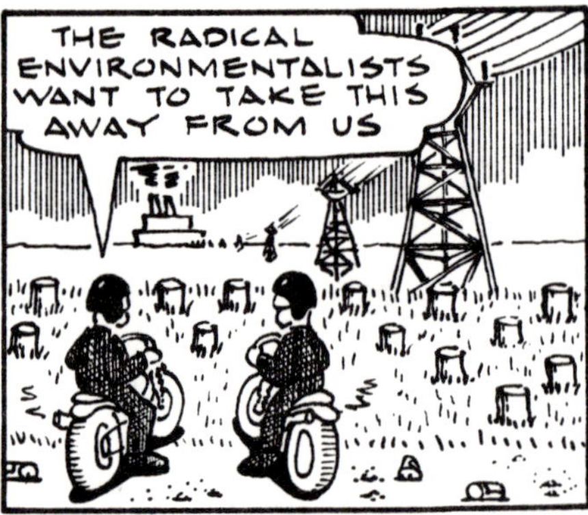
THE RADICAL ENVIRONMENTALISTS WANT TO TAKE THIS AWAY FROM US

b. von alten

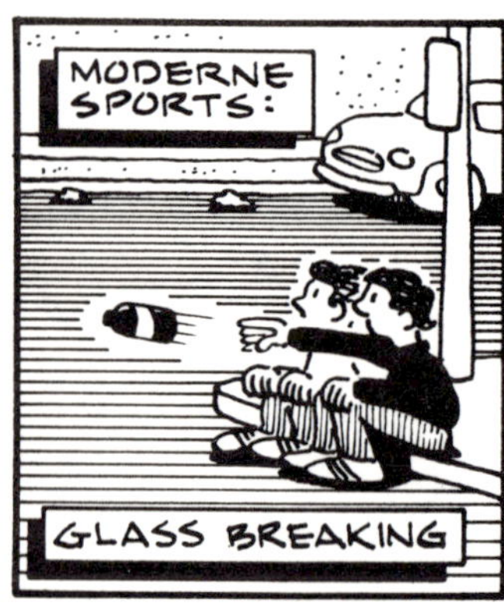
MODERNE SPORTS:
GLASS BREAKING
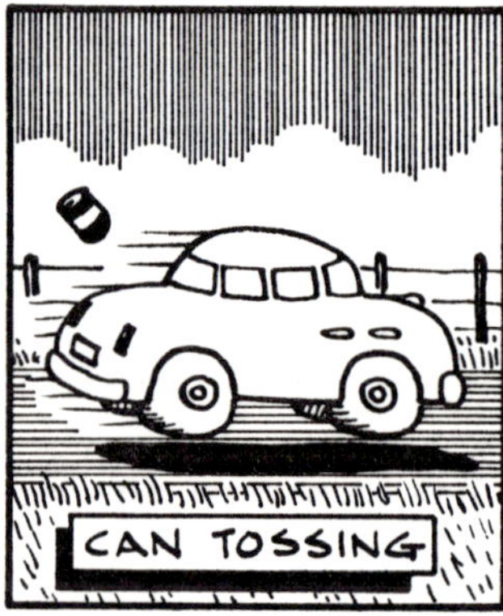
CAN TOSSING
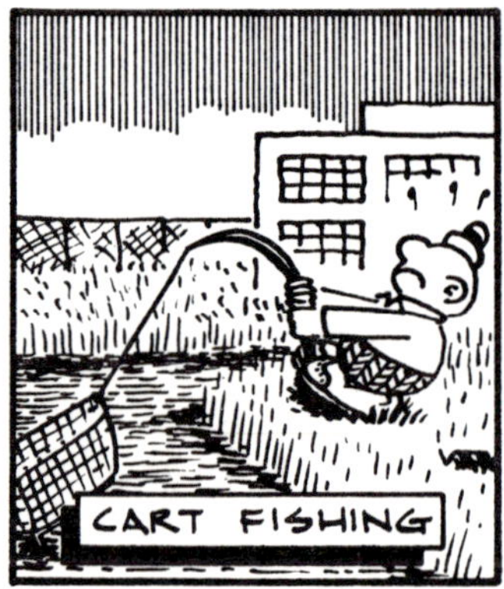
CART FISHING
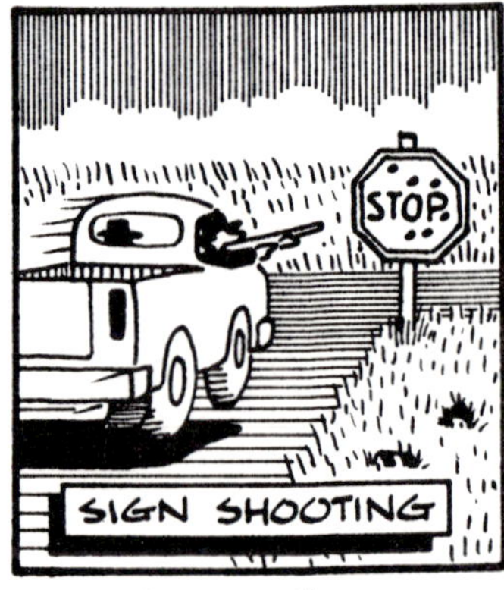
STOP
SIGN SHOOTING

b. von alten

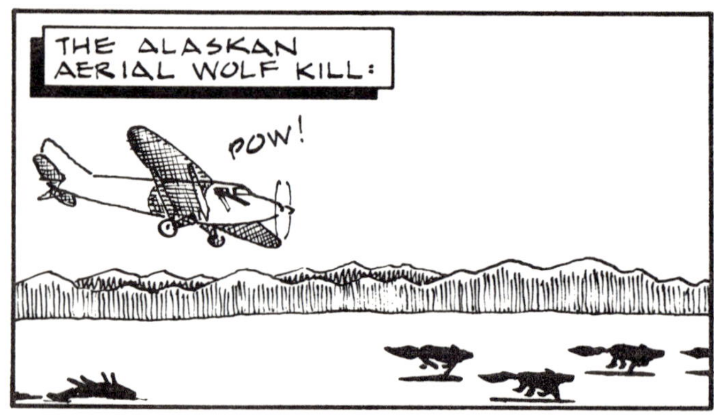
THE ALASKAN AERIAL WOLF KILL:
POW!
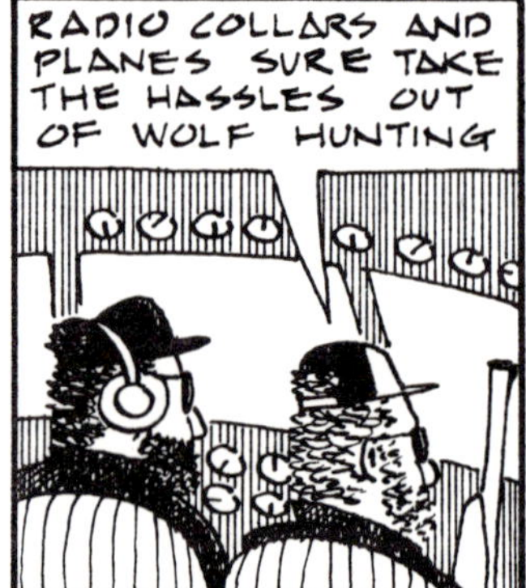
RADIO COLLARS AND PLANES SURE TAKE THE HASSLES OUT OF WOLF HUNTING
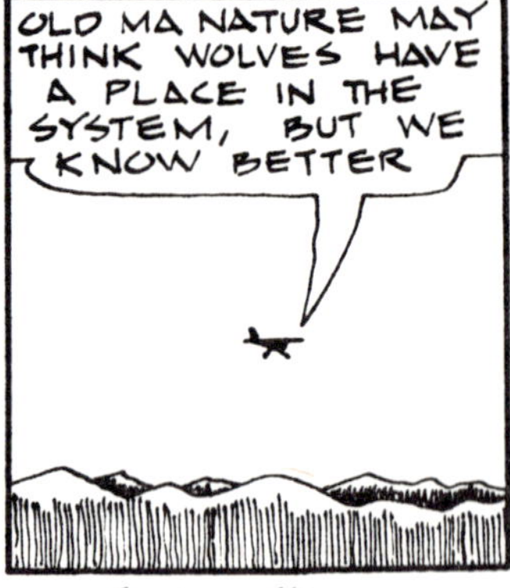
OLD MA NATURE MAY THINK WOLVES HAVE A PLACE IN THE SYSTEM, BUT WE KNOW BETTER

b. von alten

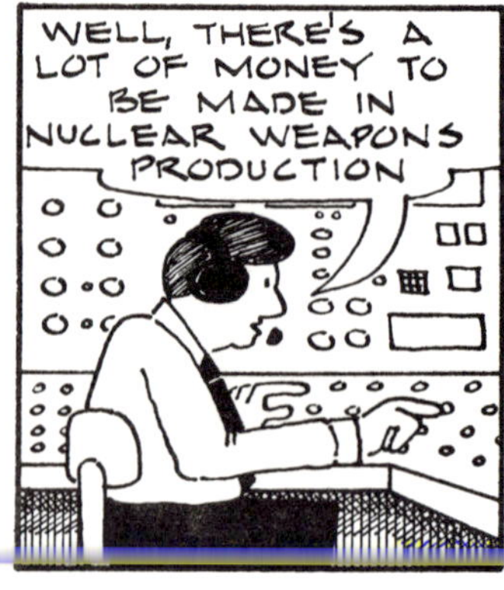
WELL, THERE'S A LOT OF MONEY TO BE MADE IN NUCLEAR WEAPONS PRODUCTION
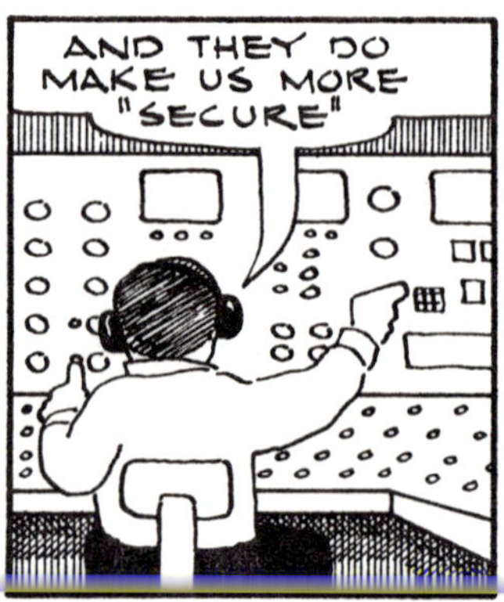
AND THEY DO MAKE US MORE "SECURE"
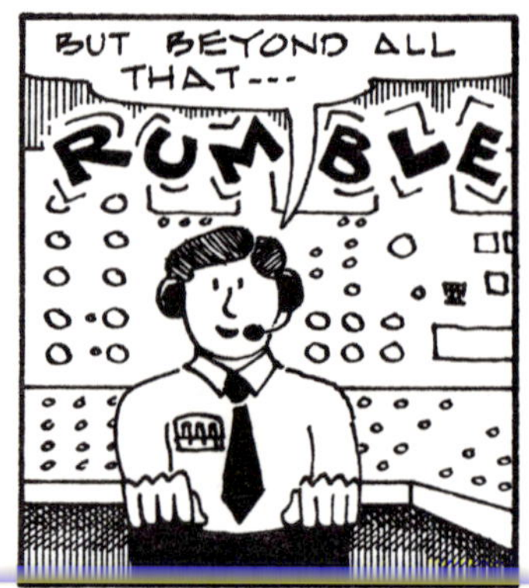
BUT BEYOND ALL THAT---
RUMBLE
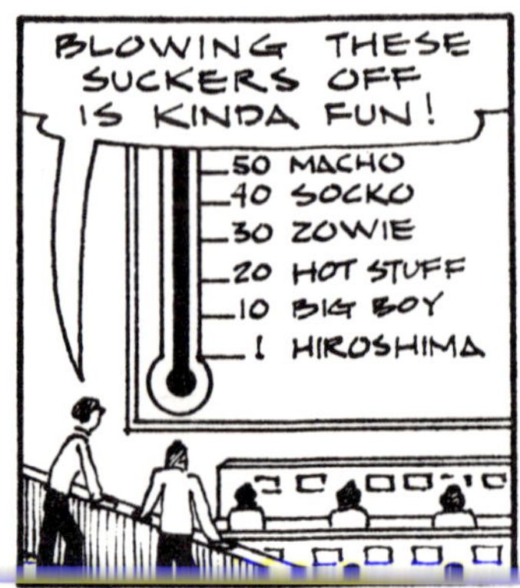
BLOWING THESE SUCKERS OFF IS KINDA FUN!
50 MACHO
40 SOCKO
30 ZOWIE
20 HOT STUFF
10 BIG BOY
1 HIROSHIMA

b. von alten

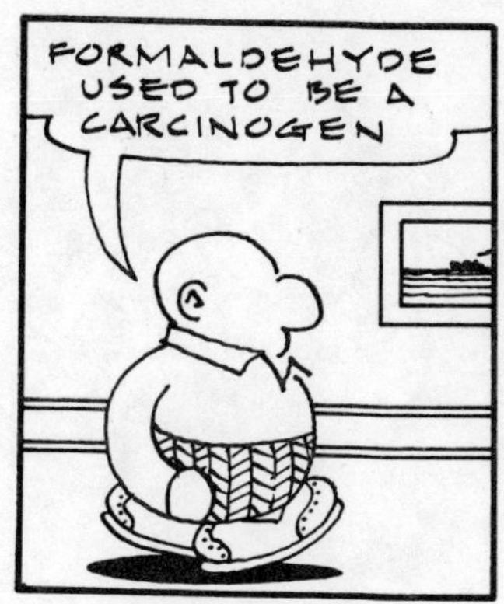
FORMALDEHYDE USED TO BE A CARCINOGEN

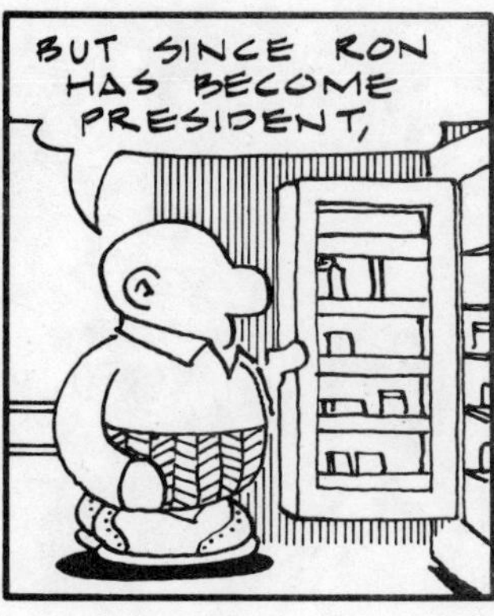
BUT SINCE RON HAS BECOME PRESIDENT,

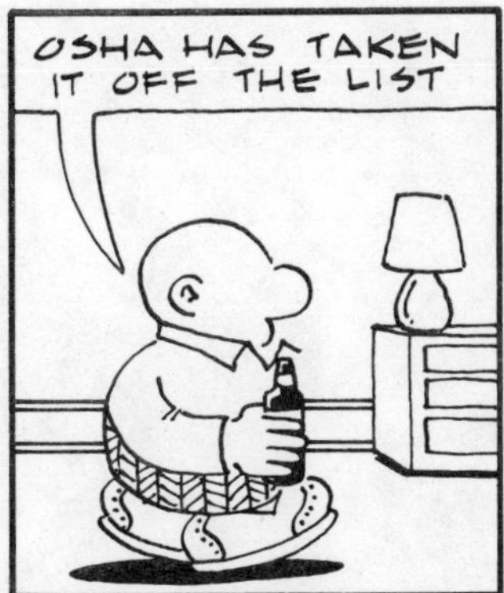
OSHA HAS TAKEN IT OFF THE LIST

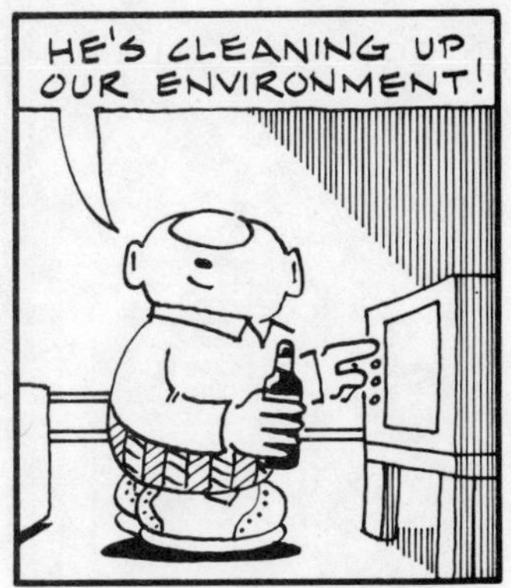
HE'S CLEANING UP OUR ENVIRONMENT!

b. von alten

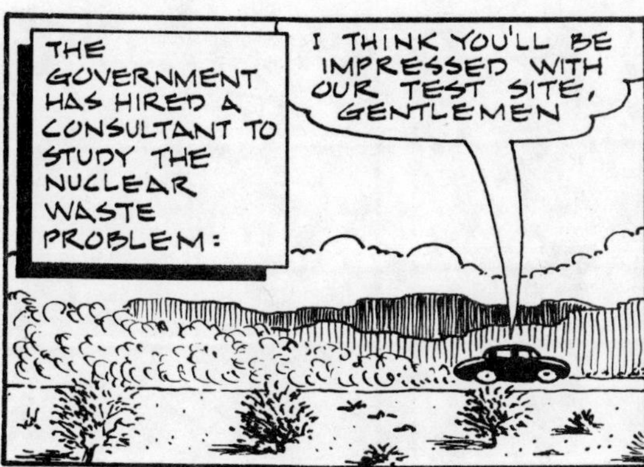
THE GOVERNMENT HAS HIRED A CONSULTANT TO STUDY THE NUCLEAR WASTE PROBLEM:
I THINK YOU'LL BE IMPRESSED WITH OUR TEST SITE, GENTLEMEN

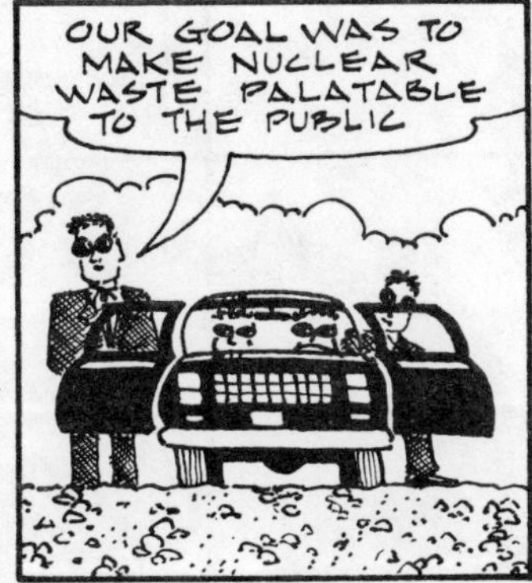
OUR GOAL WAS TO MAKE NUCLEAR WASTE PALATABLE TO THE PUBLIC

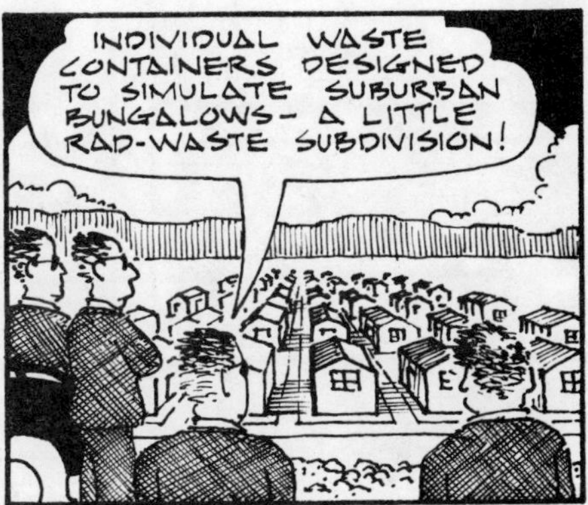
INDIVIDUAL WASTE CONTAINERS DESIGNED TO SIMULATE SUBURBAN BUNGALOWS— A LITTLE RAD-WASTE SUBDIVISION!

b. von alten

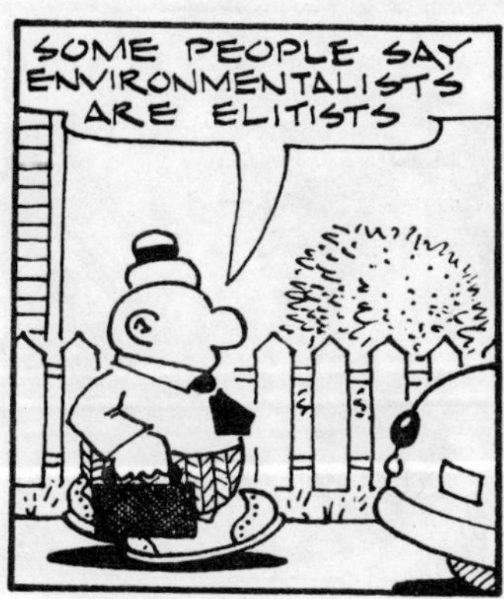
SOME PEOPLE SAY ENVIRONMENTALISTS ARE ELITISTS

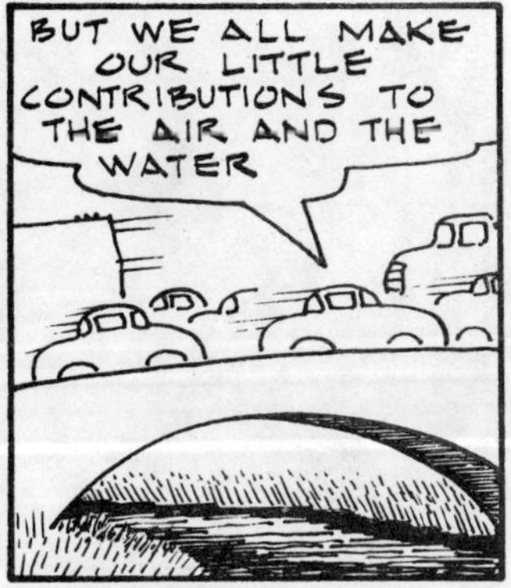
BUT WE ALL MAKE OUR LITTLE CONTRIBUTIONS TO THE AIR AND THE WATER

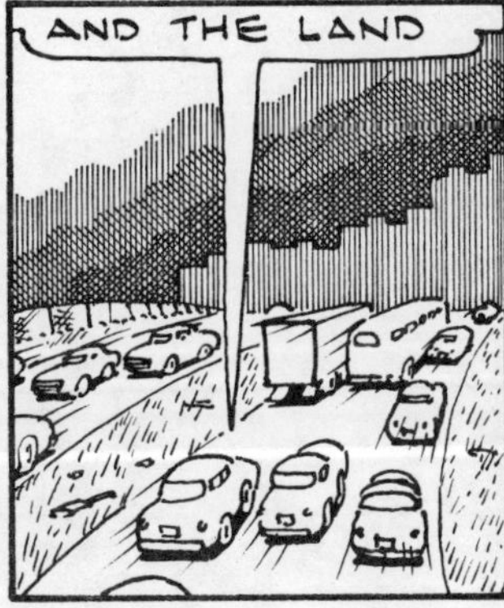
AND THE LAND

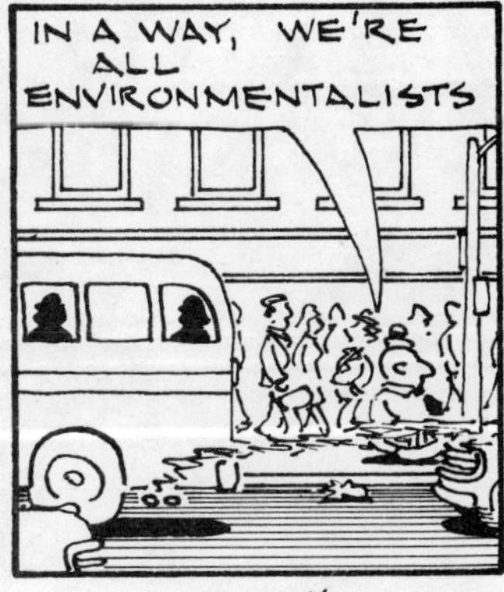
IN A WAY, WE'RE ALL ENVIRONMENTALISTS

b. von alten

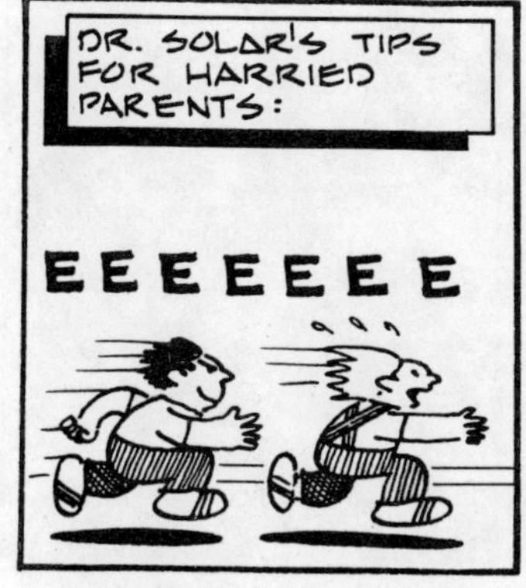
DR. SOLAR'S TIPS FOR HARRIED PARENTS:
EEEEEEE

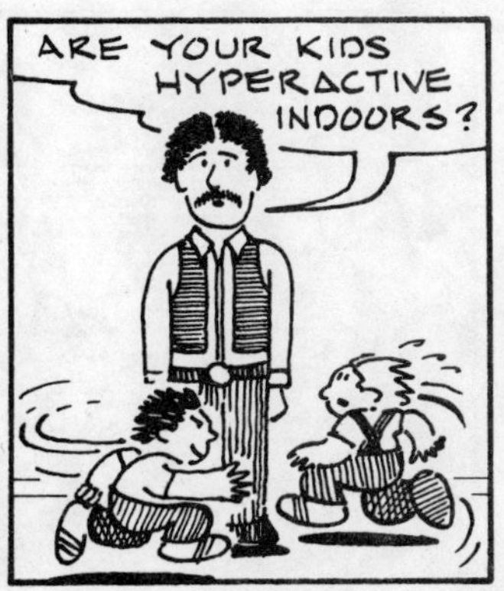
ARE YOUR KIDS HYPERACTIVE INDOORS?

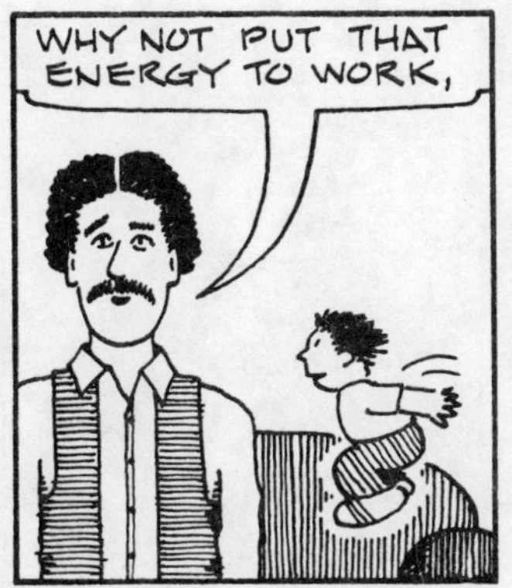
WHY NOT PUT THAT ENERGY TO WORK,

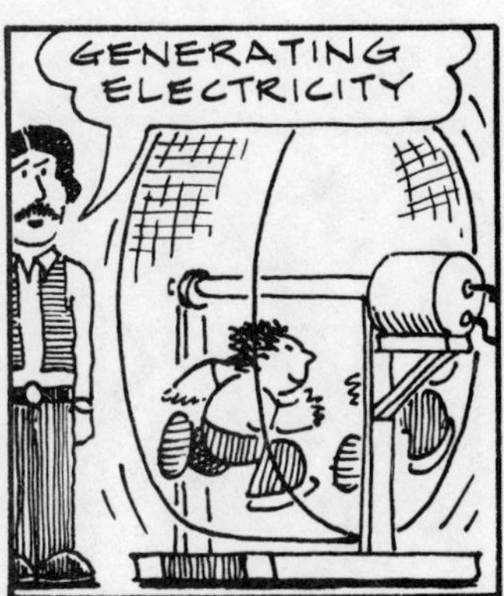
GENERATING ELECTRICITY

b. von alten

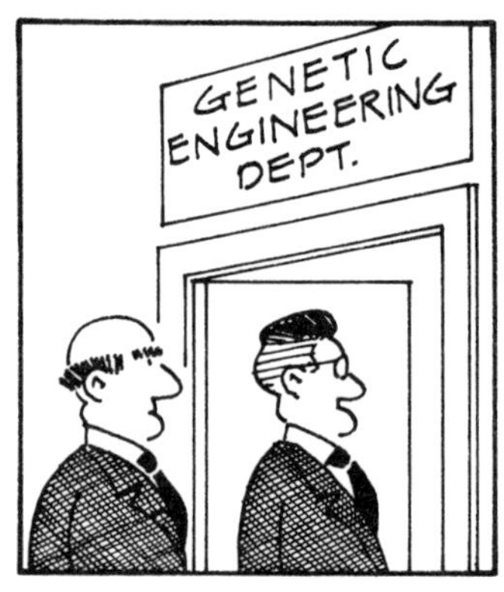
GENETIC ENGINEERING DEPT.

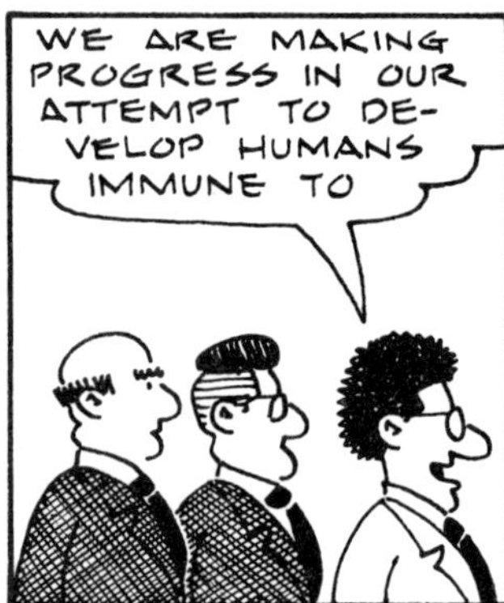
WE ARE MAKING PROGRESS IN OUR ATTEMPT TO DE-VELOP HUMANS IMMUNE TO

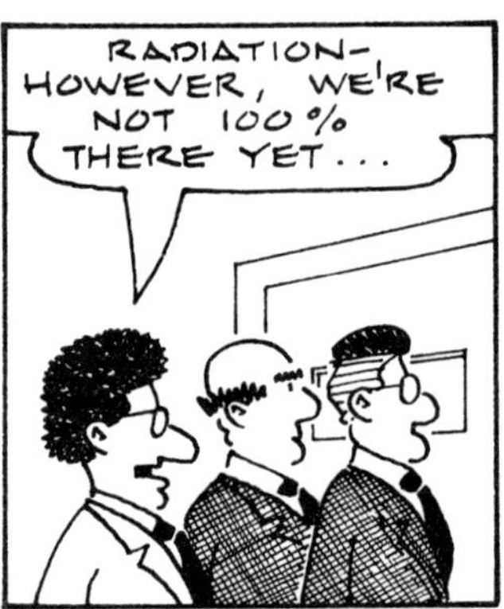
RADIATION- HOWEVER, WE'RE NOT 100% THERE YET...

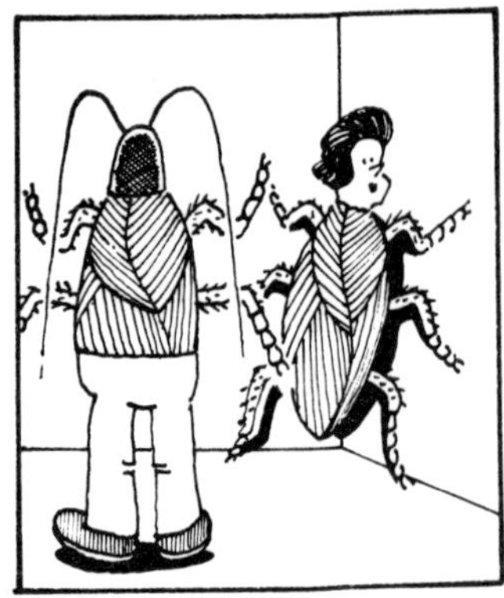

b. von alten

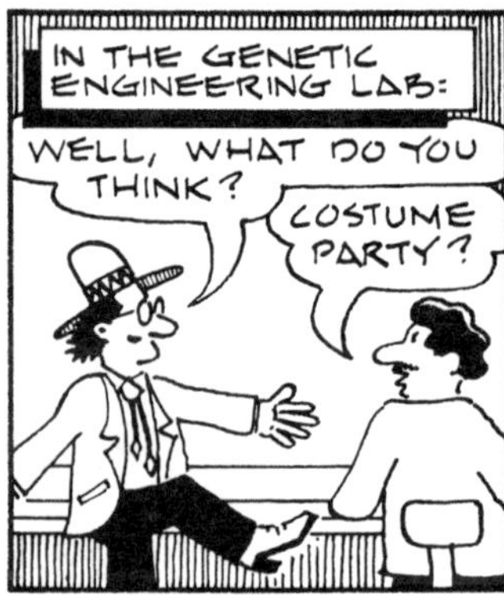
IN THE GENETIC ENGINEERING LAB:
WELL, WHAT DO YOU THINK?
COSTUME PARTY?

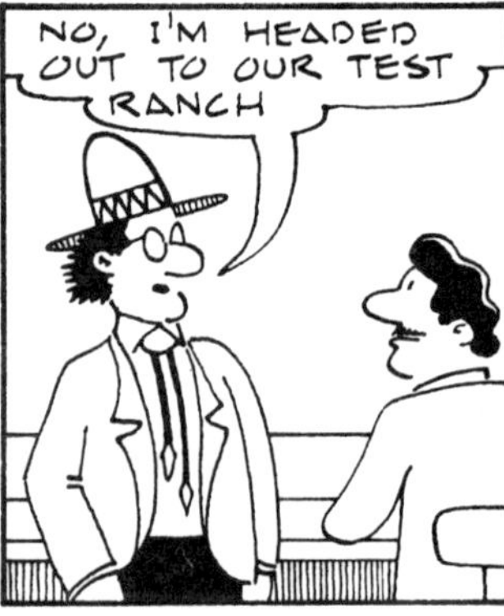
NO, I'M HEADED OUT TO OUR TEST RANCH

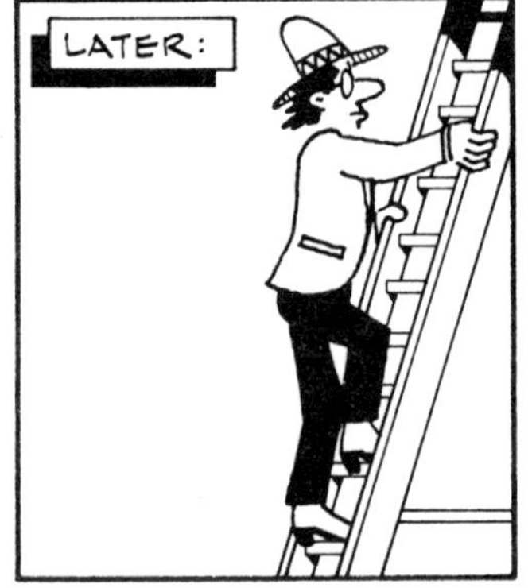
LATER:

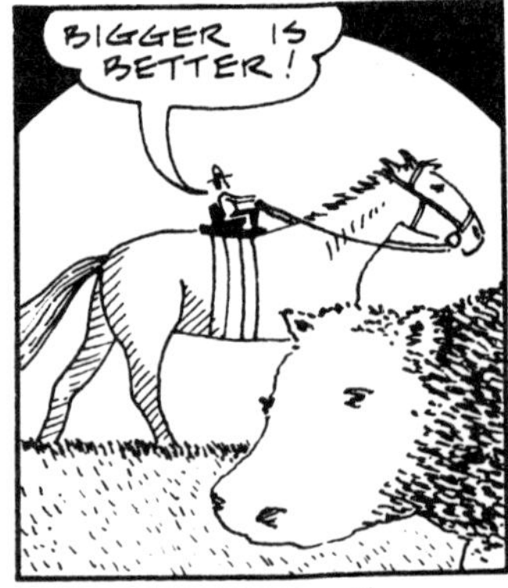
BIGGER IS BETTER!

b. von alten

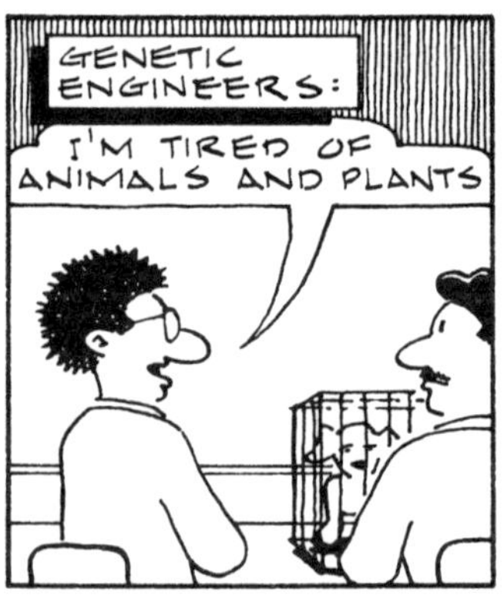
GENETIC ENGINEERS:
I'M TIRED OF ANIMALS AND PLANTS

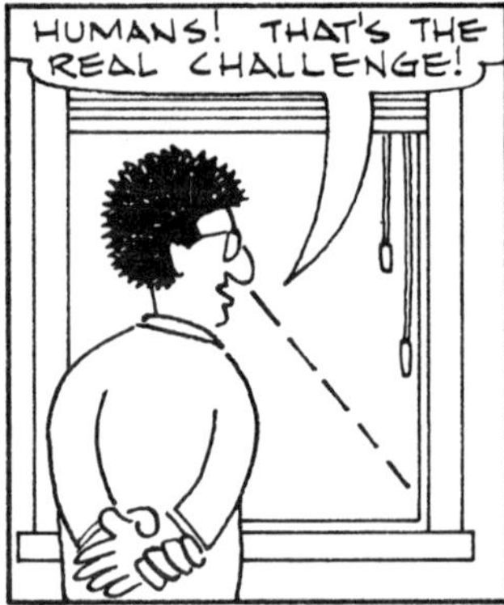
HUMANS! THAT'S THE REAL CHALLENGE!

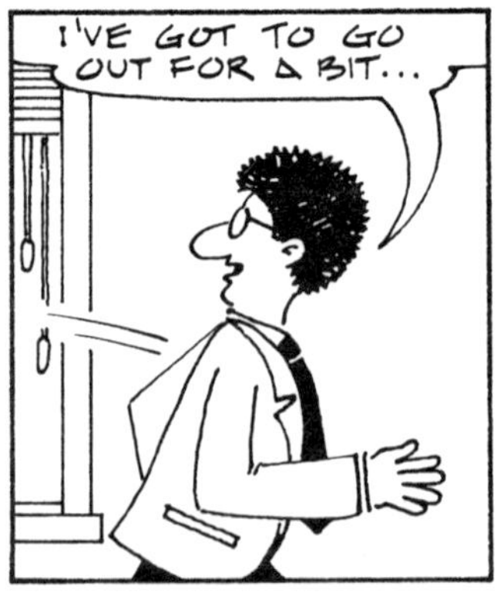
I'VE GOT TO GO OUT FOR A BIT...

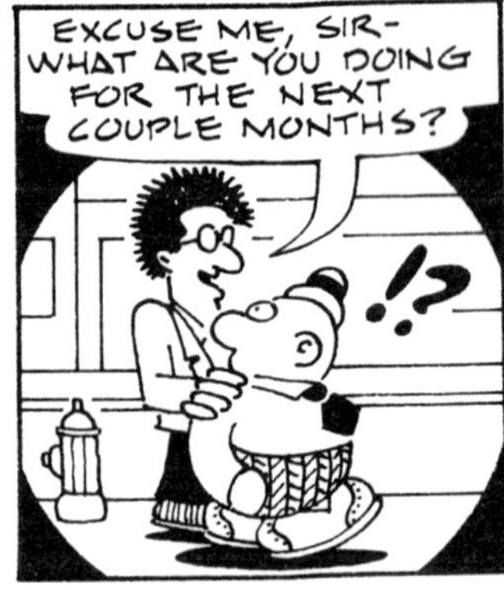
EXCUSE ME, SIR- WHAT ARE YOU DOING FOR THE NEXT COUPLE MONTHS?
!?

b. von alten

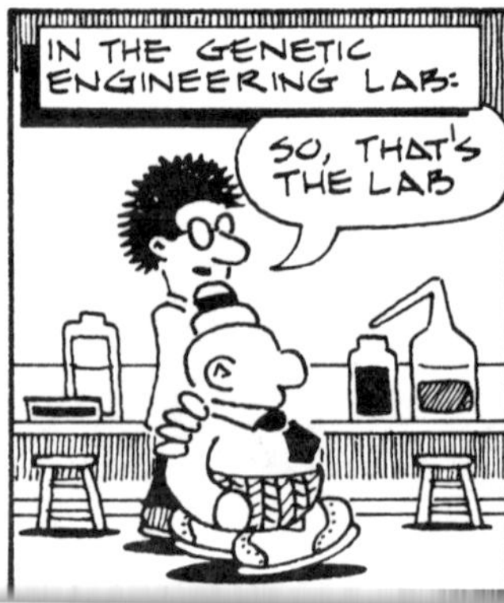
IN THE GENETIC ENGINEERING LAB:
SO, THAT'S THE LAB

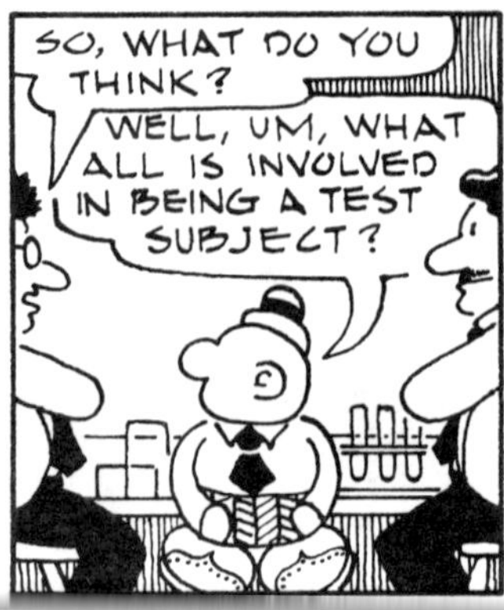
SO, WHAT DO YOU THINK?
WELL, UM, WHAT ALL IS INVOLVED IN BEING A TEST SUBJECT?

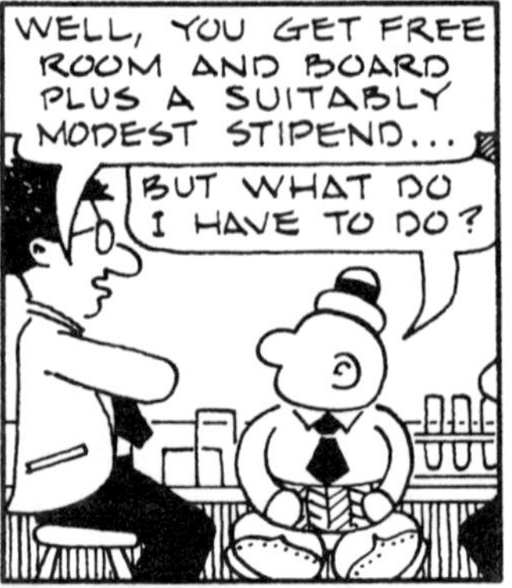
WELL, YOU GET FREE ROOM AND BOARD PLUS A SUITABLY MODEST STIPEND...
BUT WHAT DO I HAVE TO DO?

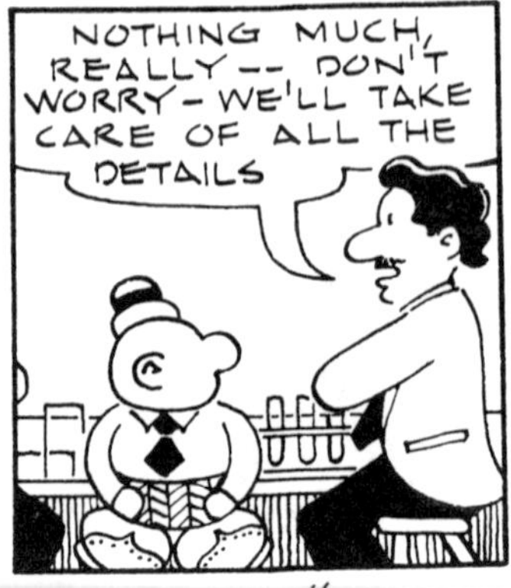
NOTHING MUCH, REALLY -- DON'T WORRY - WE'LL TAKE CARE OF ALL THE DETAILS

b. von alten

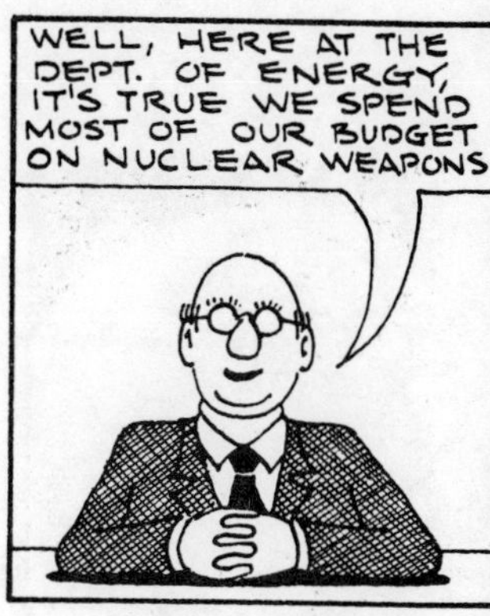
WELL, HERE AT THE DEPT. OF ENERGY, IT'S TRUE WE SPEND MOST OF OUR BUDGET ON NUCLEAR WEAPONS

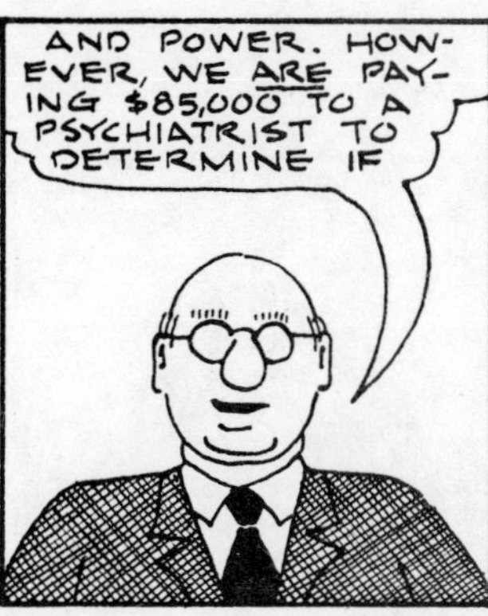
AND POWER. HOWEVER, WE ARE PAYING $85,000 TO A PSYCHIATRIST TO DETERMINE IF

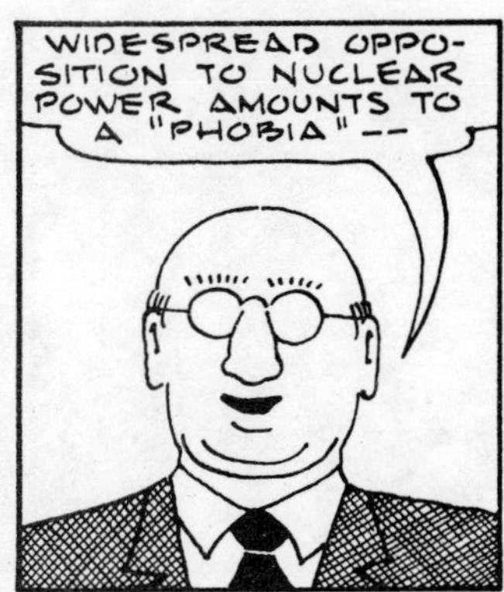
WIDESPREAD OPPOSITION TO NUCLEAR POWER AMOUNTS TO A "PHOBIA"--

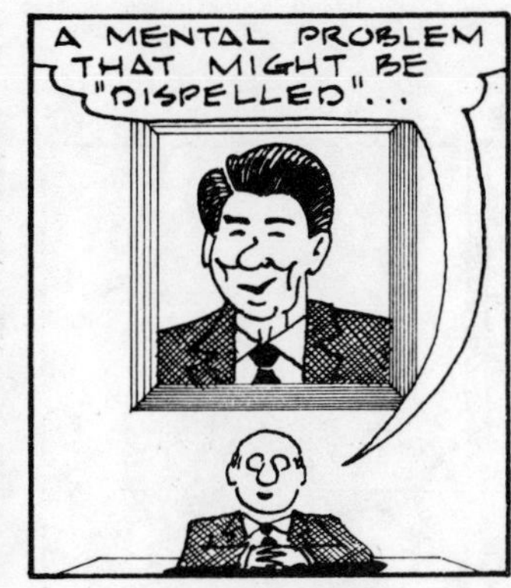
A MENTAL PROBLEM THAT MIGHT BE "DISPELLED"...

b. von alten

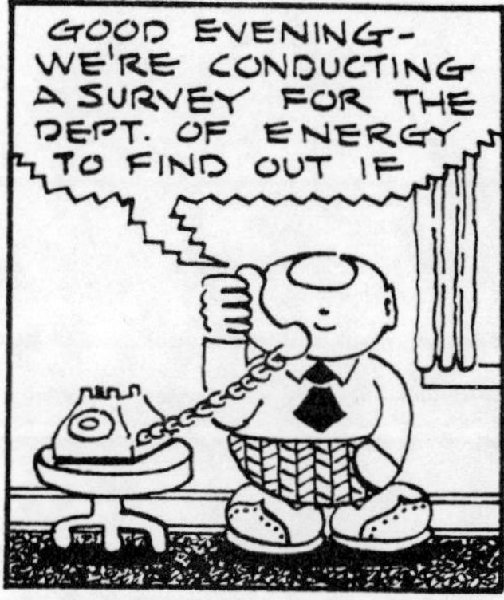
GOOD EVENING- WE'RE CONDUCTING A SURVEY FOR THE DEPT. OF ENERGY TO FIND OUT IF

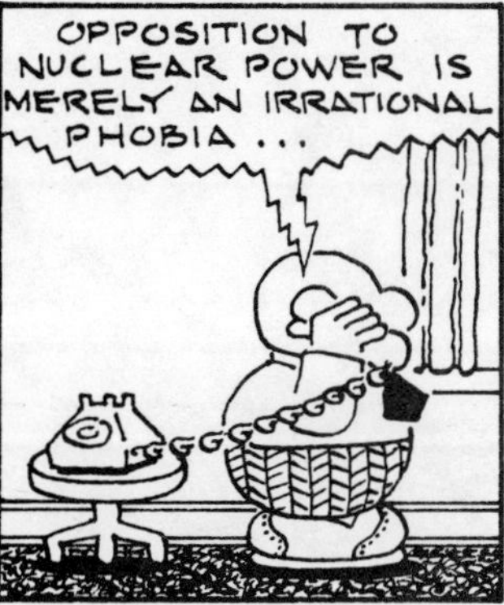
OPPOSITION TO NUCLEAR POWER IS MERELY AN IRRATIONAL PHOBIA ...

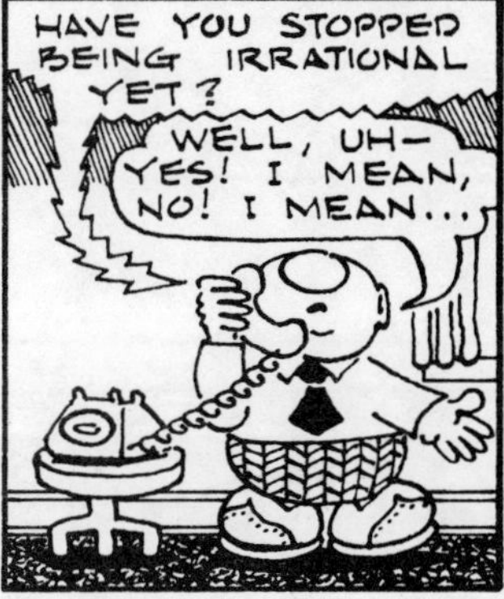
HAVE YOU STOPPED BEING IRRATIONAL YET?
WELL, UH- YES! I MEAN, NO! I MEAN...

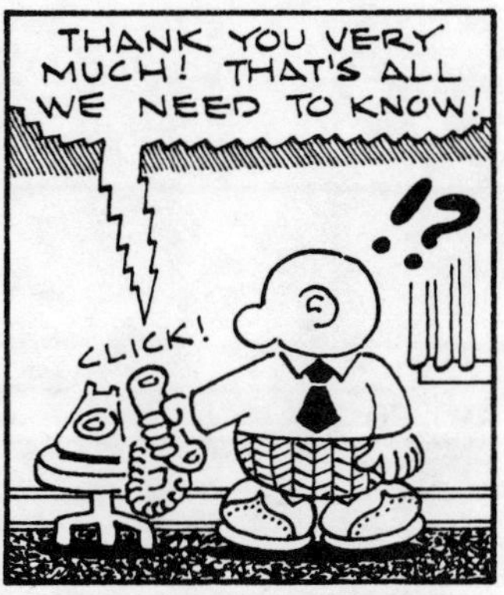
THANK YOU VERY MUCH! THAT'S ALL WE NEED TO KNOW!
CLICK!
!?

b. von alten

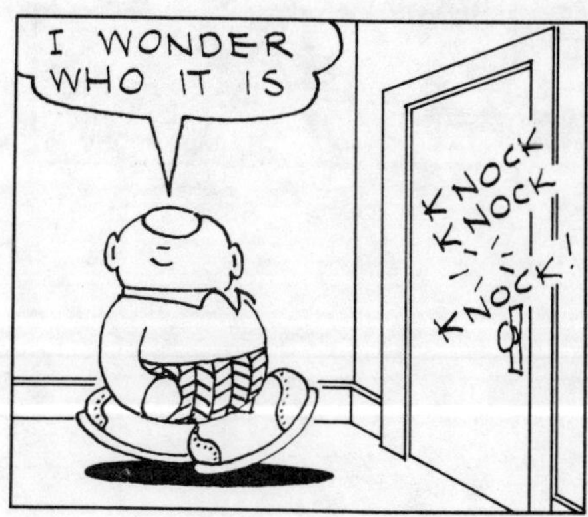
I WONDER WHO IT IS
KNOCK KNOCK KNOCK!

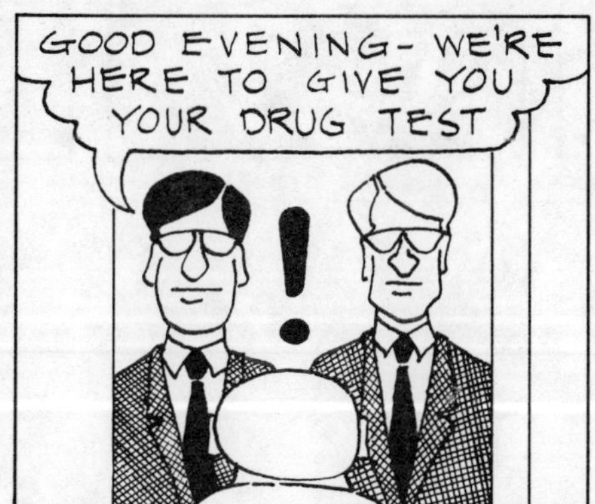
GOOD EVENING- WE'RE HERE TO GIVE YOU YOUR DRUG TEST
!

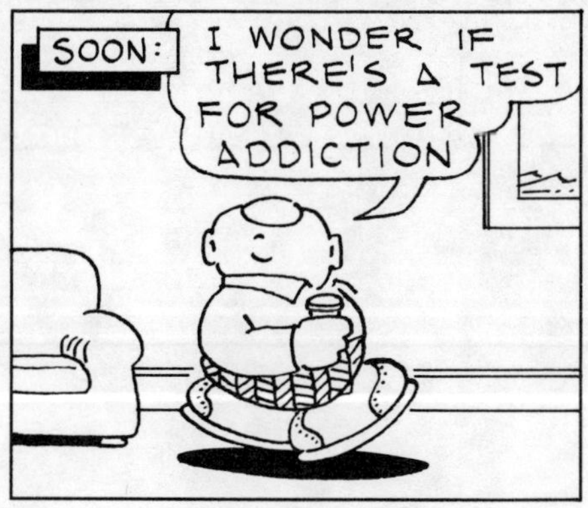
SOON:
I WONDER IF THERE'S A TEST FOR POWER ADDICTION

b. von alten

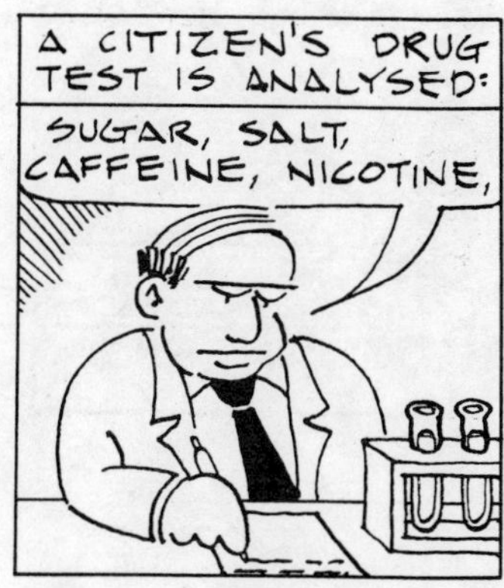
A CITIZEN'S DRUG TEST IS ANALYSED:
SUGAR, SALT, CAFFEINE, NICOTINE,

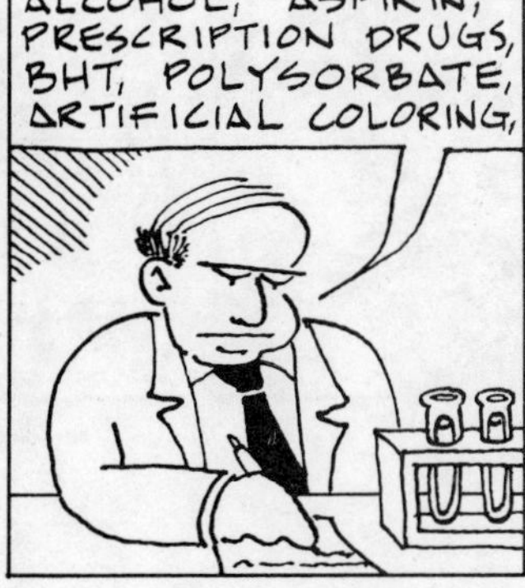
ALCOHOL, ASPIRIN, PRESCRIPTION DRUGS, BHT, POLYSORBATE, ARTIFICIAL COLORING,

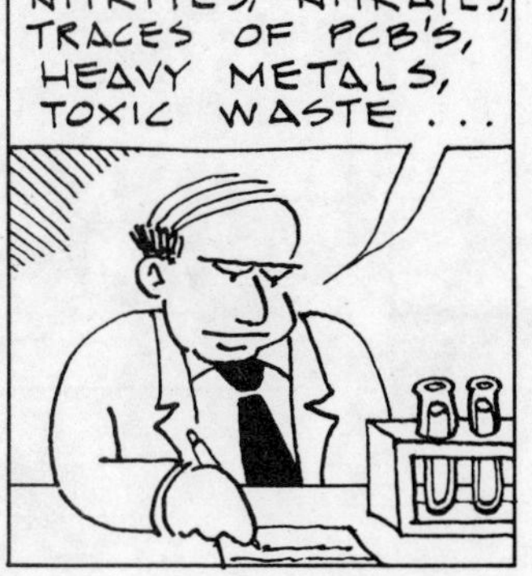
NITRITES, NITRATES, TRACES OF PCB'S, HEAVY METALS, TOXIC WASTE ...

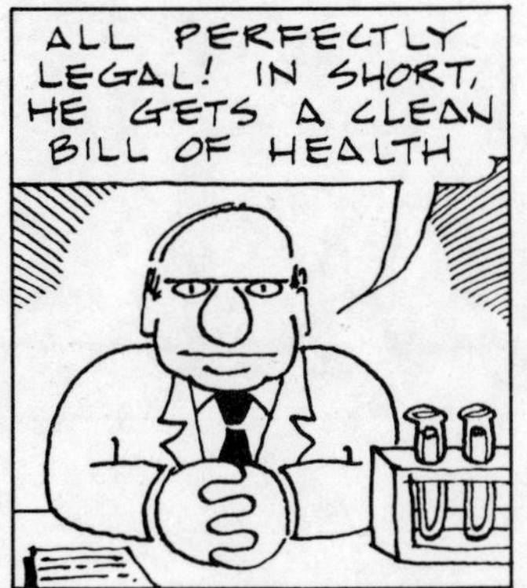
ALL PERFECTLY LEGAL! IN SHORT, HE GETS A CLEAN BILL OF HEALTH

b. von alten

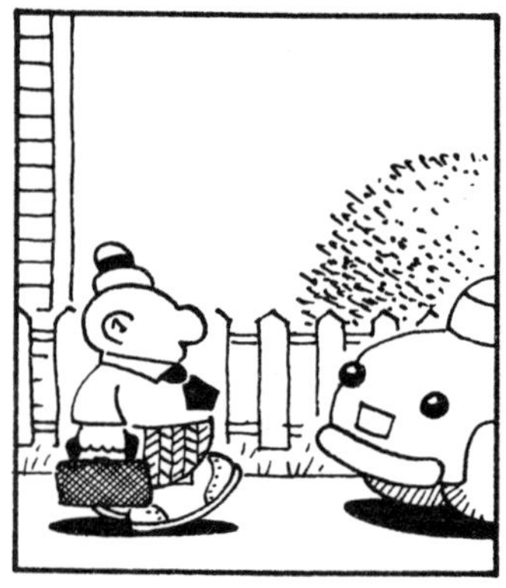
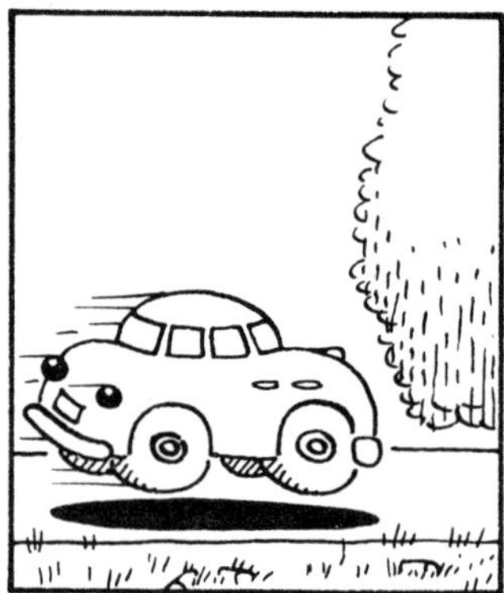
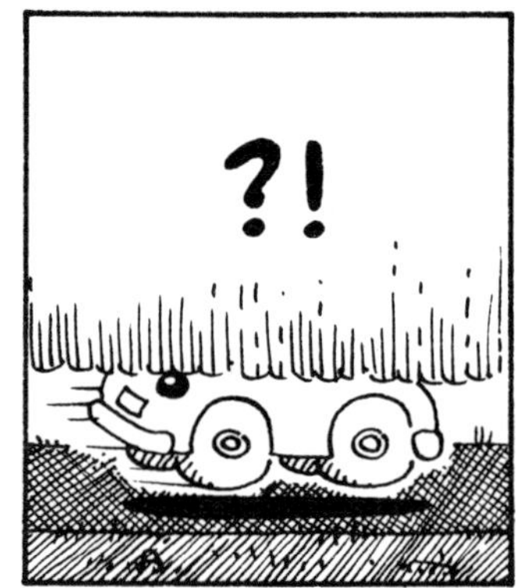
?!
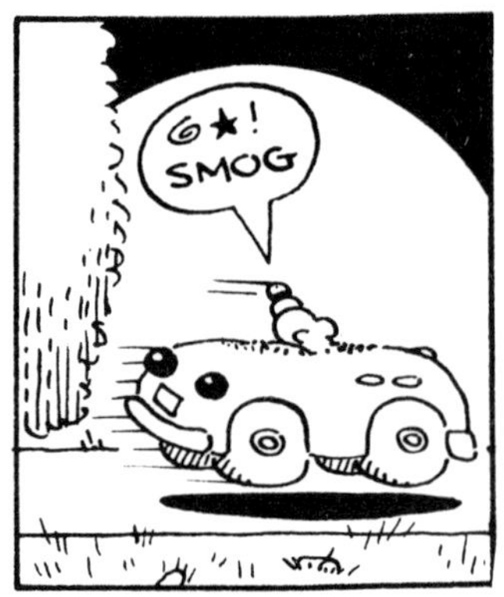
G★!
SMOG

b. von alten

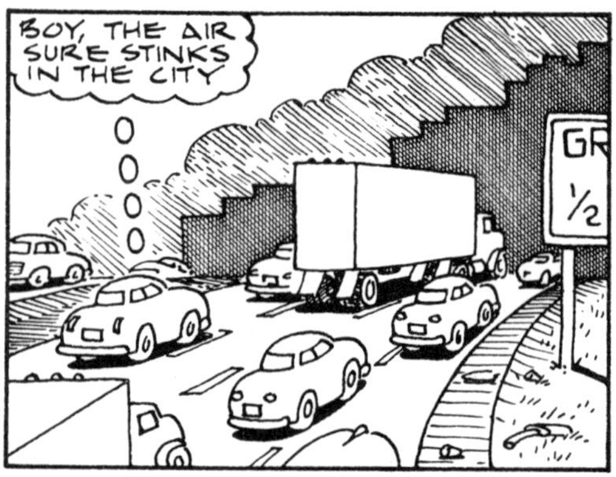
BOY, THE AIR SURE STINKS IN THE CITY
GR
1/2
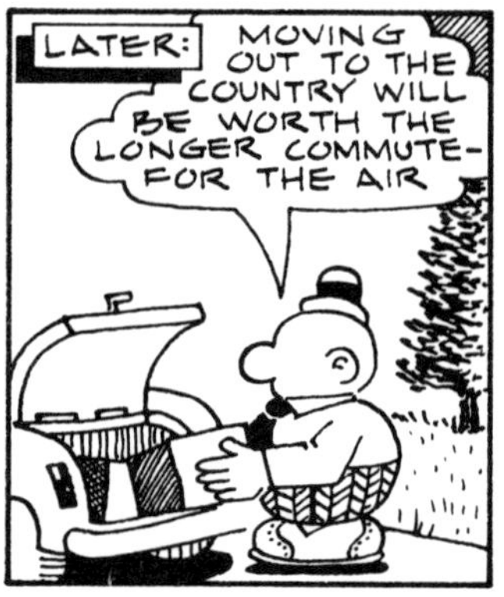
LATER:
MOVING OUT TO THE COUNTRY WILL BE WORTH THE LONGER COMMUTE- FOR THE AIR
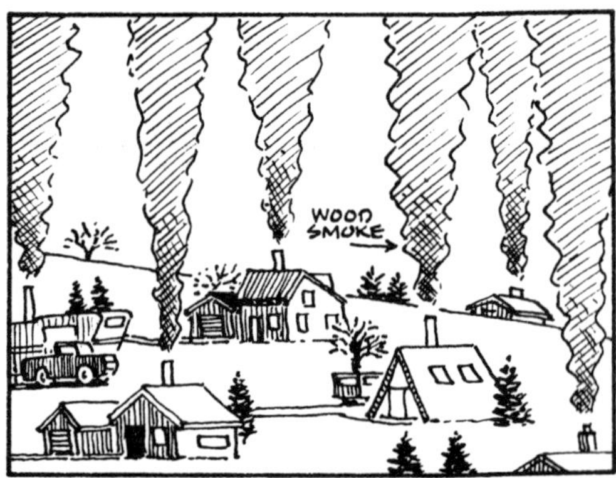
WOOD SMOKE

b. von alten

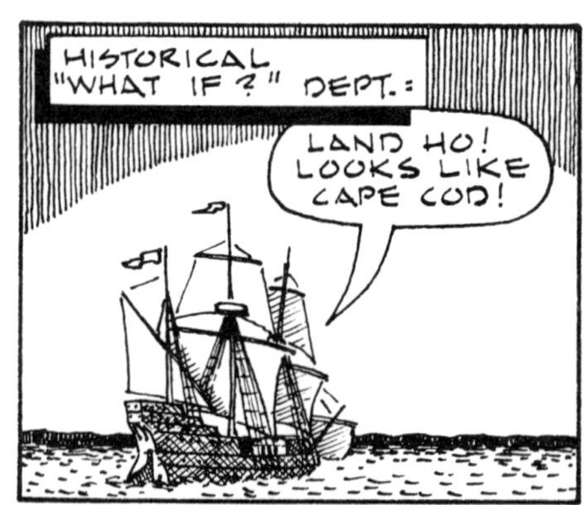
HISTORICAL "WHAT IF?" DEPT.:
LAND HO! LOOKS LIKE CAPE COD!
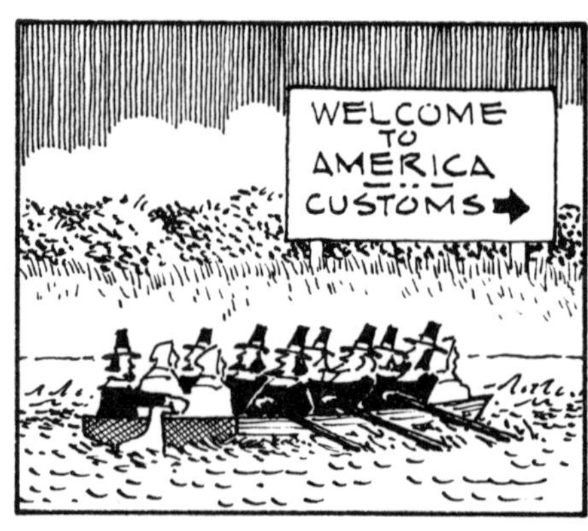
WELCOME TO AMERICA
CUSTOMS
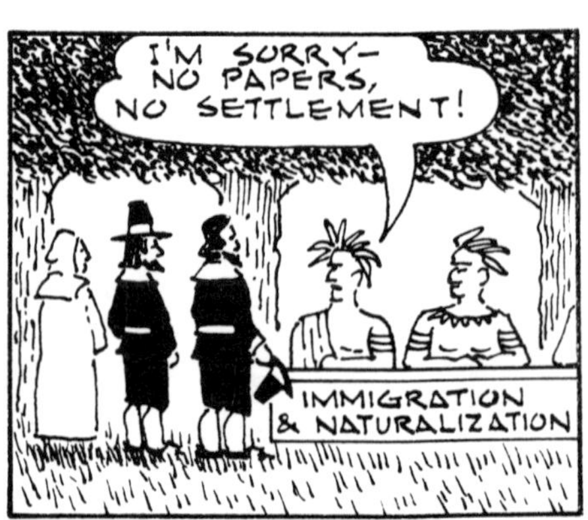
I'M SORRY- NO PAPERS, NO SETTLEMENT!
IMMIGRATION & NATURALIZATION

p. campbell, b. von alten

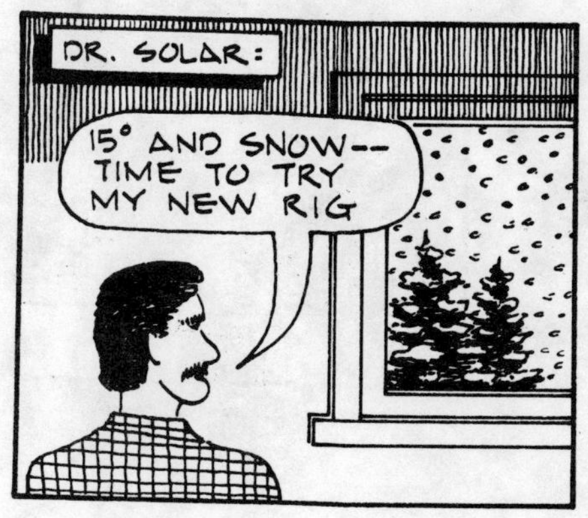
DR. SOLAR:
15° AND SNOW-- TIME TO TRY MY NEW RIG

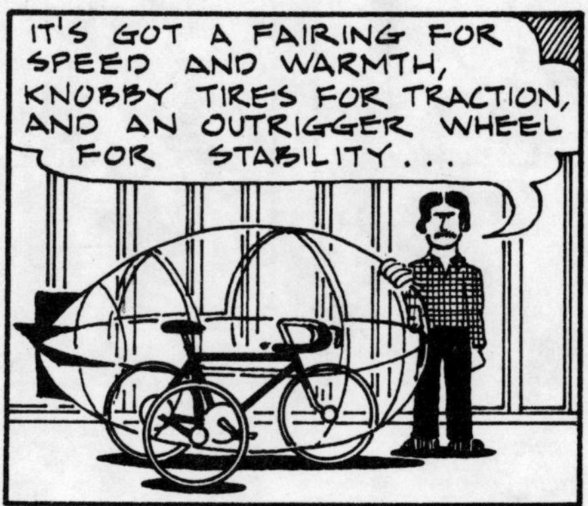
IT'S GOT A FAIRING FOR SPEED AND WARMTH, KNOBBY TIRES FOR TRACTION, AND AN OUTRIGGER WHEEL FOR STABILITY...

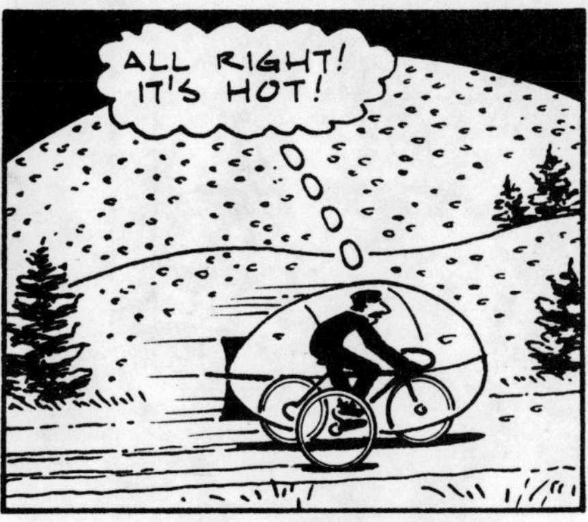
ALL RIGHT! IT'S HOT!

b. von alten

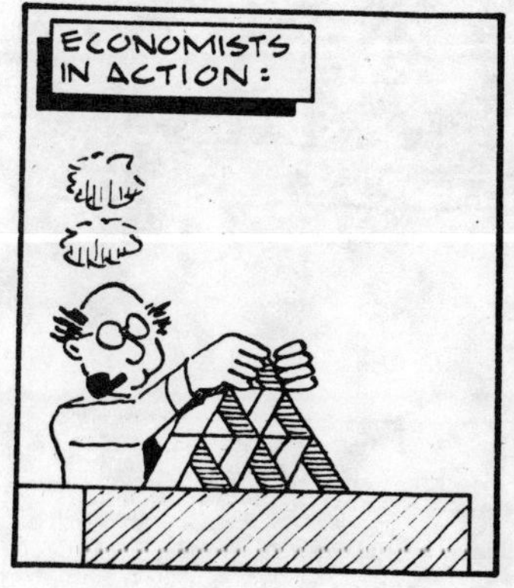
ECONOMISTS IN ACTION:

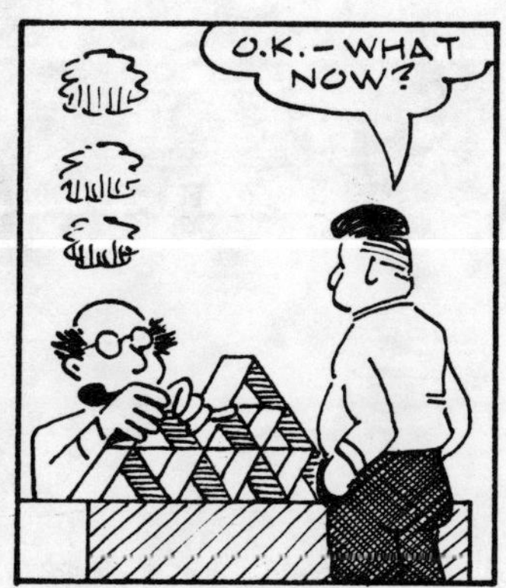
O.K.-WHAT NOW?

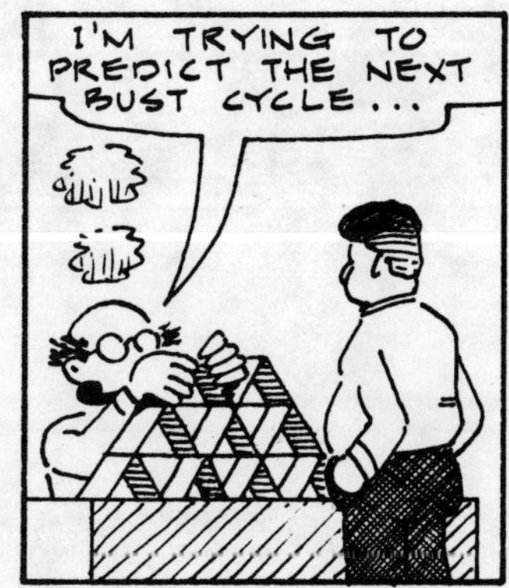
I'M TRYING TO PREDICT THE NEXT BUST CYCLE...

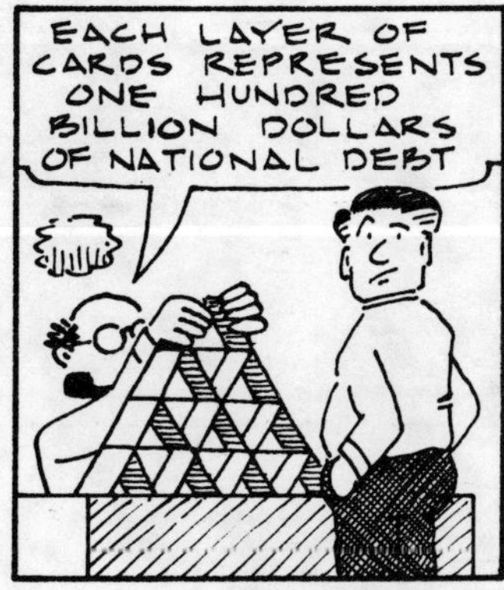
EACH LAYER OF CARDS REPRESENTS ONE HUNDRED BILLION DOLLARS OF NATIONAL DEBT

b. von alten

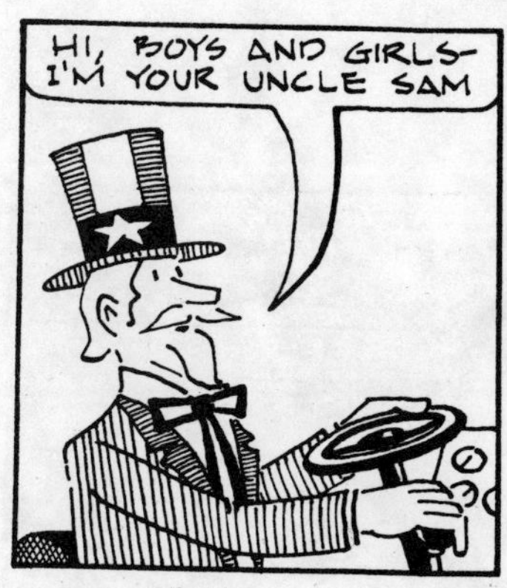
HI, BOYS AND GIRLS- I'M YOUR UNCLE SAM

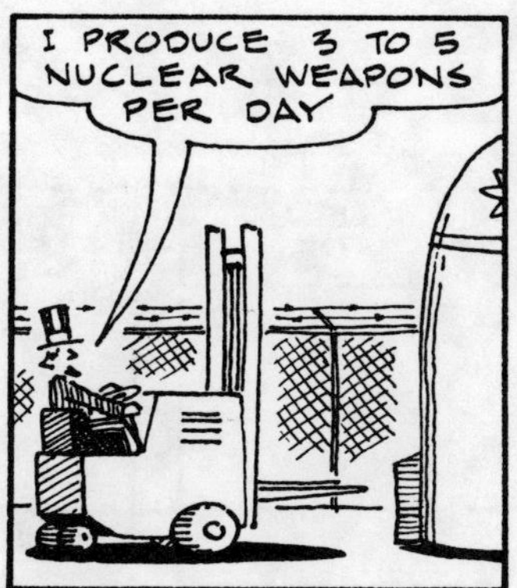
I PRODUCE 3 TO 5 NUCLEAR WEAPONS PER DAY

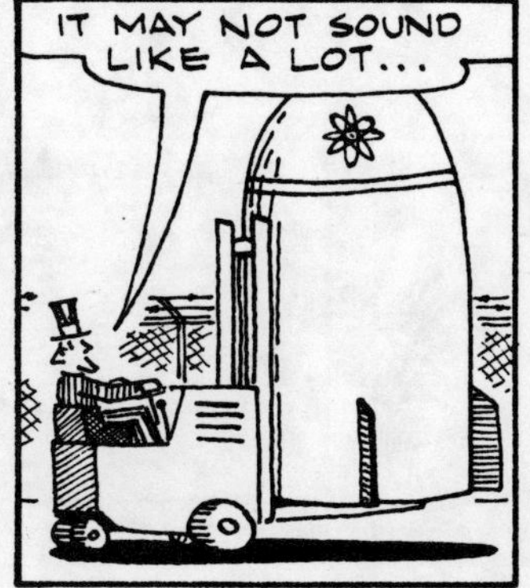
IT MAY NOT SOUND LIKE A LOT...

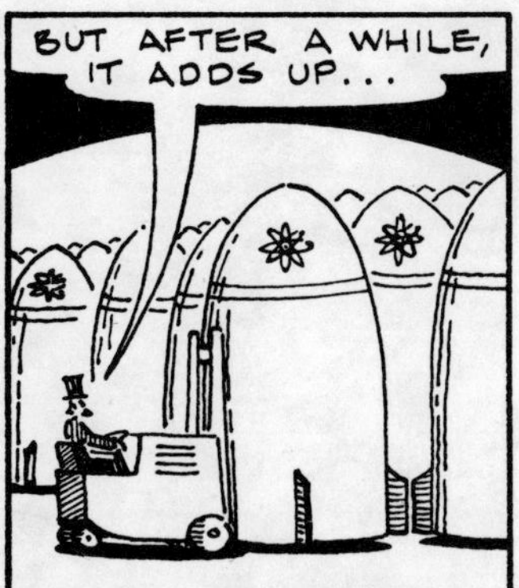
BUT AFTER A WHILE, IT ADDS UP...

b. von alten

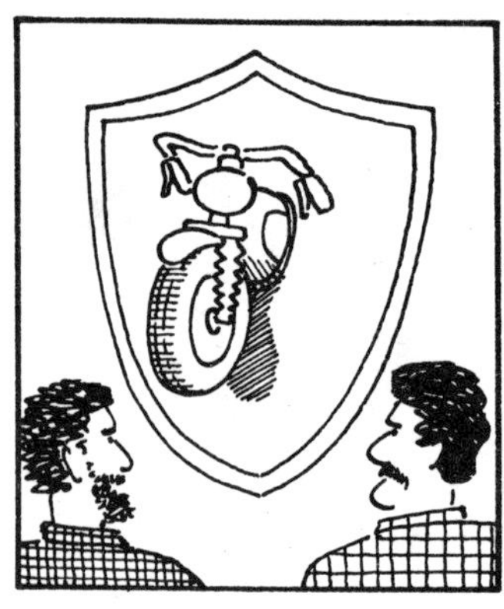
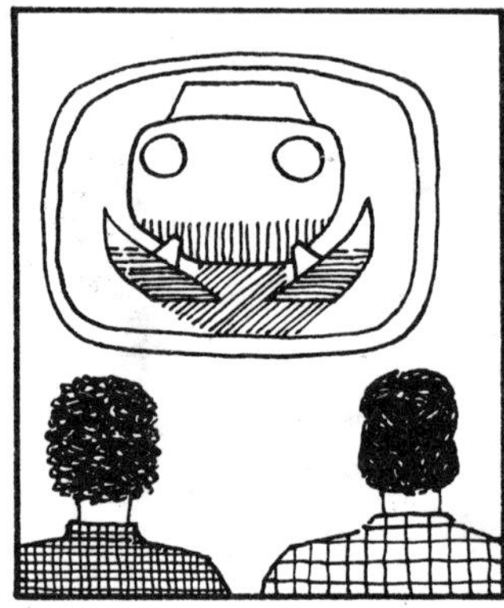
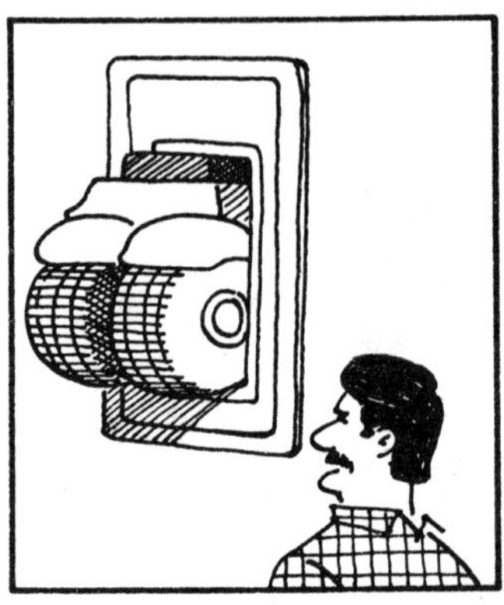
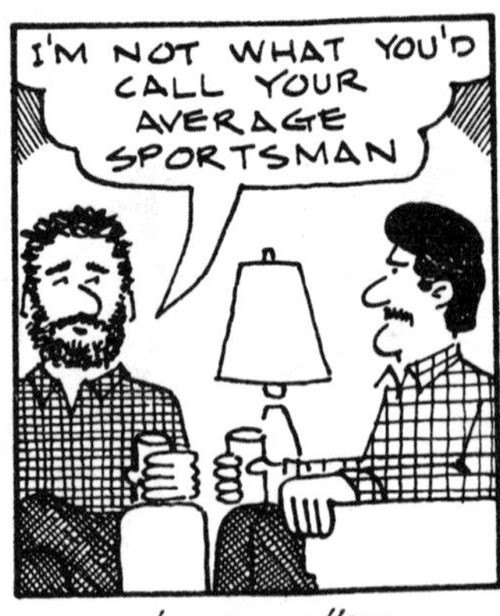
I'M NOT WHAT YOU'D CALL YOUR AVERAGE SPORTSMAN

b. von alten

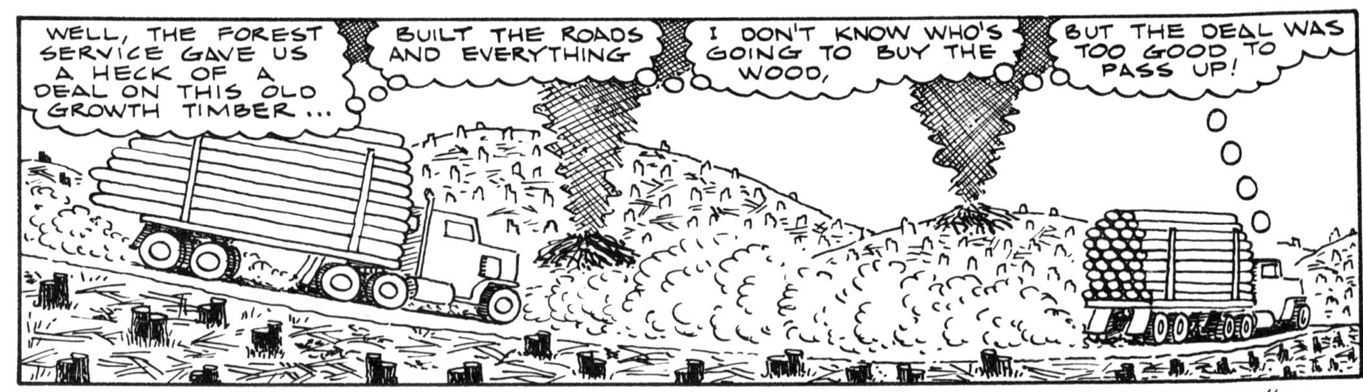
WELL, THE FOREST SERVICE GAVE US A HECK OF A DEAL ON THIS OLD GROWTH TIMBER...
BUILT THE ROADS AND EVERYTHING
I DON'T KNOW WHO'S GOING TO BUY THE WOOD,
BUT THE DEAL WAS TOO GOOD TO PASS UP!

b. von alten

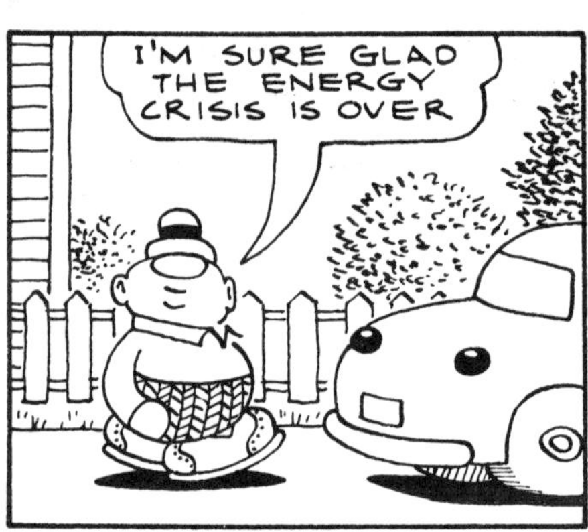
I'M SURE GLAD THE ENERGY CRISIS IS OVER
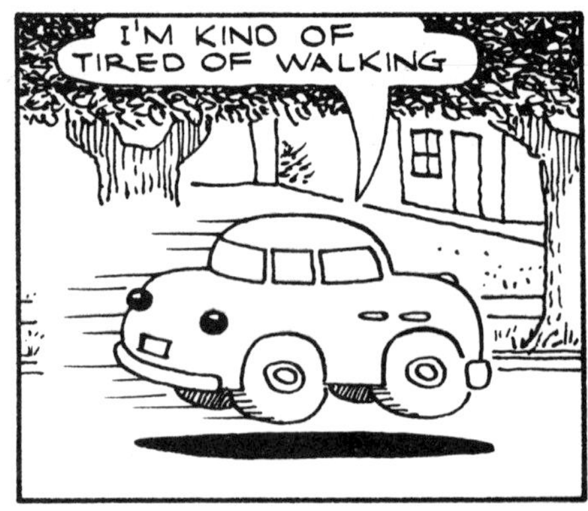
I'M KIND OF TIRED OF WALKING
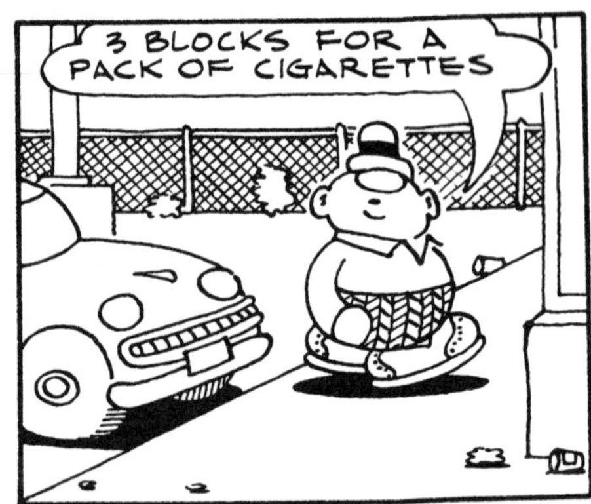
3 BLOCKS FOR A PACK OF CIGARETTES

b. von alten

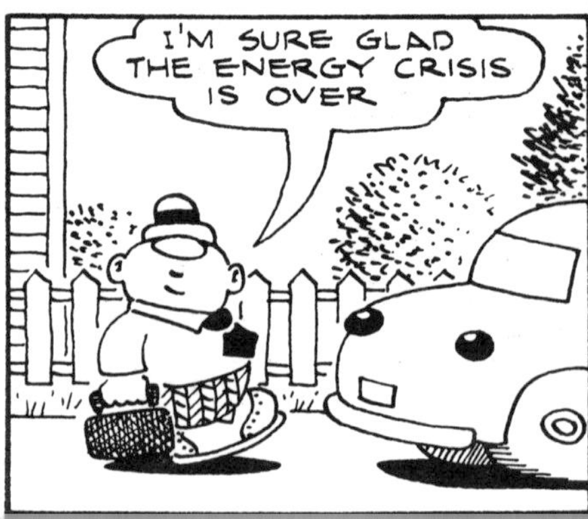
I'M SURE GLAD THE ENERGY CRISIS IS OVER
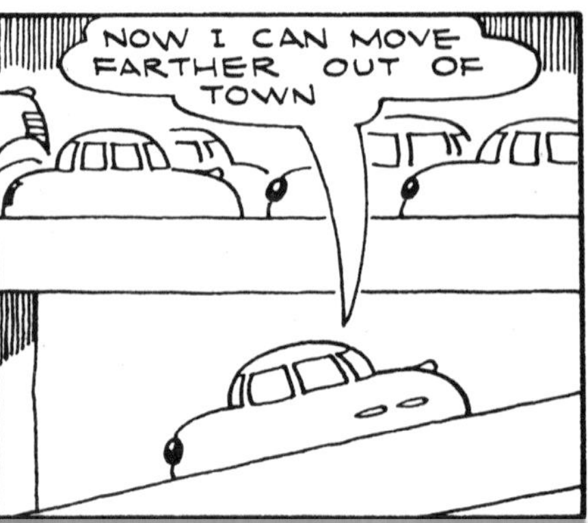
NOW I CAN MOVE FARTHER OUT OF TOWN
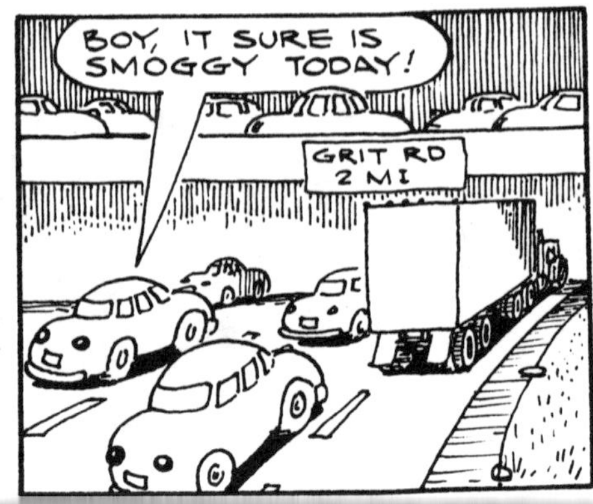
BOY, IT SURE IS SMOGGY TODAY!
GRIT RD
2 MI

b. von alten

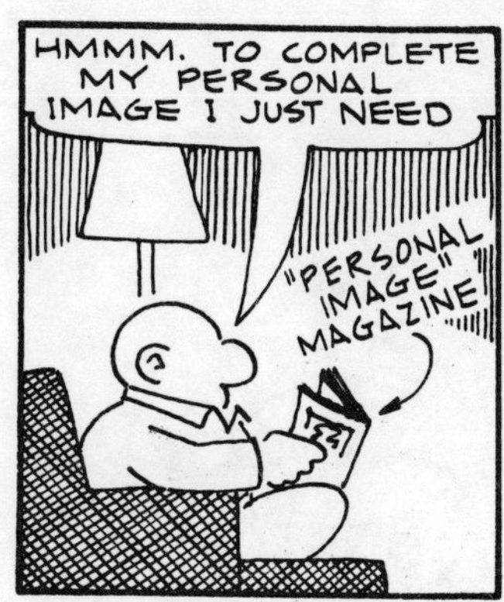
HMMM. TO COMPLETE MY PERSONAL IMAGE I JUST NEED
"PERSONAL IMAGE" MAGAZINE

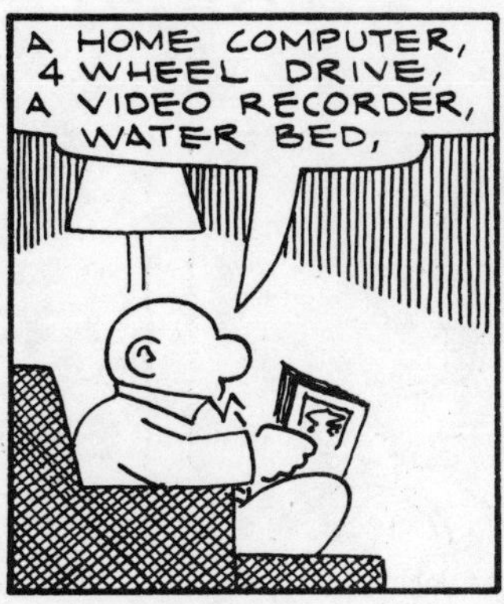
A HOME COMPUTER, 4 WHEEL DRIVE, A VIDEO RECORDER, WATER BED,

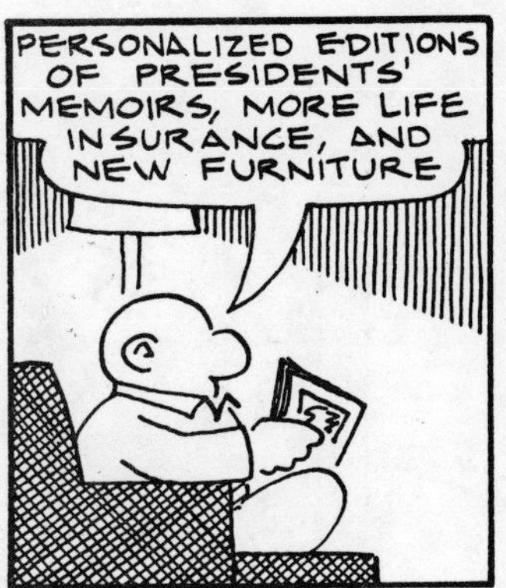
PERSONALIZED EDITIONS OF PRESIDENTS' MEMOIRS, MORE LIFE INSURANCE, AND NEW FURNITURE

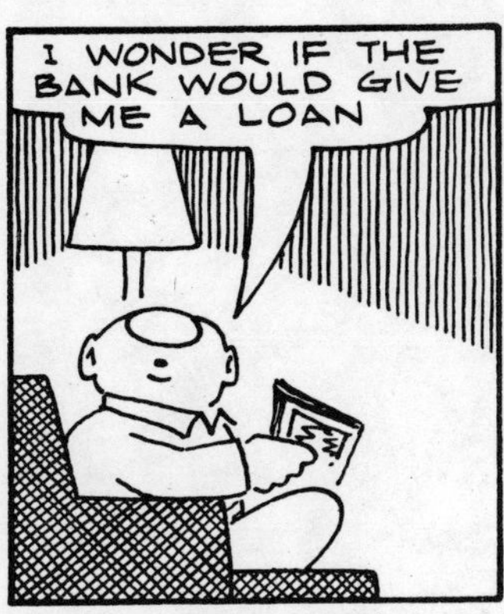
I WONDER IF THE BANK WOULD GIVE ME A LOAN

b. von alten

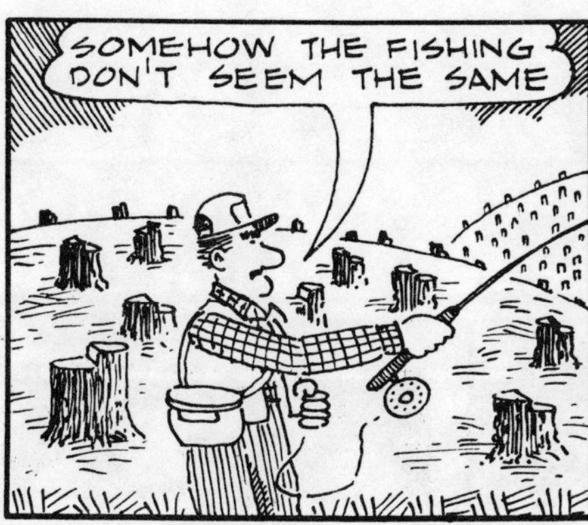
SOMEHOW THE FISHING DON'T SEEM THE SAME

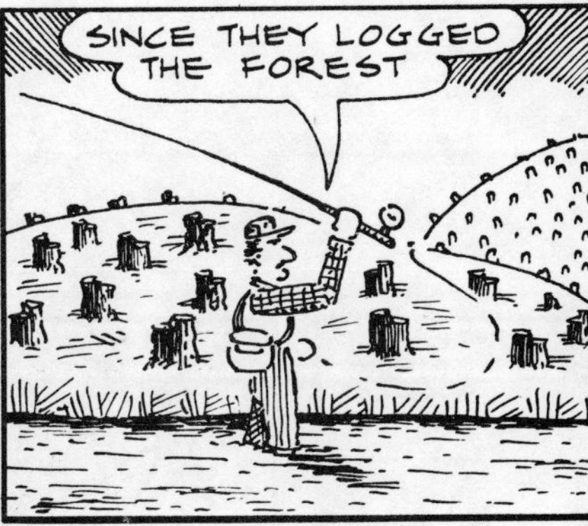
SINCE THEY LOGGED THE FOREST

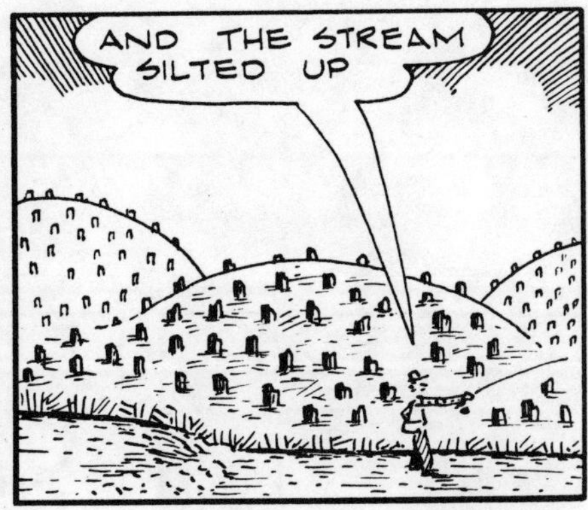
AND THE STREAM SILTED UP

b. von alten

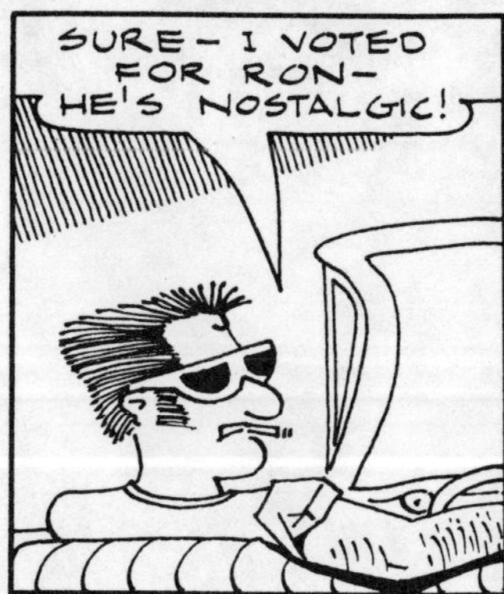
SURE– I VOTED FOR RON– HE'S NOSTALGIC!

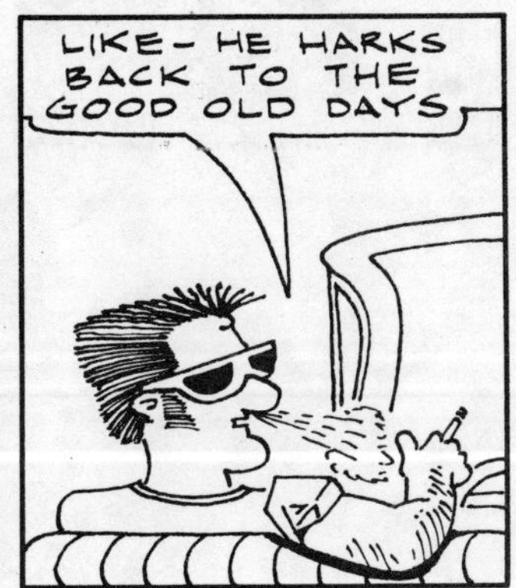
LIKE– HE HARKS BACK TO THE GOOD OLD DAYS

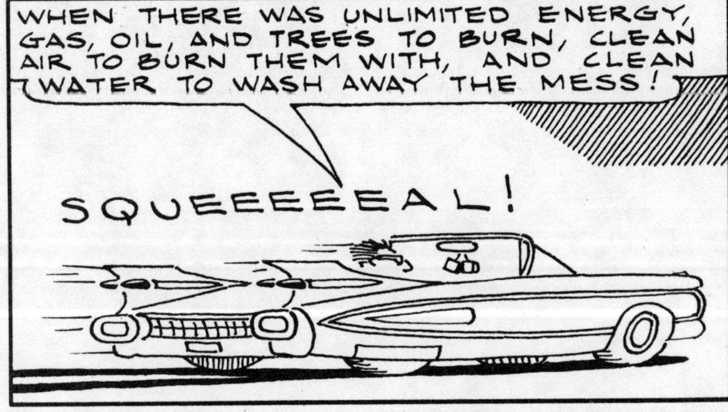
WHEN THERE WAS UNLIMITED ENERGY, GAS, OIL, AND TREES TO BURN, CLEAN AIR TO BURN THEM WITH, AND CLEAN WATER TO WASH AWAY THE MESS!
SQUEEEEEEAL!

b. von alten

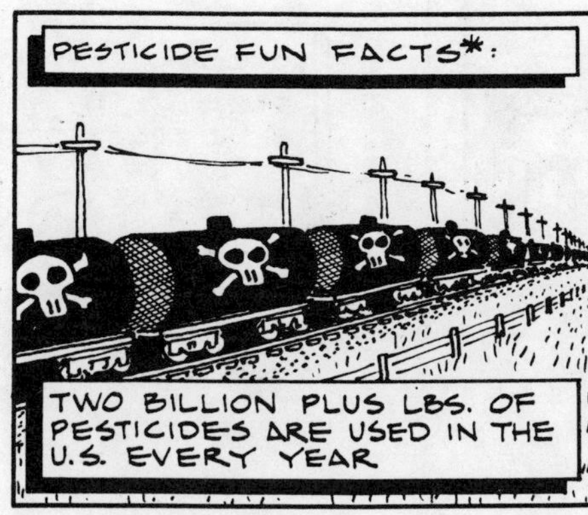
PESTICIDE FUN FACTS*:
TWO BILLION PLUS LBS. OF PESTICIDES ARE USED IN THE U.S. EVERY YEAR

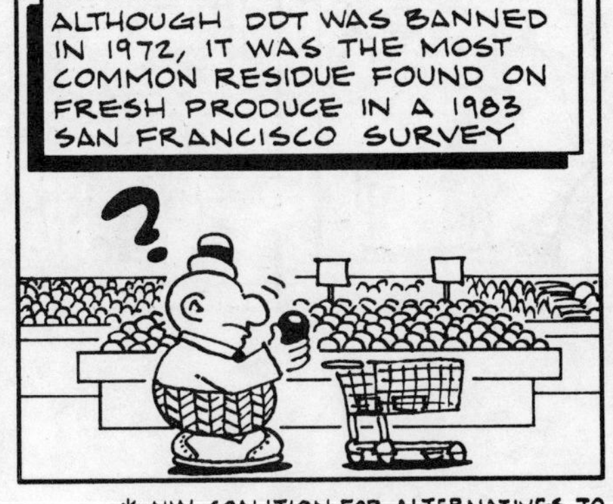
ALTHOUGH DDT WAS BANNED IN 1972, IT WAS THE MOST COMMON RESIDUE FOUND ON FRESH PRODUCE IN A 1983 SAN FRANCISCO SURVEY
?

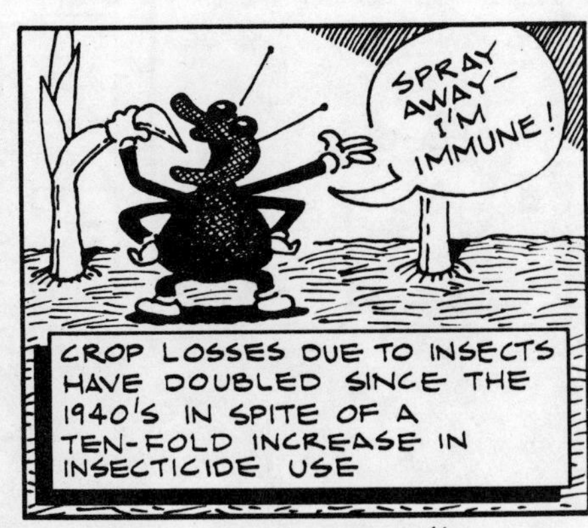
SPRAY AWAY– I'M IMMUNE!
CROP LOSSES DUE TO INSECTS HAVE DOUBLED SINCE THE 1940'S IN SPITE OF A TEN-FOLD INCREASE IN INSECTICIDE USE

b. von alten

* NW COALITION FOR ALTERNATIVES TO PESTICIDES · BOX 1393 · EUGENE, OR 97440

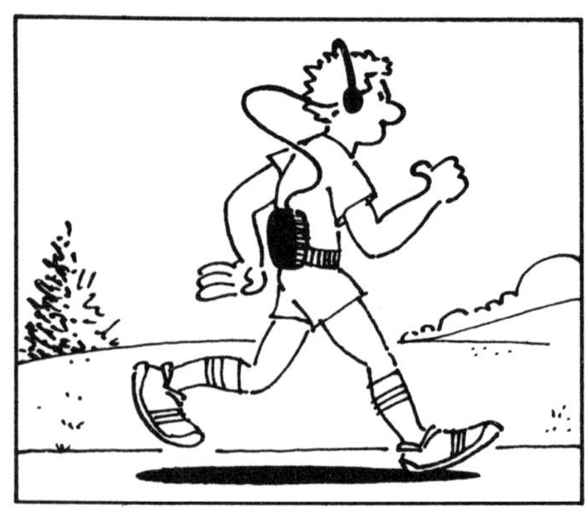

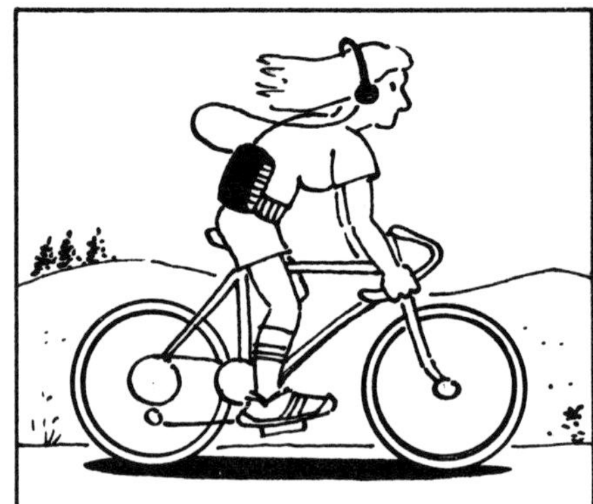

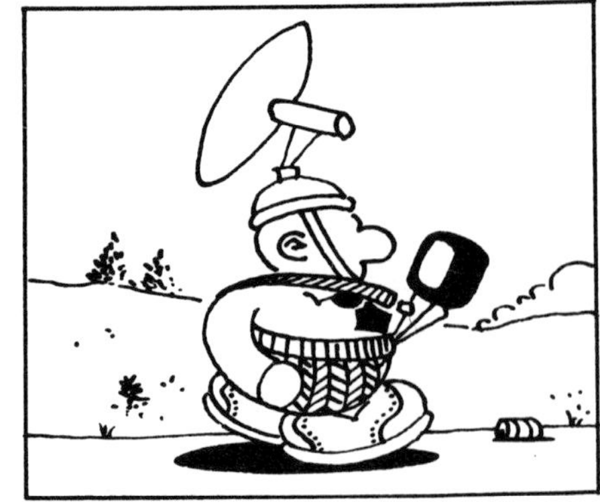

b. von alten

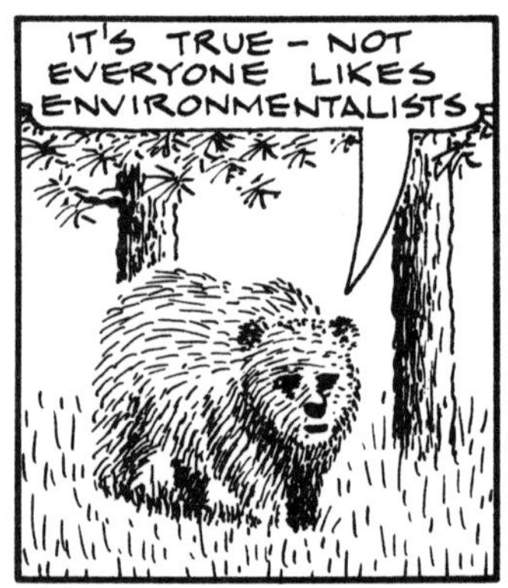
IT'S TRUE - NOT EVERYONE LIKES ENVIRONMENTALISTS

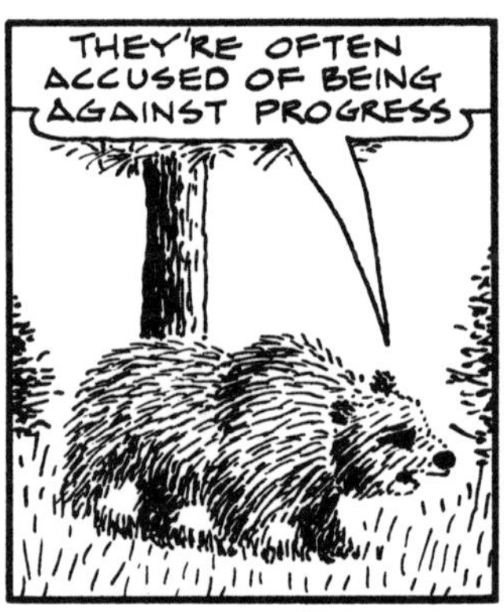
THEY'RE OFTEN ACCUSED OF BEING AGAINST PROGRESS

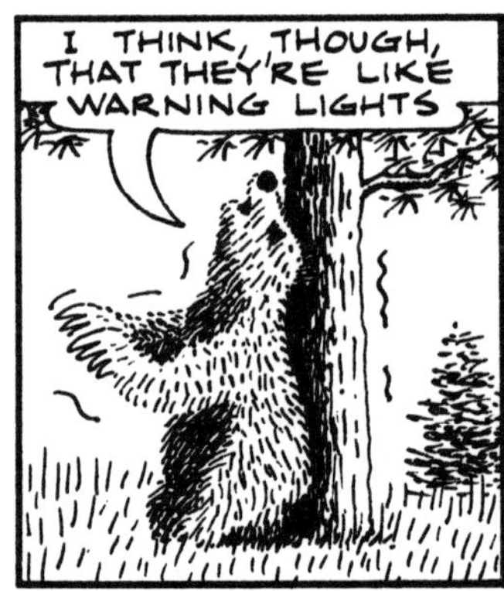
I THINK, THOUGH, THAT THEY'RE LIKE WARNING LIGHTS

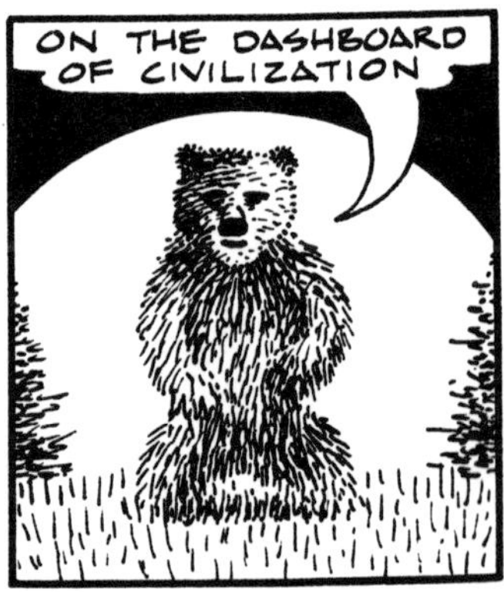
ON THE DASHBOARD OF CIVILIZATION

b. von alten

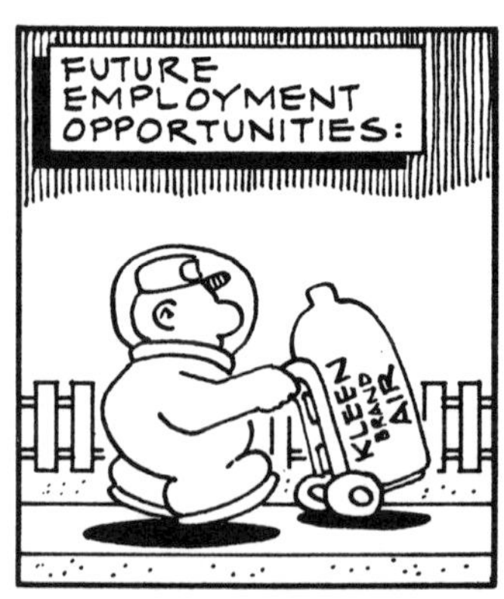
FUTURE EMPLOYMENT OPPORTUNITIES:
KLEEN BRAND AIR

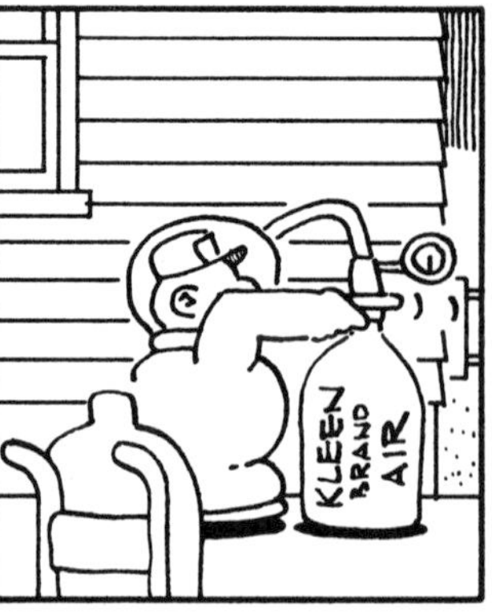
KLEEN BRAND AIR

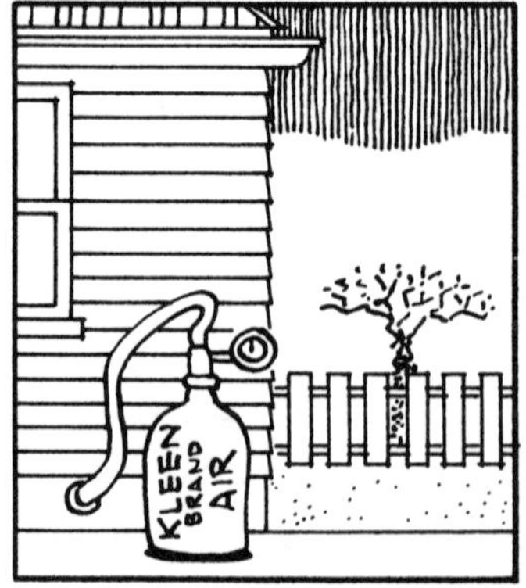
KLEEN BRAND AIR

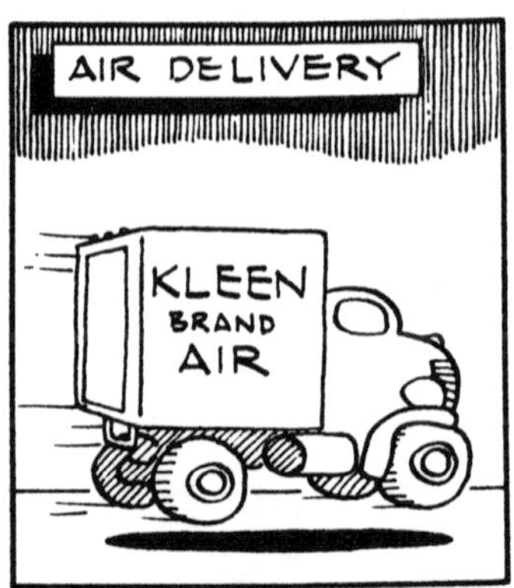
AIR DELIVERY
KLEEN BRAND AIR

b. von alten

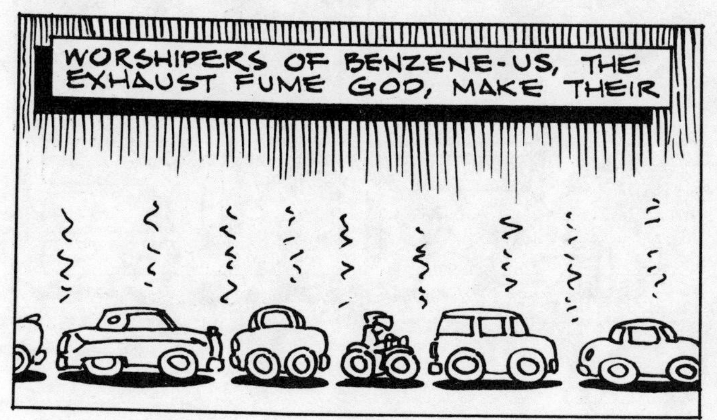
WORSHIPERS OF BENZENE-US, THE EXHAUST FUME GOD, MAKE THEIR

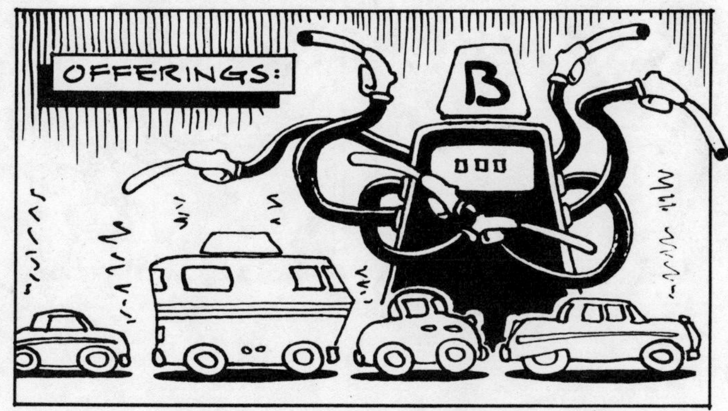
OFFERINGS:
B
b. von alten

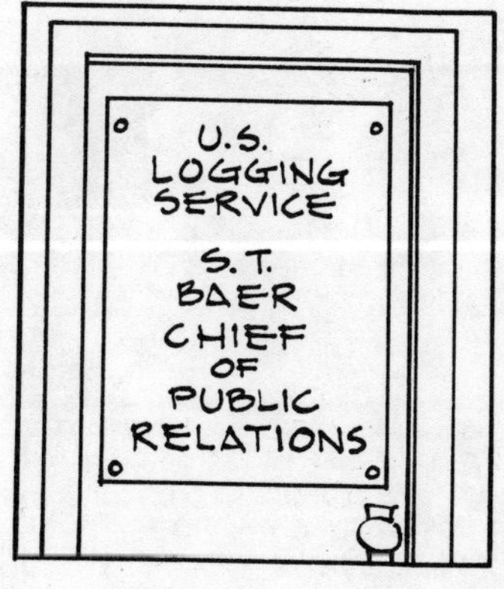
U.S. LOGGING SERVICE
S.T. BAER CHIEF OF PUBLIC RELATIONS

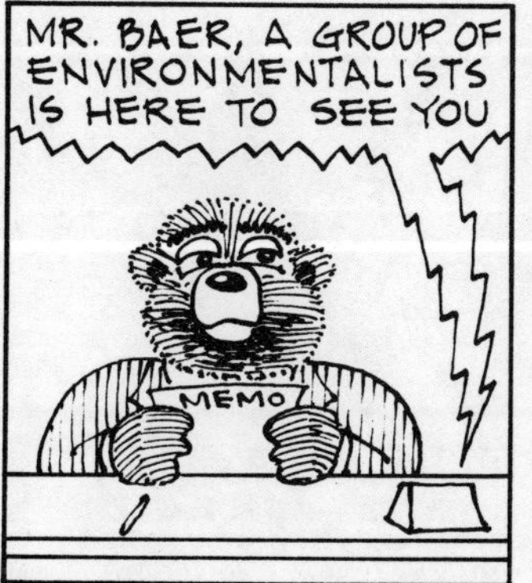
MR. BAER, A GROUP OF ENVIRONMENTALISTS IS HERE TO SEE YOU
MEMO

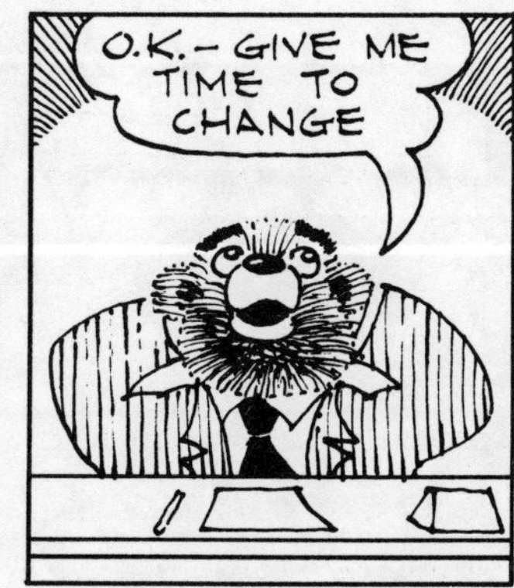
O.K.- GIVE ME TIME TO CHANGE

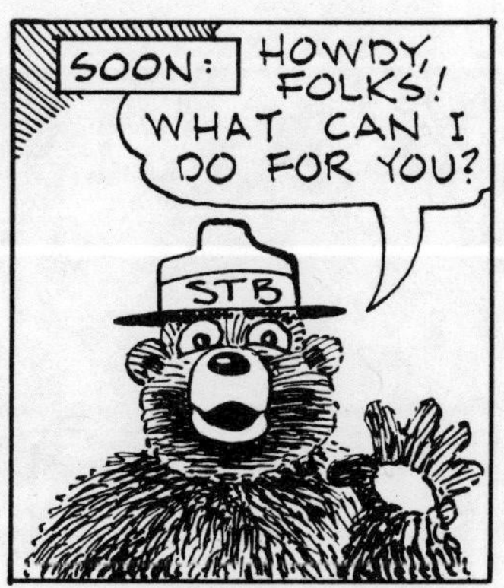
SOON:
HOWDY, FOLKS! WHAT CAN I DO FOR YOU?
STB
b. von alten

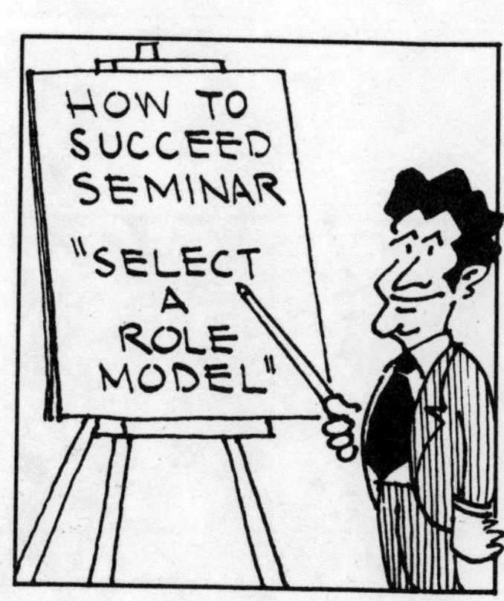
HOW TO SUCCEED SEMINAR
"SELECT A ROLE MODEL"

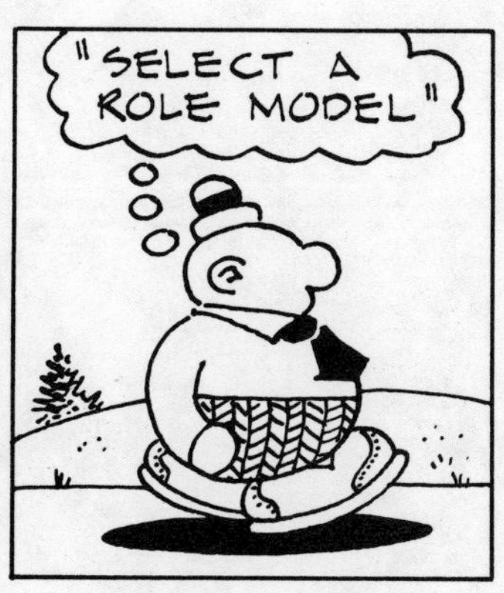
"SELECT A ROLE MODEL"

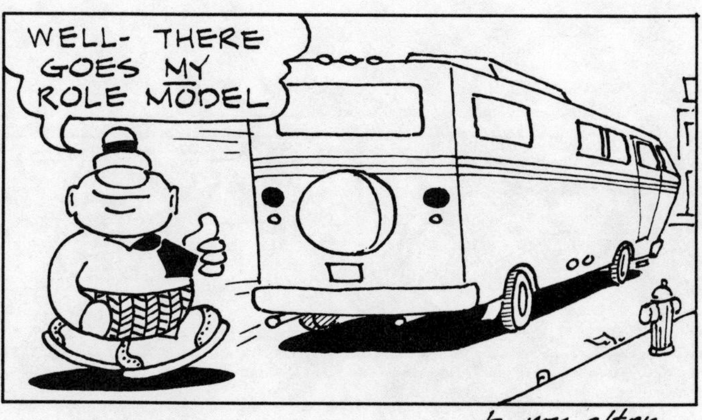
WELL- THERE GOES MY ROLE MODEL
b. von alten

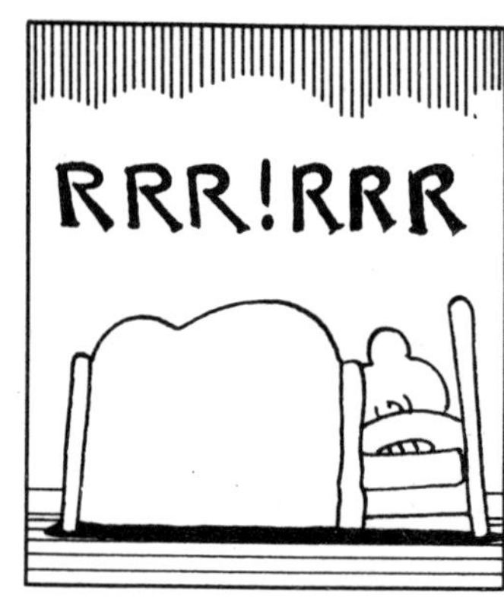
RRR!RRR
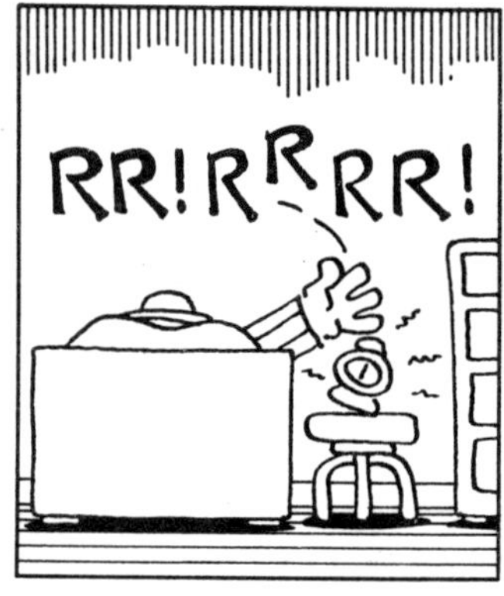
RR!RRRR!
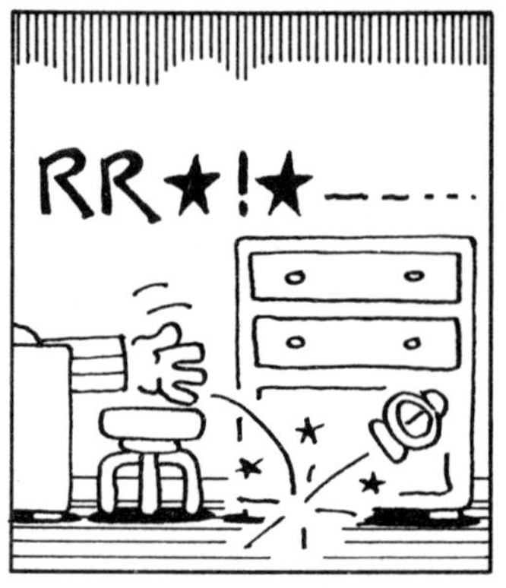
RR★!★
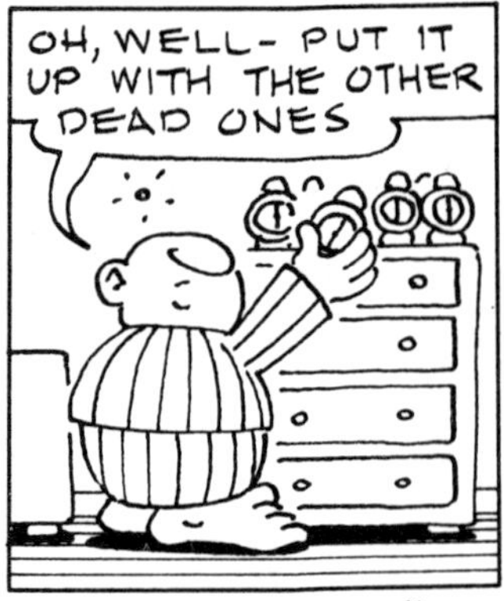
OH, WELL- PUT IT UP WITH THE OTHER DEAD ONES

b. von alten

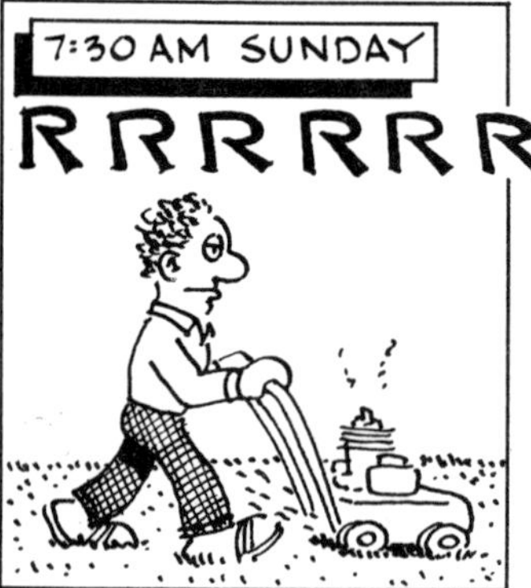
7:30 AM SUNDAY
RRRRRR
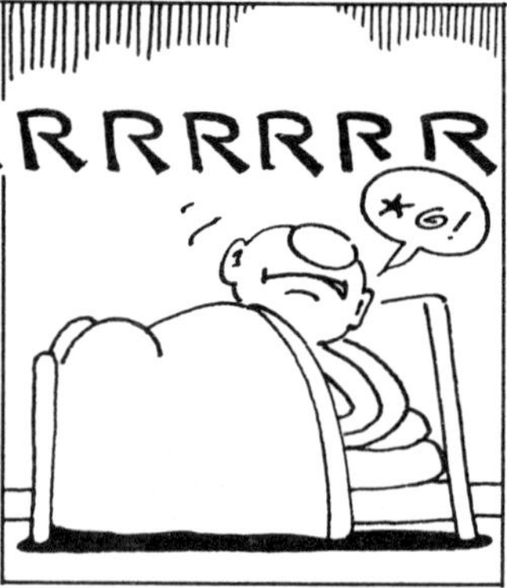
RRRRRRR
★G!
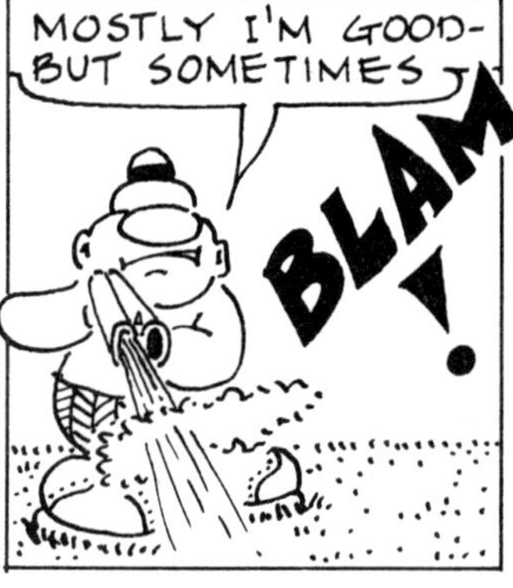
MOSTLY I'M GOOD- BUT SOMETIMES
BLAM!
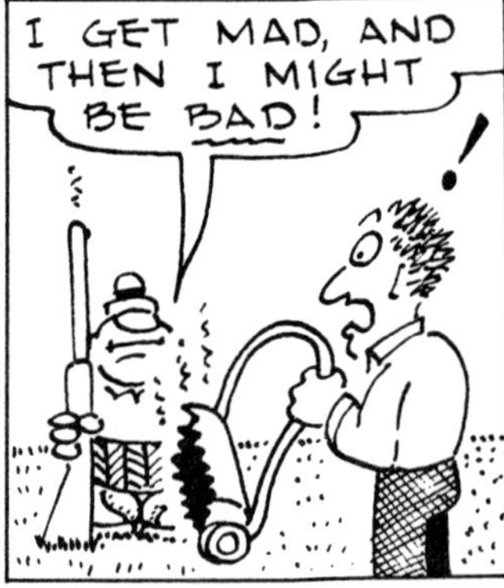
I GET MAD, AND THEN I MIGHT BE BAD!
!

b. von alten

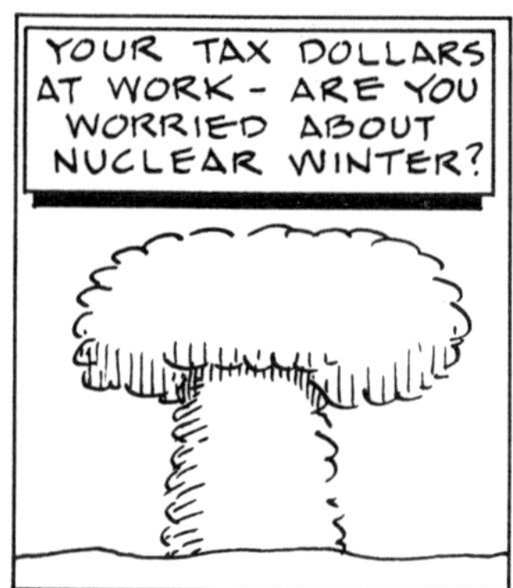
YOUR TAX DOLLARS AT WORK - ARE YOU WORRIED ABOUT NUCLEAR WINTER?
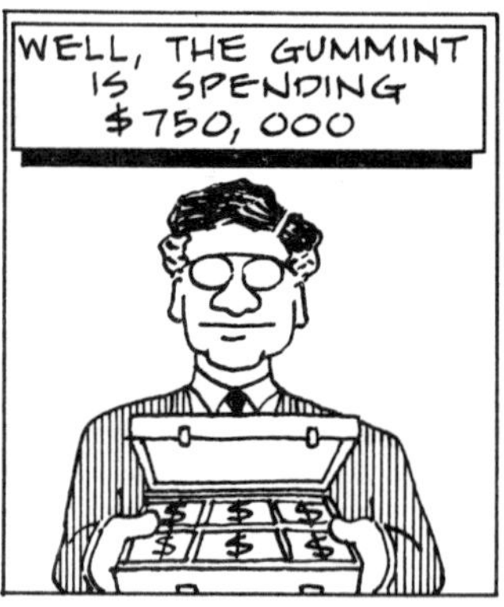
WELL, THE GUMMINT IS SPENDING $750,000
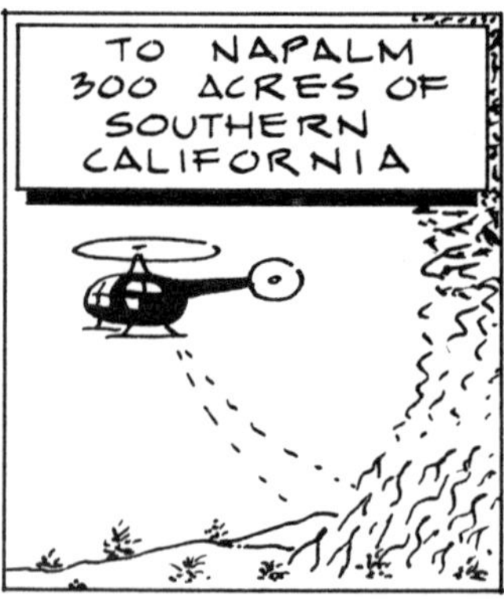
TO NAPALM 300 ACRES OF SOUTHERN CALIFORNIA
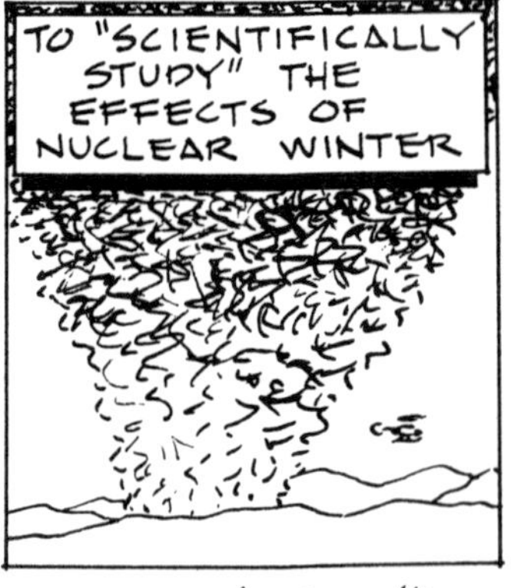
TO "SCIENTIFICALLY STUDY" THE EFFECTS OF NUCLEAR WINTER

b. von alten

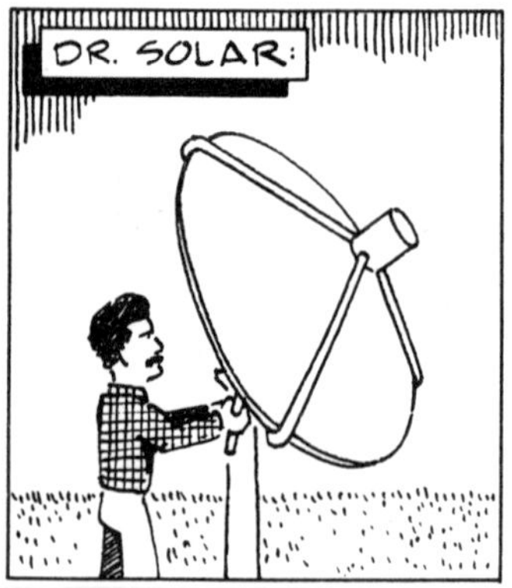
DR. SOLAR:
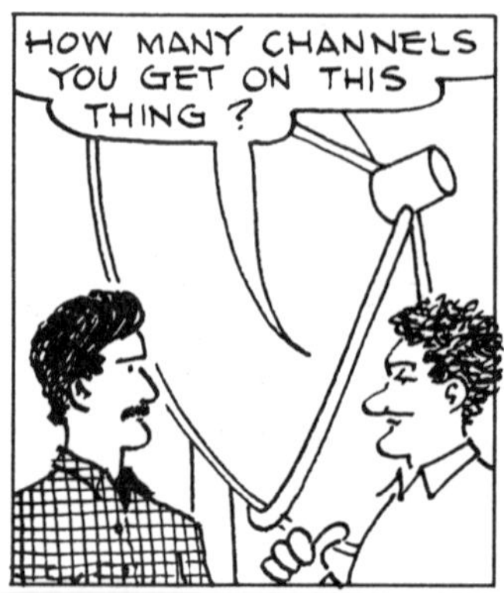
HOW MANY CHANNELS YOU GET ON THIS THING ?
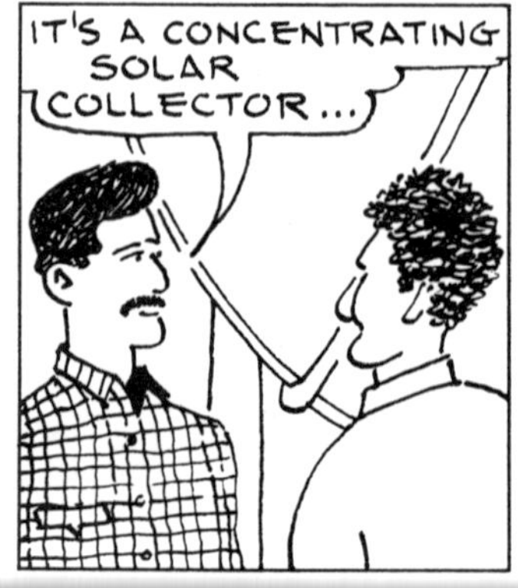
IT'S A CONCENTRATING SOLAR COLLECTOR...
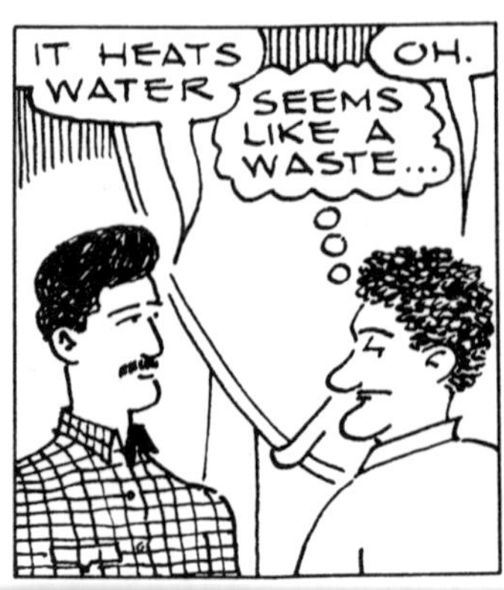
IT HEATS WATER
OH.
SEEMS LIKE A WASTE...

b. von alten

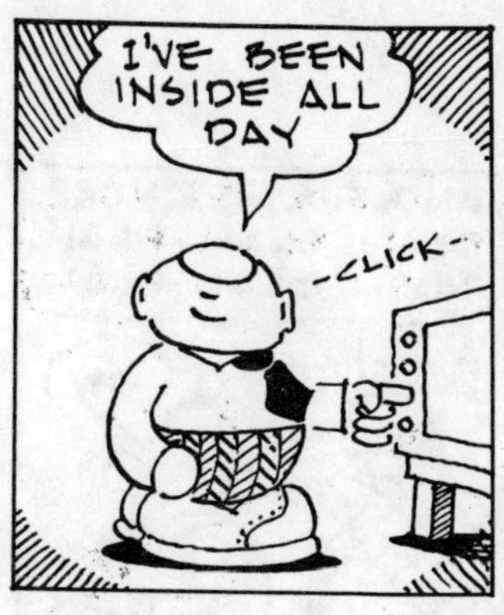
I'VE BEEN INSIDE ALL DAY
-CLICK-
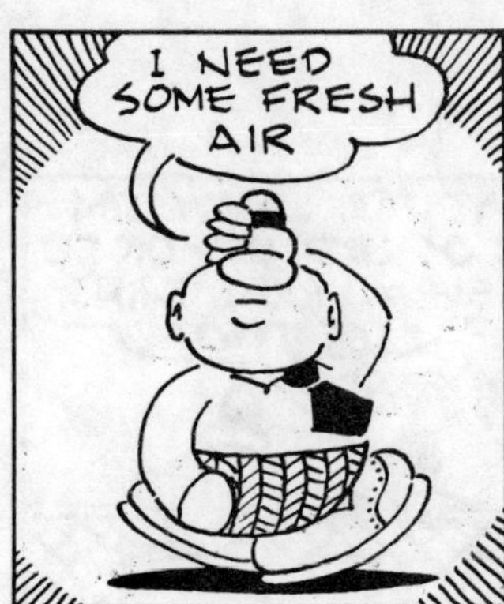
I NEED SOME FRESH AIR
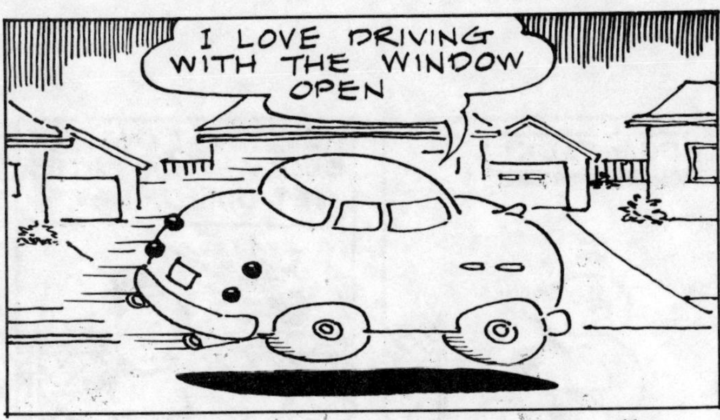
I LOVE DRIVING WITH THE WINDOW OPEN

b. von alten

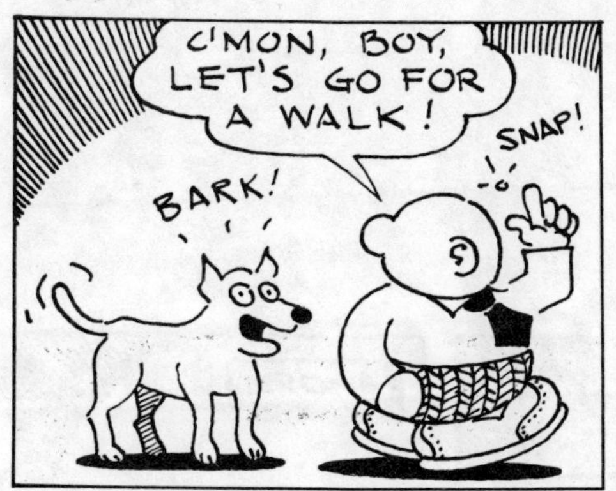
C'MON, BOY, LET'S GO FOR A WALK!
SNAP!
BARK!
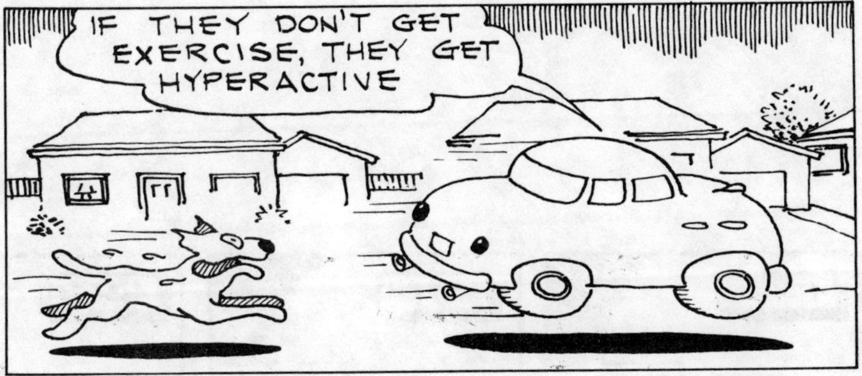
IF THEY DON'T GET EXERCISE, THEY GET HYPERACTIVE

b. von alten

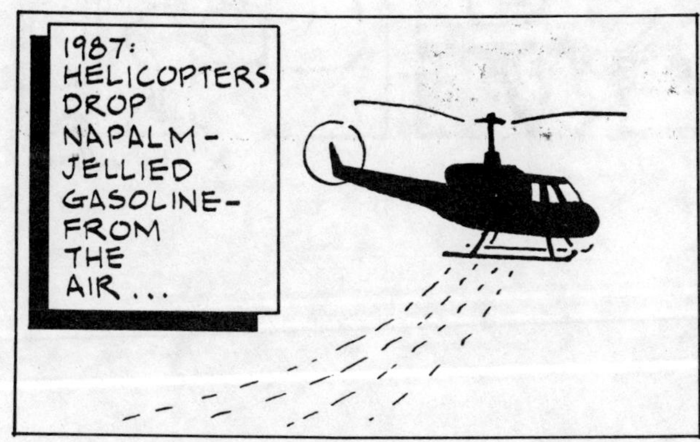
1987: HELICOPTERS DROP NAPALM-JELLIED GASOLINE-FROM THE AIR...
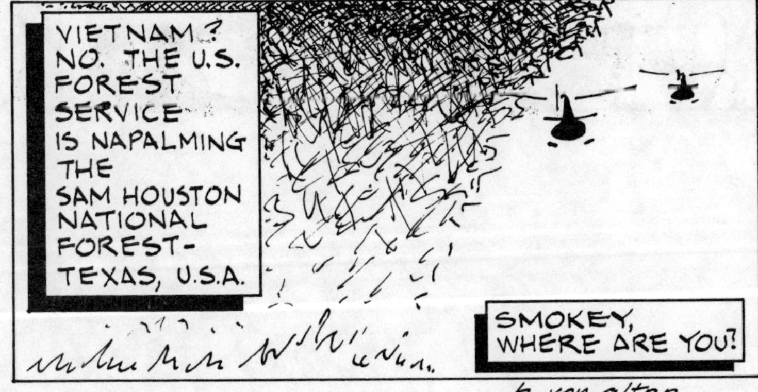
VIETNAM? NO. THE U.S. FOREST SERVICE IS NAPALMING THE SAM HOUSTON NATIONAL FOREST-TEXAS, U.S.A.
SMOKEY, WHERE ARE YOU?

b. von alten

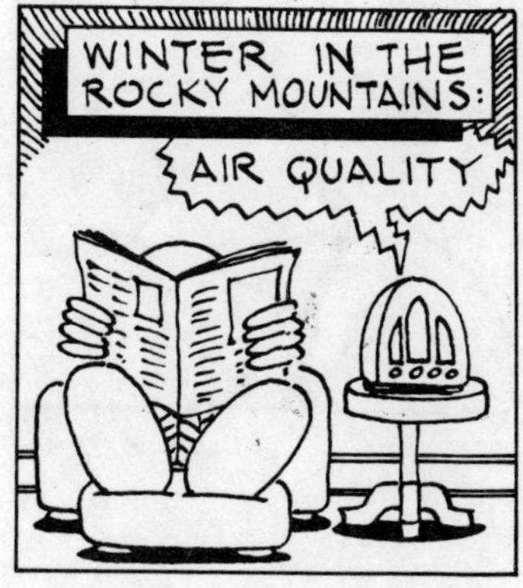
WINTER IN THE ROCKY MOUNTAINS:
AIR QUALITY
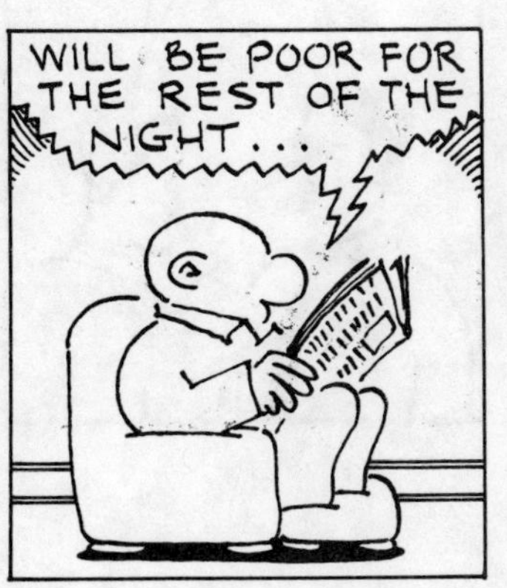
WILL BE POOR FOR THE REST OF THE NIGHT...
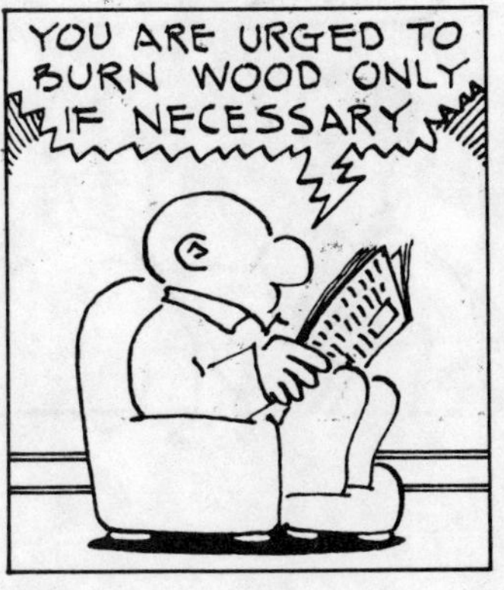
YOU ARE URGED TO BURN WOOD ONLY IF NECESSARY
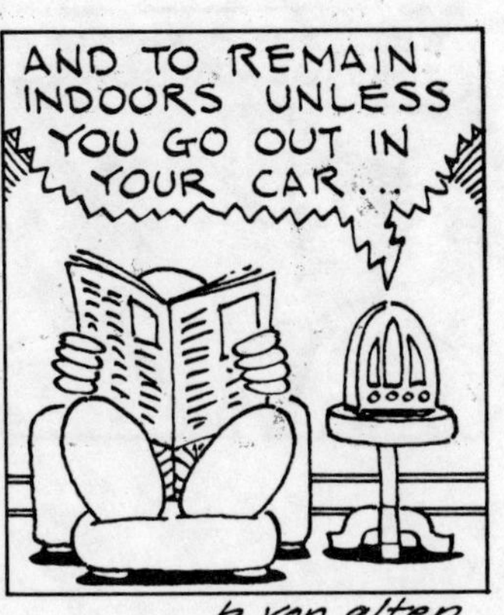
AND TO REMAIN INDOORS UNLESS YOU GO OUT IN YOUR CAR...

b. von alten

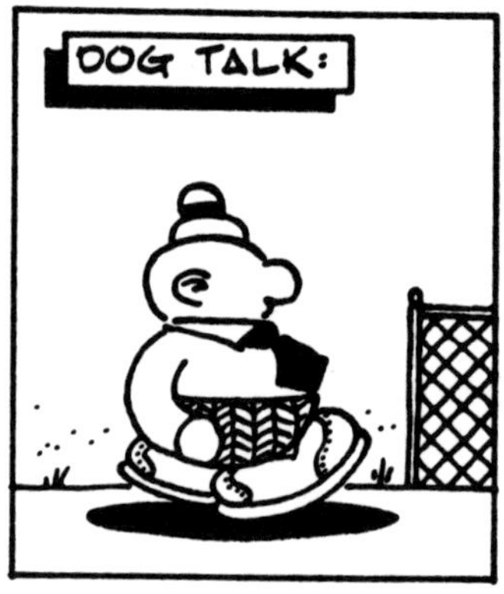
DOG TALK:

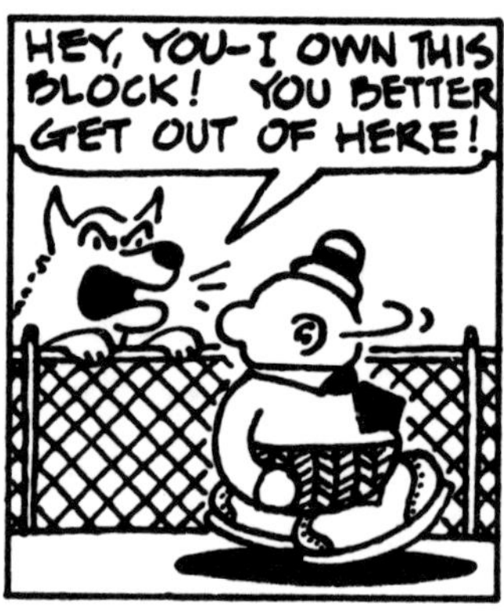
HEY, YOU- I OWN THIS BLOCK! YOU BETTER GET OUT OF HERE!

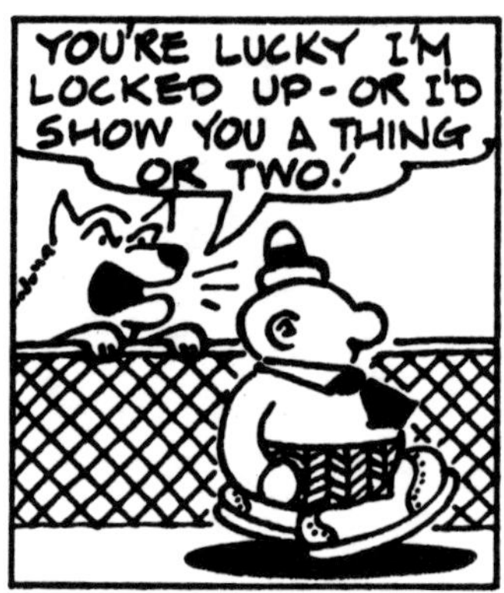
YOU'RE LUCKY I'M LOCKED UP- OR I'D SHOW YOU A THING OR TWO!

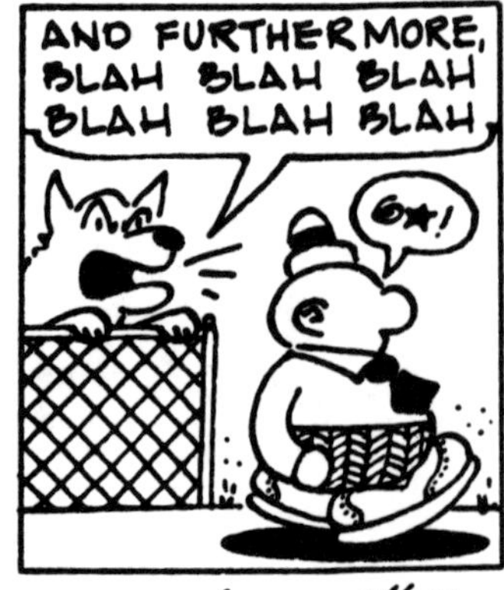
AND FURTHERMORE, BLAH BLAH BLAH BLAH BLAH BLAH

b. von alten

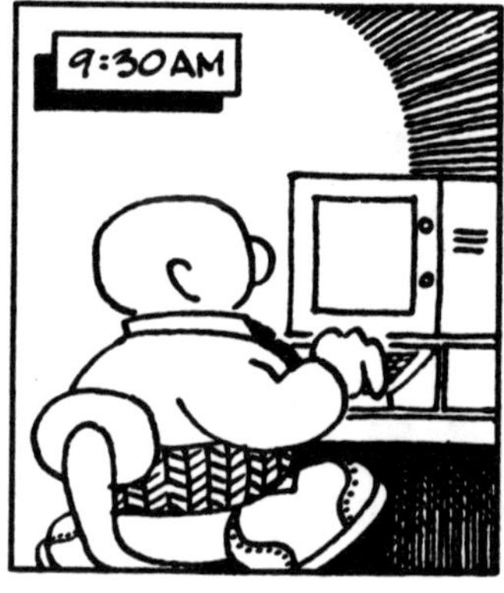
9:30AM

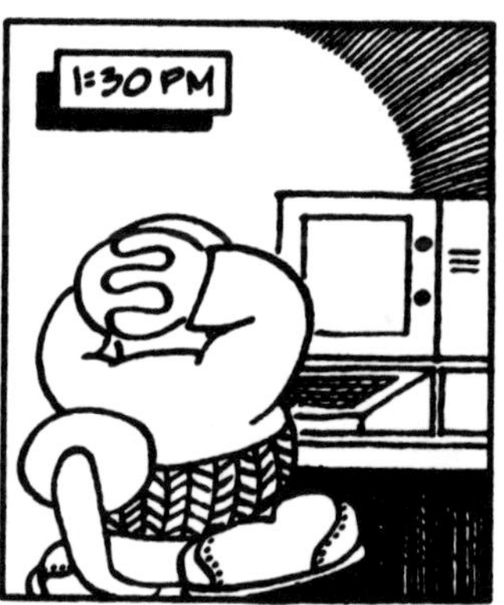
1:30PM

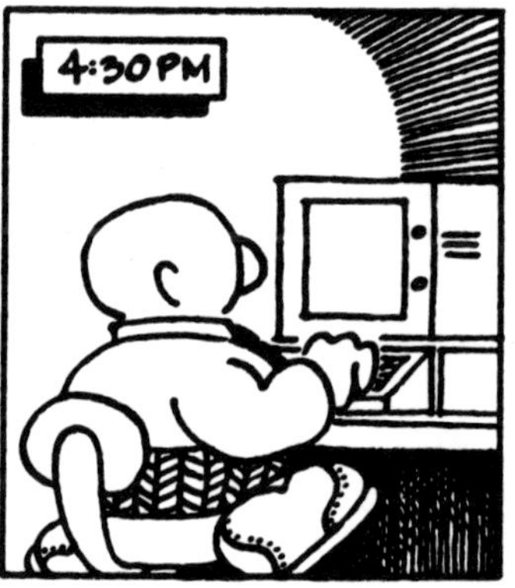
4:30PM

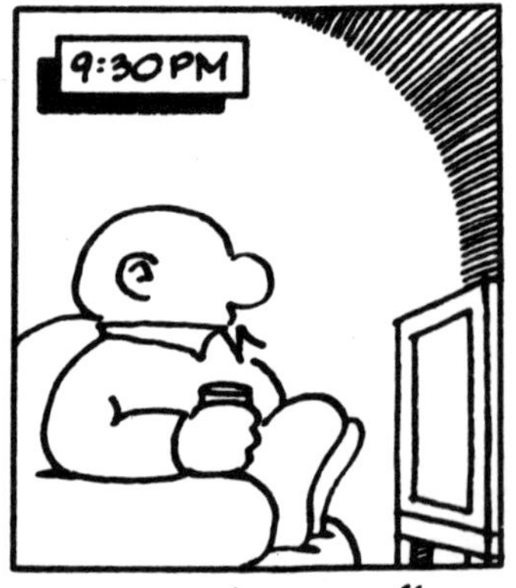
9:30PM

b. von alten

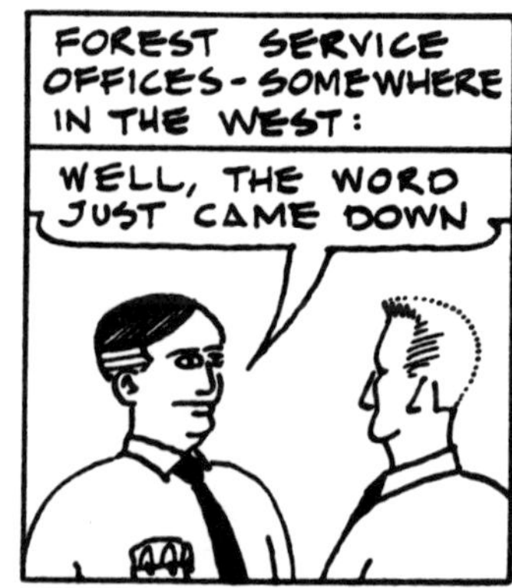
FOREST SERVICE OFFICES- SOMEWHERE IN THE WEST:
WELL, THE WORD JUST CAME DOWN

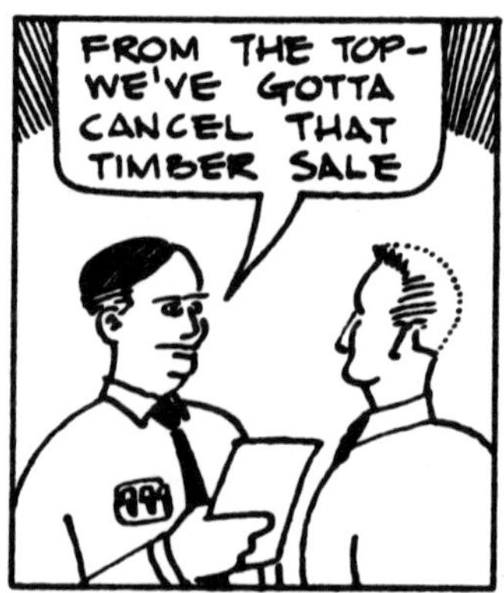
FROM THE TOP- WE'VE GOTTA CANCEL THAT TIMBER SALE

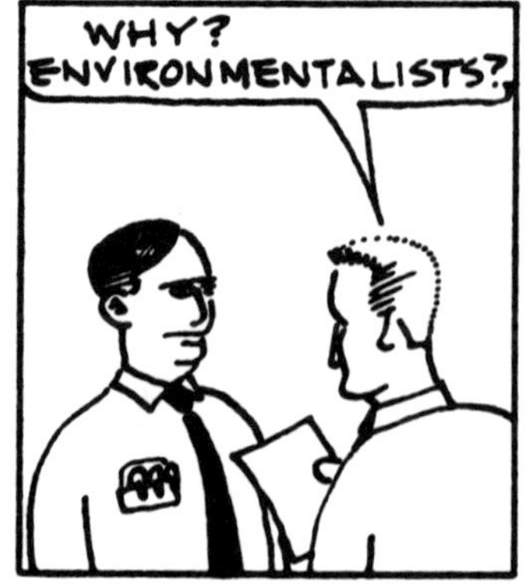
WHY? ENVIRONMENTALISTS?

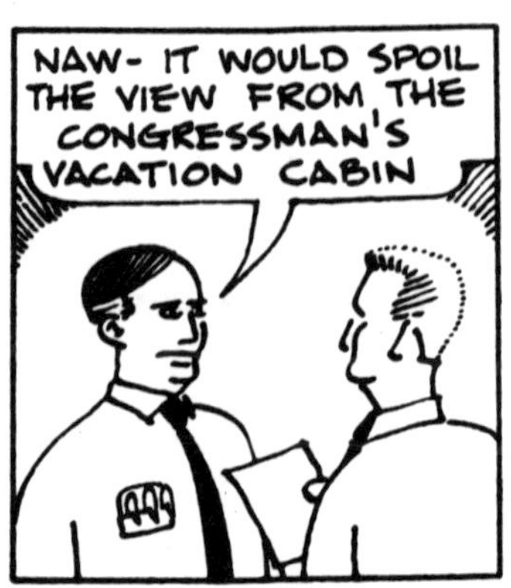
NAW- IT WOULD SPOIL THE VIEW FROM THE CONGRESSMAN'S VACATION CABIN

b. von alten

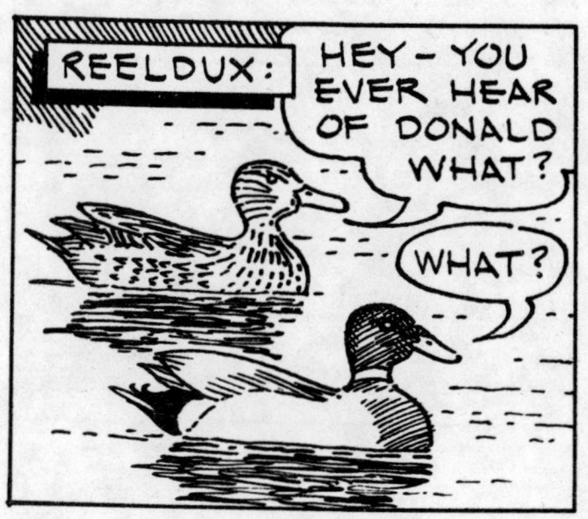
REELDUX:
HEY - YOU EVER HEAR OF DONALD WHAT?
WHAT?

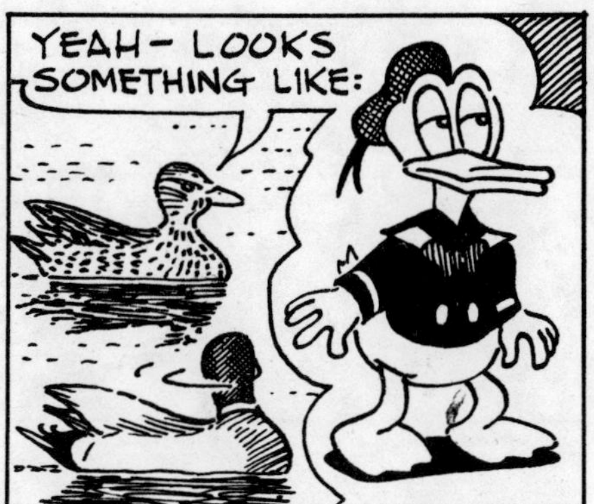
YEAH - LOOKS SOMETHING LIKE:

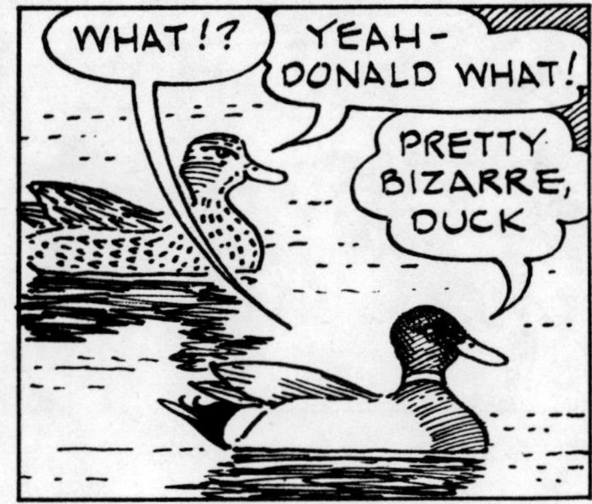
WHAT!?
YEAH - DONALD WHAT!
PRETTY BIZARRE, DUCK

b. von alten

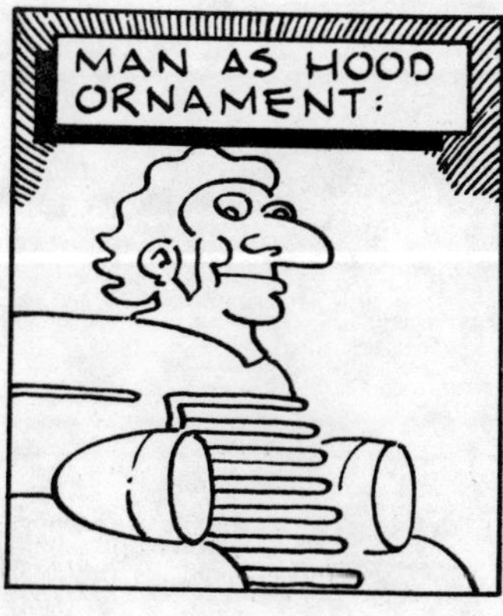
MAN AS HOOD ORNAMENT:

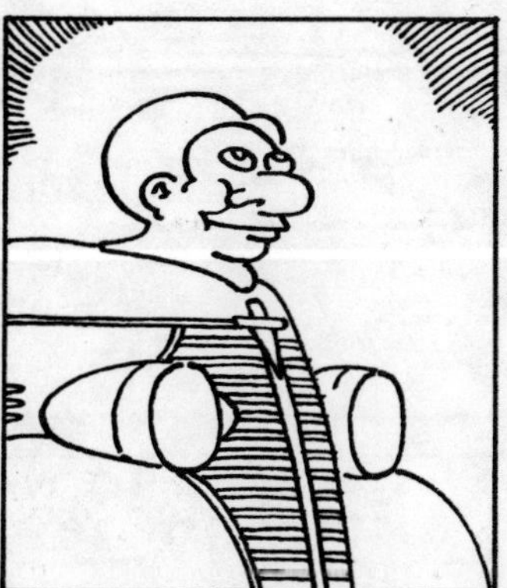

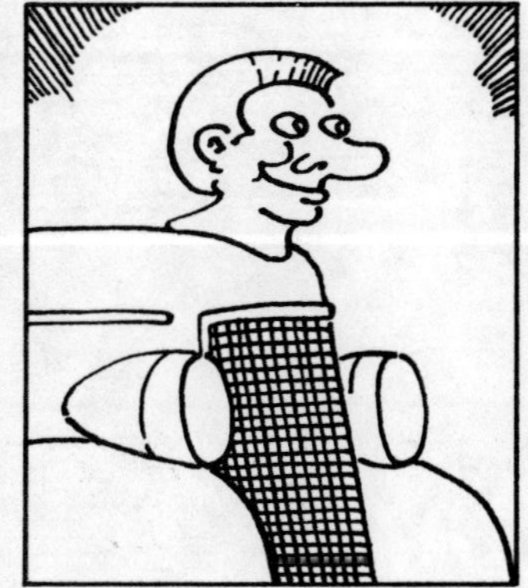

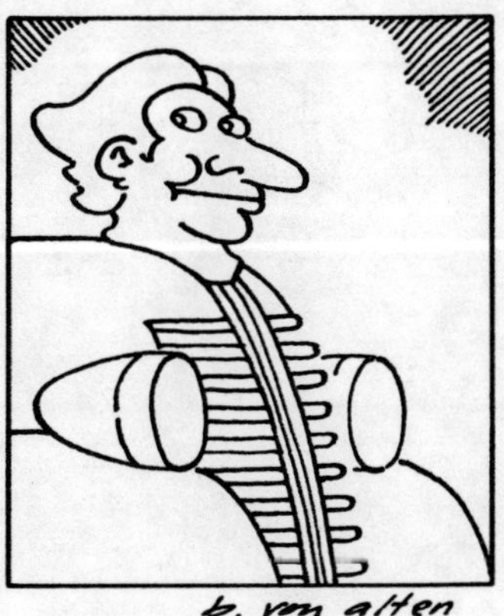

b. von alten

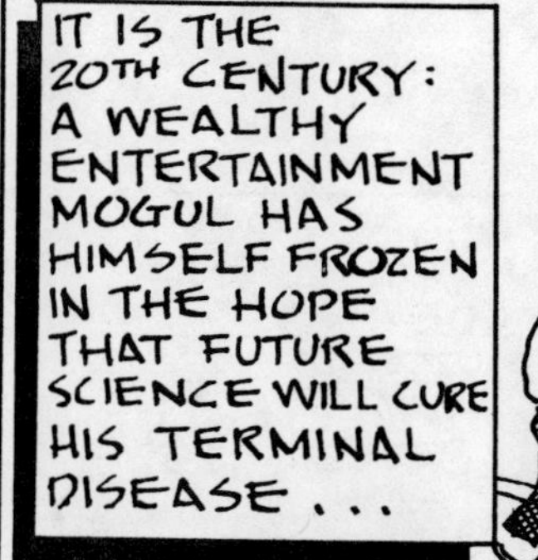
IT IS THE 20TH CENTURY: A WEALTHY ENTERTAINMENT MOGUL HAS HIMSELF FROZEN IN THE HOPE THAT FUTURE SCIENCE WILL CURE HIS TERMINAL DISEASE . . .

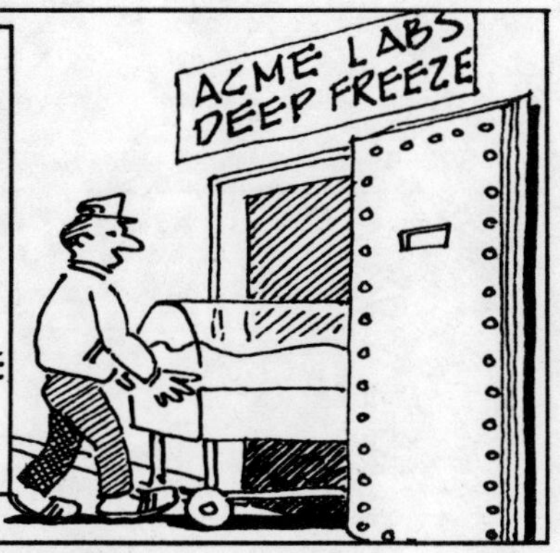
ACME LABS DEEP FREEZE

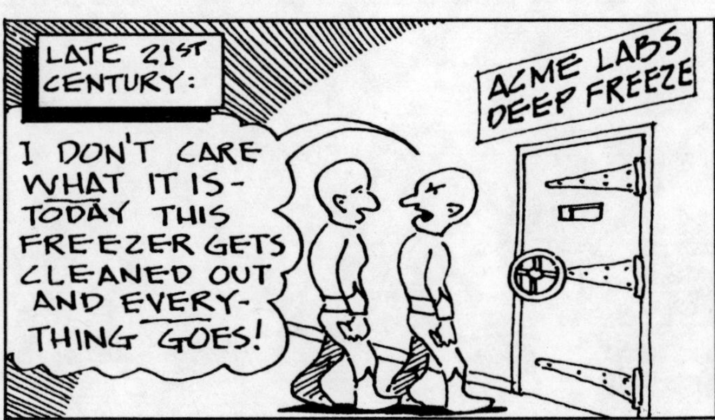
LATE 21ST CENTURY:
ACME LABS DEEP FREEZE
I DON'T CARE WHAT IT IS - TODAY THIS FREEZER GETS CLEANED OUT AND EVERYTHING GOES!

b. von alten

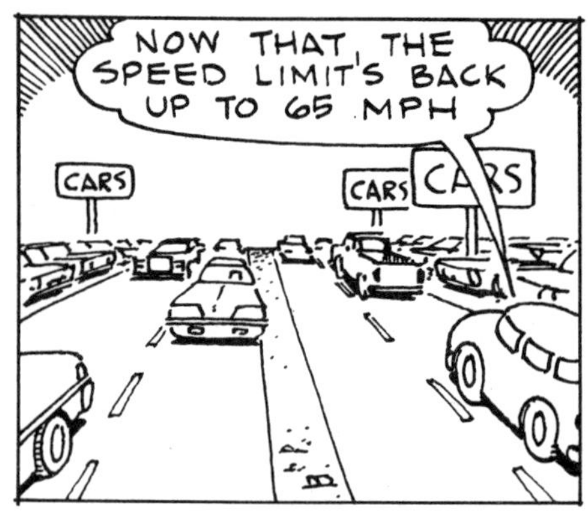
NOW THAT THE SPEED LIMIT'S BACK UP TO 65 MPH
CARS
CARS
CARS

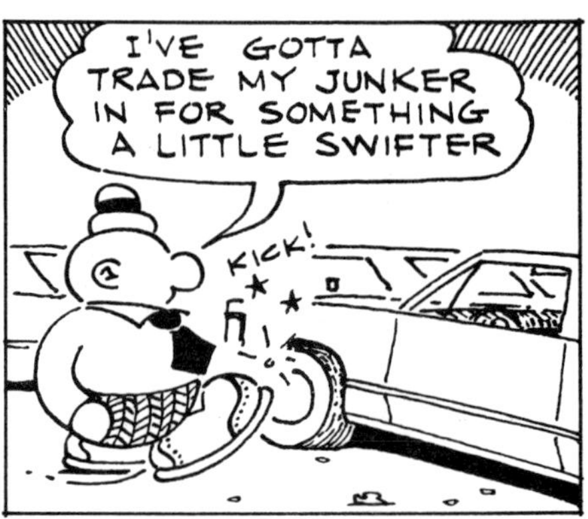
I'VE GOTTA TRADE MY JUNKER IN FOR SOMETHING A LITTLE SWIFTER
KICK!

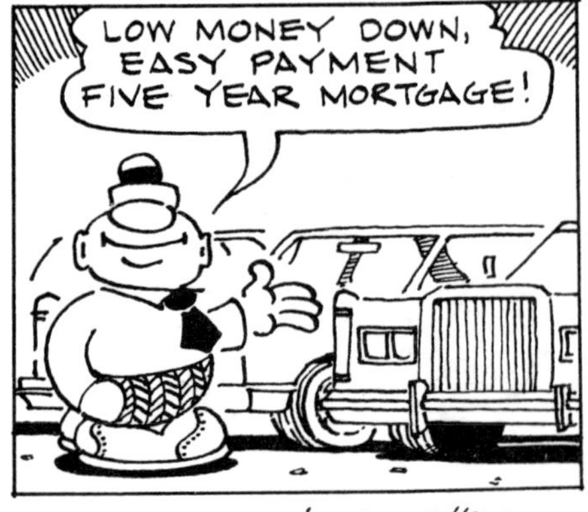
LOW MONEY DOWN, EASY PAYMENT FIVE YEAR MORTGAGE!

b. von alten

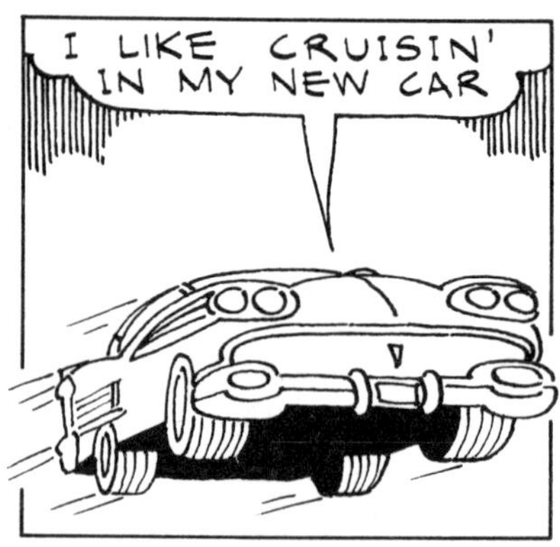
I LIKE CRUISIN' IN MY NEW CAR

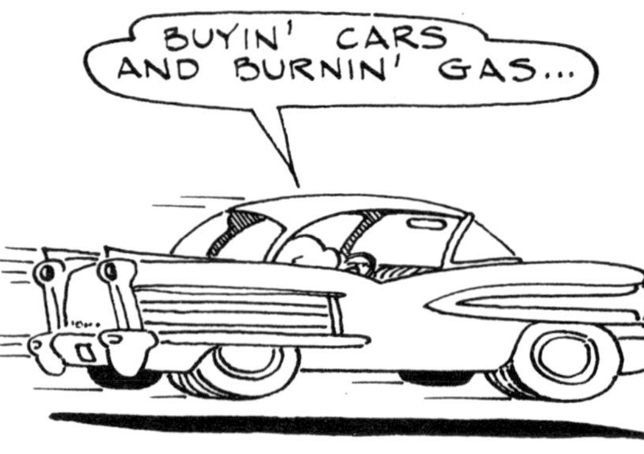
BUYIN' CARS AND BURNIN' GAS...

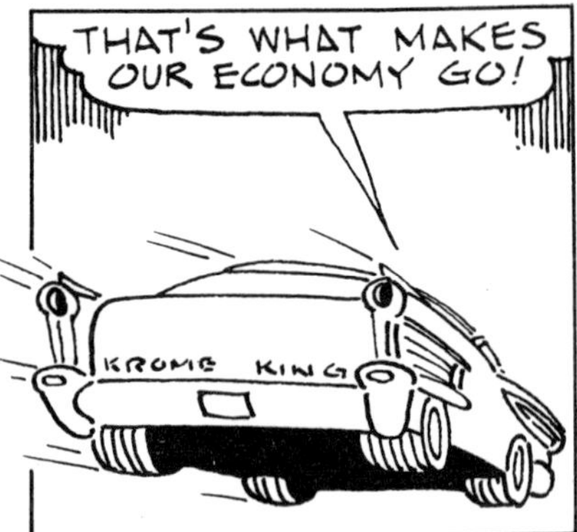
THAT'S WHAT MAKES OUR ECONOMY GO!
KROME KING

b. von alten

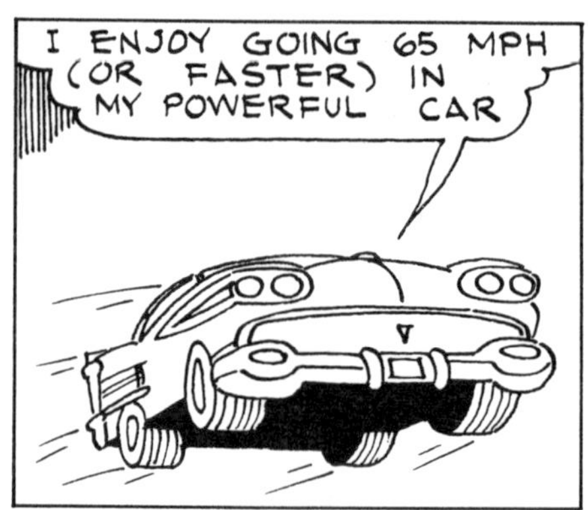
I ENJOY GOING 65 MPH (OR FASTER) IN MY POWERFUL CAR

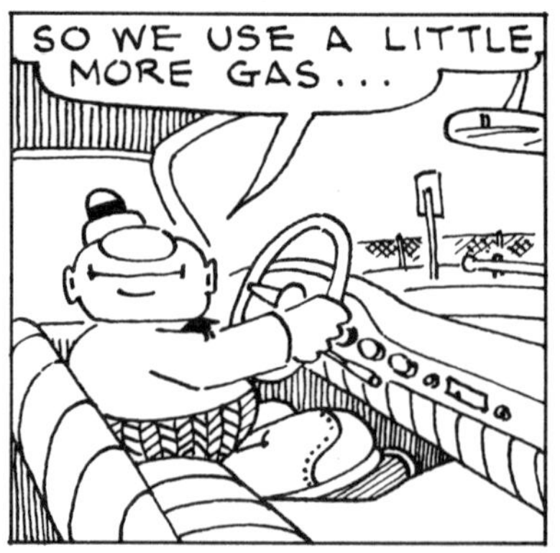
SO WE USE A LITTLE MORE GAS...

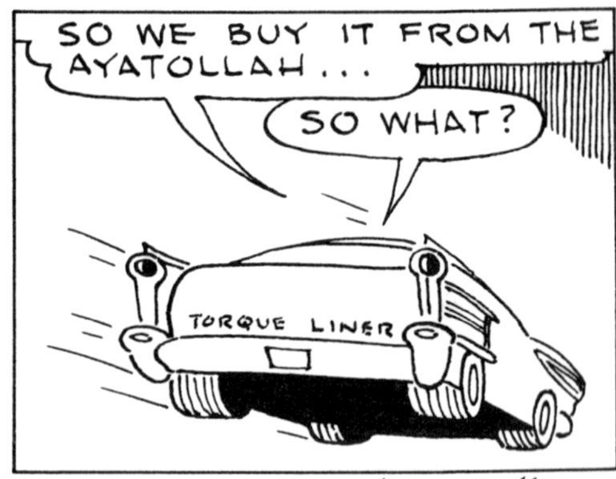
SO WE BUY IT FROM THE AYATOLLAH...
SO WHAT?
TORQUE LINER

b. von alten

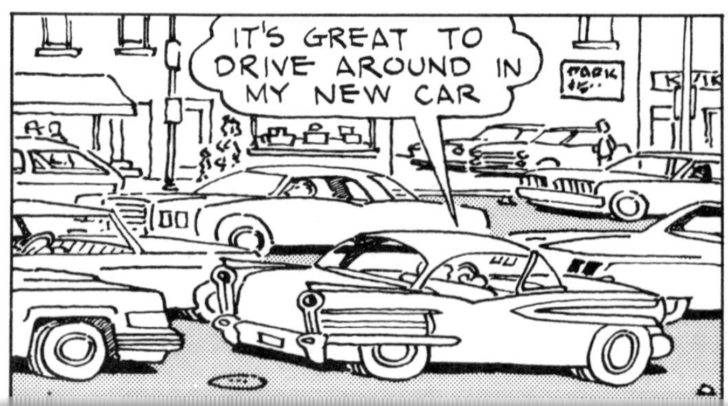
IT'S GREAT TO DRIVE AROUND IN MY NEW CAR

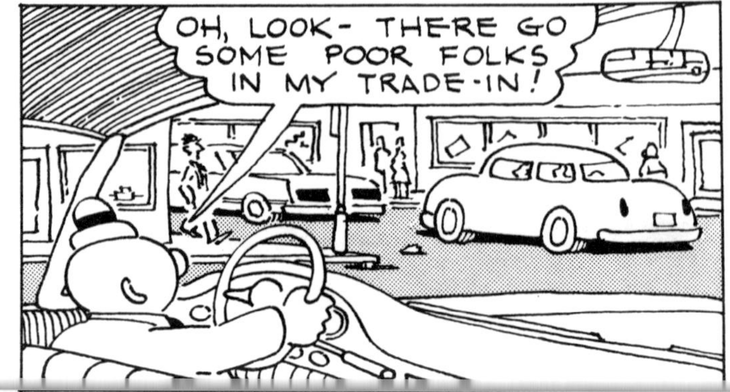
OH, LOOK- THERE GO SOME POOR FOLKS IN MY TRADE-IN!

b. von alten

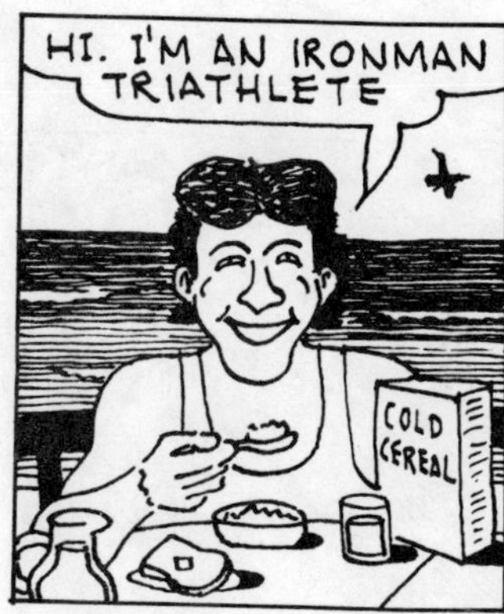
HI. I'M AN IRONMAN TRIATHLETE
COLD CEREAL

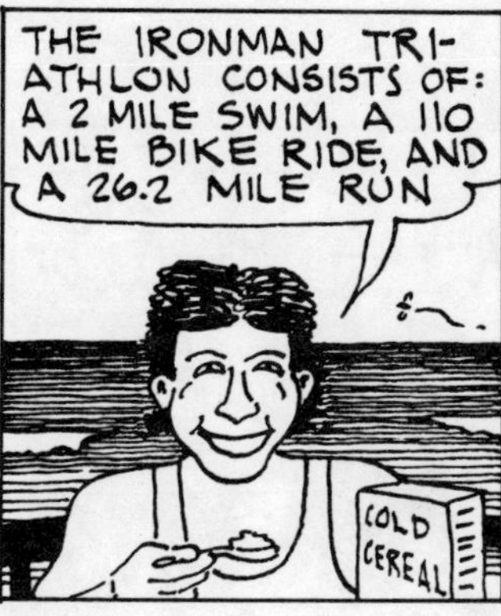
THE IRONMAN TRI-ATHLON CONSISTS OF: A 2 MILE SWIM, A 110 MILE BIKE RIDE, AND A 26.2 MILE RUN
COLD CEREAL

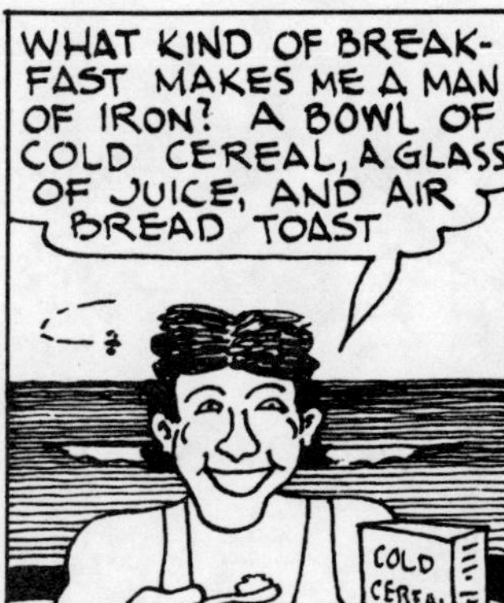
WHAT KIND OF BREAK-FAST MAKES ME A MAN OF IRON? A BOWL OF COLD CEREAL, A GLASS OF JUICE, AND AIR BREAD TOAST

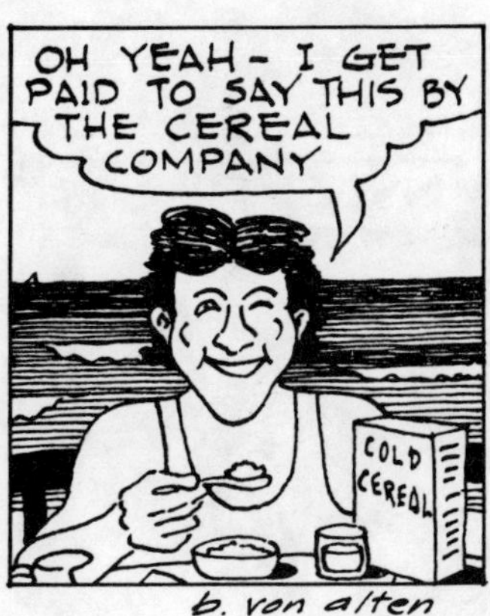
OH YEAH - I GET PAID TO SAY THIS BY THE CEREAL COMPANY
COLD CEREAL

b. von alten

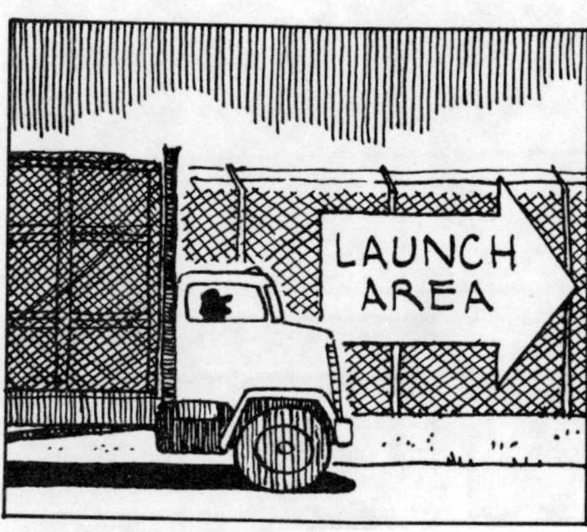
LAUNCH AREA

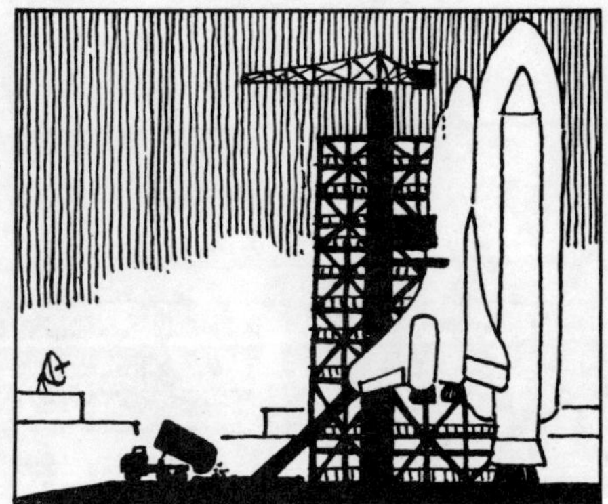

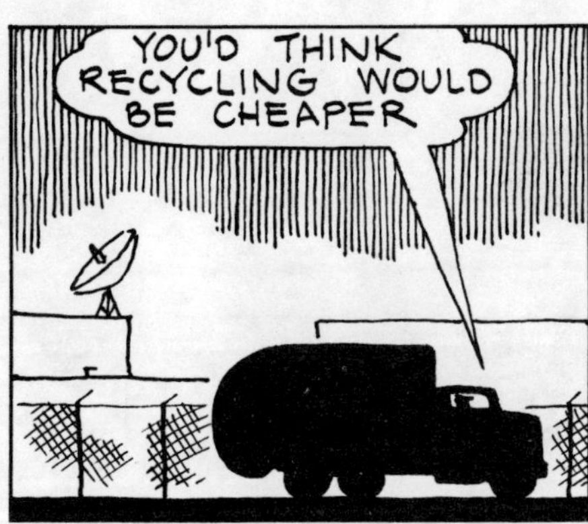
YOU'D THINK RECYCLING WOULD BE CHEAPER

b. von alten

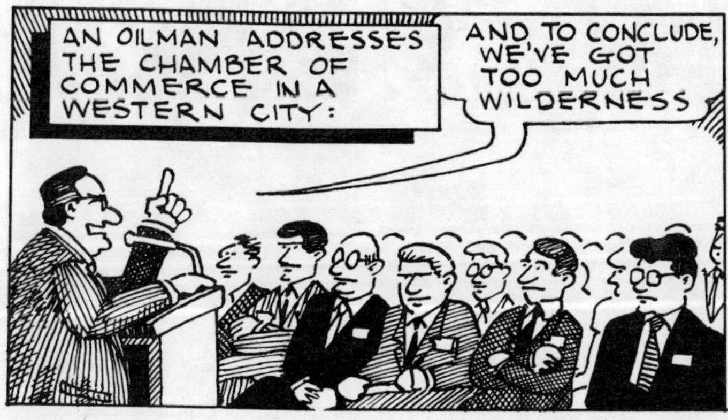
AN OILMAN ADDRESSES THE CHAMBER OF COMMERCE IN A WESTERN CITY:
AND TO CONCLUDE, WE'VE GOT TOO MUCH WILDERNESS

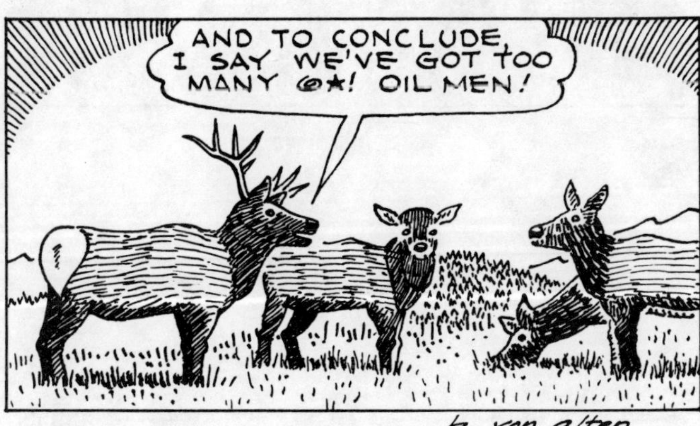
AND TO CONCLUDE, I SAY WE'VE GOT TOO MANY @*! OIL MEN!

b. von alten

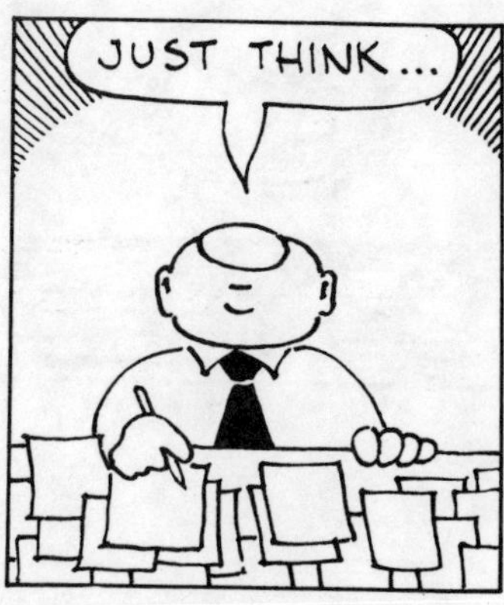
JUST THINK...

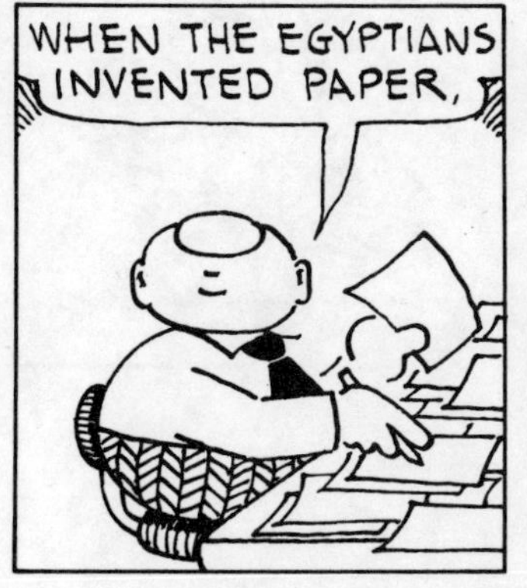
WHEN THE EGYPTIANS INVENTED PAPER,

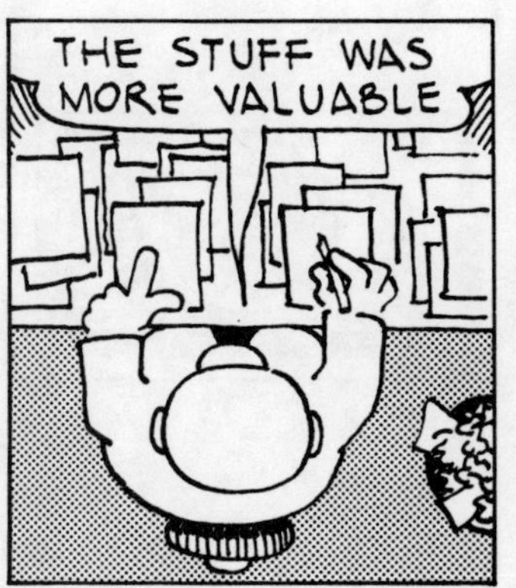
THE STUFF WAS MORE VALUABLE

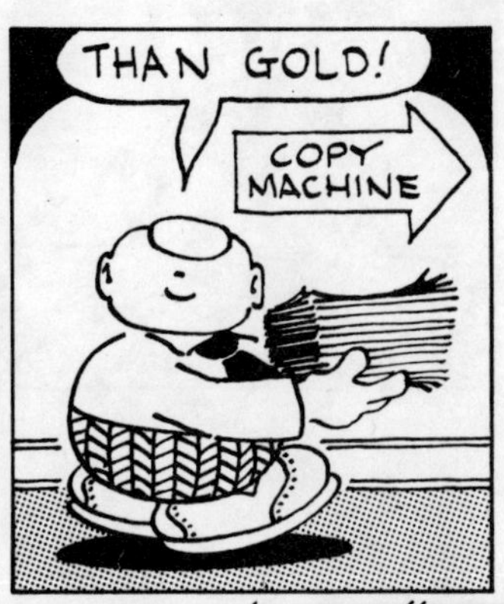
THAN GOLD!
COPY MACHINE

b. von alten

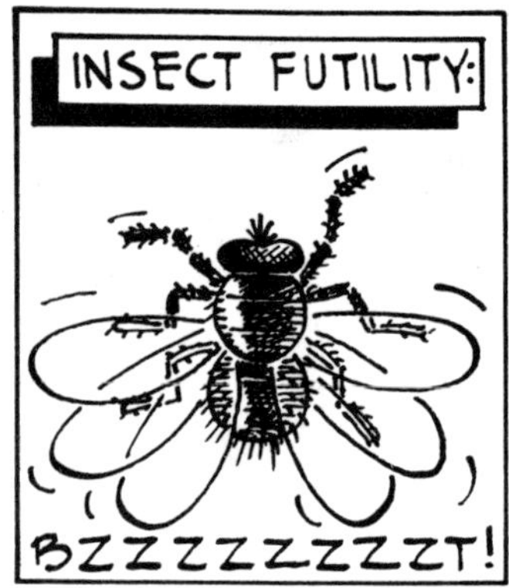
INSECT FUTILITY:
BZZZZZZZZT!

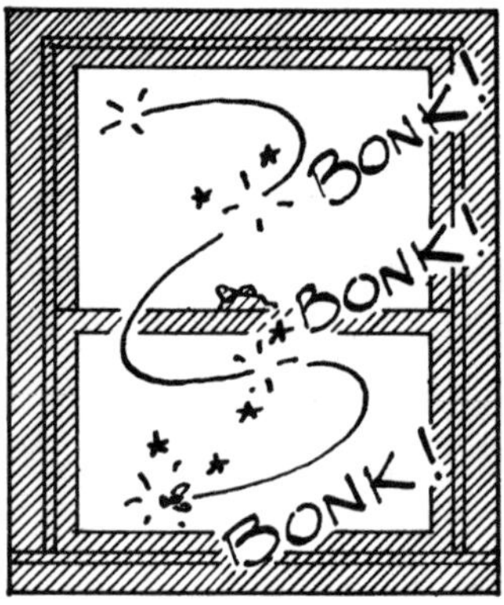
BONK!
BONK!
BONK!

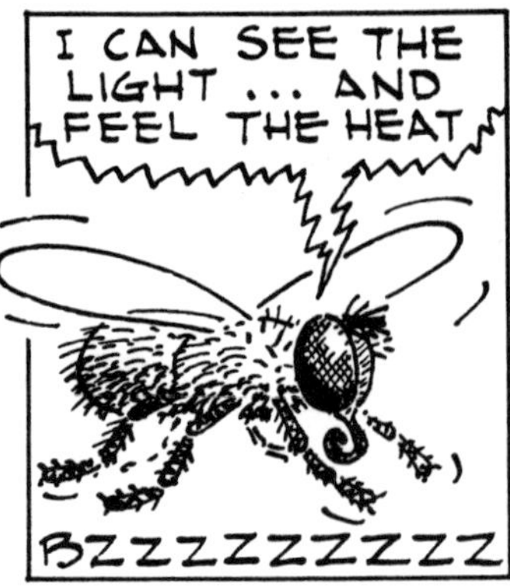
I CAN SEE THE LIGHT ... AND FEEL THE HEAT
BZZZZZZZZZ

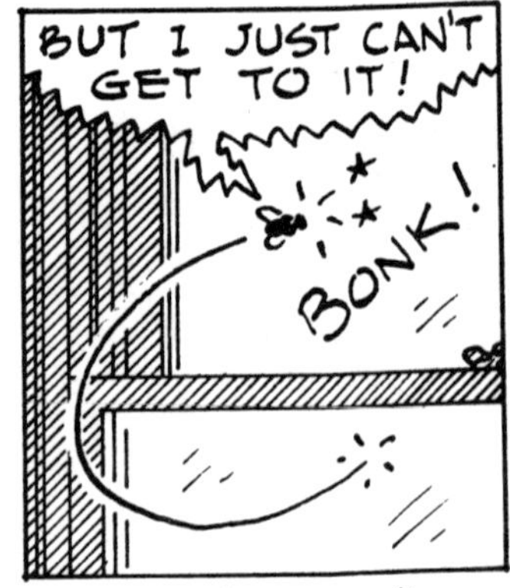
BUT I JUST CAN'T GET TO IT!
BONK!
b. von alten

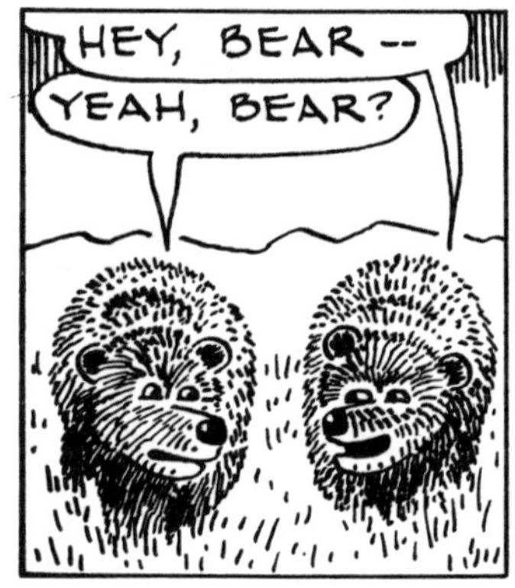
HEY, BEAR --
YEAH, BEAR?

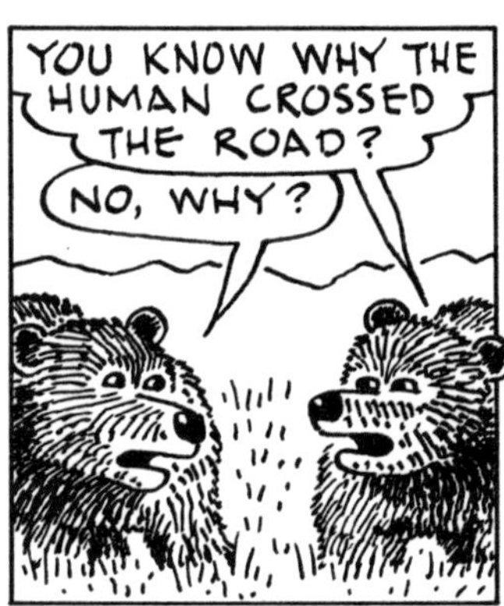
YOU KNOW WHY THE HUMAN CROSSED THE ROAD?
NO, WHY?

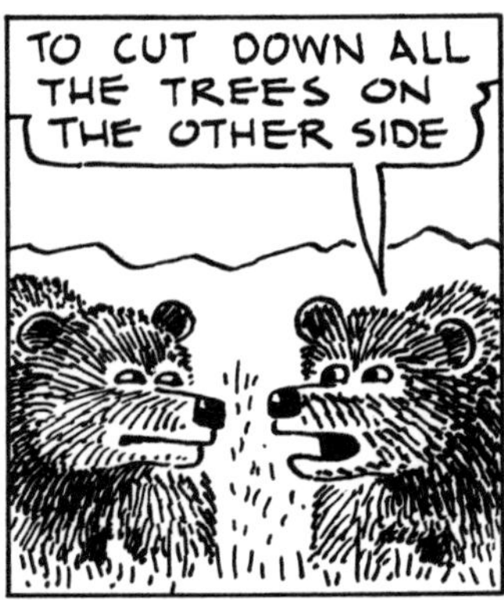
TO CUT DOWN ALL THE TREES ON THE OTHER SIDE

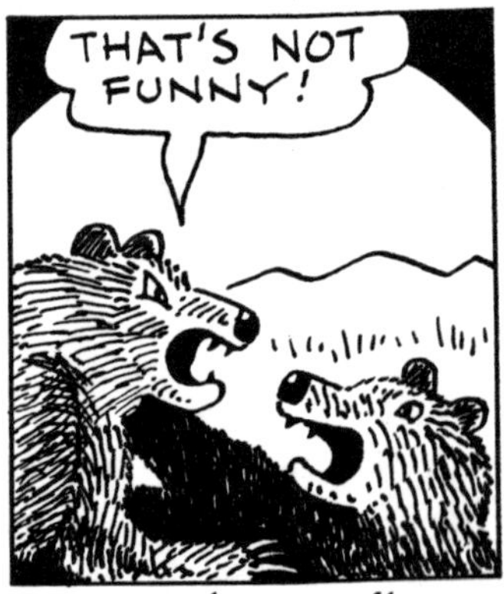
THAT'S NOT FUNNY!
b. von alten

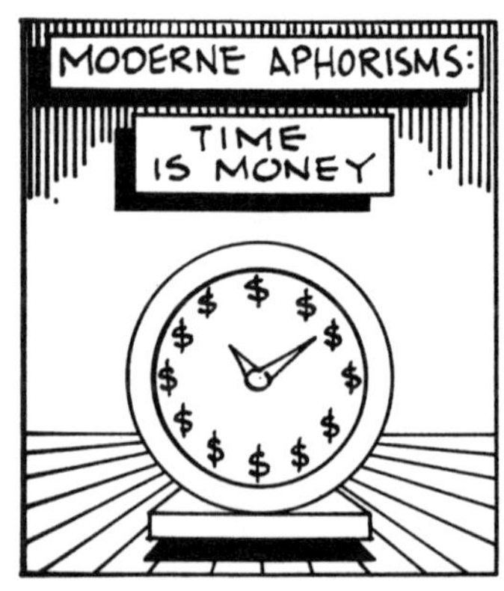
MODERNE APHORISMS:
TIME IS MONEY

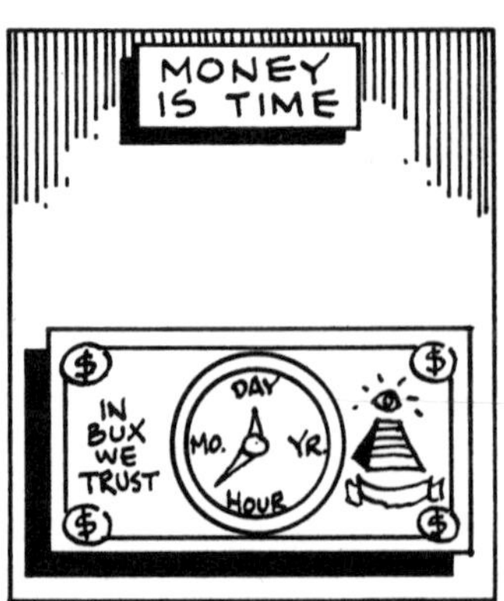
MONEY IS TIME
IN BUX WE TRUST
DAY
MO.
YR.
HOUR

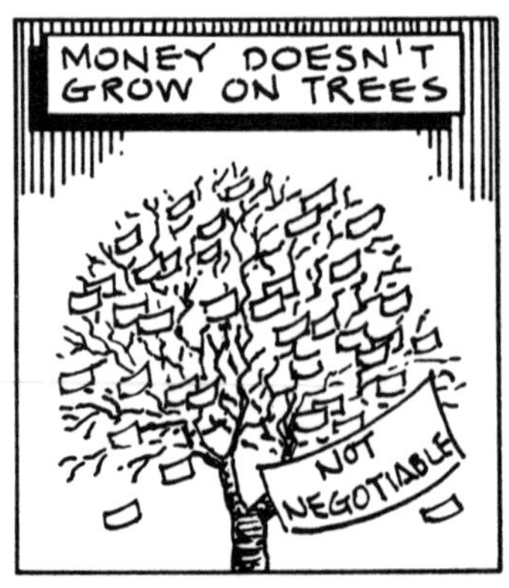
MONEY DOESN'T GROW ON TREES
NOT NEGOTIABLE

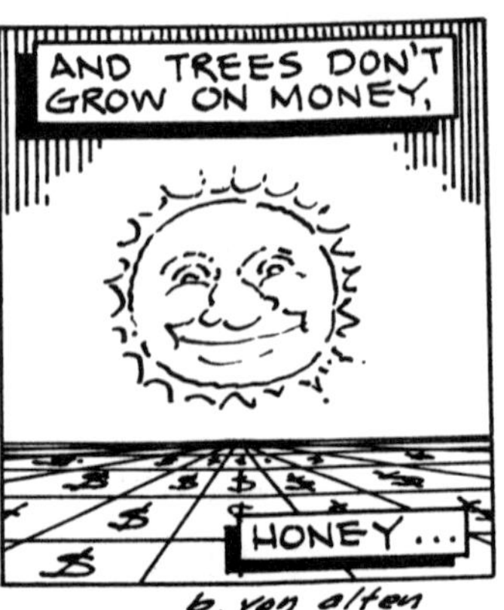
AND TREES DON'T GROW ON MONEY,
HONEY...
b. von alten

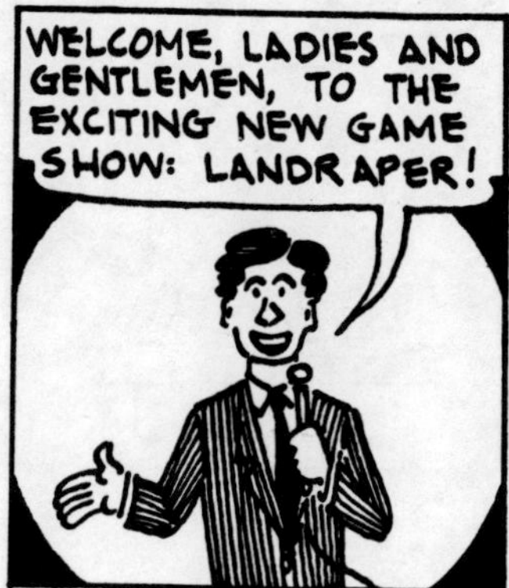
WELCOME, LADIES AND GENTLEMEN, TO THE EXCITING NEW GAME SHOW: LANDRAPER!
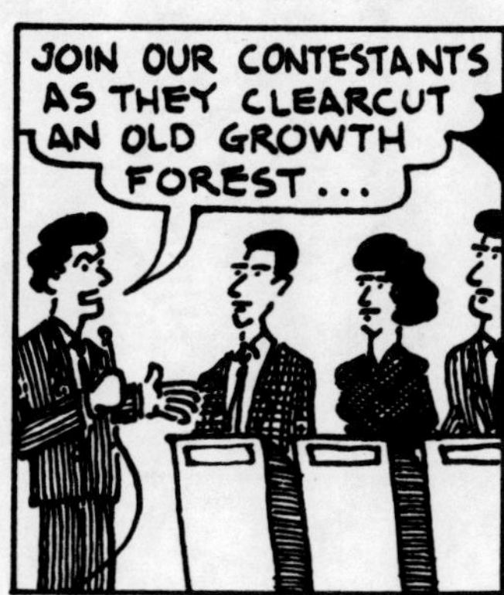
JOIN OUR CONTESTANTS AS THEY CLEARCUT AN OLD GROWTH FOREST...
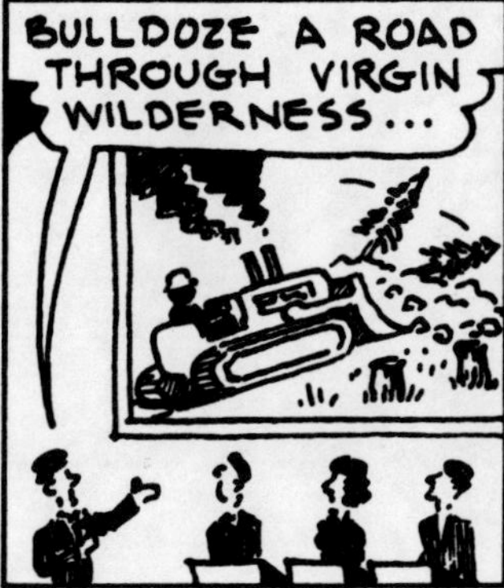
BULLDOZE A ROAD THROUGH VIRGIN WILDERNESS...
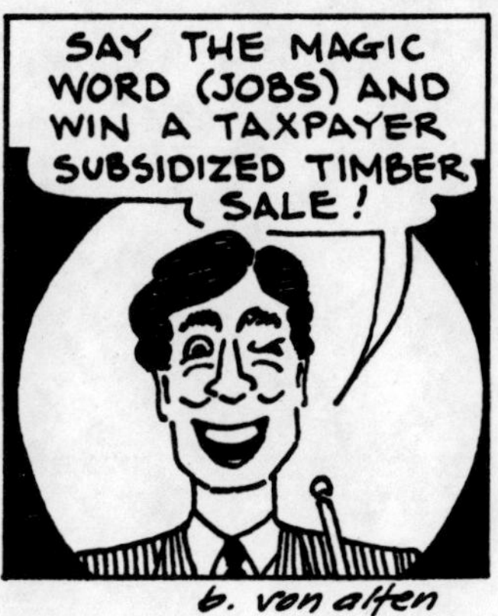
SAY THE MAGIC WORD (JOBS) AND WIN A TAXPAYER SUBSIDIZED TIMBER SALE!

b. von alten

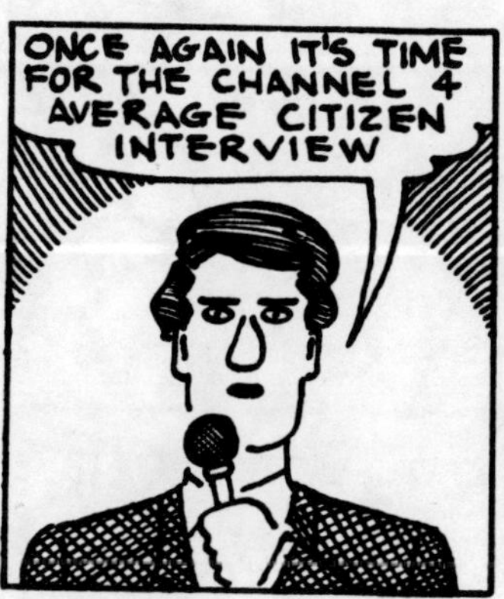
ONCE AGAIN IT'S TIME FOR THE CHANNEL 4 AVERAGE CITIZEN INTERVIEW
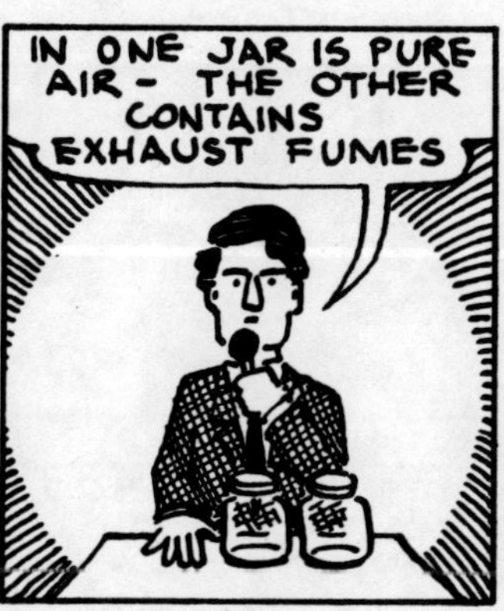
IN ONE JAR IS PURE AIR - THE OTHER CONTAINS EXHAUST FUMES
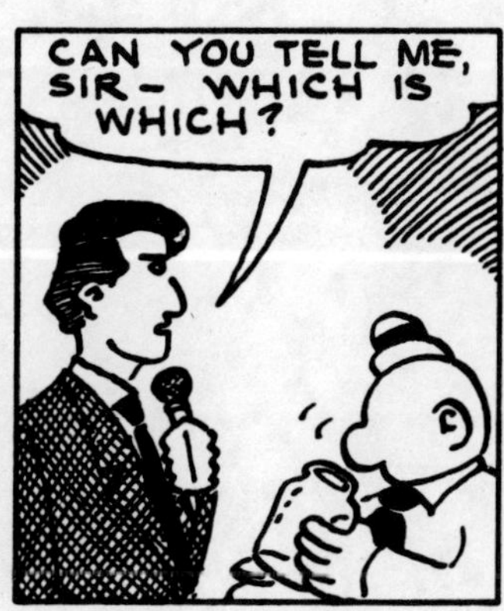
CAN YOU TELL ME, SIR - WHICH IS WHICH?
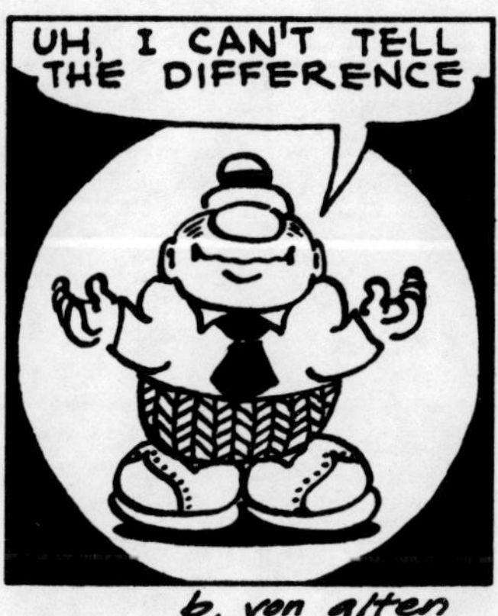
UH, I CAN'T TELL THE DIFFERENCE

b. von alten

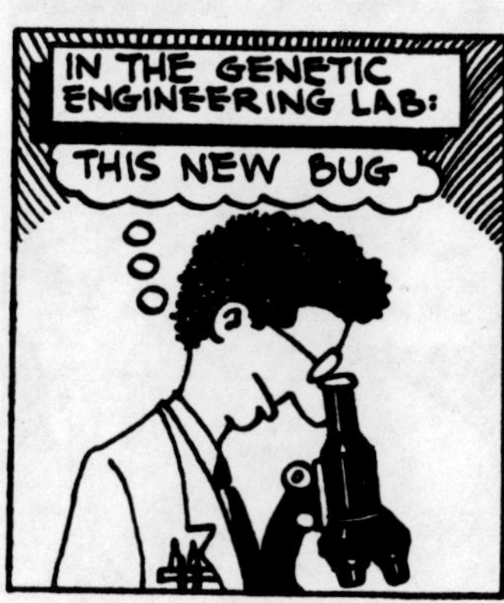
IN THE GENETIC ENGINEERING LAB:
THIS NEW BUG
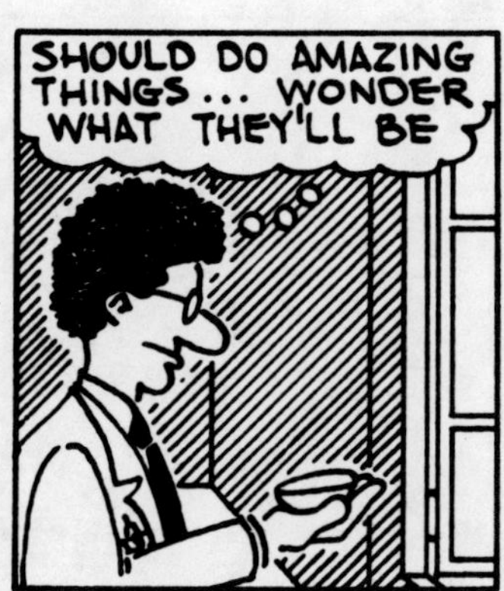
SHOULD DO AMAZING THINGS... WONDER WHAT THEY'LL BE
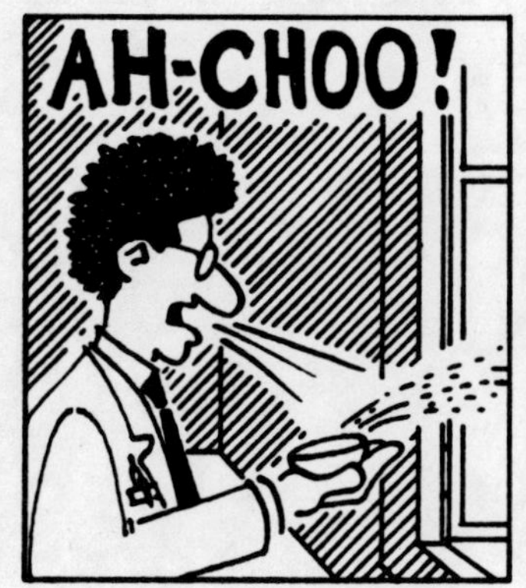
AH-CHOO!
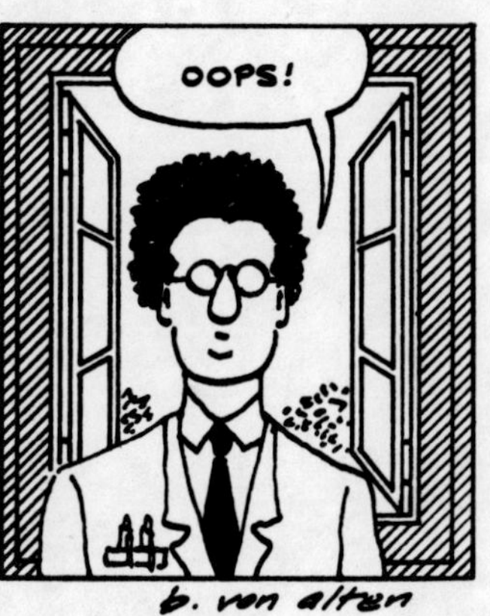
OOPS!

b. von alten

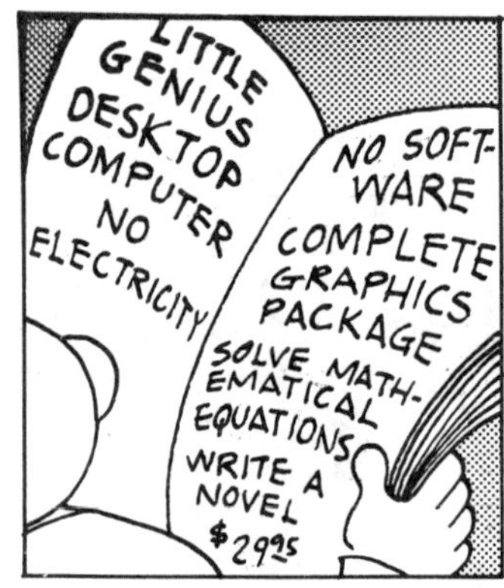
LITTLE GENIUS DESKTOP COMPUTER
NO ELECTRICITY
NO SOFTWARE
COMPLETE GRAPHICS PACKAGE
SOLVE MATHEMATICAL EQUATIONS
WRITE A NOVEL
$29.95

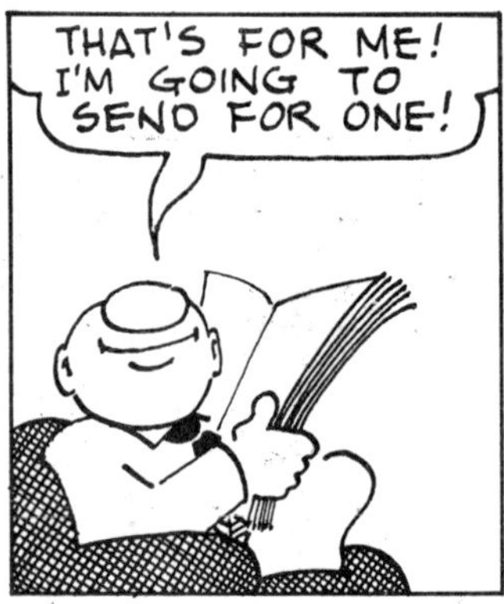
THAT'S FOR ME! I'M GOING TO SEND FOR ONE!

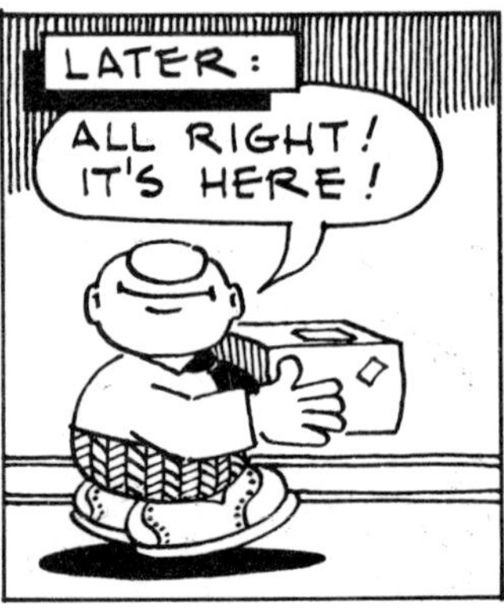
LATER:
ALL RIGHT! IT'S HERE!

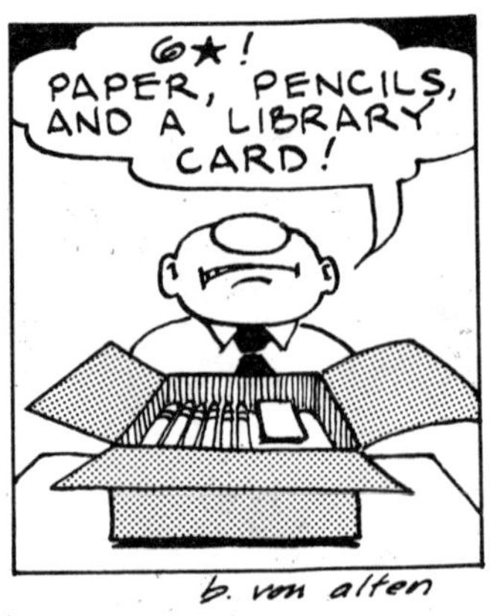
G★! PAPER, PENCILS, AND A LIBRARY CARD!
b. von alten

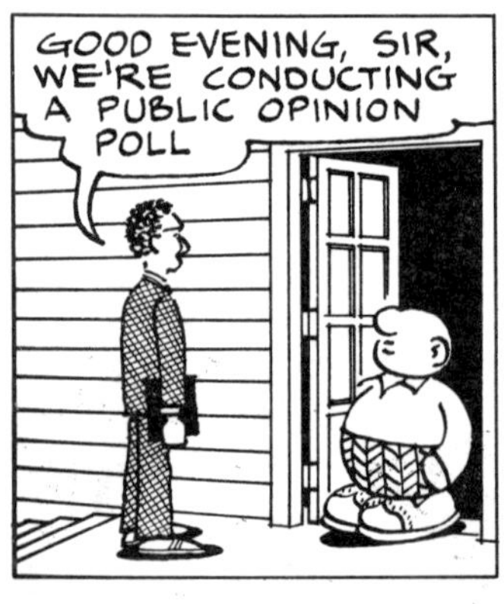
GOOD EVENING, SIR, WE'RE CONDUCTING A PUBLIC OPINION POLL

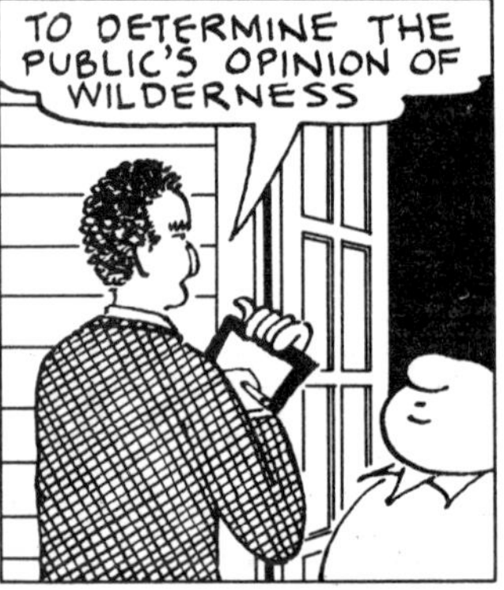
TO DETERMINE THE PUBLIC'S OPINION OF WILDERNESS

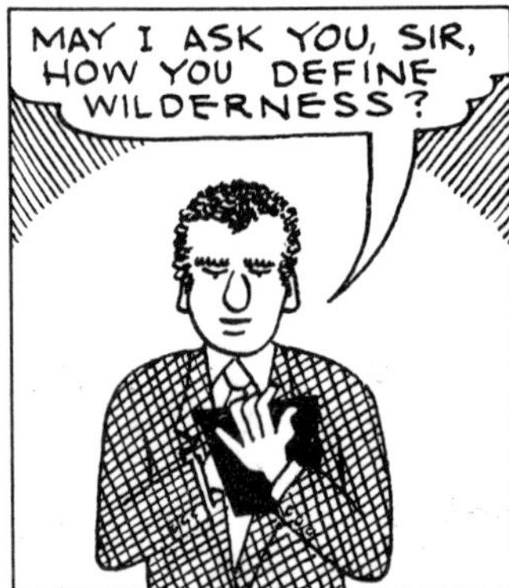
MAY I ASK YOU, SIR, HOW YOU DEFINE WILDERNESS?

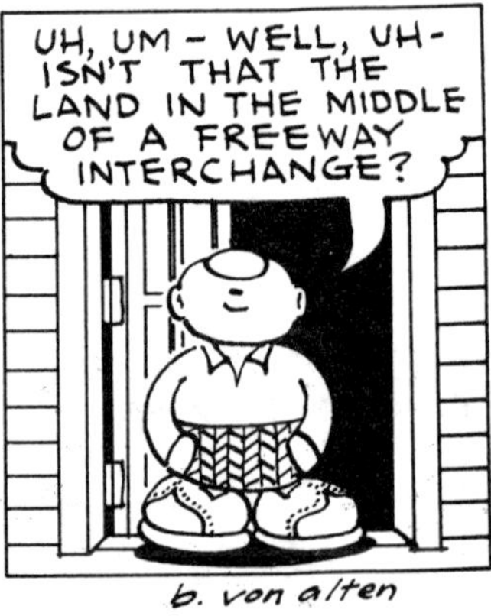
UH, UM - WELL, UH - ISN'T THAT THE LAND IN THE MIDDLE OF A FREEWAY INTERCHANGE?
b. von alten

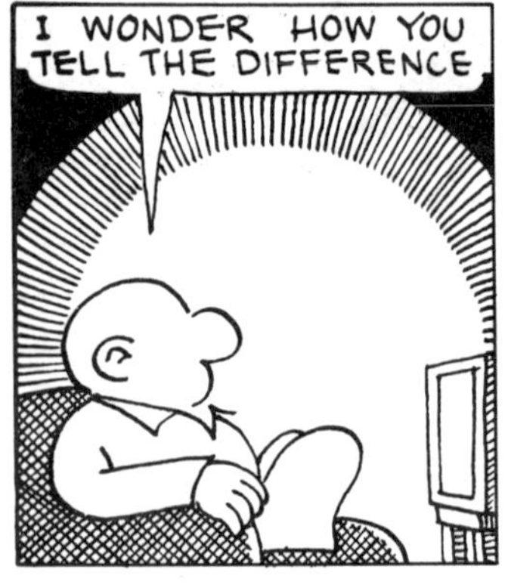
I WONDER HOW YOU TELL THE DIFFERENCE

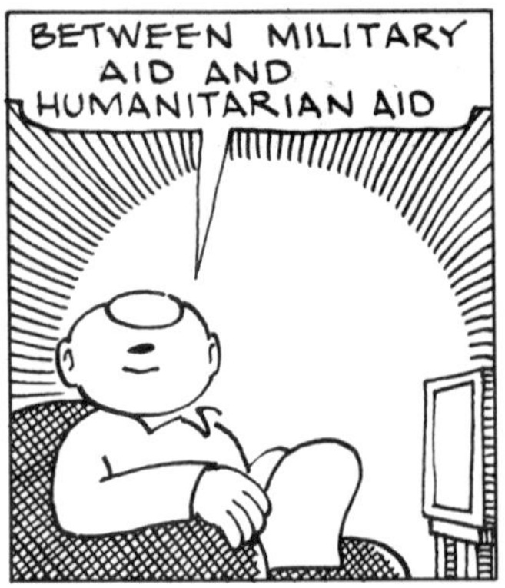
BETWEEN MILITARY AID AND HUMANITARIAN AID

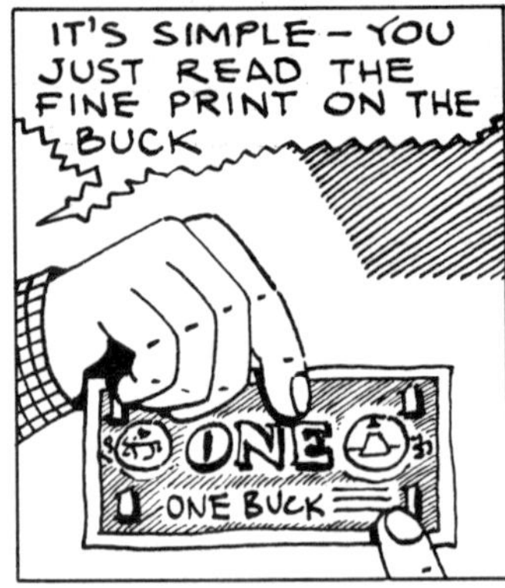
IT'S SIMPLE - YOU JUST READ THE FINE PRINT ON THE BUCK
ONE
ONE BUCK

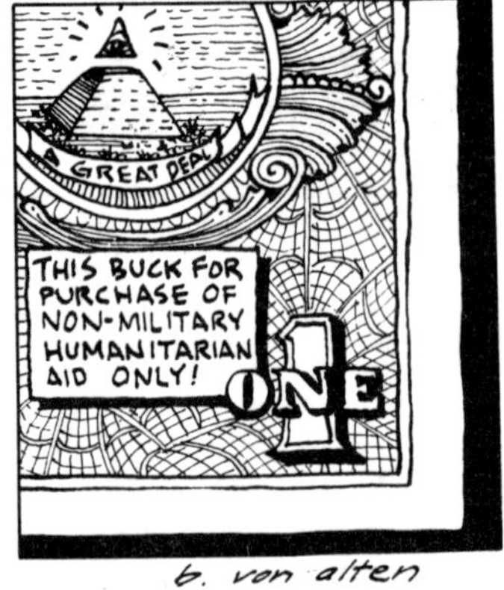
A GREAT DEAL
THIS BUCK FOR PURCHASE OF NON-MILITARY HUMANITARIAN AID ONLY!
ONE
b. von alten

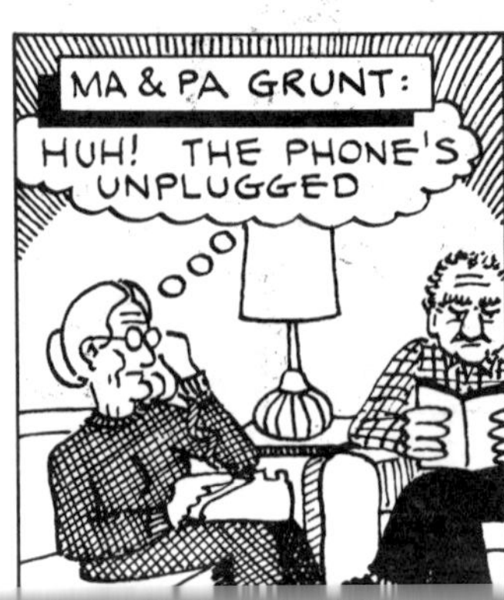
MA & PA GRUNT:
HUH! THE PHONE'S UNPLUGGED

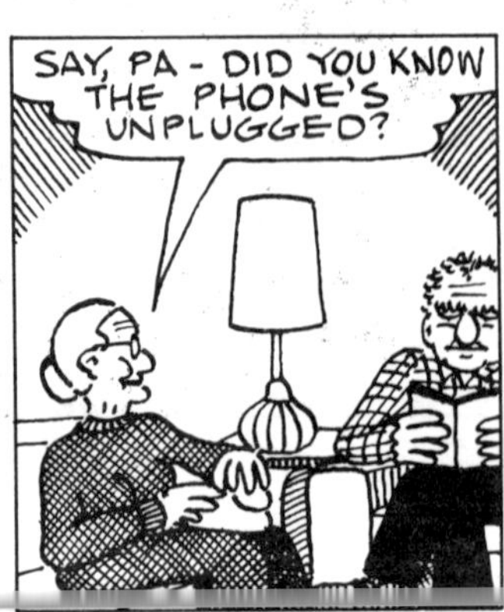
SAY, PA - DID YOU KNOW THE PHONE'S UNPLUGGED?

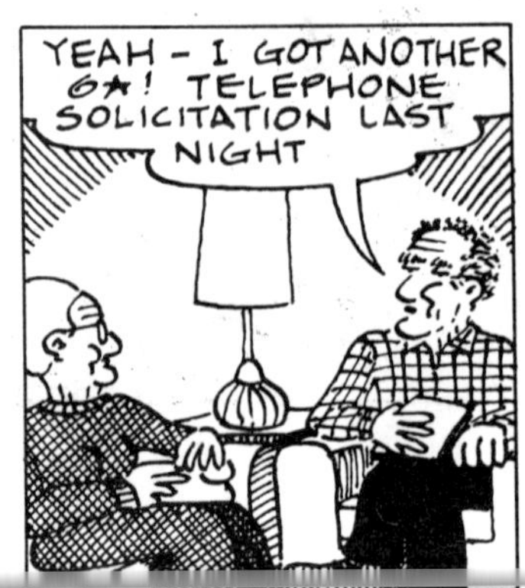
YEAH - I GOT ANOTHER G★! TELEPHONE SOLICITATION LAST NIGHT

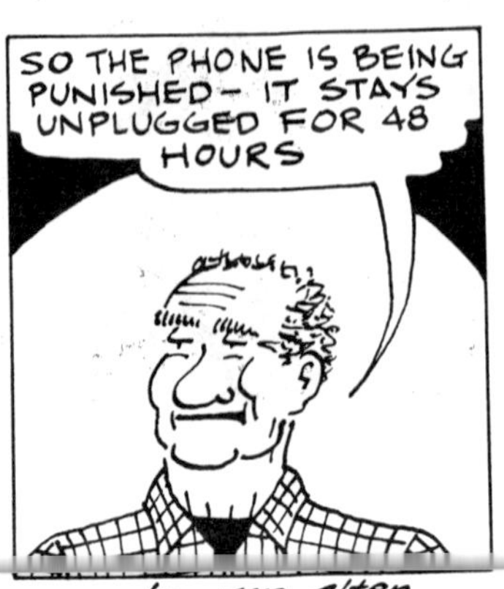
SO THE PHONE IS BEING PUNISHED - IT STAYS UNPLUGGED FOR 48 HOURS
b. von alten

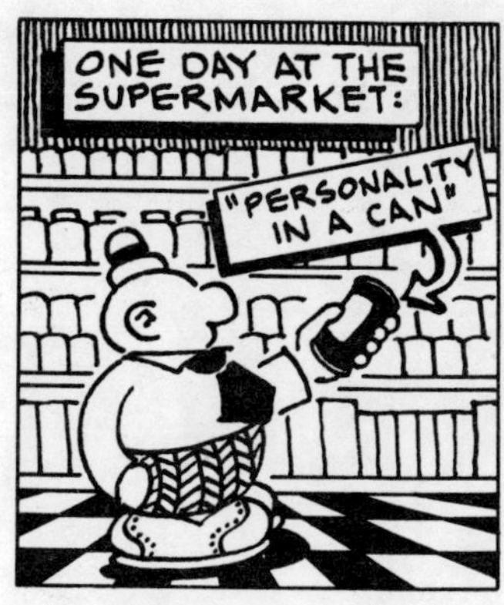
ONE DAY AT THE SUPERMARKET:
"PERSONALITY IN A CAN"

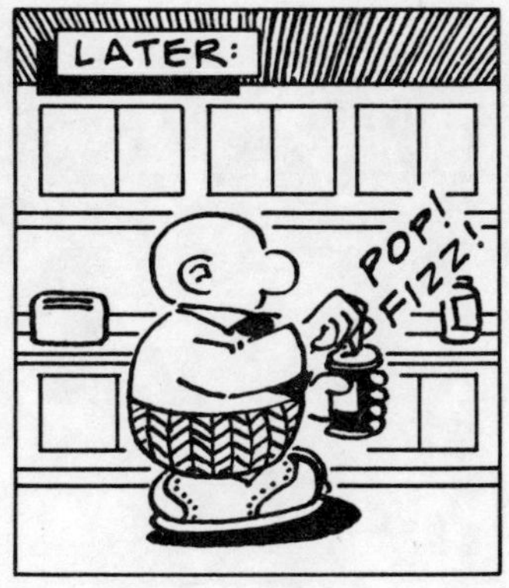
LATER:
POP! FIZZ!

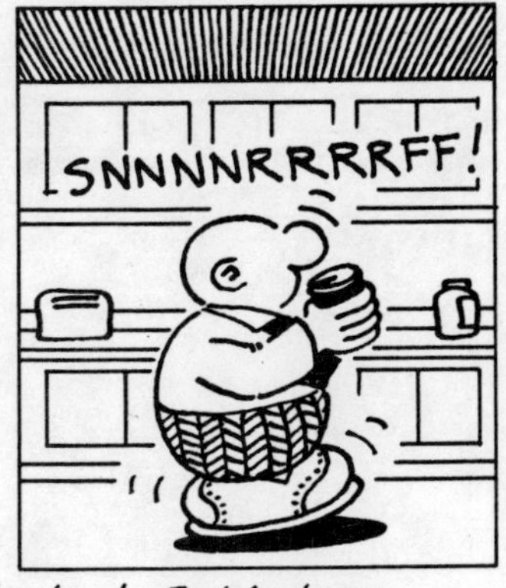
SNNNNRRRRFF!

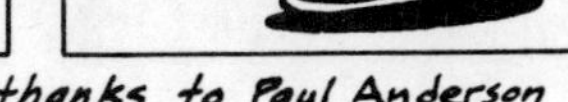
thanks to Paul Anderson

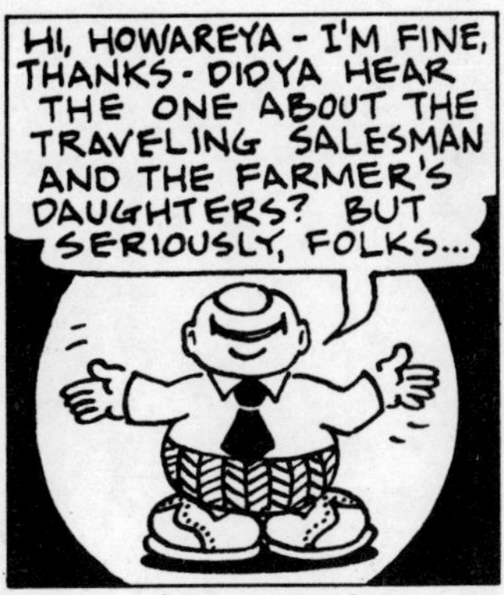
HI, HOWAREYA - I'M FINE, THANKS - DIDYA HEAR THE ONE ABOUT THE TRAVELING SALESMAN AND THE FARMER'S DAUGHTERS? BUT SERIOUSLY, FOLKS...

b. von alten

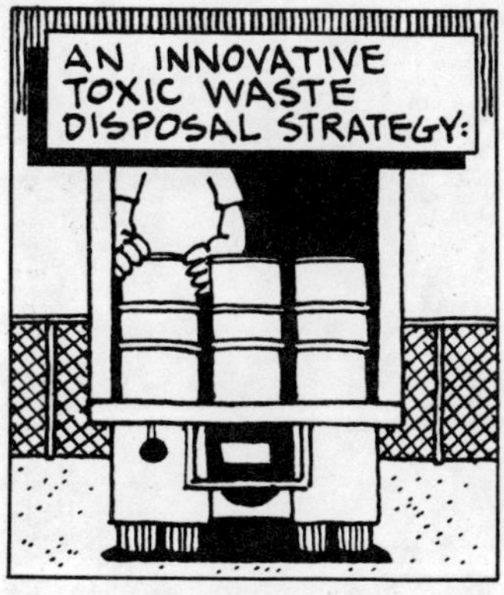
AN INNOVATIVE TOXIC WASTE DISPOSAL STRATEGY:

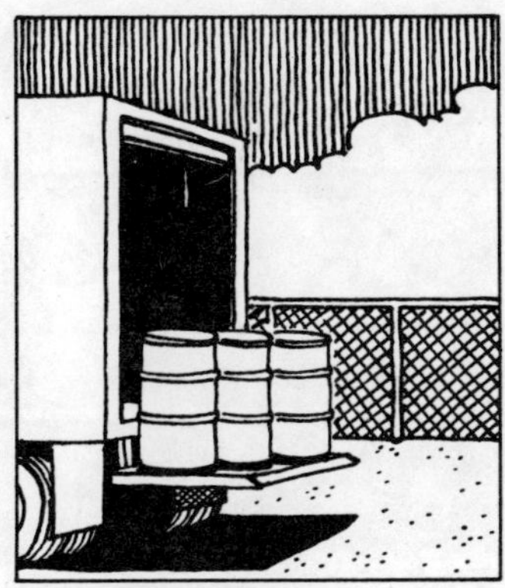

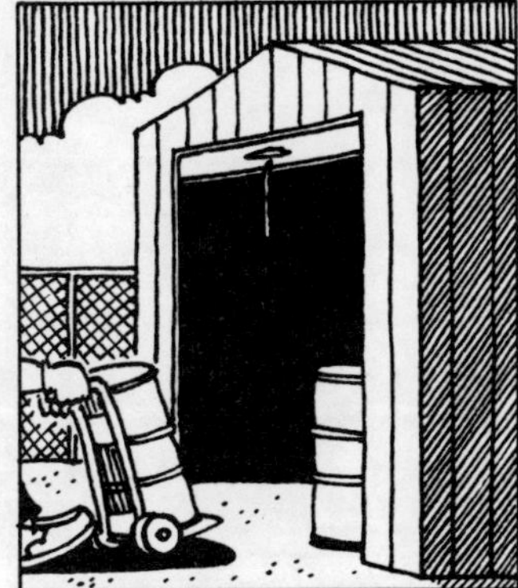

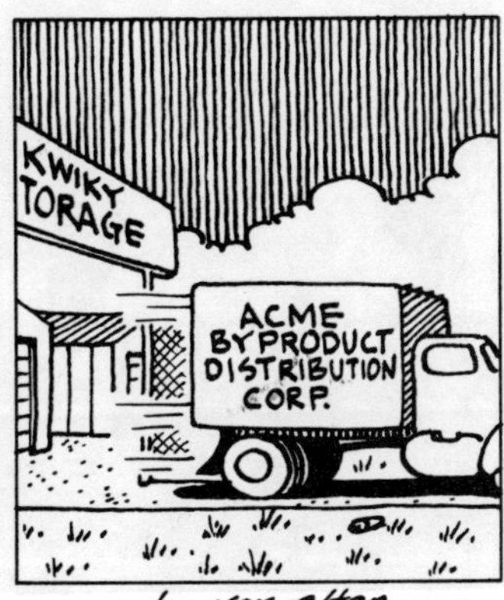
KWIKY TORAGE
ACME BYPRODUCT DISTRIBUTION CORP.

b. von alten

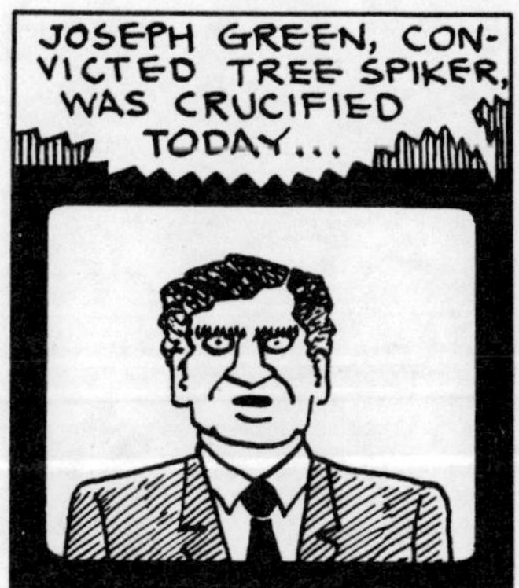
JOSEPH GREEN, CONVICTED TREE SPIKER, WAS CRUCIFIED TODAY...

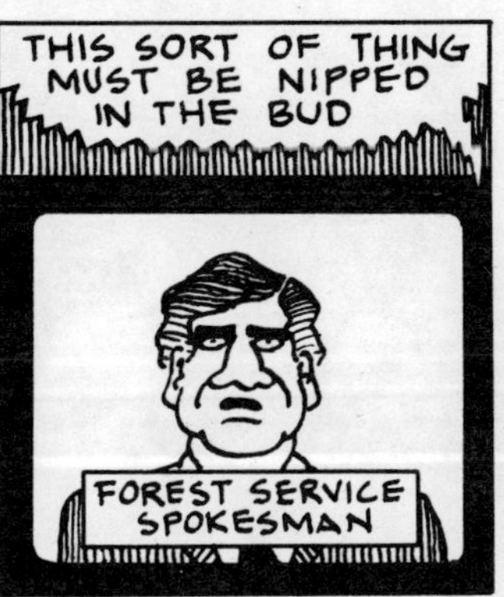
THIS SORT OF THING MUST BE NIPPED IN THE BUD
FOREST SERVICE SPOKESMAN

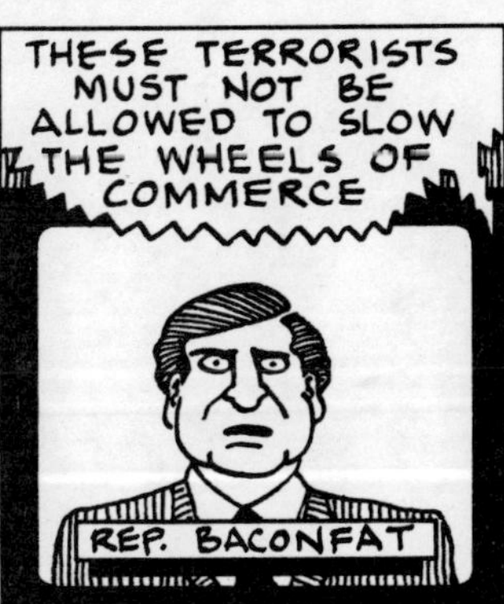
THESE TERRORISTS MUST NOT BE ALLOWED TO SLOW THE WHEELS OF COMMERCE
REP. BACONFAT

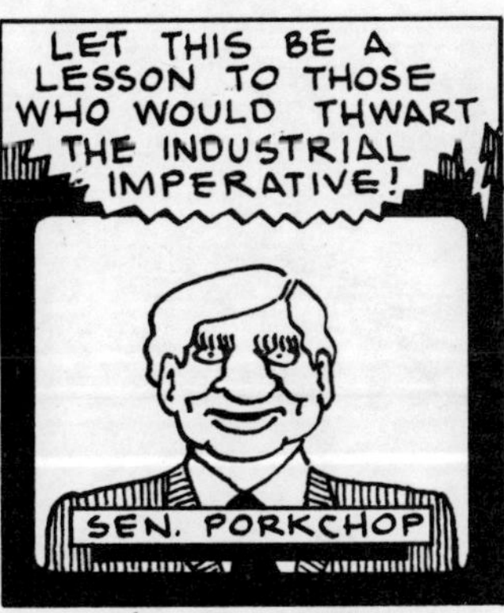
LET THIS BE A LESSON TO THOSE WHO WOULD THWART THE INDUSTRIAL IMPERATIVE!
SEN. PORKCHOP

b. von alten

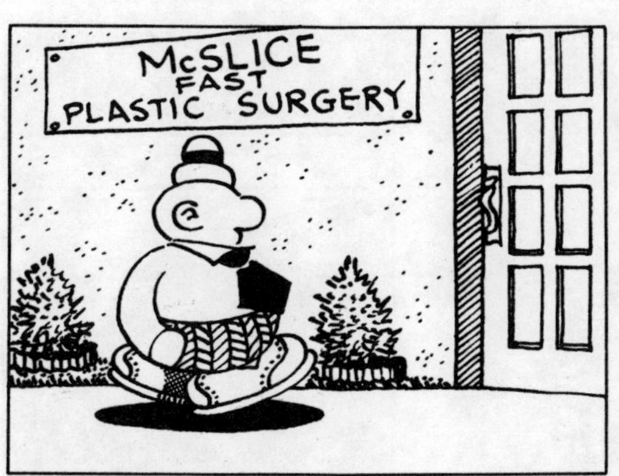
McSLICE FAST PLASTIC SURGERY

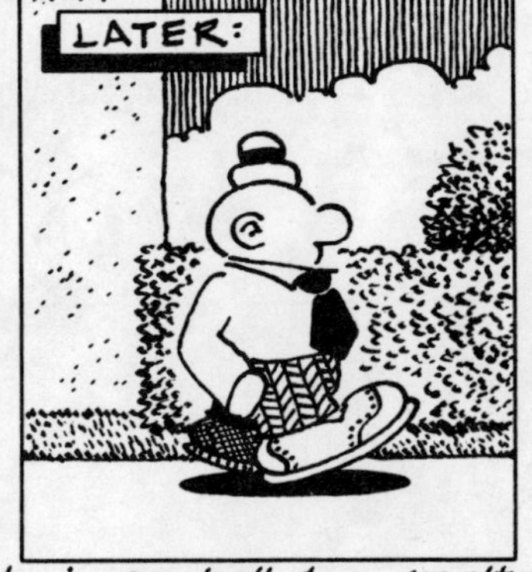
LATER:

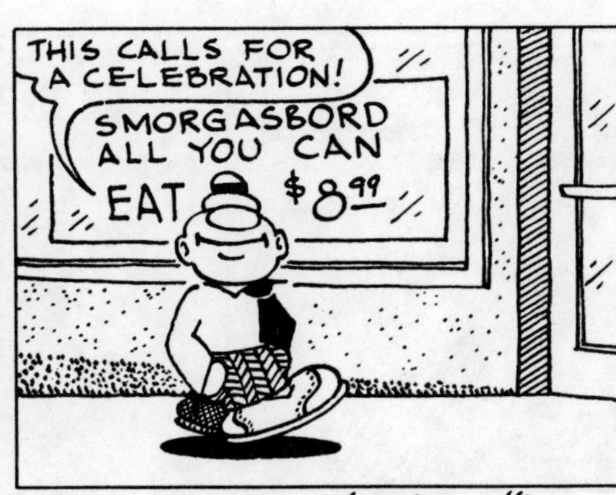
THIS CALLS FOR A CELEBRATION!
SMORGASBORD ALL YOU CAN EAT $8.99

thanks to j. campbell & p. von alten

b. von alten

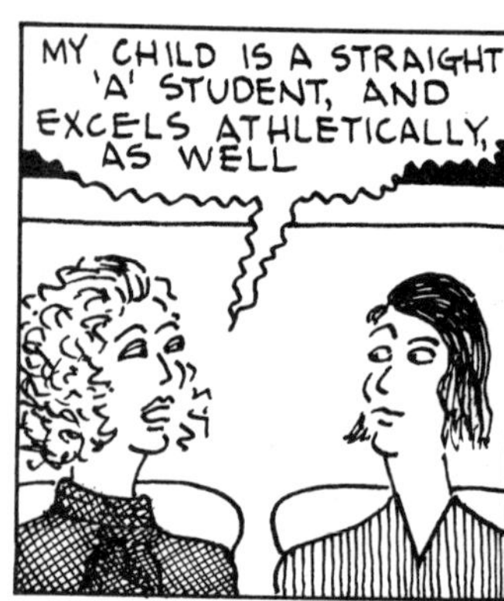
MY CHILD IS A STRAIGHT 'A' STUDENT, AND EXCELS ATHLETICALLY, AS WELL

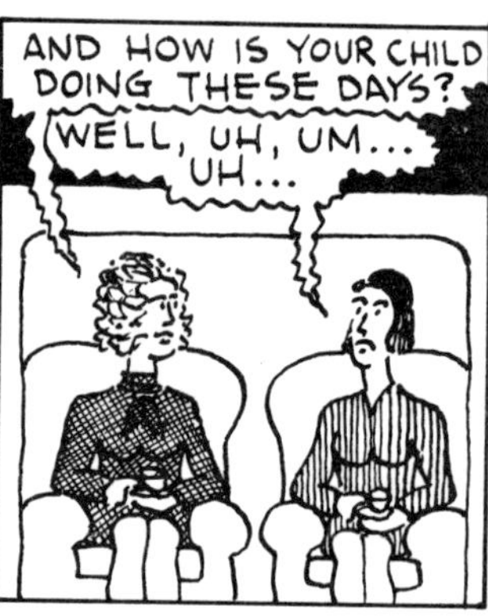
AND HOW IS YOUR CHILD DOING THESE DAYS?
WELL, UH, UM... UH...

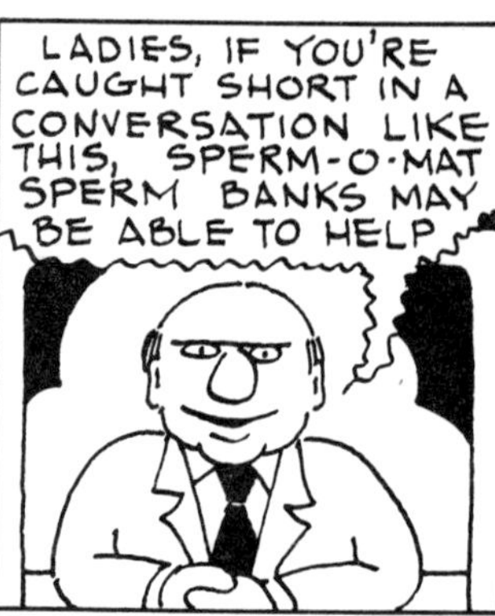
LADIES, IF YOU'RE CAUGHT SHORT IN A CONVERSATION LIKE THIS, SPERM-O-MAT SPERM BANKS MAY BE ABLE TO HELP

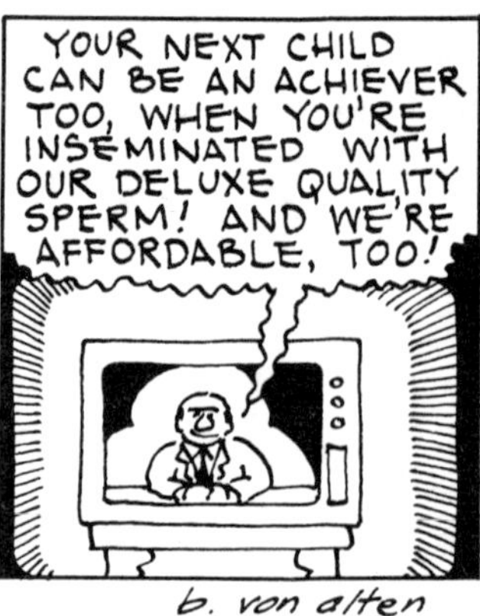
YOUR NEXT CHILD CAN BE AN ACHIEVER TOO, WHEN YOU'RE INSEMINATED WITH OUR DELUXE QUALITY SPERM! AND WE'RE AFFORDABLE, TOO!

b. von alten

AT SPERM-O-MAT SPERM BANKS, OUR DONORS ARE SELECTED

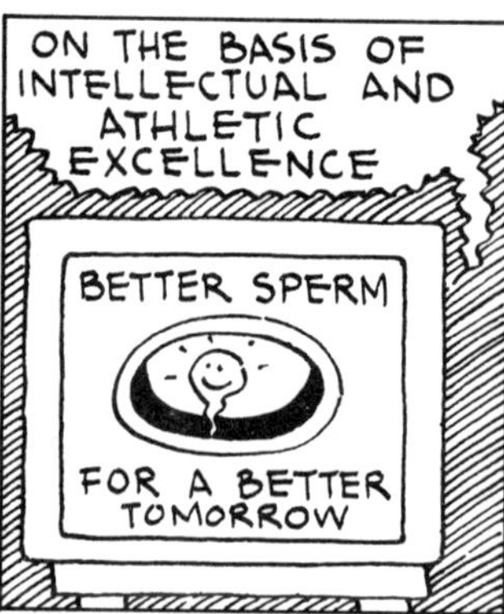
ON THE BASIS OF INTELLECTUAL AND ATHLETIC EXCELLENCE
BETTER SPERM
FOR A BETTER TOMORROW

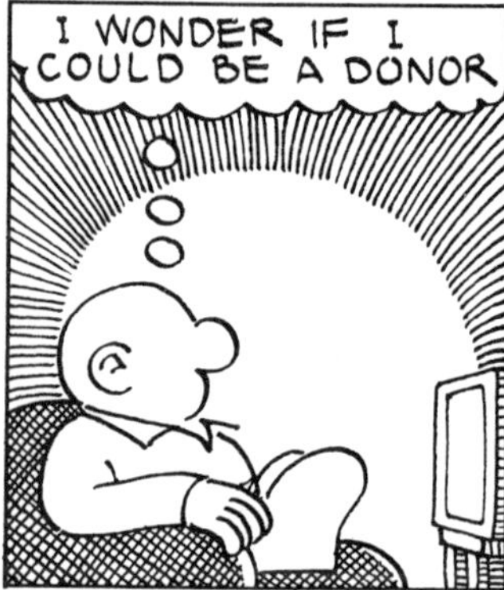
I WONDER IF I COULD BE A DONOR

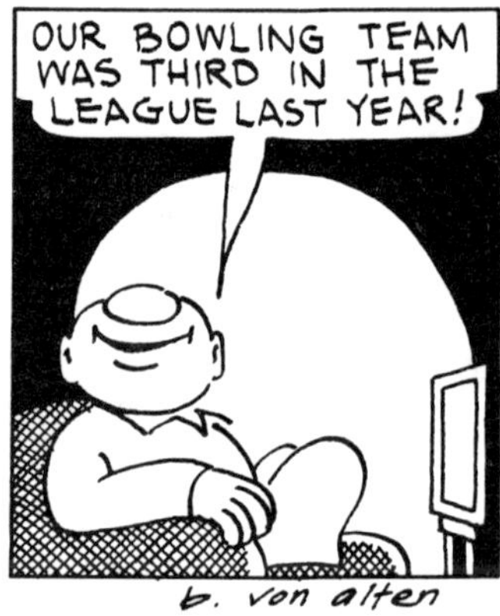
OUR BOWLING TEAM WAS THIRD IN THE LEAGUE LAST YEAR!

b. von alten

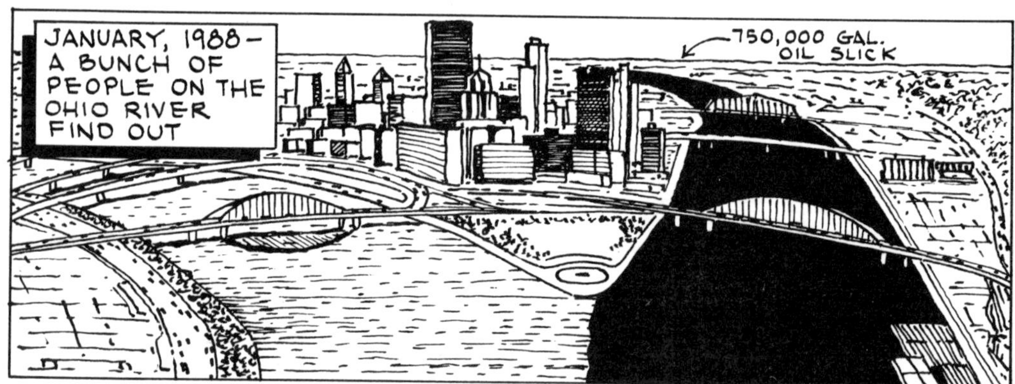
JANUARY, 1988 – A BUNCH OF PEOPLE ON THE OHIO RIVER FIND OUT
750,000 GAL. OIL SLICK

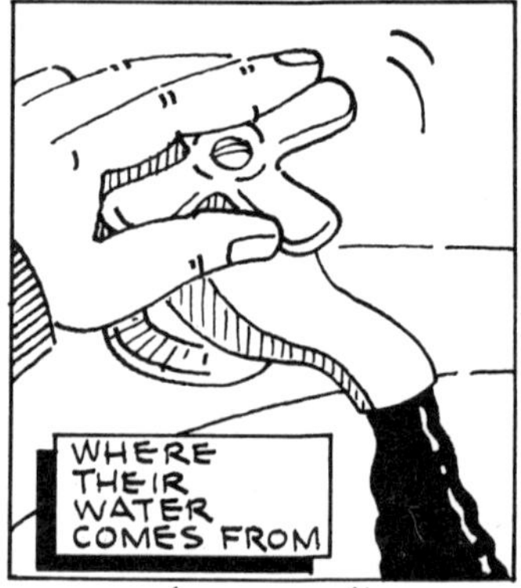
WHERE THEIR WATER COMES FROM

b. von alten

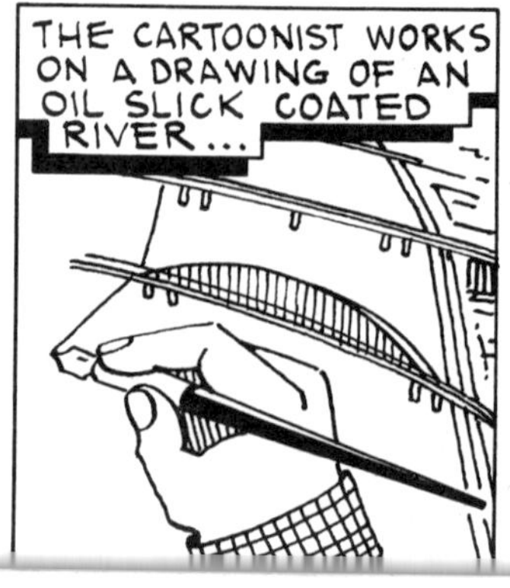
THE CARTOONIST WORKS ON A DRAWING OF AN OIL SLICK COATED RIVER...

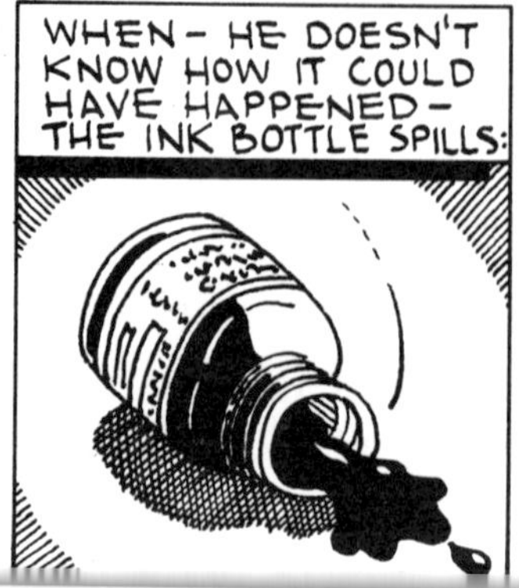
WHEN – HE DOESN'T KNOW HOW IT COULD HAVE HAPPENED – THE INK BOTTLE SPILLS:

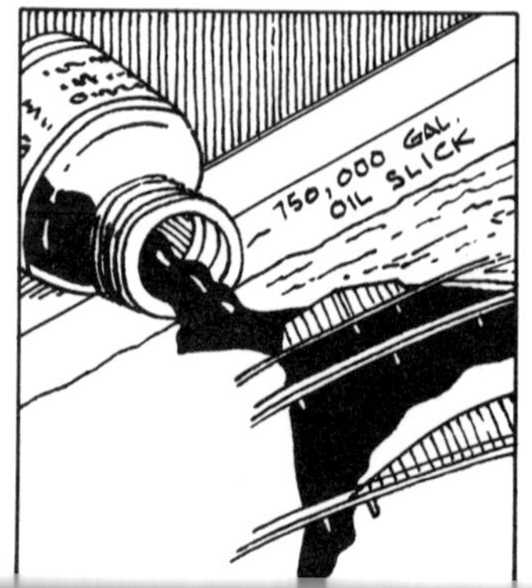
750,000 GAL. OIL SLICK

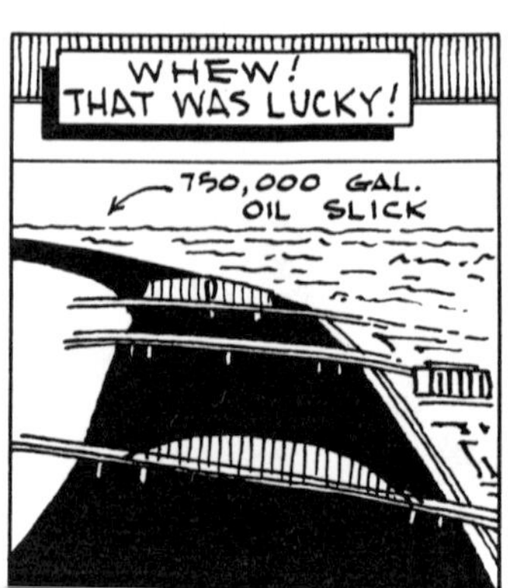
WHEW! THAT WAS LUCKY!
750,000 GAL. OIL SLICK

b. von alten

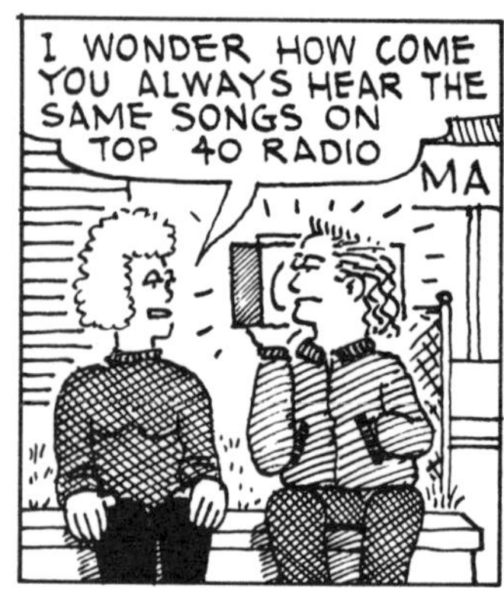
I WONDER HOW COME YOU ALWAYS HEAR THE SAME SONGS ON TOP 40 RADIO
MA
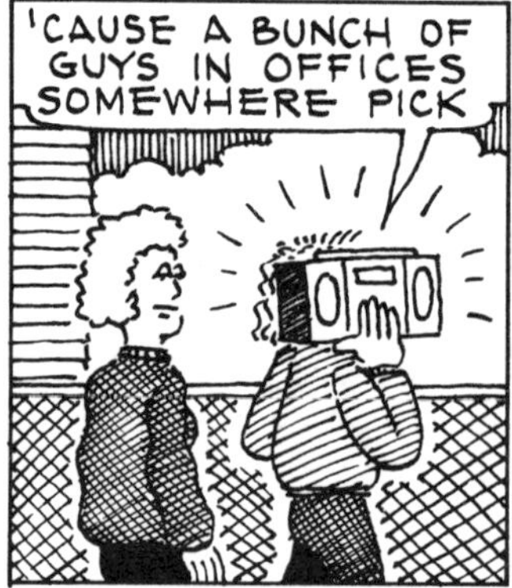
'CAUSE A BUNCH OF GUYS IN OFFICES SOMEWHERE PICK
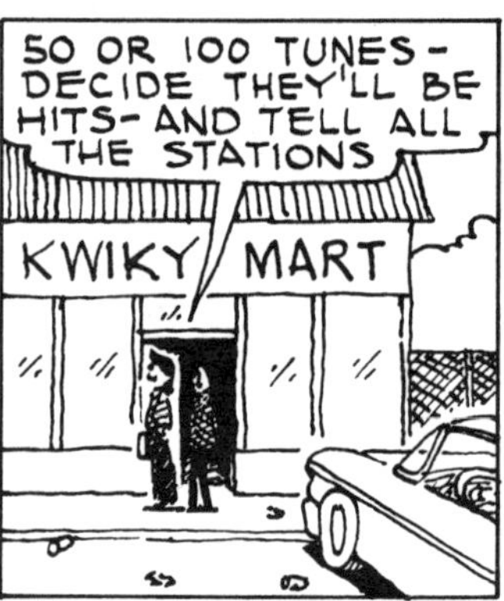
50 OR 100 TUNES - DECIDE THEY'LL BE HITS - AND TELL ALL THE STATIONS
KWIKY MART
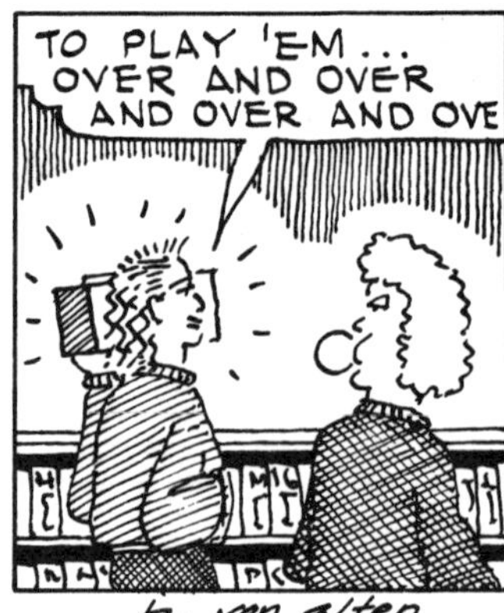
TO PLAY 'EM ... OVER AND OVER AND OVER AND OVE

b. von alten

1. 14. 88

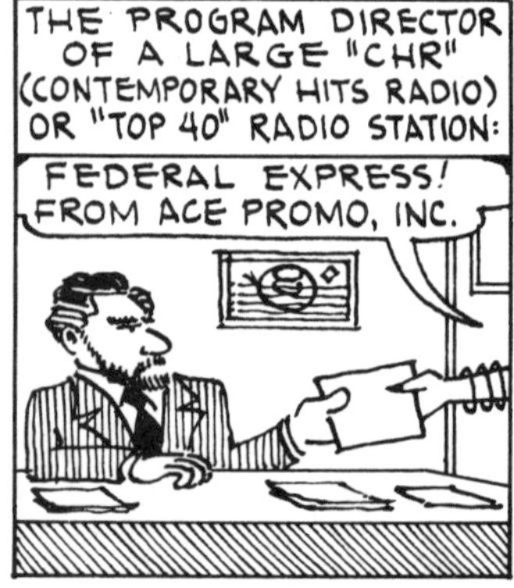
THE PROGRAM DIRECTOR OF A LARGE "CHR" (CONTEMPORARY HITS RADIO) OR "TOP 40" RADIO STATION:
FEDERAL EXPRESS! FROM ACE PROMO, INC.
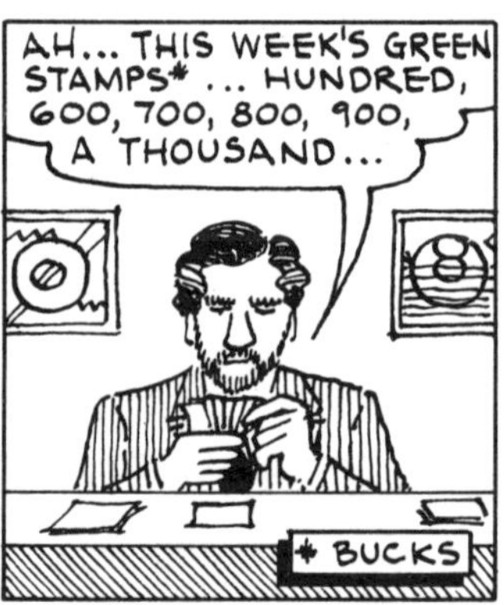
AH... THIS WEEK'S GREEN STAMPS* ... HUNDRED, 600, 700, 800, 900, A THOUSAND...
* BUCKS
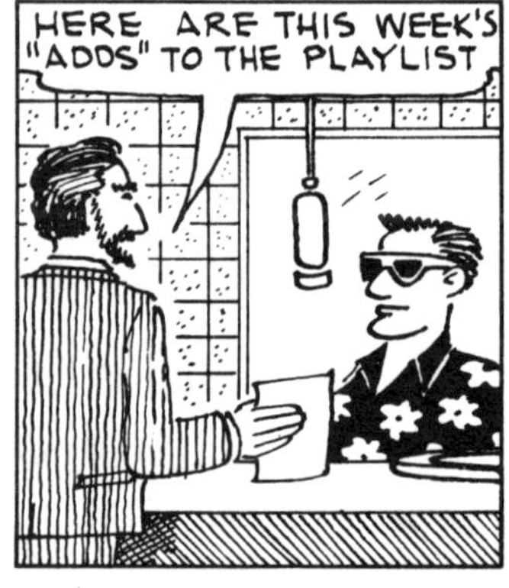
HERE ARE THIS WEEK'S "ADDS" TO THE PLAYLIST
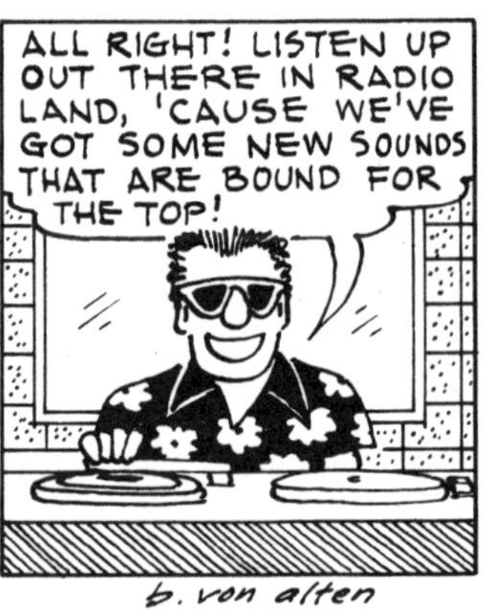
ALL RIGHT! LISTEN UP OUT THERE IN RADIO LAND, 'CAUSE WE'VE GOT SOME NEW SOUNDS THAT ARE BOUND FOR THE TOP!

b. von alten

1. 8. 88

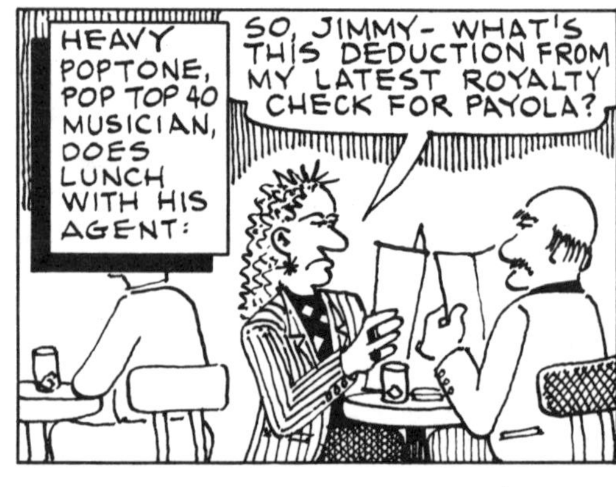
HEAVY POPTONE, POP TOP 40 MUSICIAN, DOES LUNCH WITH HIS AGENT:
SO, JIMMY - WHAT'S THIS DEDUCTION FROM MY LATEST ROYALTY CHECK FOR PAYOLA?
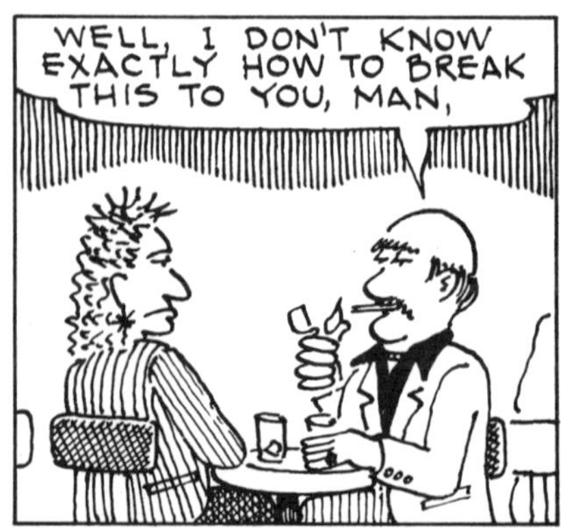
WELL, I DON'T KNOW EXACTLY HOW TO BREAK THIS TO YOU, MAN,
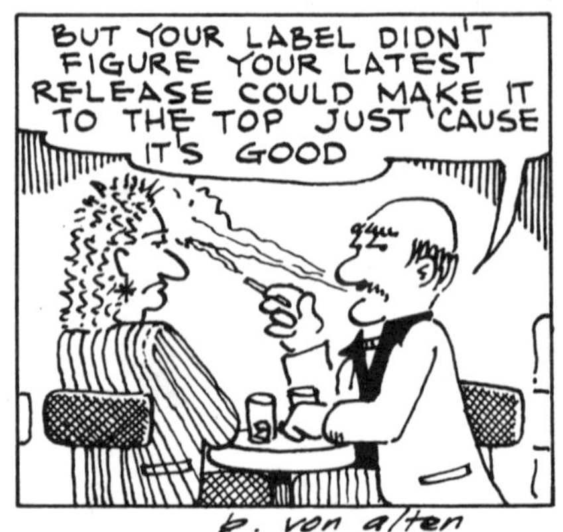
BUT YOUR LABEL DIDN'T FIGURE YOUR LATEST RELEASE COULD MAKE IT TO THE TOP JUST 'CAUSE IT'S GOOD

b. von alten

1. 13. 88

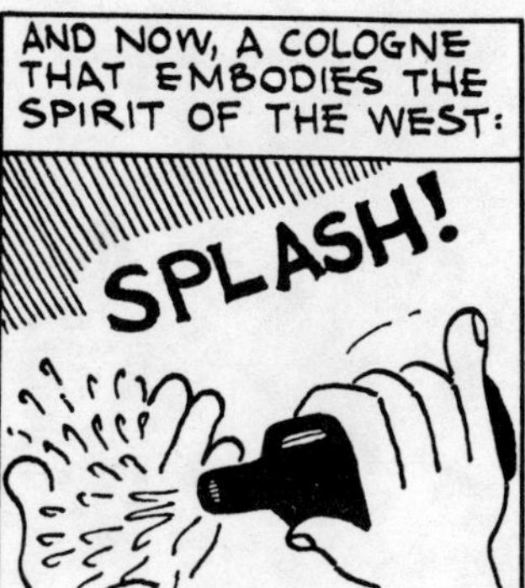
AND NOW, A COLOGNE THAT EMBODIES THE SPIRIT OF THE WEST:
SPLASH!

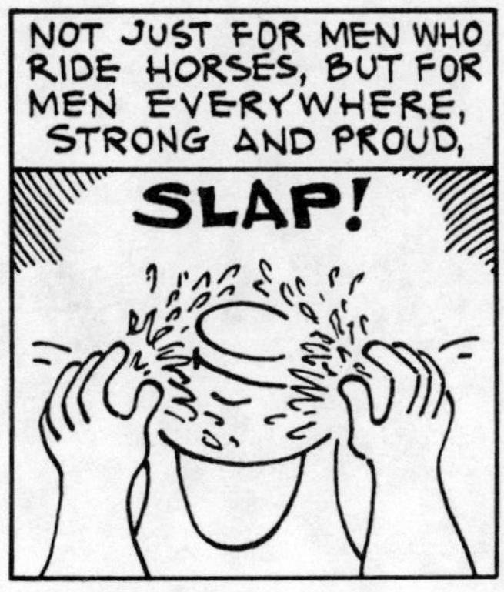
NOT JUST FOR MEN WHO RIDE HORSES, BUT FOR MEN EVERYWHERE, STRONG AND PROUD,
SLAP!

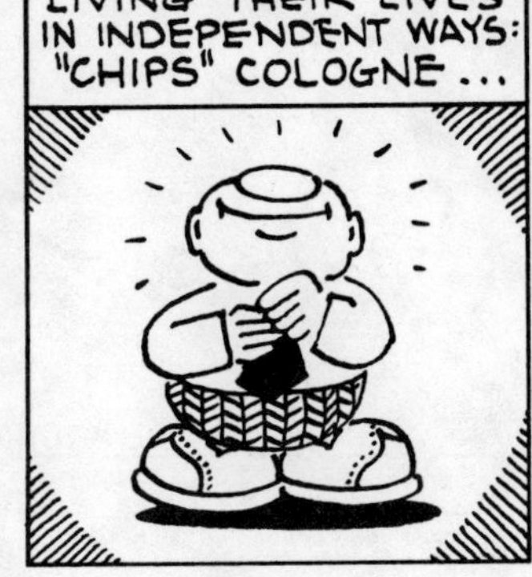
LIVING THEIR LIVES IN INDEPENDENT WAYS: "CHIPS" COLOGNE ...

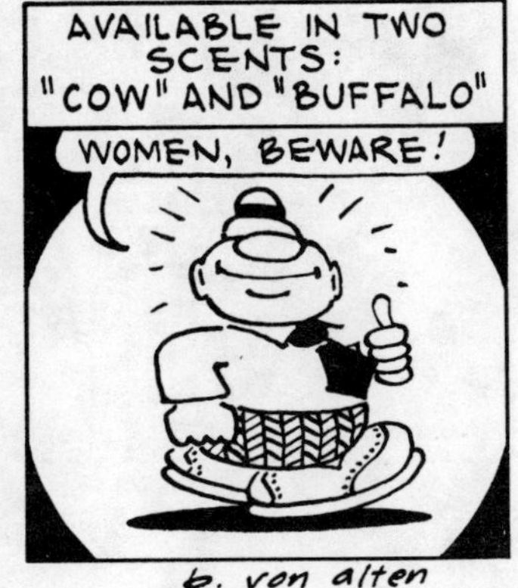
AVAILABLE IN TWO SCENTS: "COW" AND "BUFFALO"
WOMEN, BEWARE!

b. von alten

1-6-88

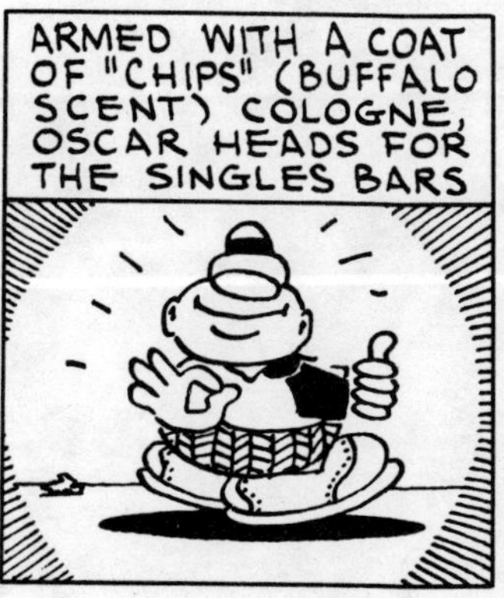
ARMED WITH A COAT OF "CHIPS" (BUFFALO SCENT) COLOGNE, OSCAR HEADS FOR THE SINGLES BARS

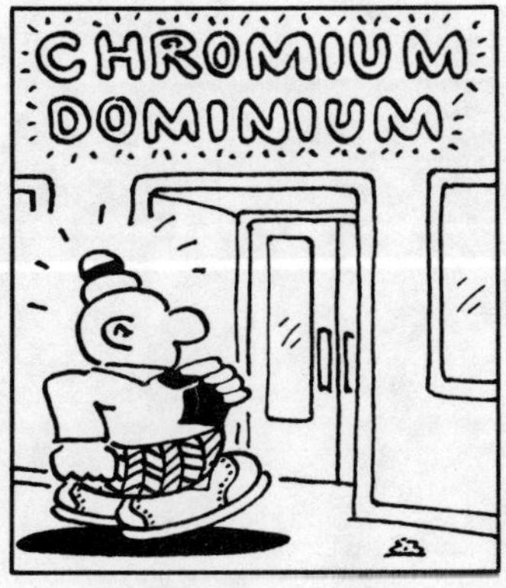
CHROMIUM DOMINIUM

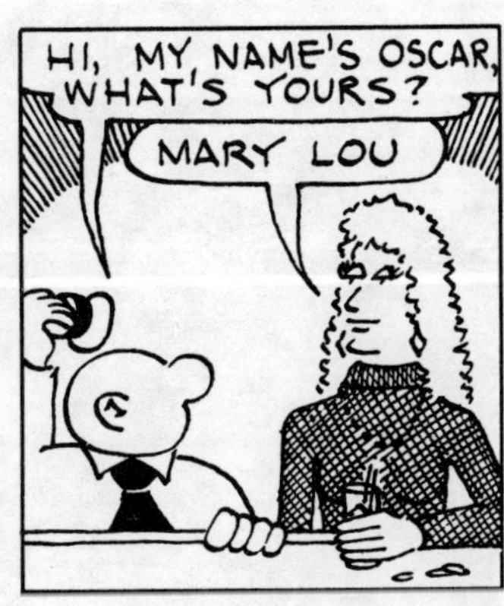
HI, MY NAME'S OSCAR, WHAT'S YOURS?
MARY LOU

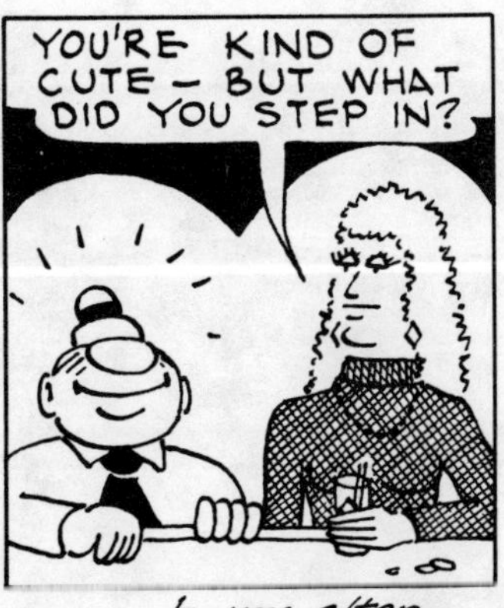
YOU'RE KIND OF CUTE — BUT WHAT DID YOU STEP IN?

b. von alten

1-18-88

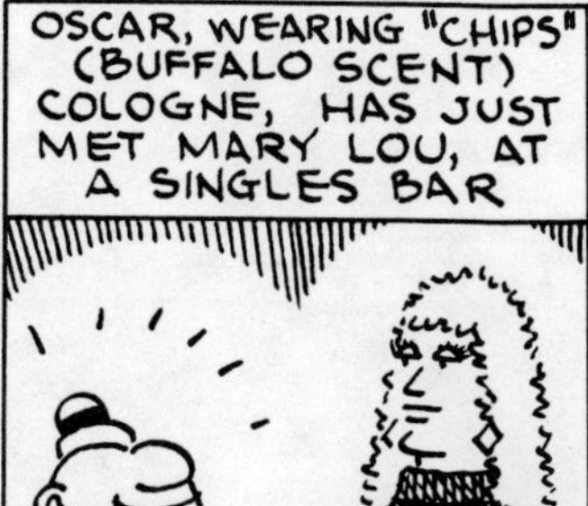
OSCAR, WEARING "CHIPS" (BUFFALO SCENT) COLOGNE, HAS JUST MET MARY LOU, AT A SINGLES BAR

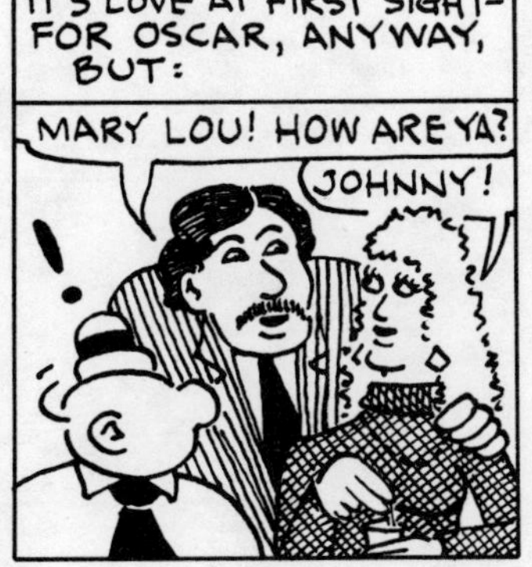
IT'S LOVE AT FIRST SIGHT— FOR OSCAR, ANYWAY, BUT:
MARY LOU! HOW ARE YA?
JOHNNY!
!

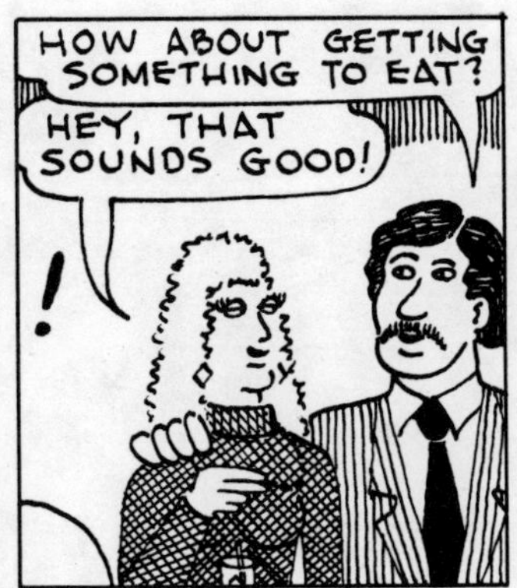
HOW ABOUT GETTING SOMETHING TO EAT?
HEY, THAT SOUNDS GOOD!
!

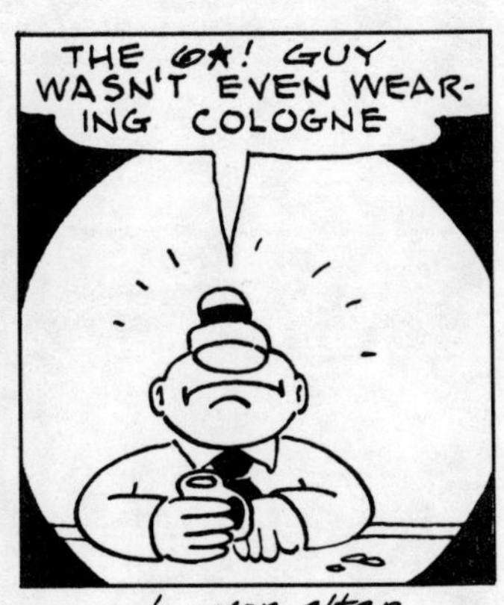
THE @★! GUY WASN'T EVEN WEARING COLOGNE

b. von alten

1-19-88

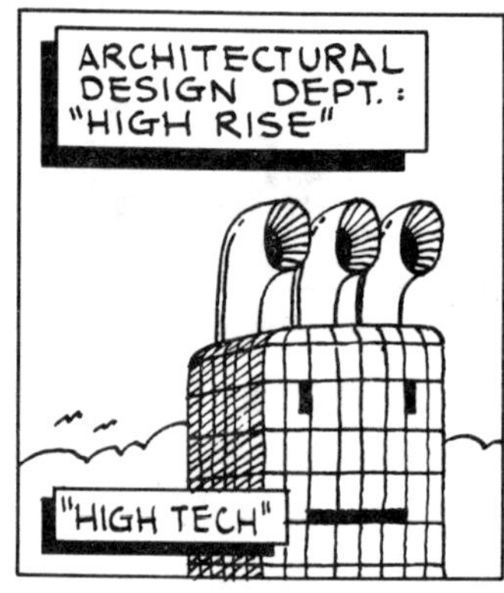
ARCHITECTURAL DESIGN DEPT.: "HIGH RISE"
"HIGH TECH"

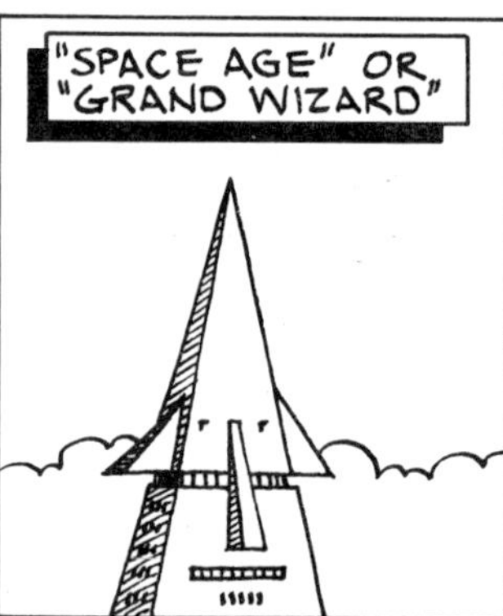
"SPACE AGE" OR "GRAND WIZARD"

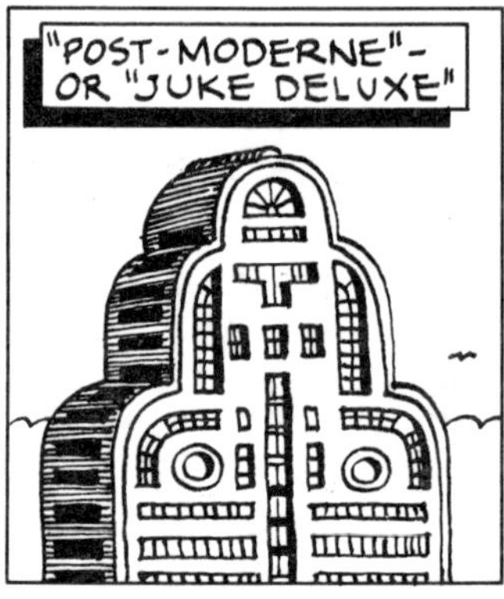
"POST-MODERNE"- OR "JUKE DELUXE"

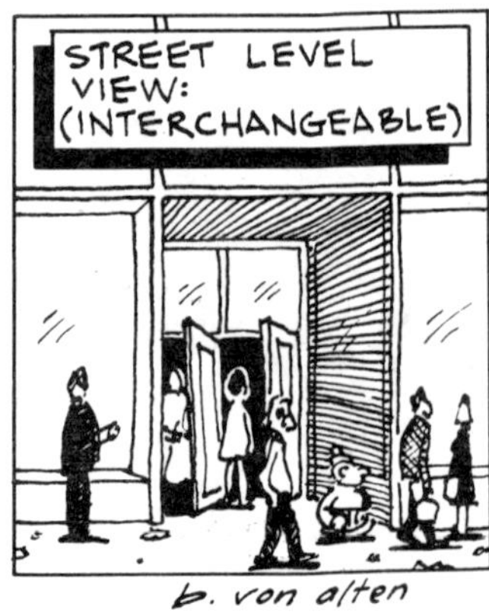
STREET LEVEL VIEW: (INTERCHANGEABLE)

b. von alten

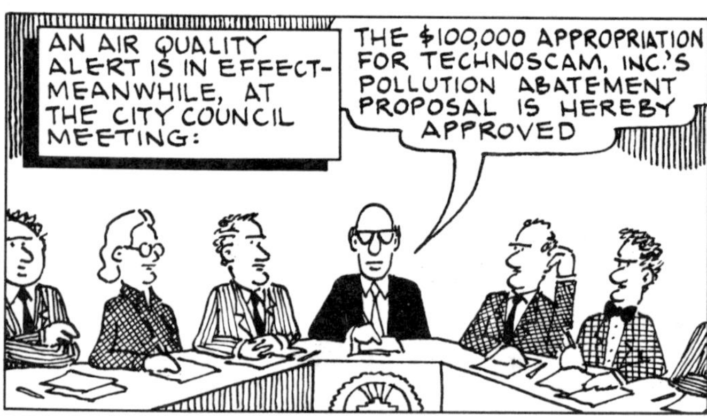
AN AIR QUALITY ALERT IS IN EFFECT- MEANWHILE, AT THE CITY COUNCIL MEETING:
THE $100,000 APPROPRIATION FOR TECHNOSCAM, INC.'S POLLUTION ABATEMENT PROPOSAL IS HEREBY APPROVED

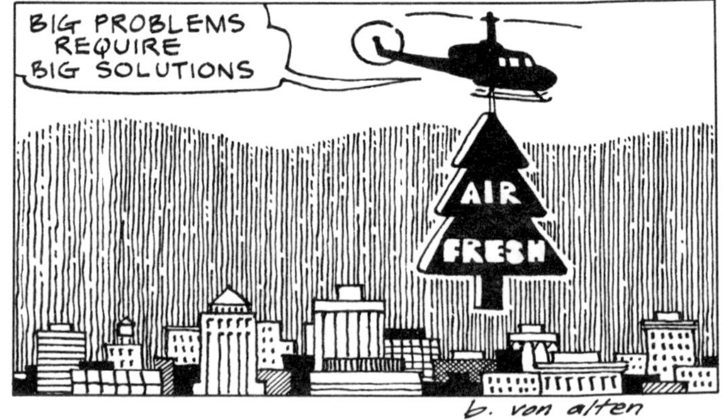
BIG PROBLEMS REQUIRE BIG SOLUTIONS
AIR FRESH

b. von alten

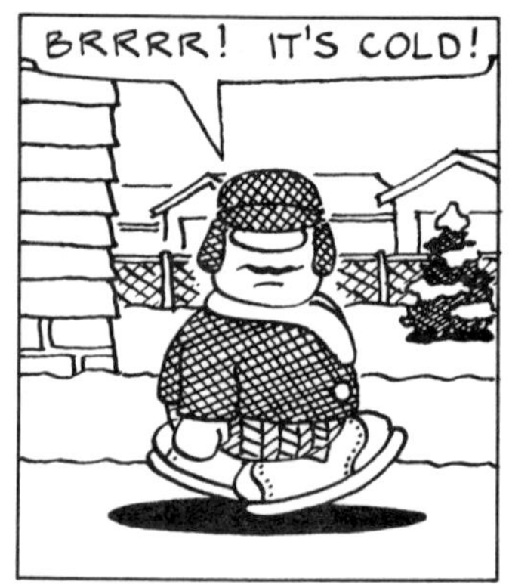
BRRRR! IT'S COLD!

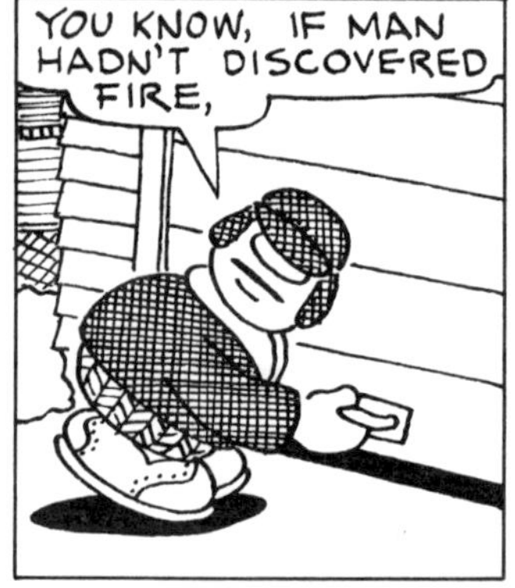
YOU KNOW, IF MAN HADN'T DISCOVERED FIRE,

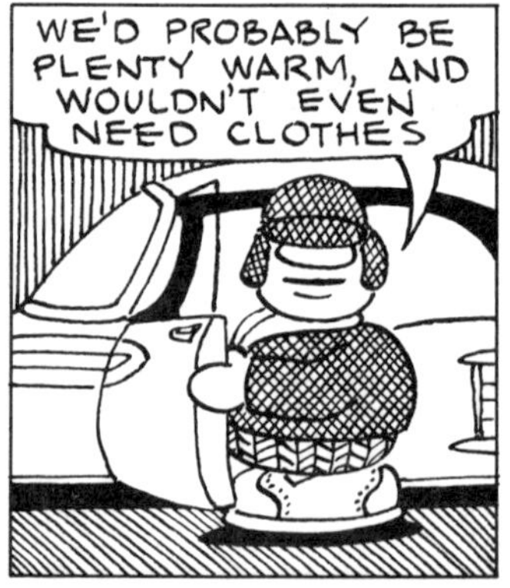
WE'D PROBABLY BE PLENTY WARM, AND WOULDN'T EVEN NEED CLOTHES

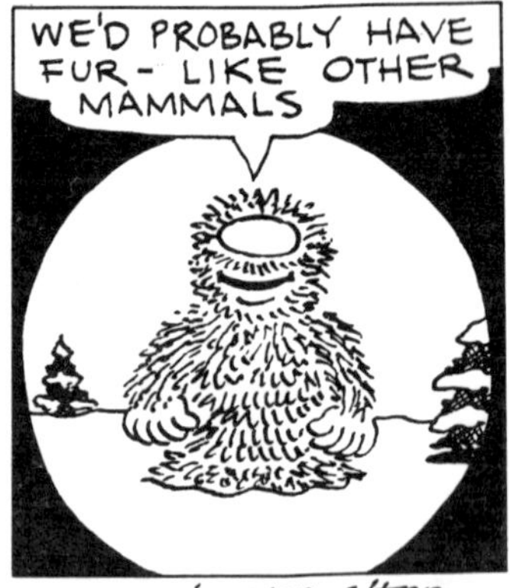
WE'D PROBABLY HAVE FUR- LIKE OTHER MAMMALS

b. von alten

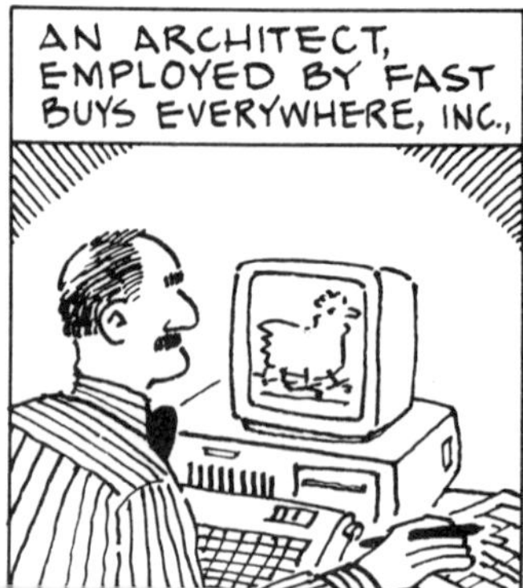
AN ARCHITECT, EMPLOYED BY FAST BUYS EVERYWHERE, INC.,

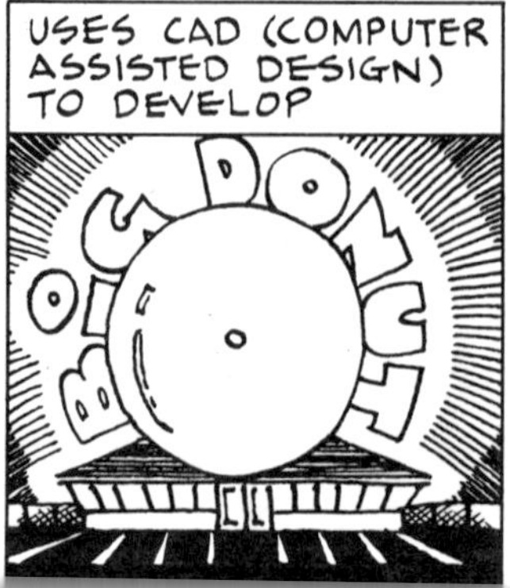
USES CAD (COMPUTER ASSISTED DESIGN) TO DEVELOP
BIG DONUT

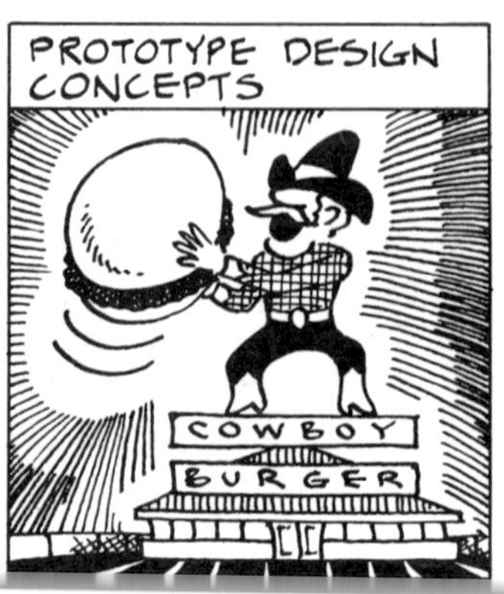
PROTOTYPE DESIGN CONCEPTS
COWBOY
BURGER

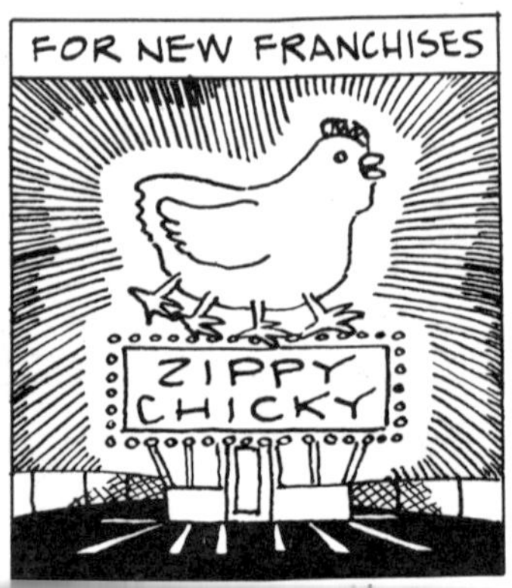
FOR NEW FRANCHISES
ZIPPY CHICKY

b. von alten

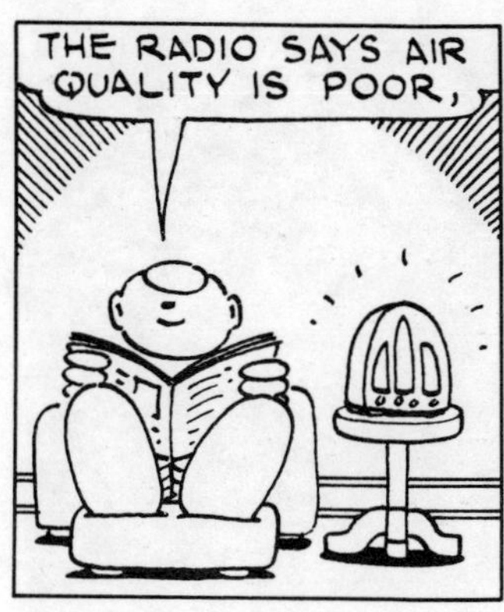
THE RADIO SAYS AIR QUALITY IS POOR,
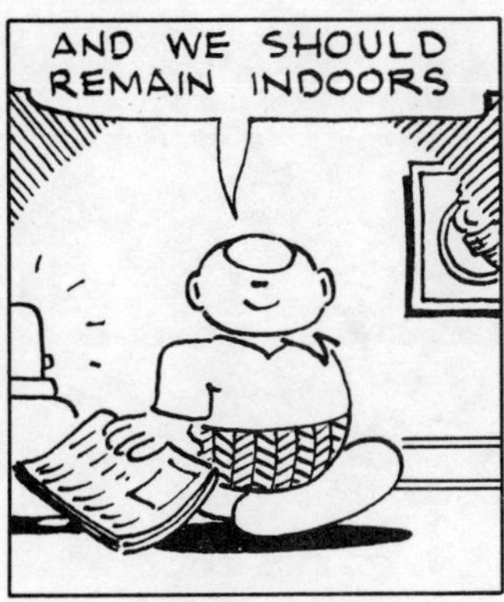
AND WE SHOULD REMAIN INDOORS
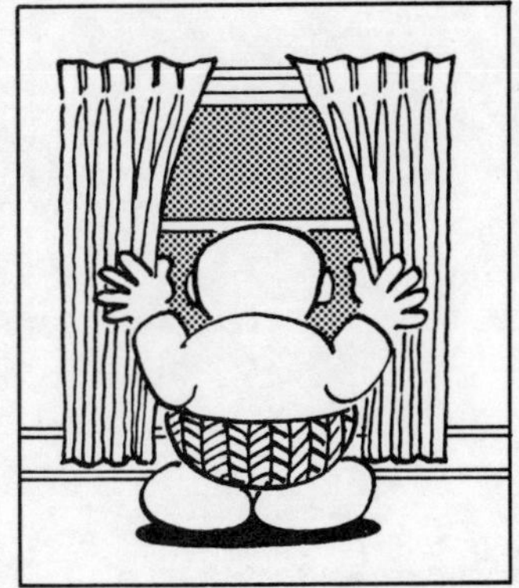
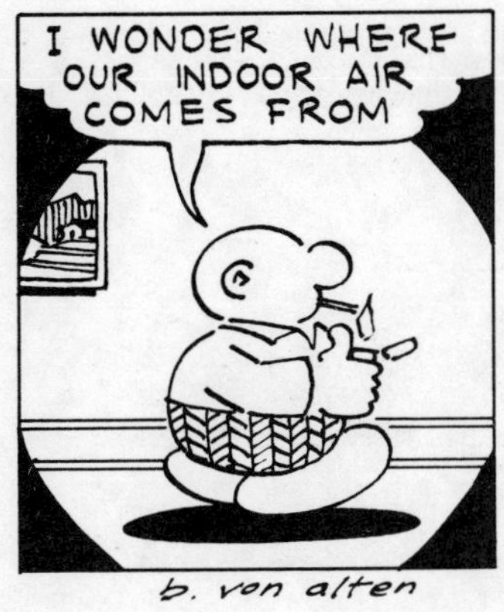
I WONDER WHERE OUR INDOOR AIR COMES FROM
b. von alten
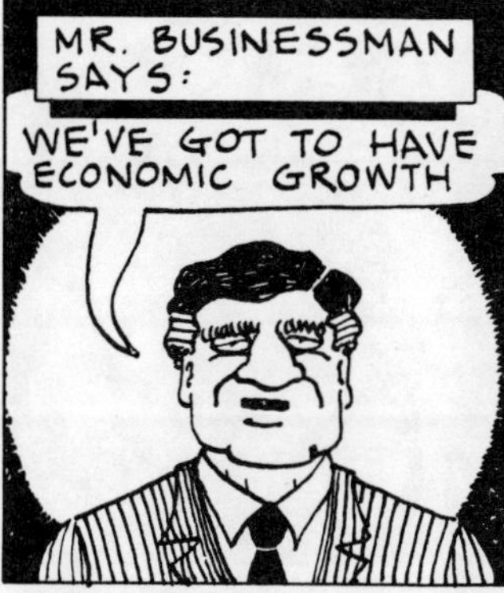
MR. BUSINESSMAN SAYS:
WE'VE GOT TO HAVE ECONOMIC GROWTH
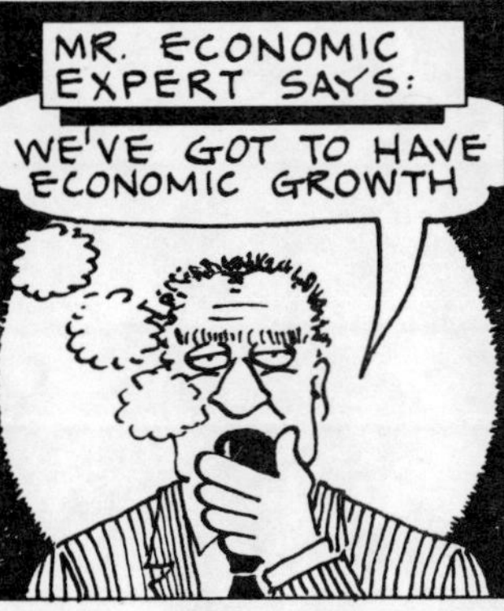
MR. ECONOMIC EXPERT SAYS:
WE'VE GOT TO HAVE ECONOMIC GROWTH
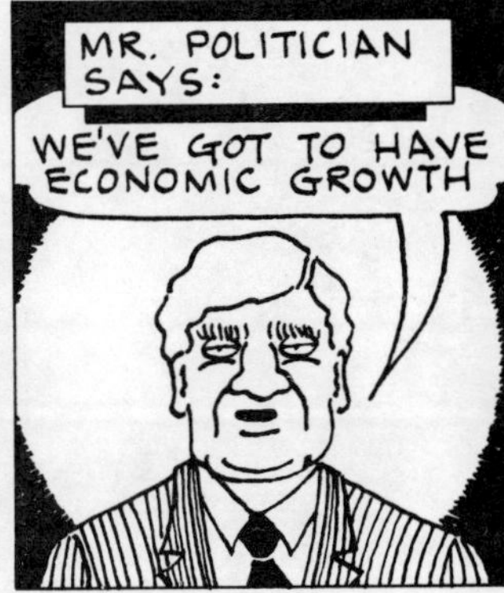
MR. POLITICIAN SAYS:
WE'VE GOT TO HAVE ECONOMIC GROWTH
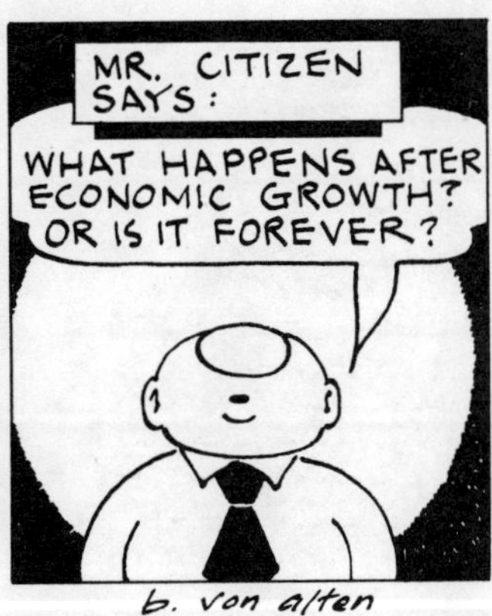
MR. CITIZEN SAYS:
WHAT HAPPENS AFTER ECONOMIC GROWTH? OR IS IT FOREVER?
b. von alten
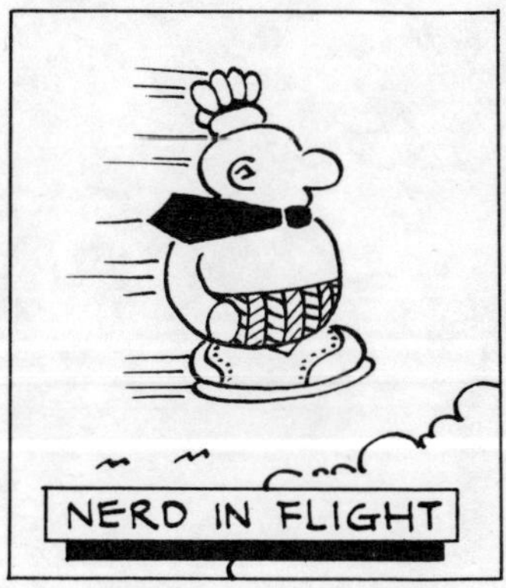
NERD IN FLIGHT
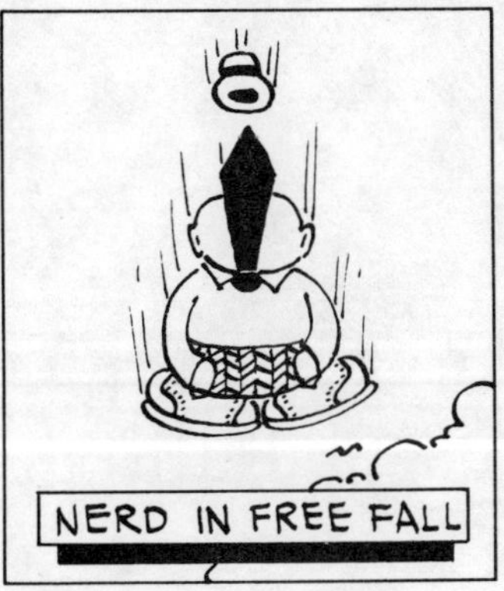
NERD IN FREE FALL
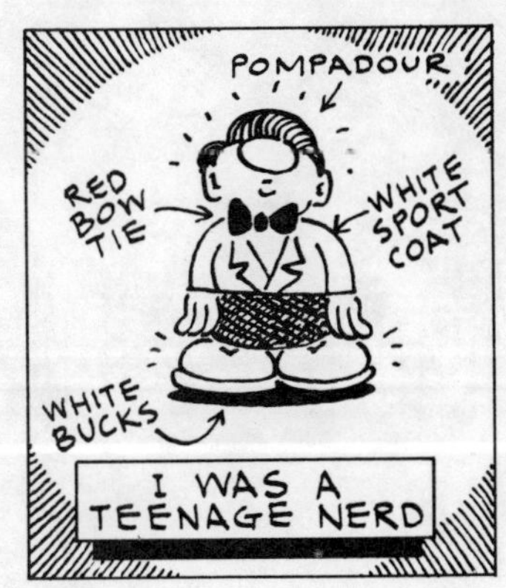
POMPADOUR
RED BOW TIE
WHITE SPORT COAT
WHITE BUCKS
I WAS A TEENAGE NERD
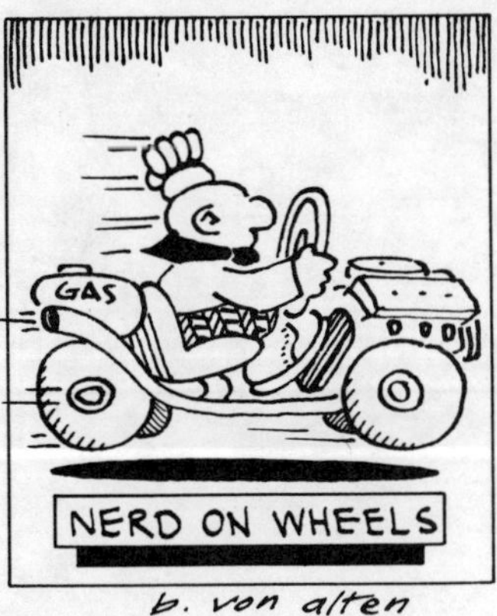
GAS
NERD ON WHEELS
b. von alten
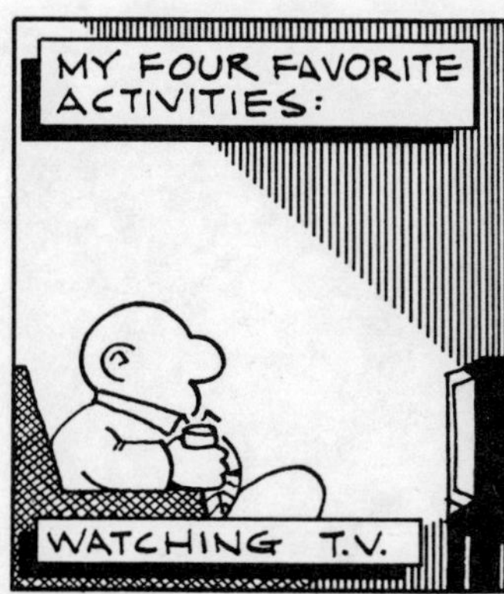
MY FOUR FAVORITE ACTIVITIES:
WATCHING T.V.
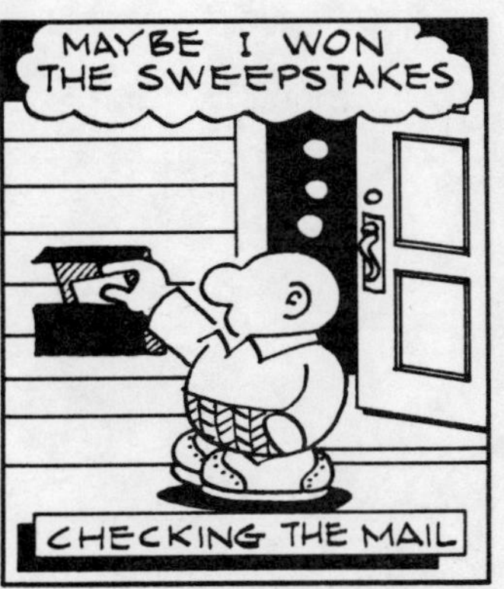
MAYBE I WON THE SWEEPSTAKES
CHECKING THE MAIL
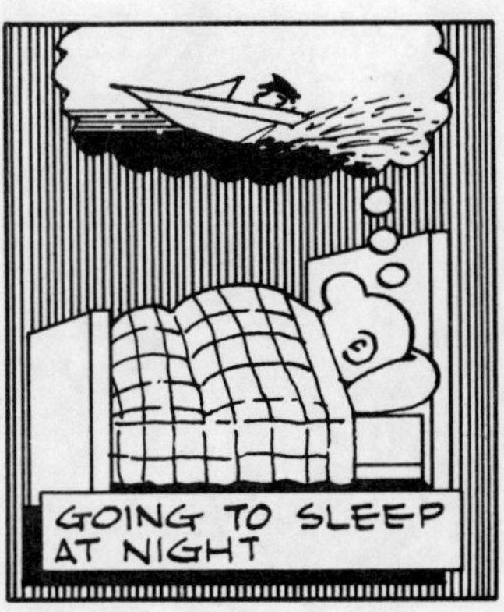
GOING TO SLEEP AT NIGHT
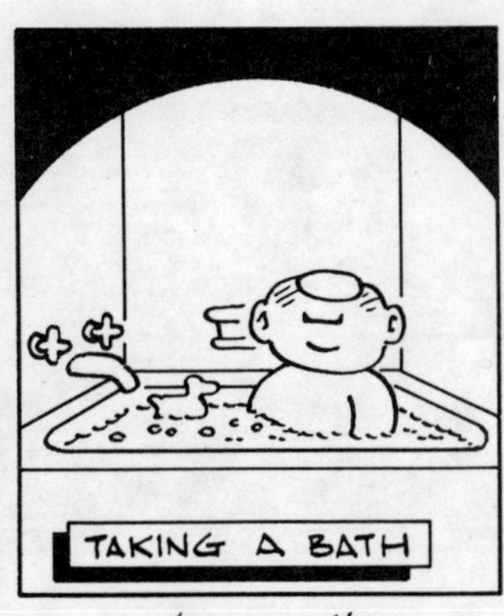
TAKING A BATH
b. von alten

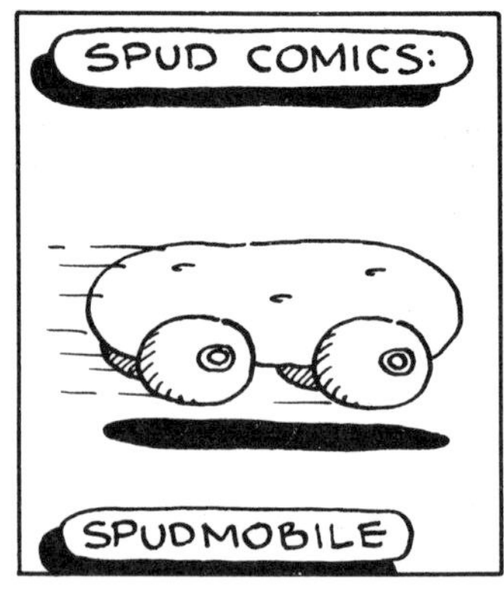
SPUD COMICS:
SPUDMOBILE
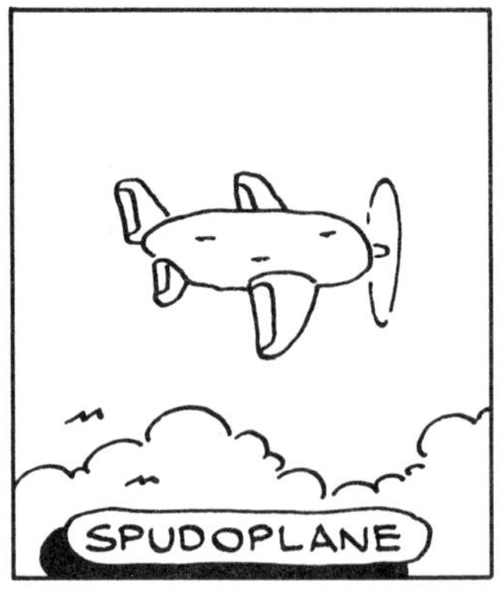
SPUDOPLANE
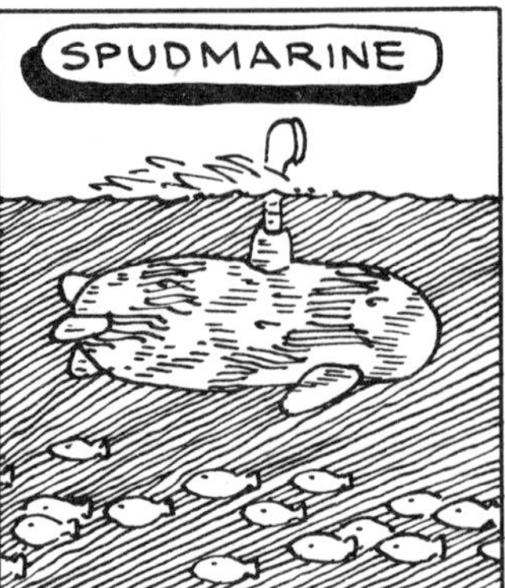
SPUDMARINE
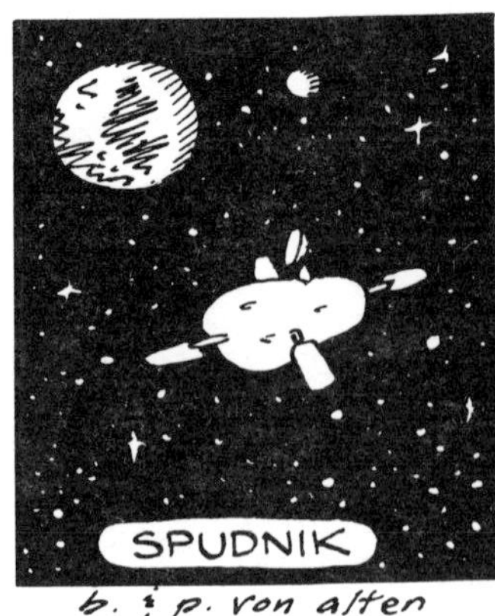
SPUDNIK

b. & p. von alten

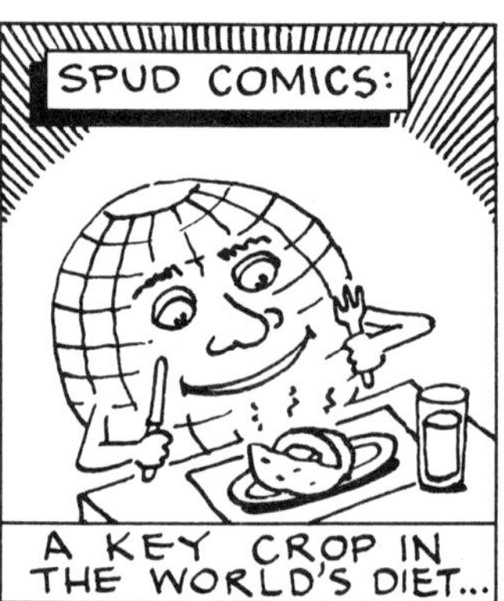
SPUD COMICS:
A KEY CROP IN THE WORLD'S DIET...
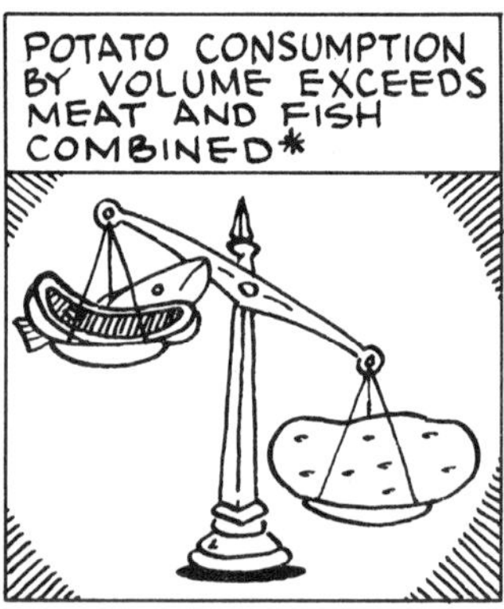
POTATO CONSUMPTION BY VOLUME EXCEEDS MEAT AND FISH COMBINED*
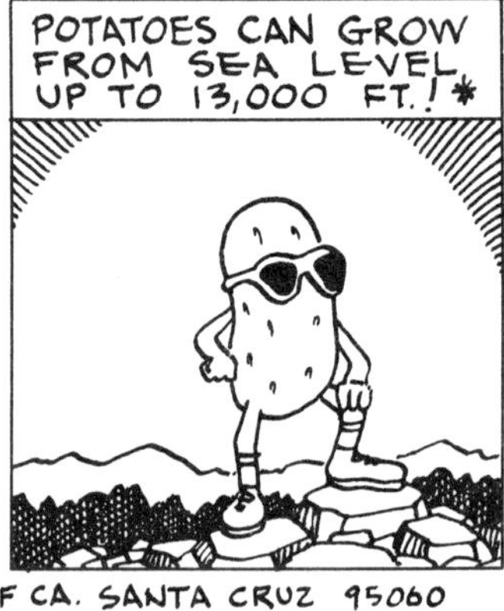
POTATOES CAN GROW FROM SEA LEVEL UP TO 13,000 FT.!*
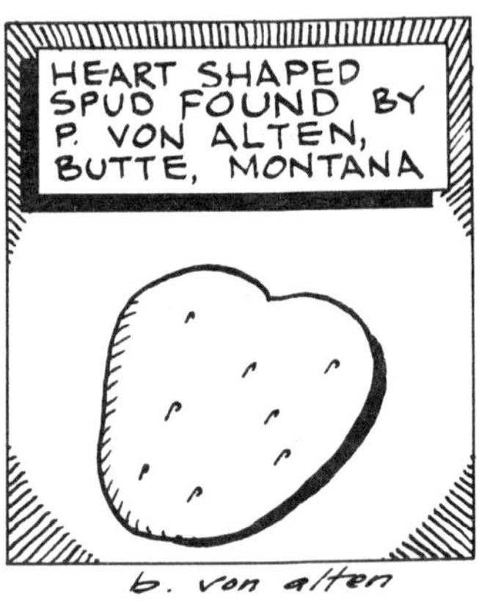
HEART SHAPED SPUD FOUND BY P. VON ALTEN, BUTTE, MONTANA

* "CULTIVAR" · VOL. 6 NO. 1 · U. OF CA. SANTA CRUZ 95060

b. von alten

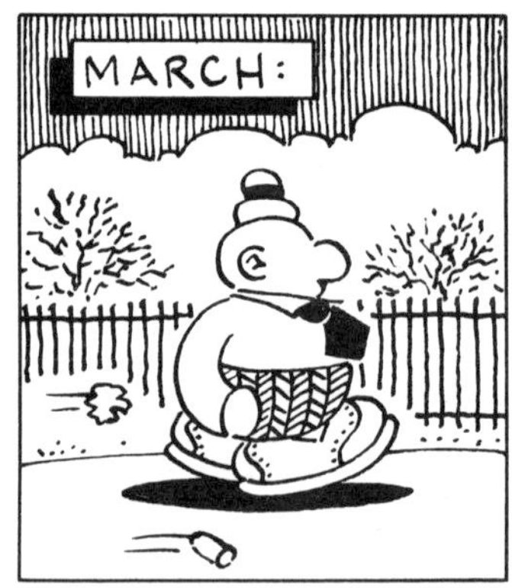
MARCH:
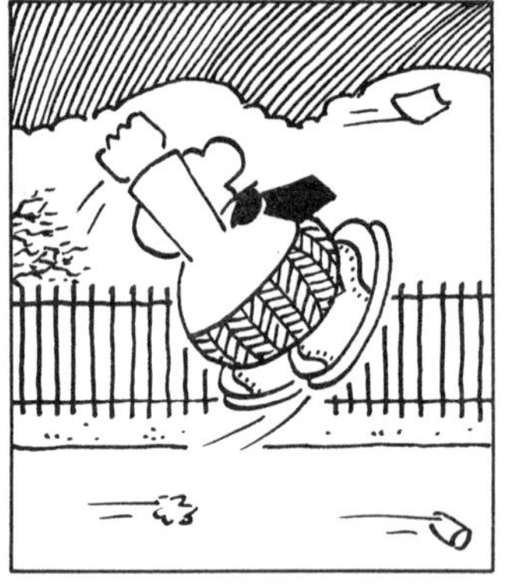
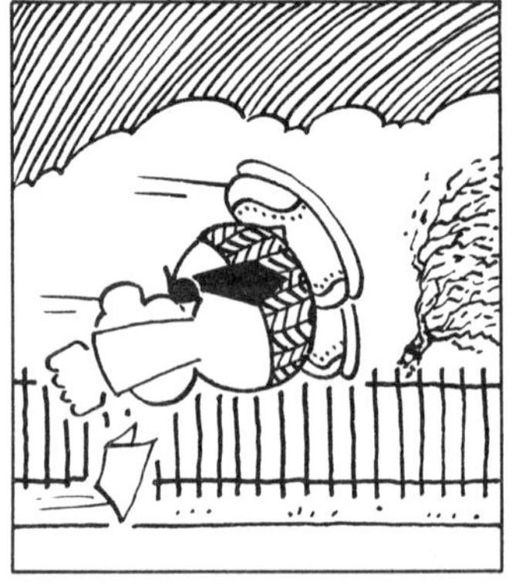
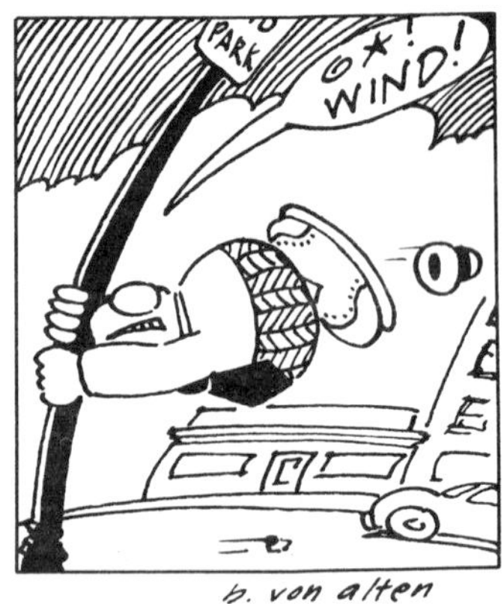
PARK
@*! WIND!

b. von alten

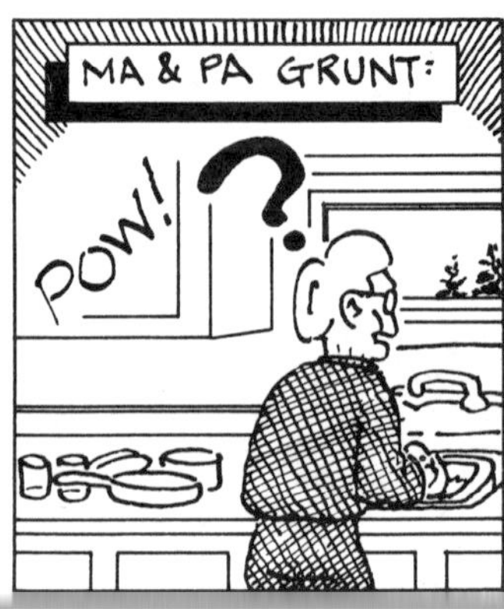
MA & PA GRUNT:
POW!
?
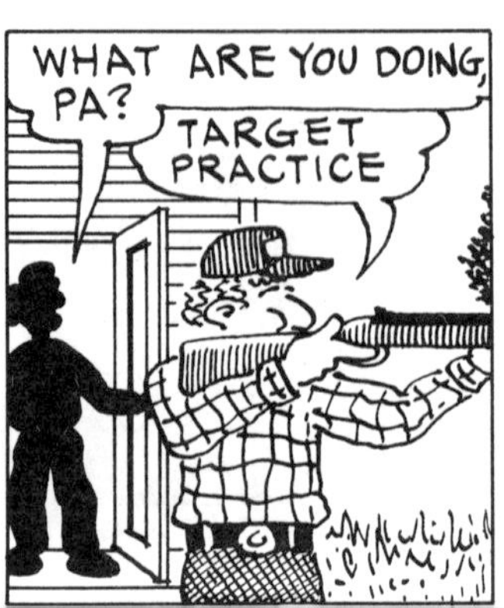
WHAT ARE YOU DOING, PA?
TARGET PRACTICE
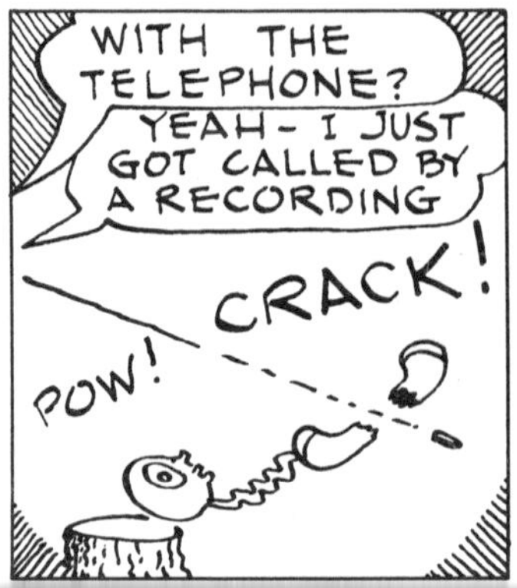
WITH THE TELEPHONE?
YEAH - I JUST GOT CALLED BY A RECORDING
CRACK!
POW!
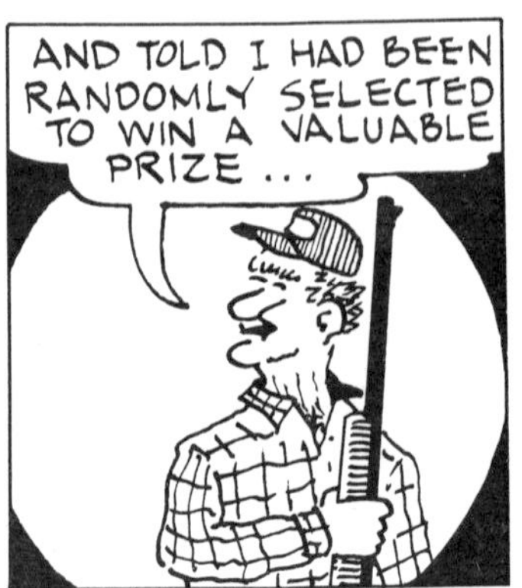
AND TOLD I HAD BEEN RANDOMLY SELECTED TO WIN A VALUABLE PRIZE ...

b. von alten

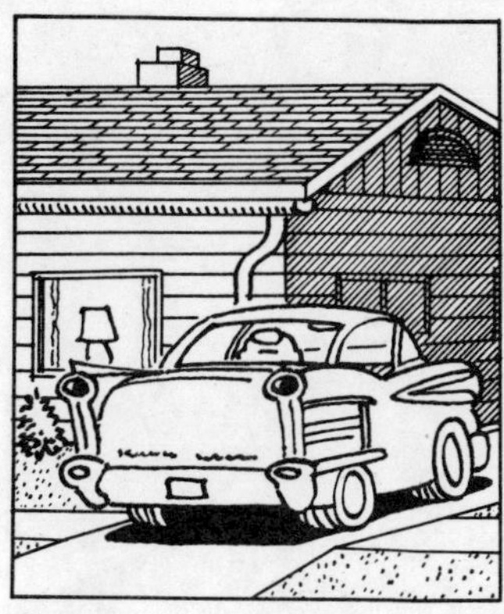
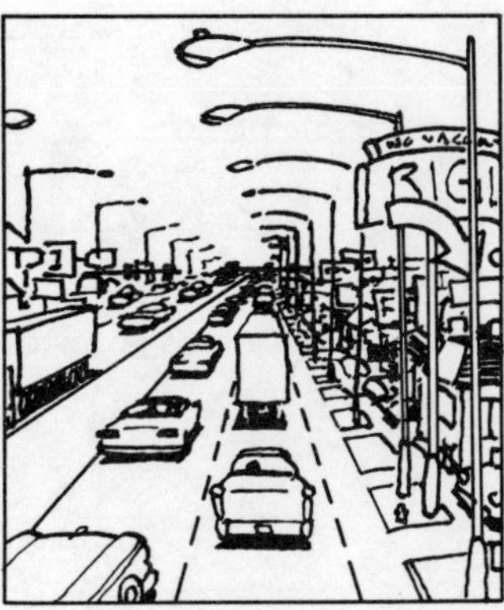
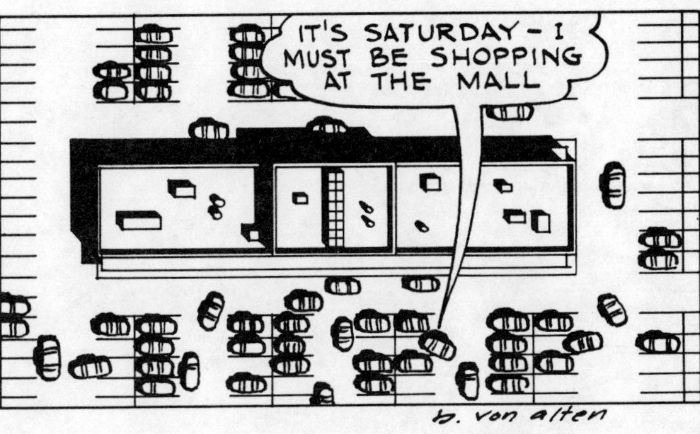
IT'S SATURDAY - I MUST BE SHOPPING AT THE MALL
b. von alten

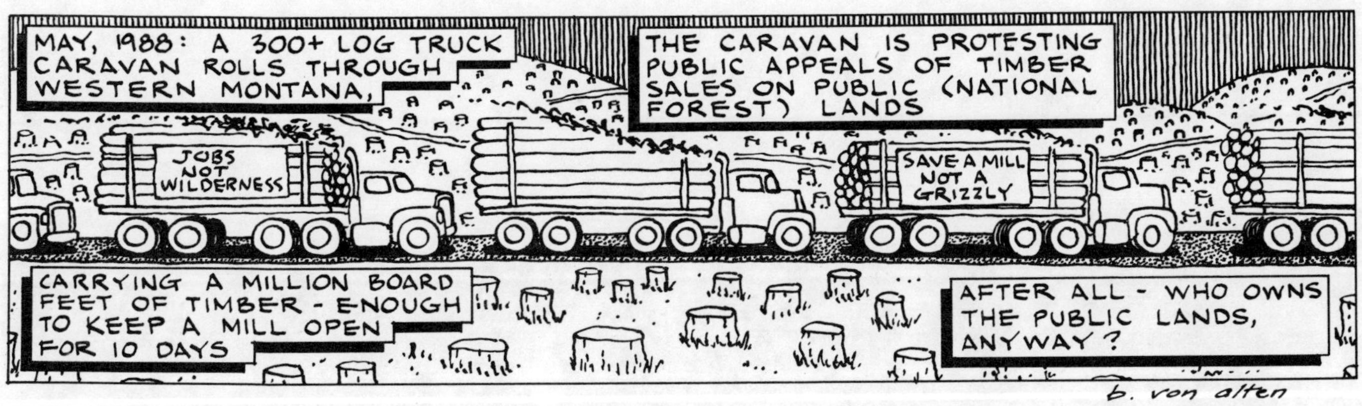
MAY, 1988: A 300+ LOG TRUCK CARAVAN ROLLS THROUGH WESTERN MONTANA,
THE CARAVAN IS PROTESTING PUBLIC APPEALS OF TIMBER SALES ON PUBLIC (NATIONAL FOREST) LANDS
JOBS NOT WILDERNESS
SAVE A MILL NOT A GRIZZLY
CARRYING A MILLION BOARD FEET OF TIMBER - ENOUGH TO KEEP A MILL OPEN FOR 10 DAYS
AFTER ALL - WHO OWNS THE PUBLIC LANDS, ANYWAY?
b. von alten

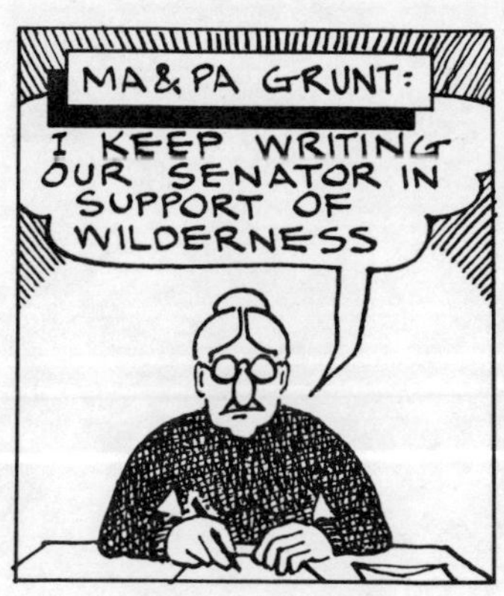
MA & PA GRUNT:
I KEEP WRITING OUR SENATOR IN SUPPORT OF WILDERNESS
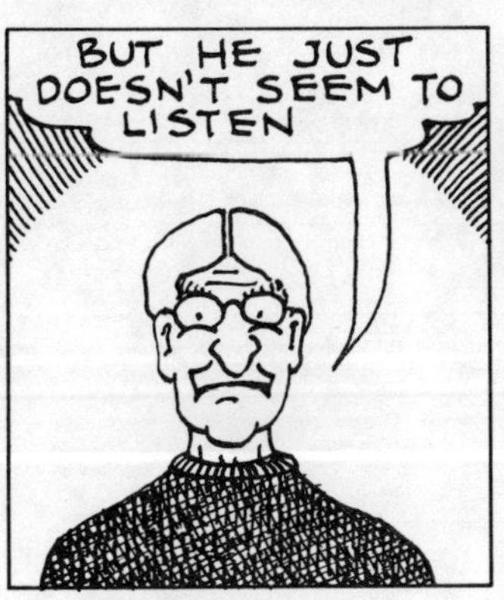
BUT HE JUST DOESN'T SEEM TO LISTEN
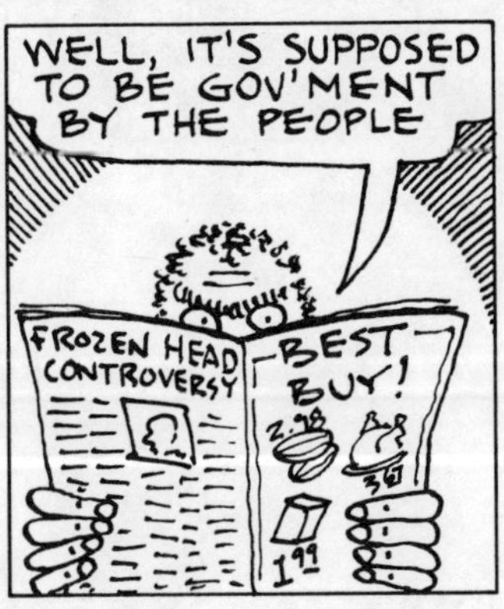
WELL, IT'S SUPPOSED TO BE GOV'MENT BY THE PEOPLE
FROZEN HEAD CONTROVERSY
BEST BUY!
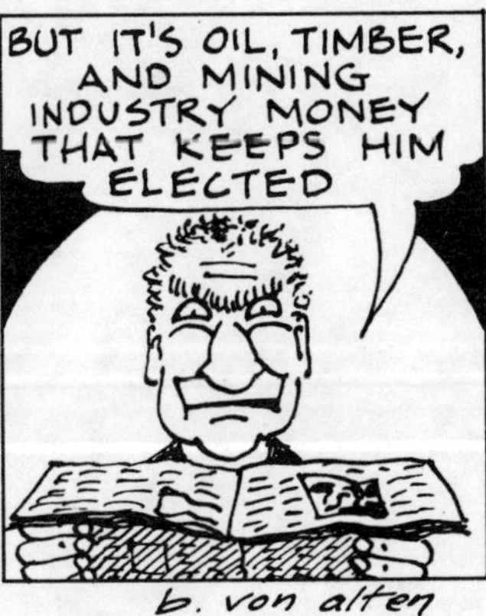
BUT IT'S OIL, TIMBER, AND MINING INDUSTRY MONEY THAT KEEPS HIM ELECTED
b. von alten

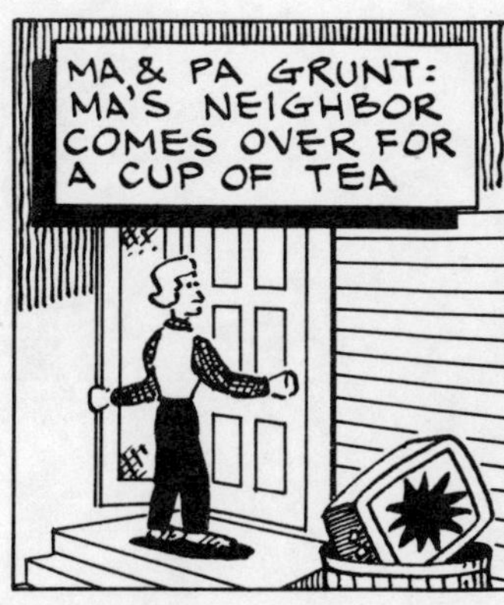
MA & PA GRUNT: MA'S NEIGHBOR COMES OVER FOR A CUP OF TEA
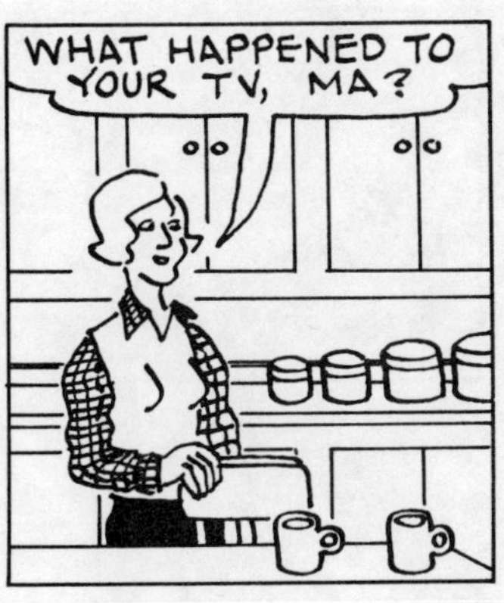
WHAT HAPPENED TO YOUR TV, MA?
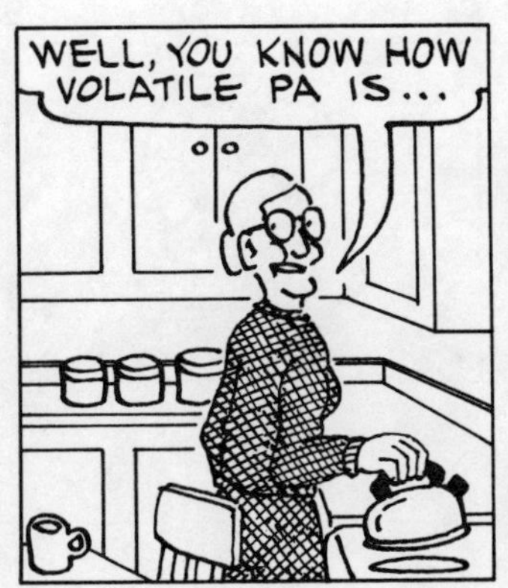
WELL, YOU KNOW HOW VOLATILE PA IS...
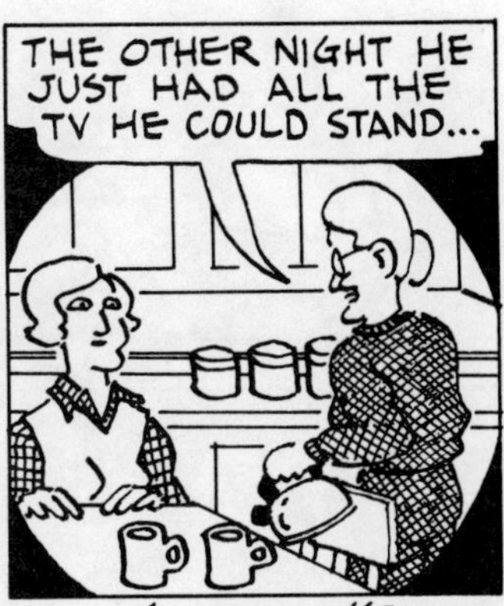
THE OTHER NIGHT HE JUST HAD ALL THE TV HE COULD STAND...
b. von alten

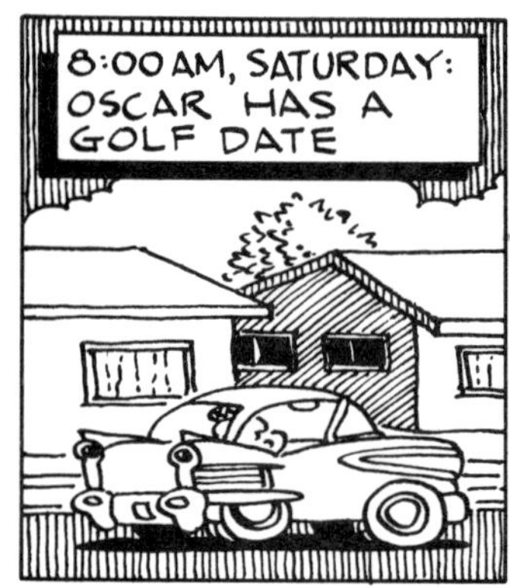
8:00 AM, SATURDAY:
OSCAR HAS A
GOLF DATE

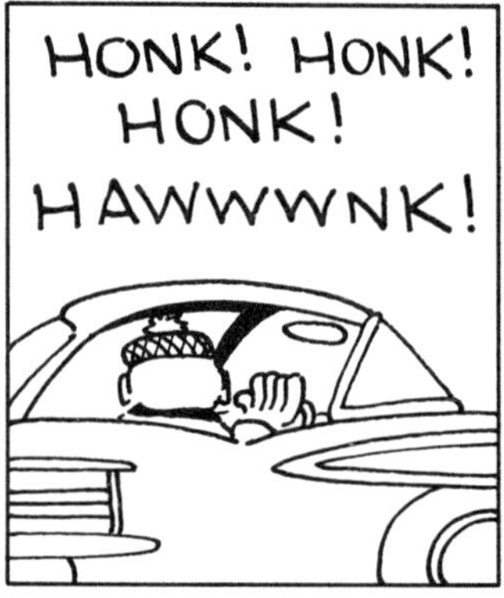
HONK! HONK!
HONK!
HAWWWNK!

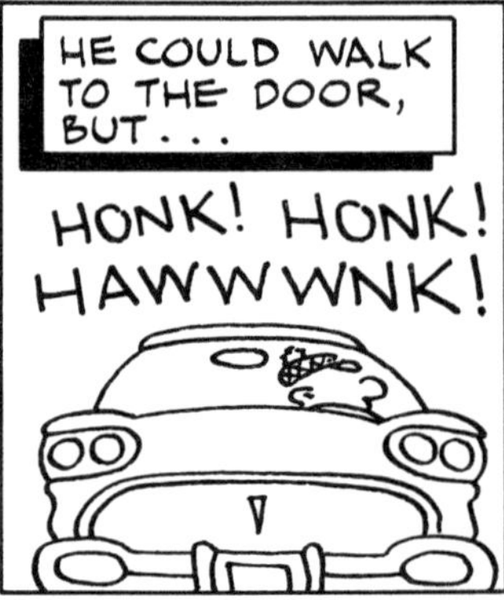
HE COULD WALK
TO THE DOOR,
BUT...
HONK! HONK!
HAWWWNK!

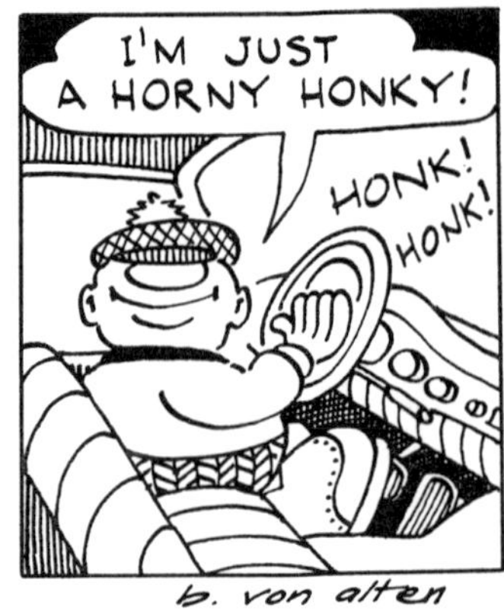
I'M JUST
A HORNY HONKY!
HONK!
HONK!
b. von alten

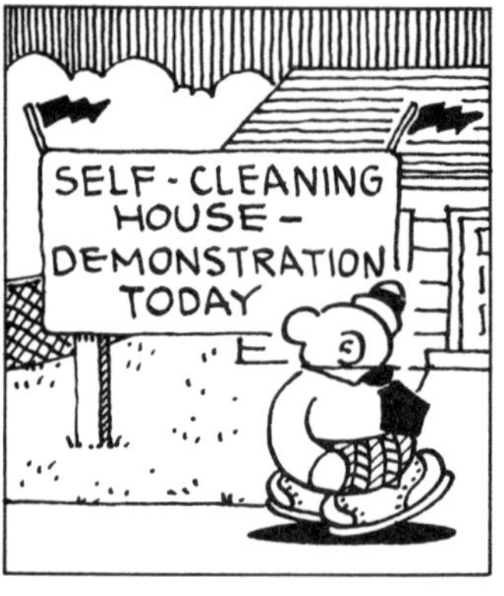
SELF-CLEANING
HOUSE-
DEMONSTRATION
TODAY

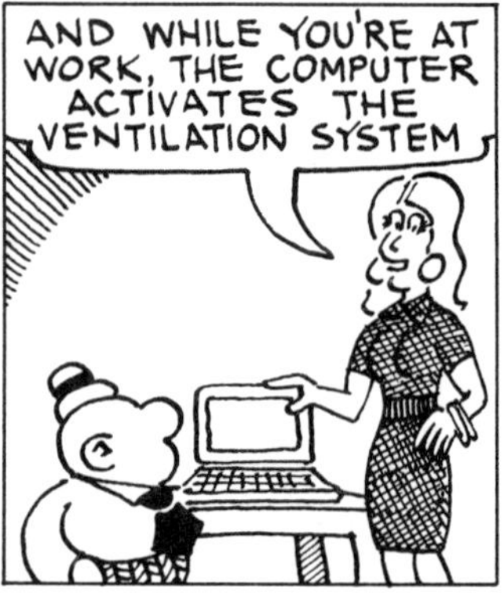
AND WHILE YOU'RE AT
WORK, THE COMPUTER
ACTIVATES THE
VENTILATION SYSTEM

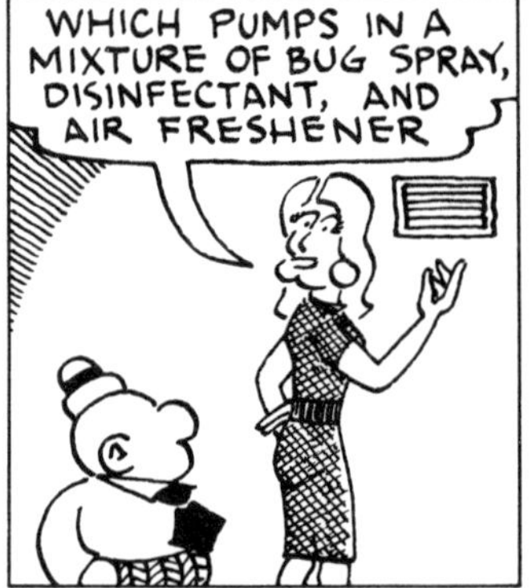
WHICH PUMPS IN A
MIXTURE OF BUG SPRAY,
DISINFECTANT, AND
AIR FRESHENER

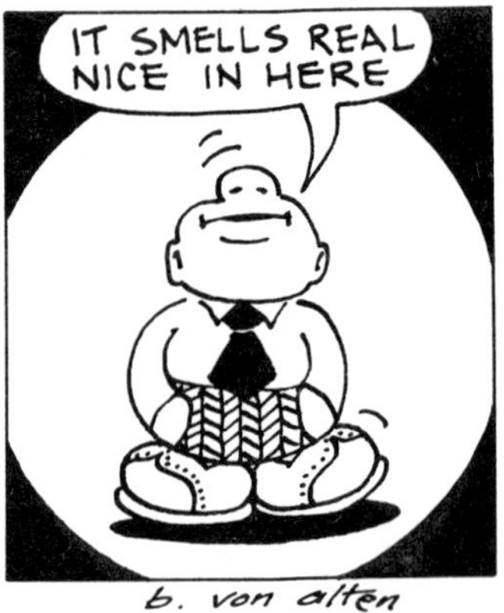
IT SMELLS REAL
NICE IN HERE
b. von alten

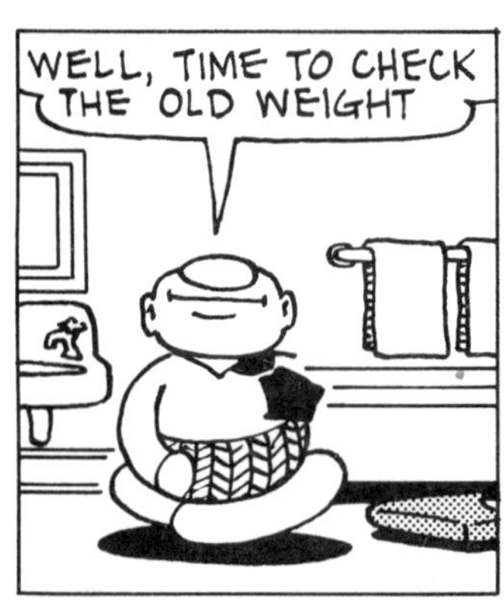
WELL, TIME TO CHECK
THE OLD WEIGHT

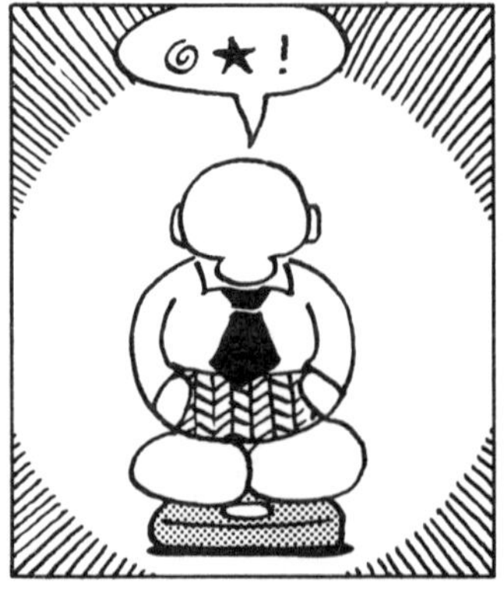

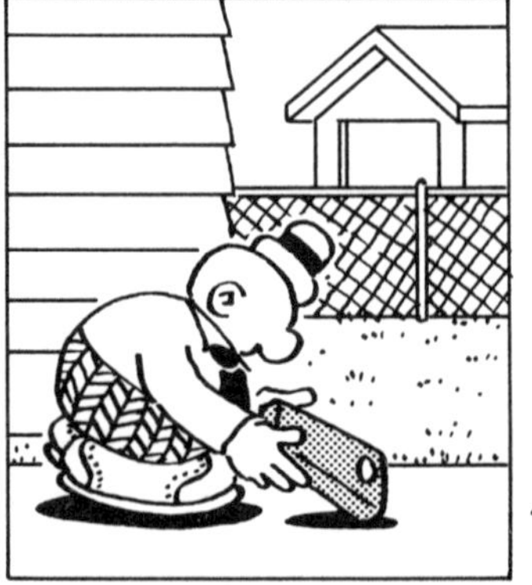

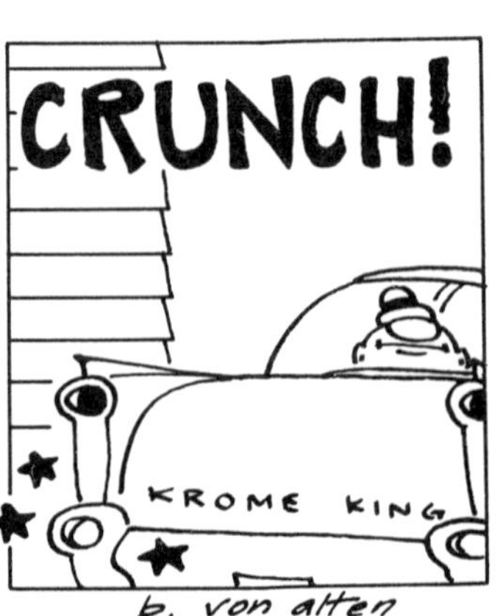
CRUNCH!
KROME KING
b. von alten

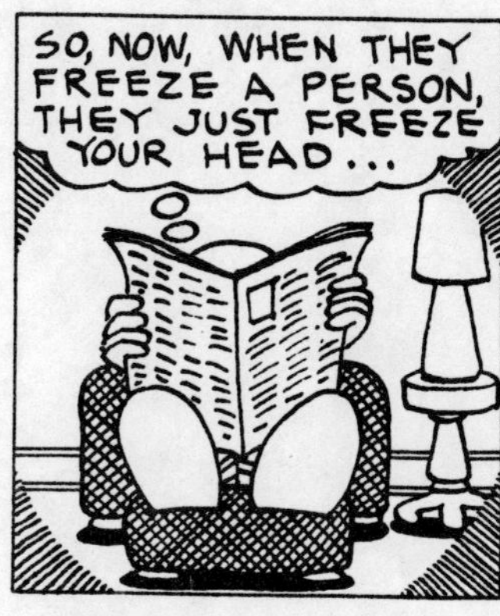
SO, NOW, WHEN THEY FREEZE A PERSON, THEY JUST FREEZE YOUR HEAD...

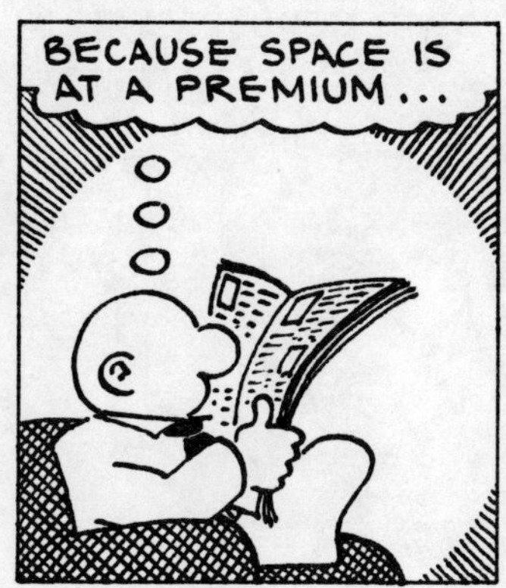
BECAUSE SPACE IS AT A PREMIUM...

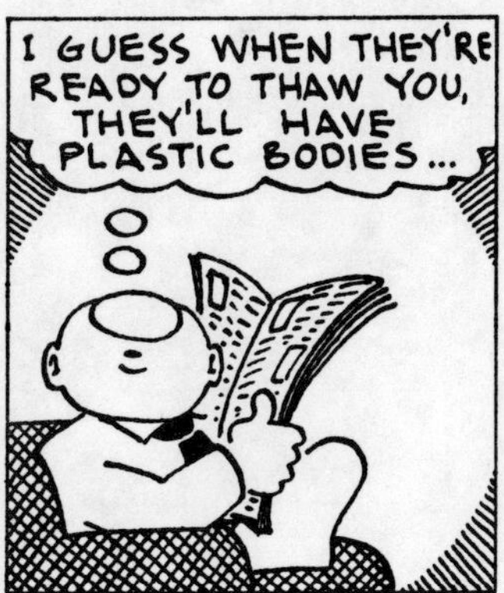
I GUESS WHEN THEY'RE READY TO THAW YOU, THEY'LL HAVE PLASTIC BODIES...

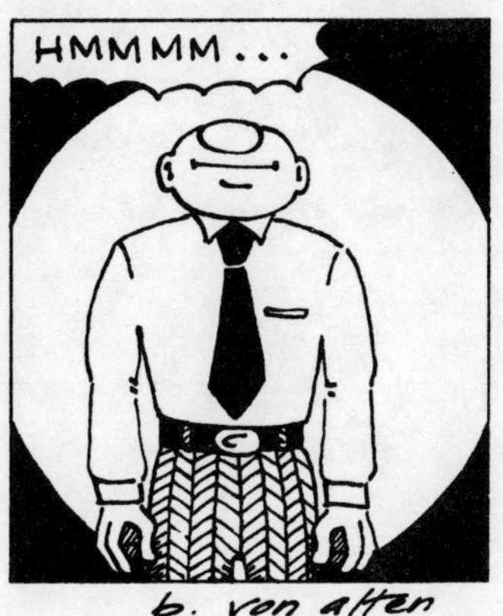
HMMMM...
b. von alten

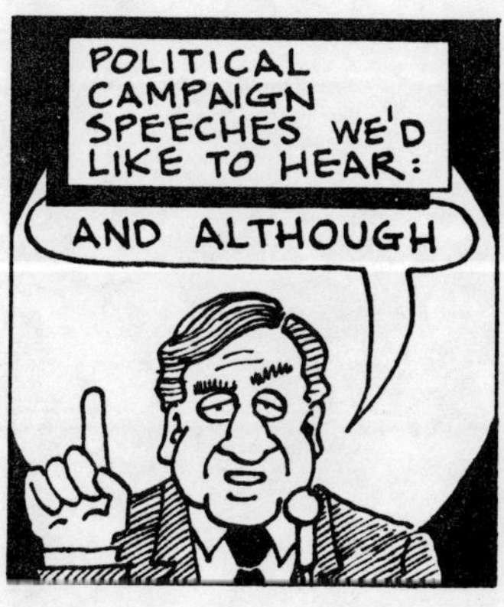
POLITICAL CAMPAIGN SPEECHES WE'D LIKE TO HEAR:
AND ALTHOUGH

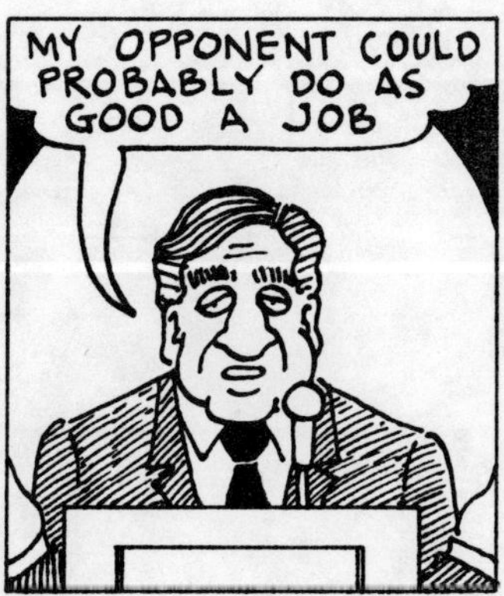
MY OPPONENT COULD PROBABLY DO AS GOOD A JOB

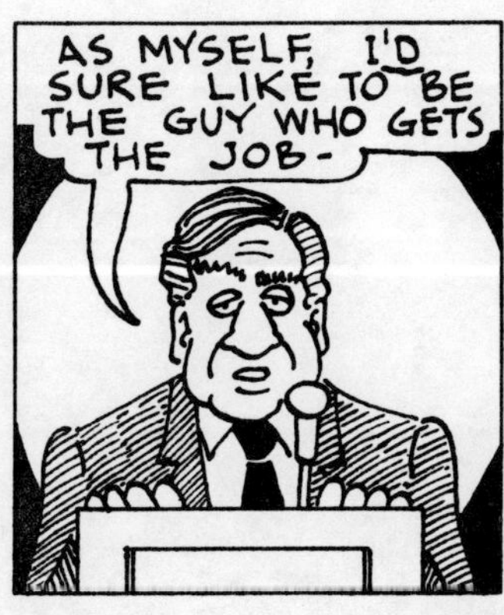
AS MYSELF, I'D SURE LIKE TO BE THE GUY WHO GETS THE JOB-

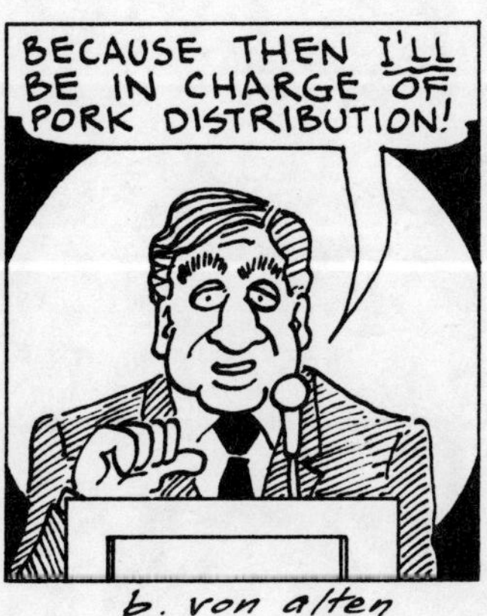
BECAUSE THEN I'LL BE IN CHARGE OF PORK DISTRIBUTION!
b. von alten

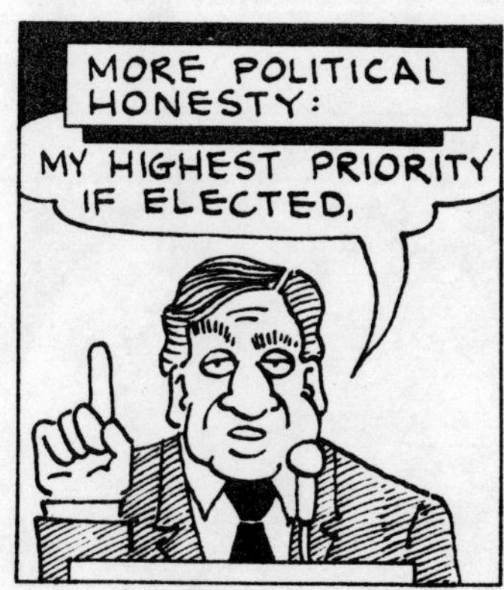
MORE POLITICAL HONESTY:
MY HIGHEST PRIORITY IF ELECTED,

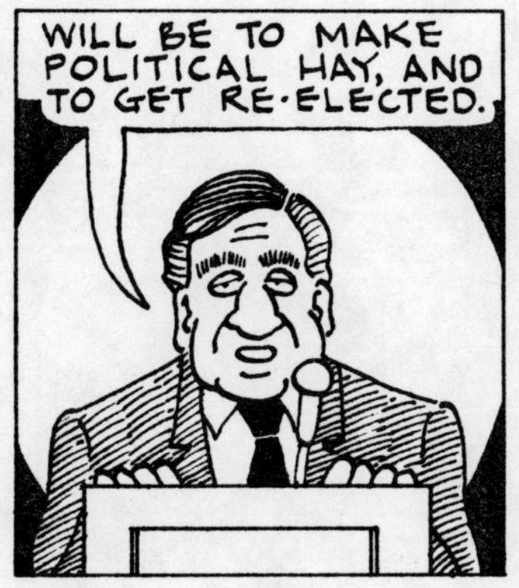
WILL BE TO MAKE POLITICAL HAY, AND TO GET RE-ELECTED.

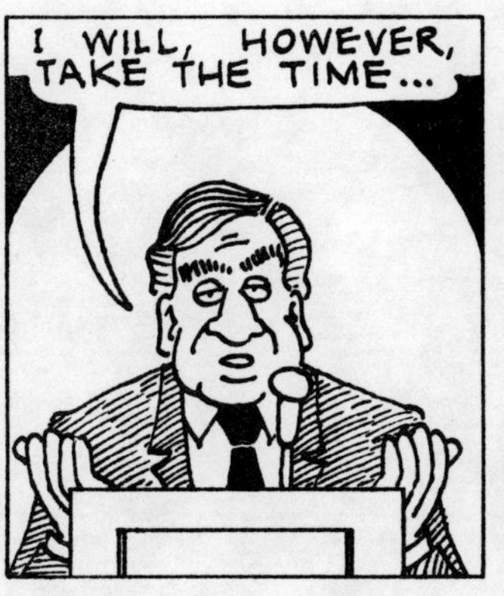
I WILL, HOWEVER, TAKE THE TIME...

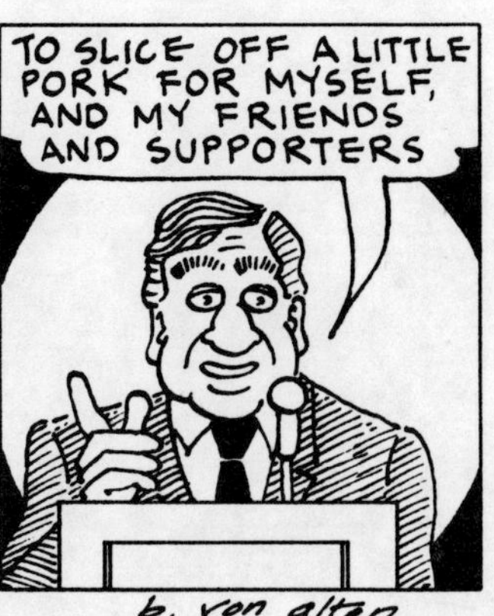
TO SLICE OFF A LITTLE PORK FOR MYSELF, AND MY FRIENDS AND SUPPORTERS
b. von alten

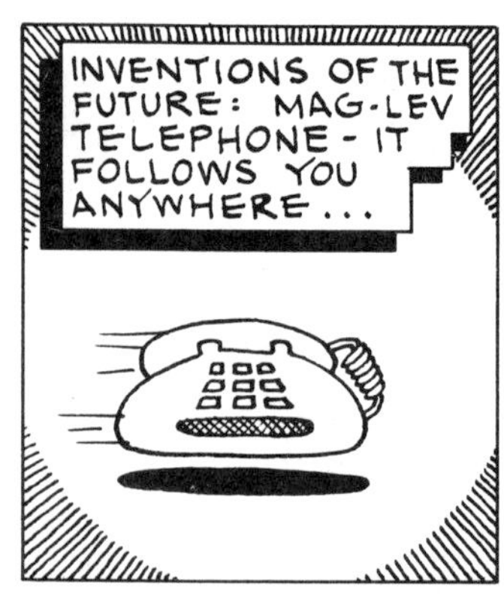
INVENTIONS OF THE FUTURE: MAG-LEV TELEPHONE - IT FOLLOWS YOU ANYWHERE...

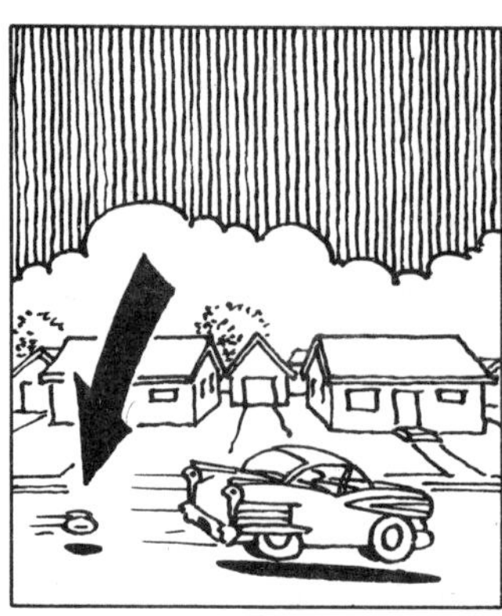

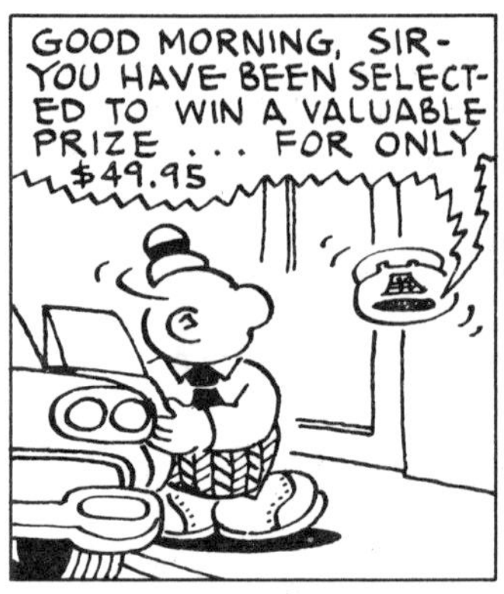
GOOD MORNING, SIR- YOU HAVE BEEN SELECTED TO WIN A VALUABLE PRIZE ... FOR ONLY $49.95

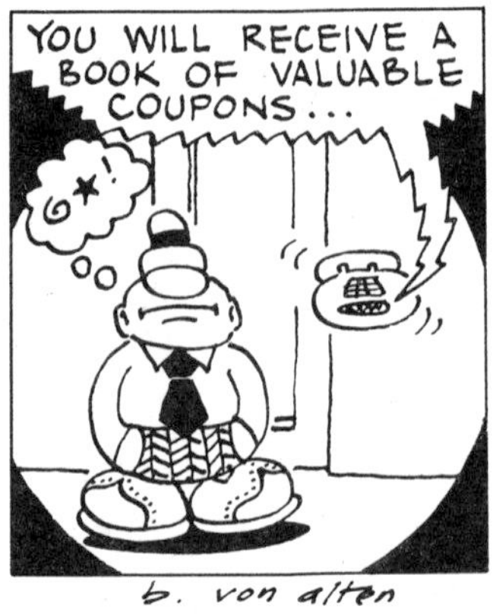
YOU WILL RECEIVE A BOOK OF VALUABLE COUPONS...
G★!
b. von alten

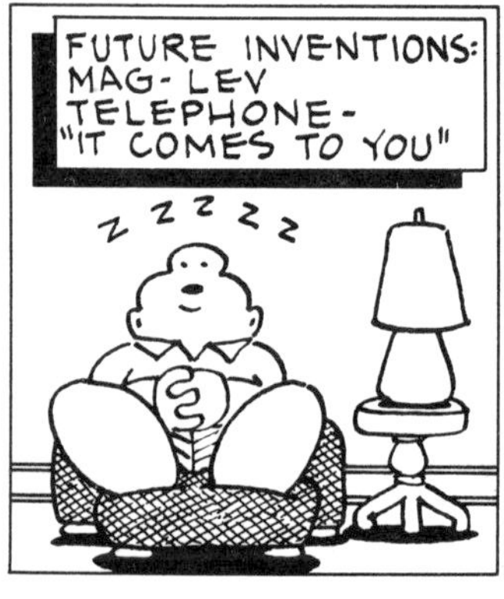
FUTURE INVENTIONS: MAG-LEV TELEPHONE- "IT COMES TO YOU"
Z Z Z Z Z

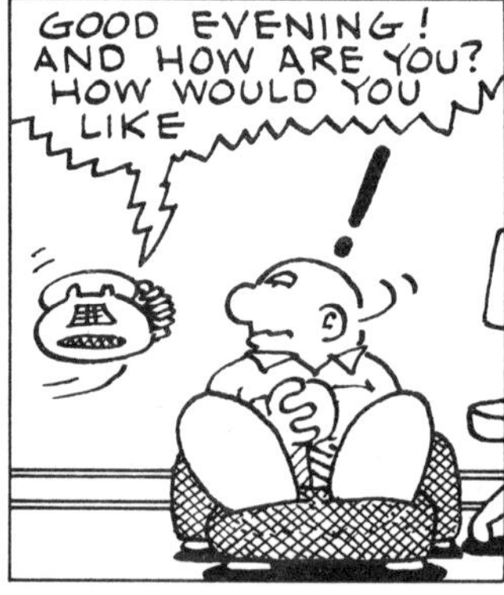
GOOD EVENING! AND HOW ARE YOU? HOW WOULD YOU LIKE
!

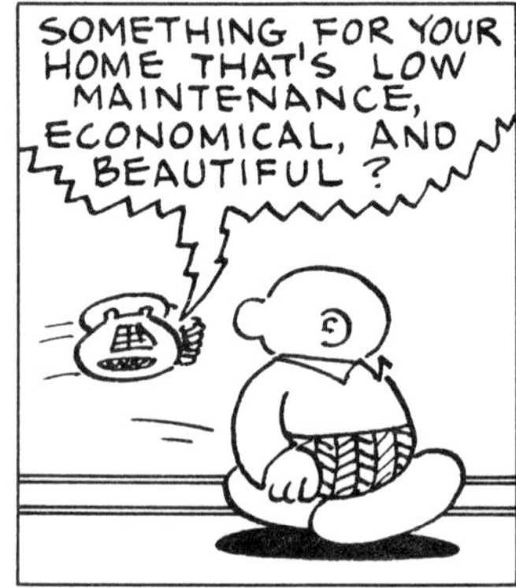
SOMETHING FOR YOUR HOME THAT'S LOW MAINTENANCE, ECONOMICAL, AND BEAUTIFUL?

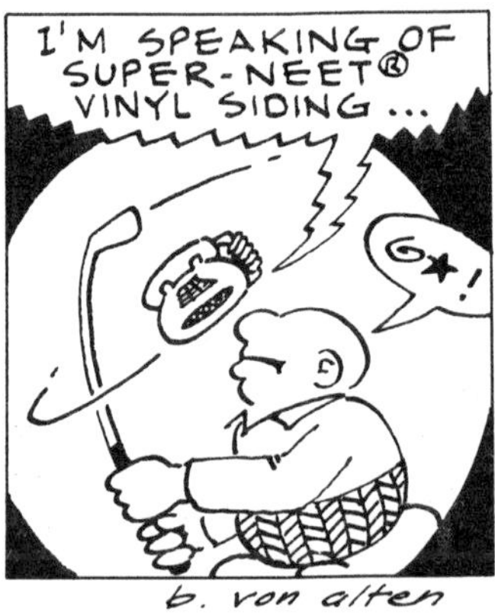
I'M SPEAKING OF SUPER-NEET® VINYL SIDING...
G★!
b. von alten

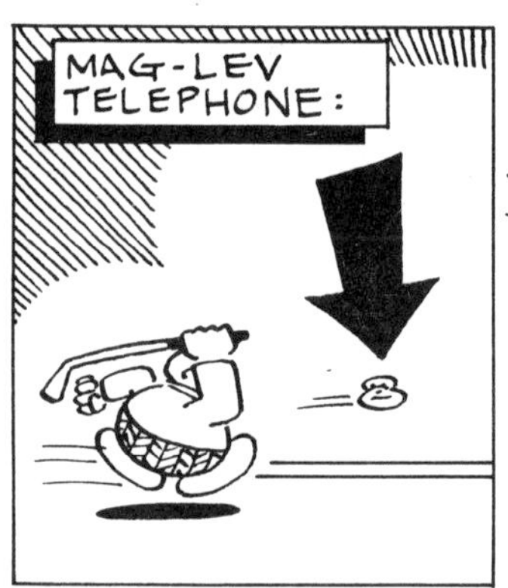
MAG-LEV TELEPHONE:

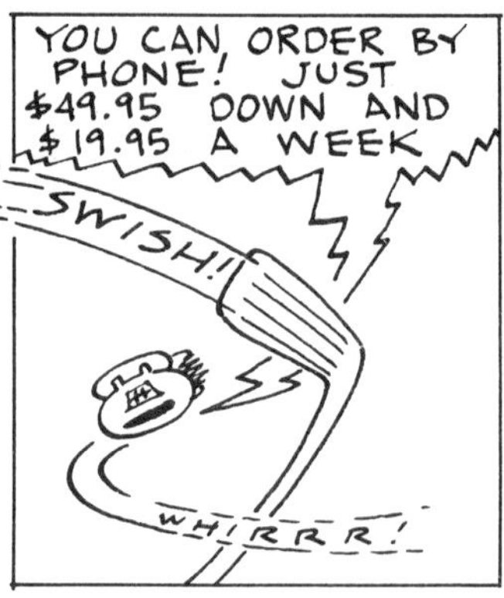
YOU CAN ORDER BY PHONE! JUST $49.95 DOWN AND $19.95 A WEEK
SWISH!
WHIRRRR!

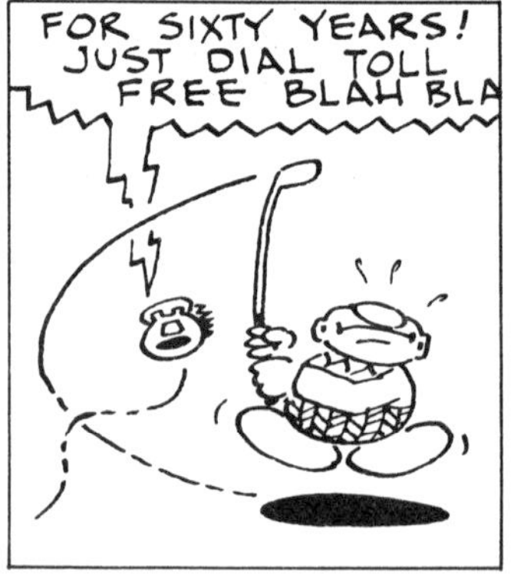
FOR SIXTY YEARS! JUST DIAL TOLL FREE BLAH BLA

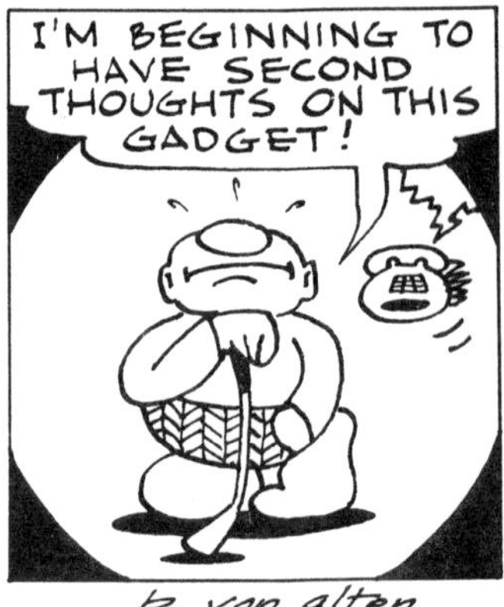
I'M BEGINNING TO HAVE SECOND THOUGHTS ON THIS GADGET!
b. von alten

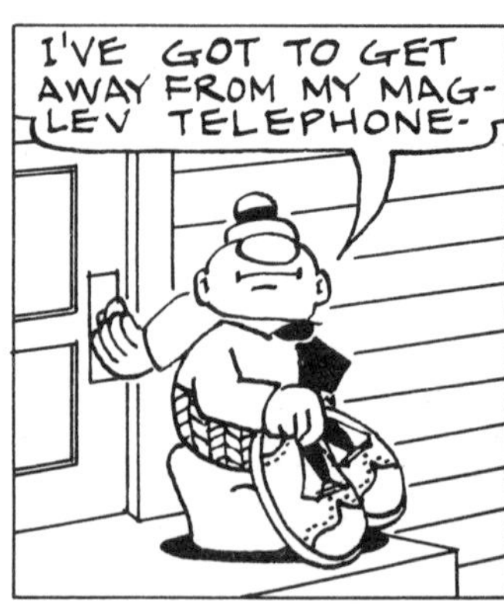
I'VE GOT TO GET AWAY FROM MY MAG-LEV TELEPHONE-

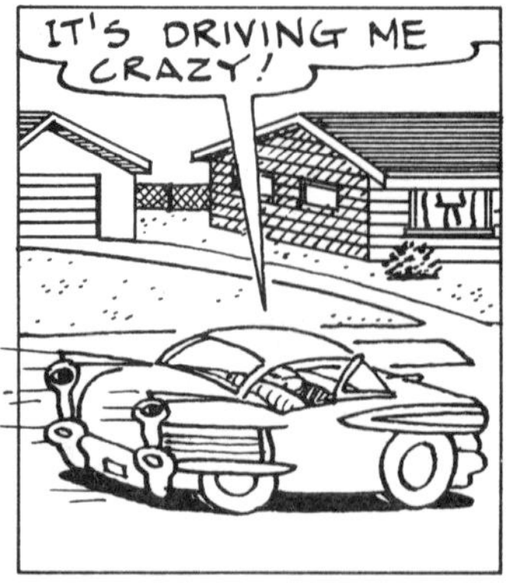
IT'S DRIVING ME CRAZY!

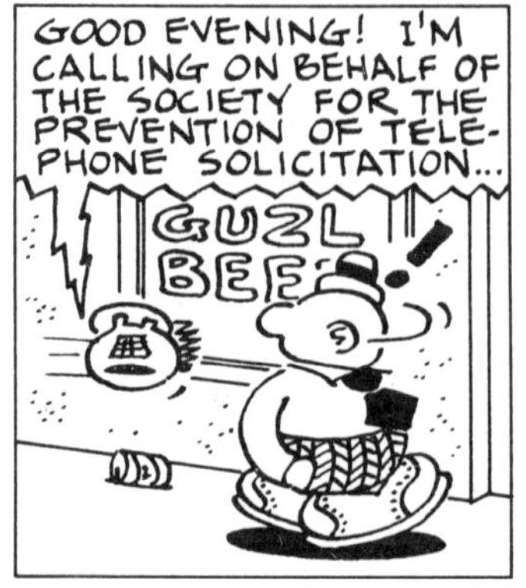
GOOD EVENING! I'M CALLING ON BEHALF OF THE SOCIETY FOR THE PREVENTION OF TELEPHONE SOLICITATION...
GUZL BEE
!

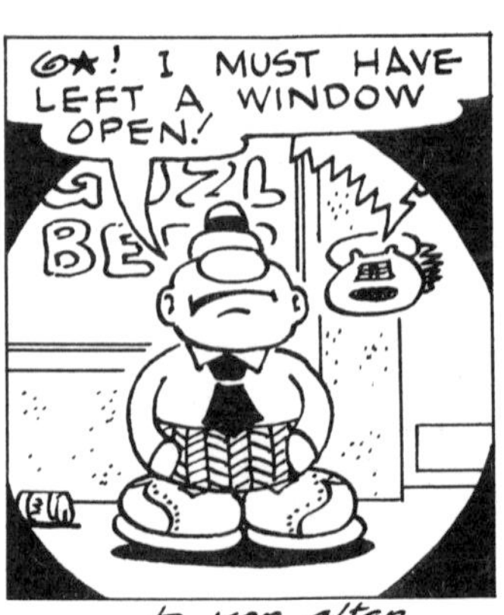
G★! I MUST HAVE LEFT A WINDOW OPEN!
b. von alten

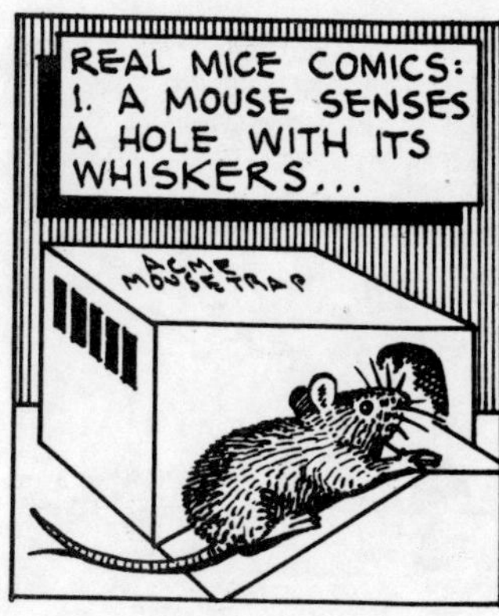
REAL MICE COMICS:
1. A MOUSE SENSES A HOLE WITH ITS WHISKERS...
ACME MOUSETRAP

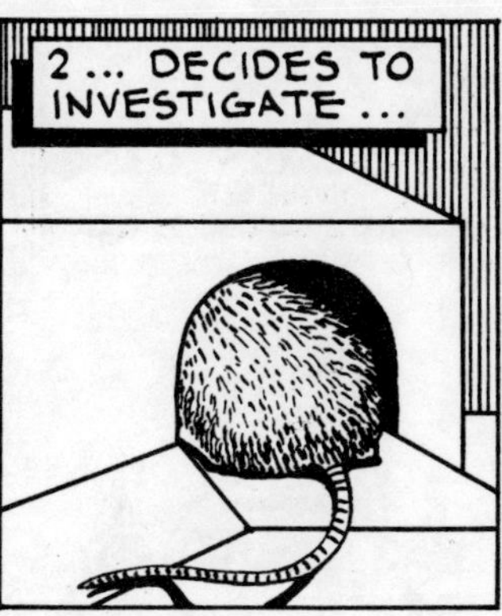
2 ... DECIDES TO INVESTIGATE ...

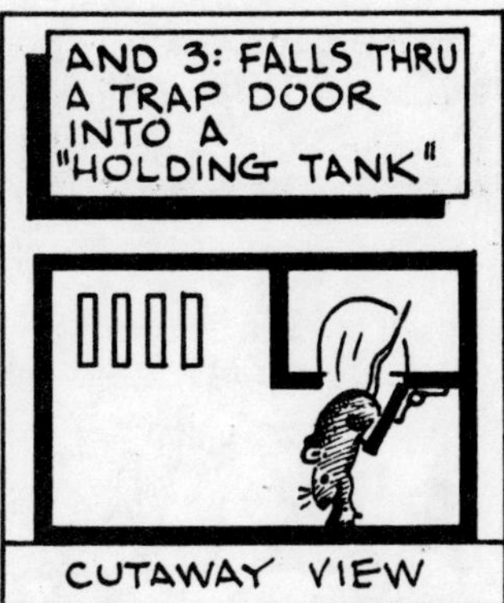
AND 3: FALLS THRU A TRAP DOOR INTO A "HOLDING TANK"
CUTAWAY VIEW

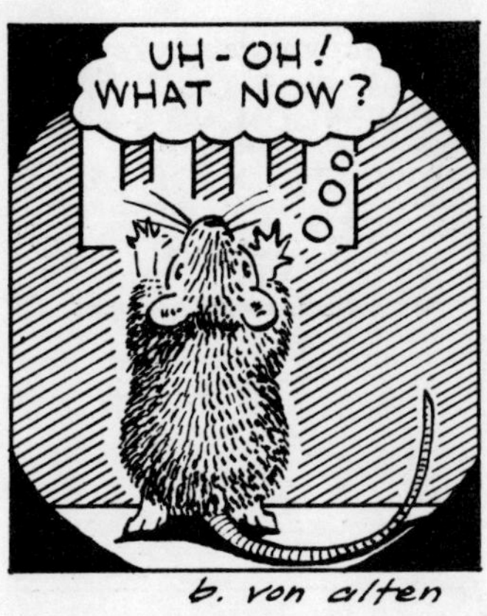
UH-OH! WHAT NOW?

b. von alten

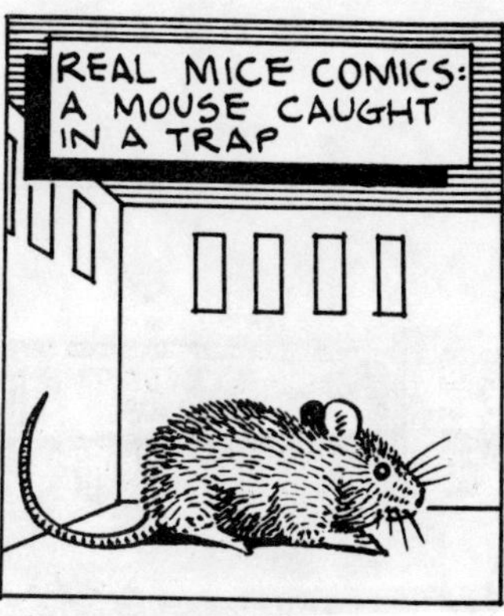
REAL MICE COMICS: A MOUSE CAUGHT IN A TRAP

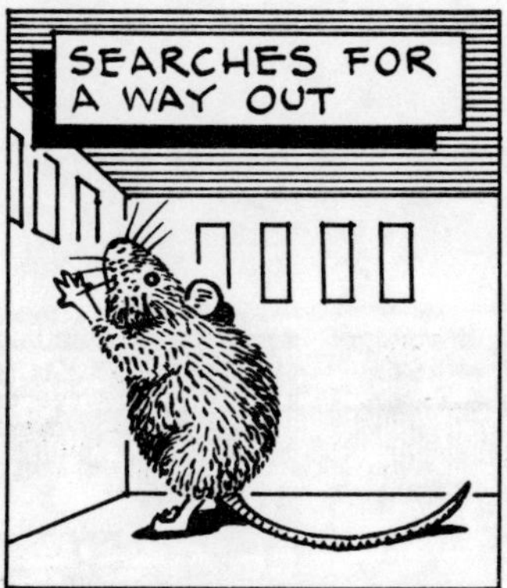
SEARCHES FOR A WAY OUT

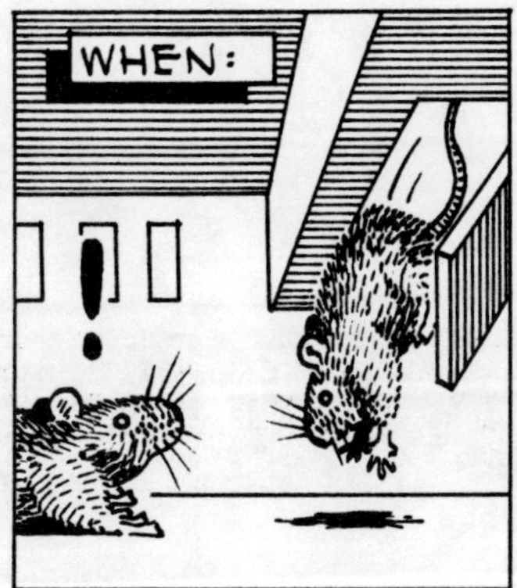
WHEN:

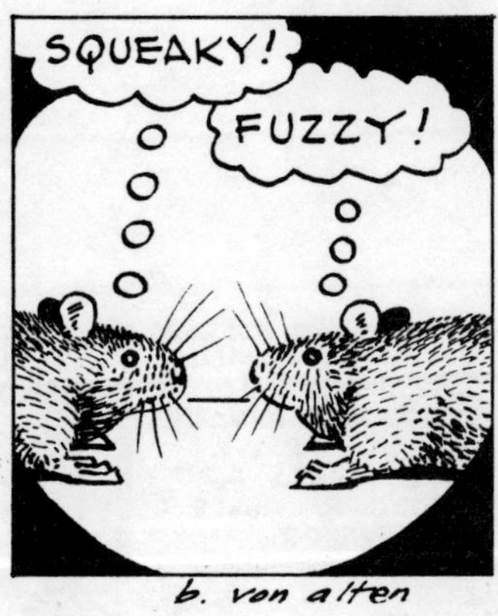
SQUEAKY!
FUZZY!

b. von alten

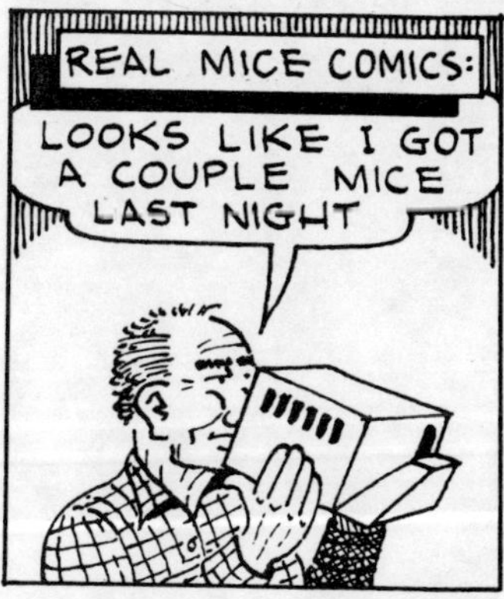
REAL MICE COMICS:
LOOKS LIKE I GOT A COUPLE MICE LAST NIGHT

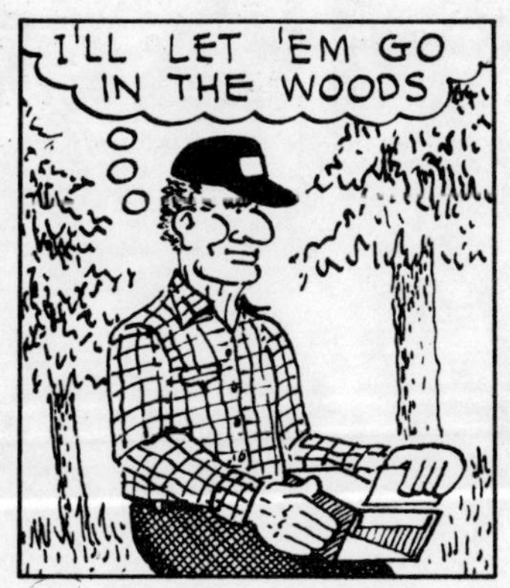
I'LL LET 'EM GO IN THE WOODS

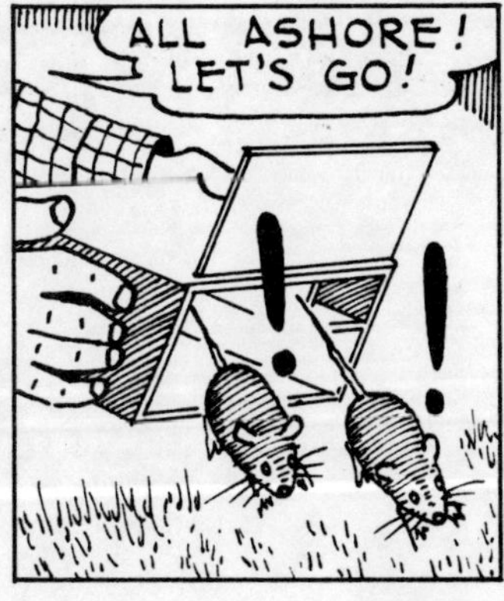
ALL ASHORE! LET'S GO!

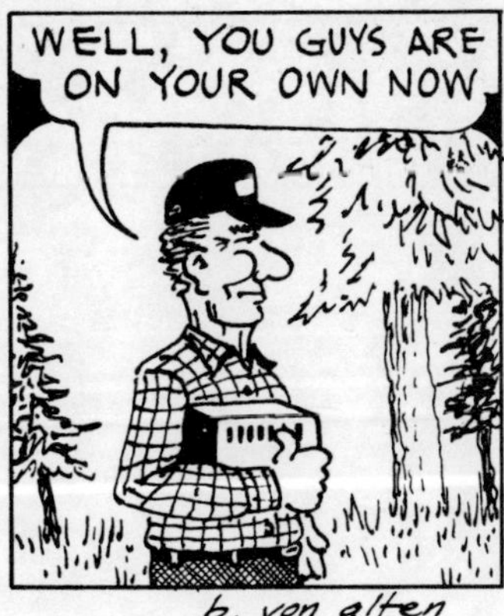
WELL, YOU GUYS ARE ON YOUR OWN NOW

b. von alten

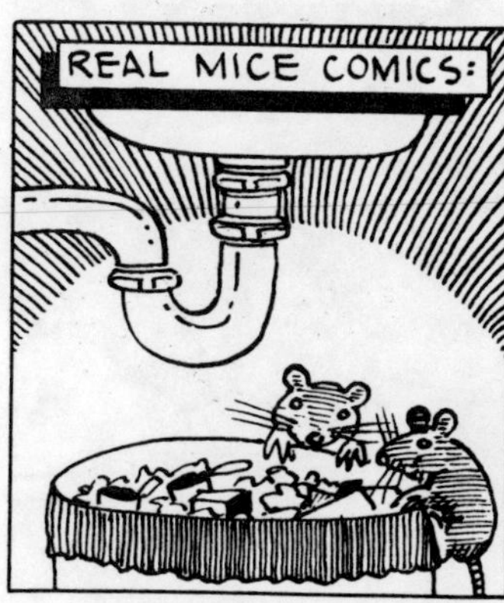
REAL MICE COMICS:

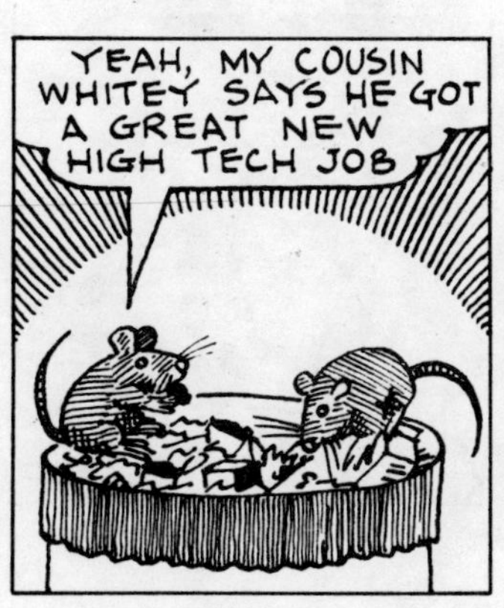
YEAH, MY COUSIN WHITEY SAYS HE GOT A GREAT NEW HIGH TECH JOB

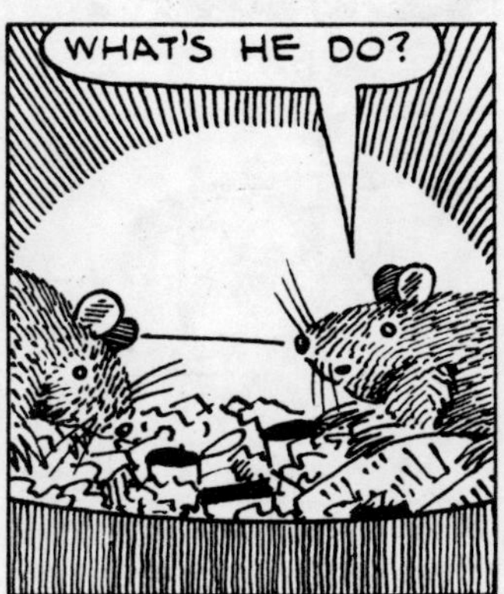
WHAT'S HE DO?

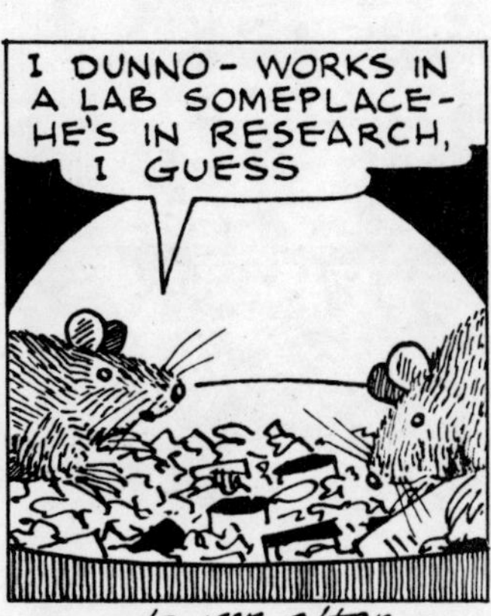
I DUNNO - WORKS IN A LAB SOMEPLACE - HE'S IN RESEARCH, I GUESS

b. von alten

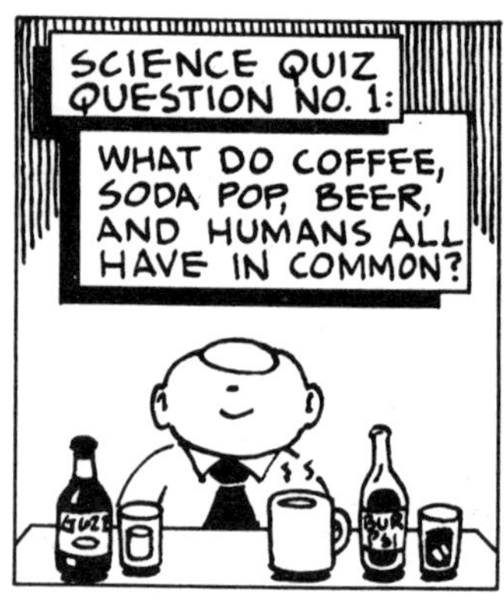
SCIENCE QUIZ QUESTION NO. 1:
WHAT DO COFFEE, SODA POP, BEER, AND HUMANS ALL HAVE IN COMMON?

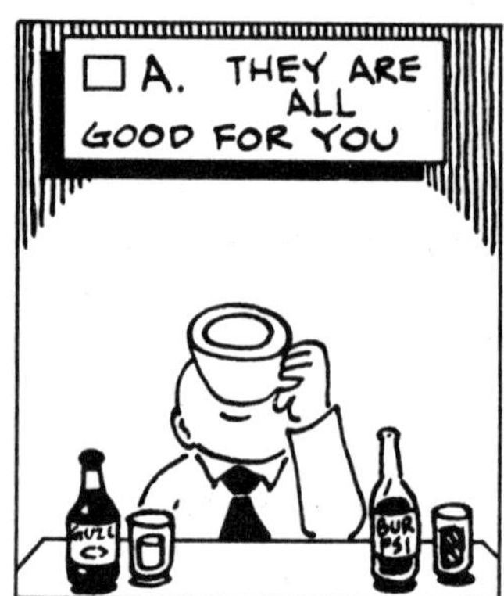
☐ A. THEY ARE ALL GOOD FOR YOU

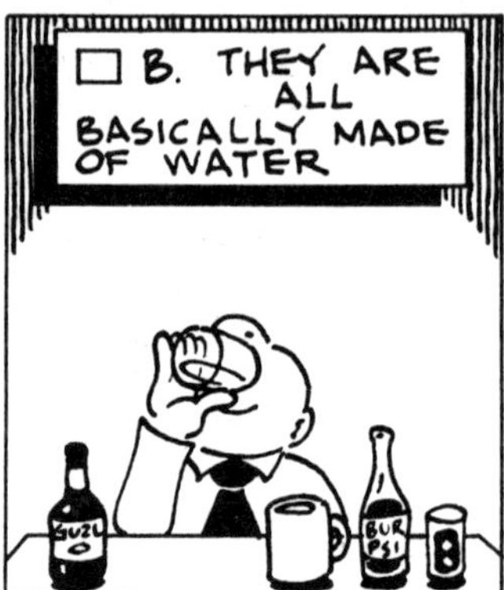
☐ B. THEY ARE ALL BASICALLY MADE OF WATER

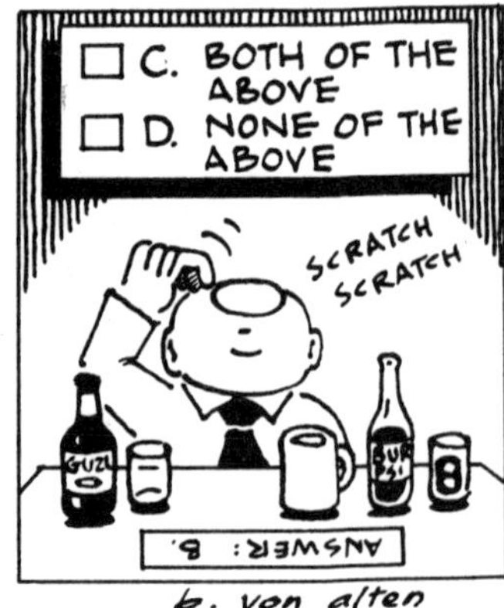
☐ C. BOTH OF THE ABOVE
☐ D. NONE OF THE ABOVE
SCRATCH SCRATCH
ANSWER: B.

b. von alten

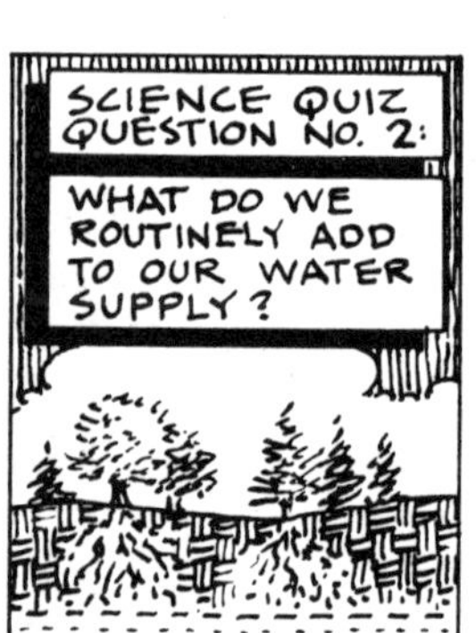
SCIENCE QUIZ QUESTION NO. 2:
WHAT DO WE ROUTINELY ADD TO OUR WATER SUPPLY?
GROUNDWATER (WATER TABLE)

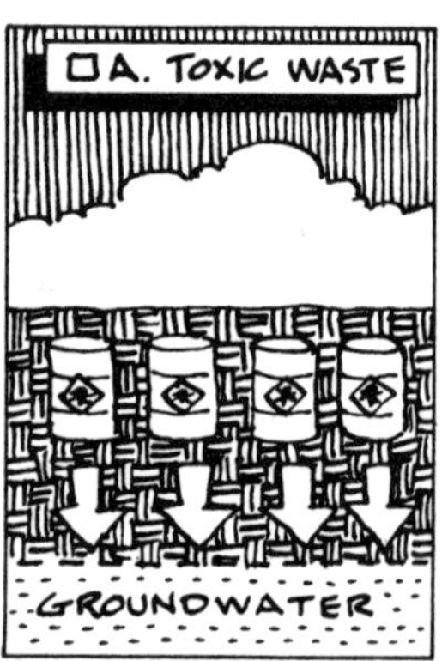
☐ A. TOXIC WASTE
GROUNDWATER

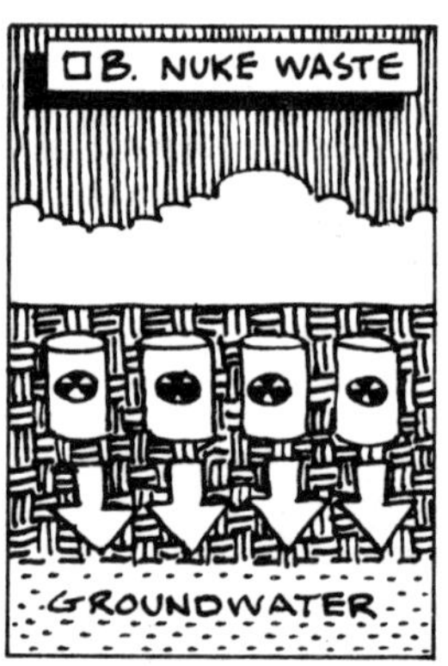
☐ B. NUKE WASTE
GROUNDWATER

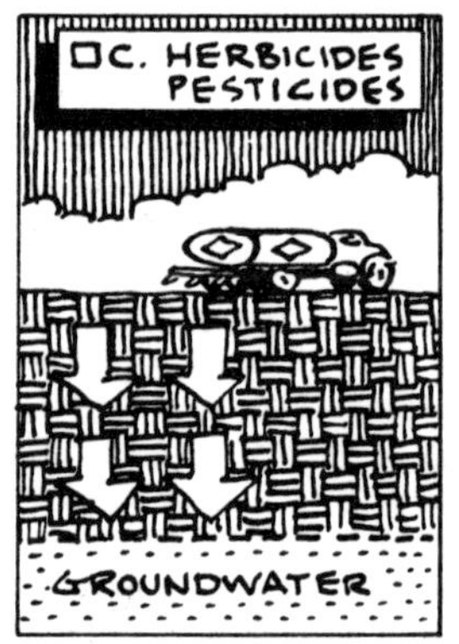
☐ C. HERBICIDES PESTICIDES
GROUNDWATER

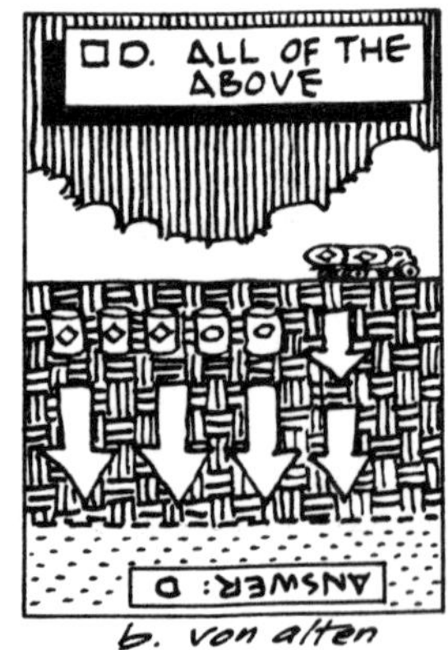
☐ D. ALL OF THE ABOVE
ANSWER: D

b. von alten

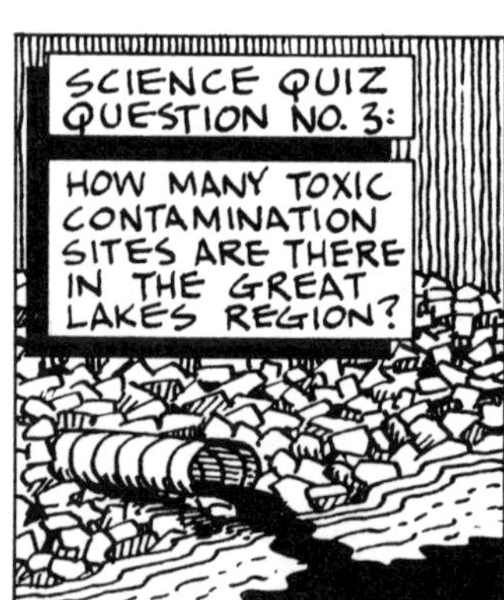
SCIENCE QUIZ QUESTION NO. 3:
HOW MANY TOXIC CONTAMINATION SITES ARE THERE IN THE GREAT LAKES REGION?

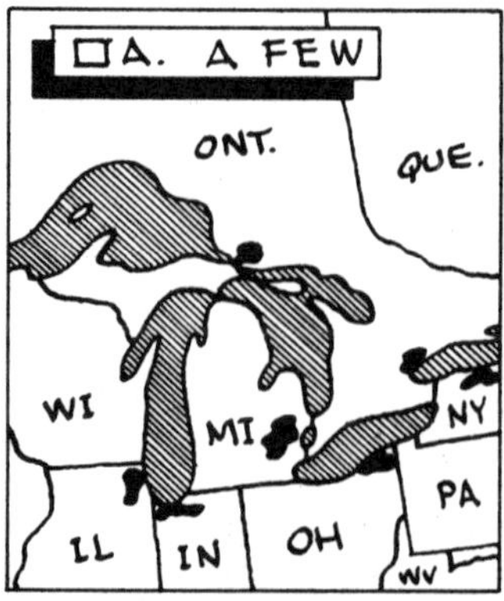
☐ A. A FEW
ONT.
QUE.
WI
MI
NY
PA
IL
IN
OH
WV

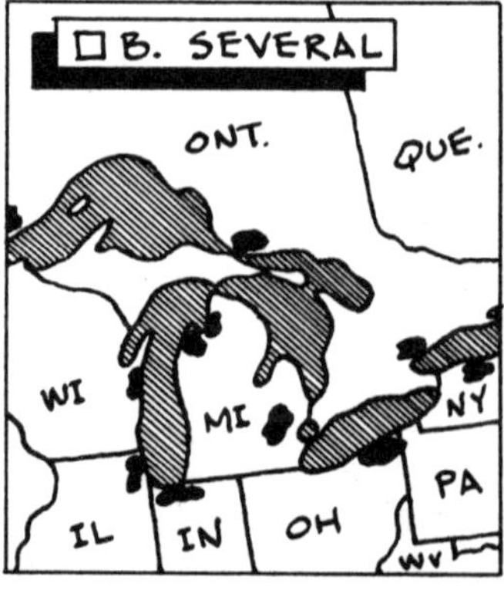
☐ B. SEVERAL
ONT.
QUE.
WI
MI
NY
PA
IL
IN
OH
WV

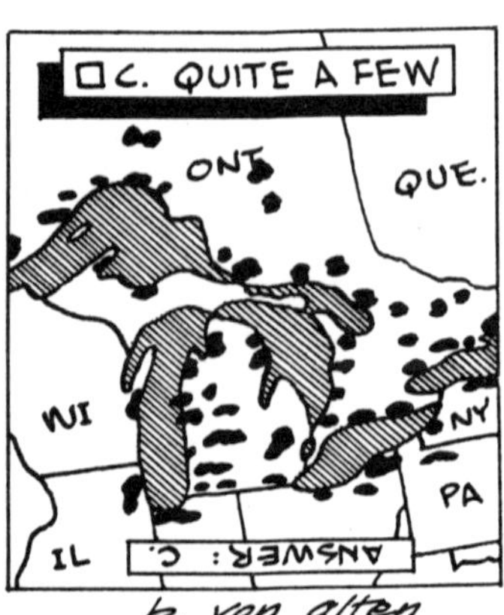
☐ C. QUITE A FEW
ONT.
QUE.
WI
NY
PA
IL
ANSWER: C.

b. von alten

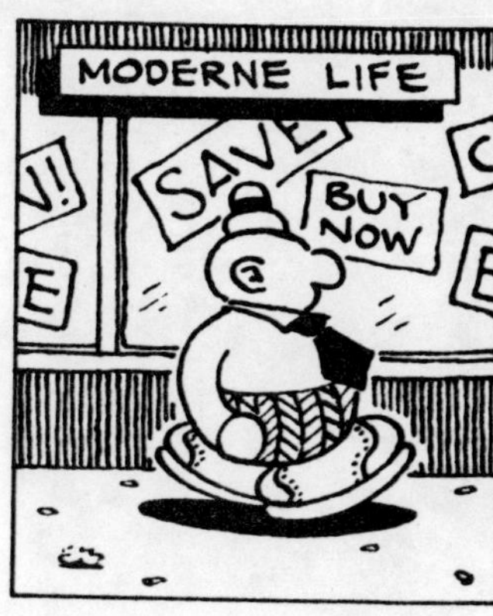
MODERNE LIFE
SAVE
BUY NOW

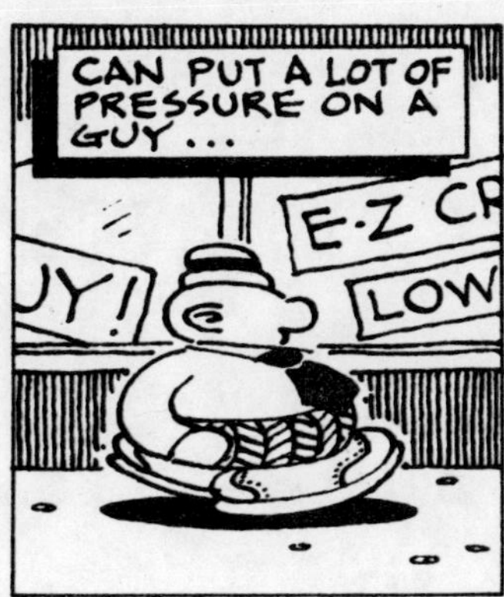
CAN PUT A LOT OF PRESSURE ON A GUY ...
E-Z CR
LOW

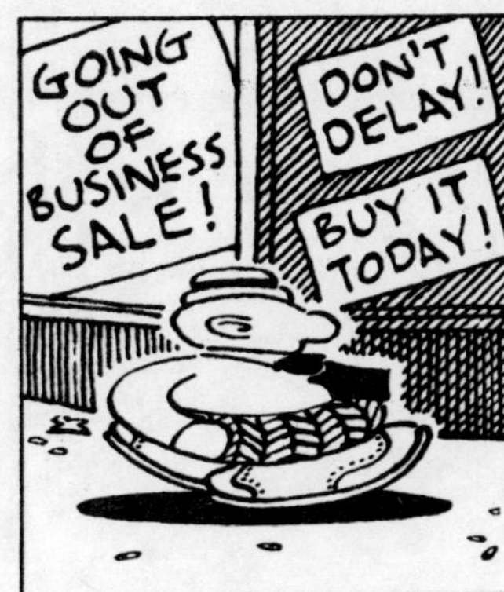
GOING OUT OF BUSINESS SALE!
DON'T DELAY!
BUY IT TODAY!

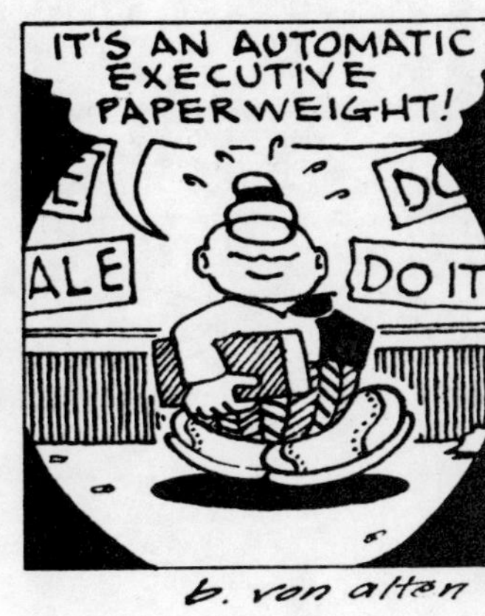
IT'S AN AUTOMATIC EXECUTIVE PAPERWEIGHT!
ALE
DO IT

b. von alten

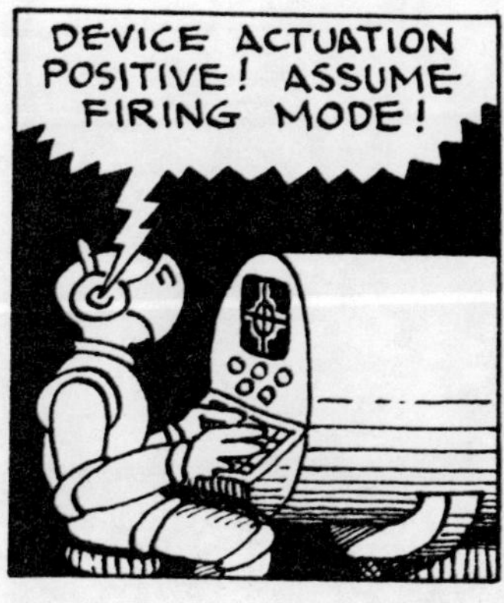
DEVICE ACTUATION POSITIVE! ASSUME FIRING MODE!

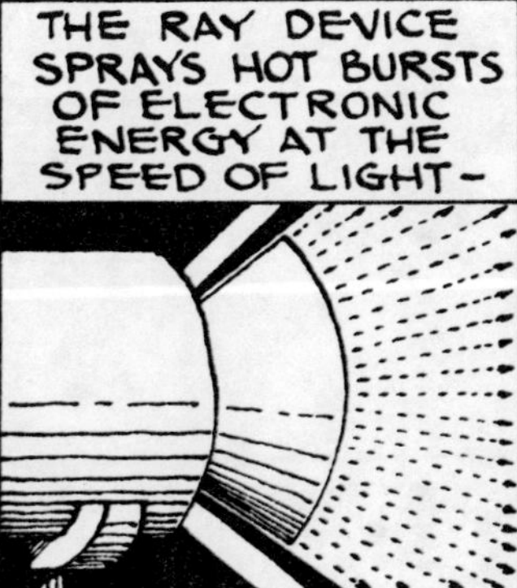
THE RAY DEVICE SPRAYS HOT BURSTS OF ELECTRONIC ENERGY AT THE SPEED OF LIGHT-

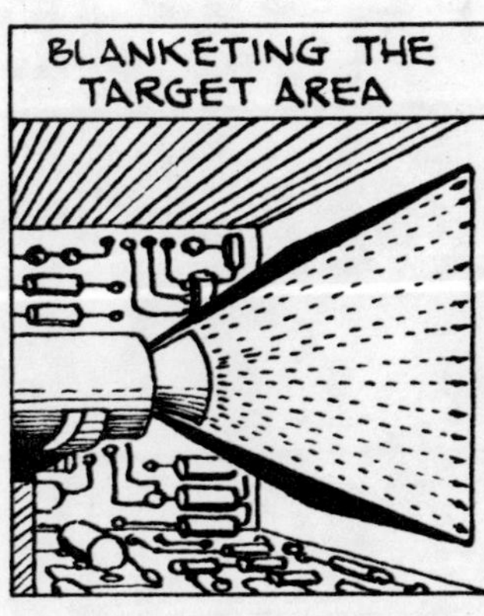
BLANKETING THE TARGET AREA

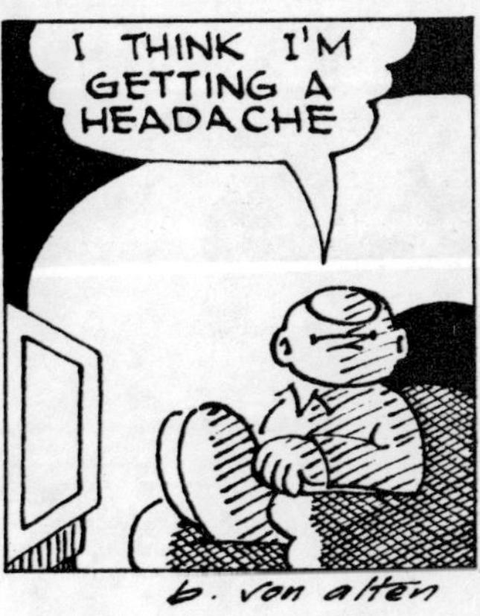
I THINK I'M GETTING A HEADACHE

b. von alten

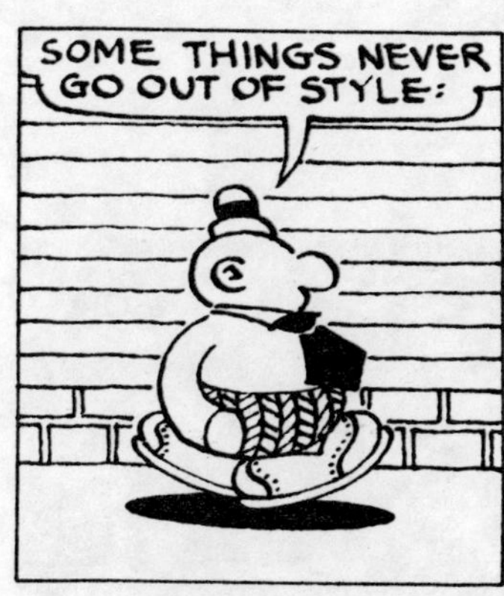
SOME THINGS NEVER GO OUT OF STYLE:

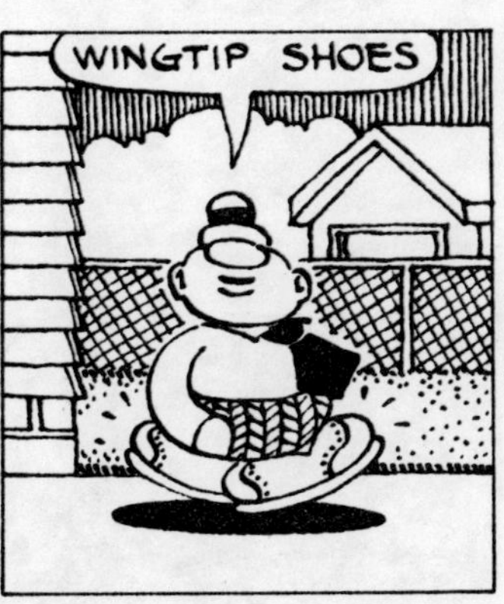
WINGTIP SHOES

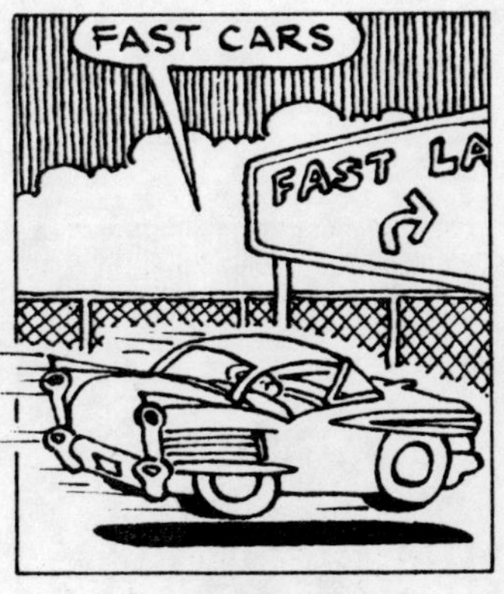
FAST CARS
FAST LA

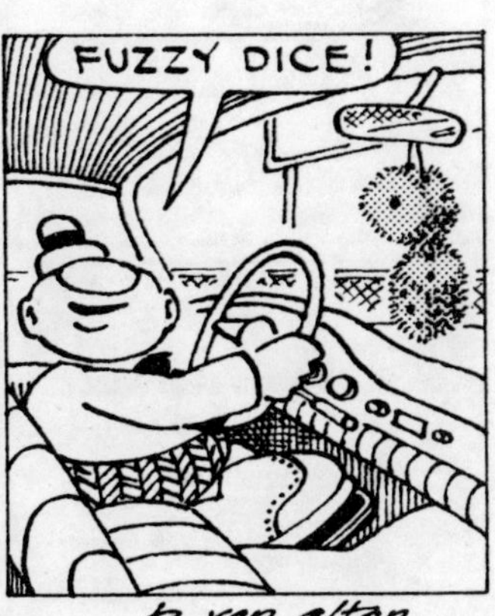
FUZZY DICE!

b. von alten

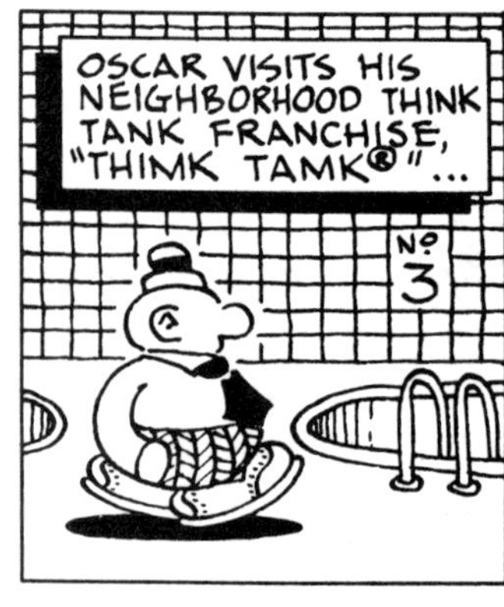
OSCAR VISITS HIS NEIGHBORHOOD THINK TANK FRANCHISE, "THIMK TAMK®"...
NO 3

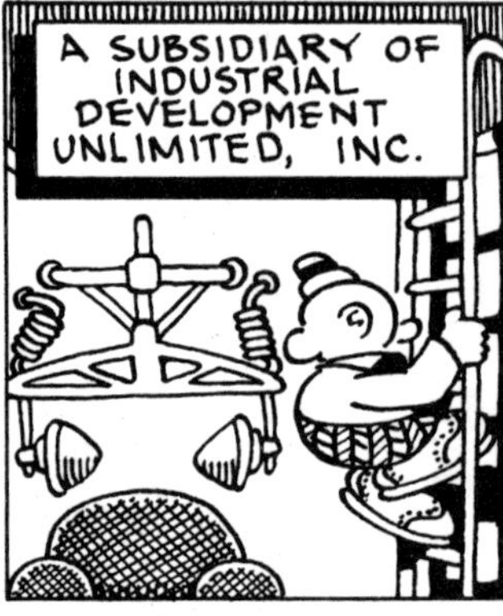
A SUBSIDIARY OF INDUSTRIAL DEVELOPMENT UNLIMITED, INC.

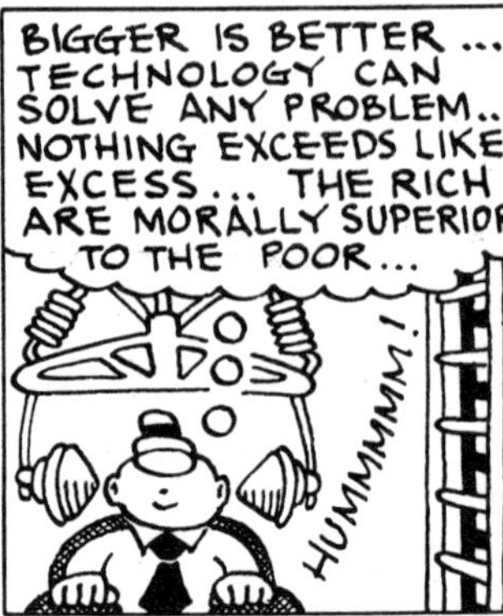
BIGGER IS BETTER ... TECHNOLOGY CAN SOLVE ANY PROBLEM... NOTHING EXCEEDS LIKE EXCESS ... THE RICH ARE MORALLY SUPERIOR TO THE POOR ...
HUMMMMM!

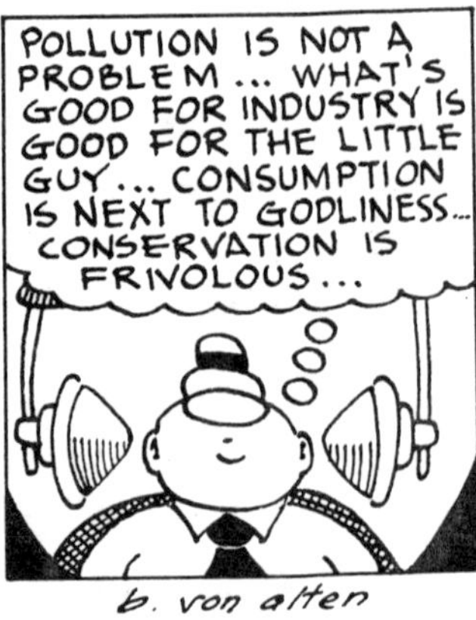
POLLUTION IS NOT A PROBLEM ... WHAT'S GOOD FOR INDUSTRY IS GOOD FOR THE LITTLE GUY ... CONSUMPTION IS NEXT TO GODLINESS... CONSERVATION IS FRIVOLOUS ...

b. von alten

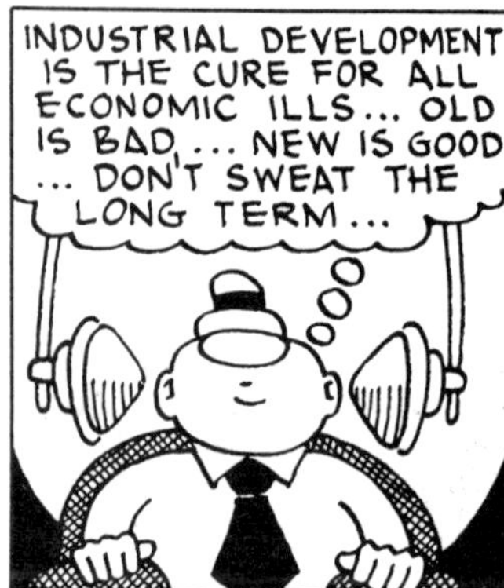
INDUSTRIAL DEVELOPMENT IS THE CURE FOR ALL ECONOMIC ILLS ... OLD IS BAD, ... NEW IS GOOD ... DON'T SWEAT THE LONG TERM ...

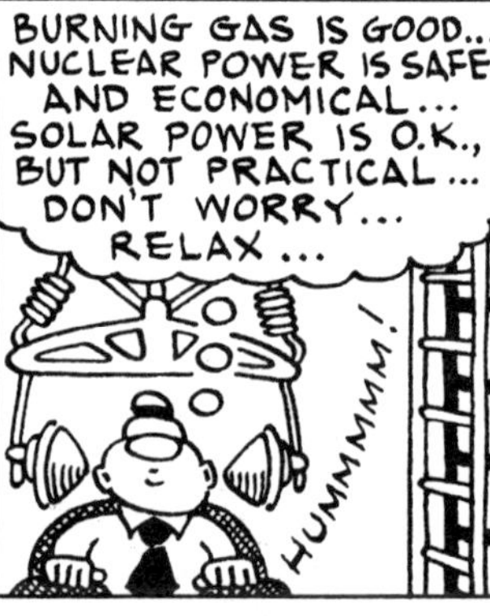
BURNING GAS IS GOOD... NUCLEAR POWER IS SAFE AND ECONOMICAL ... SOLAR POWER IS O.K., BUT NOT PRACTICAL ... DON'T WORRY ... RELAX ...
HUMMMMM!

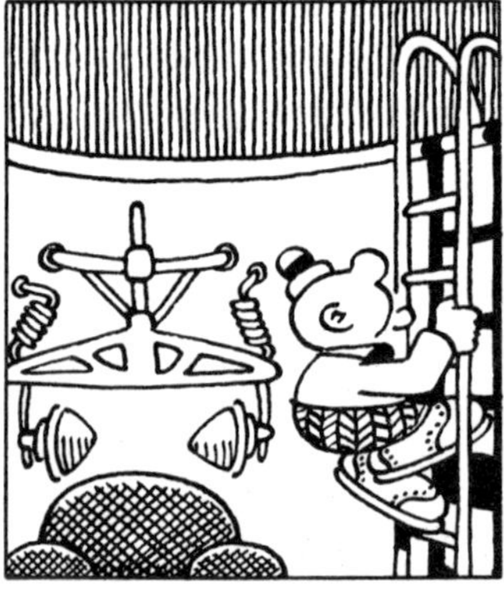

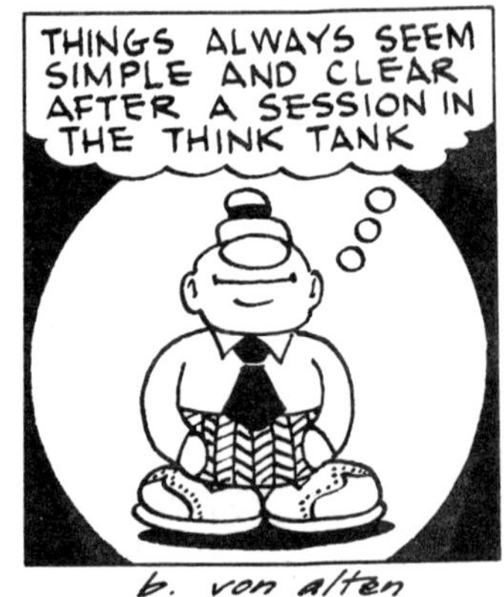
THINGS ALWAYS SEEM SIMPLE AND CLEAR AFTER A SESSION IN THE THINK TANK

b. von alten

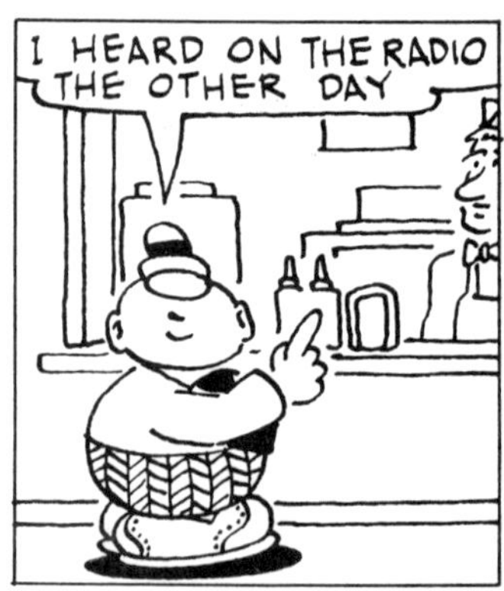
I HEARD ON THE RADIO THE OTHER DAY

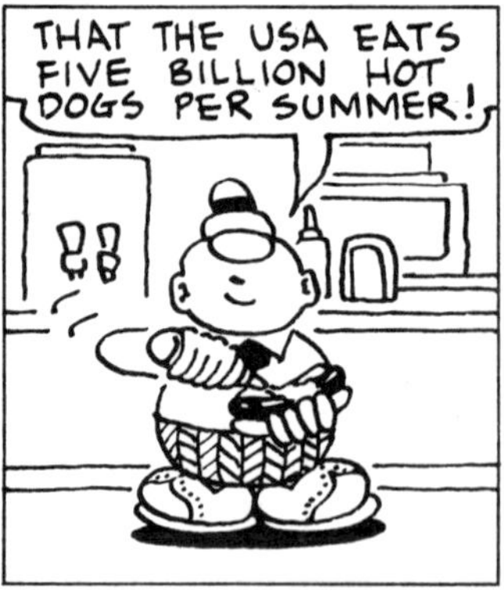
THAT THE USA EATS FIVE BILLION HOT DOGS PER SUMMER!

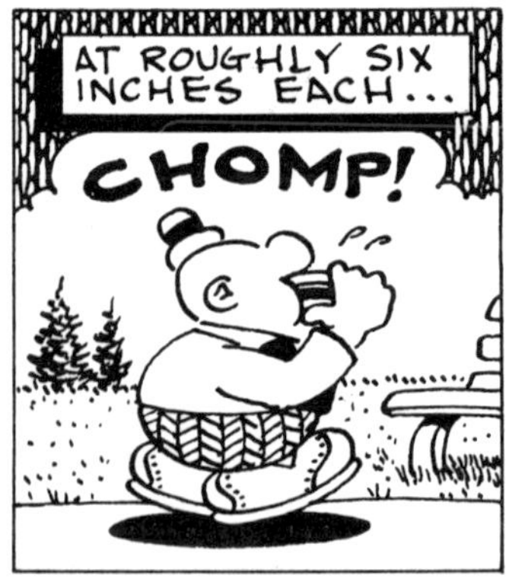
AT ROUGHLY SIX INCHES EACH ...
CHOMP!

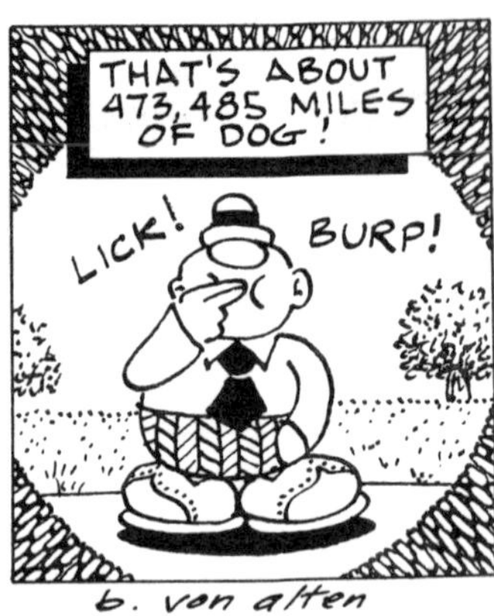
THAT'S ABOUT 473,485 MILES OF DOG!
LICK!
BURP!

b. von alten

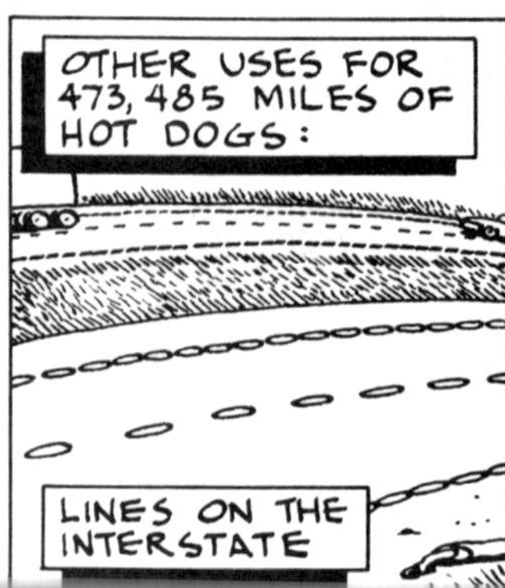
OTHER USES FOR 473,485 MILES OF HOT DOGS:
LINES ON THE INTERSTATE

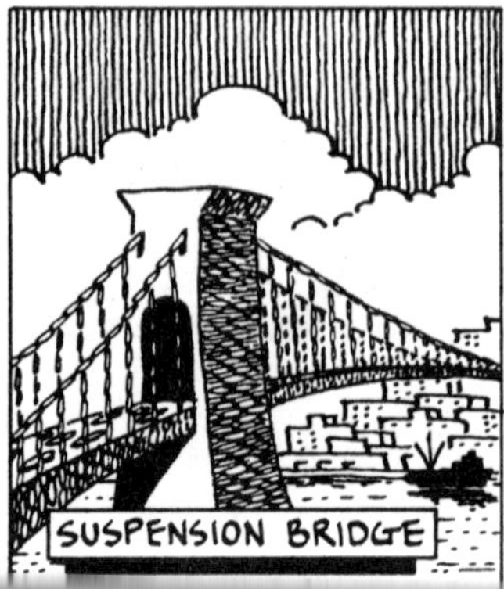
SUSPENSION BRIDGE

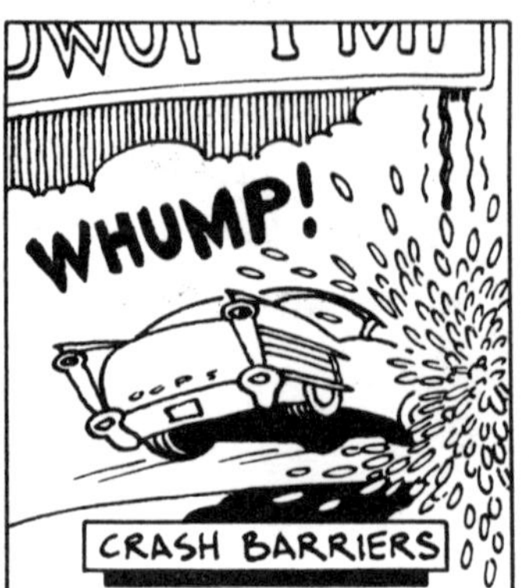
WHUMP!
CRASH BARRIERS

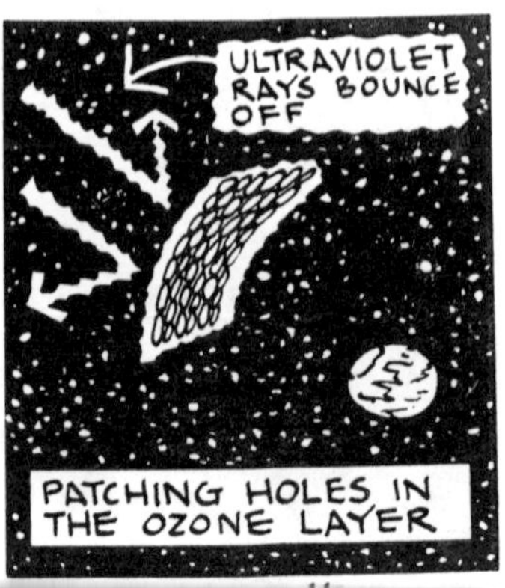
ULTRAVIOLET RAYS BOUNCE OFF
PATCHING HOLES IN THE OZONE LAYER

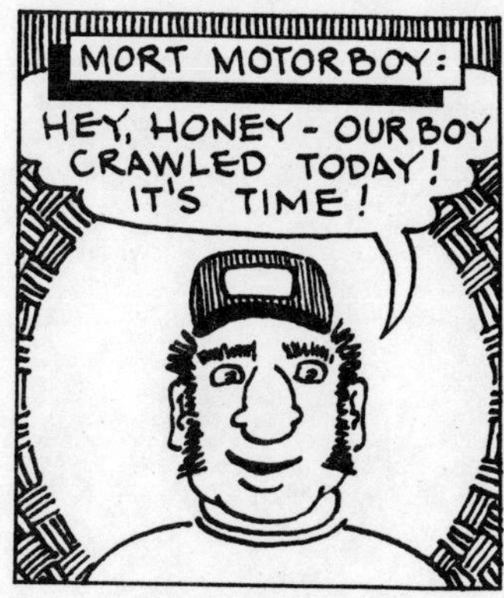
MORT MOTORBOY:
HEY, HONEY - OUR BOY CRAWLED TODAY! IT'S TIME!

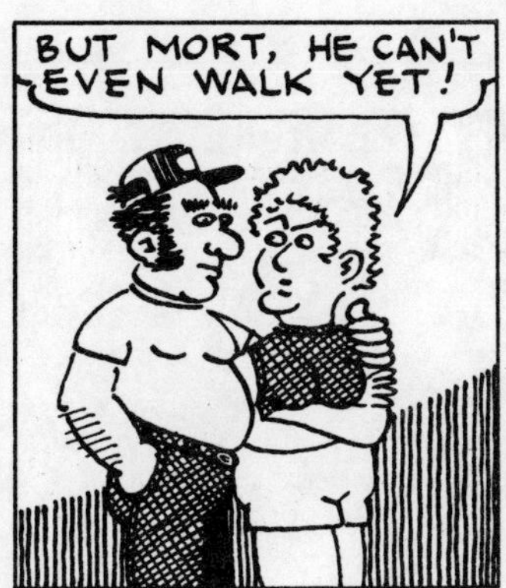
BUT MORT, HE CAN'T EVEN WALK YET!

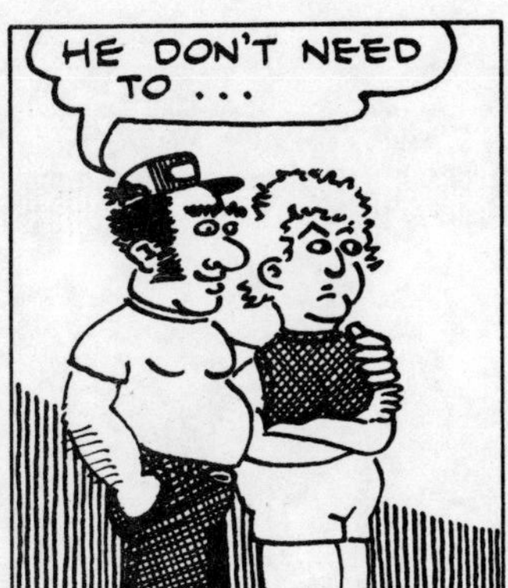
HE DON'T NEED TO ...

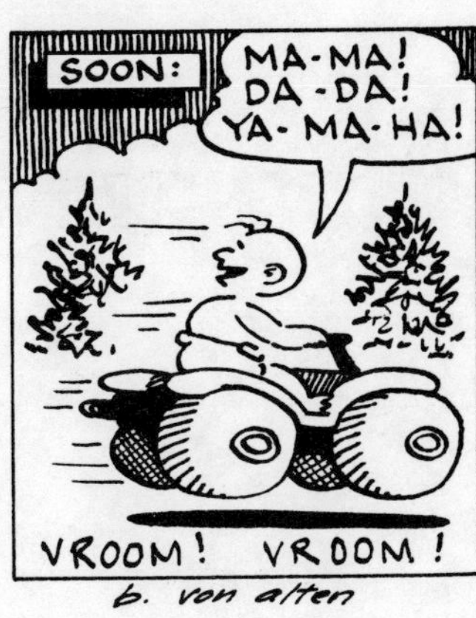
SOON:
MA-MA! DA-DA! YA-MA-HA!
VROOM! VROOM!
b. von alten

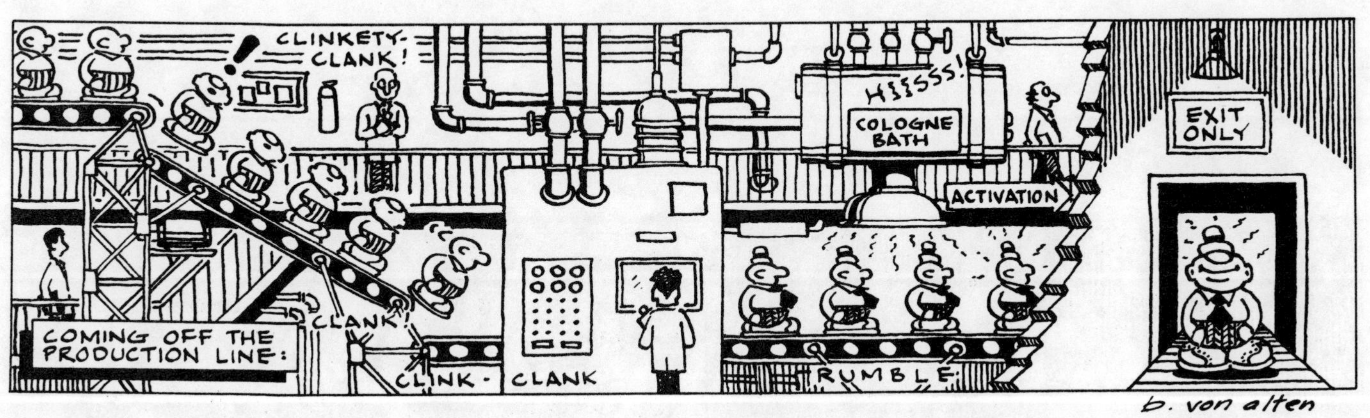
CLINKETY-CLANK!
HISSSS!
COLOGNE BATH
ACTIVATION
EXIT ONLY
CLANK!
COMING OFF THE PRODUCTION LINE:
CLINK-
CLANK
RUMBLE
b. von alten

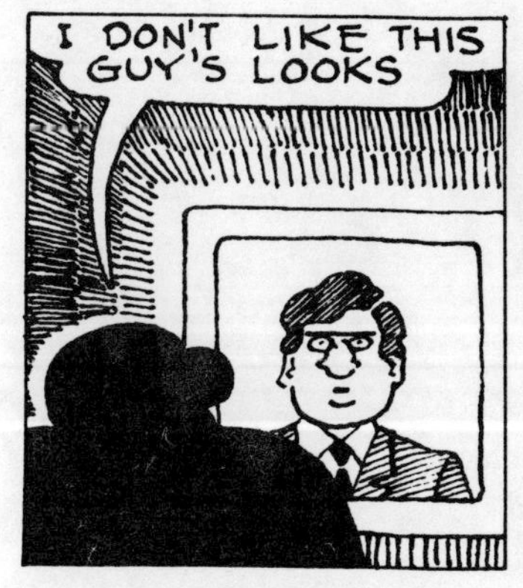
I DON'T LIKE THIS GUY'S LOOKS

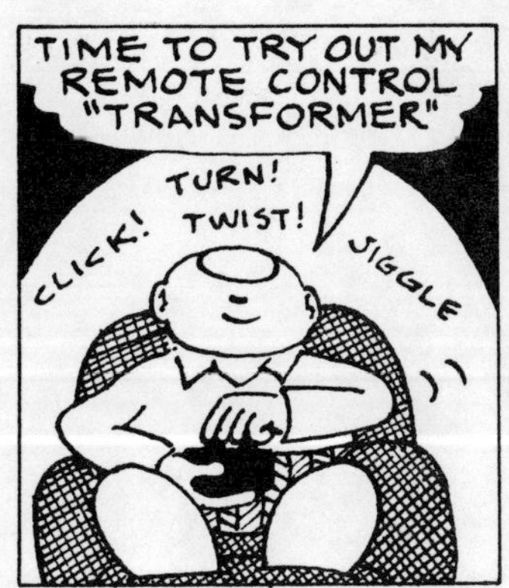
TIME TO TRY OUT MY REMOTE CONTROL "TRANSFORMER"
TURN!
TWIST!
CLICK!
JIGGLE

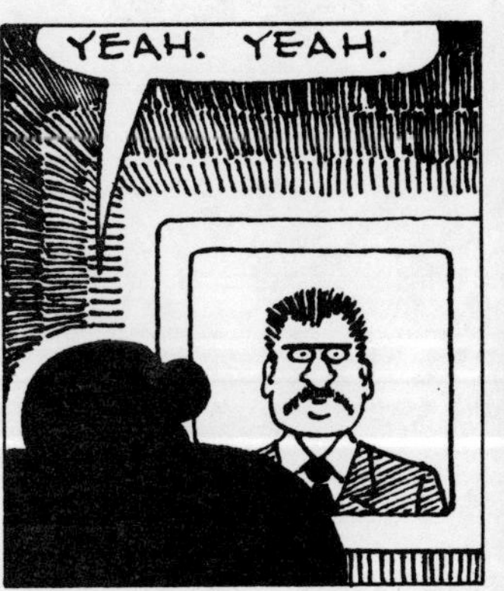
YEAH. YEAH.

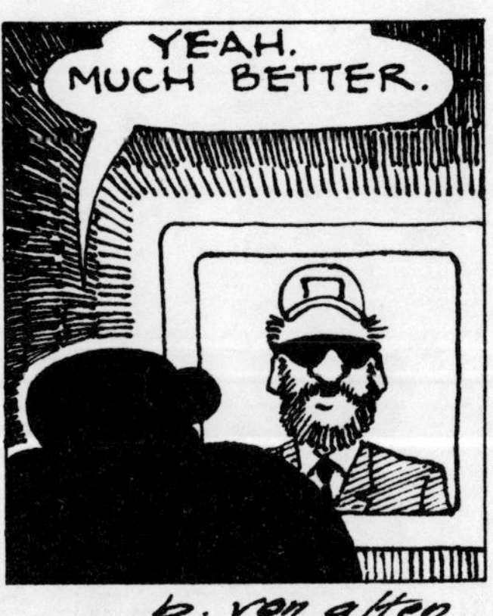
YEAH. MUCH BETTER.
b. von alten

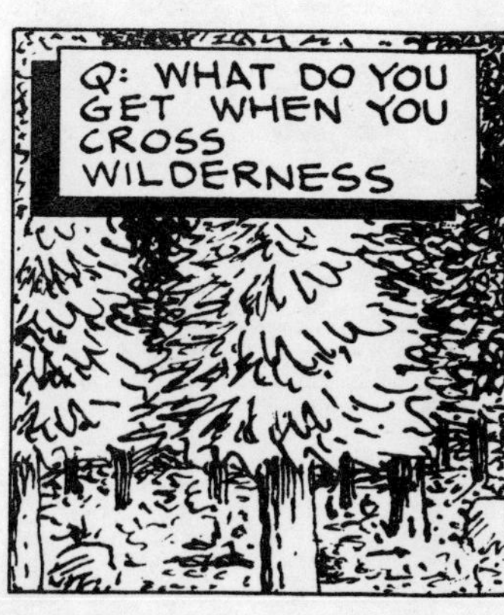
Q: WHAT DO YOU GET WHEN YOU CROSS WILDERNESS

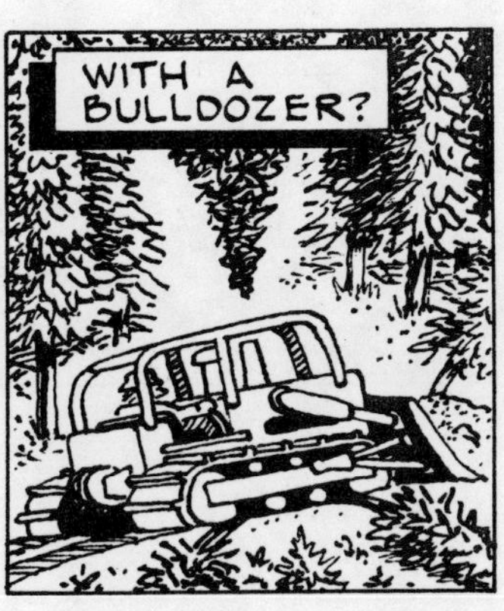
WITH A BULLDOZER?

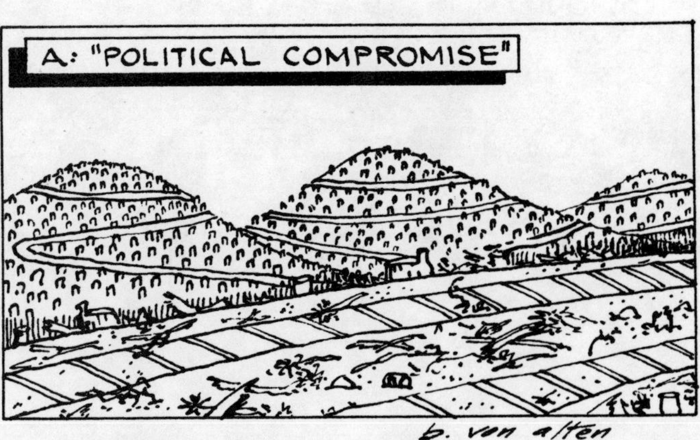
A: "POLITICAL COMPROMISE"
b. von alten

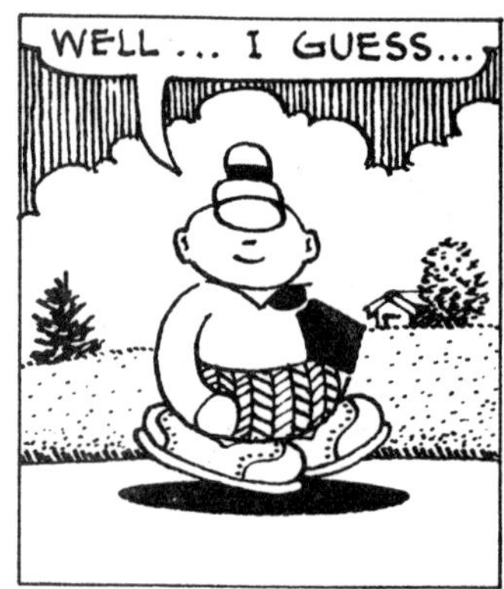
WELL ... I GUESS...

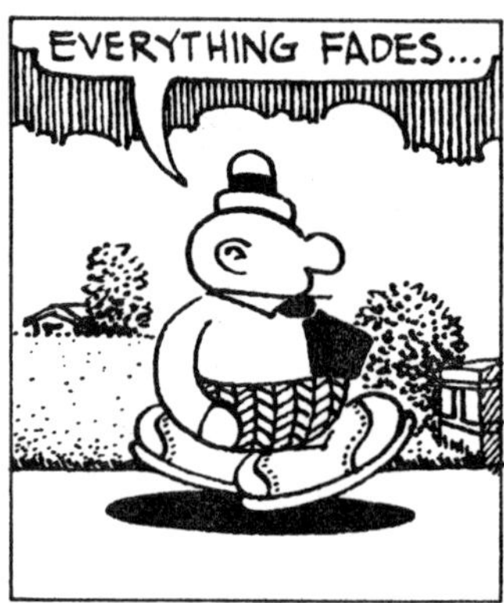
EVERYTHING FADES...

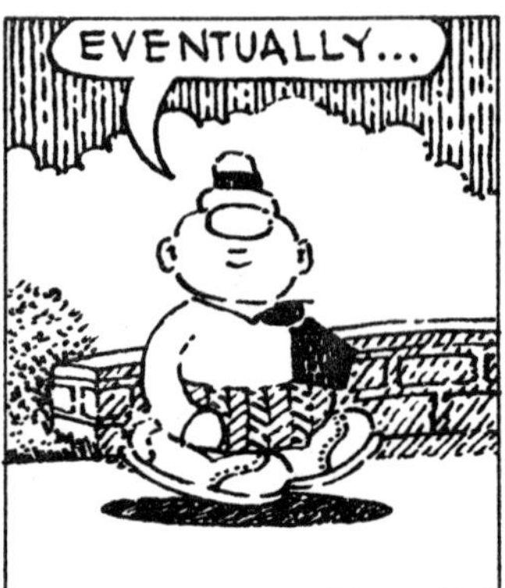
EVENTUALLY...

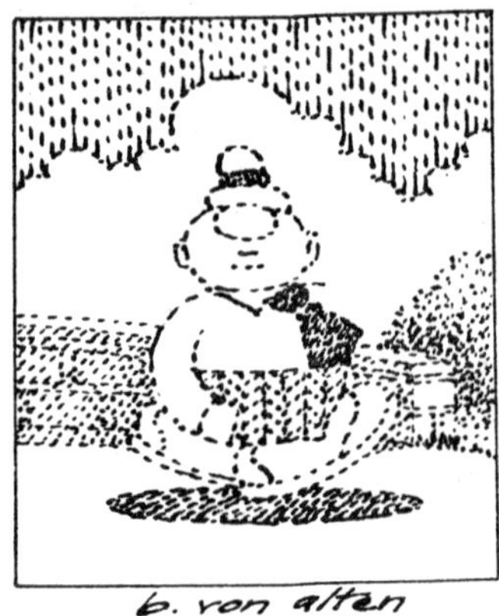

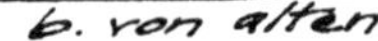
b. von alten

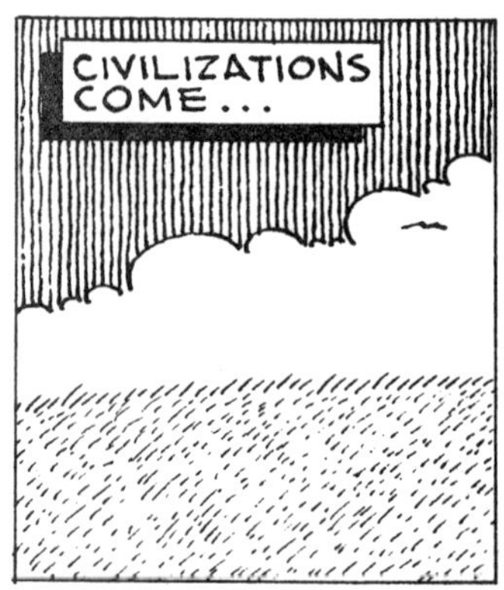
CIVILIZATIONS
COME...

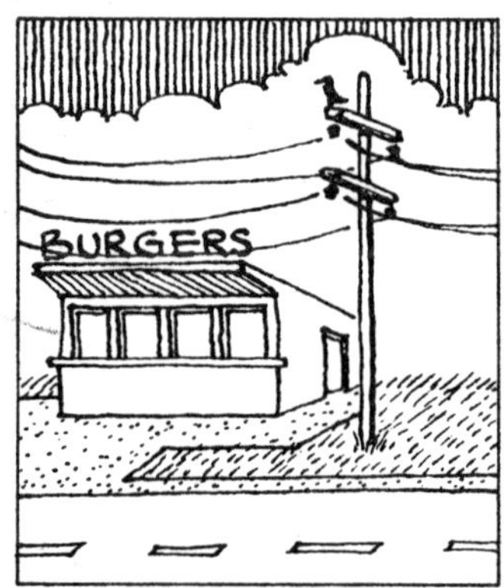
BURGERS

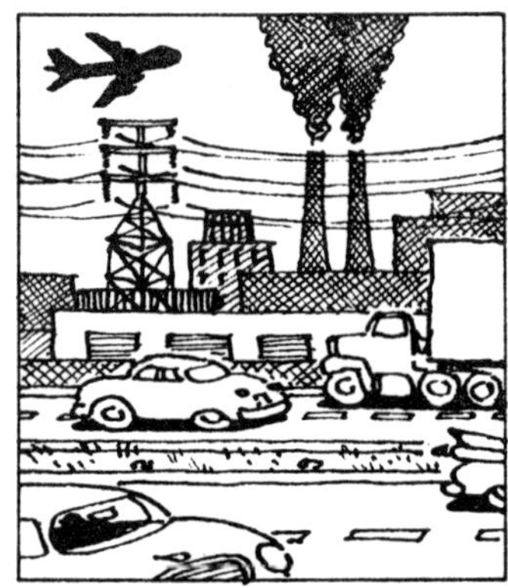

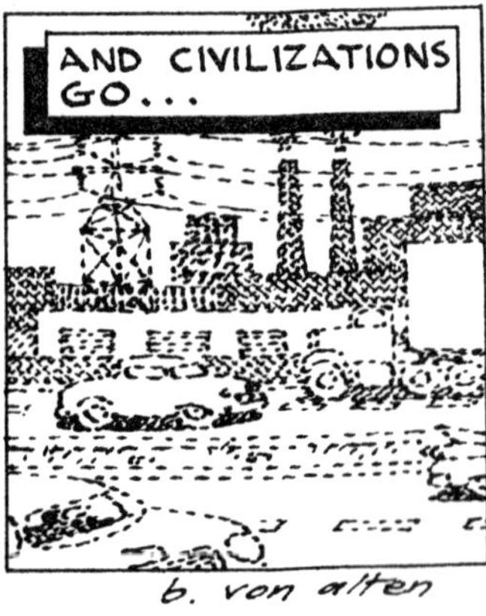
AND CIVILIZATIONS
GO...

b. von alten

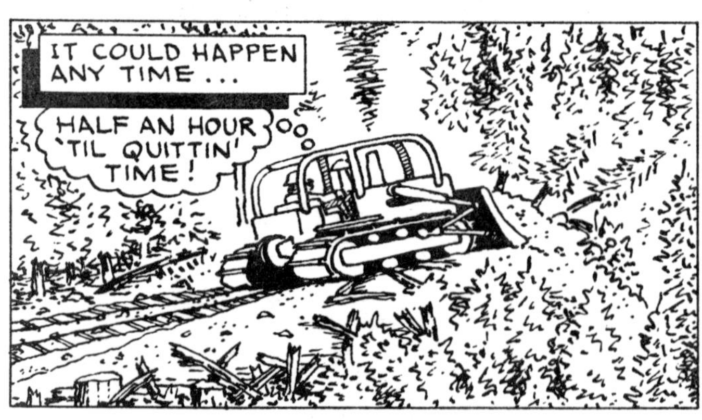
IT COULD HAPPEN
ANY TIME...
HALF AN HOUR
'TIL QUITTIN'
TIME!

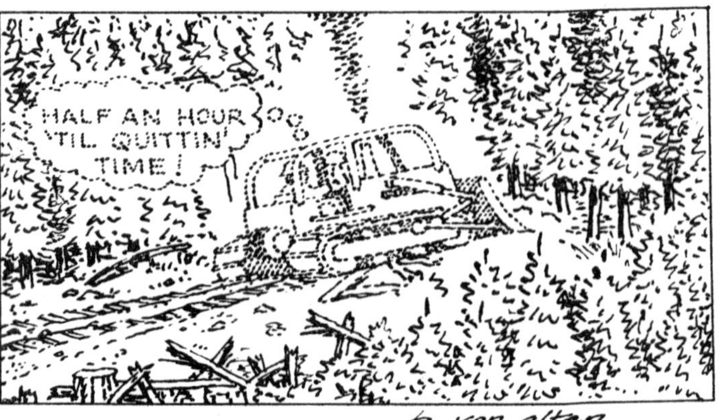
HALF AN HOUR
'TIL QUITTIN'
TIME!

b. von alten

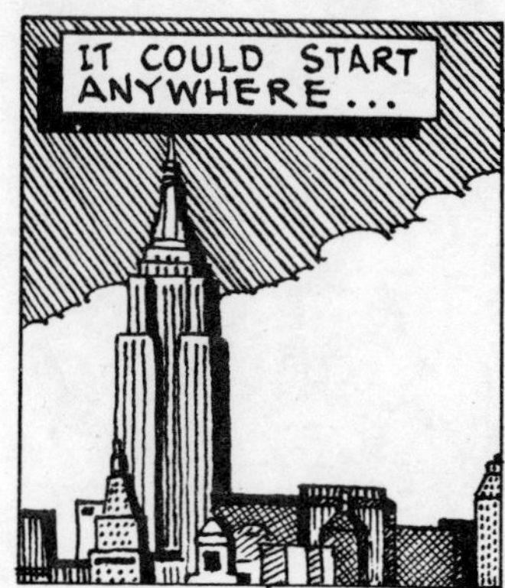
IT COULD START ANYWHERE...

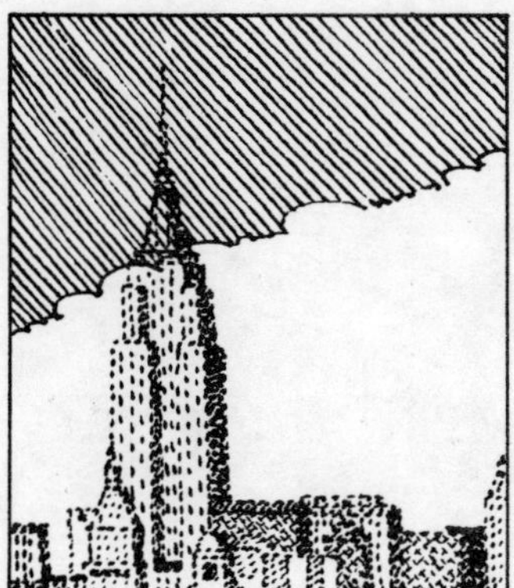

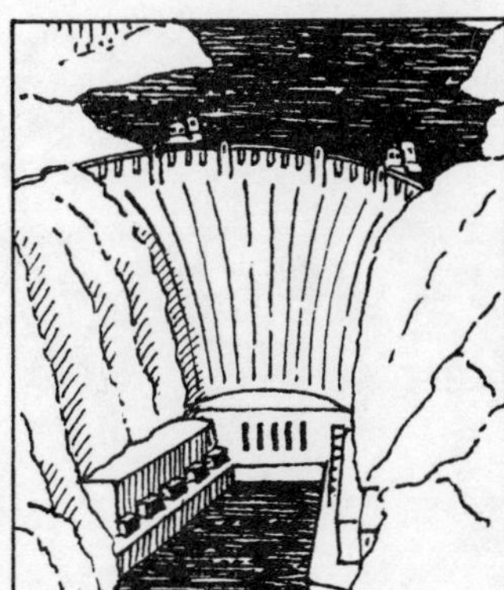

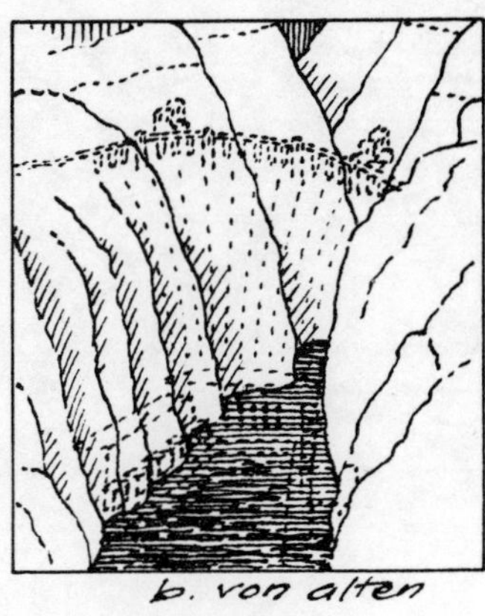
b. von alten

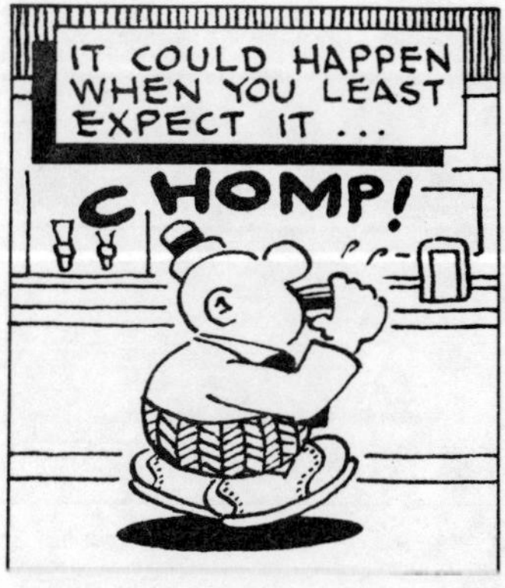
IT COULD HAPPEN WHEN YOU LEAST EXPECT IT...
CHOMP!

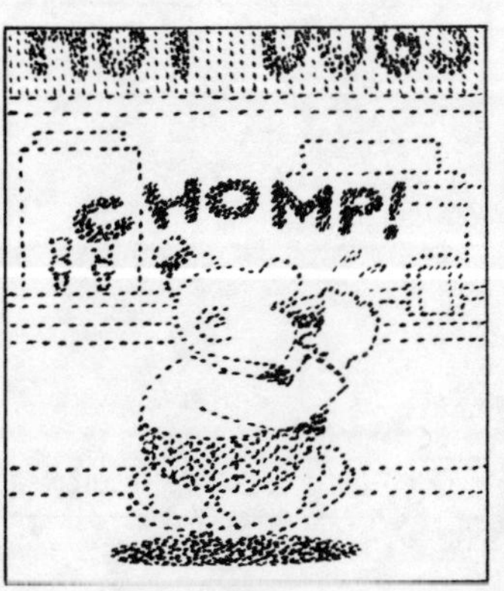
CHOMP!

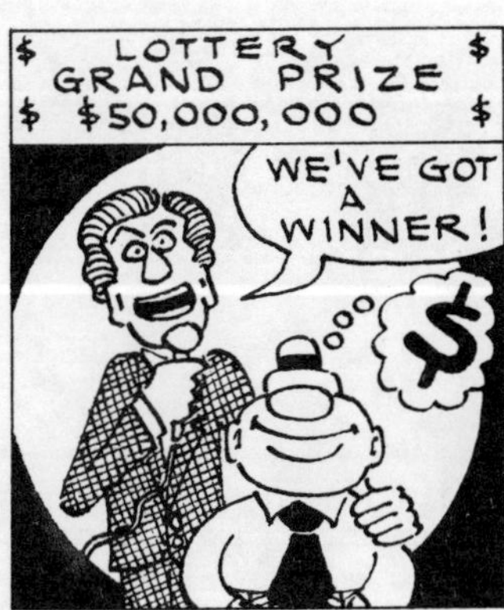
$ LOTTERY GRAND PRIZE $50,000,000 $
WE'VE GOT A WINNER!
$

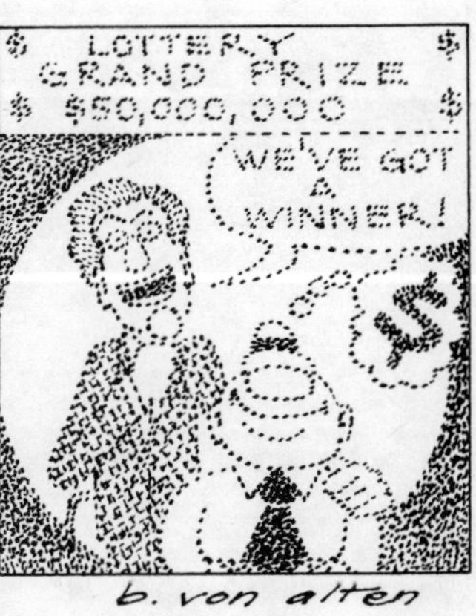
$ LOTTERY GRAND PRIZE $50,000,000 $
WE'VE GOT A WINNER!
$
b. von alten

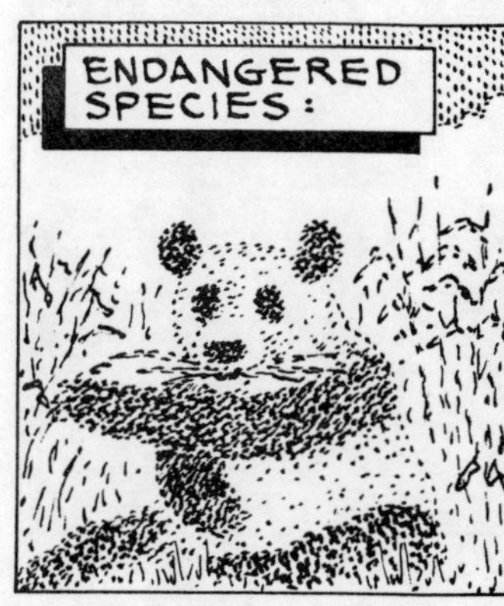
ENDANGERED SPECIES:

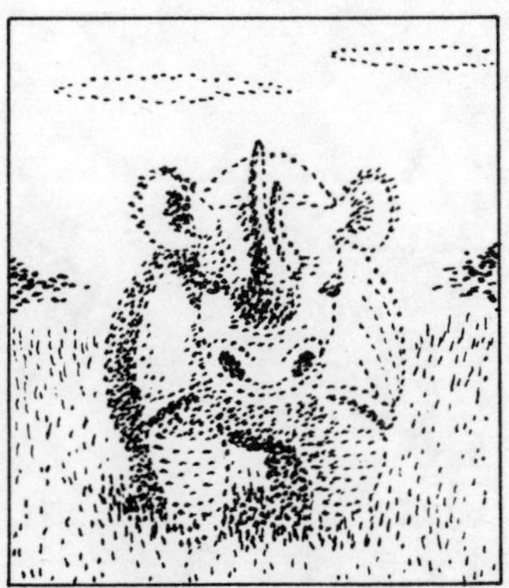

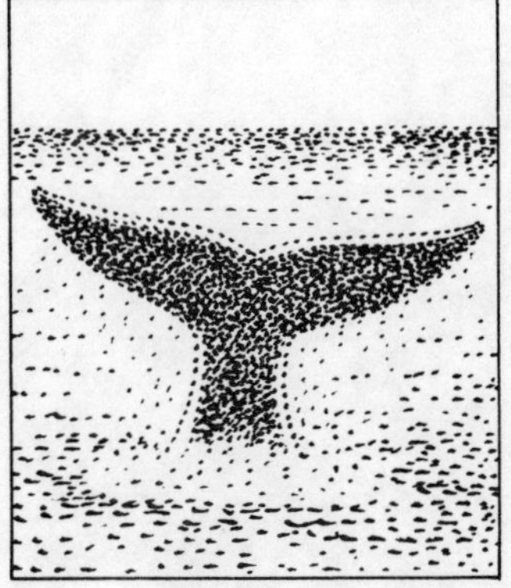

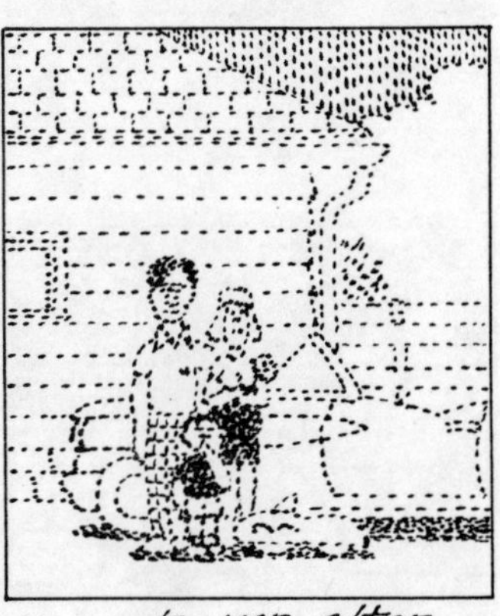
b. von alten

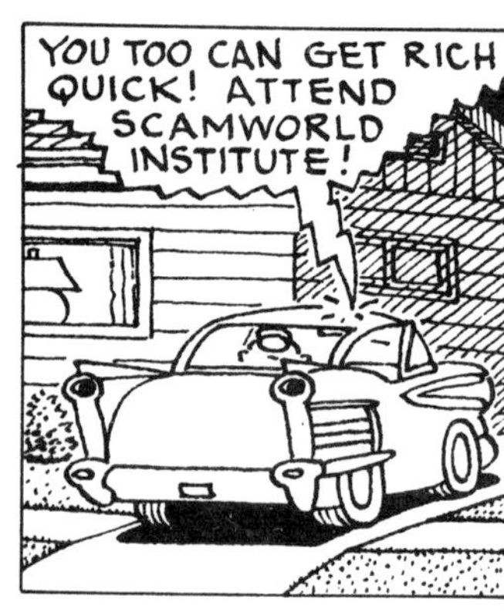
YOU TOO CAN GET RICH QUICK! ATTEND SCAMWORLD INSTITUTE!
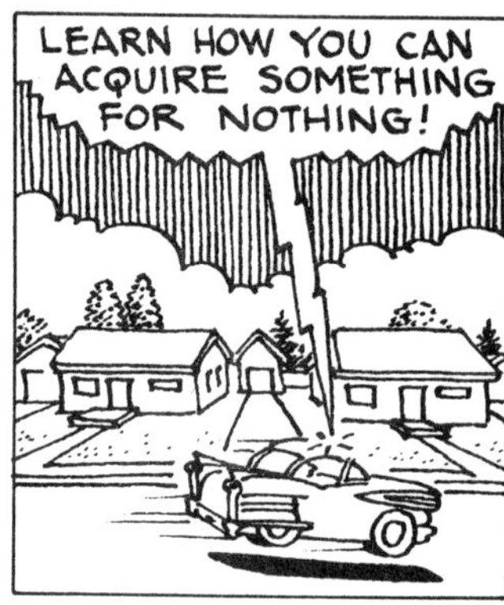
LEARN HOW YOU CAN ACQUIRE SOMETHING FOR NOTHING!
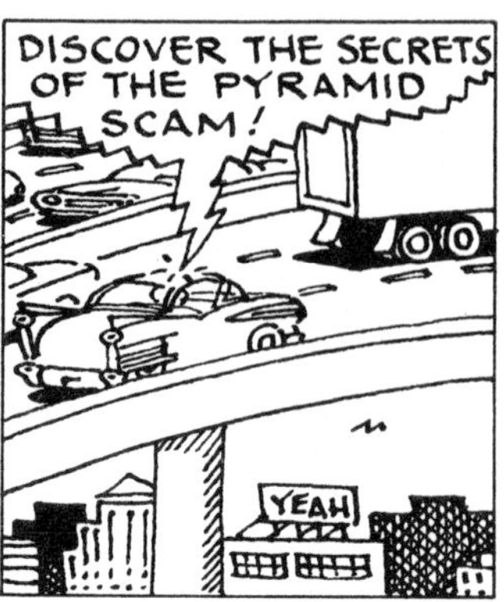
DISCOVER THE SECRETS OF THE PYRAMID SCAM!
YEAH
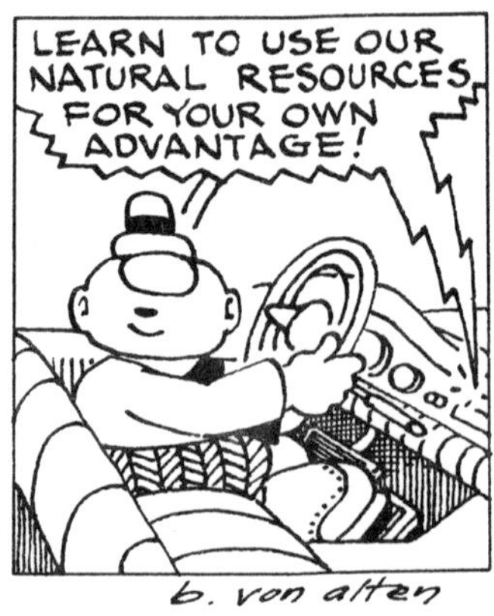
LEARN TO USE OUR NATURAL RESOURCES FOR YOUR OWN ADVANTAGE!

b. von alten

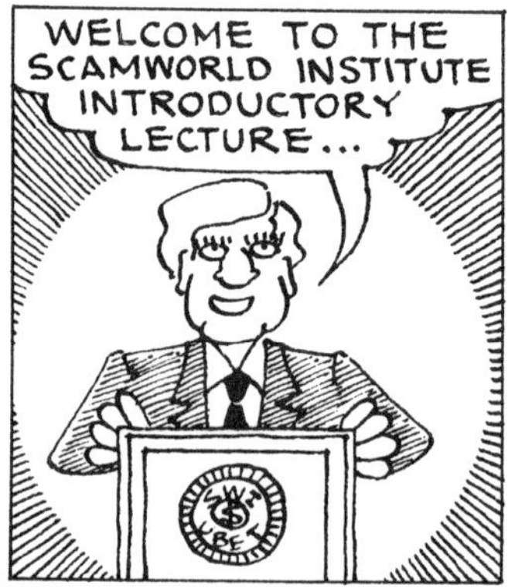
WELCOME TO THE SCAMWORLD INSTITUTE INTRODUCTORY LECTURE...
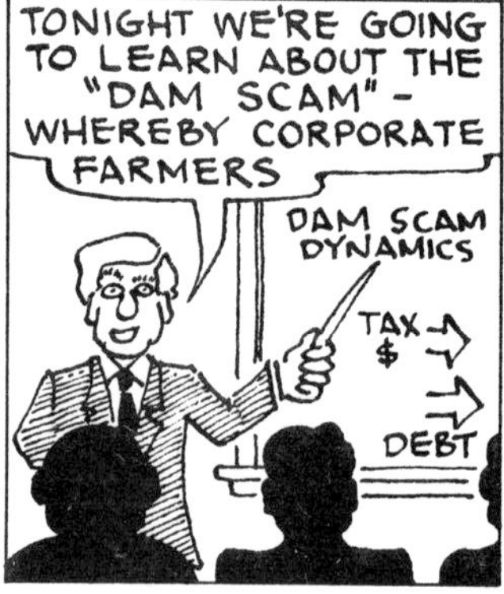
TONIGHT WE'RE GOING TO LEARN ABOUT THE "DAM SCAM" - WHEREBY CORPORATE FARMERS
DAM SCAM DYNAMICS
TAX $
DEBT
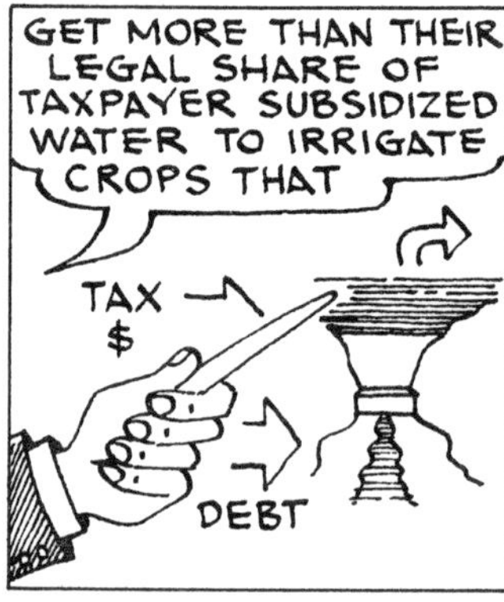
GET MORE THAN THEIR LEGAL SHARE OF TAXPAYER SUBSIDIZED WATER TO IRRIGATE CROPS THAT
TAX $
DEBT
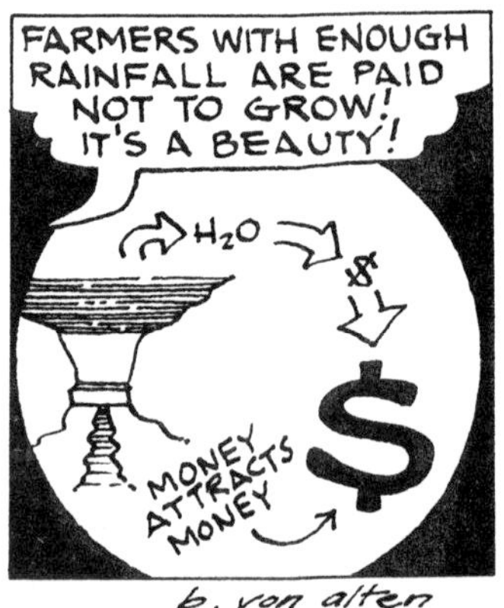
FARMERS WITH ENOUGH RAINFALL ARE PAID NOT TO GROW! IT'S A BEAUTY!
H2O
$
MONEY ATTRACTS MONEY

b. von alten

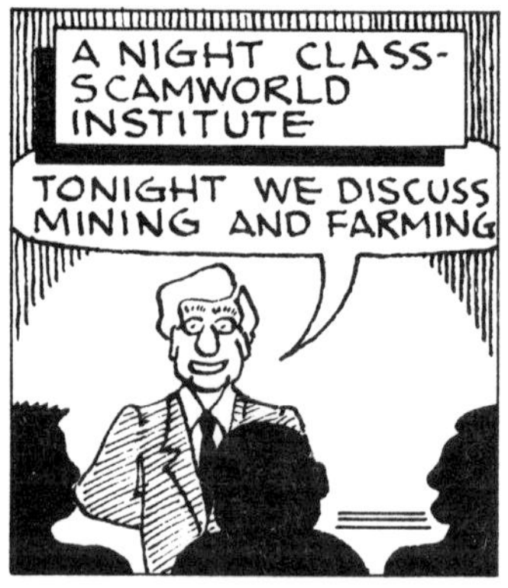
A NIGHT CLASS- SCAMWORLD INSTITUTE
TONIGHT WE DISCUSS MINING AND FARMING
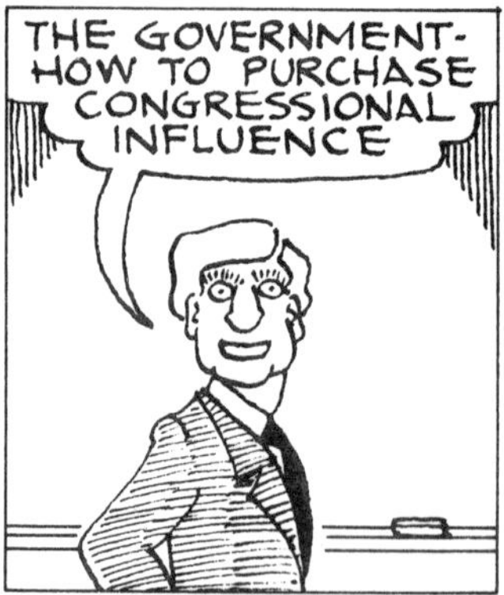
THE GOVERNMENT- HOW TO PURCHASE CONGRESSIONAL INFLUENCE
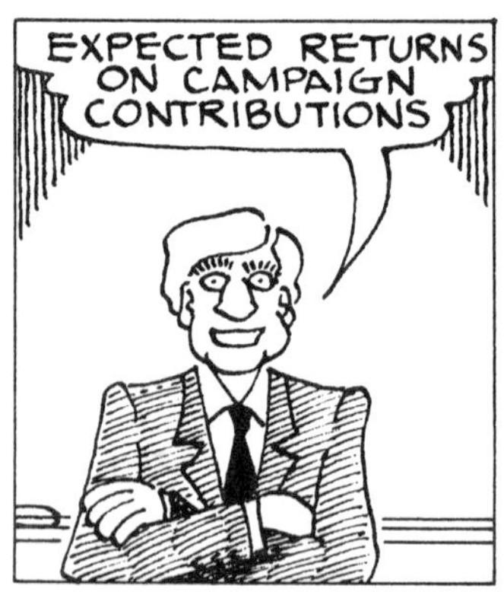
EXPECTED RETURNS ON CAMPAIGN CONTRIBUTIONS
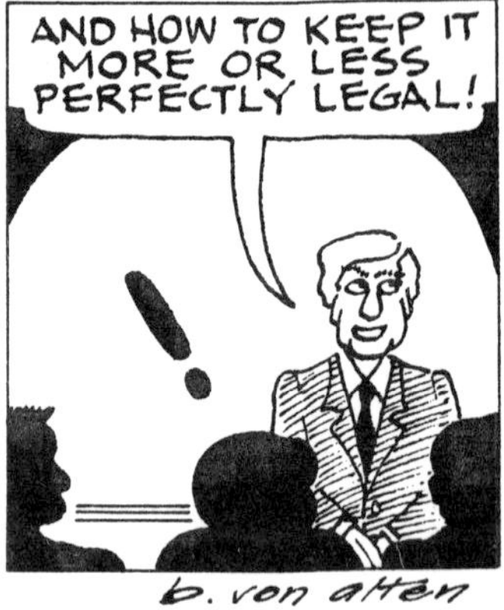
AND HOW TO KEEP IT MORE OR LESS PERFECTLY LEGAL!
!

b. von alten

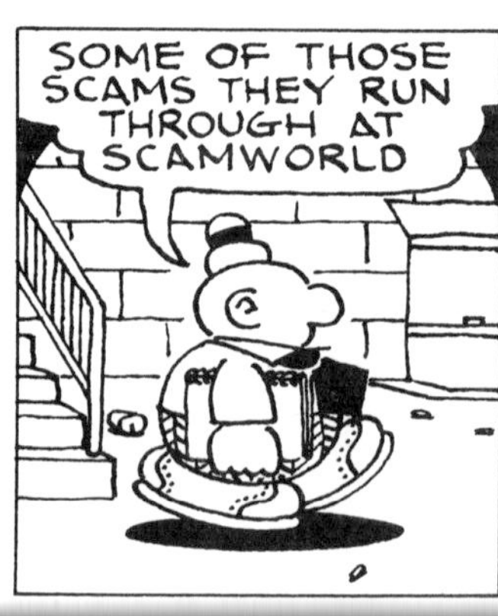
SOME OF THOSE SCAMS THEY RUN THROUGH AT SCAMWORLD
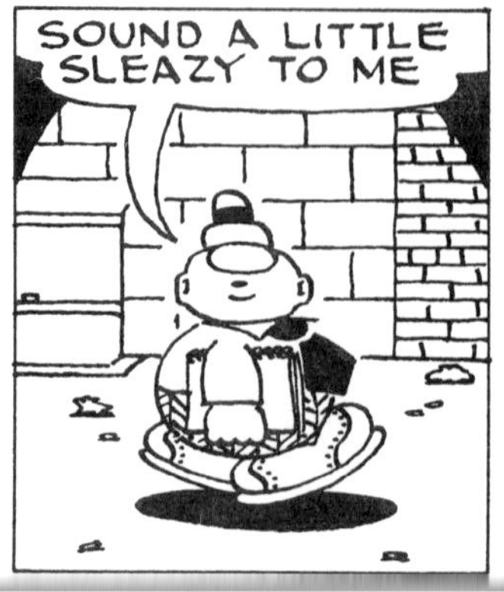
SOUND A LITTLE SLEAZY TO ME
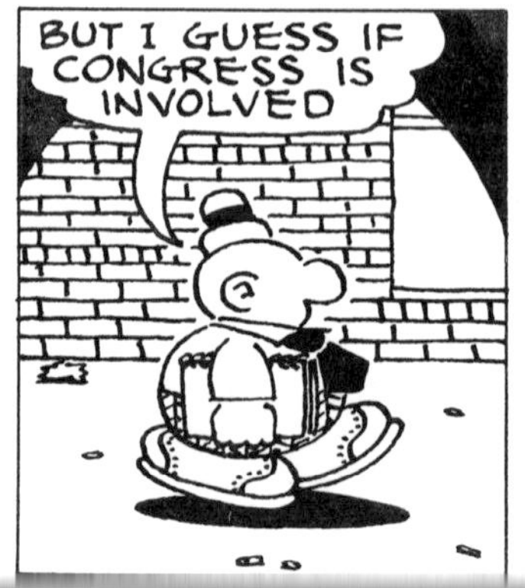
BUT I GUESS IF CONGRESS IS INVOLVED
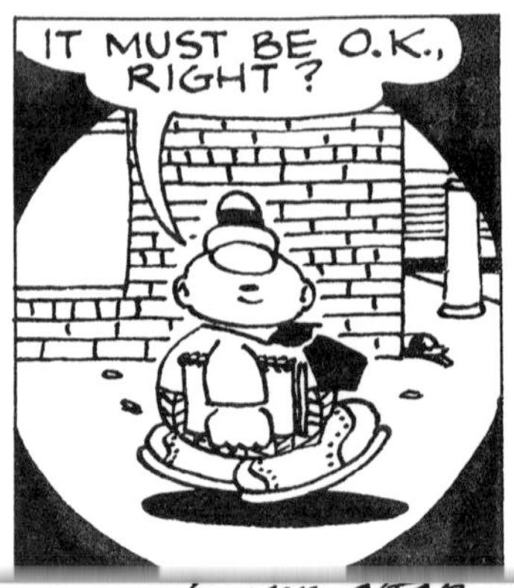
IT MUST BE O.K., RIGHT?

b. von alten

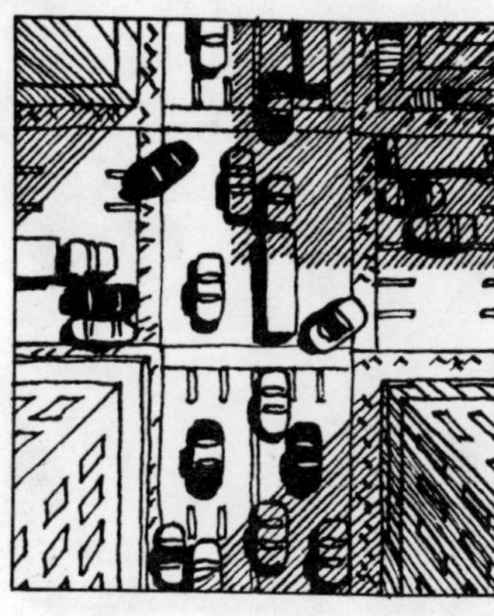
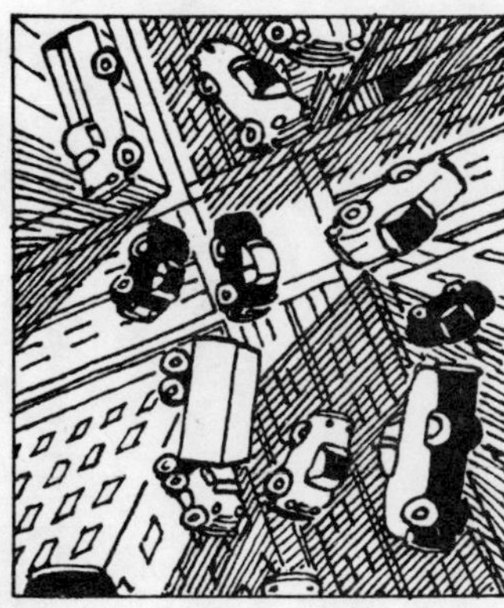
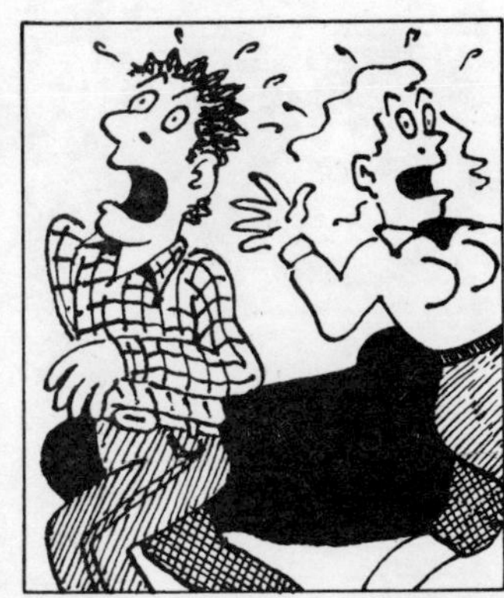
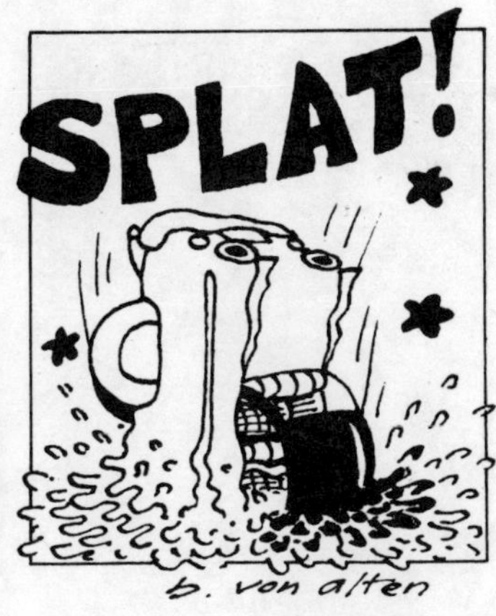
SPLAT!

b. von alten

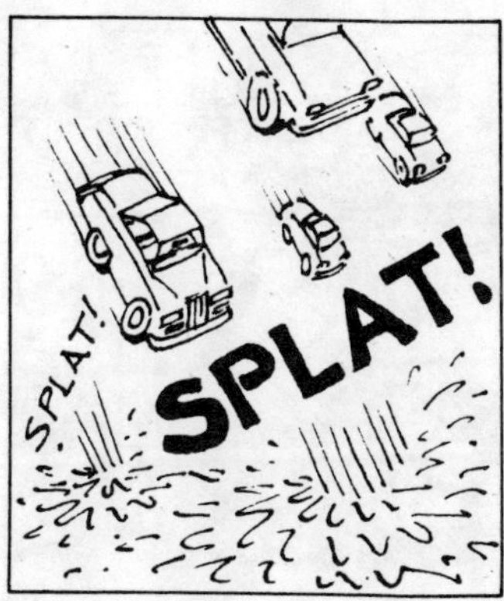
SPLAT!
SPLAT!
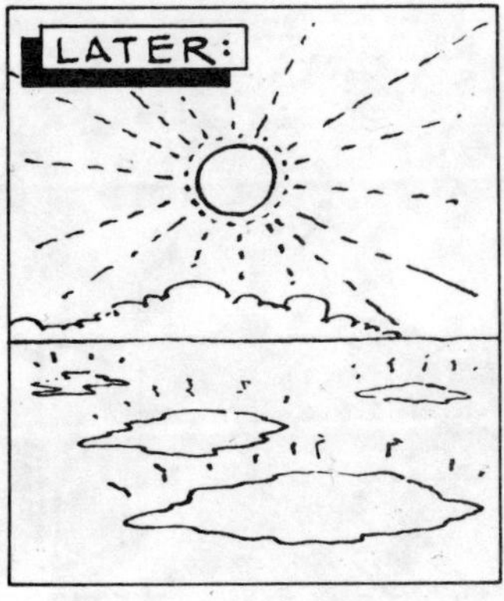
LATER:
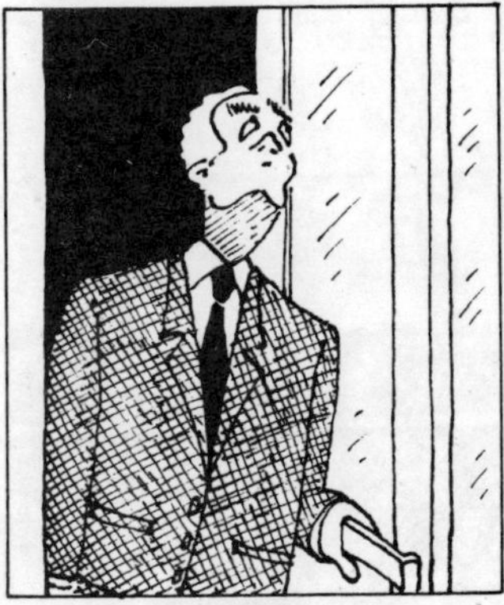
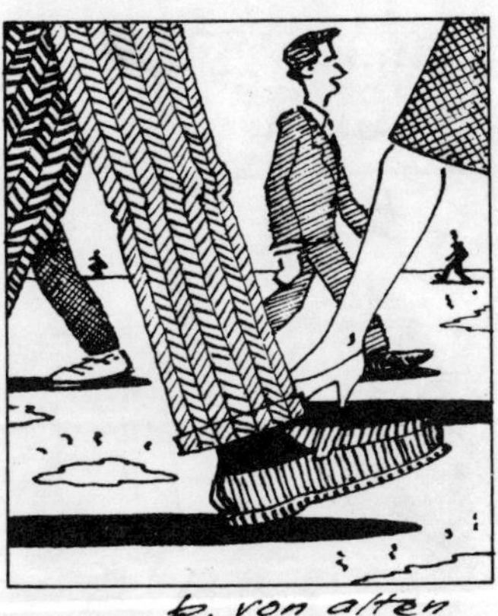

b. von alten

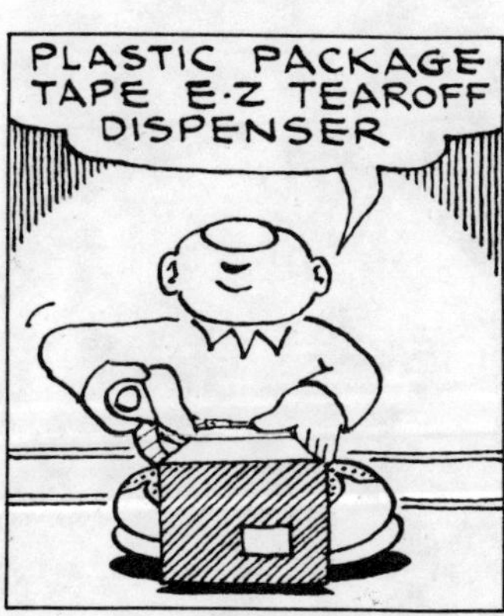
PLASTIC PACKAGE TAPE E-Z TEAROFF DISPENSER
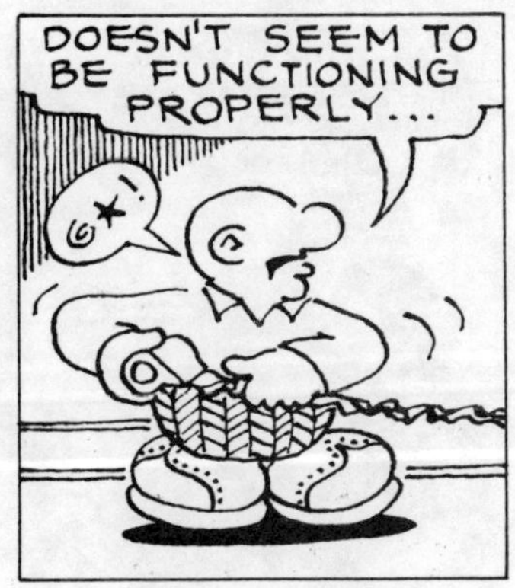
DOESN'T SEEM TO BE FUNCTIONING PROPERLY...
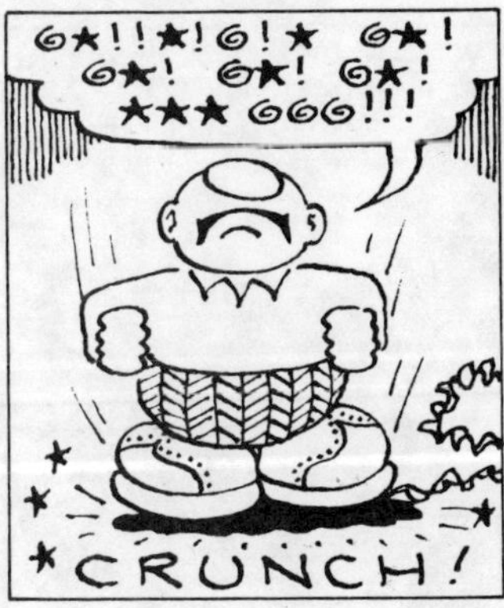
CRUNCH!
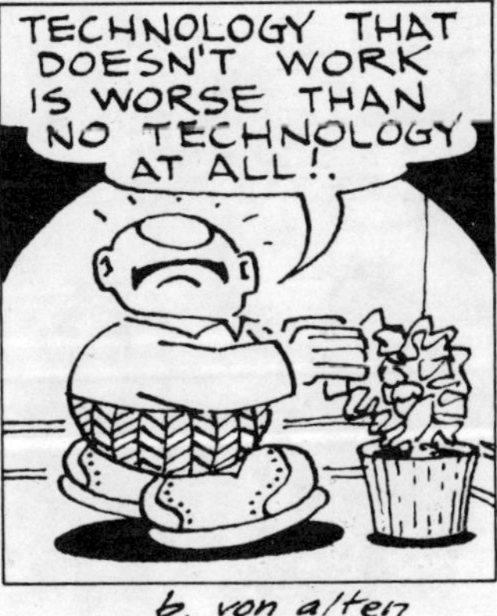
TECHNOLOGY THAT DOESN'T WORK IS WORSE THAN NO TECHNOLOGY AT ALL!.

b. von alten

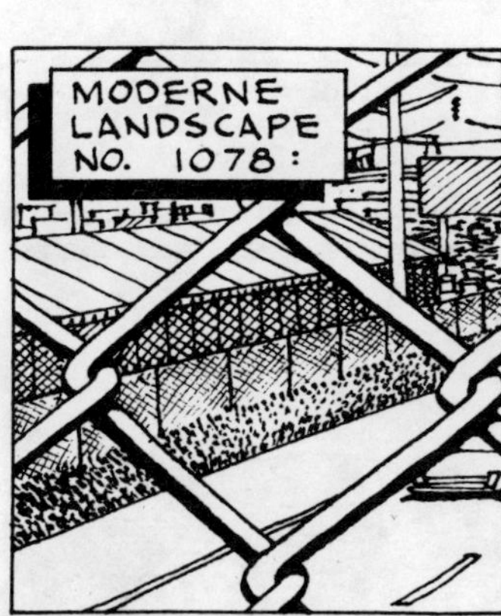
MODERNE LANDSCAPE NO. 1078:
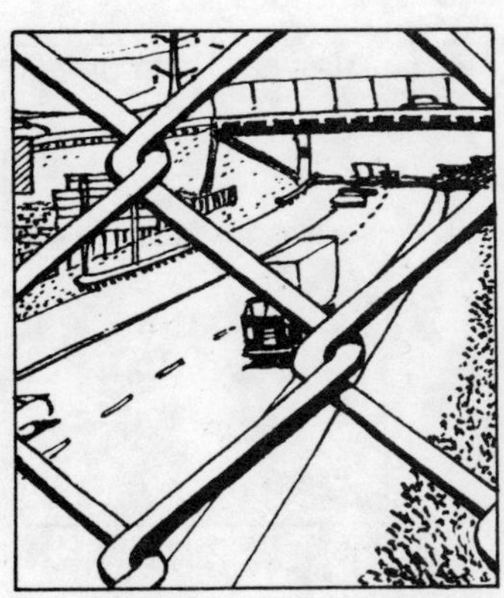
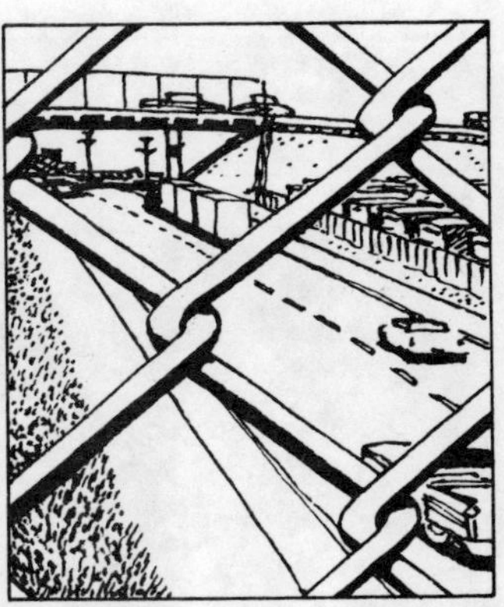
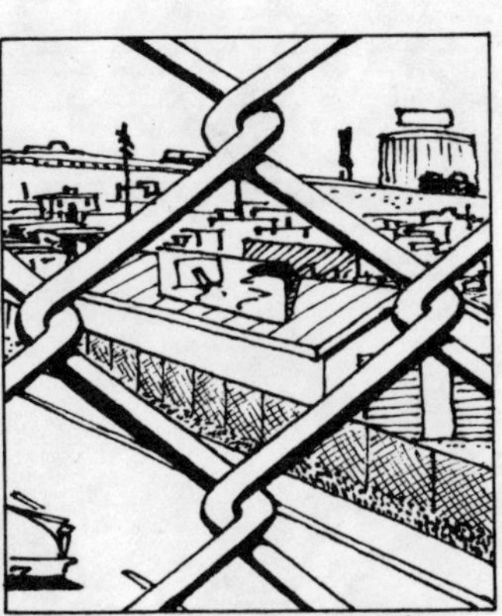

b. von alten

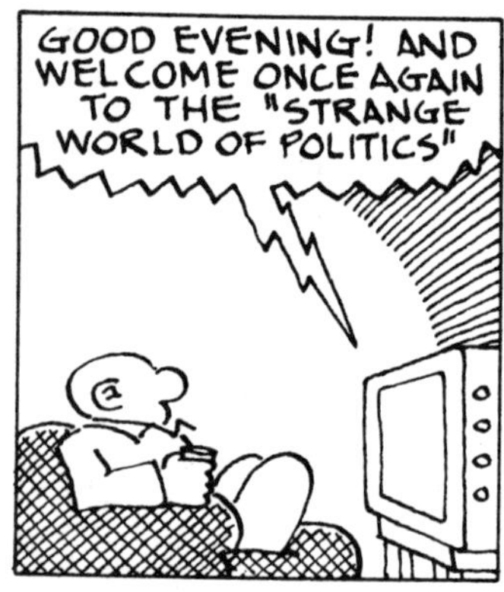
GOOD EVENING! AND WELCOME ONCE AGAIN TO THE "STRANGE WORLD OF POLITICS"
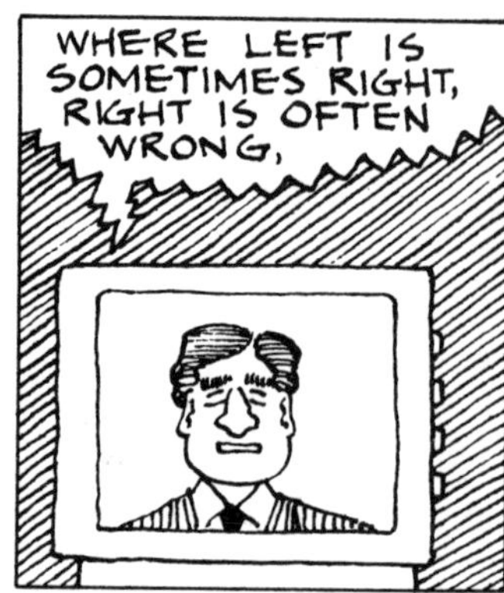
WHERE LEFT IS SOMETIMES RIGHT, RIGHT IS OFTEN WRONG,
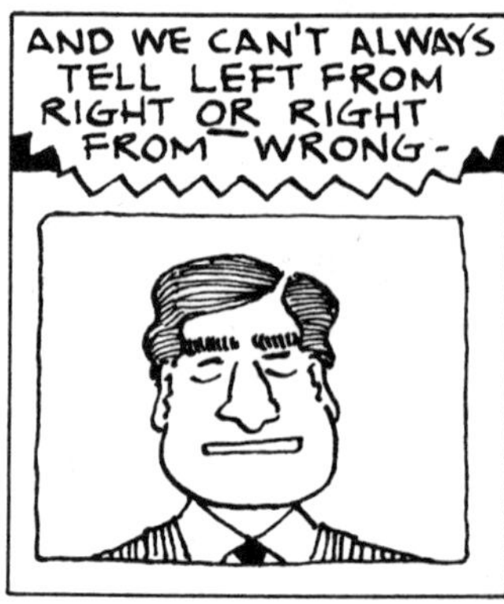
AND WE CAN'T ALWAYS TELL LEFT FROM RIGHT OR RIGHT FROM WRONG -
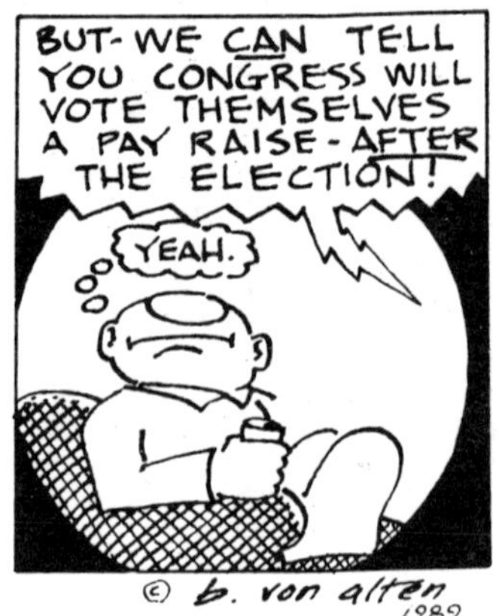
BUT- WE CAN TELL YOU CONGRESS WILL VOTE THEMSELVES A PAY RAISE - AFTER THE ELECTION!
YEAH.

© b. von alten 1989

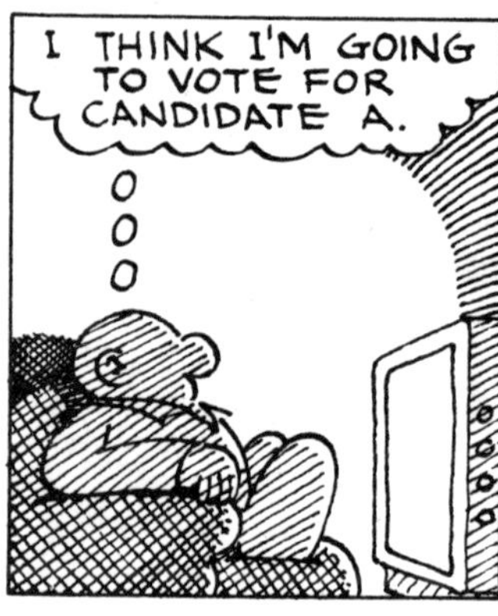
I THINK I'M GOING TO VOTE FOR CANDIDATE A.
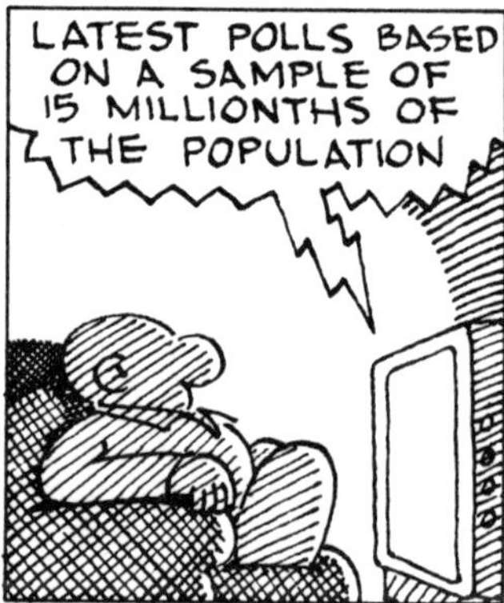
LATEST POLLS BASED ON A SAMPLE OF 15 MILLIONTHS OF THE POPULATION
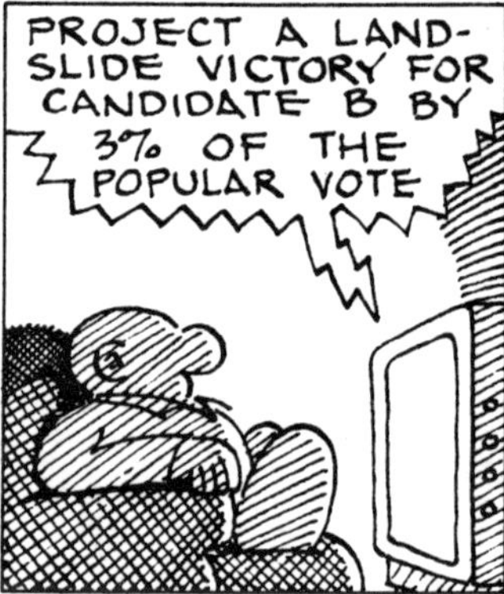
PROJECT A LAND-SLIDE VICTORY FOR CANDIDATE B BY 3% OF THE POPULAR VOTE
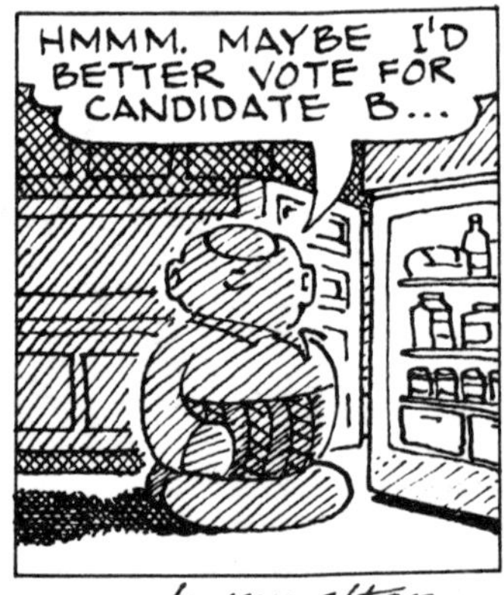
HMMM. MAYBE I'D BETTER VOTE FOR CANDIDATE B...

b. von alten

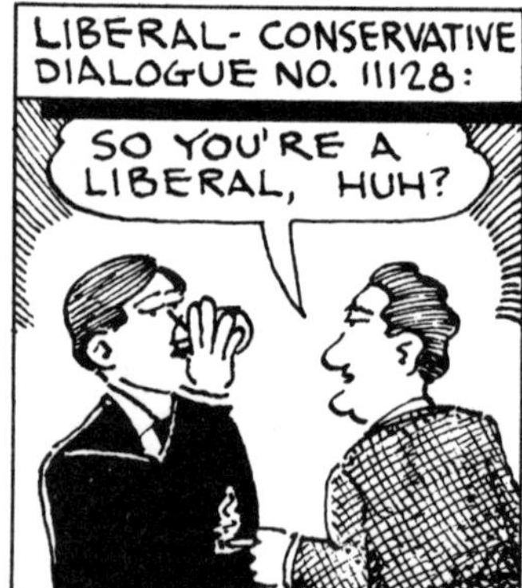
LIBERAL- CONSERVATIVE DIALOGUE NO. 11128:
SO YOU'RE A LIBERAL, HUH?
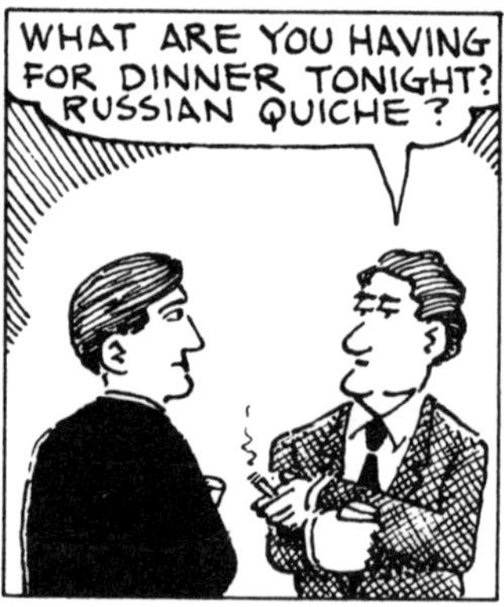
WHAT ARE YOU HAVING FOR DINNER TONIGHT? RUSSIAN QUICHE?
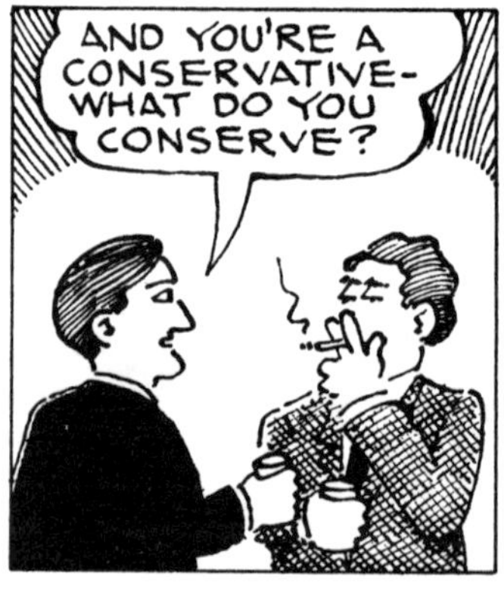
AND YOU'RE A CONSERVATIVE- WHAT DO YOU CONSERVE?
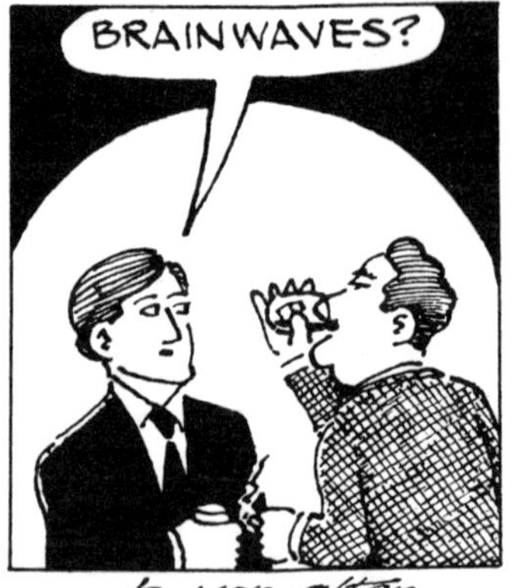
BRAINWAVES?

b. von alten

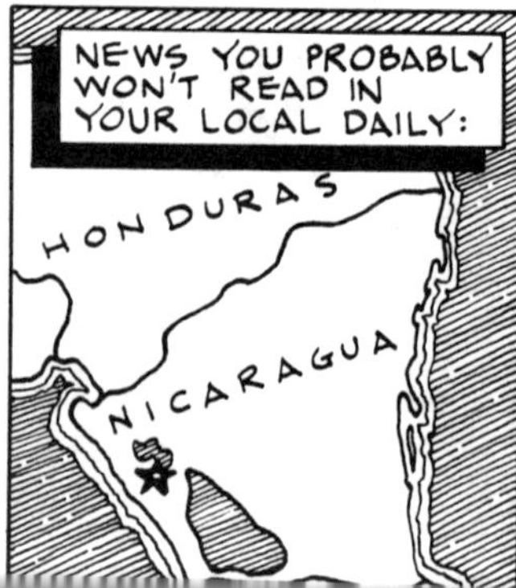
NEWS YOU PROBABLY WON'T READ IN YOUR LOCAL DAILY:
HONDURAS
NICARAGUA
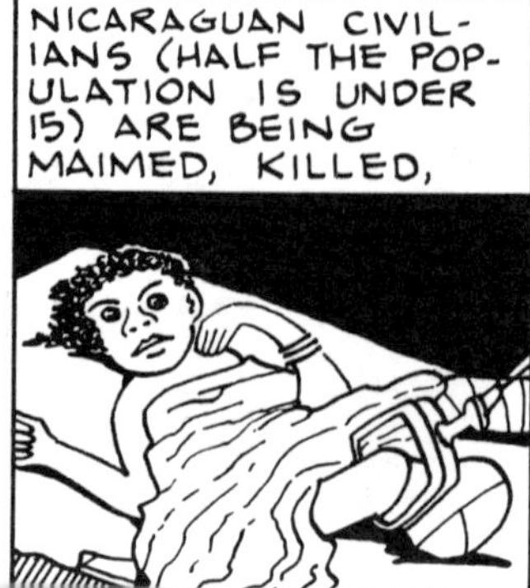
NICARAGUAN CIVIL-IANS (HALF THE POP-ULATION IS UNDER 15) ARE BEING MAIMED, KILLED,
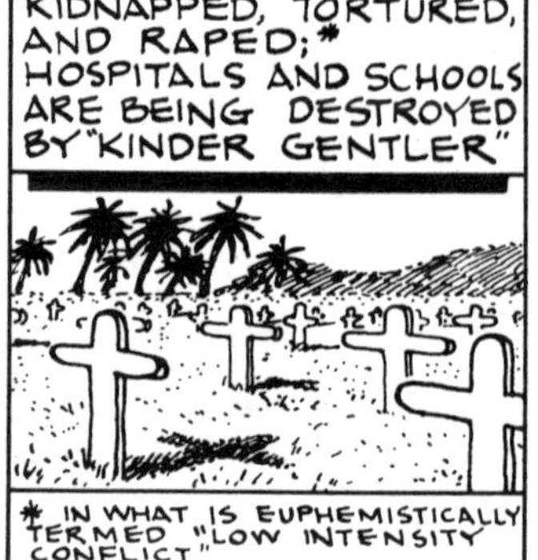
KIDNAPPED, TORTURED, AND RAPED;* HOSPITALS AND SCHOOLS ARE BEING DESTROYED BY "KINDER GENTLER"
* IN WHAT IS EUPHEMISTICALLY TERMED "LOW INTENSITY CONFLICT"
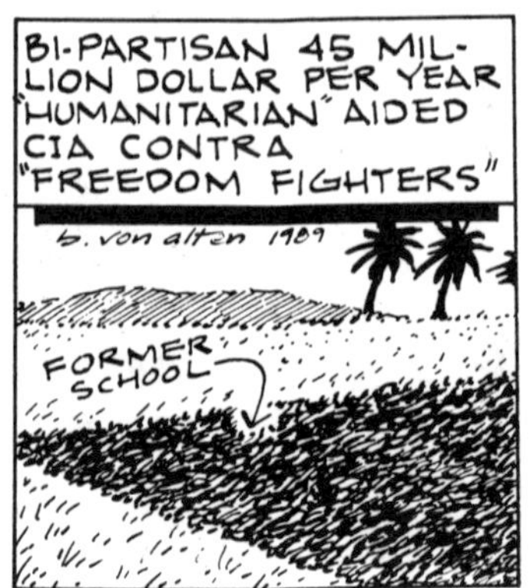
BI-PARTISAN 45 MIL-LION DOLLAR PER YEAR "HUMANITARIAN" AIDED CIA CONTRA "FREEDOM FIGHTERS"
b. von alten 1989
FORMER SCHOOL

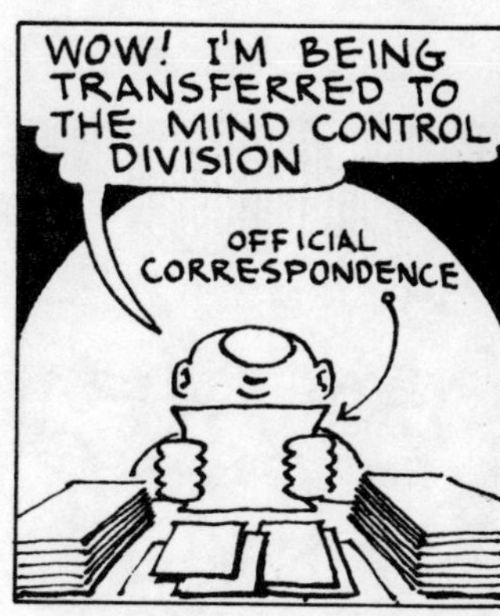
WOW! I'M BEING TRANSFERRED TO THE MIND CONTROL DIVISION
OFFICIAL CORRESPONDENCE

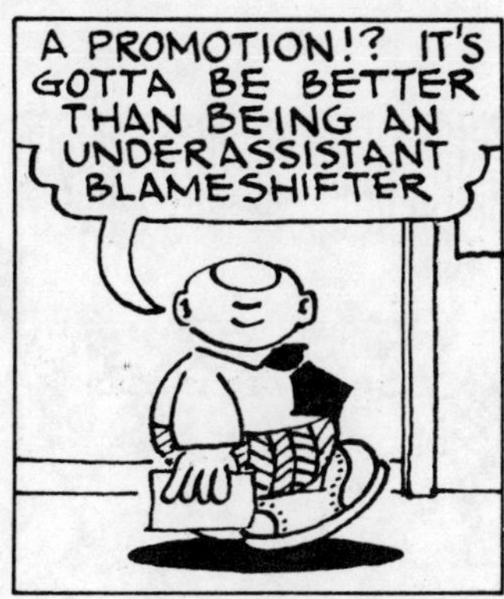
A PROMOTION!? IT'S GOTTA BE BETTER THAN BEING AN UNDERASSISTANT BLAMESHIFTER

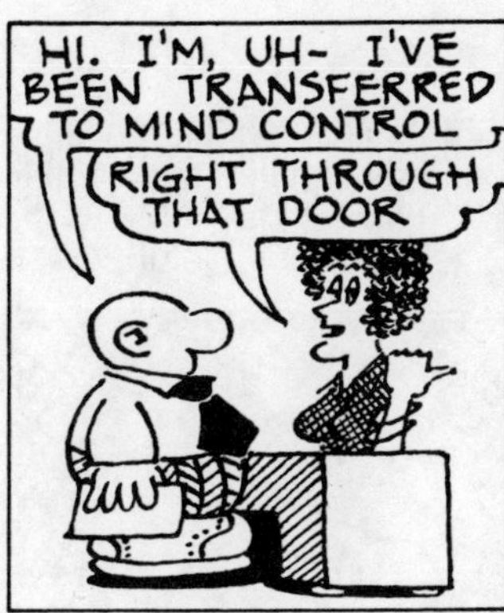
HI. I'M, UH- I'VE BEEN TRANSFERRED TO MIND CONTROL
RIGHT THROUGH THAT DOOR

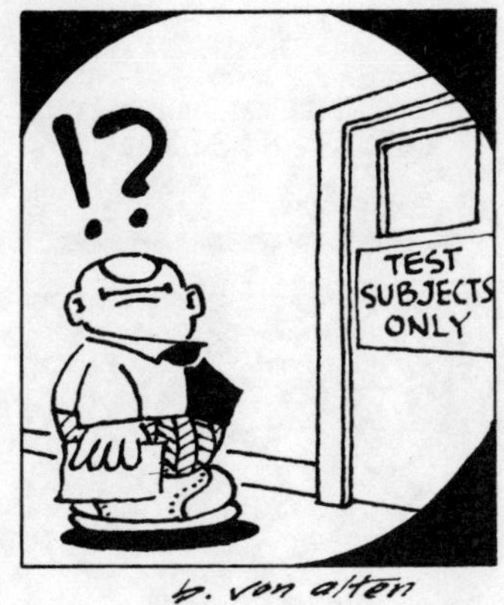
!?
TEST SUBJECTS ONLY
b. von alten

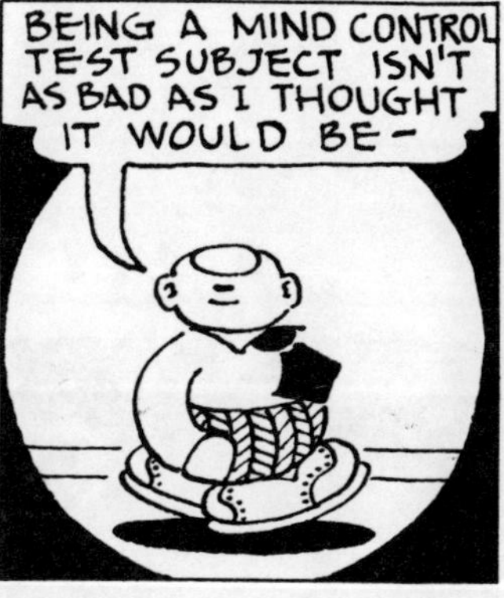
BEING A MIND CONTROL TEST SUBJECT ISN'T AS BAD AS I THOUGHT IT WOULD BE-

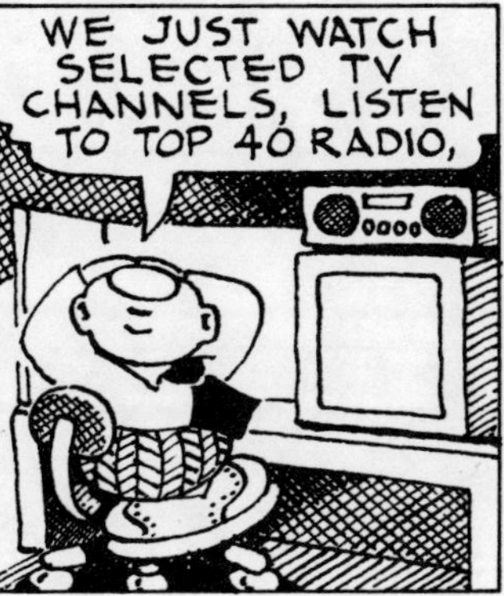
WE JUST WATCH SELECTED TV CHANNELS, LISTEN TO TOP 40 RADIO,

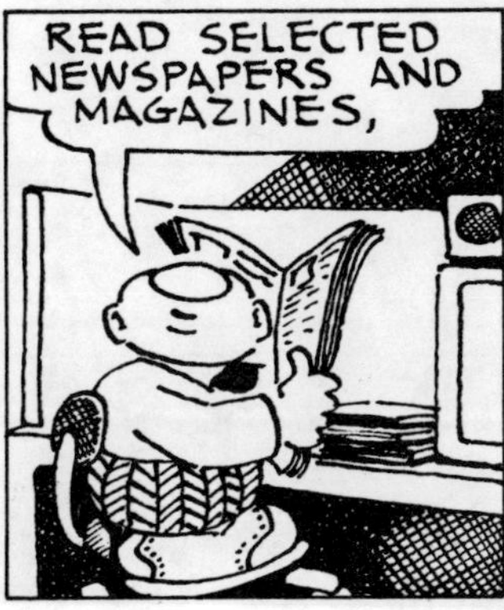
READ SELECTED NEWSPAPERS AND MAGAZINES,

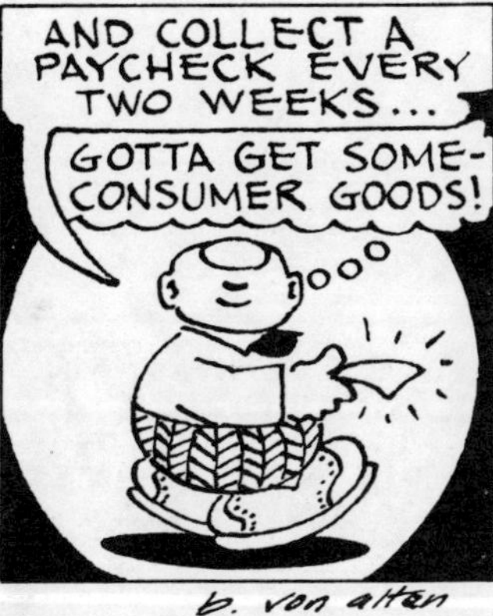
AND COLLECT A PAYCHECK EVERY TWO WEEKS...
GOTTA GET SOME-CONSUMER GOODS!
b. von alten

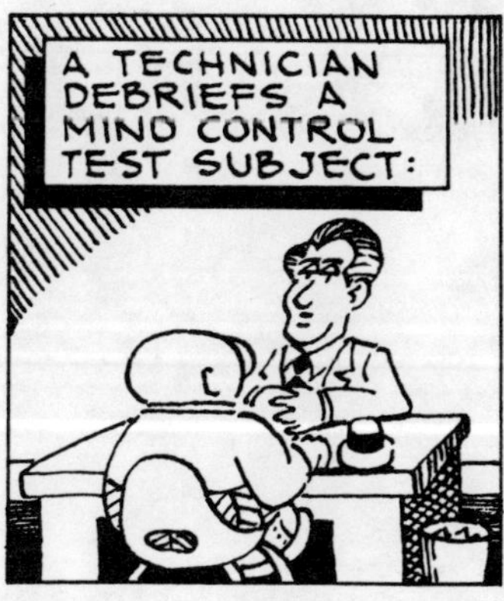
A TECHNICIAN DEBRIEFS A MIND CONTROL TEST SUBJECT:

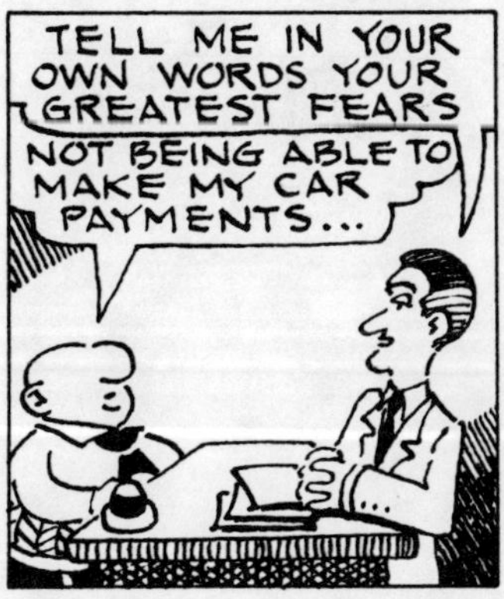
TELL ME IN YOUR OWN WORDS YOUR GREATEST FEARS
NOT BEING ABLE TO MAKE MY CAR PAYMENTS...

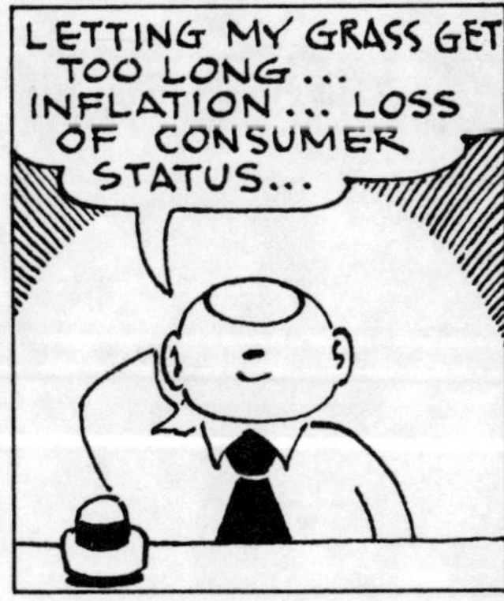
LETTING MY GRASS GET TOO LONG... INFLATION... LOSS OF CONSUMER STATUS...

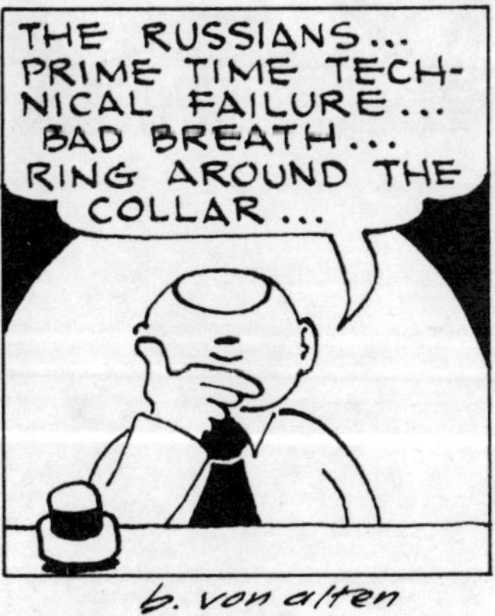
THE RUSSIANS... PRIME TIME TECH-NICAL FAILURE... BAD BREATH... RING AROUND THE COLLAR...
b. von alten

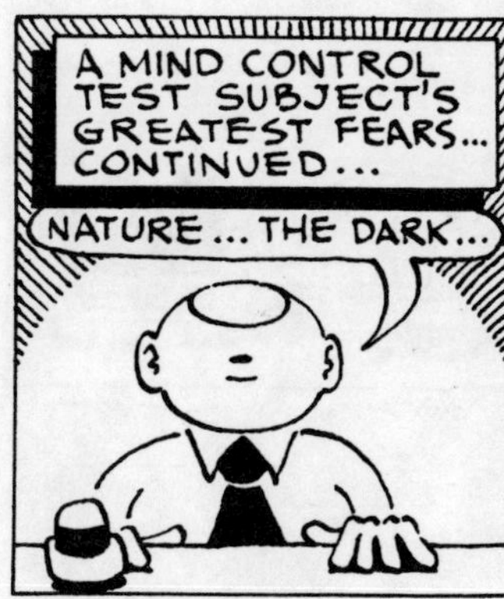
A MIND CONTROL TEST SUBJECT'S GREATEST FEARS... CONTINUED...
NATURE... THE DARK...

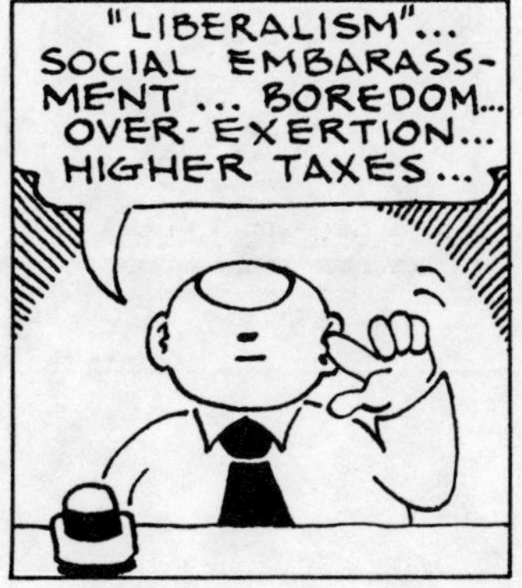
"LIBERALISM"... SOCIAL EMBARASS-MENT... BOREDOM... OVER-EXERTION... HIGHER TAXES...

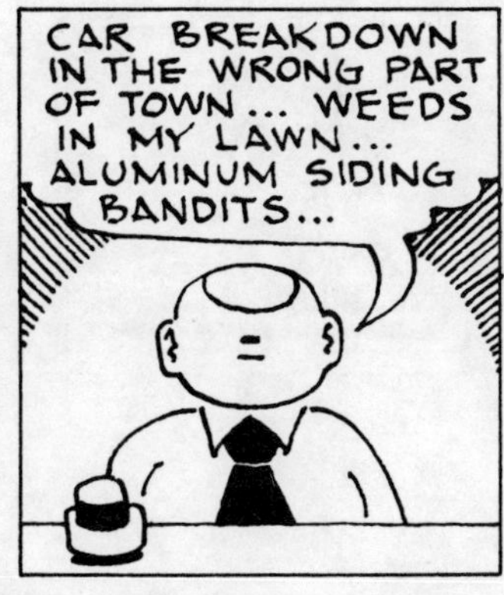
CAR BREAKDOWN IN THE WRONG PART OF TOWN... WEEDS IN MY LAWN... ALUMINUM SIDING BANDITS...

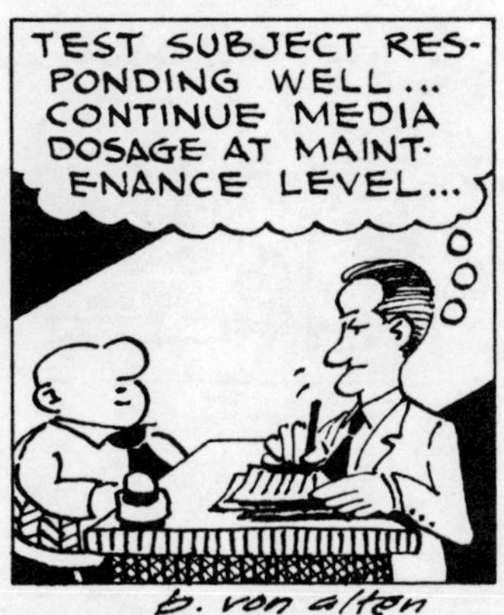
TEST SUBJECT RES-PONDING WELL... CONTINUE MEDIA DOSAGE AT MAINT-ENANCE LEVEL...
b. von alten

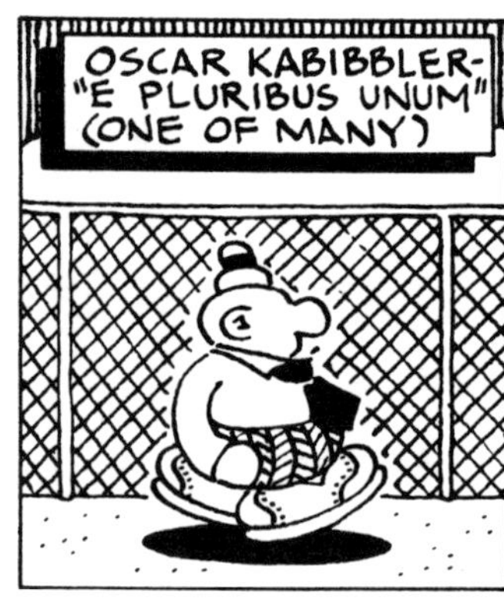
OSCAR KABIBBLER-
"E PLURIBUS UNUM"
(ONE OF MANY)
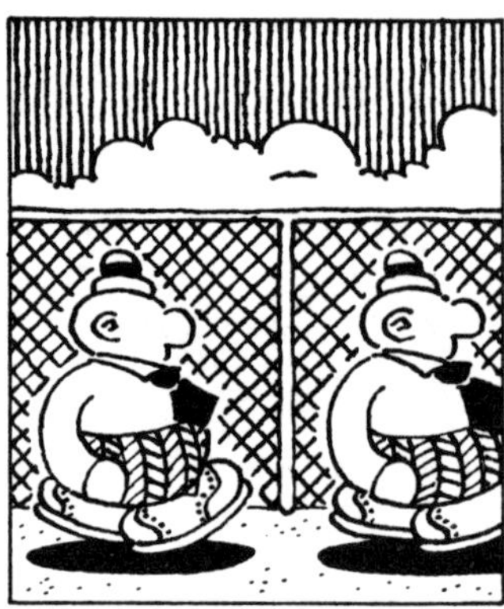
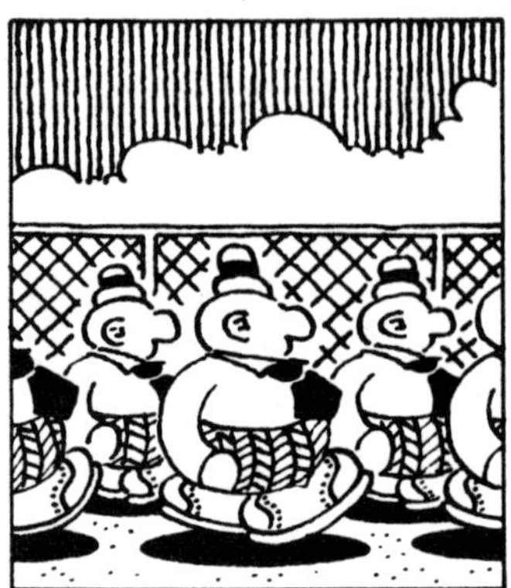
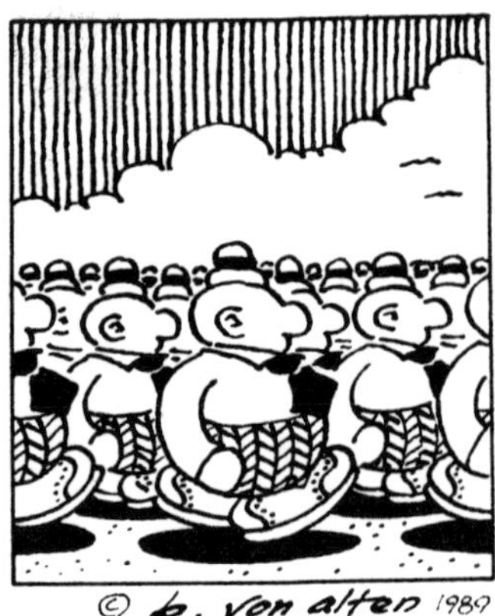
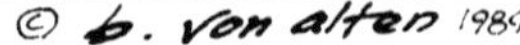
© b. von alten 1989

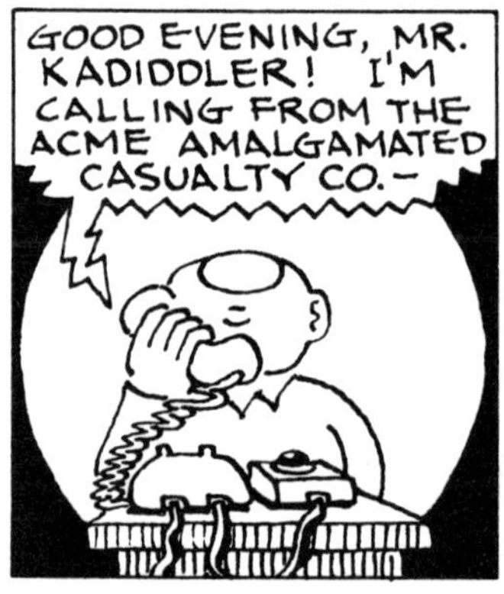
GOOD EVENING, MR. KADIDDLER! I'M CALLING FROM THE ACME AMALGAMATED CASUALTY CO.-
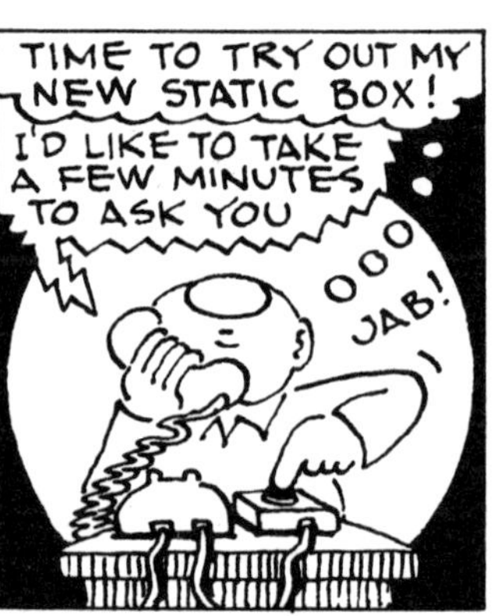
TIME TO TRY OUT MY NEW STATIC BOX!
I'D LIKE TO TAKE A FEW MINUTES TO ASK YOU
OOO
JAB!
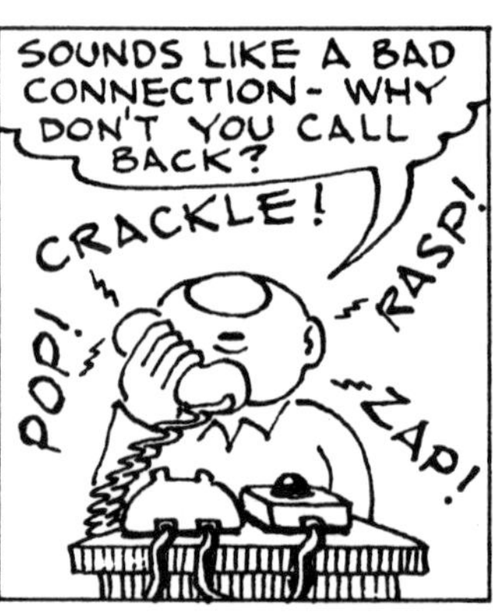
SOUNDS LIKE A BAD CONNECTION- WHY DON'T YOU CALL BACK?
CRACKLE!
RASP!
POP!
ZAP!
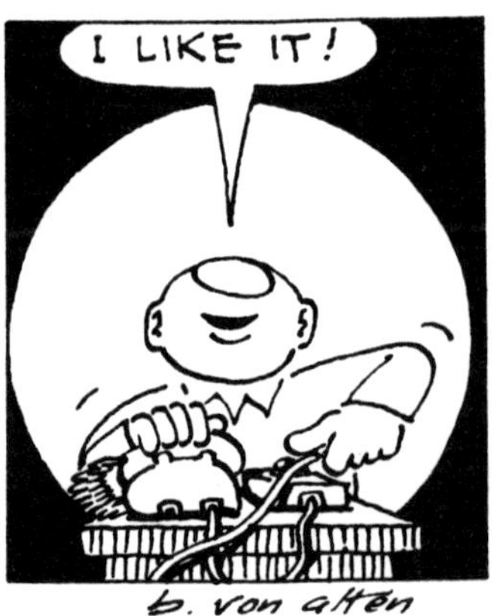
I LIKE IT!
b. von alten

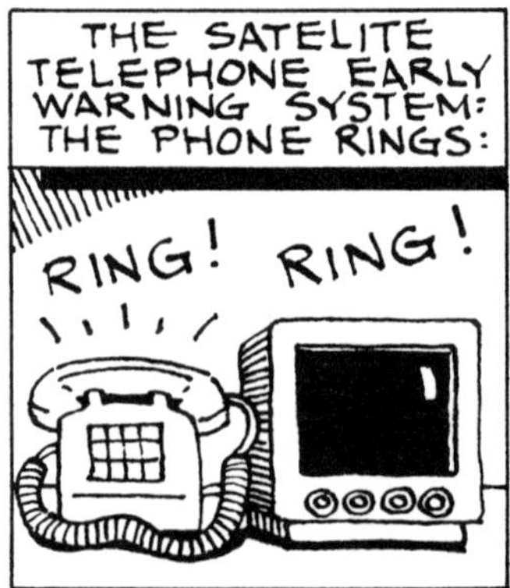
THE SATELITE TELEPHONE EARLY WARNING SYSTEM: THE PHONE RINGS:
RING! RING!
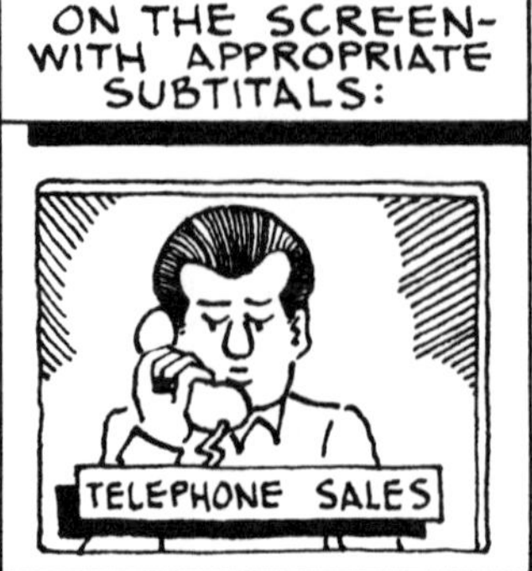
A PICTURE FLASHES ON THE SCREEN- WITH APPROPRIATE SUBTITALS:
TELEPHONE SALES
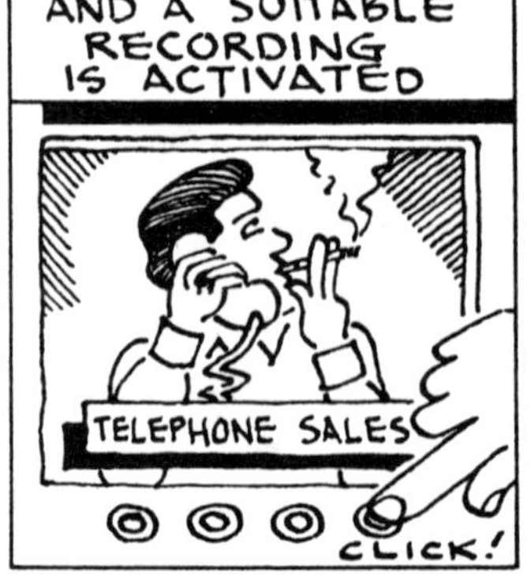
AND A SUITABLE RECORDING IS ACTIVATED
TELEPHONE SALES
CLICK!
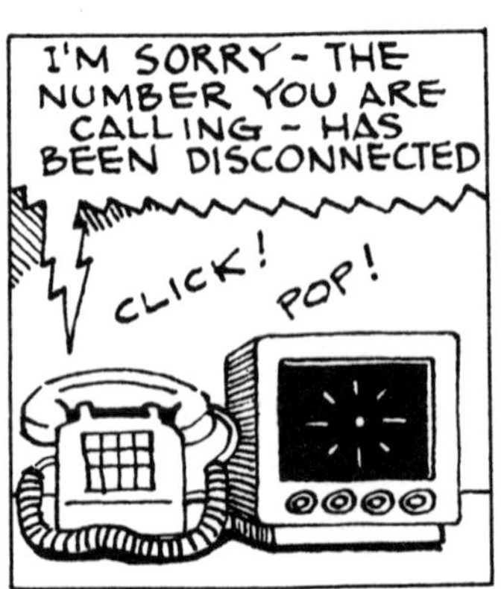
I'M SORRY - THE NUMBER YOU ARE CALLING - HAS BEEN DISCONNECTED
CLICK!
POP!
© b. von alten 1989

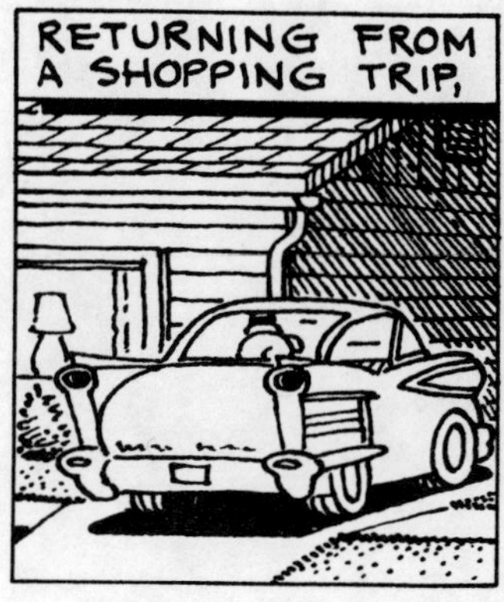
RETURNING FROM A SHOPPING TRIP,

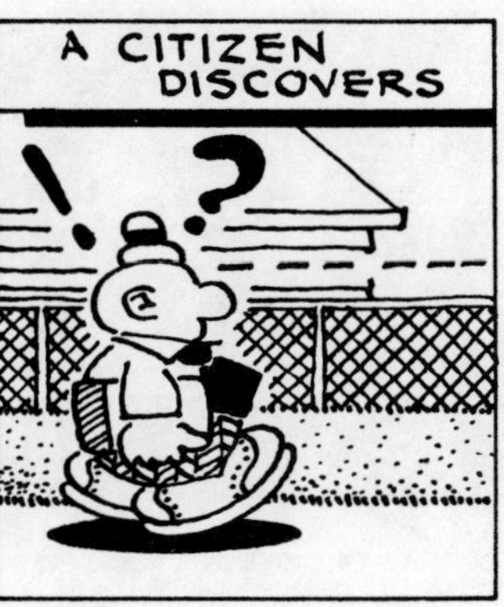
A CITIZEN DISCOVERS
! ?

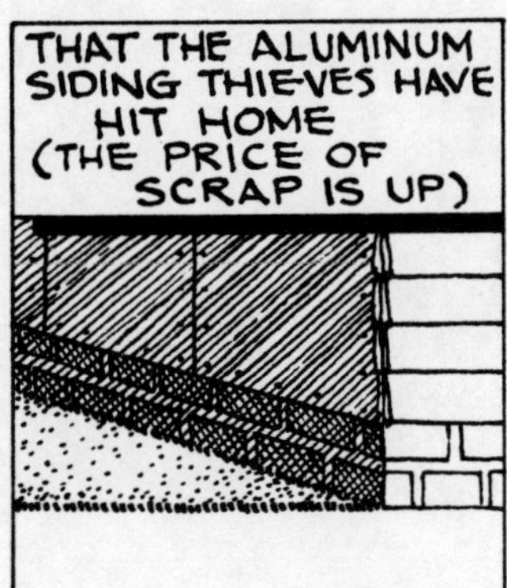
THAT THE ALUMINUM SIDING THIEVES HAVE HIT HOME (THE PRICE OF SCRAP IS UP)

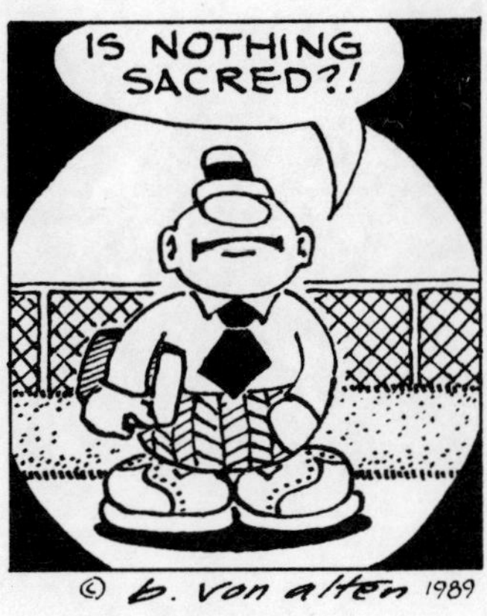
IS NOTHING SACRED?!

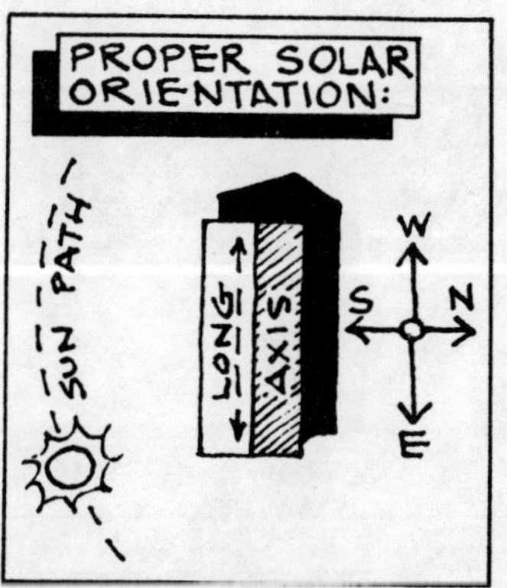
PROPER SOLAR ORIENTATION:
SUN PATH
LONG AXIS
W
S
N
E

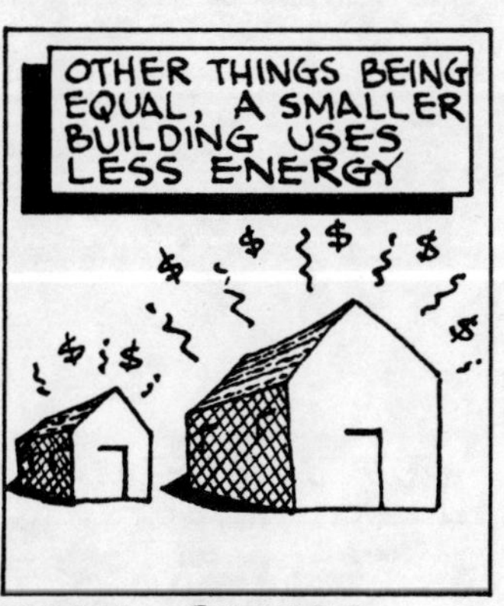
OTHER THINGS BEING EQUAL, A SMALLER BUILDING USES LESS ENERGY
$ $ $ $
$ $ $ $

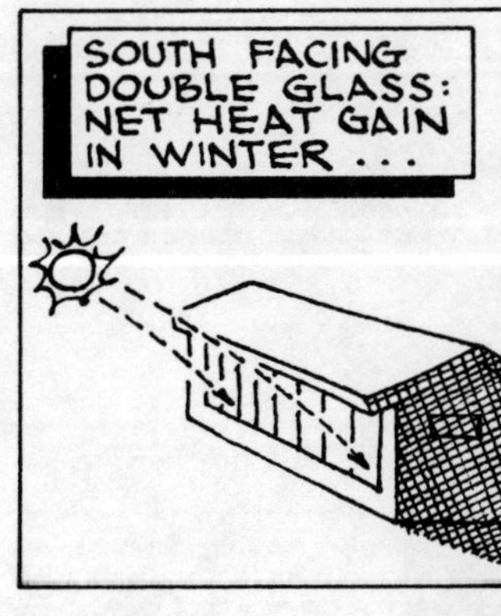
SOUTH FACING DOUBLE GLASS: NET HEAT GAIN IN WINTER ...

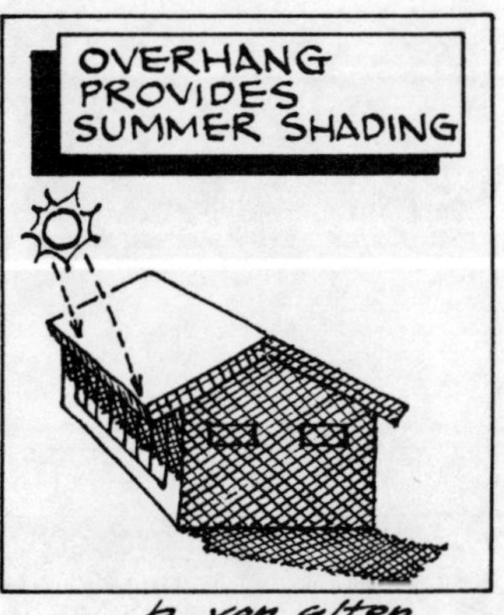
OVERHANG PROVIDES SUMMER SHADING

ARCHITECTURAL DESIGN BASICS

b. von alten

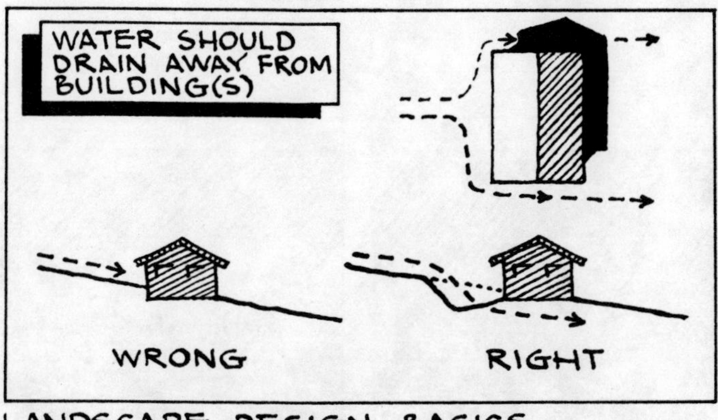
WATER SHOULD DRAIN AWAY FROM BUILDING(S)
WRONG
RIGHT

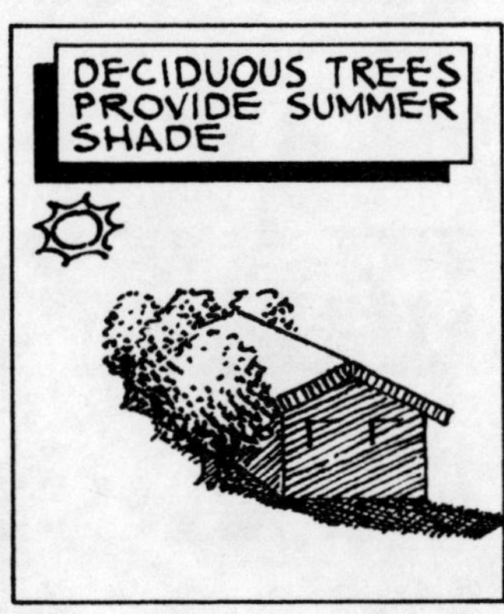
DECIDUOUS TREES PROVIDE SUMMER SHADE

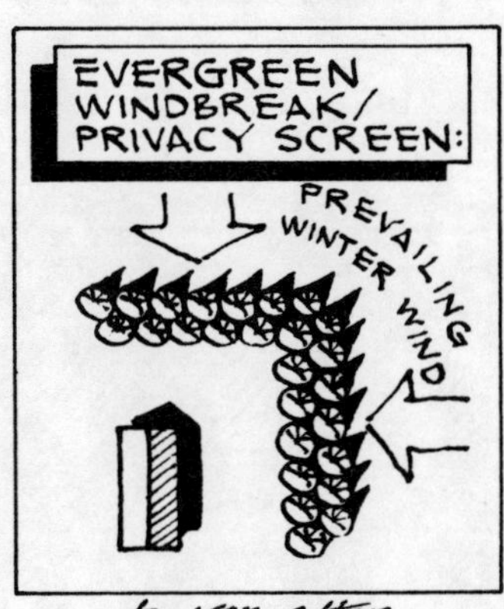
EVERGREEN WINDBREAK/ PRIVACY SCREEN:
PREVAILING WINTER WIND

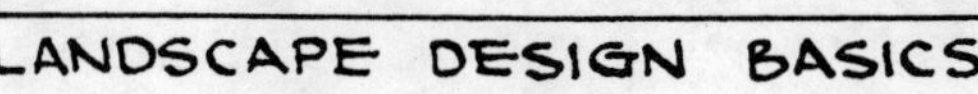
LANDSCAPE DESIGN BASICS

b. von alten

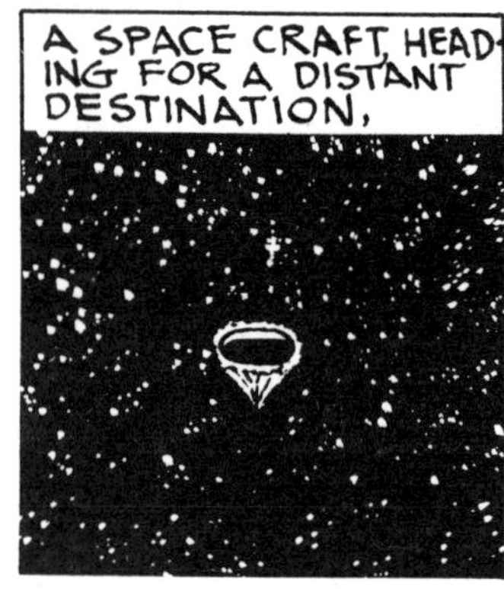
A SPACE CRAFT, HEADING FOR A DISTANT DESTINATION,
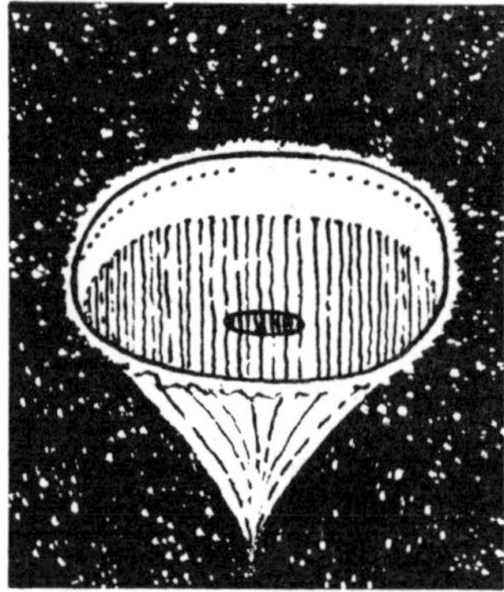
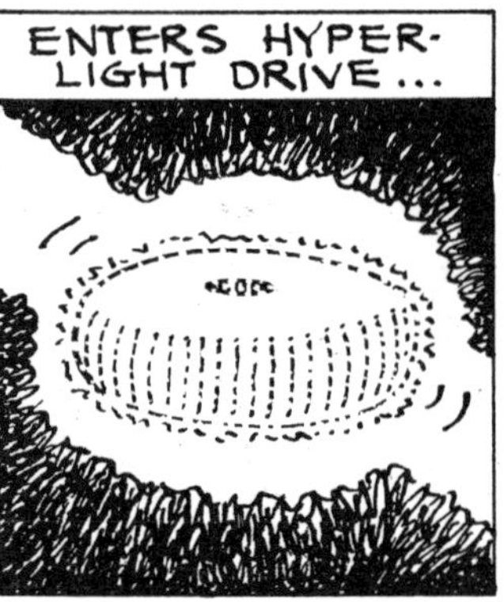
ENTERS HYPER-LIGHT DRIVE...
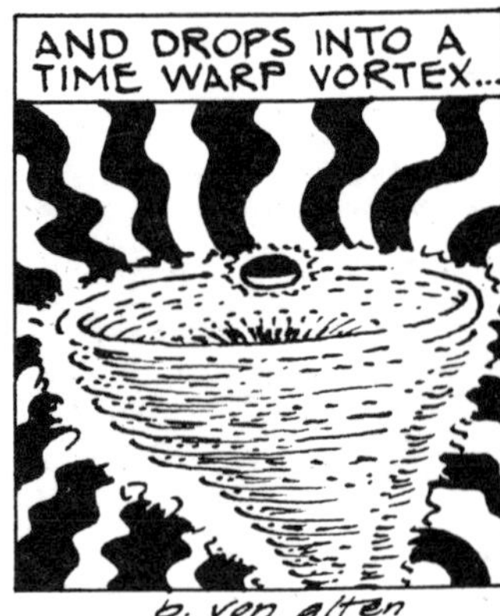
AND DROPS INTO A TIME WARP VORTEX...
b. von alten
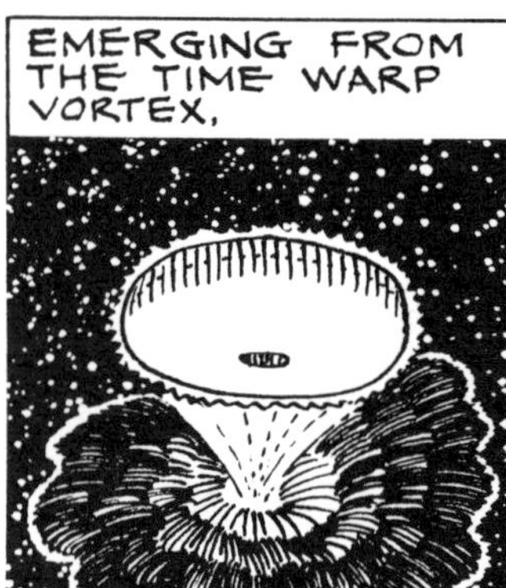
EMERGING FROM THE TIME WARP VORTEX,
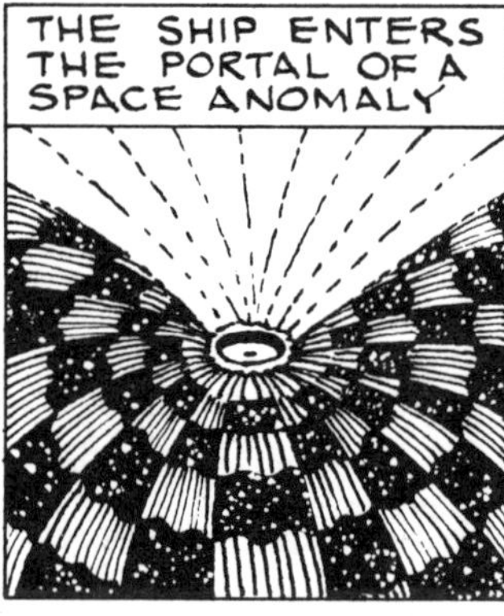
THE SHIP ENTERS THE PORTAL OF A SPACE ANOMALY
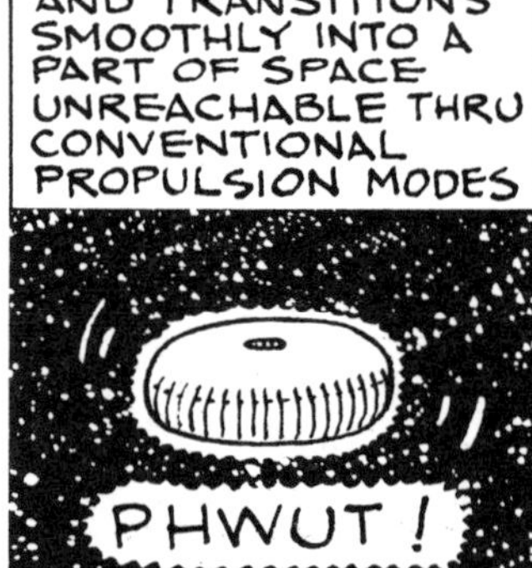
AND TRANSITIONS SMOOTHLY INTO A PART OF SPACE UNREACHABLE THRU CONVENTIONAL PROPULSION MODES
PHWUT!
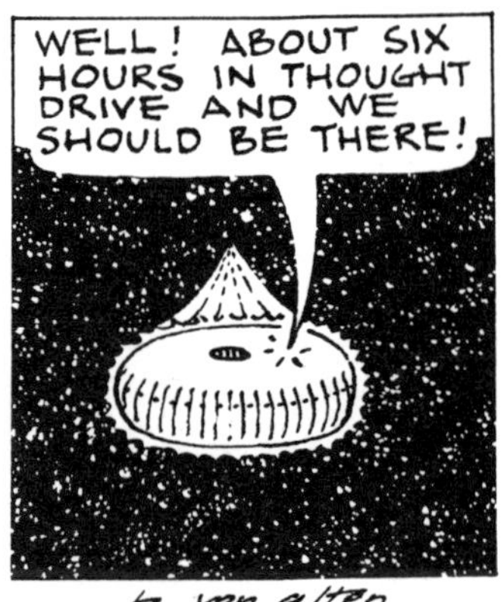
WELL! ABOUT SIX HOURS IN THOUGHT DRIVE AND WE SHOULD BE THERE!
b. von alten
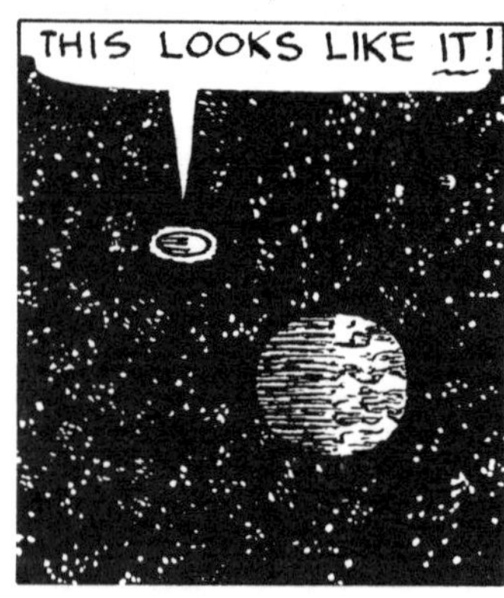
THIS LOOKS LIKE IT!
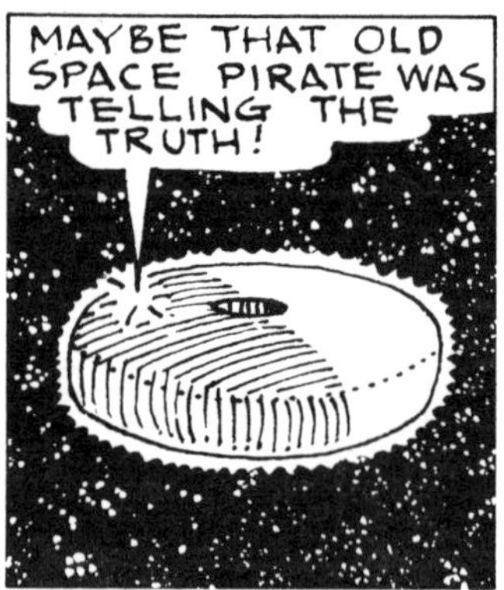
MAYBE THAT OLD SPACE PIRATE WAS TELLING THE TRUTH!
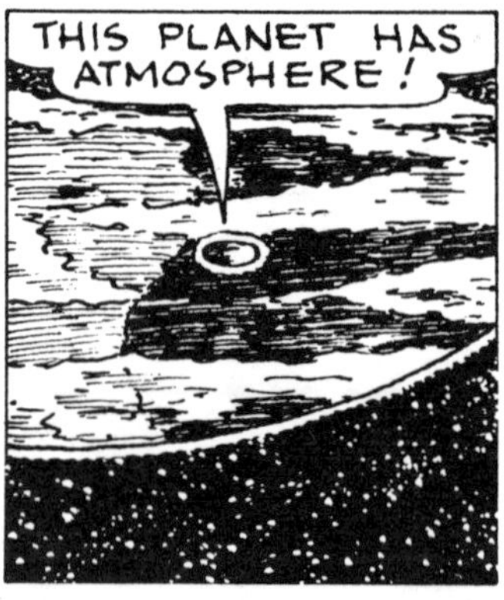
THIS PLANET HAS ATMOSPHERE!
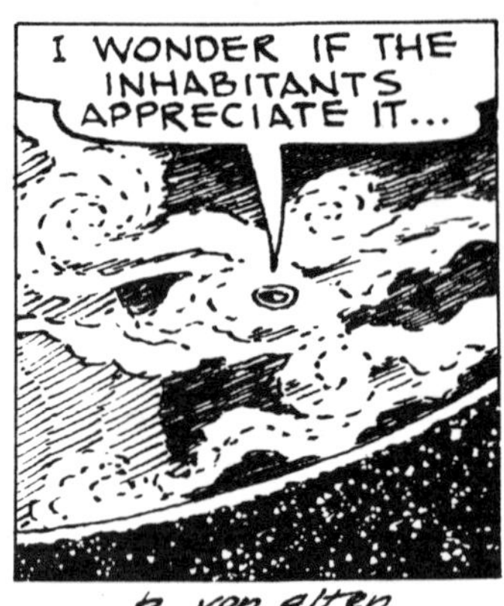
I WONDER IF THE INHABITANTS APPRECIATE IT...
b. von alten
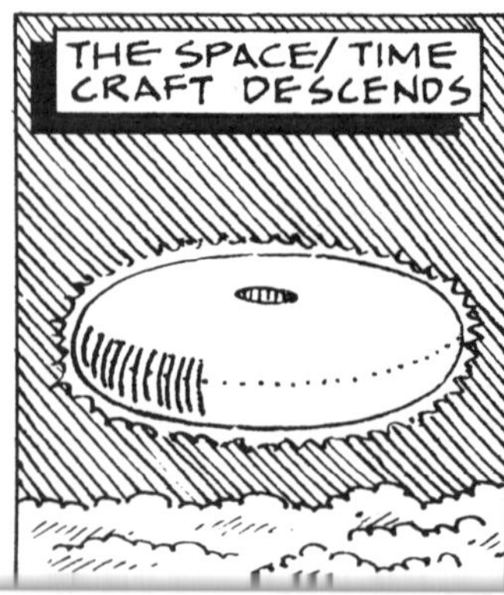
THE SPACE/TIME CRAFT DESCENDS
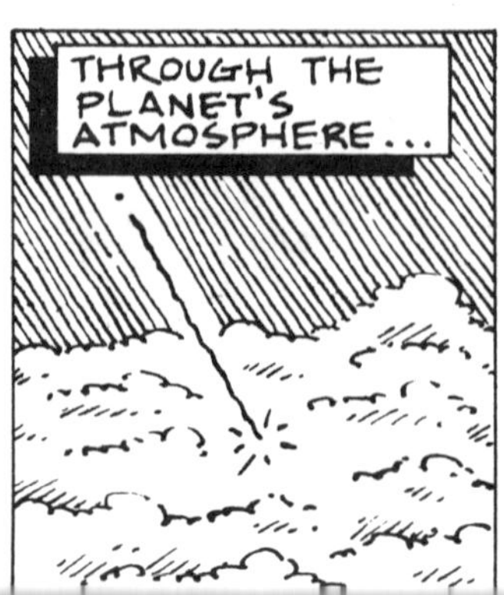
THROUGH THE PLANET'S ATMOSPHERE...
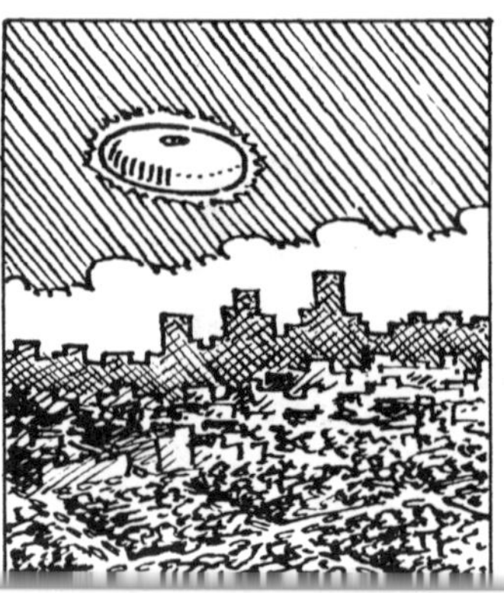
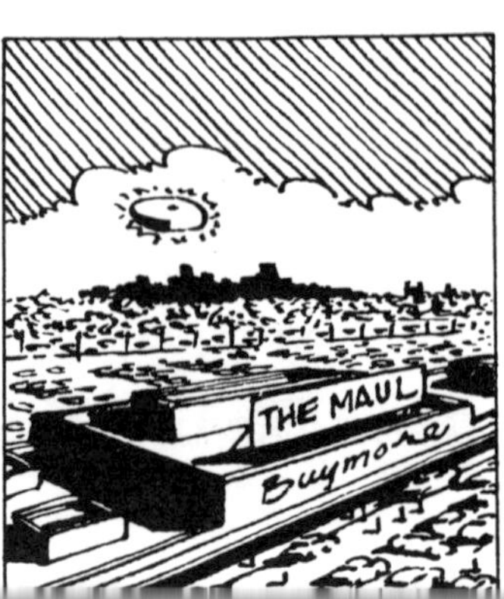
THE MAUL
Buymore

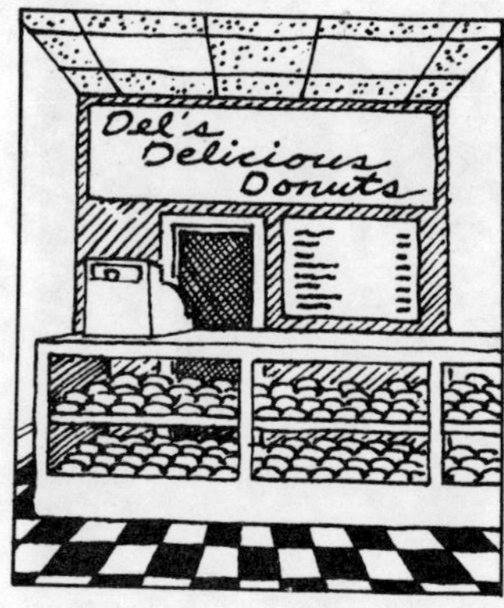
Del's Delicious Donuts
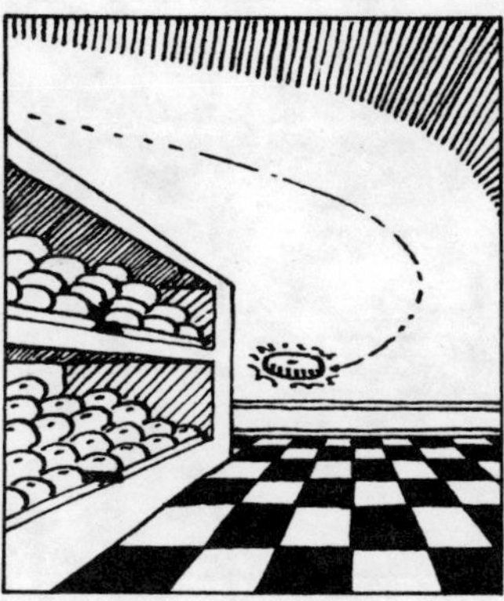
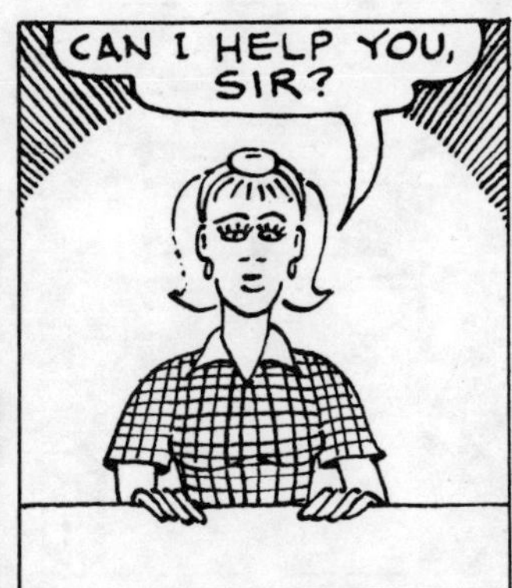
CAN I HELP YOU, SIR?
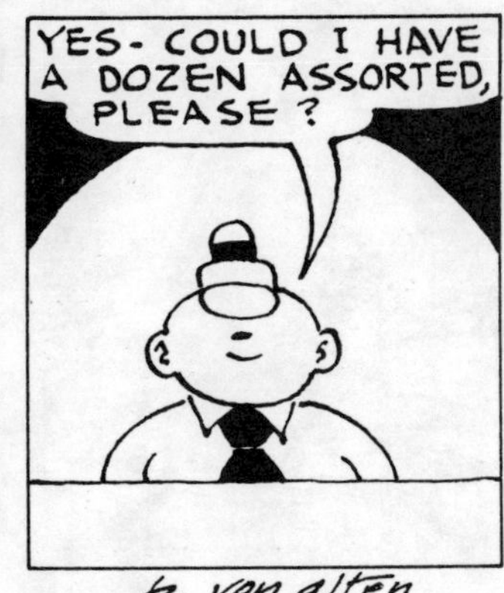
YES- COULD I HAVE A DOZEN ASSORTED, PLEASE ?

b. von alten

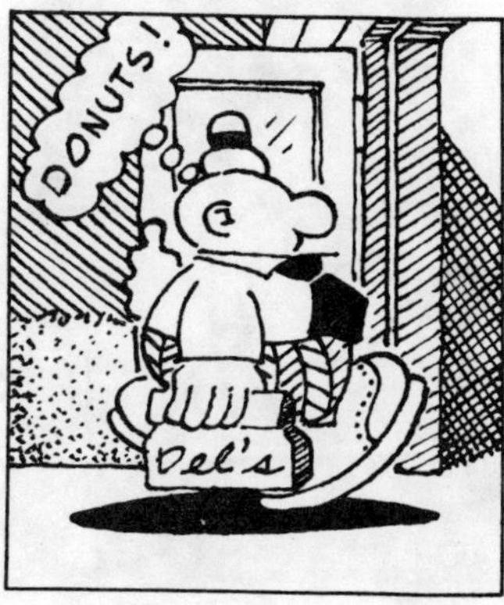
DONUTS!
Del's
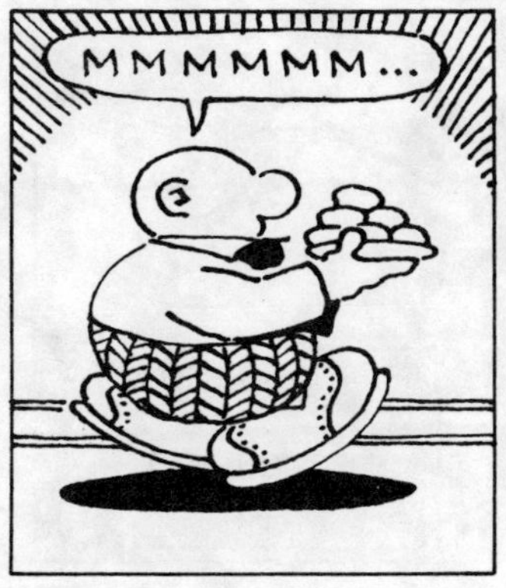
MMMMMM...
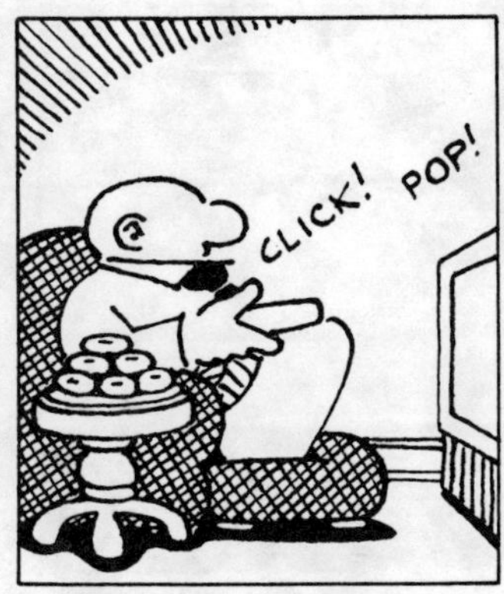
CLICK! POP!
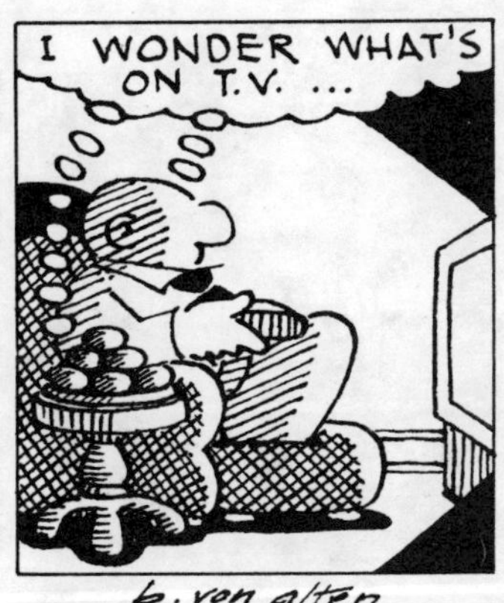
I WONDER WHAT'S ON T.V. ...

b. von alten

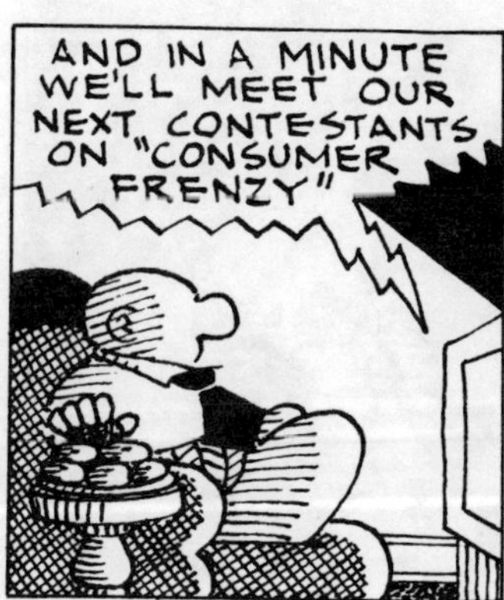
AND IN A MINUTE WE'LL MEET OUR NEXT CONTESTANTS ON "CONSUMER FRENZY"
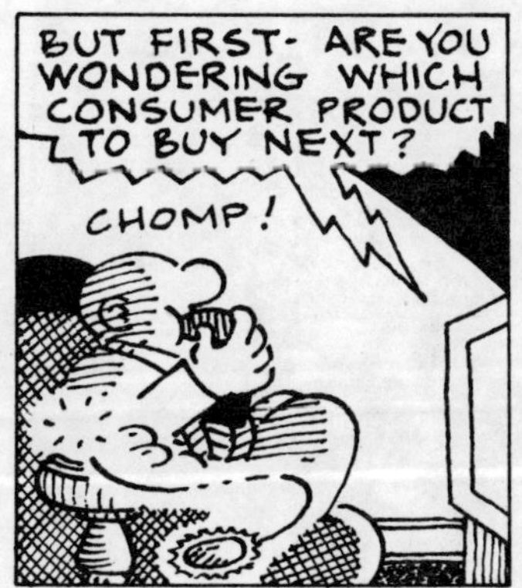
BUT FIRST- ARE YOU WONDERING WHICH CONSUMER PRODUCT TO BUY NEXT?
CHOMP!
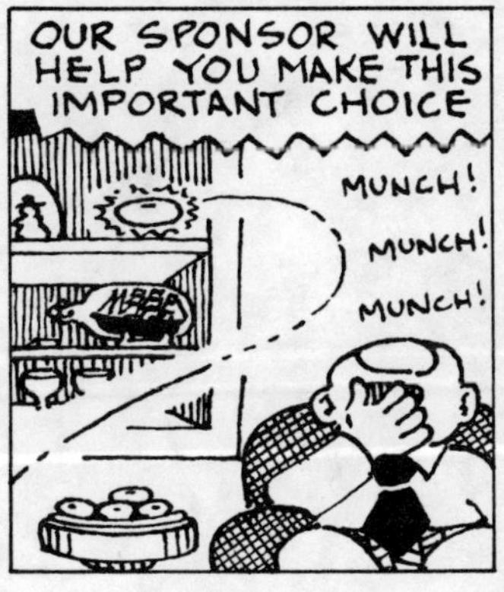
OUR SPONSOR WILL HELP YOU MAKE THIS IMPORTANT CHOICE
MUNCH!
MUNCH!
MUNCH!
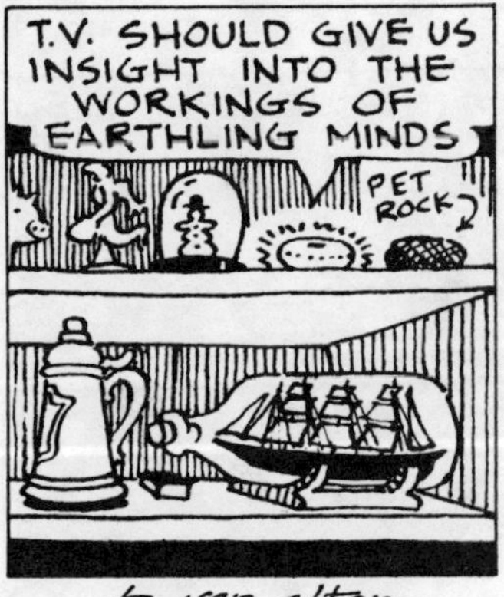
T.V. SHOULD GIVE US INSIGHT INTO THE WORKINGS OF EARTHLING MINDS
PET ROCK

b. von alten

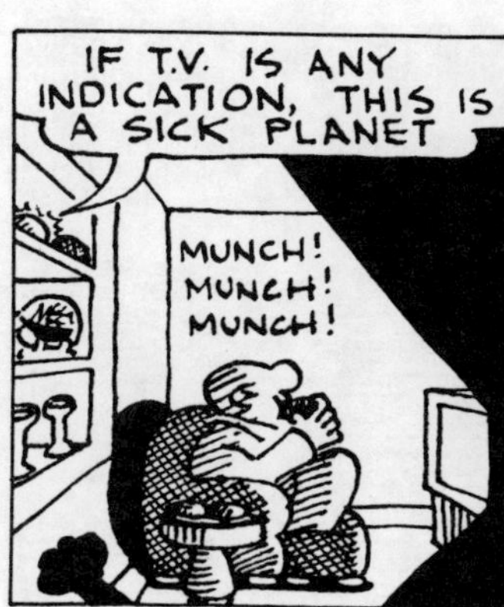
IF T.V. IS ANY INDICATION, THIS IS A SICK PLANET
MUNCH!
MUNCH!
MUNCH!
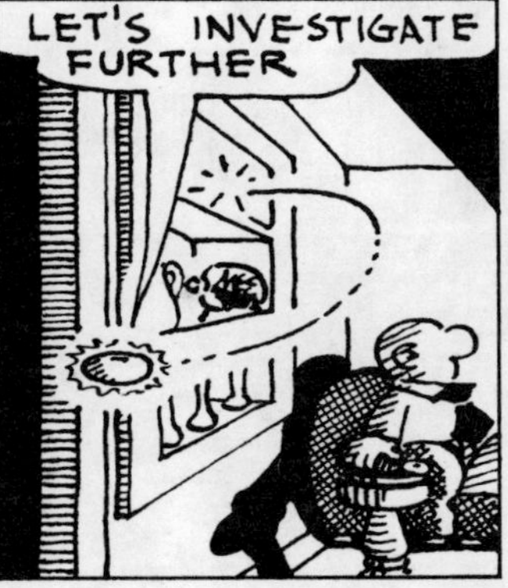
LET'S INVESTIGATE FURTHER
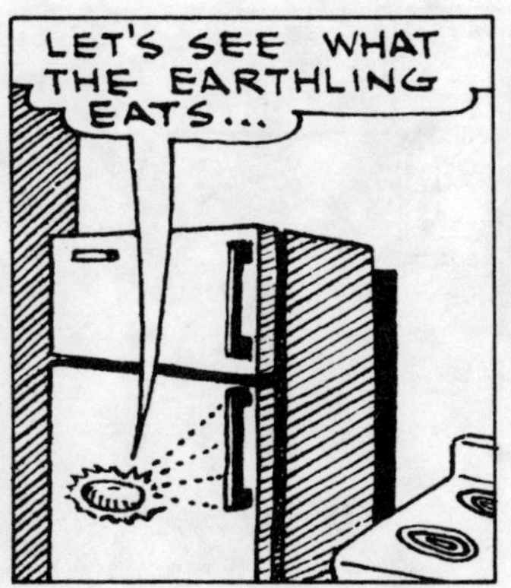
LET'S SEE WHAT THE EARTHLING EATS...
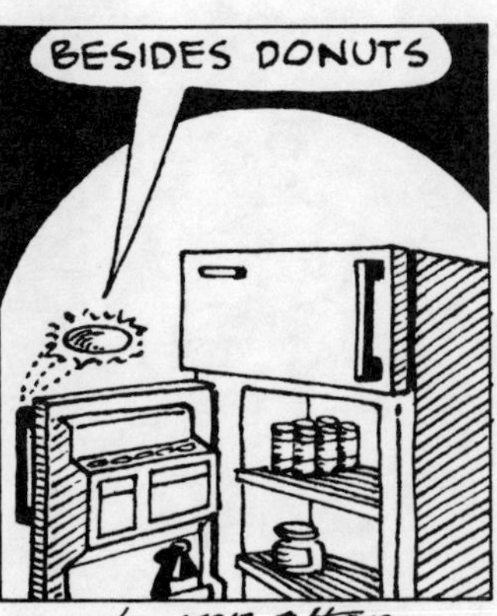
BESIDES DONUTS

b. von alten

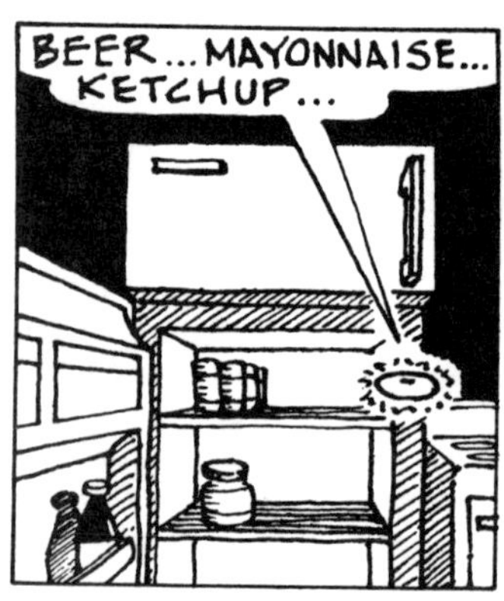
BEER...MAYONNAISE...
KETCHUP...
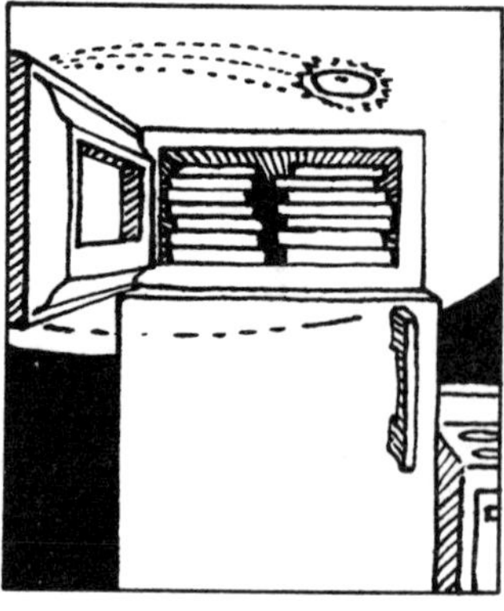
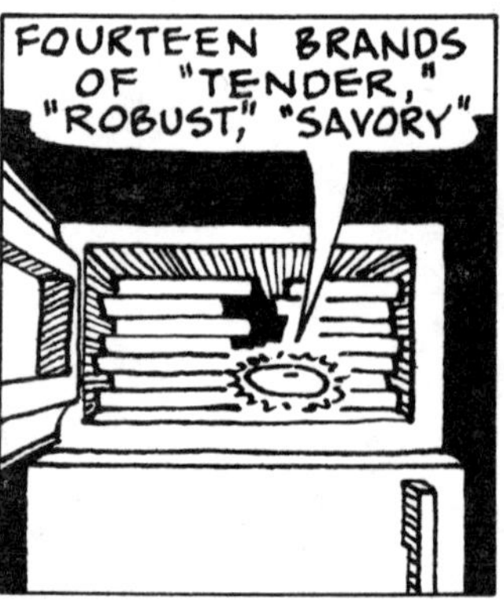
FOURTEEN BRANDS OF "TENDER," "ROBUST," "SAVORY"
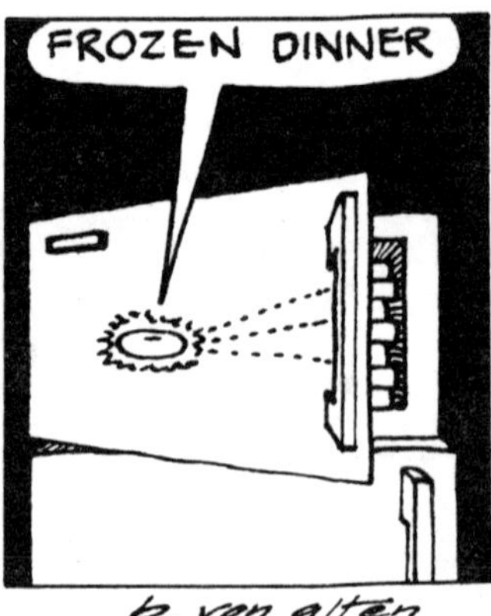
FROZEN DINNER
b. von alten
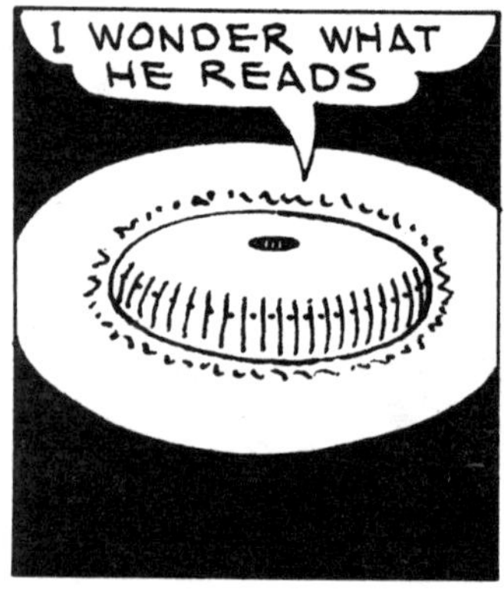
I WONDER WHAT HE READS
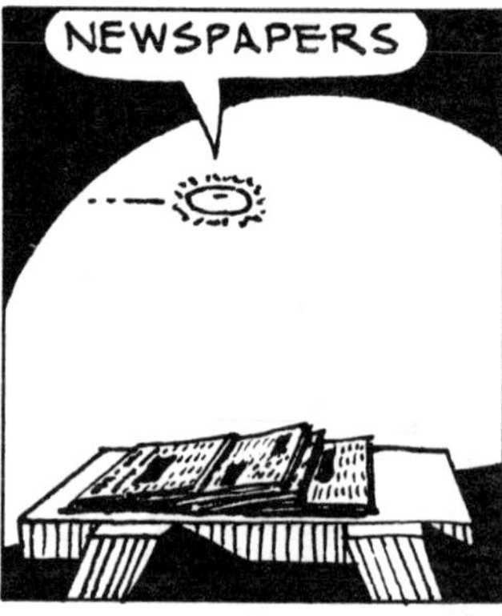
NEWSPAPERS
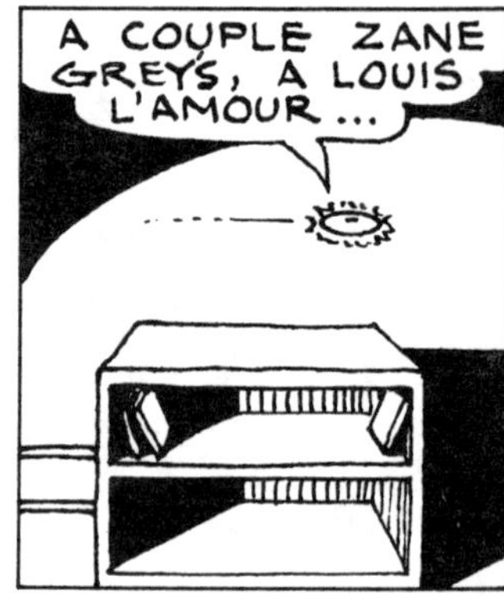
A COUPLE ZANE GREY'S, A LOUIS L'AMOUR...
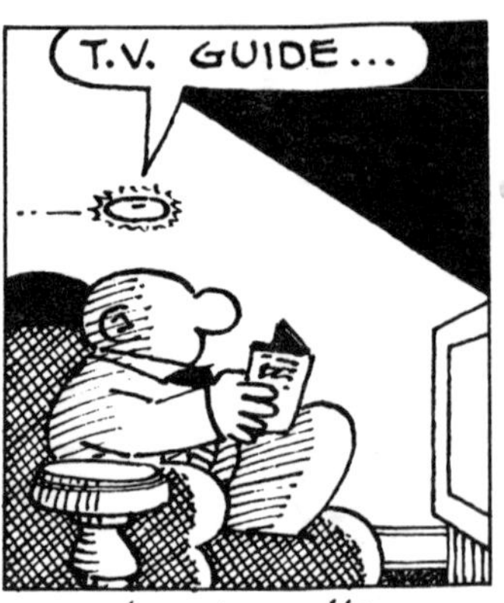
T.V. GUIDE...
b. von alten
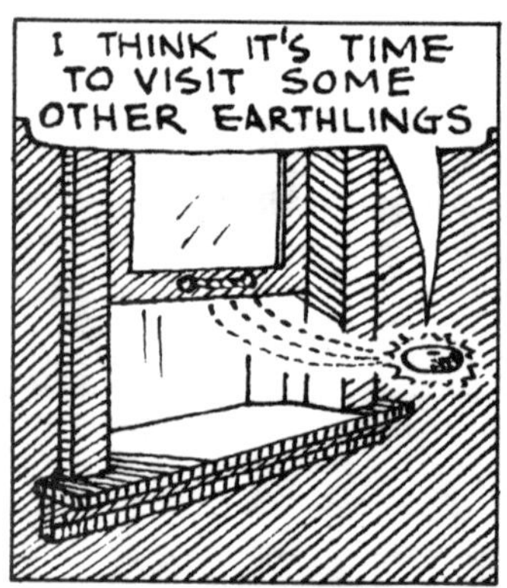
I THINK IT'S TIME TO VISIT SOME OTHER EARTHLINGS
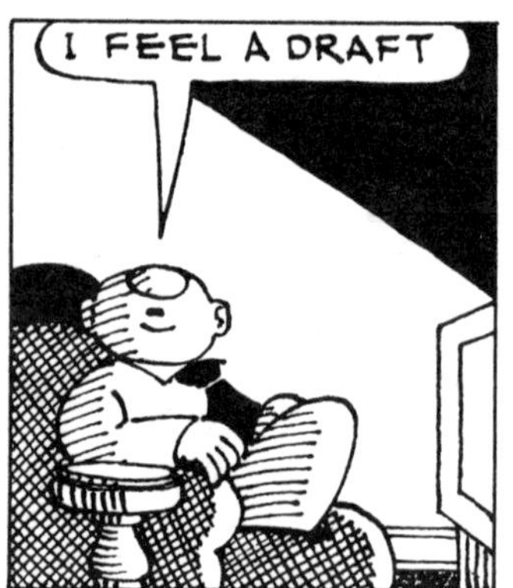
I FEEL A DRAFT
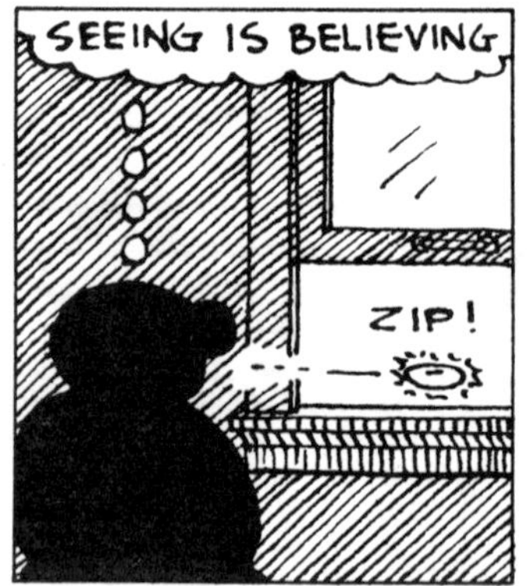
SEEING IS BELIEVING
ZIP!
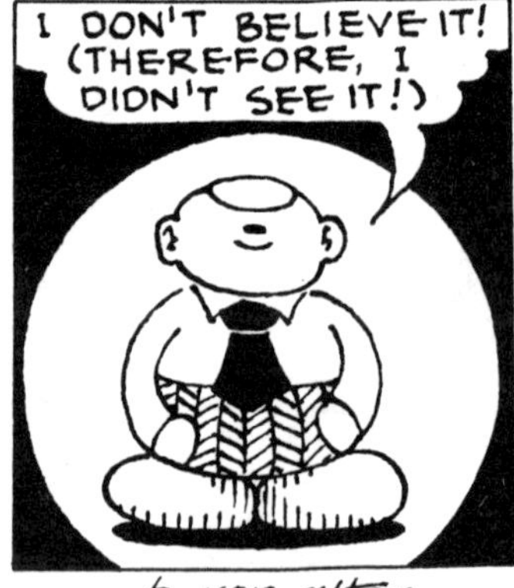
I DON'T BELIEVE IT! (THEREFORE, I DIDN'T SEE IT!)
b. von alten
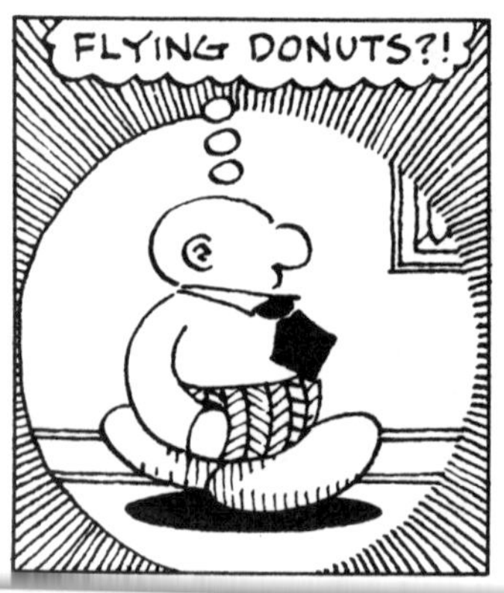
FLYING DONUTS?!
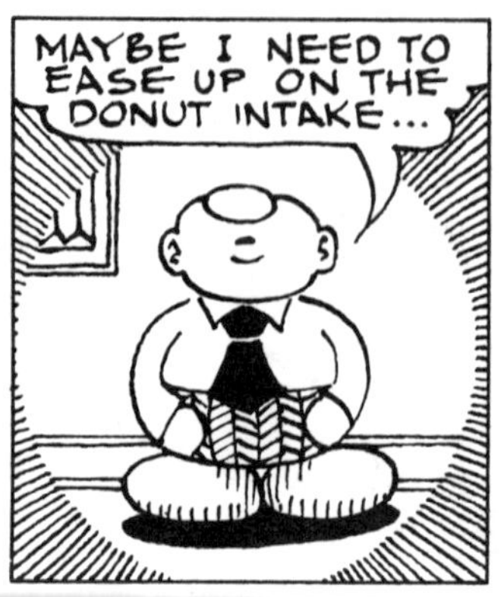
MAYBE I NEED TO EASE UP ON THE DONUT INTAKE...
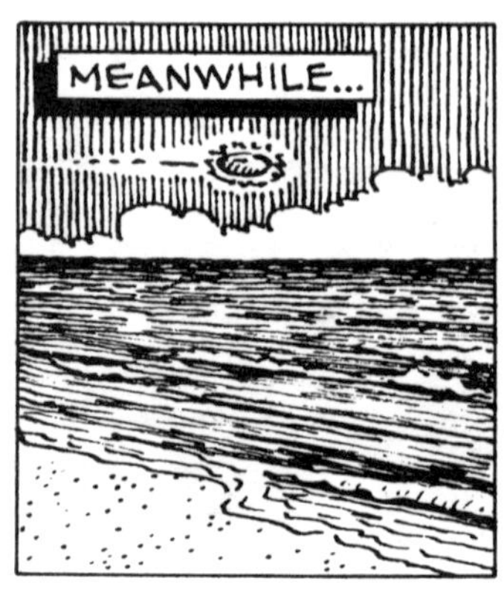
MEANWHILE...
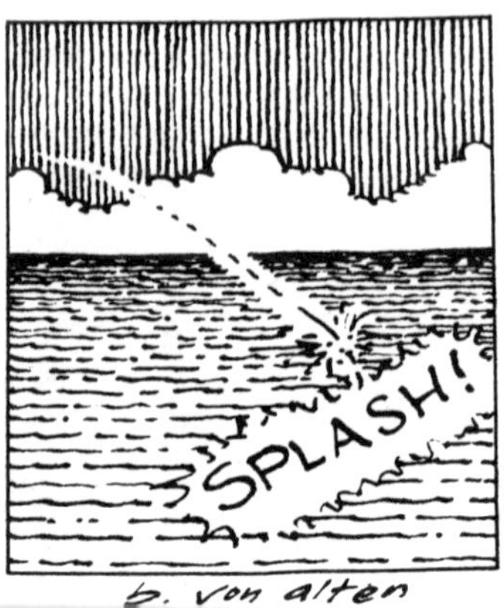
SPLASH!
b. von alten

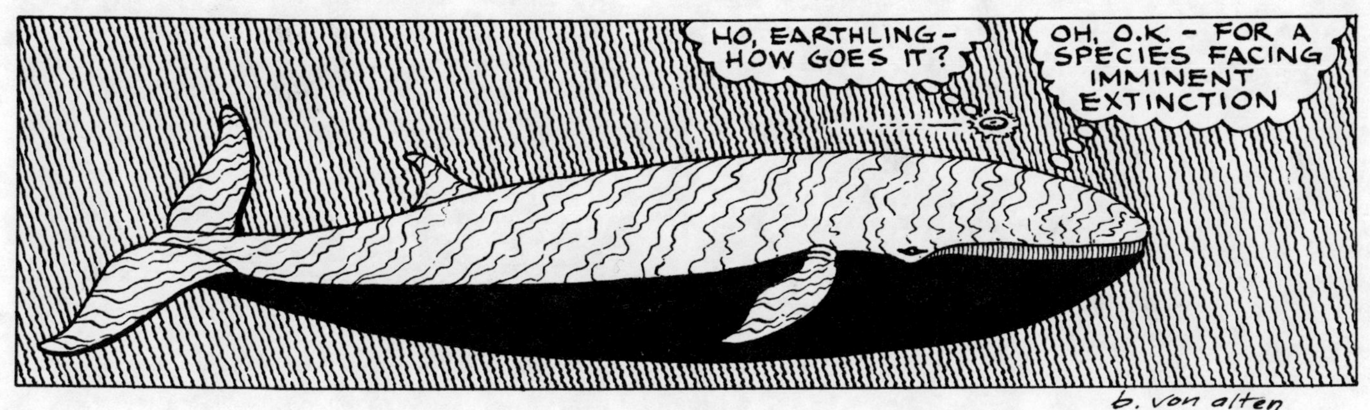
HO, EARTHLING - HOW GOES IT?
OH, O.K. - FOR A SPECIES FACING IMMINENT EXTINCTION

b. von alten

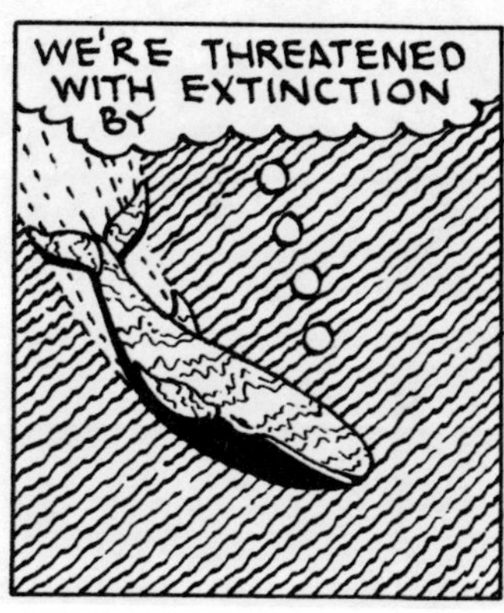
WE'RE THREATENED WITH EXTINCTION BY
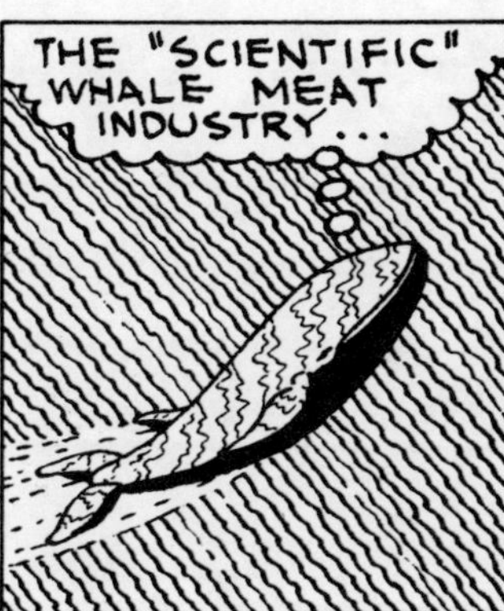
THE "SCIENTIFIC" WHALE MEAT INDUSTRY...
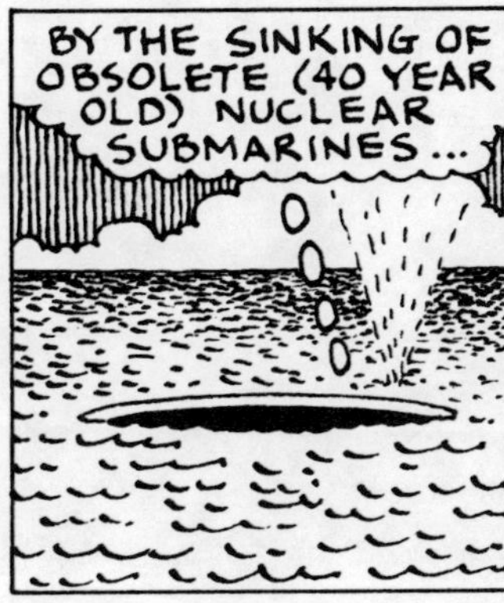
BY THE SINKING OF OBSOLETE (40 YEAR OLD) NUCLEAR SUBMARINES...
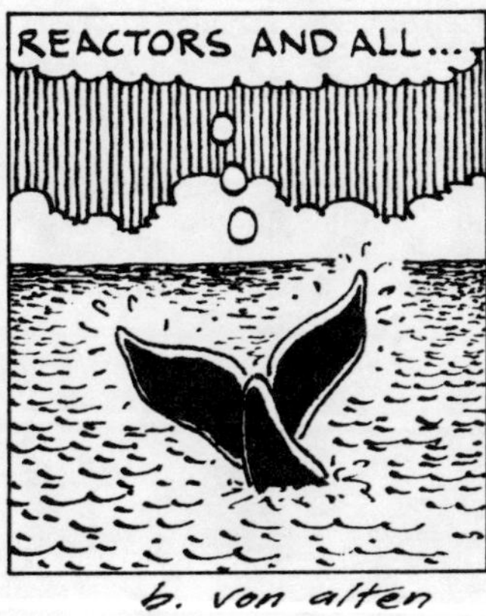
REACTORS AND ALL...

b. von alten

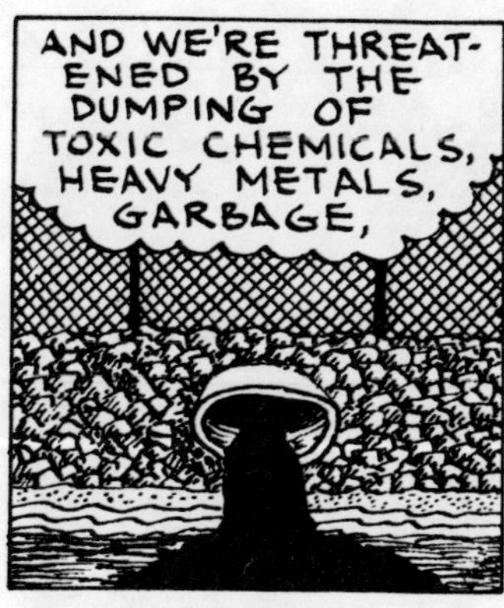
AND WE'RE THREATENED BY THE DUMPING OF TOXIC CHEMICALS, HEAVY METALS, GARBAGE,
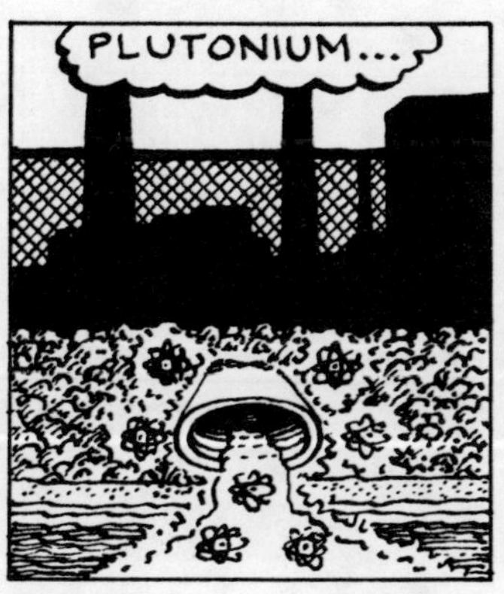
PLUTONIUM...
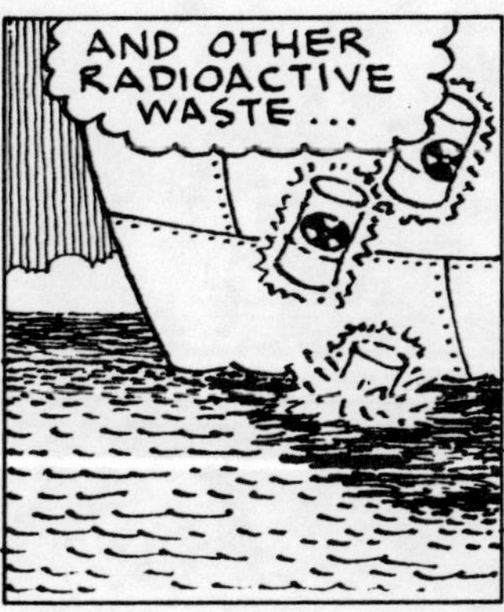
AND OTHER RADIOACTIVE WASTE...
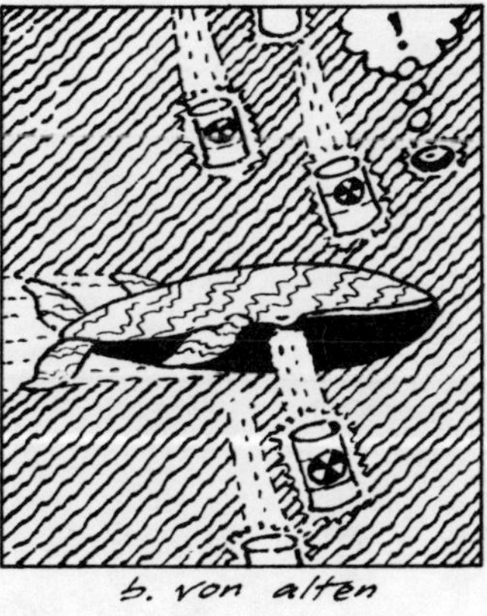
!

b. von alten

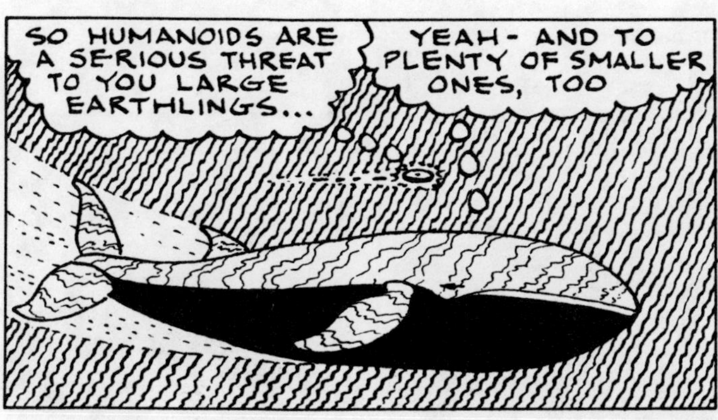
SO HUMANOIDS ARE A SERIOUS THREAT TO YOU LARGE EARTHLINGS...
YEAH - AND TO PLENTY OF SMALLER ONES, TOO
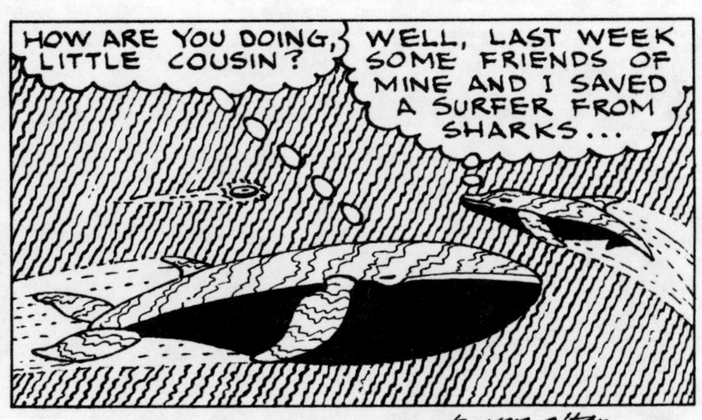
HOW ARE YOU DOING, LITTLE COUSIN?
WELL, LAST WEEK SOME FRIENDS OF MINE AND I SAVED A SURFER FROM SHARKS...

b. von alten

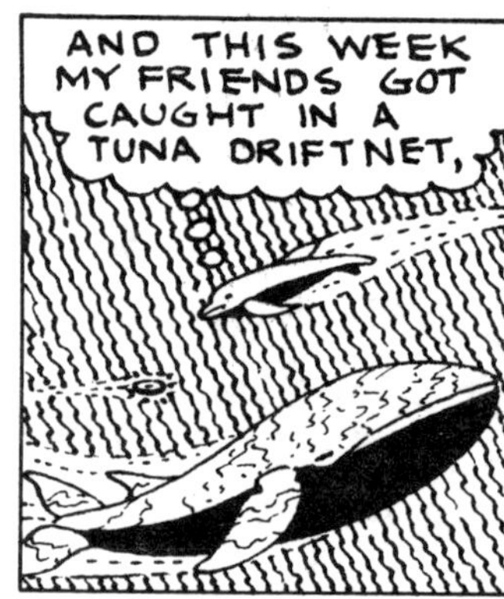
AND THIS WEEK MY FRIENDS GOT CAUGHT IN A TUNA DRIFTNET,
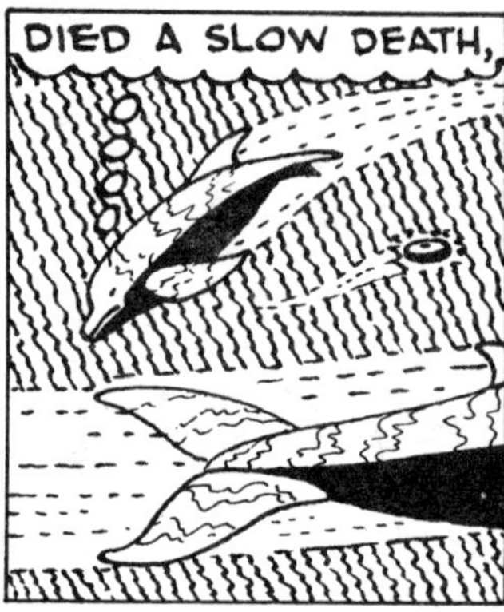
DIED A SLOW DEATH,
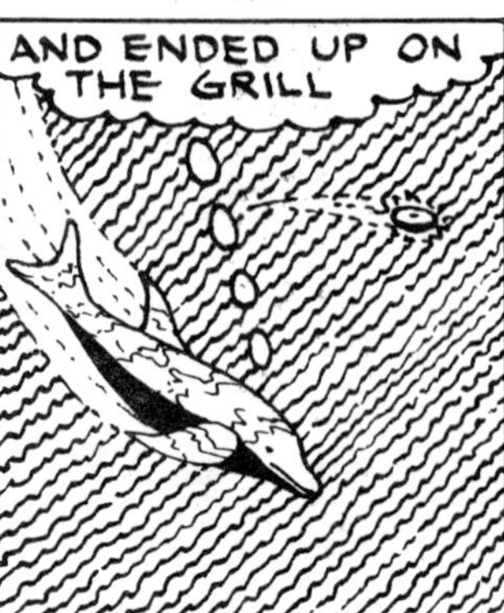
AND ENDED UP ON THE GRILL
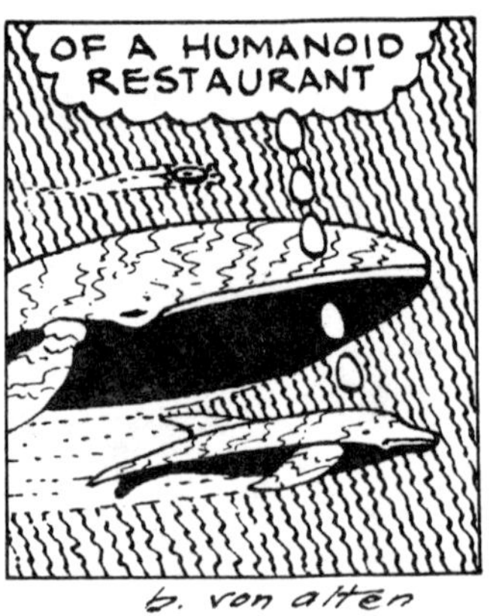
OF A HUMANOID RESTAURANT
b. von alten
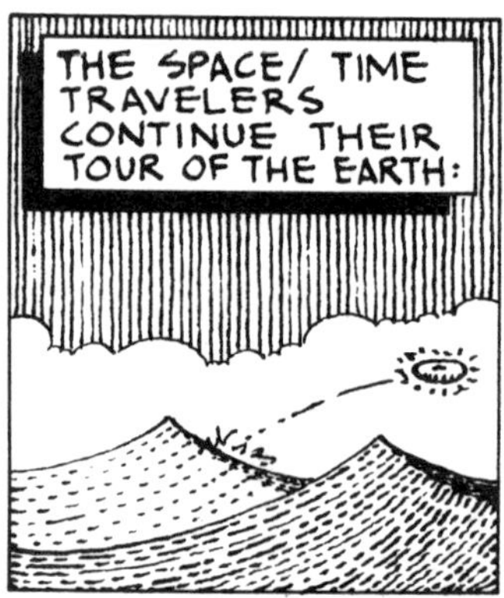
THE SPACE/ TIME TRAVELERS CONTINUE THEIR TOUR OF THE EARTH:
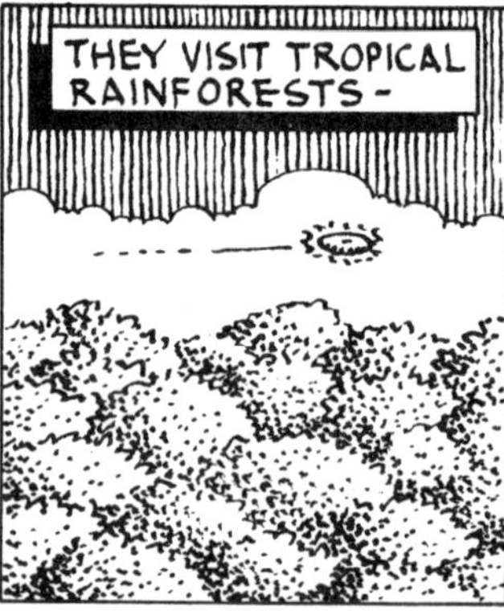
THEY VISIT TROPICAL RAINFORESTS -
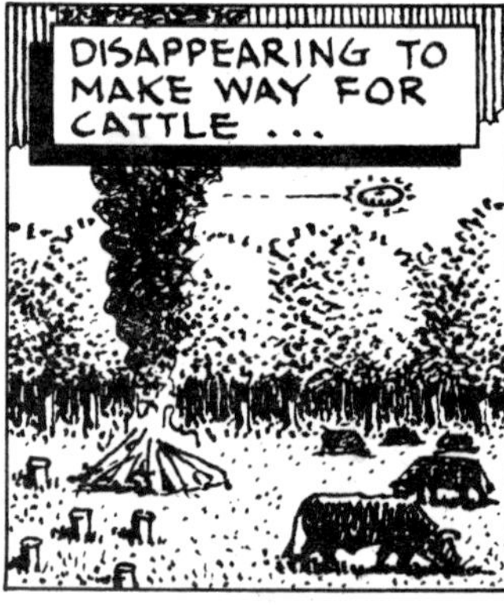
DISAPPEARING TO MAKE WAY FOR CATTLE ...
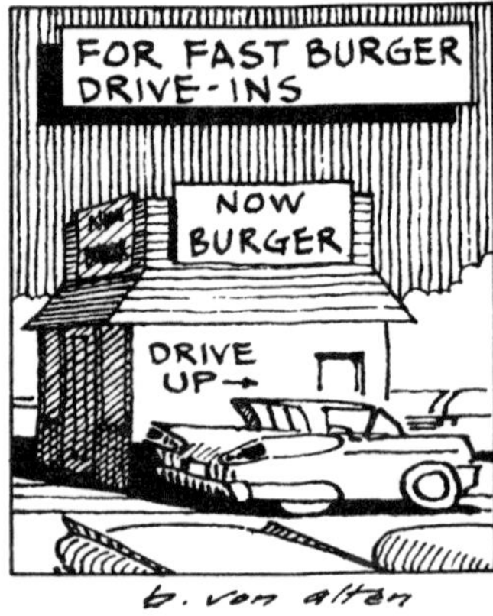
FOR FAST BURGER DRIVE-INS
NOW BURGER
DRIVE UP →
b. von alten
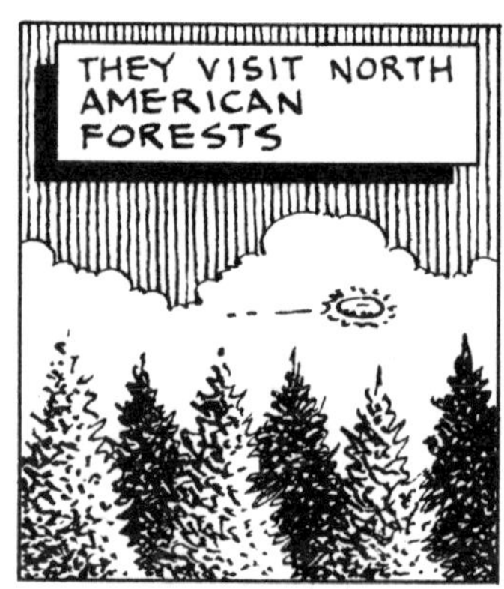
THEY VISIT NORTH AMERICAN FORESTS
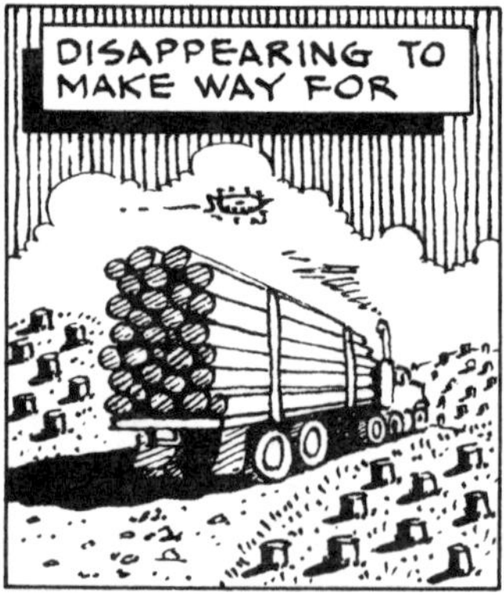
DISAPPEARING TO MAKE WAY FOR
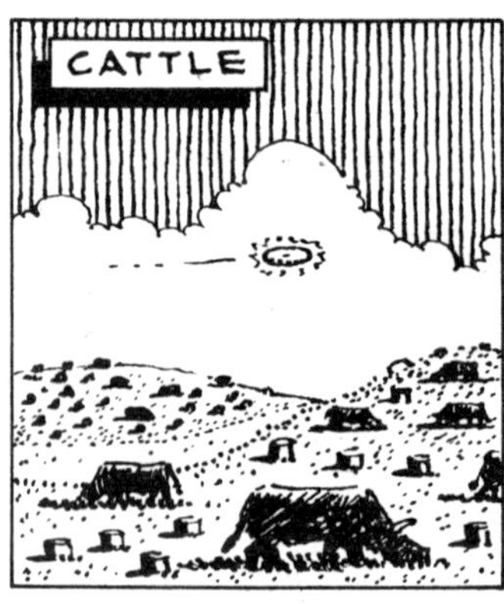
CATTLE
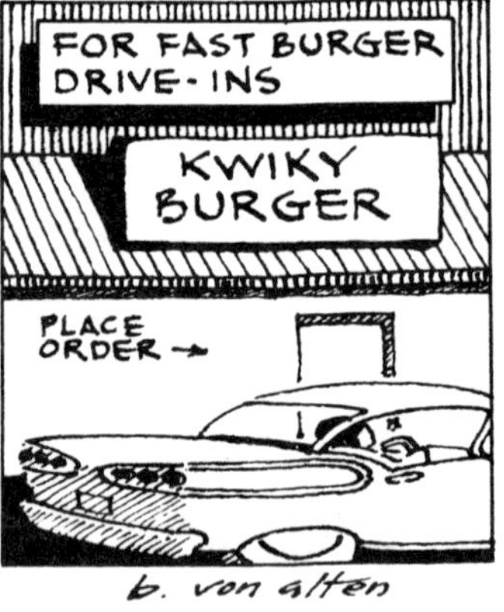
FOR FAST BURGER DRIVE-INS
KWIKY BURGER
PLACE ORDER →
b. von alten
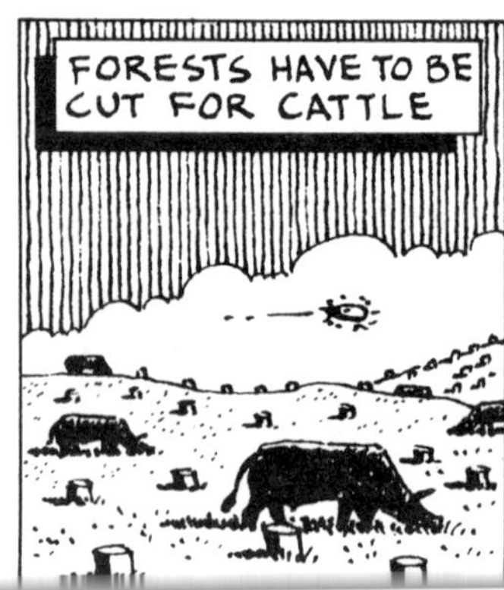
FORESTS HAVE TO BE CUT FOR CATTLE
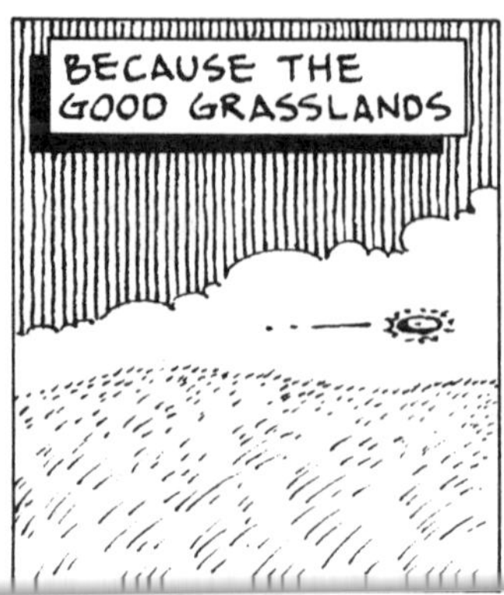
BECAUSE THE GOOD GRASSLANDS
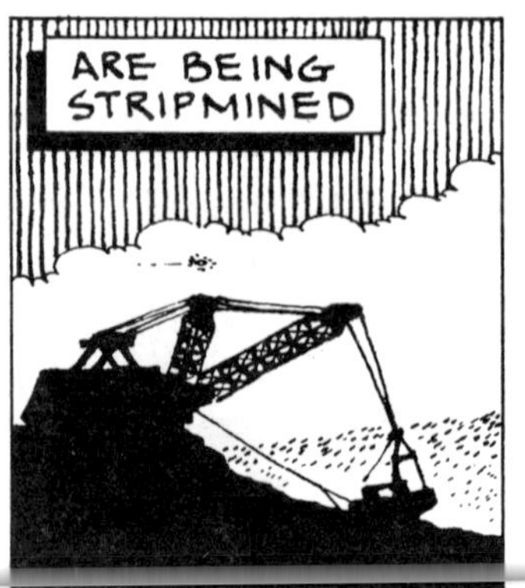
ARE BEING STRIPMINED
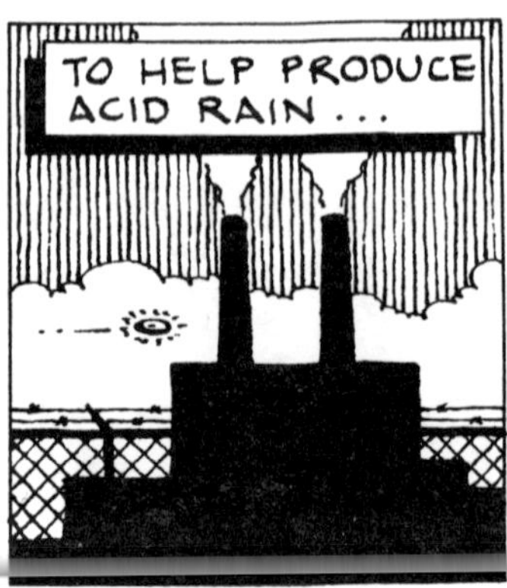
TO HELP PRODUCE ACID RAIN ...
b. von alten

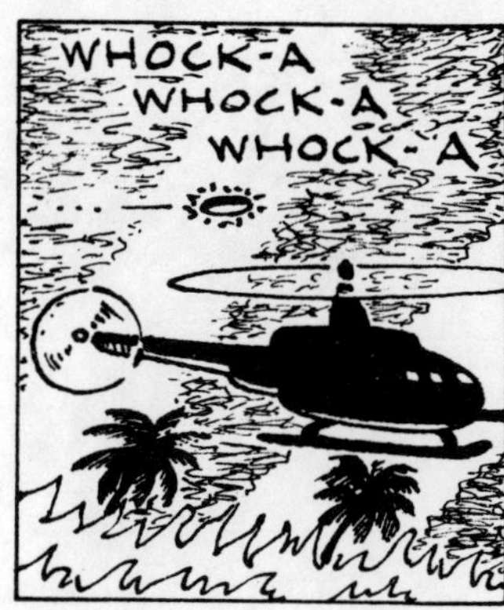
WHOCK-A
WHOCK-A
WHOCK-A

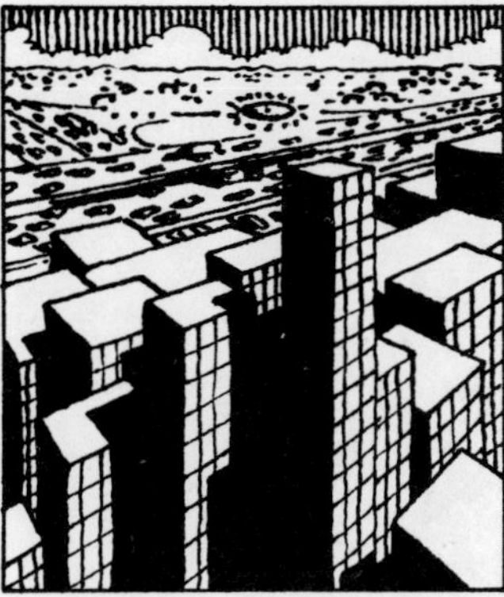

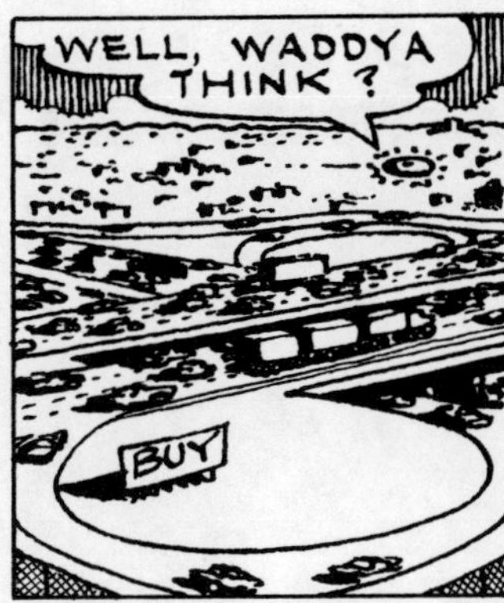
WELL, WADDYA THINK ?
BUY

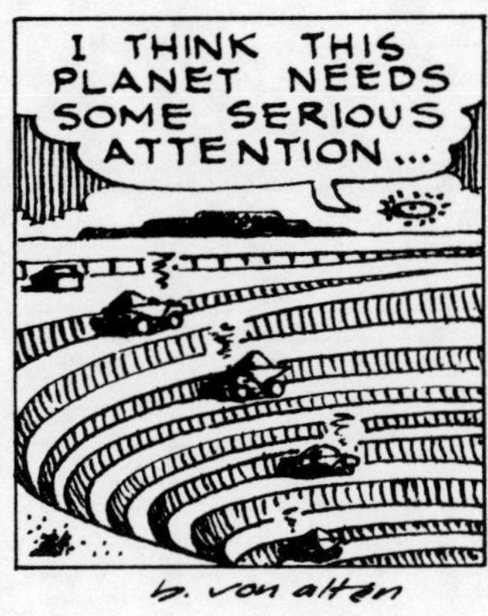
I THINK THIS PLANET NEEDS SOME SERIOUS ATTENTION...
b. von alten

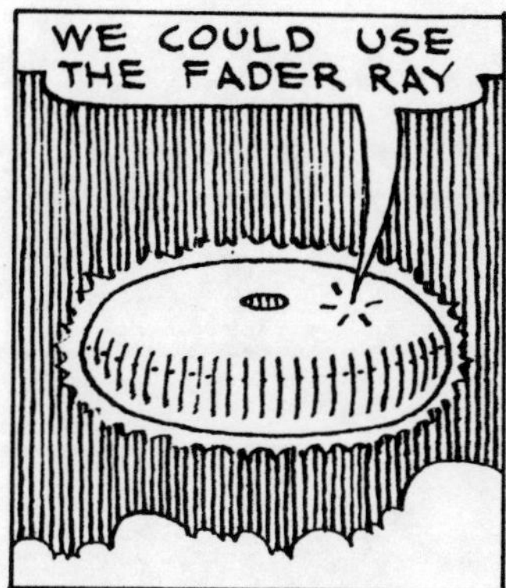
WE COULD USE THE FADER RAY

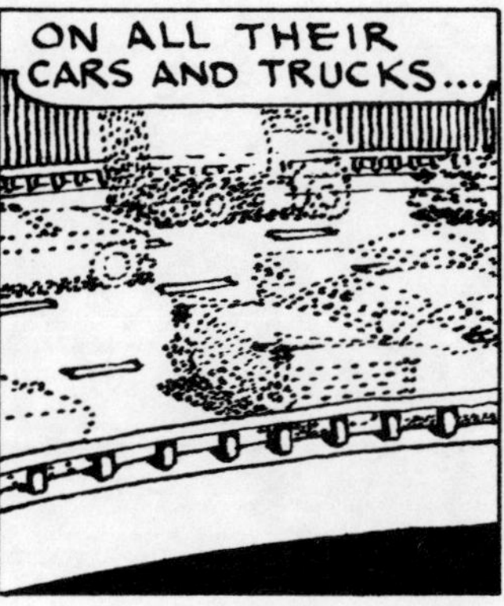
ON ALL THEIR CARS AND TRUCKS...

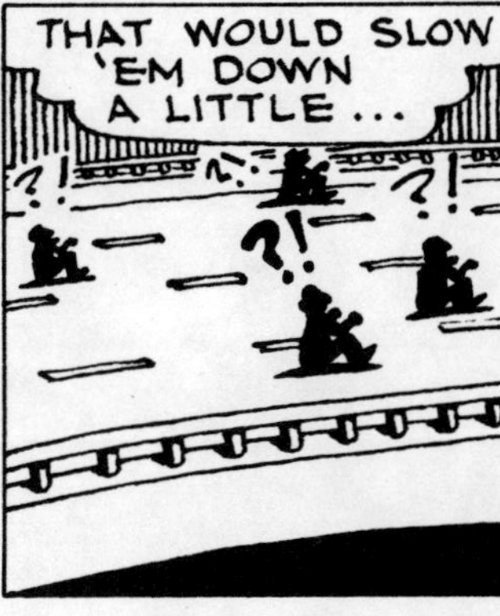
THAT WOULD SLOW 'EM DOWN A LITTLE...
?!
?!
?!
?!

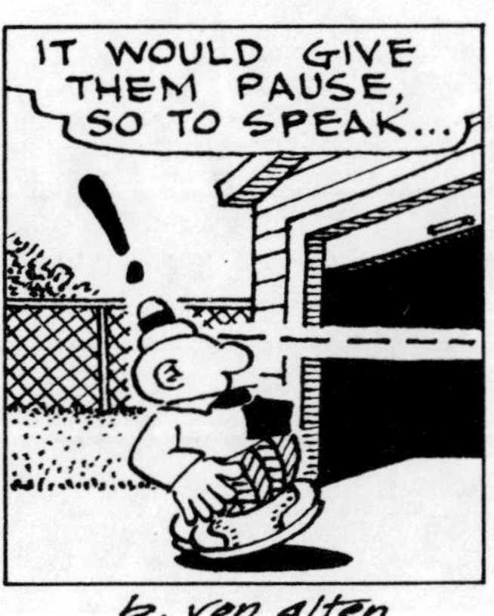
IT WOULD GIVE THEM PAUSE, SO TO SPEAK...
!
b. von alten

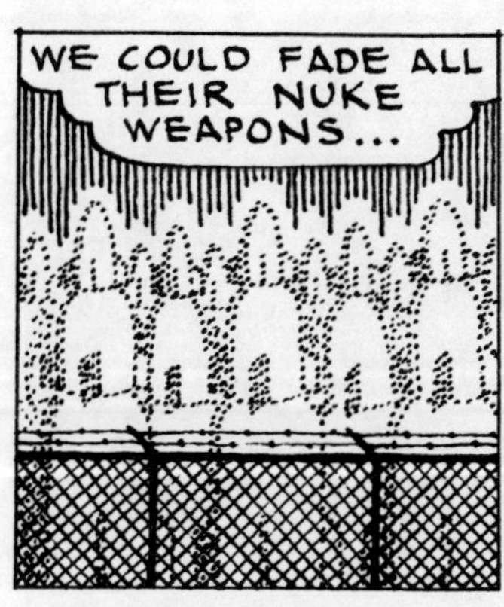
WE COULD FADE ALL THEIR NUKE WEAPONS...

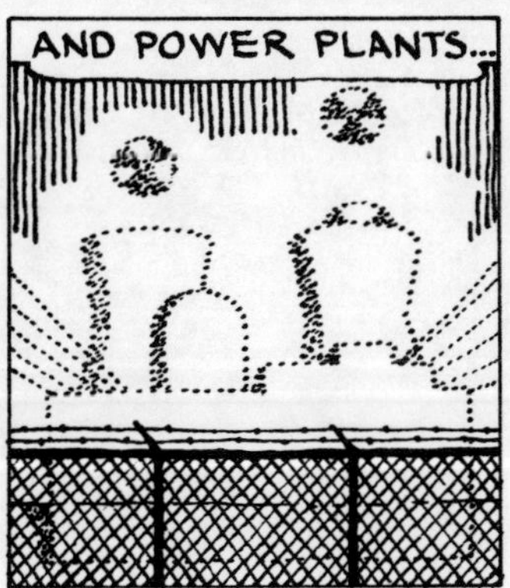
AND POWER PLANTS...

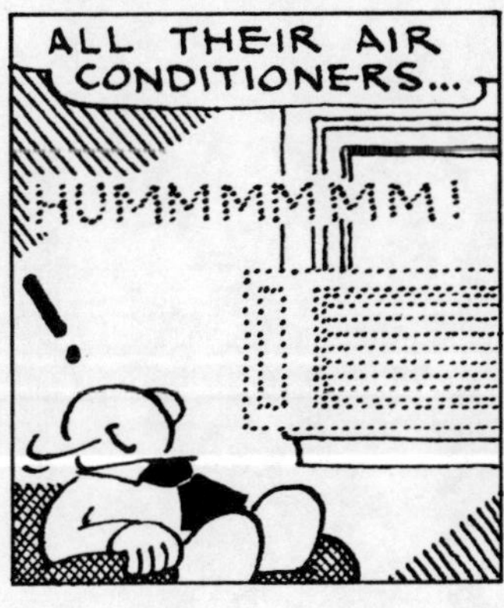
ALL THEIR AIR CONDITIONERS...
HUMMMMMMM!
!

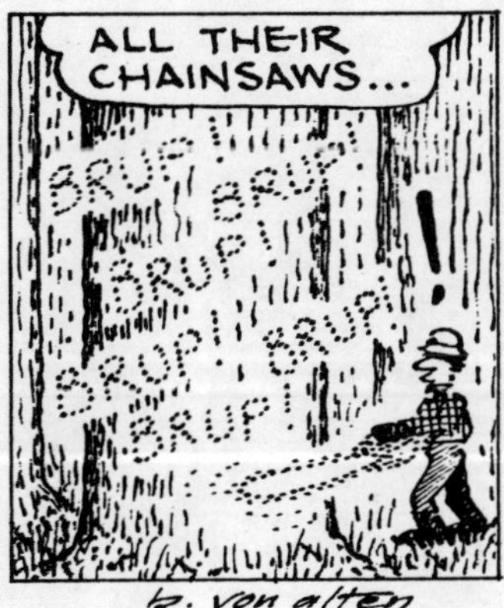
ALL THEIR CHAINSAWS...
BRUP!
BRUP!
BRUP!
BRUP!
BRUP!
BRUP!
BRUP!
!
b. von alten

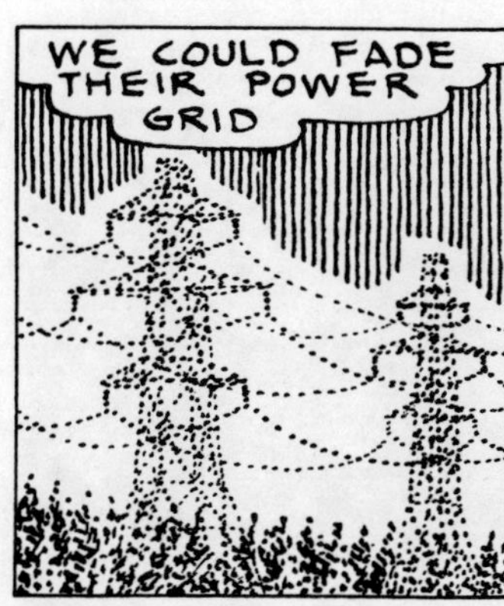
WE COULD FADE THEIR POWER GRID

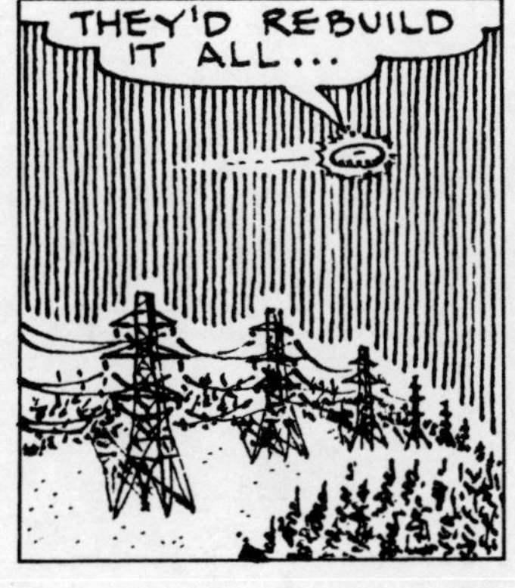
THEY'D REBUILD IT ALL...

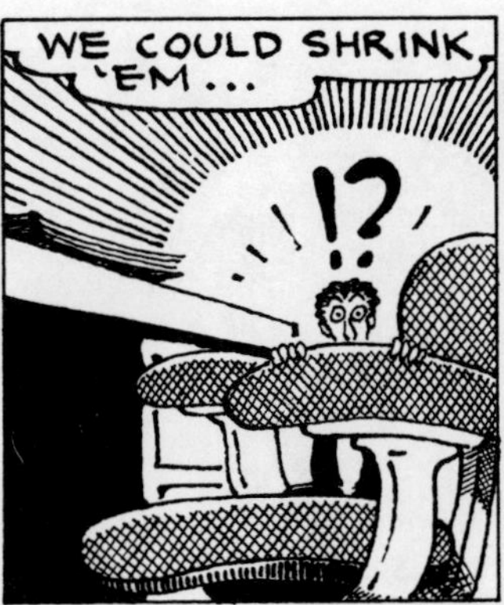
WE COULD SHRINK 'EM...
!?

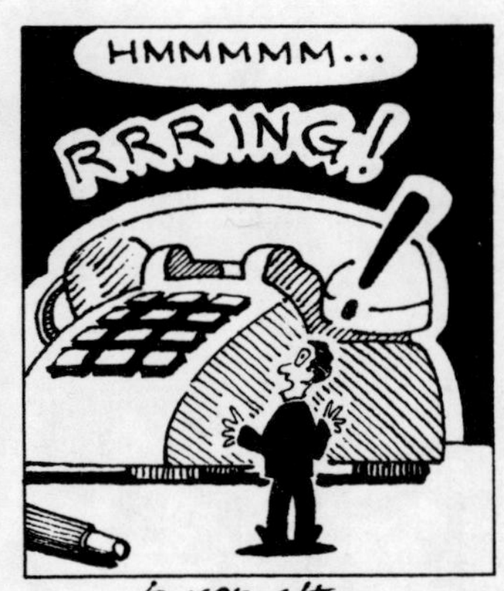
HMMMMM...
RRRING!
!
b. von alten

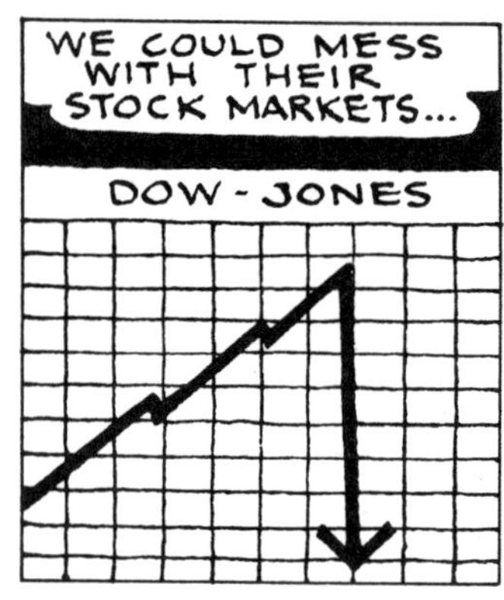
WE COULD MESS WITH THEIR STOCK MARKETS...
DOW-JONES

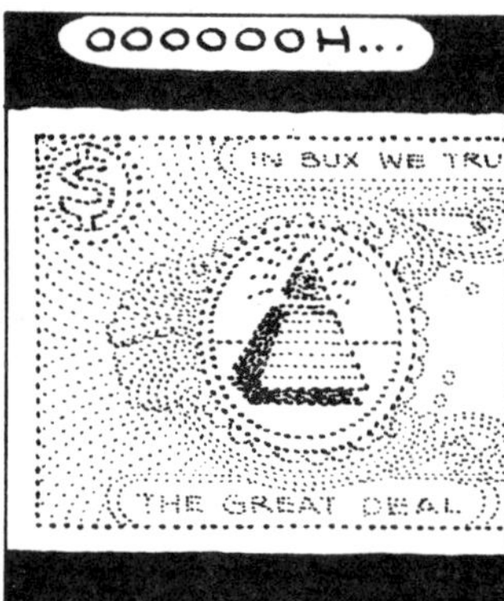
OOOOOOH...
IN BUX WE TRU
THE GREAT DEAL

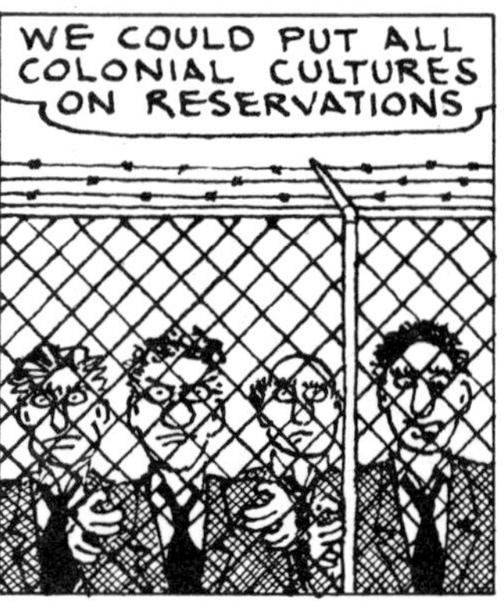
WE COULD PUT ALL COLONIAL CULTURES ON RESERVATIONS

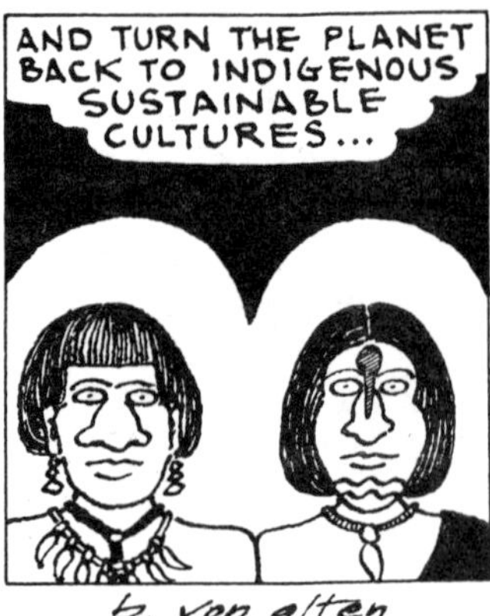
AND TURN THE PLANET BACK TO INDIGENOUS SUSTAINABLE CULTURES...

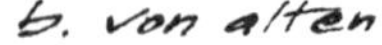
b. von alten

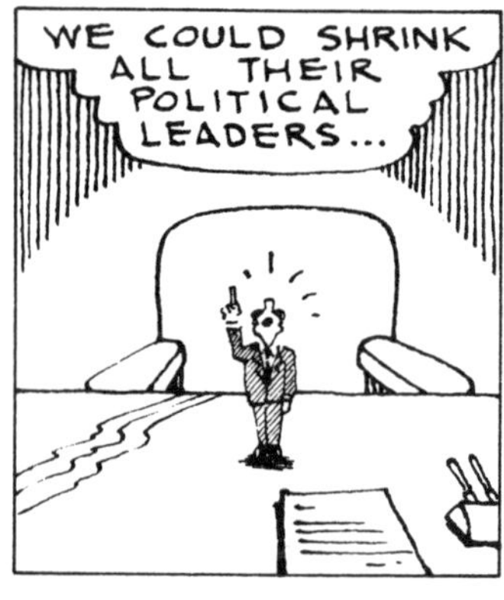
WE COULD SHRINK ALL THEIR POLITICAL LEADERS...

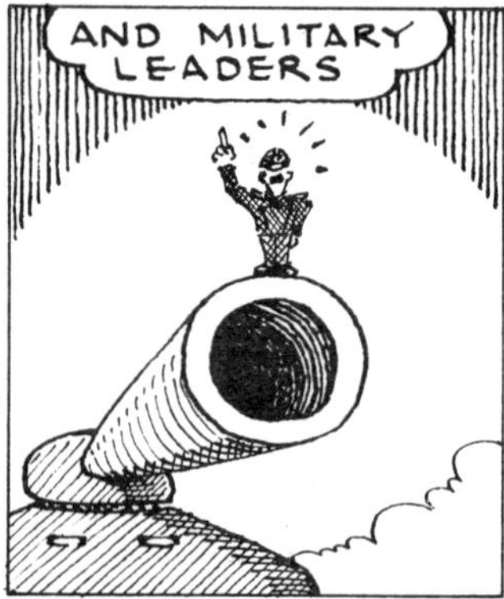
AND MILITARY LEADERS

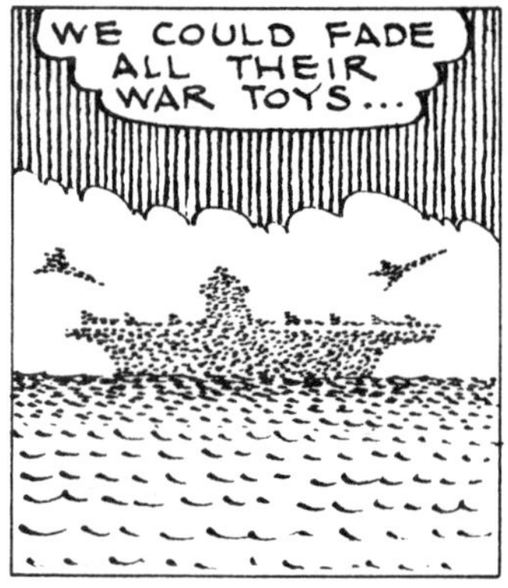
WE COULD FADE ALL THEIR WAR TOYS...

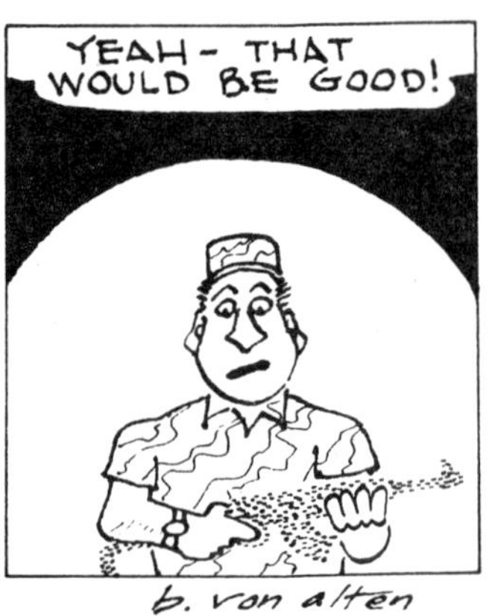
YEAH - THAT WOULD BE GOOD!
b. von alten

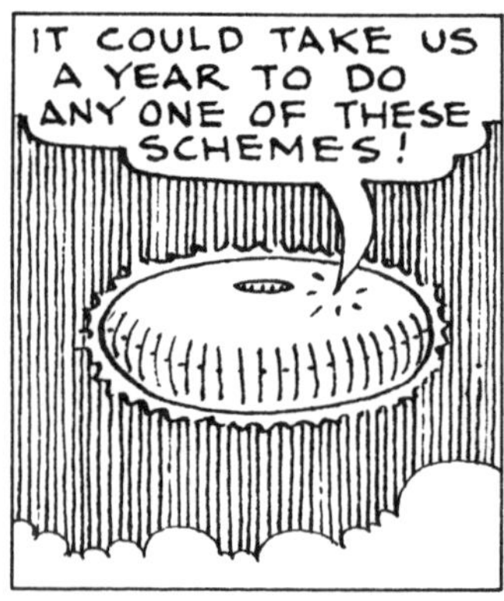
IT COULD TAKE US A YEAR TO DO ANY ONE OF THESE SCHEMES!

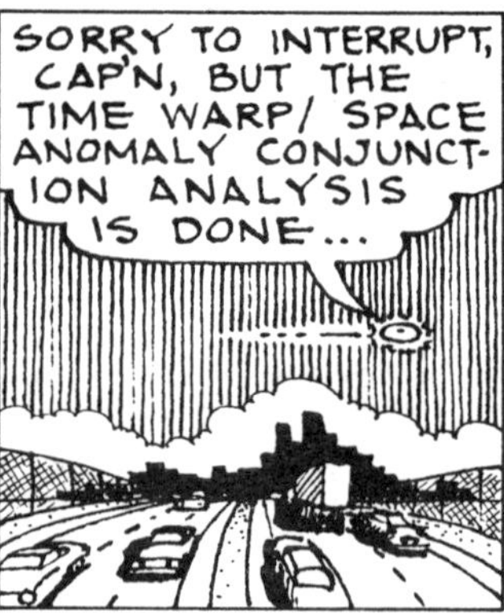
SORRY TO INTERRUPT, CAP'N, BUT THE TIME WARP/ SPACE ANOMALY CONJUNCTION ANALYSIS IS DONE...

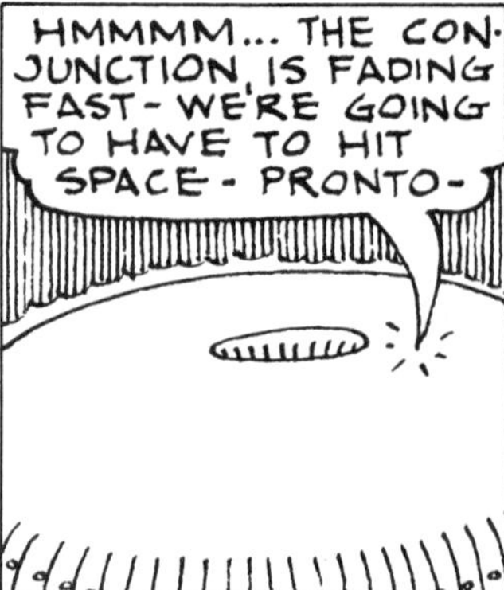
HMMMM... THE CONJUNCTION IS FADING FAST- WE'RE GOING TO HAVE TO HIT SPACE- PRONTO-

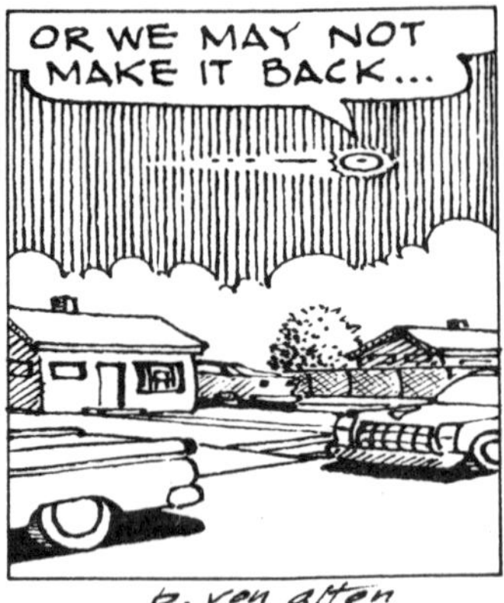
OR WE MAY NOT MAKE IT BACK...
b. von alten

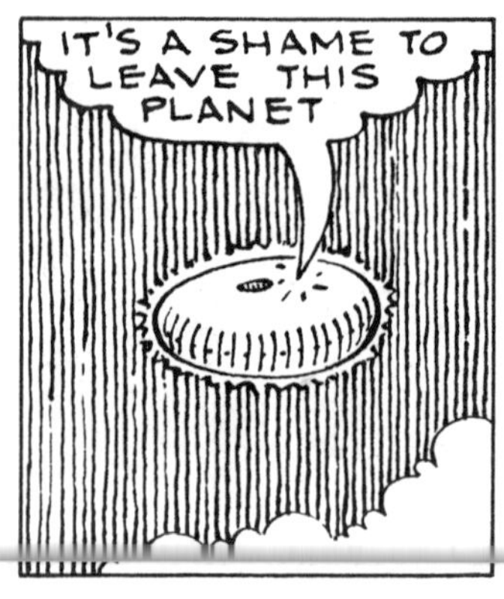
IT'S A SHAME TO LEAVE THIS PLANET

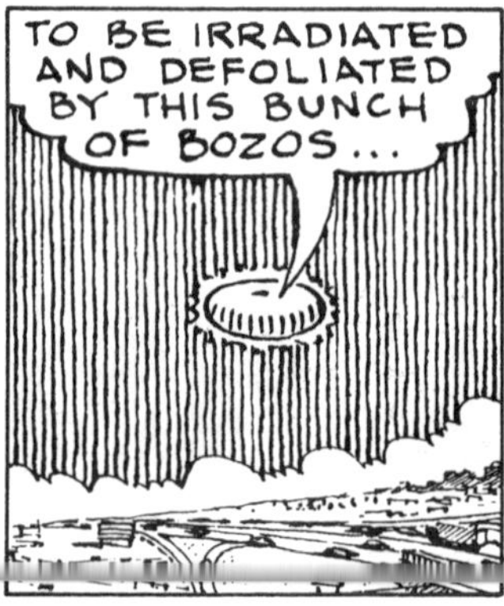
TO BE IRRADIATED AND DEFOLIATED BY THIS BUNCH OF BOZOS...

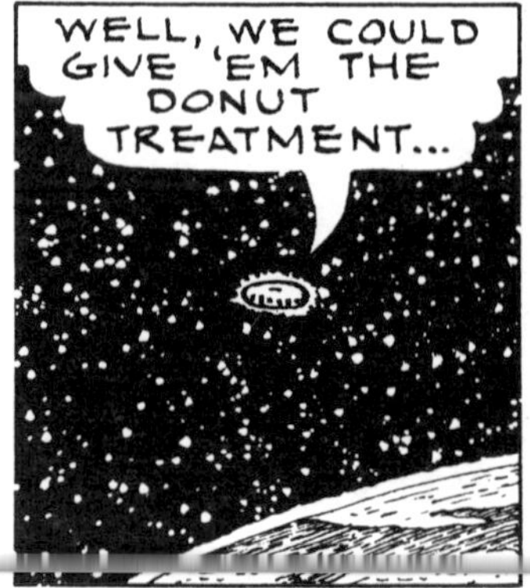
WELL, WE COULD GIVE 'EM THE DONUT TREATMENT...

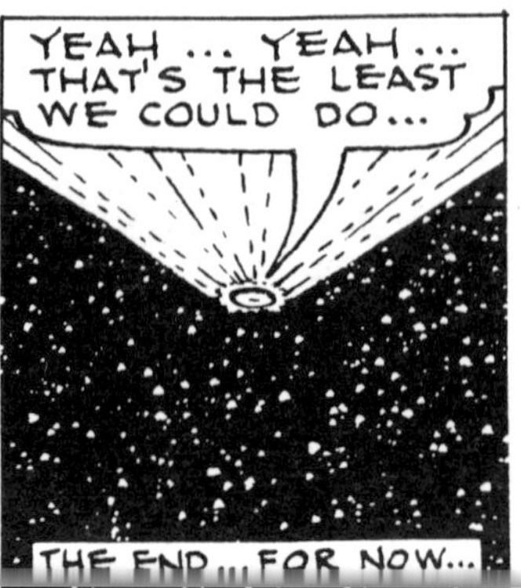
YEAH ... YEAH ... THAT'S THE LEAST WE COULD DO...
THE END... FOR NOW...

b. von alten

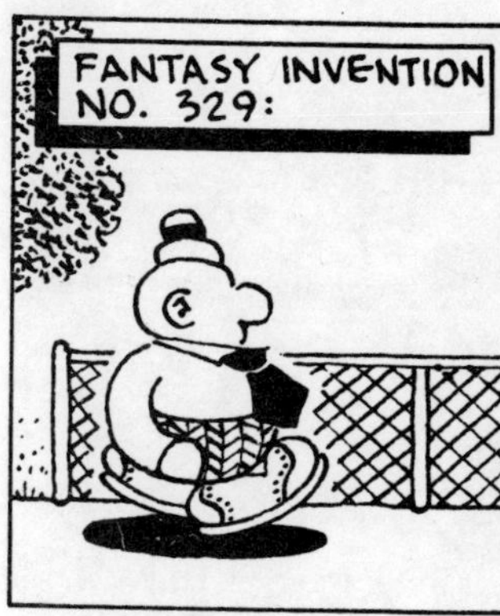
FANTASY INVENTION NO. 329:

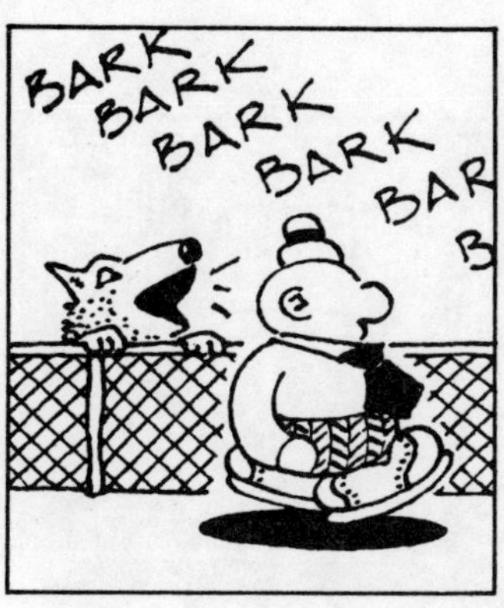
BARK
BARK
BARK
BARK
BAR
B

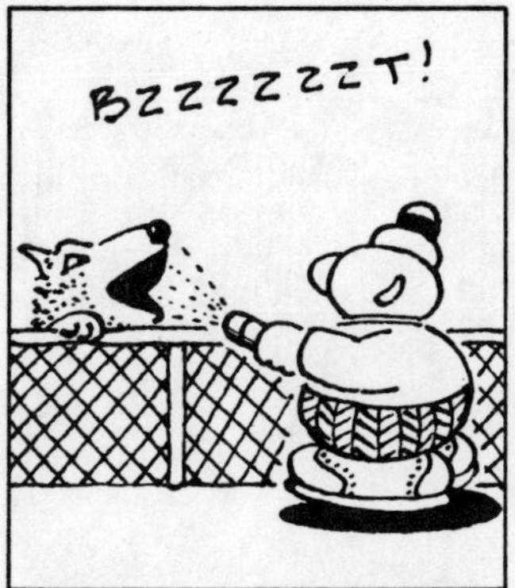
BZZZZZZT!

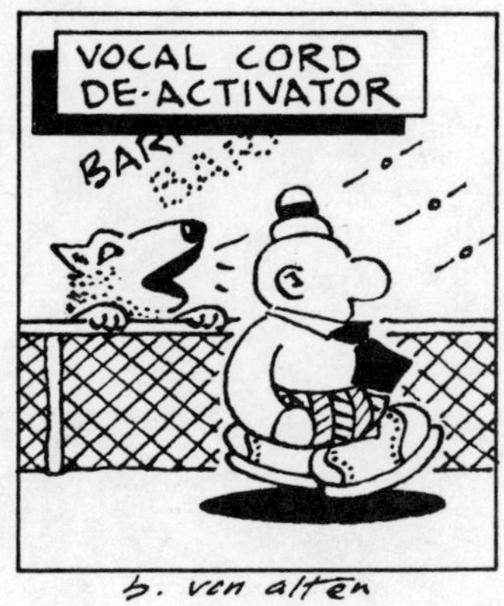
VOCAL CORD DE-ACTIVATOR
b. von alten

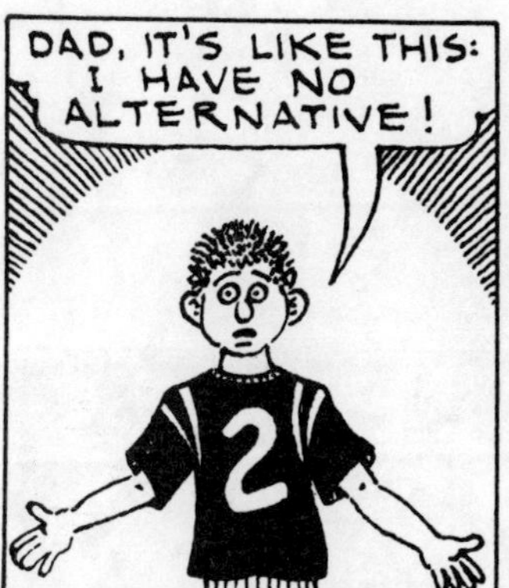
DAD, IT'S LIKE THIS: I HAVE NO ALTERNATIVE!

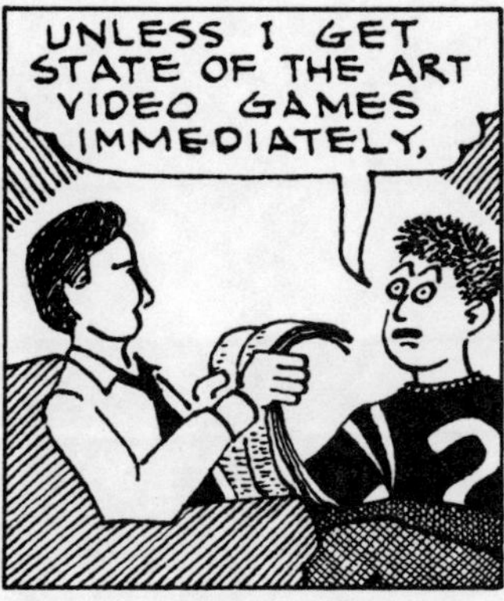
UNLESS I GET STATE OF THE ART VIDEO GAMES IMMEDIATELY,

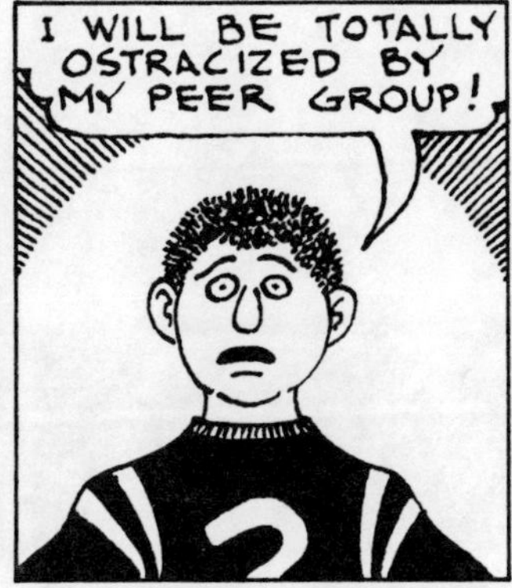
I WILL BE TOTALLY OSTRACIZED BY MY PEER GROUP!

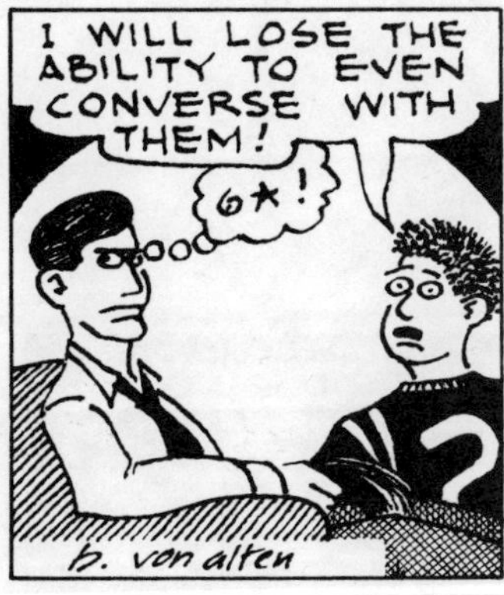
I WILL LOSE THE ABILITY TO EVEN CONVERSE WITH THEM!
b. von alten

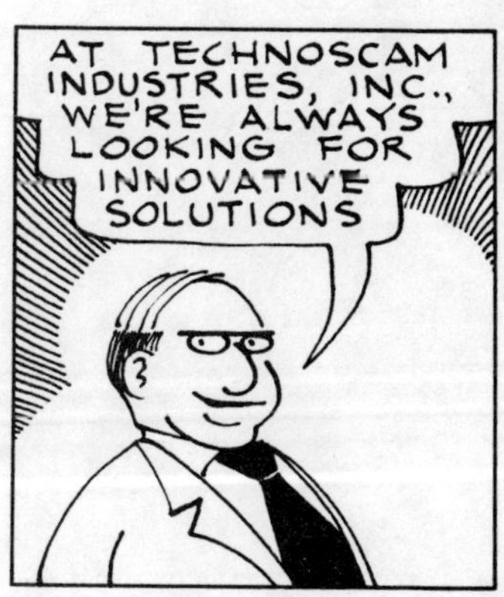
AT TECHNOSCAM INDUSTRIES, INC., WE'RE ALWAYS LOOKING FOR INNOVATIVE SOLUTIONS

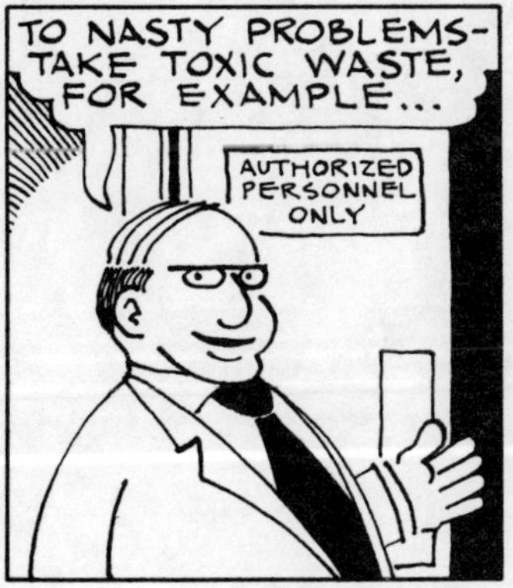
TO NASTY PROBLEMS-TAKE TOXIC WASTE, FOR EXAMPLE...
AUTHORIZED PERSONNEL ONLY

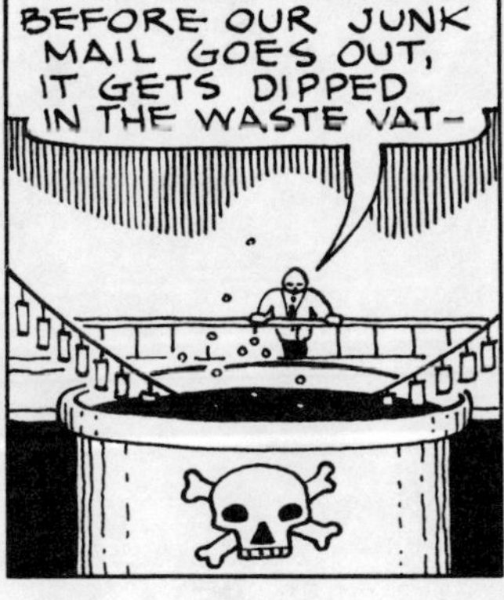
BEFORE OUR JUNK MAIL GOES OUT, IT GETS DIPPED IN THE WASTE VAT-

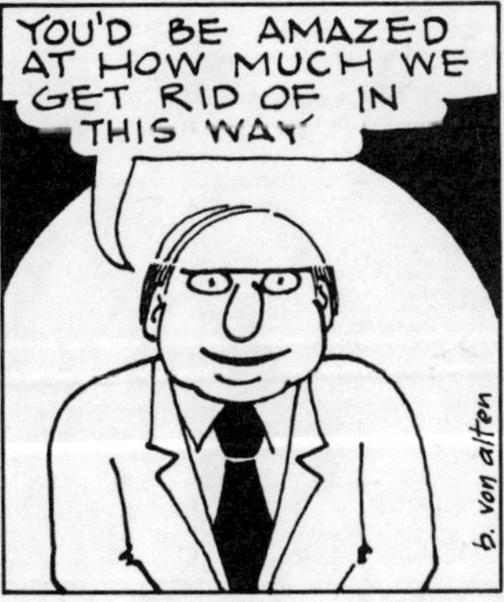
YOU'D BE AMAZED AT HOW MUCH WE GET RID OF IN THIS WAY
b. von alten

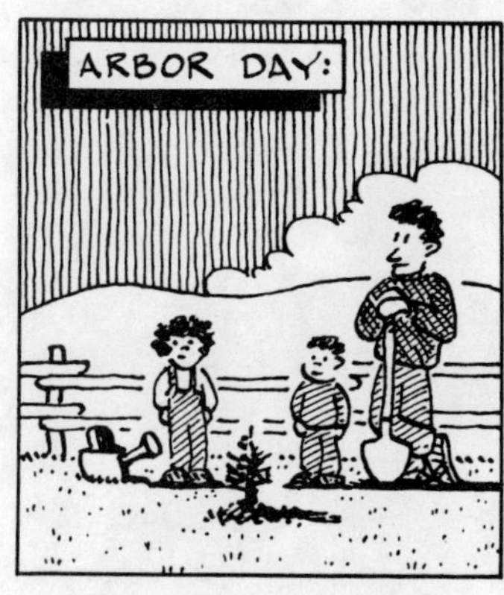
ARBOR DAY:

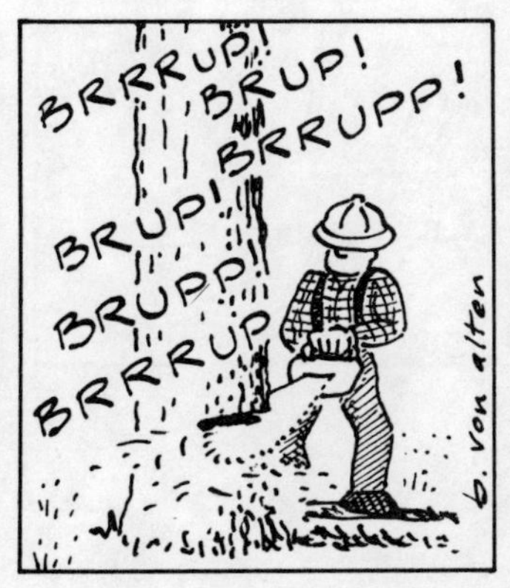
BRRRUP!
BRUP!
BRRUPP!
BRUP!
BRUPP!
BRRRUP
b. von alten

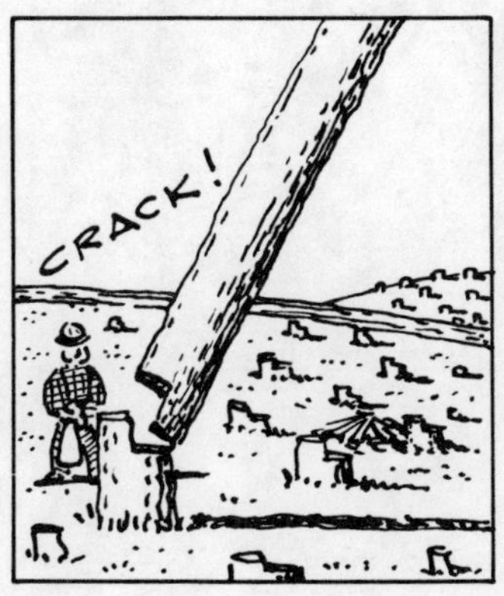
CRACK!

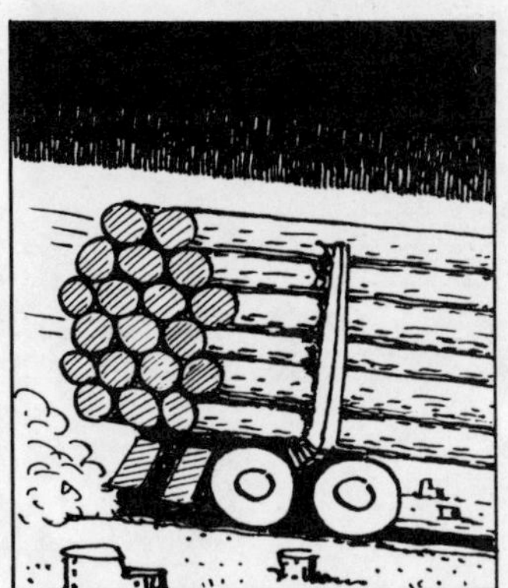

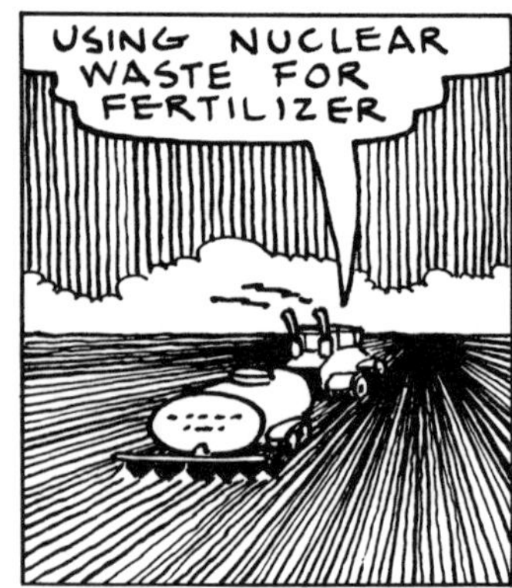
USING NUCLEAR WASTE FOR FERTILIZER
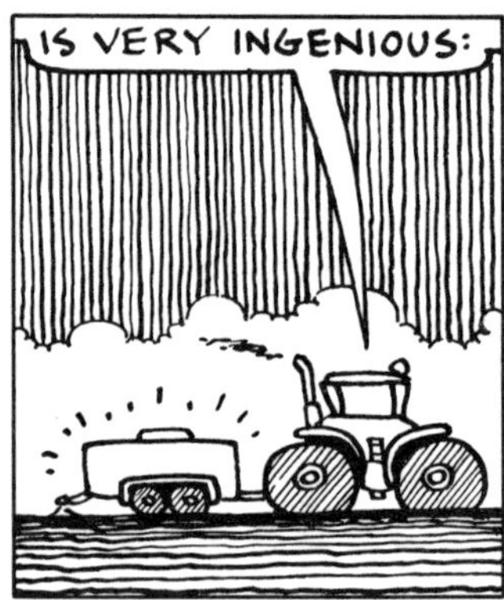
IS VERY INGENIOUS:
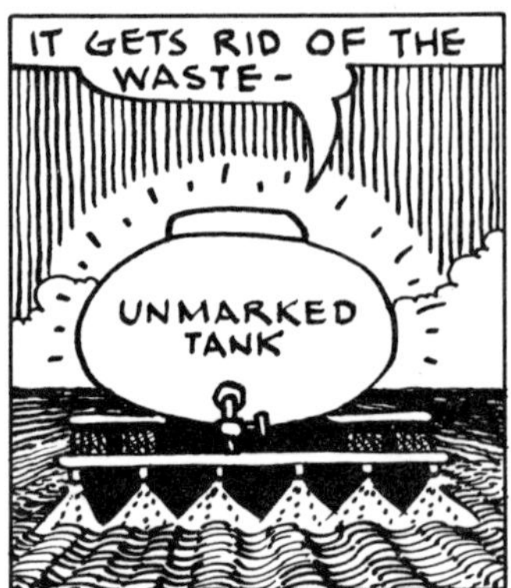
IT GETS RID OF THE WASTE-
UNMARKED TANK
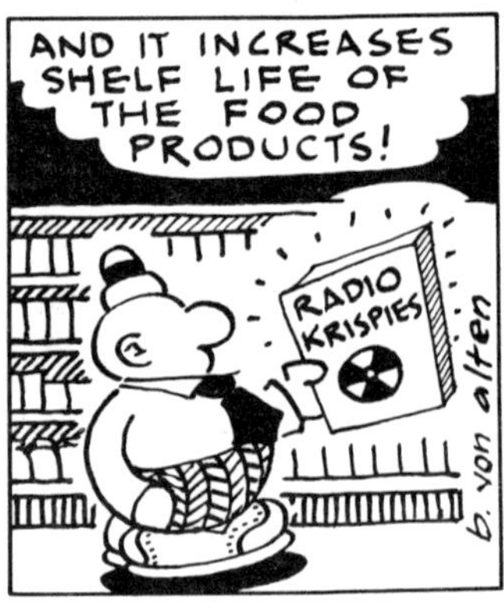
AND IT INCREASES SHELF LIFE OF THE FOOD PRODUCTS!
RADIO KRISPIES
b. von alten
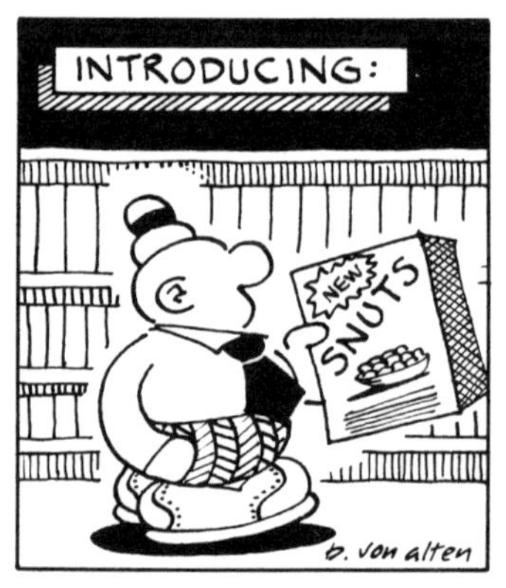
INTRODUCING:
NEW SNUTS
b. von alten
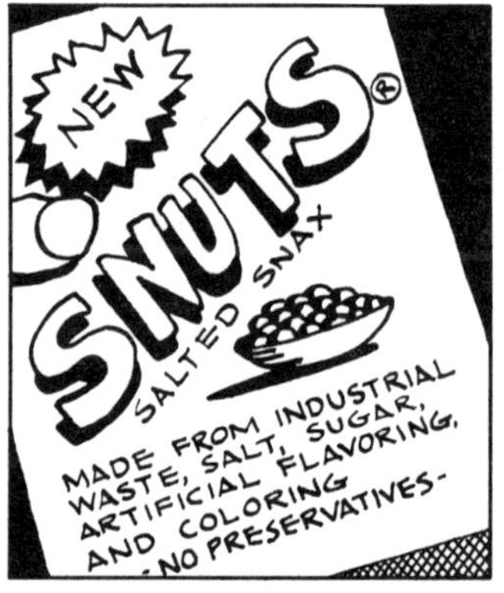
NEW
SNUTS®
SALTED SNAX
MADE FROM INDUSTRIAL WASTE, SALT, SUGAR, ARTIFICIAL FLAVORING, AND COLORING
-NO PRESERVATIVES-
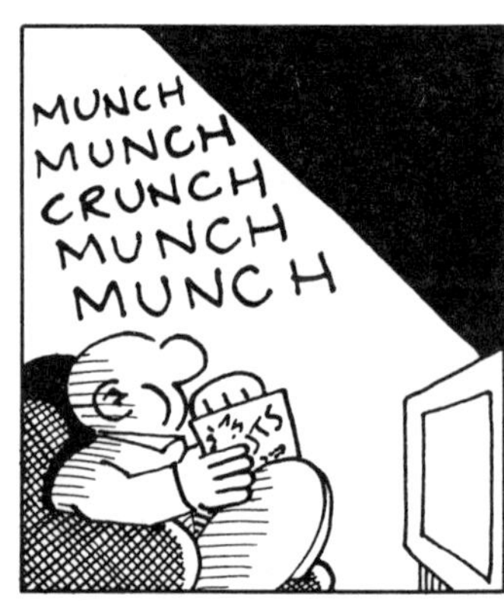
MUNCH
MUNCH
CRUNCH
MUNCH
MUNCH
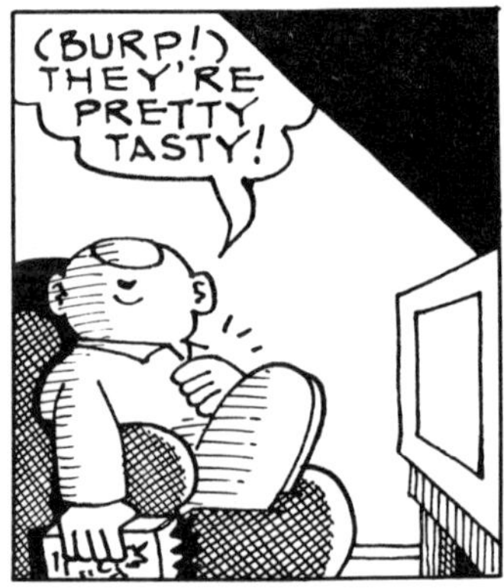
(BURP!) THEY'RE PRETTY TASTY!
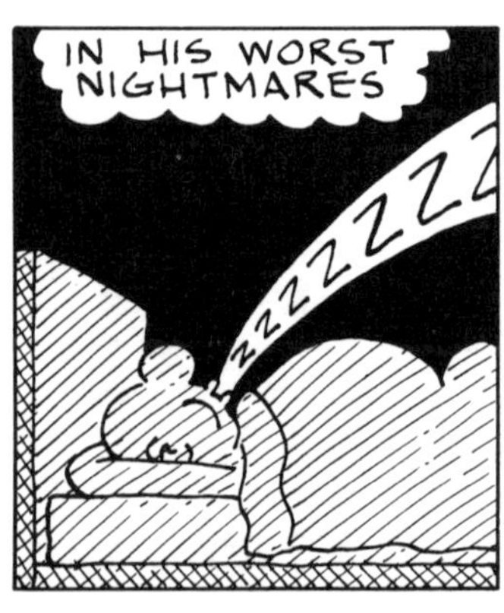
IN HIS WORST NIGHTMARES
ZZZZZZZ
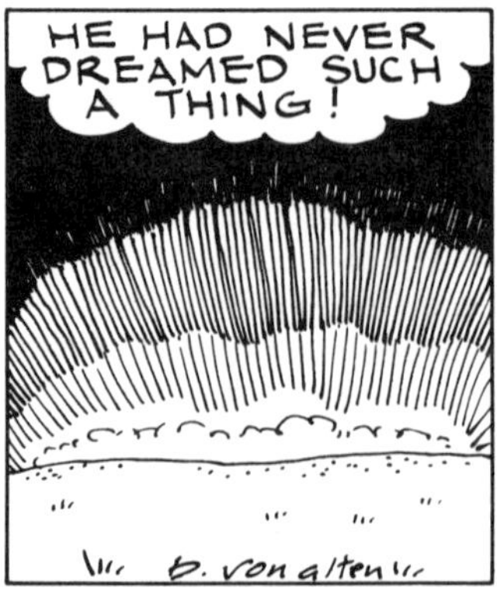
HE HAD NEVER DREAMED SUCH A THING!
b. von alten
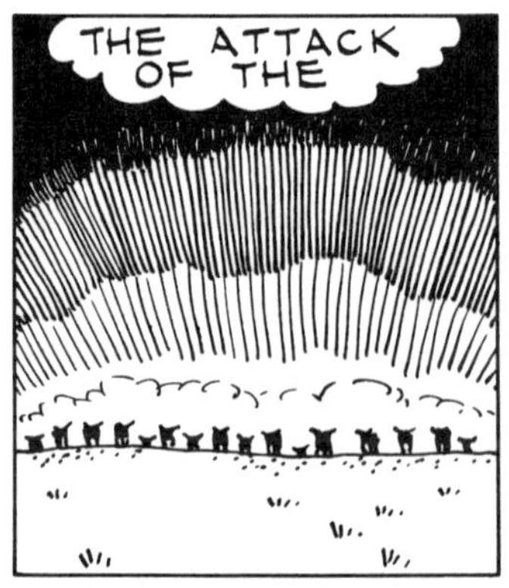
THE ATTACK OF THE
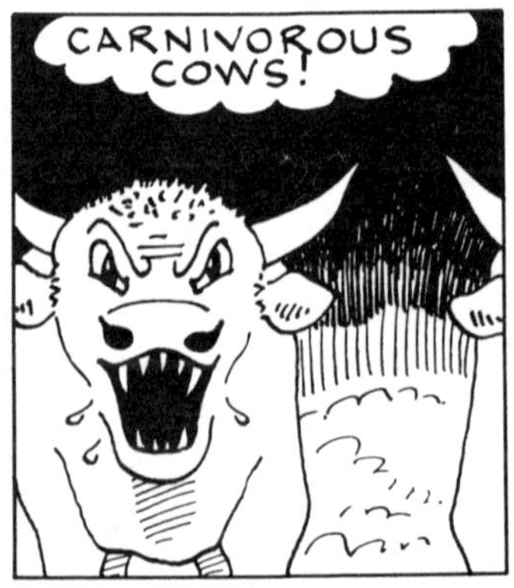
CARNIVOROUS COWS!

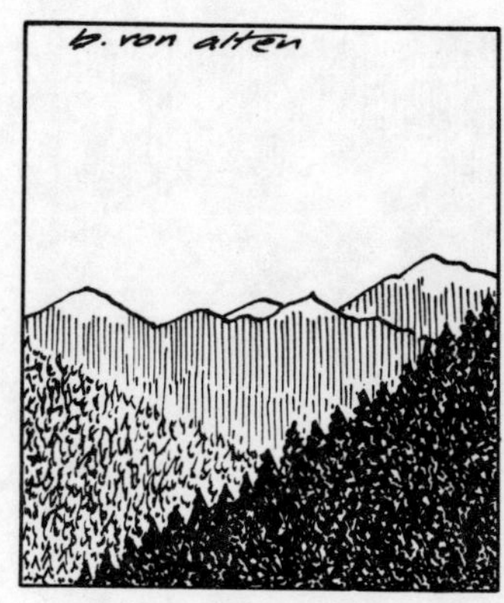
b. von alten

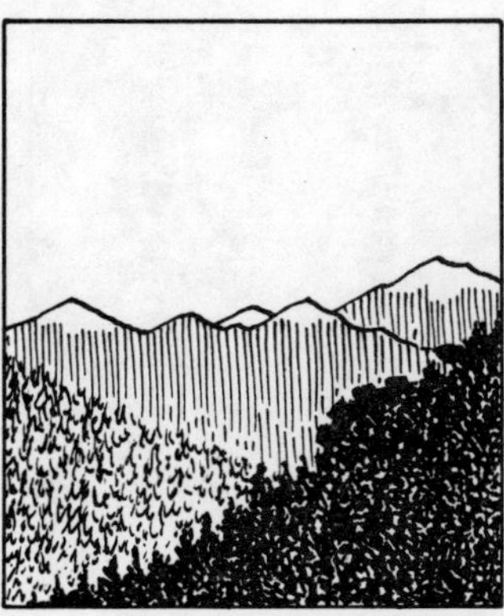

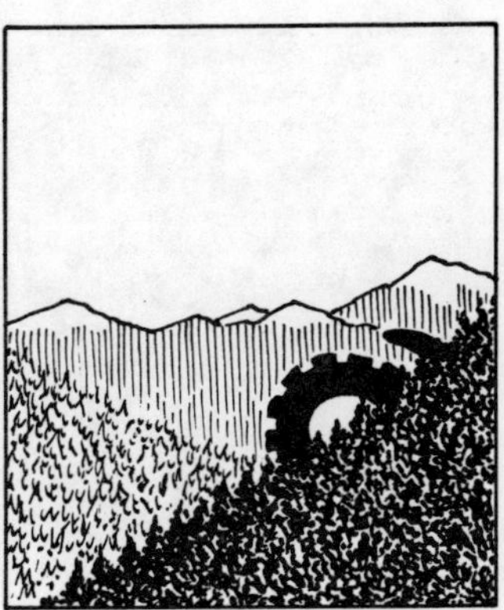

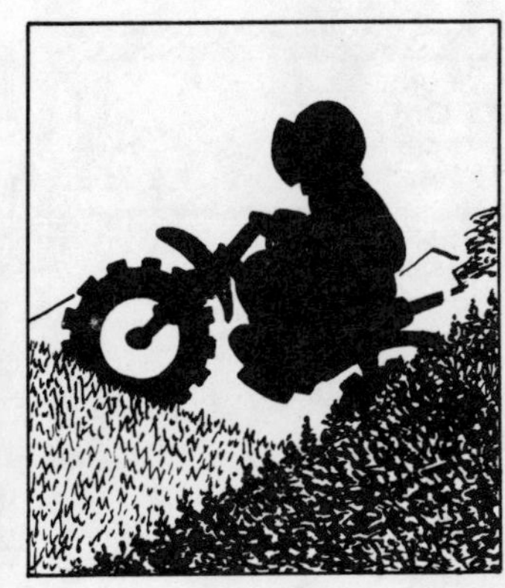

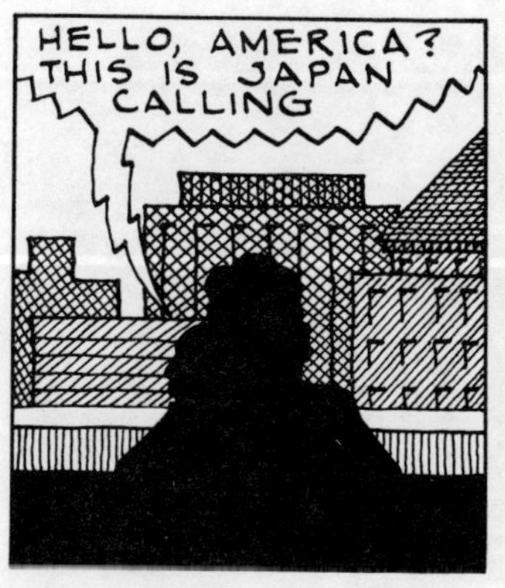
HELLO, AMERICA?
THIS IS JAPAN
CALLING

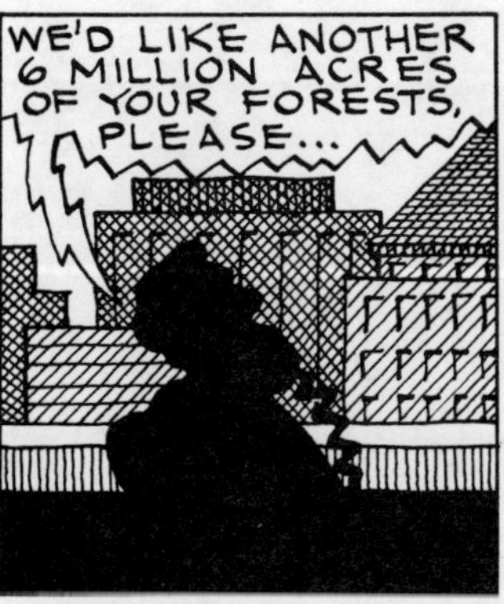
WE'D LIKE ANOTHER
6 MILLION ACRES
OF YOUR FORESTS,
PLEASE...

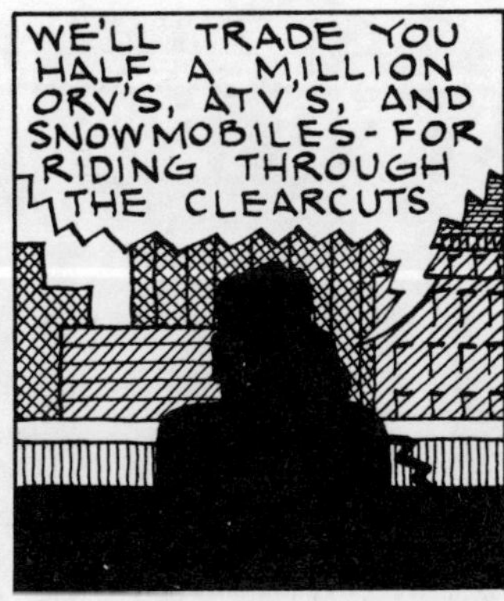
WE'LL TRADE YOU
HALF A MILLION
ORV'S, ATV'S, AND
SNOWMOBILES-FOR
RIDING THROUGH
THE CLEARCUTS

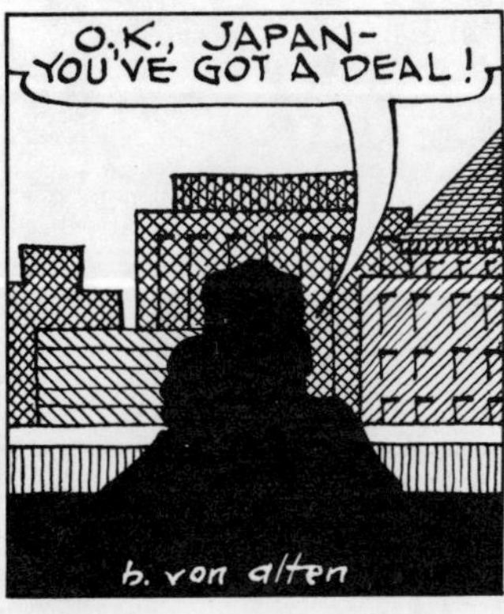
O.K., JAPAN-
YOU'VE GOT A DEAL!
b. von alten

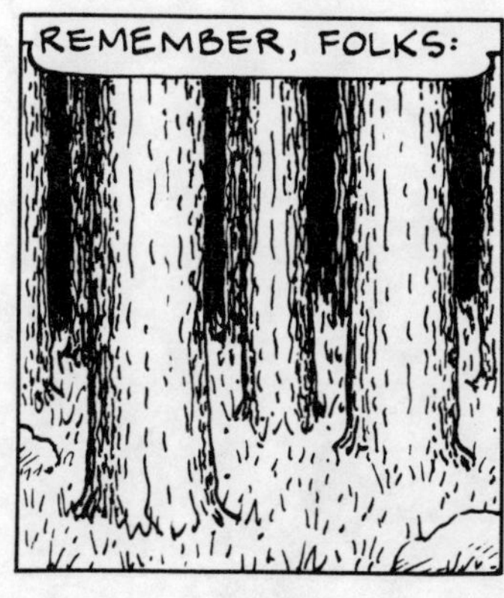
REMEMBER, FOLKS:

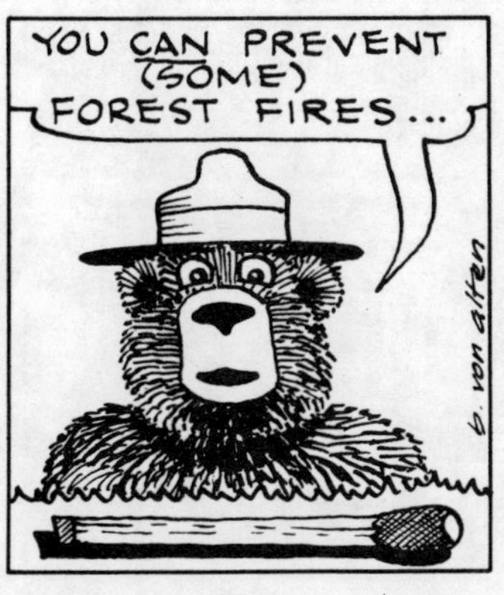
YOU CAN PREVENT
(SOME)
FOREST FIRES...
b. von alten

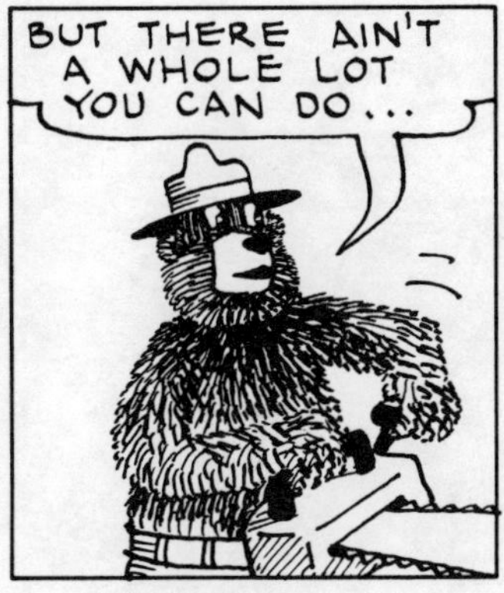
BUT THERE AIN'T
A WHOLE LOT
YOU CAN DO...

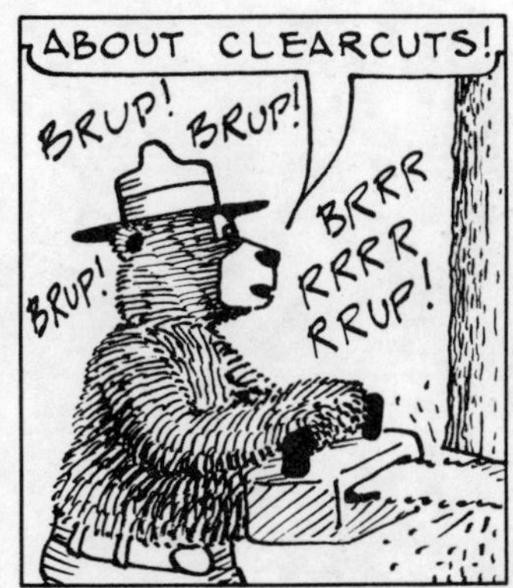
ABOUT CLEARCUTS!
BRUP!
BRUP!
BRUP!
BRRR
RRRR
RRUP!

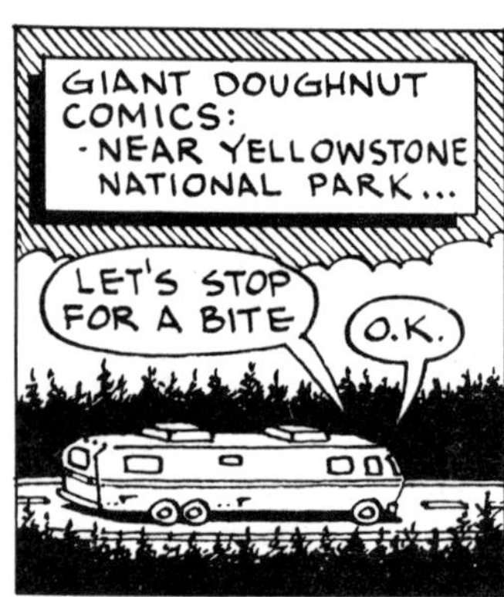
GIANT DOUGHNUT COMICS:
-NEAR YELLOWSTONE NATIONAL PARK...
LET'S STOP FOR A BITE
O.K.

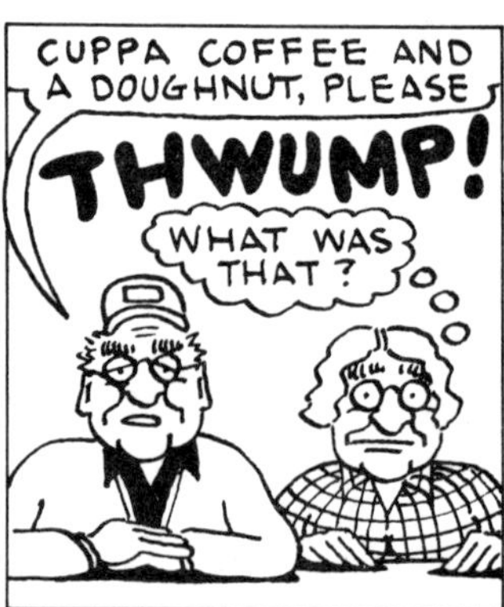
CUPPA COFFEE AND A DOUGHNUT, PLEASE
THWUMP!
WHAT WAS THAT?

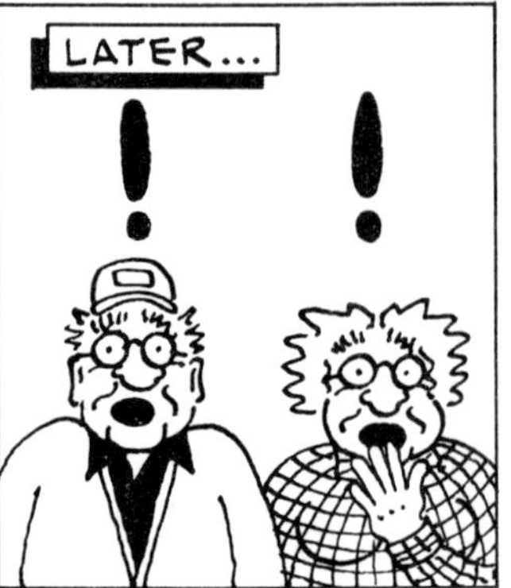
LATER...
!
!

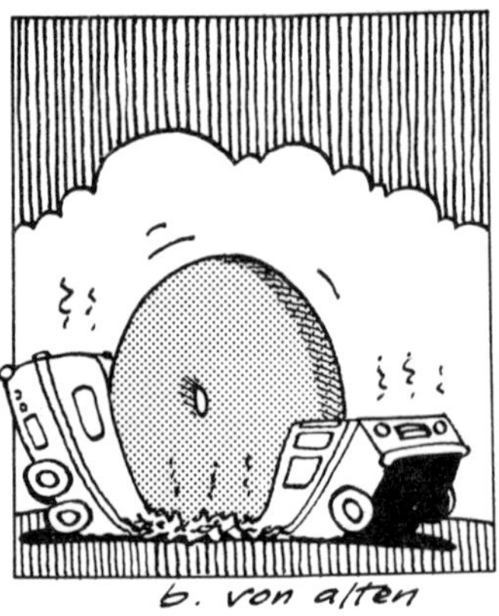

b. von alten

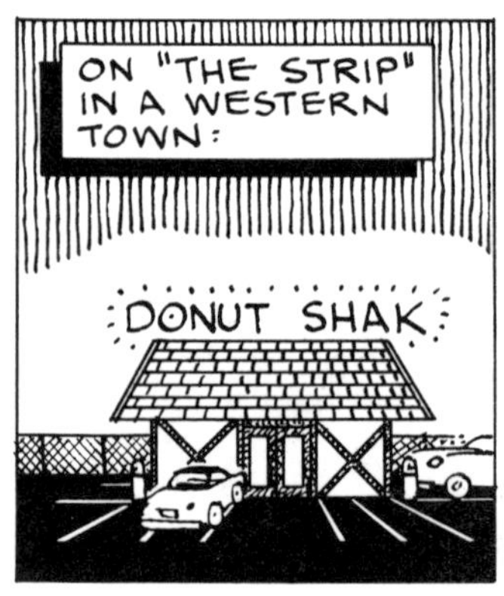
ON "THE STRIP" IN A WESTERN TOWN:
DONUT SHAK

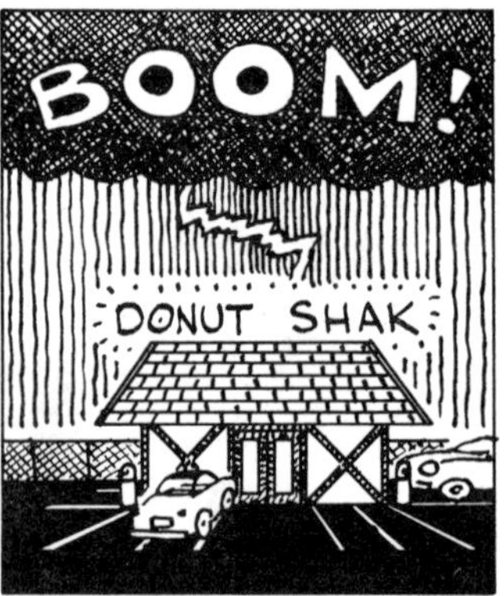
BOOM!
DONUT SHAK

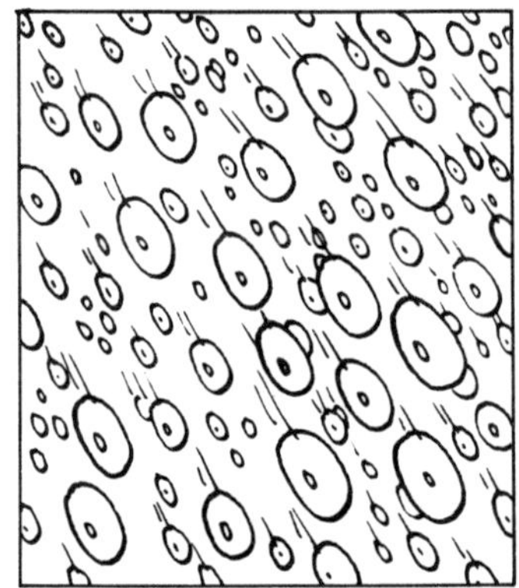

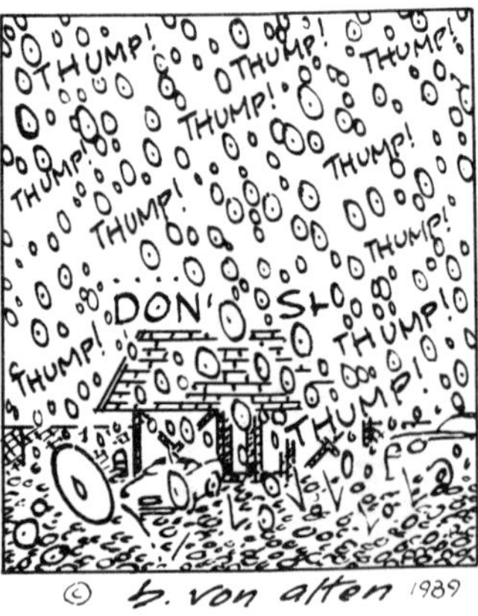
THUMP!
THUMP!
THUMP!
THUMP!
THUMP!
THUMP!
THUMP!
THUMP!
THUMP!
THUMP!
THUMP!

© b. von alten 1989

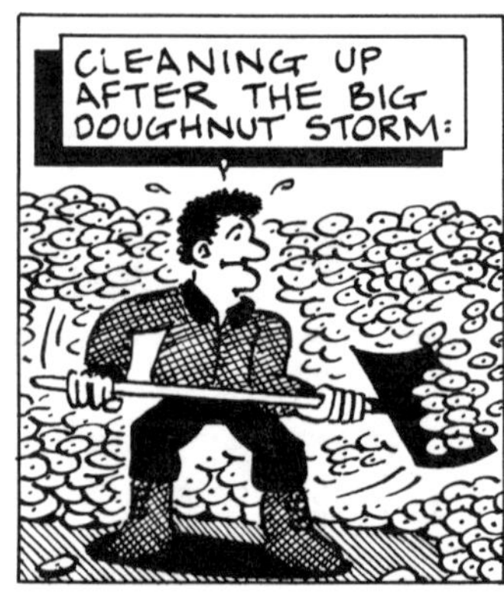
CLEANING UP AFTER THE BIG DOUGHNUT STORM:

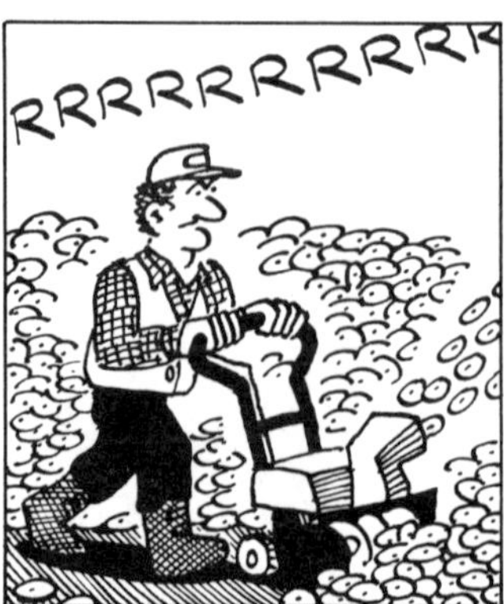
RRRRRRRRRRR

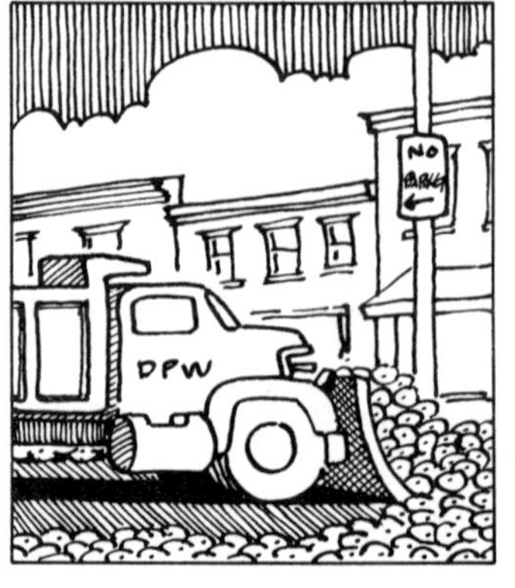
DPW

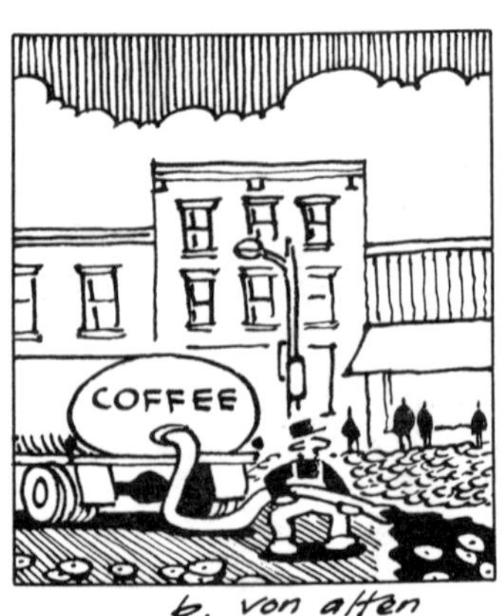
COFFEE

b. von alten

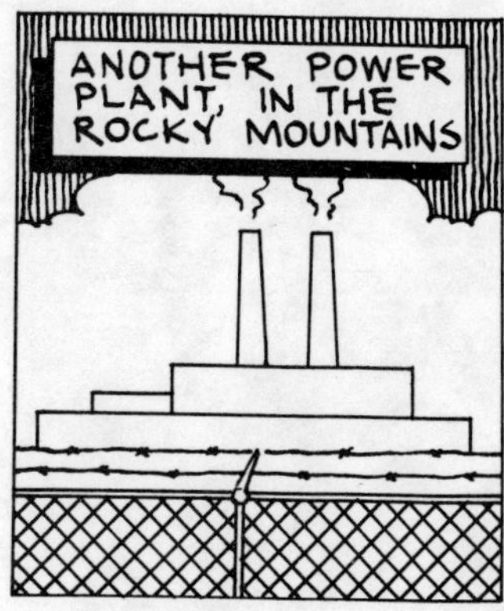
ANOTHER POWER PLANT, IN THE ROCKY MOUNTAINS

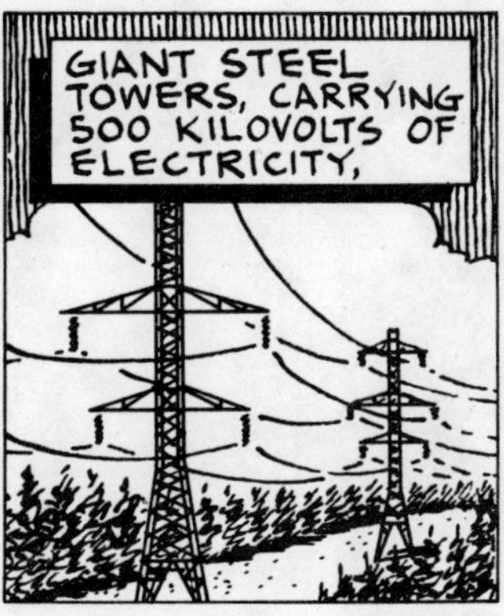
GIANT STEEL TOWERS, CARRYING 500 KILOVOLTS OF ELECTRICITY,

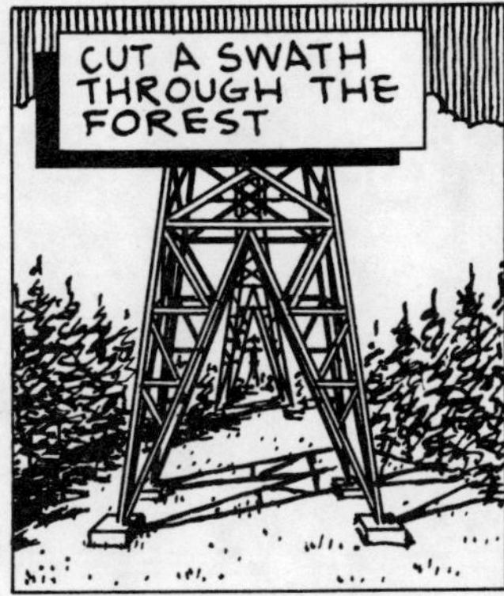
CUT A SWATH THROUGH THE FOREST

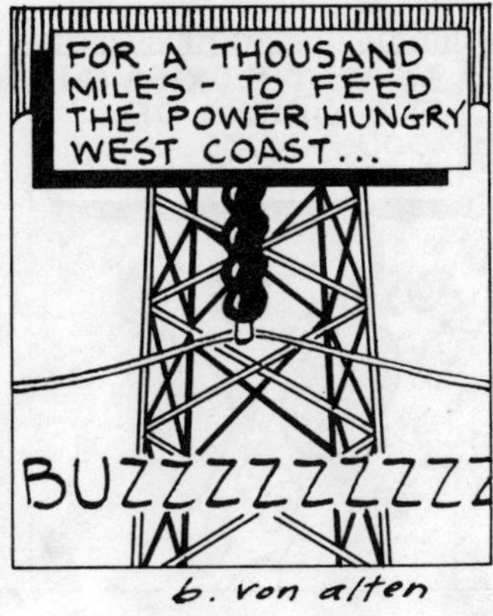
FOR A THOUSAND MILES - TO FEED THE POWER HUNGRY WEST COAST...
BUZZZZZZZZZZ

b. von alten

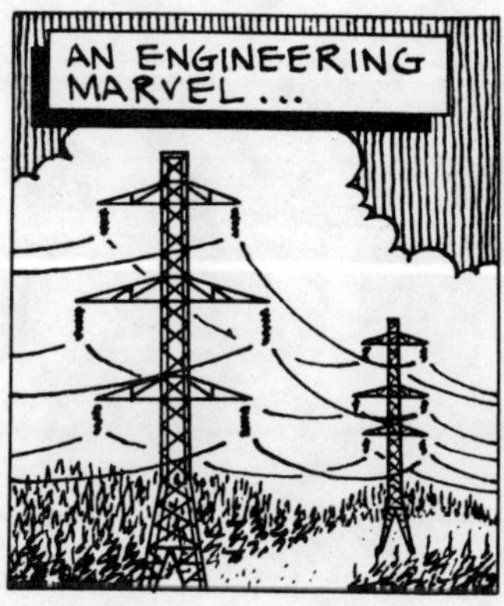
AN ENGINEERING MARVEL...

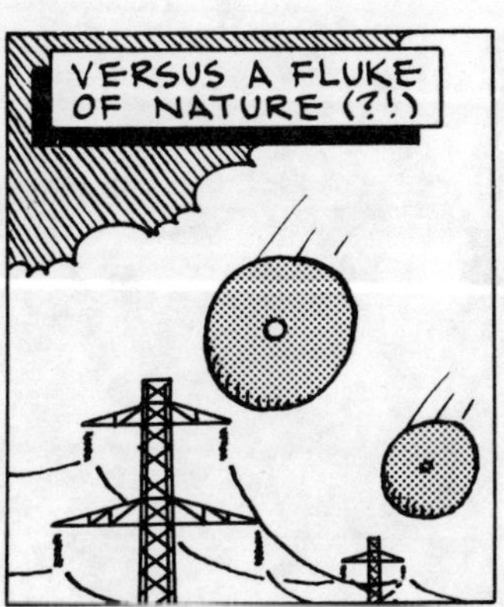
VERSUS A FLUKE OF NATURE (?!)

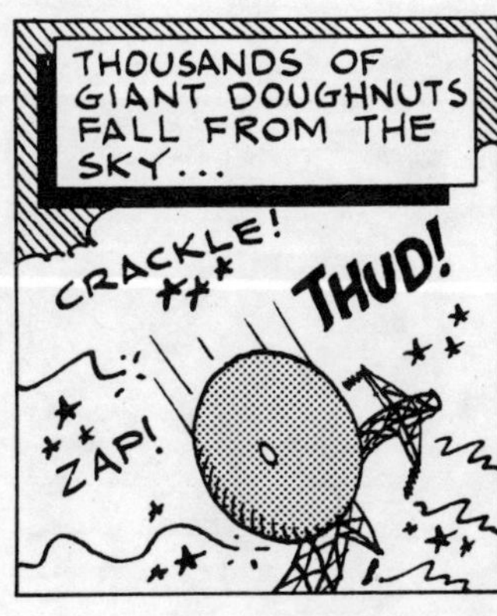
THOUSANDS OF GIANT DOUGHNUTS FALL FROM THE SKY...
CRACKLE!
THUD!
ZAP!

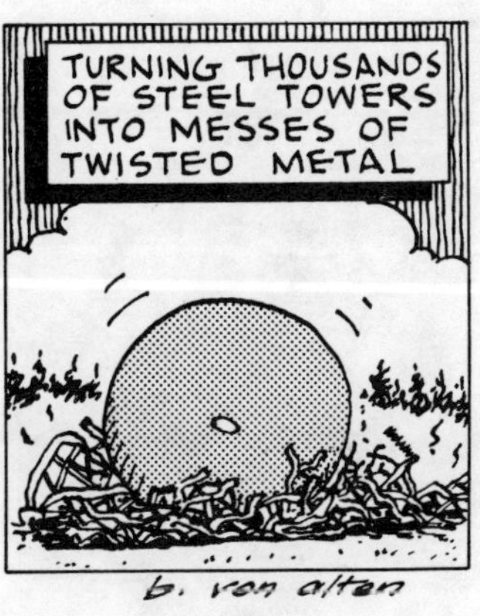
TURNING THOUSANDS OF STEEL TOWERS INTO MESSES OF TWISTED METAL

b. von alten

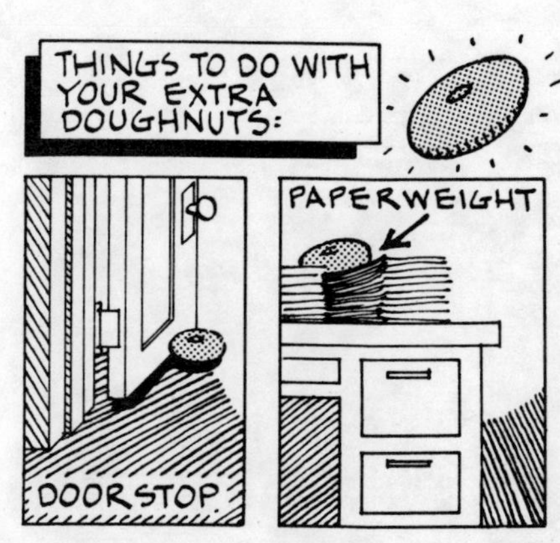
THINGS TO DO WITH YOUR EXTRA DOUGHNUTS:
DOORSTOP
PAPERWEIGHT

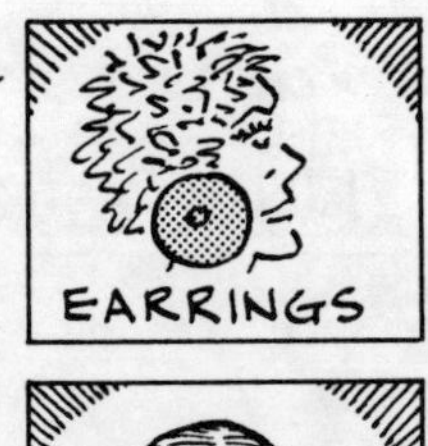
EARRINGS

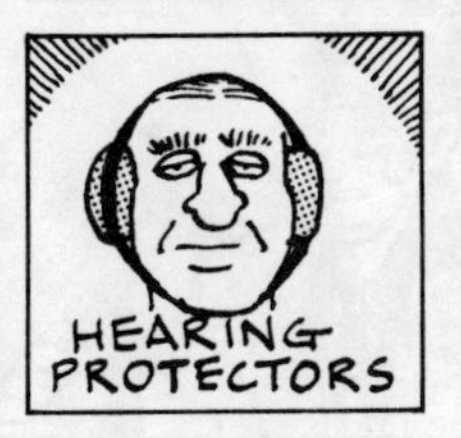
HEARING PROTECTORS

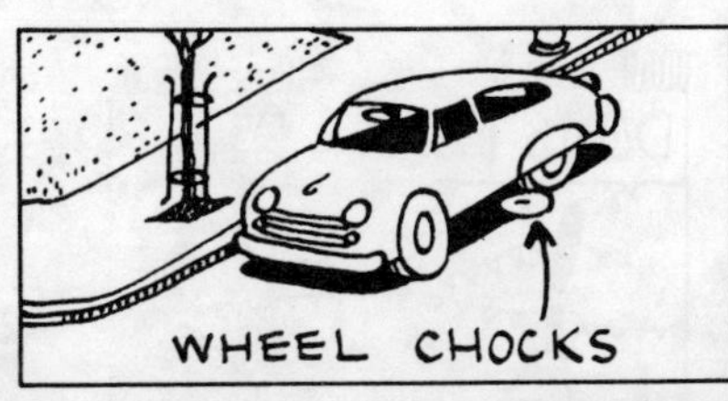
WHEEL CHOCKS

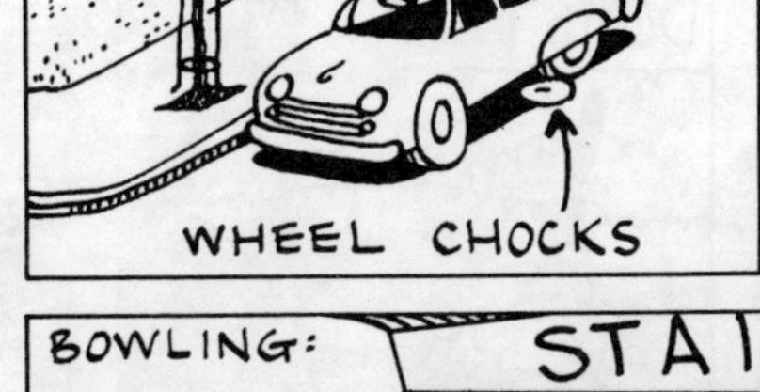
CRASH HELMET

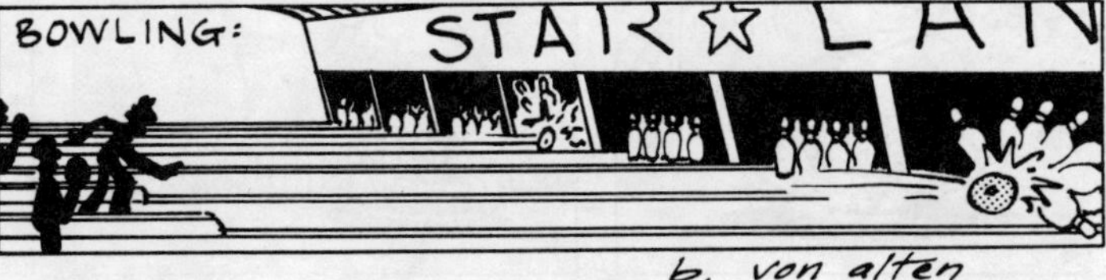
BOWLING:
STAR☆LAN

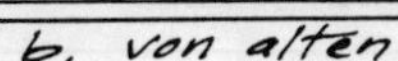
b. von alten

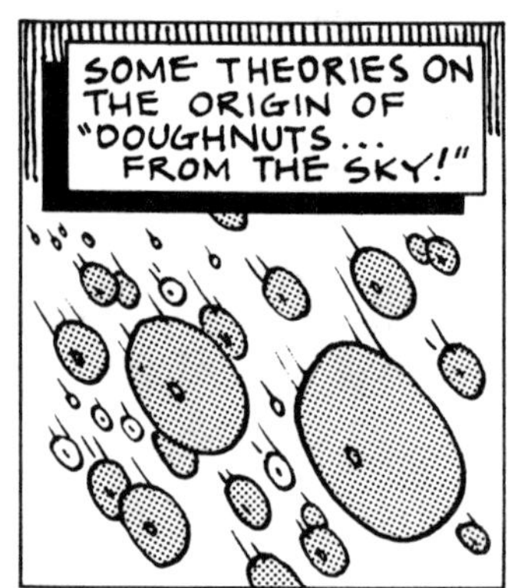
SOME THEORIES ON THE ORIGIN OF "DOUGHNUTS... FROM THE SKY!"

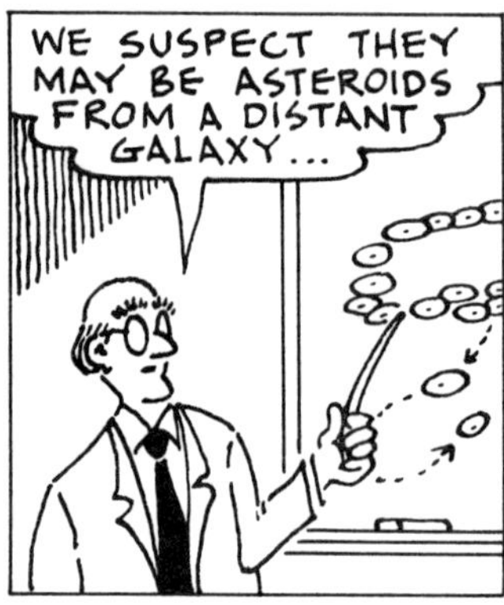
WE SUSPECT THEY MAY BE ASTEROIDS FROM A DISTANT GALAXY...

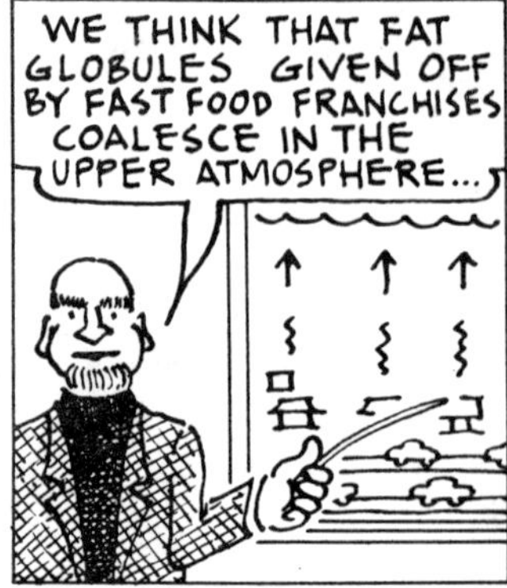
WE THINK THAT FAT GLOBULES GIVEN OFF BY FAST FOOD FRANCHISES COALESCE IN THE UPPER ATMOSPHERE...

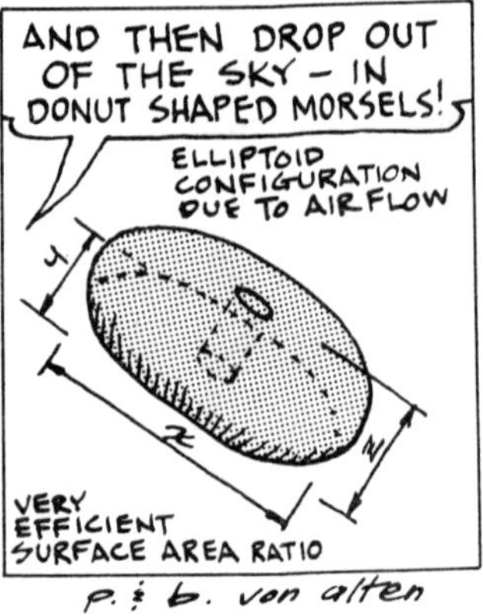
AND THEN DROP OUT OF THE SKY - IN DONUT SHAPED MORSELS!
ELLIPTOID CONFIGURATION DUE TO AIRFLOW
VERY EFFICIENT SURFACE AREA RATIO

p. & b. von alten

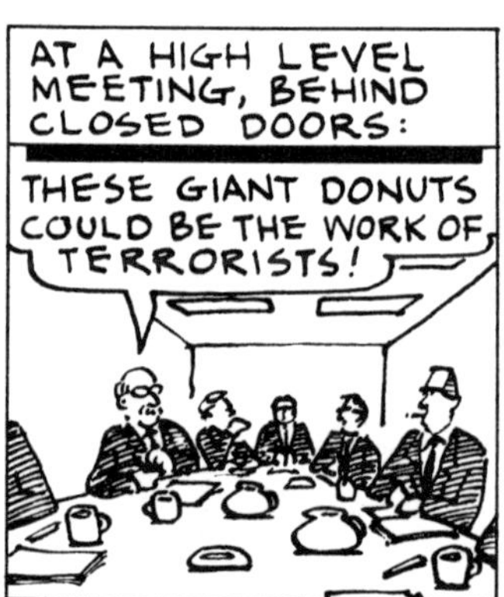
AT A HIGH LEVEL MEETING, BEHIND CLOSED DOORS:
THESE GIANT DONUTS COULD BE THE WORK OF TERRORISTS!

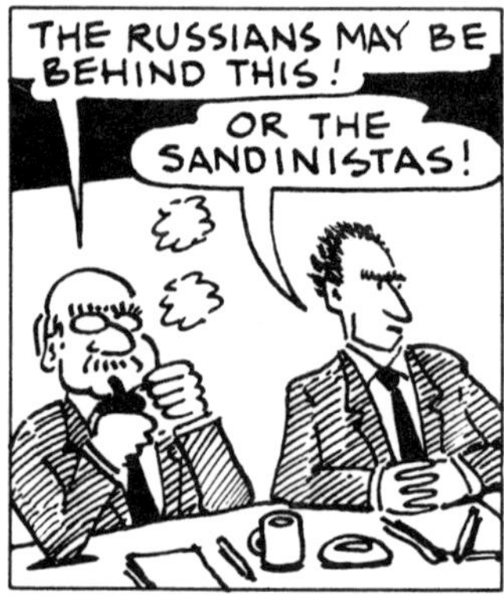
THE RUSSIANS MAY BE BEHIND THIS!
OR THE SANDINISTAS!

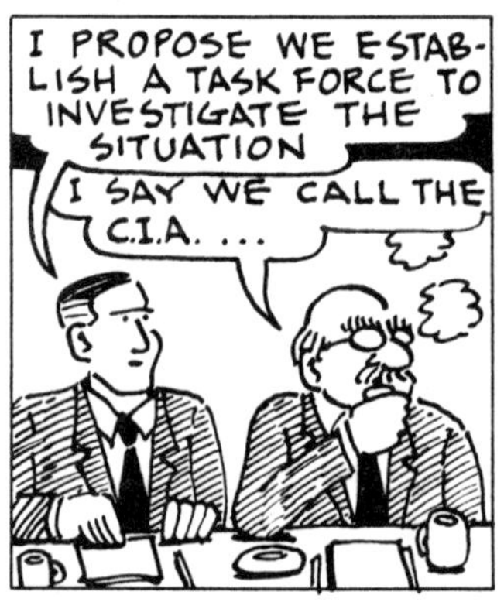
I PROPOSE WE ESTABLISH A TASK FORCE TO INVESTIGATE THE SITUATION
I SAY WE CALL THE C.I.A. ...

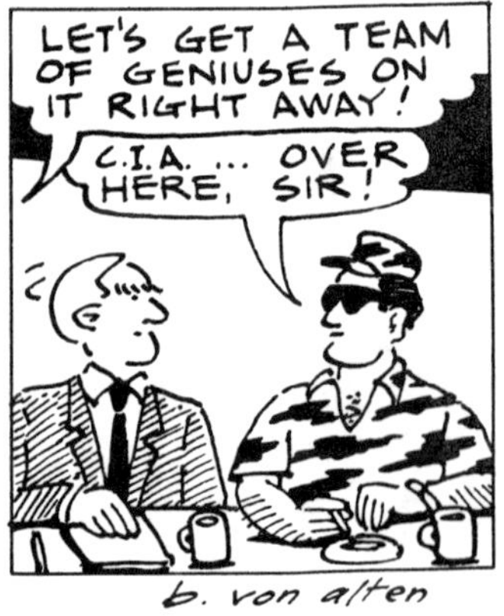
LET'S GET A TEAM OF GENIUSES ON IT RIGHT AWAY!
C.I.A. ... OVER HERE, SIR!

b. von alten

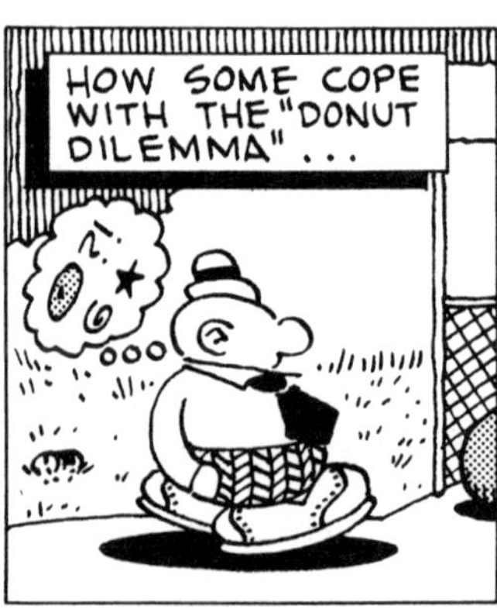
HOW SOME COPE WITH THE "DONUT DILEMMA"...

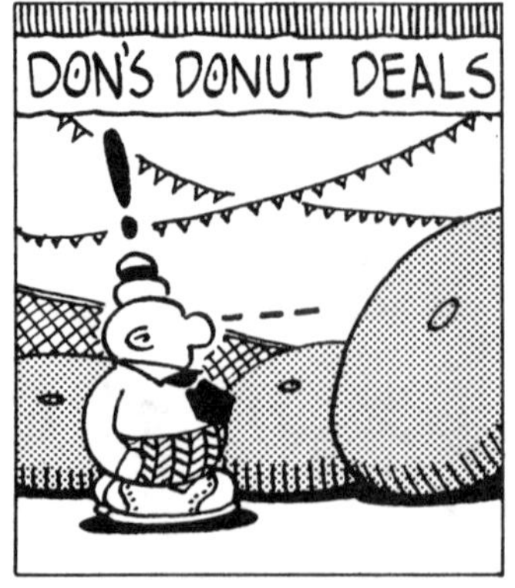
DON'S DONUT DEALS

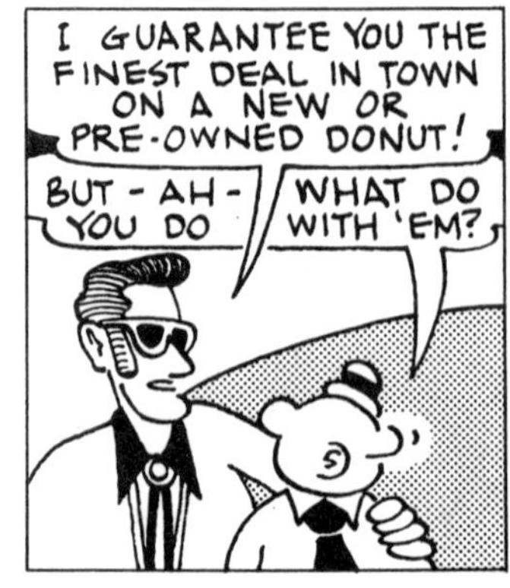
I GUARANTEE YOU THE FINEST DEAL IN TOWN ON A NEW OR PRE-OWNED DONUT!
BUT - AH - YOU DO
WHAT DO WITH 'EM?

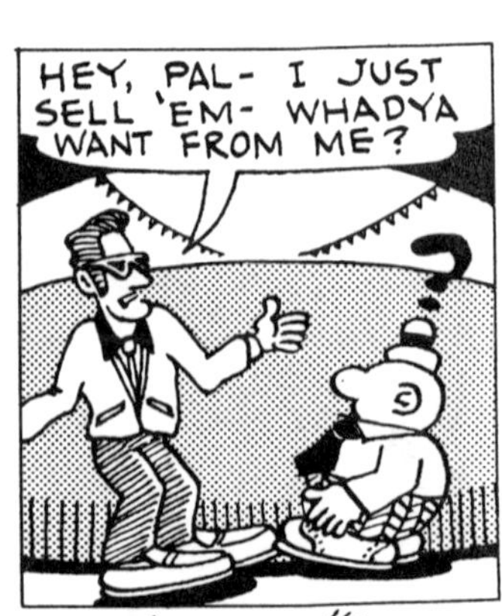
HEY, PAL- I JUST SELL 'EM- WHADYA WANT FROM ME?

b. von alten

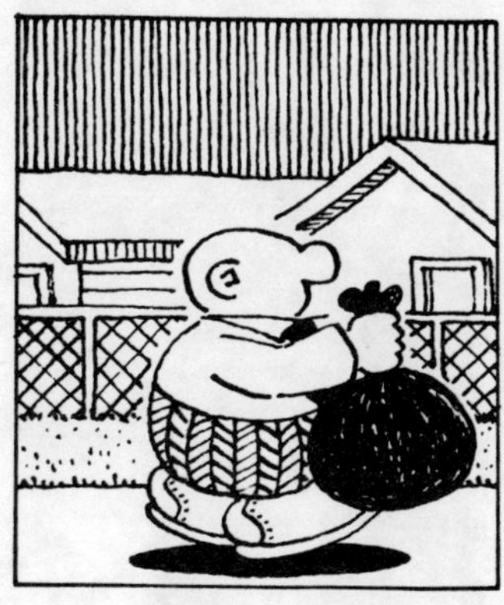
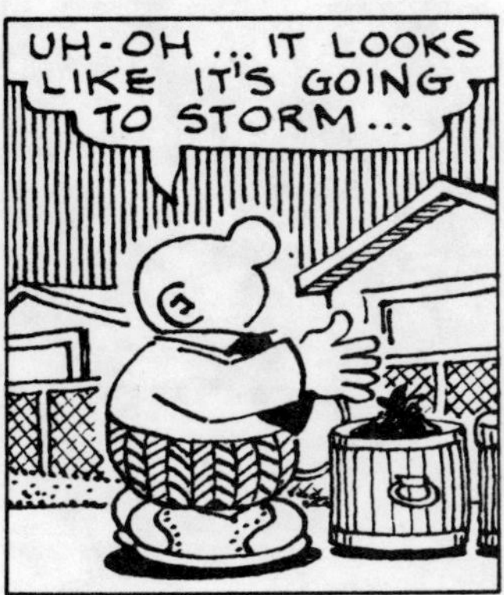
UH-OH ... IT LOOKS LIKE IT'S GOING TO STORM...
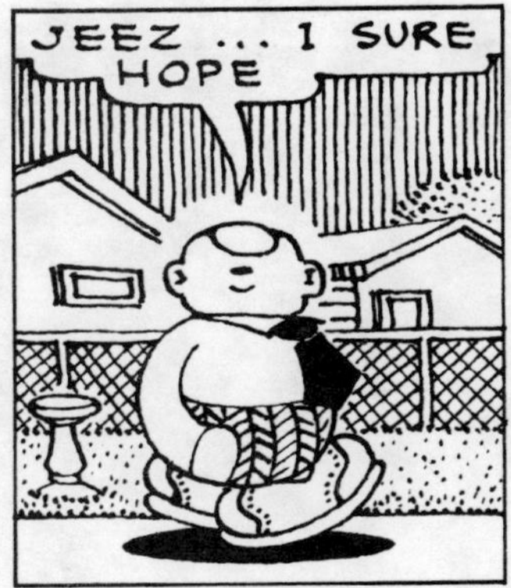
JEEZ ... I SURE HOPE
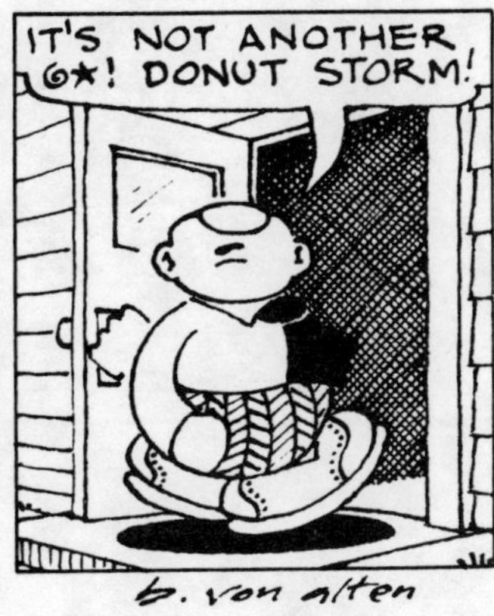
IT'S NOT ANOTHER 6★! DONUT STORM!
b. von alten
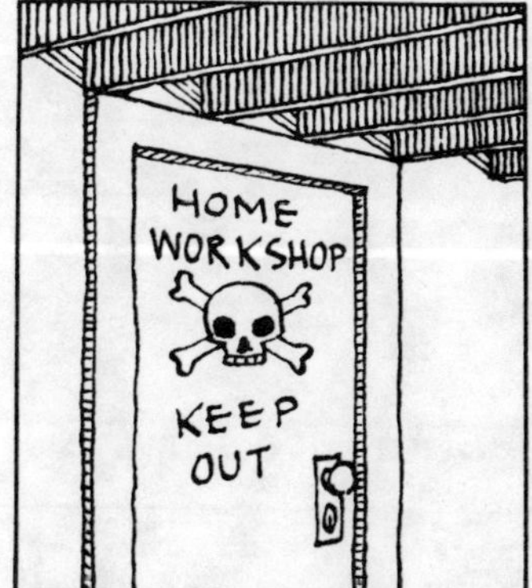
HOME WORKSHOP
KEEP OUT
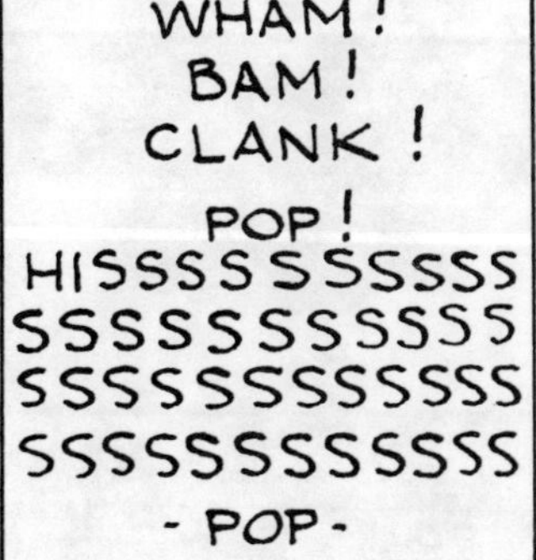
WHAM!
BAM!
CLANK!
POP!
HISSSSSSSSSS SSSSSSSSSSS SSSSSSSSSSSSS SSSSSSSSSSSS
-POP-
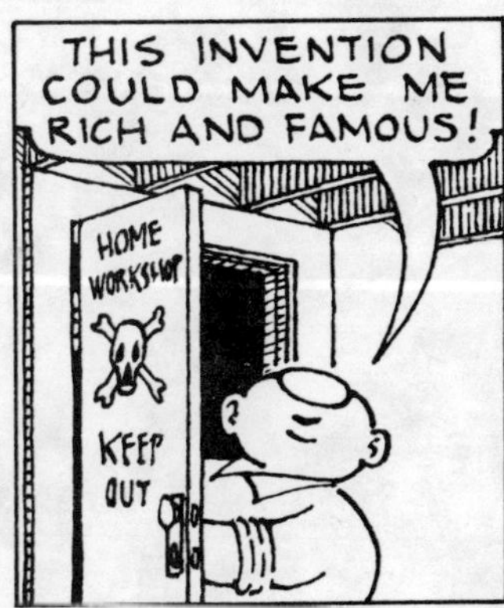
THIS INVENTION COULD MAKE ME RICH AND FAMOUS!
HOME WORKSHOP
KEEP OUT
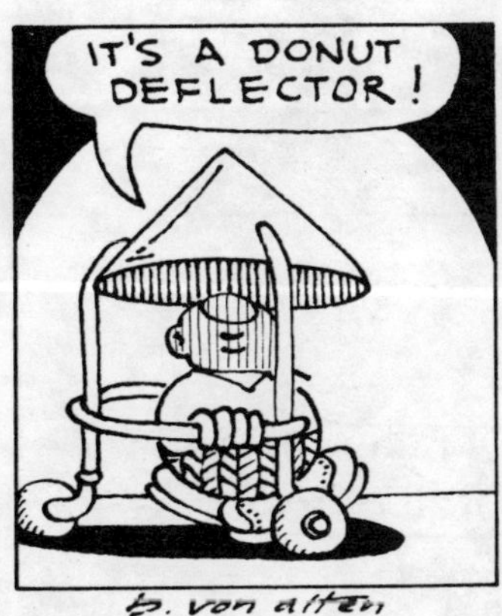
IT'S A DONUT DEFLECTOR!
b. von alten
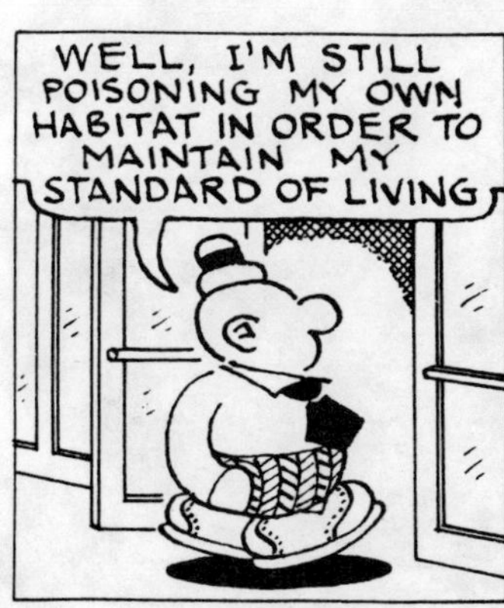
WELL, I'M STILL POISONING MY OWN HABITAT IN ORDER TO MAINTAIN MY STANDARD OF LIVING
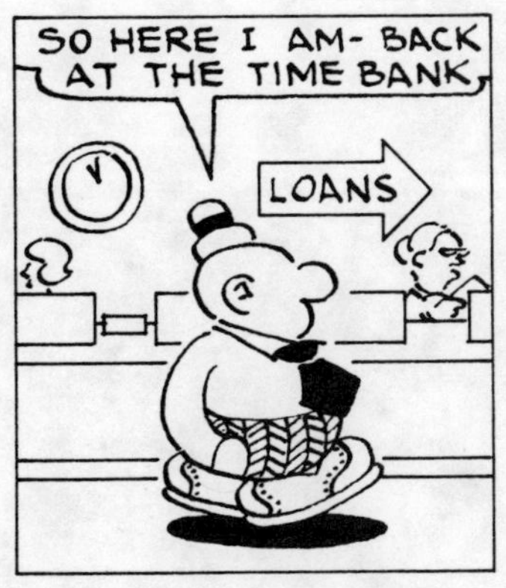
SO HERE I AM- BACK AT THE TIME BANK
LOANS
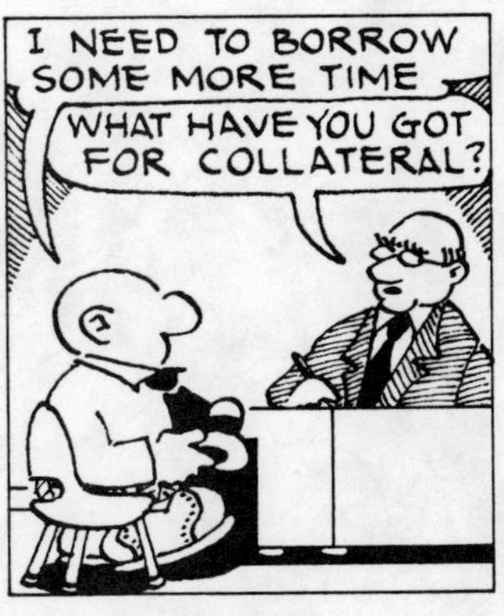
I NEED TO BORROW SOME MORE TIME
WHAT HAVE YOU GOT FOR COLLATERAL?
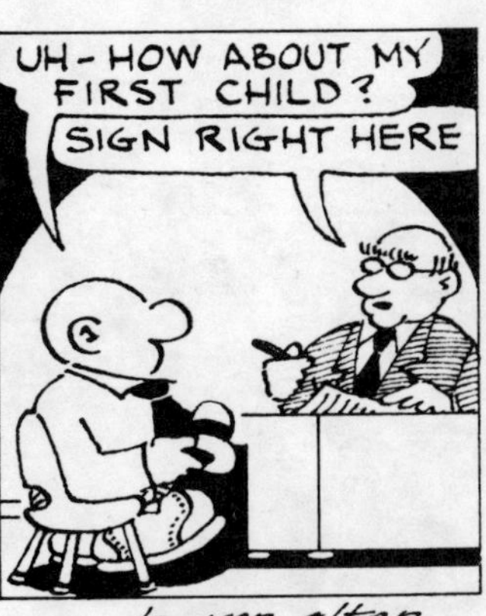
UH- HOW ABOUT MY FIRST CHILD?
SIGN RIGHT HERE
b. von alten

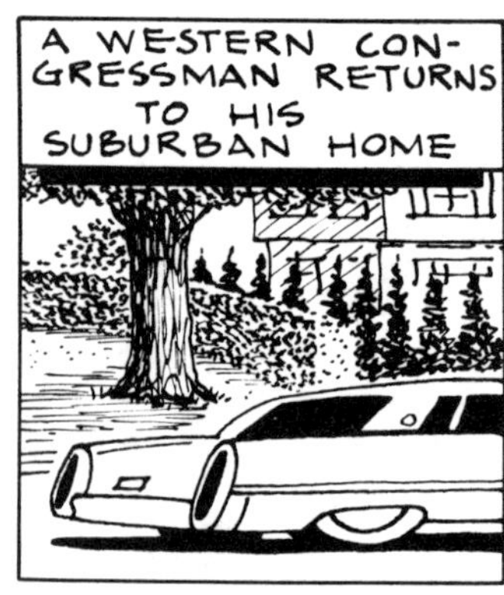
A WESTERN CONGRESSMAN RETURNS TO HIS SUBURBAN HOME

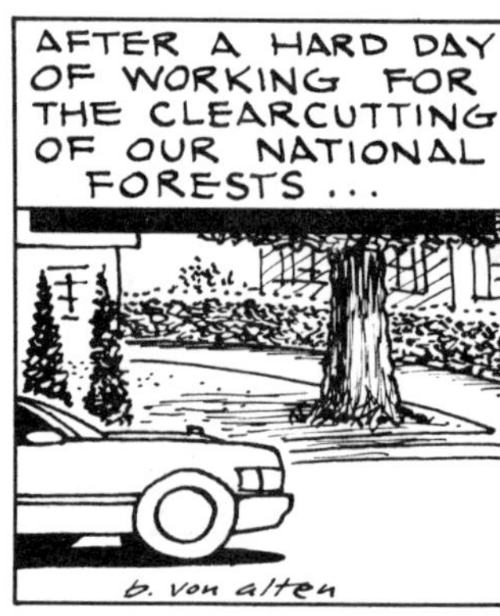
AFTER A HARD DAY OF WORKING FOR THE CLEARCUTTING OF OUR NATIONAL FORESTS ...
b. von alten

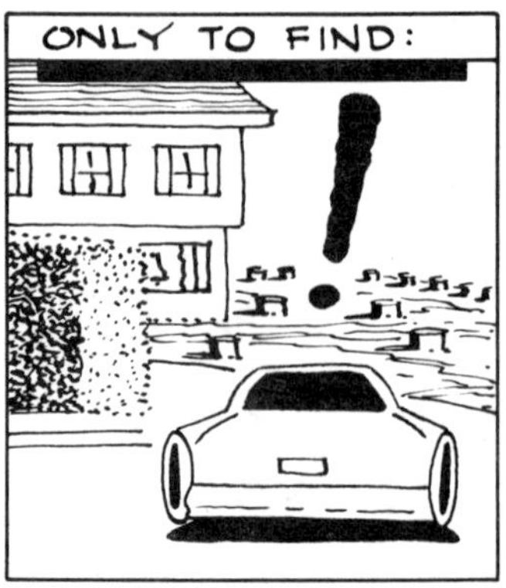
ONLY TO FIND:
!

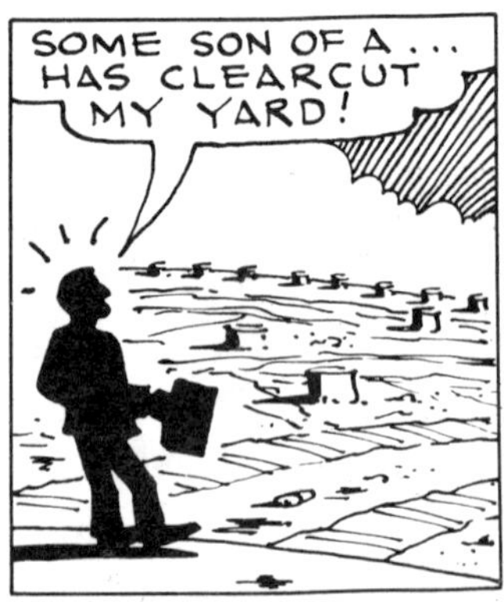
SOME SON OF A ... HAS CLEARCUT MY YARD!

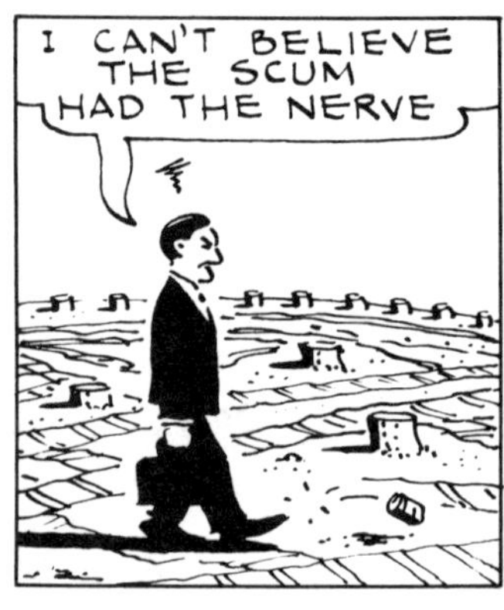
I CAN'T BELIEVE THE SCUM HAD THE NERVE

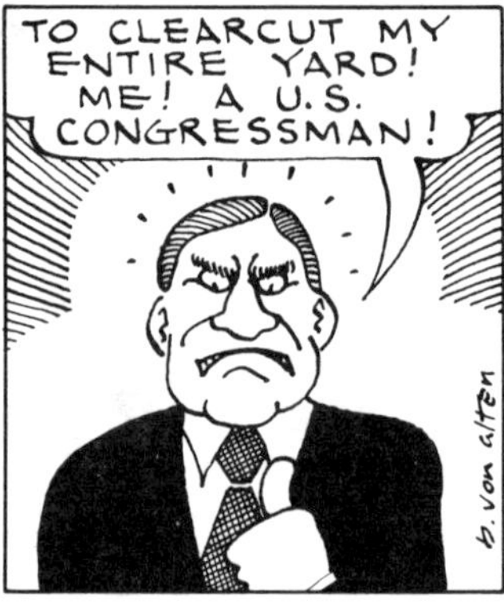
TO CLEARCUT MY ENTIRE YARD! ME! A U.S. CONGRESSMAN!
b. von alten

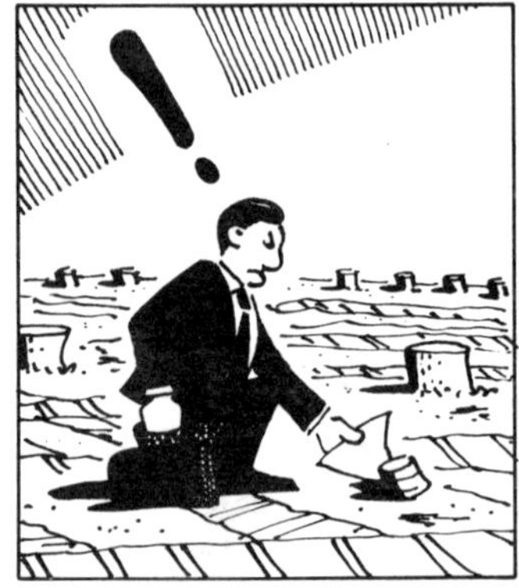
!

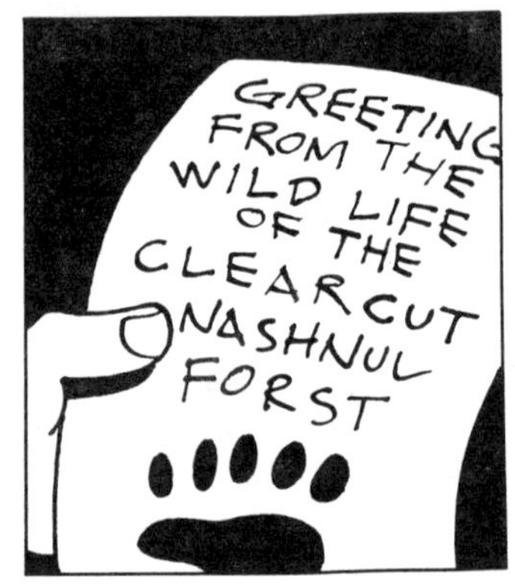
GREETING FROM THE WILD LIFE OF THE CLEARCUT NASHNUL FORST

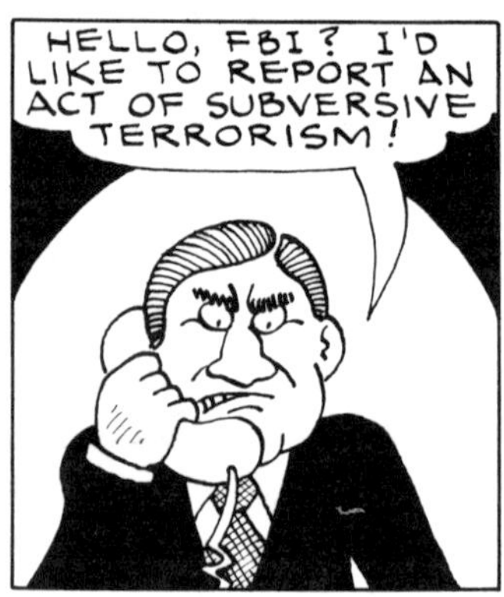
HELLO, FBI? I'D LIKE TO REPORT AN ACT OF SUBVERSIVE TERRORISM!

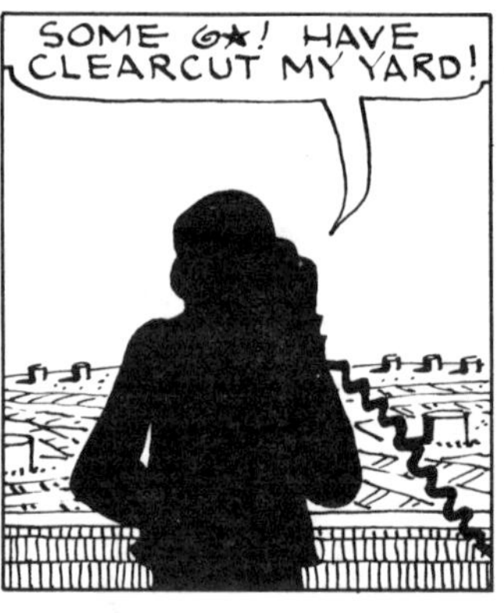
SOME G★! HAVE CLEARCUT MY YARD!

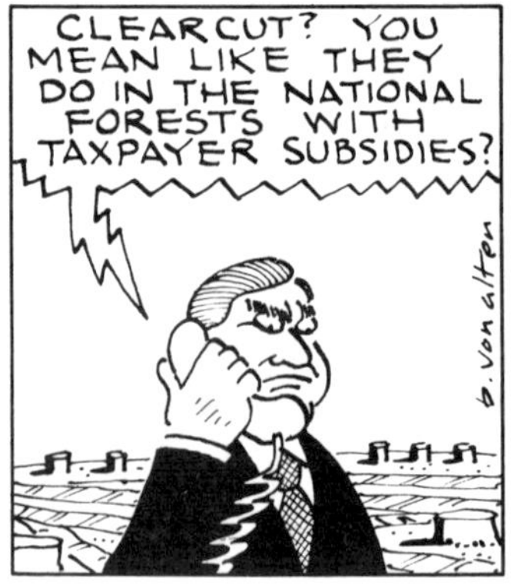
CLEARCUT? YOU MEAN LIKE THEY DO IN THE NATIONAL FORESTS WITH TAXPAYER SUBSIDIES?
b. von alten

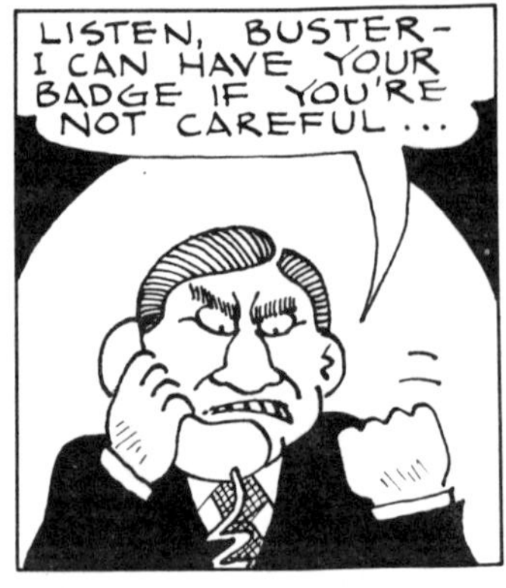
LISTEN, BUSTER- I CAN HAVE YOUR BADGE IF YOU'RE NOT CAREFUL ...

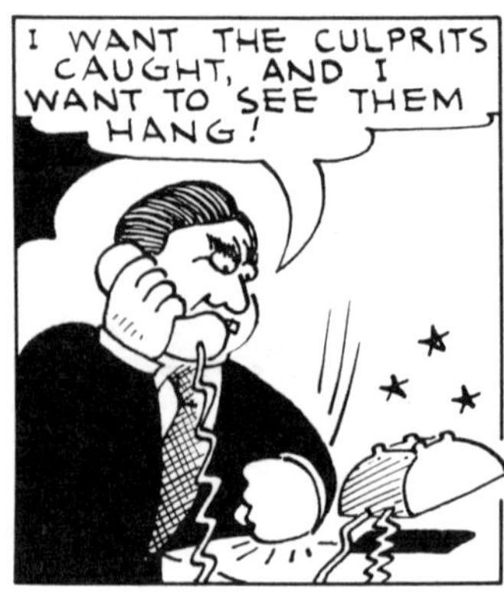
I WANT THE CULPRITS CAUGHT, AND I WANT TO SEE THEM HANG!

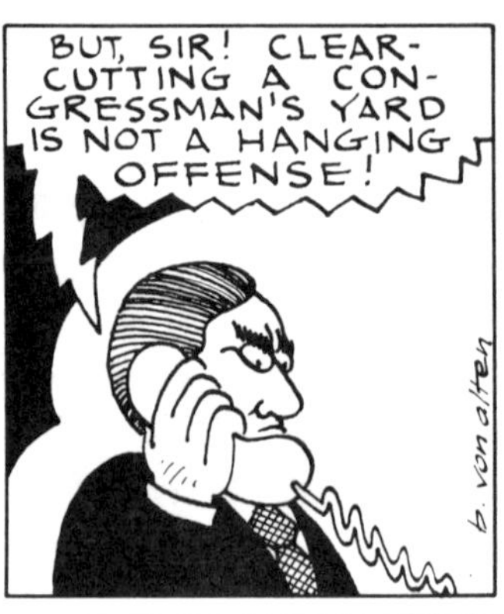
BUT, SIR! CLEARCUTTING A CONGRESSMAN'S YARD IS NOT A HANGING OFFENSE!
b. von alten

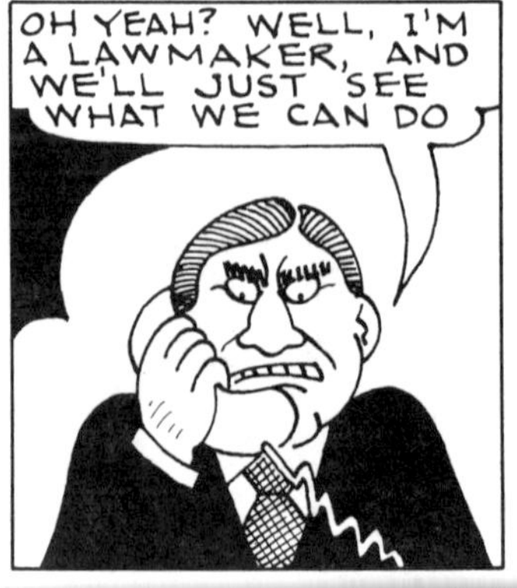
OH YEAH? WELL, I'M A LAWMAKER, AND WE'LL JUST SEE WHAT WE CAN DO

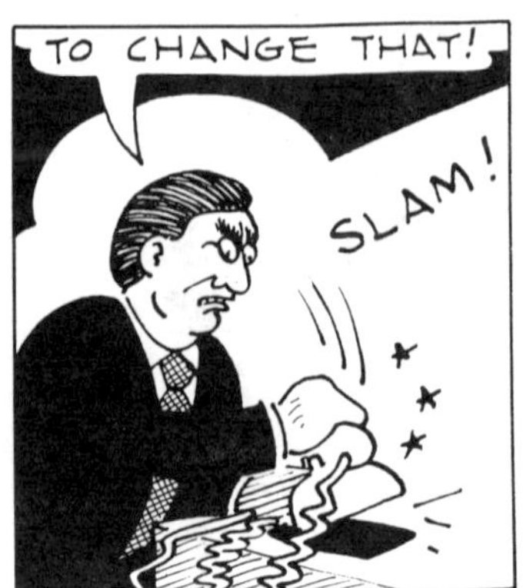
TO CHANGE THAT!
SLAM!

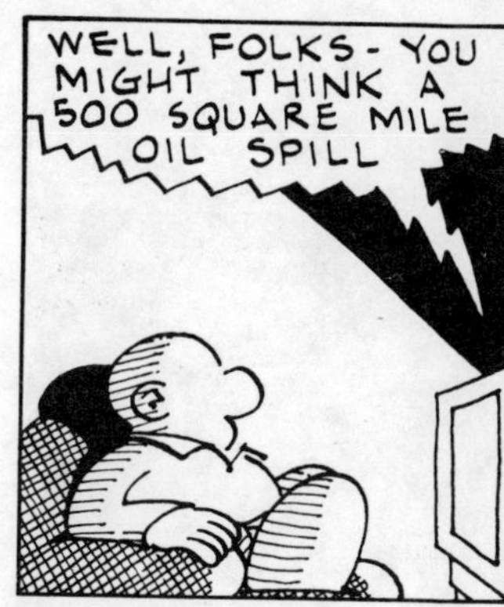
WELL, FOLKS - YOU MIGHT THINK A 500 SQUARE MILE OIL SPILL
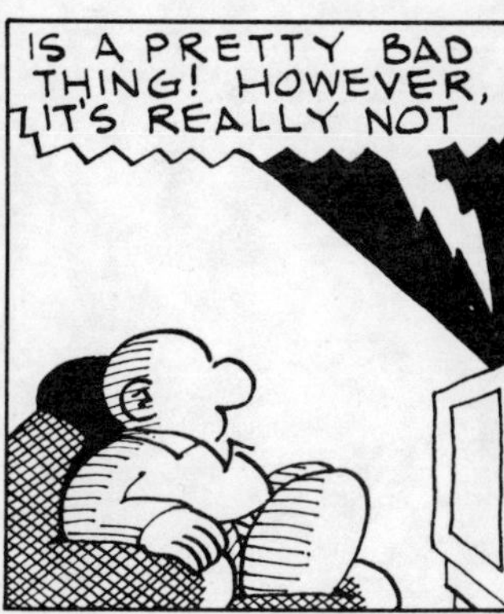
IS A PRETTY BAD THING! HOWEVER, IT'S REALLY NOT
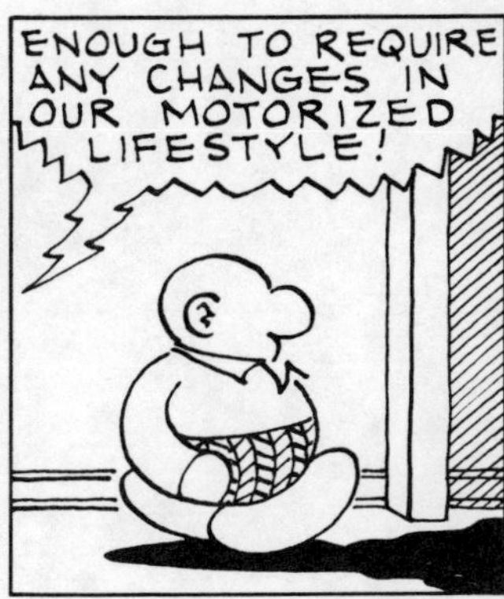
ENOUGH TO REQUIRE ANY CHANGES IN OUR MOTORIZED LIFESTYLE!
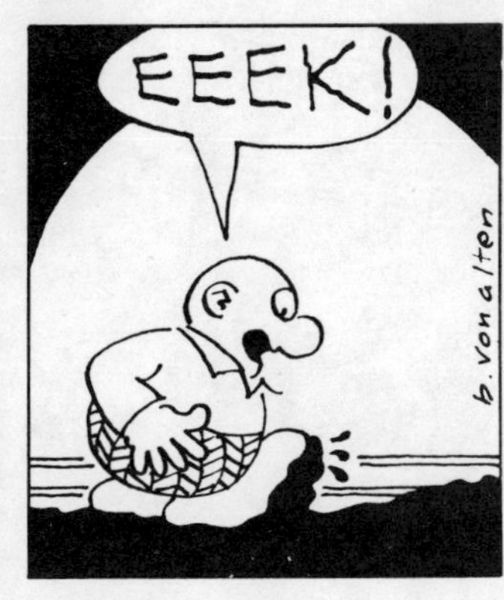
EEEK!
b. von alten
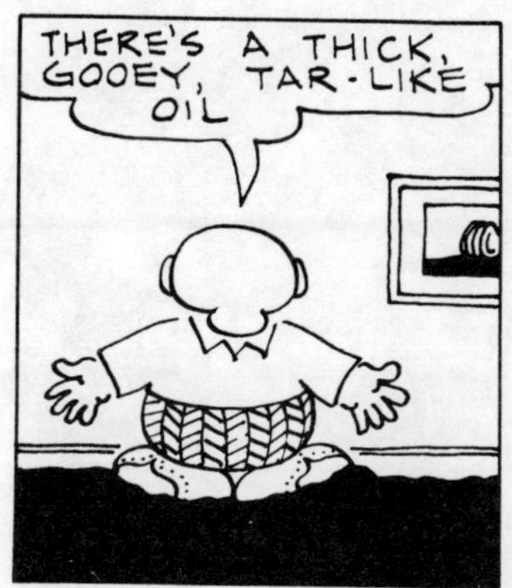
THERE'S A THICK, GOOEY, TAR-LIKE OIL
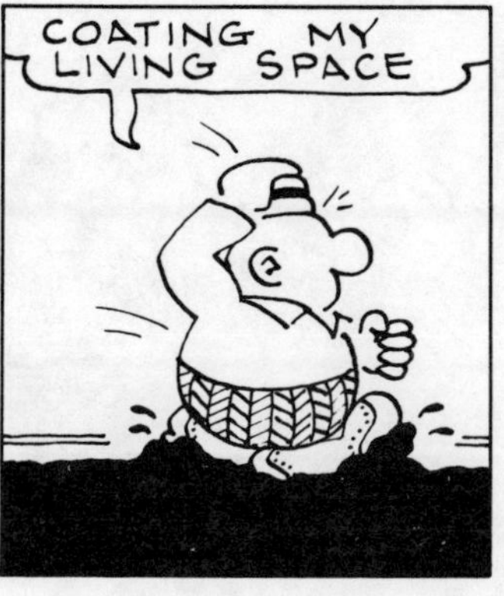
COATING MY LIVING SPACE
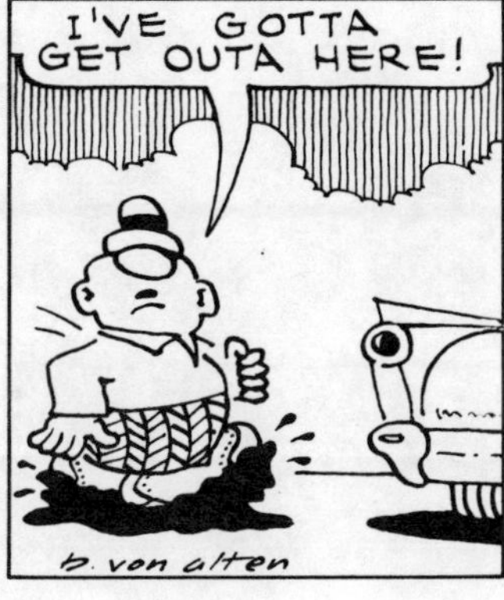
I'VE GOTTA GET OUTA HERE!
b. von alten
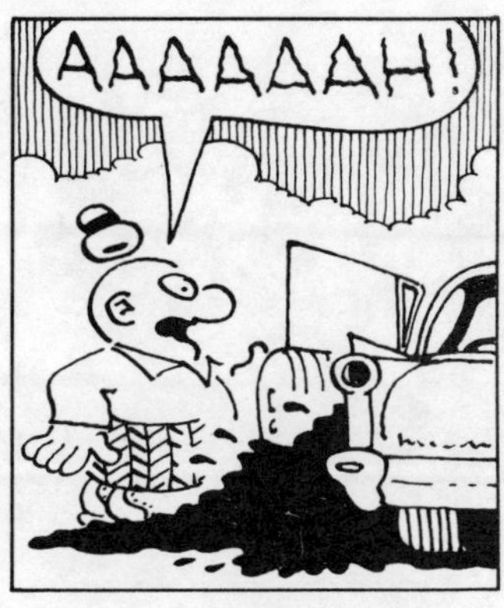
AAAAAAH!
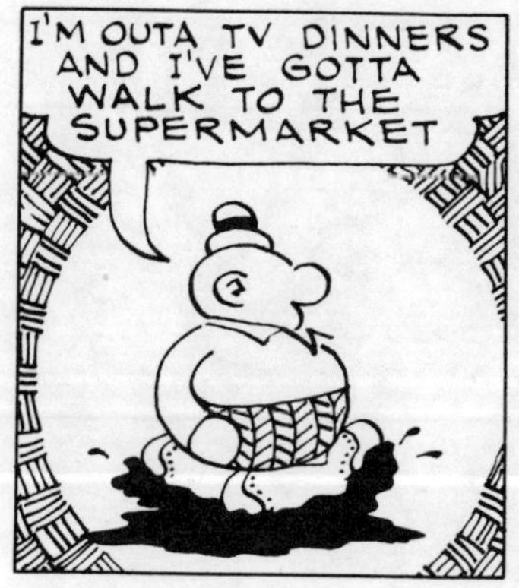
I'M OUTA TV DINNERS AND I'VE GOTTA WALK TO THE SUPERMARKET
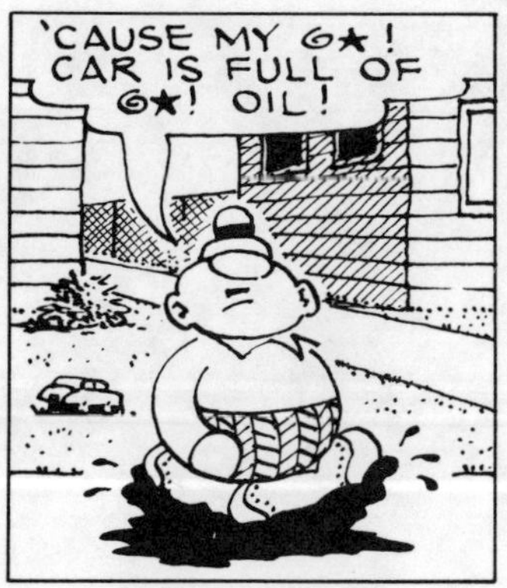
'CAUSE MY G★! CAR IS FULL OF G★! OIL!
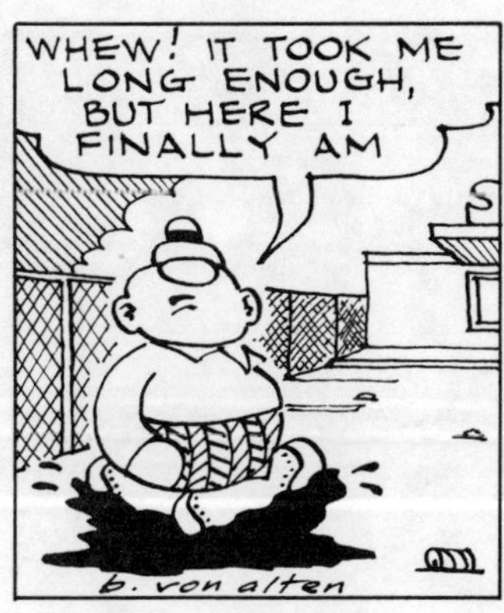
WHEW! IT TOOK ME LONG ENOUGH, BUT HERE I FINALLY AM
b. von alten
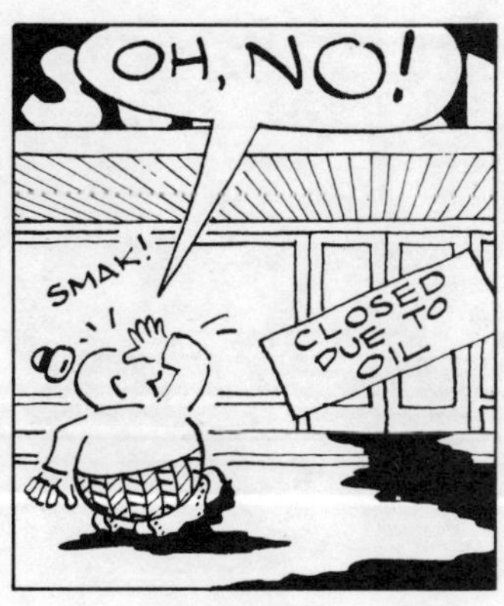
OH, NO!
SMAK!
CLOSED DUE TO OIL
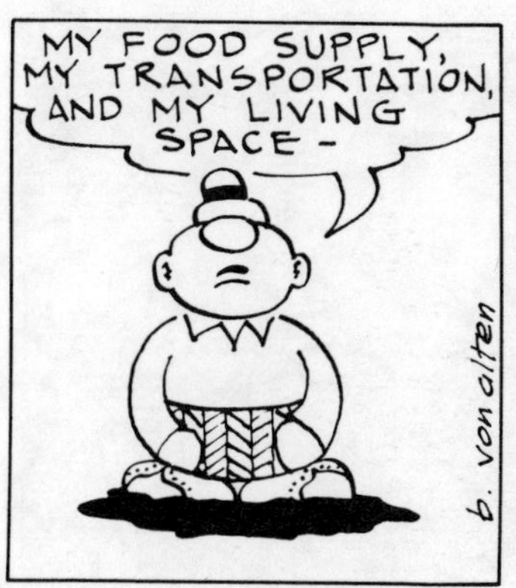
MY FOOD SUPPLY, MY TRANSPORTATION, AND MY LIVING SPACE -
b. von alten
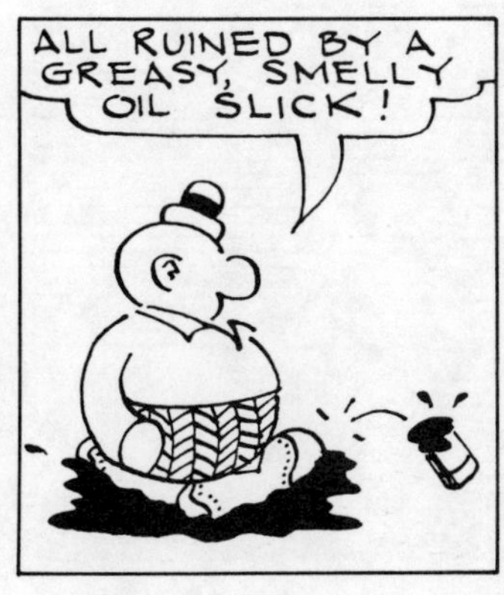
ALL RUINED BY A GREASY, SMELLY OIL SLICK!
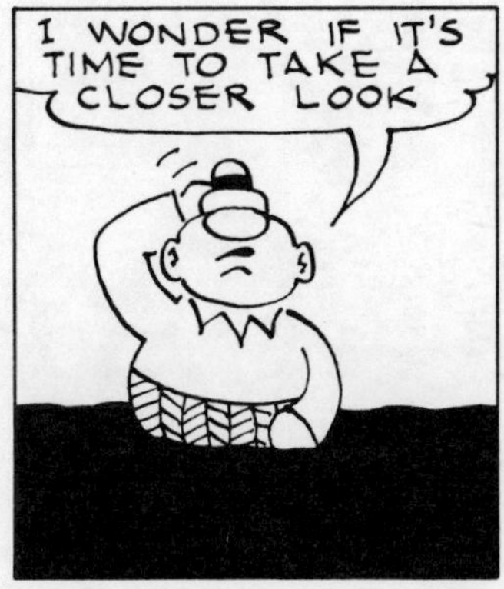
I WONDER IF IT'S TIME TO TAKE A CLOSER LOOK
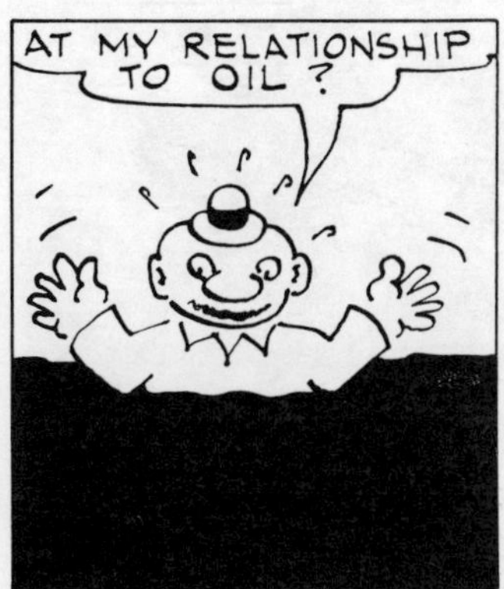
AT MY RELATIONSHIP TO OIL?

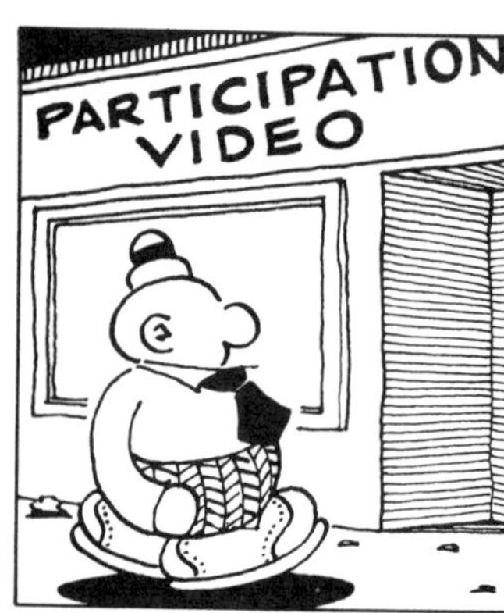
PARTICIPATION
VIDEO
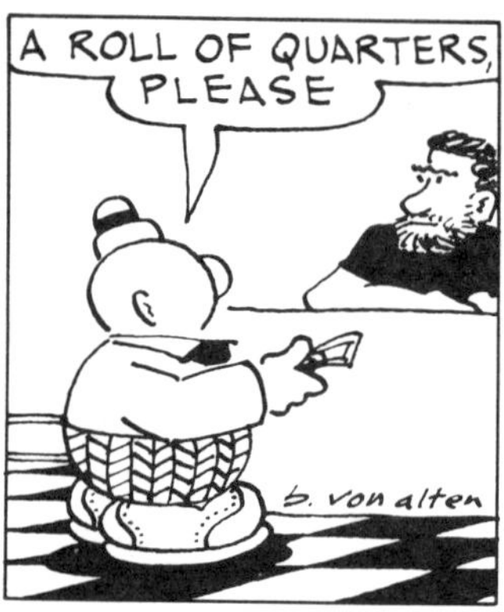
A ROLL OF QUARTERS, PLEASE
b. von alten
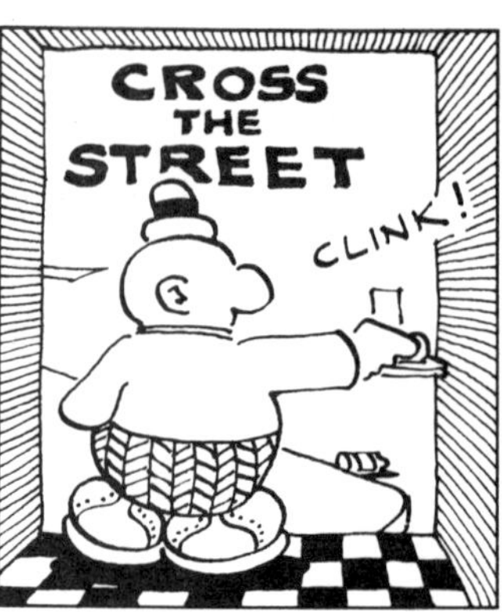
CROSS THE STREET
CLINK!
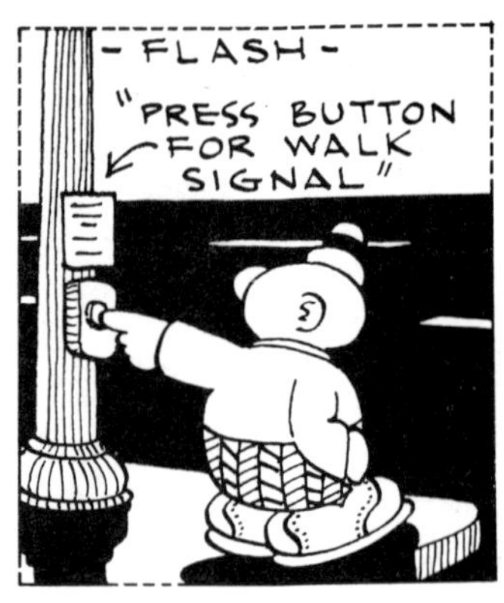
- FLASH -
"PRESS BUTTON FOR WALK SIGNAL"
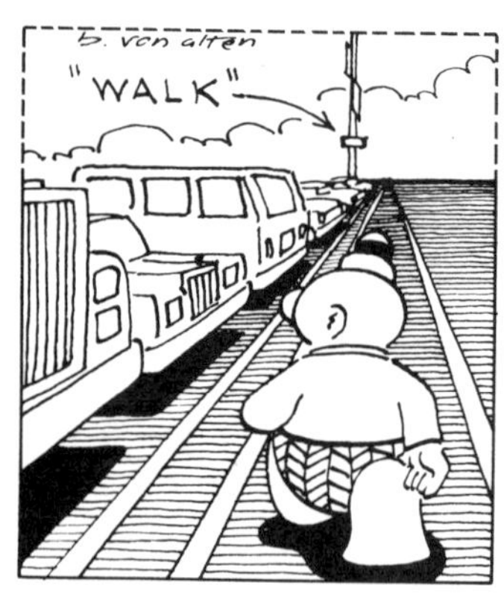
b. von alten
"WALK"
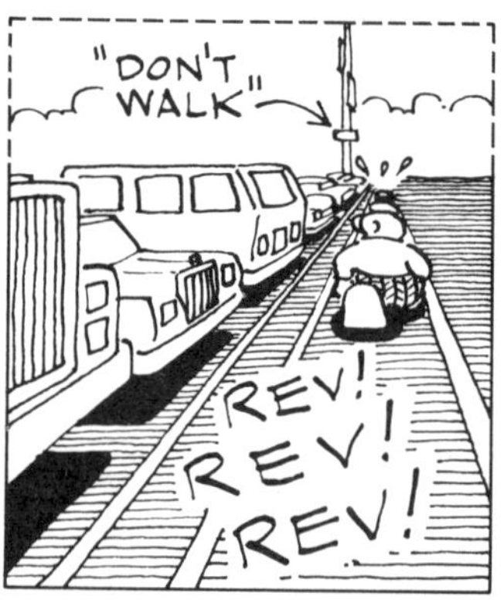
"DON'T WALK"
REV! REV! REV!
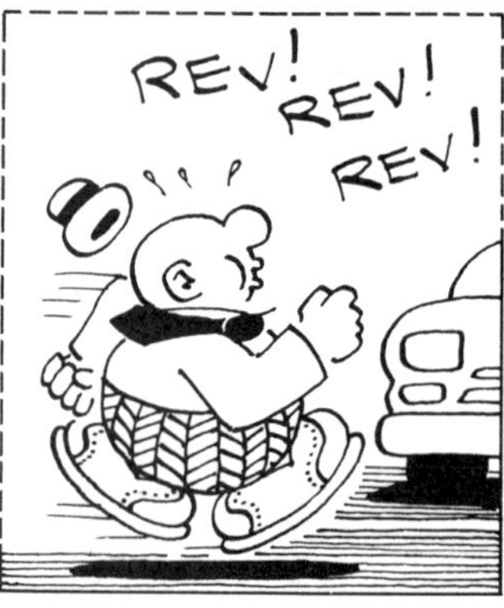
REV! REV! REV!
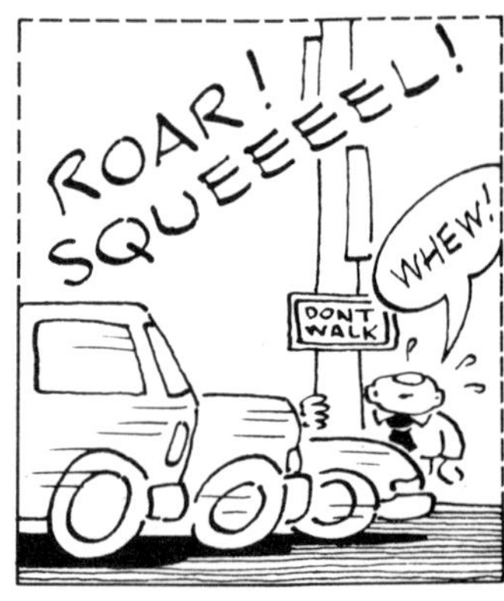
ROAR! SQUEEEEEL!
WHEW!
DONT WALK
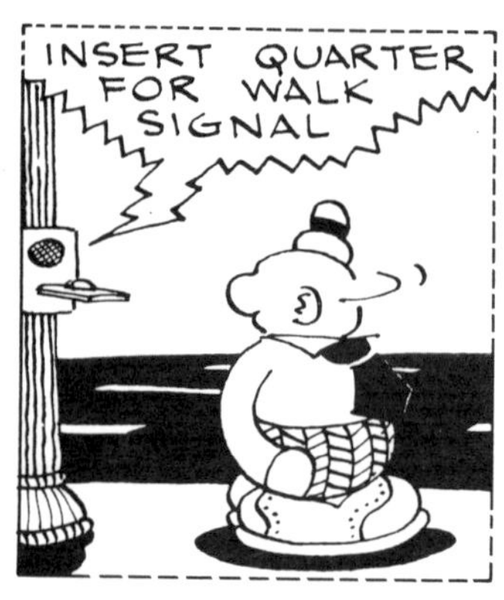
INSERT QUARTER FOR WALK SIGNAL
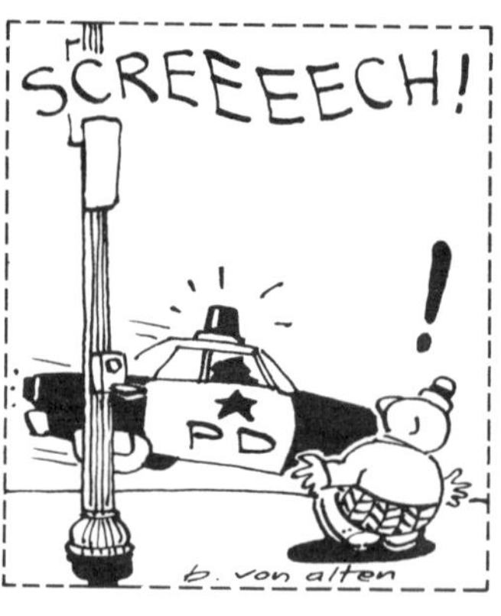
SCREEEECH!
!
PD
b. von alten
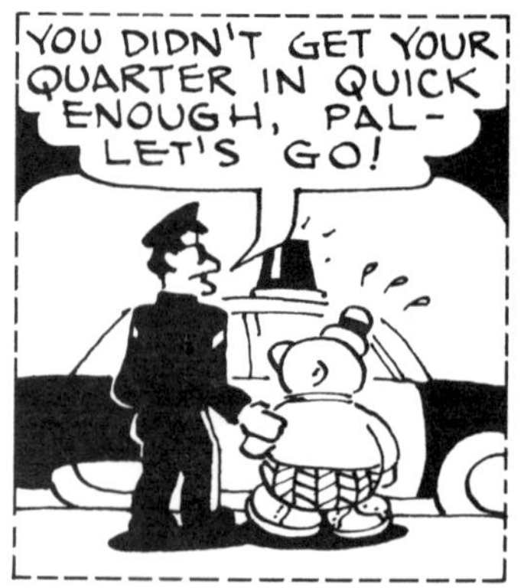
YOU DIDN'T GET YOUR QUARTER IN QUICK ENOUGH, PAL- LET'S GO!
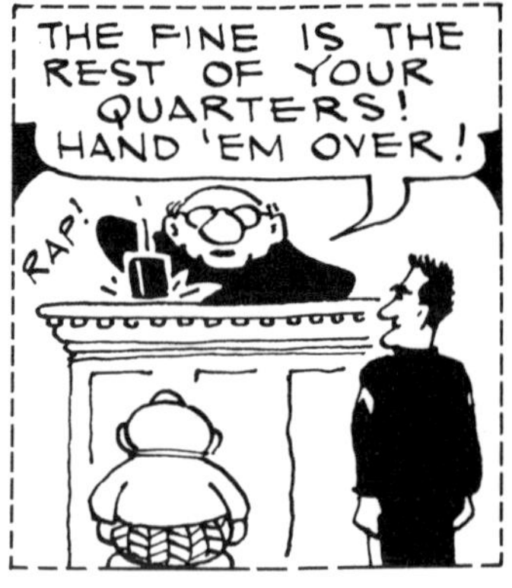
THE FINE IS THE REST OF YOUR QUARTERS! HAND 'EM OVER!
RAP!
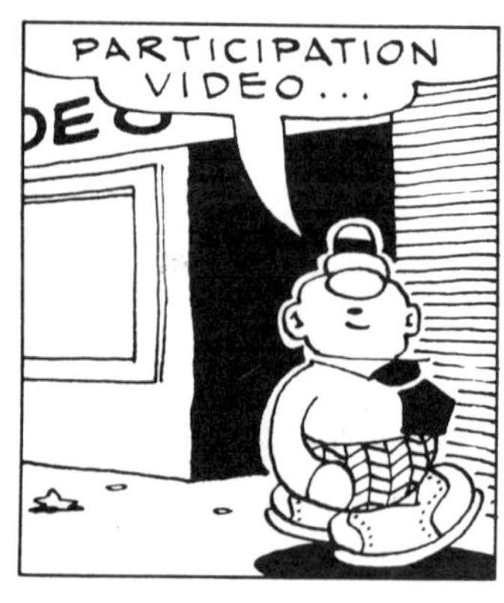
PARTICIPATION VIDEO...
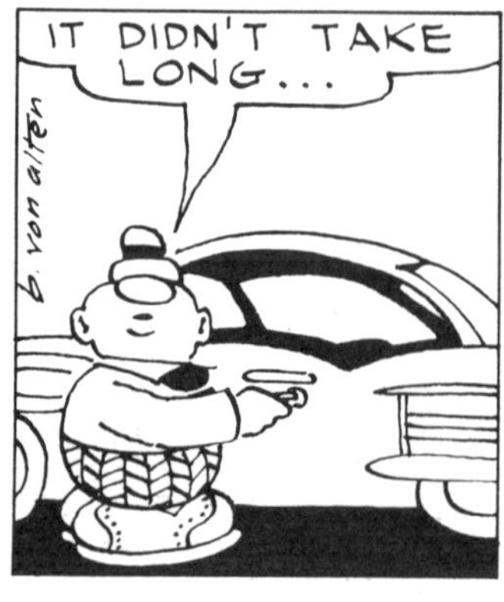
IT DIDN'T TAKE LONG...
b. von alten
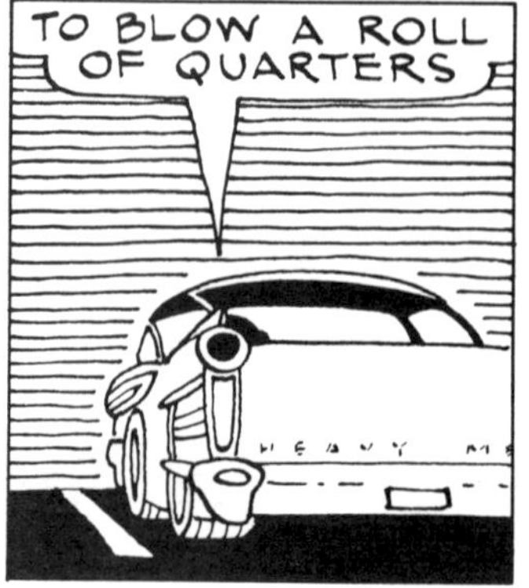
TO BLOW A ROLL OF QUARTERS
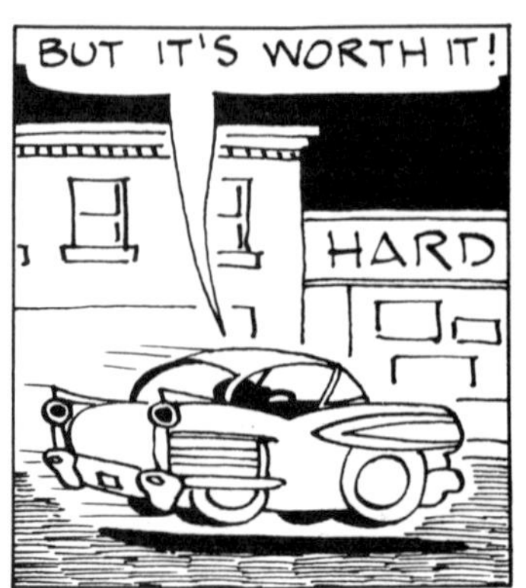
BUT IT'S WORTH IT!
HARD

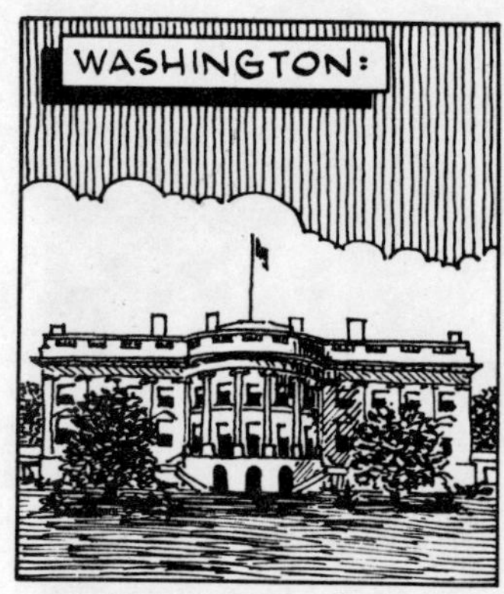
WASHINGTON:
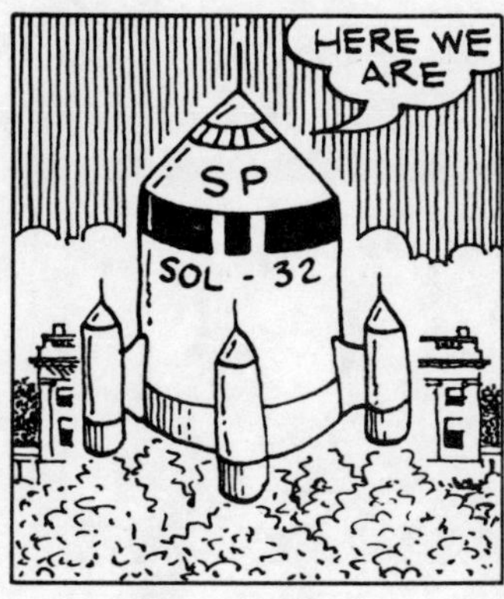
HERE WE ARE
SP
SOL - 32
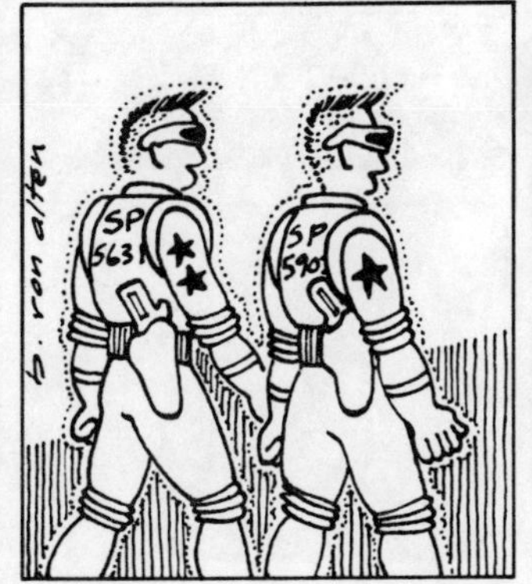
b. von alten
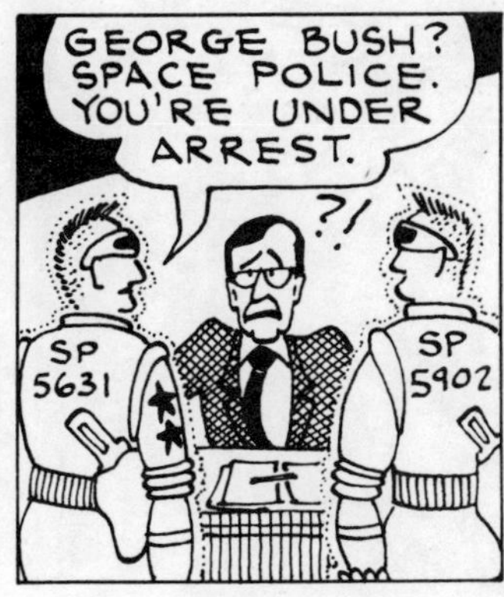
GEORGE BUSH? SPACE POLICE. YOU'RE UNDER ARREST.
?!
SP 5631
SP 5902
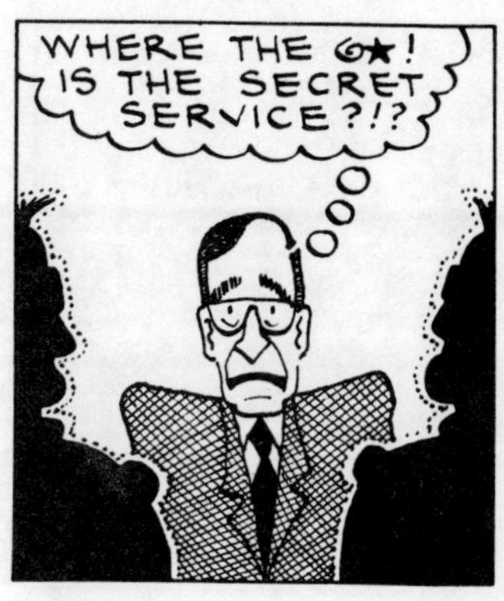
WHERE THE G★! IS THE SECRET SERVICE?!?
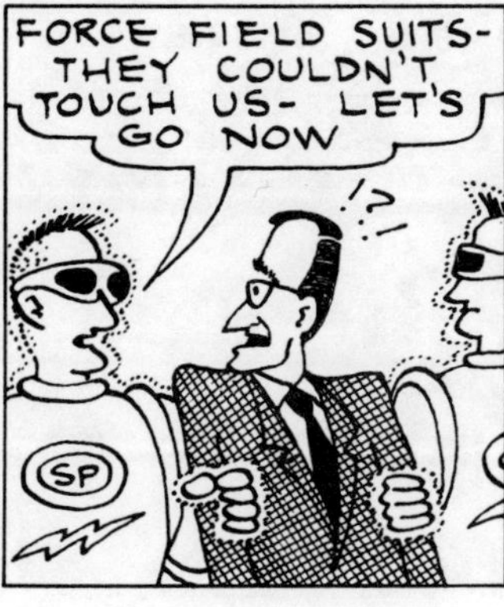
FORCE FIELD SUITS- THEY COULDN'T TOUCH US- LET'S GO NOW
!?!
SP
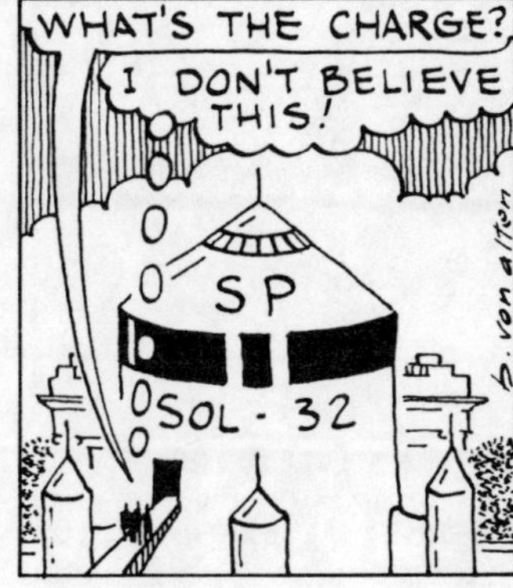
WHAT'S THE CHARGE?
I DON'T BELIEVE THIS!
SP
SOL - 32
b. von alten
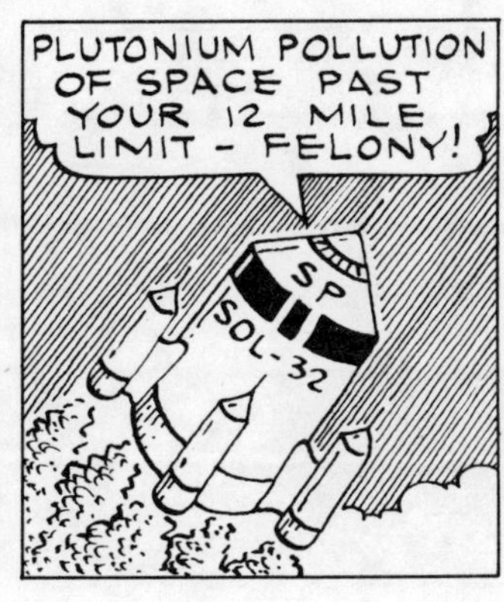
PLUTONIUM POLLUTION OF SPACE PAST YOUR 12 MILE LIMIT - FELONY!
SP
SOL-32
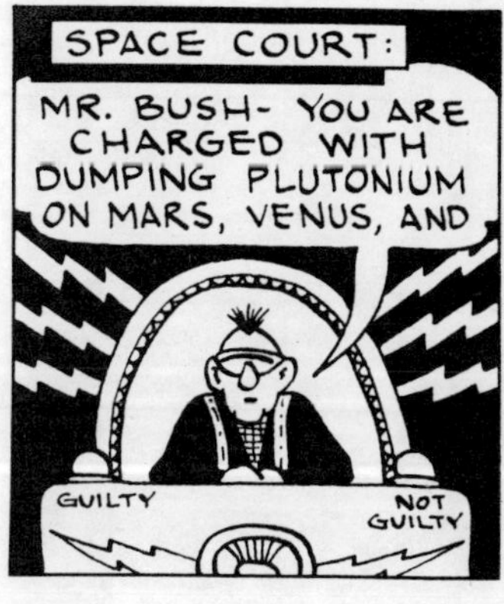
SPACE COURT:
MR. BUSH- YOU ARE CHARGED WITH DUMPING PLUTONIUM ON MARS, VENUS, AND
GUILTY
NOT GUILTY
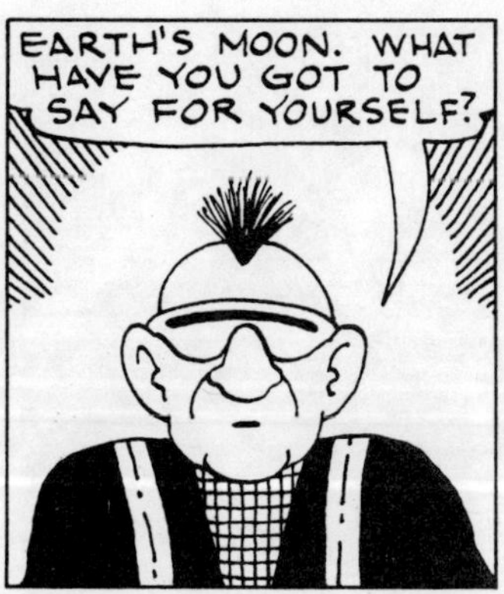
EARTH'S MOON. WHAT HAVE YOU GOT TO SAY FOR YOURSELF?
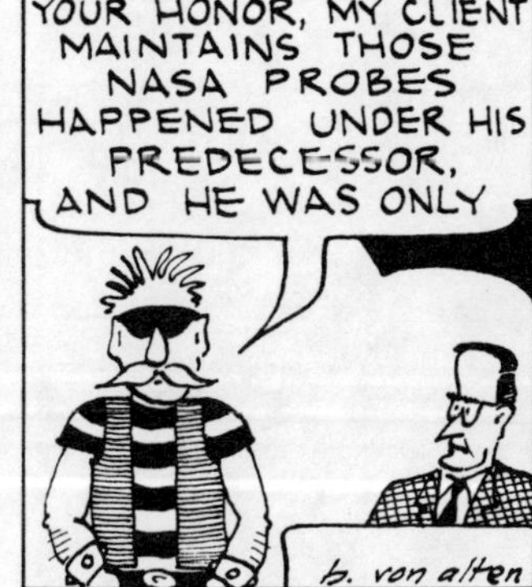
YOUR HONOR, MY CLIENT MAINTAINS THOSE NASA PROBES HAPPENED UNDER HIS PREDECESSOR, AND HE WAS ONLY
b. von alten
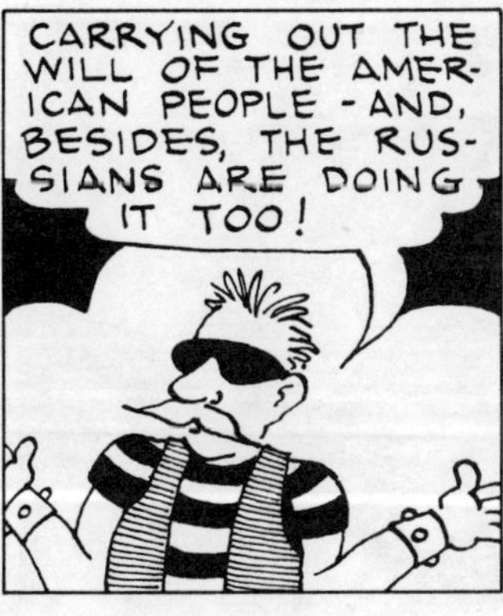
CARRYING OUT THE WILL OF THE AMERICAN PEOPLE -AND, BESIDES, THE RUSSIANS ARE DOING IT TOO!
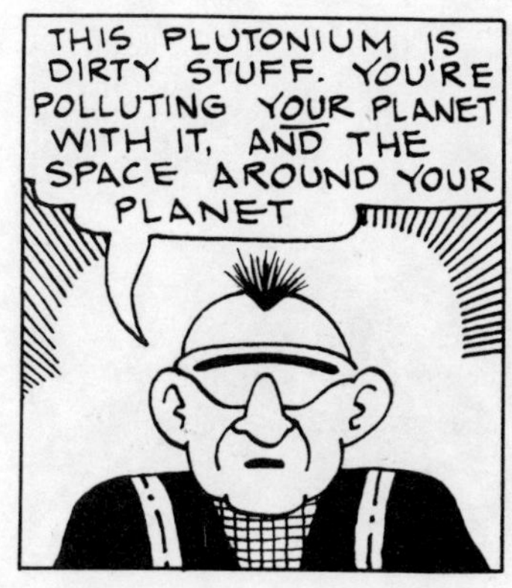
THIS PLUTONIUM IS DIRTY STUFF. YOU'RE POLLUTING YOUR PLANET WITH IT, AND THE SPACE AROUND YOUR PLANET
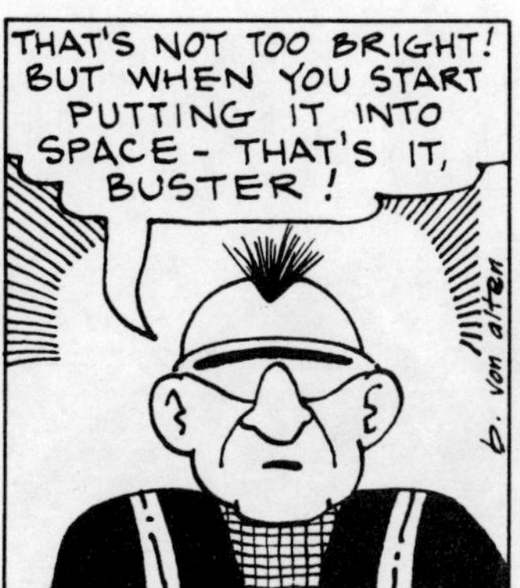
THAT'S NOT TOO BRIGHT! BUT WHEN YOU START PUTTING IT INTO SPACE - THAT'S IT, BUSTER!
b. von alten
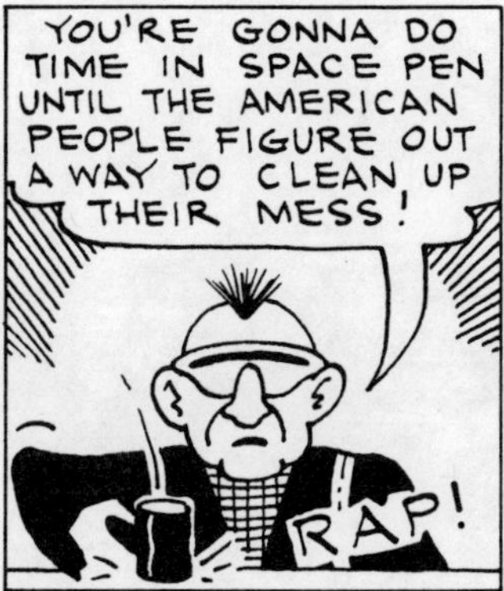
YOU'RE GONNA DO TIME IN SPACE PEN UNTIL THE AMERICAN PEOPLE FIGURE OUT A WAY TO CLEAN UP THEIR MESS!
RAP!
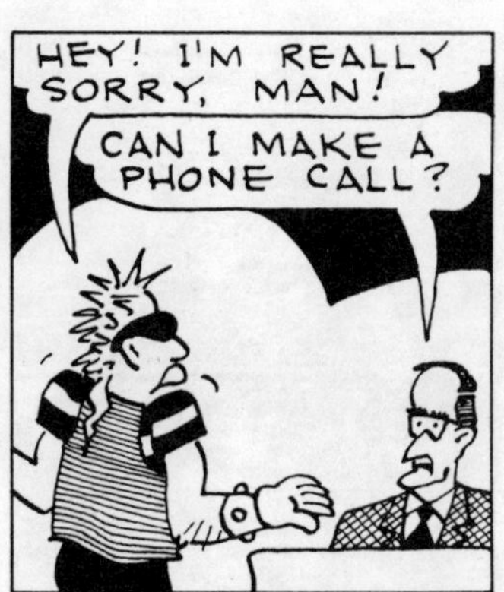
HEY! I'M REALLY SORRY, MAN!
CAN I MAKE A PHONE CALL?

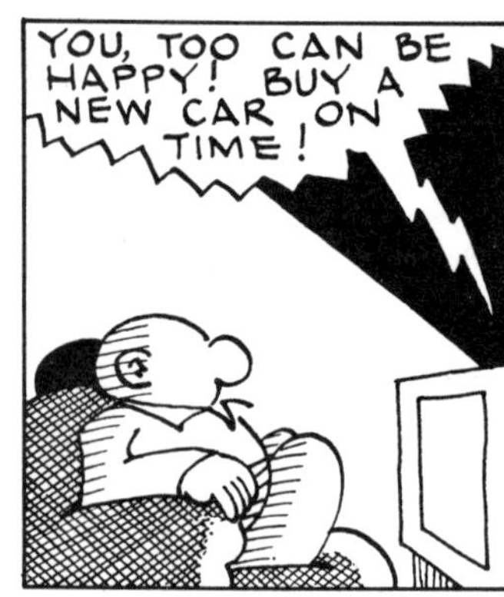
YOU, TOO CAN BE HAPPY! BUY A NEW CAR ON TIME!
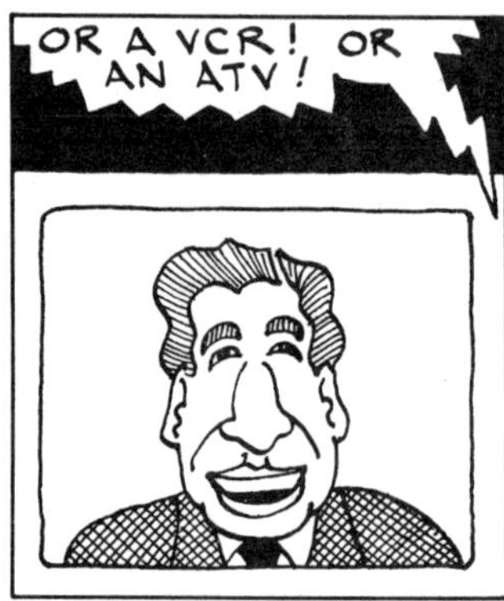
OR A VCR! OR AN ATV!
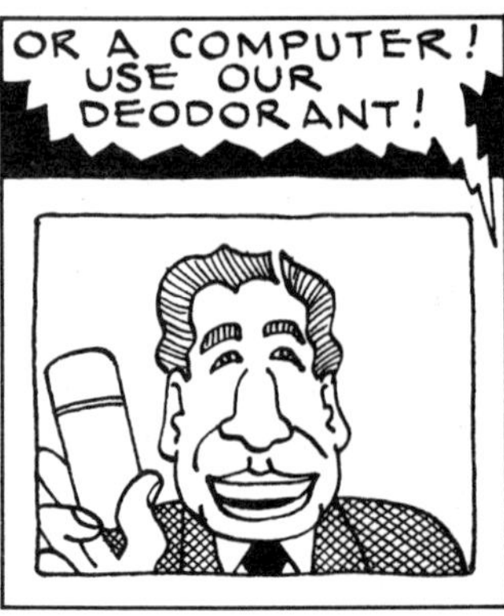
OR A COMPUTER! USE OUR DEODORANT!
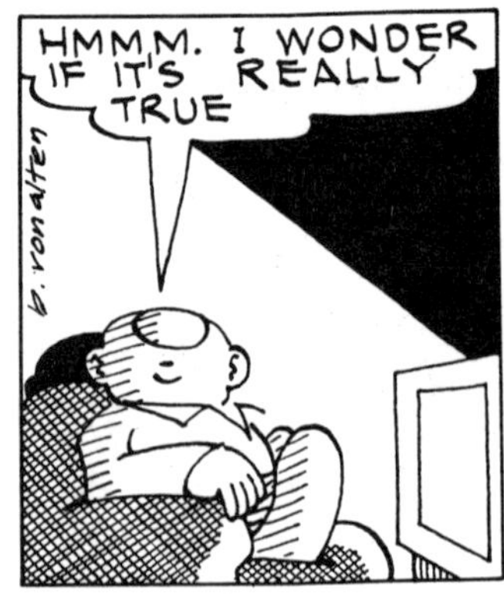
HMMM. I WONDER IF IT'S REALLY TRUE
b. von alten
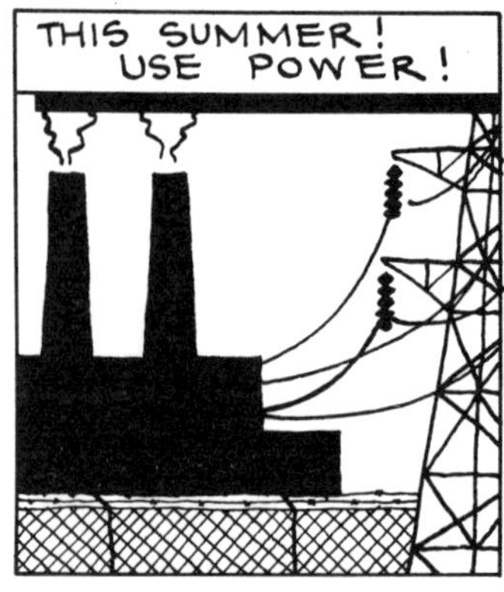
THIS SUMMER! USE POWER!
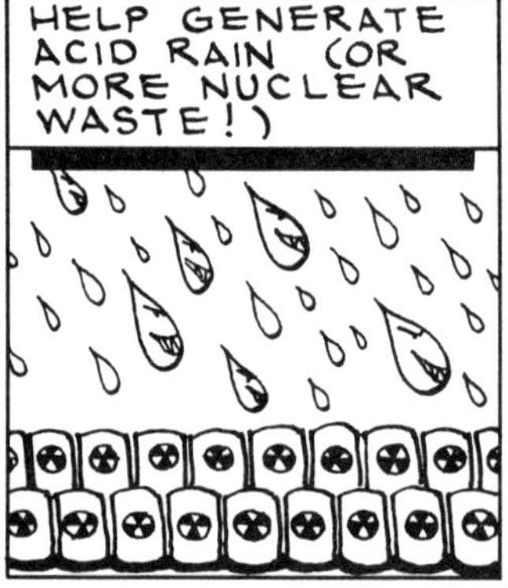
HELP GENERATE ACID RAIN (OR MORE NUCLEAR WASTE!)
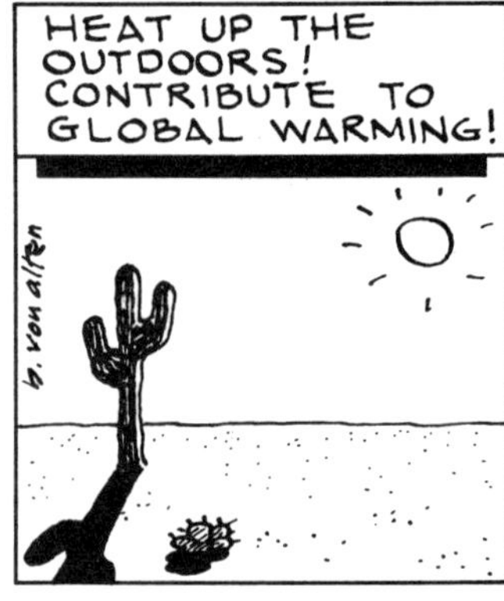
HEAT UP THE OUTDOORS! CONTRIBUTE TO GLOBAL WARMING!
b. von alten
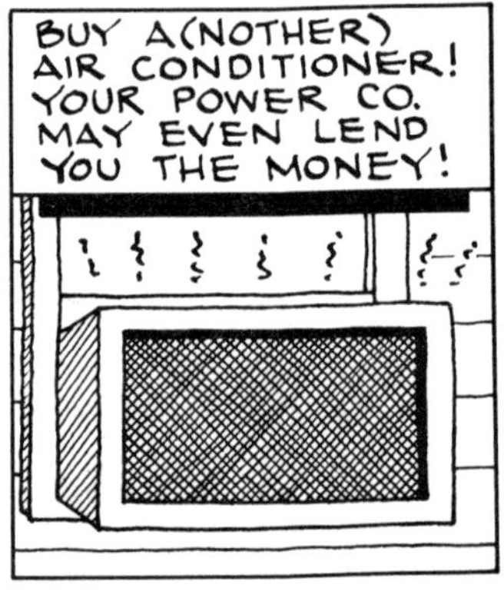
BUY A(NOTHER) AIR CONDITIONER! YOUR POWER CO. MAY EVEN LEND YOU THE MONEY!
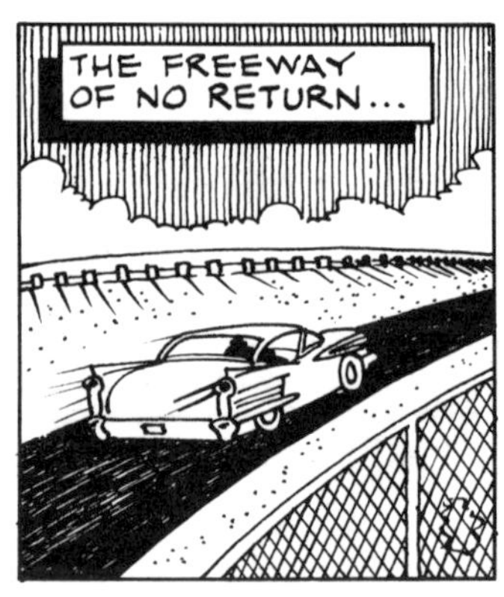
THE FREEWAY OF NO RETURN...
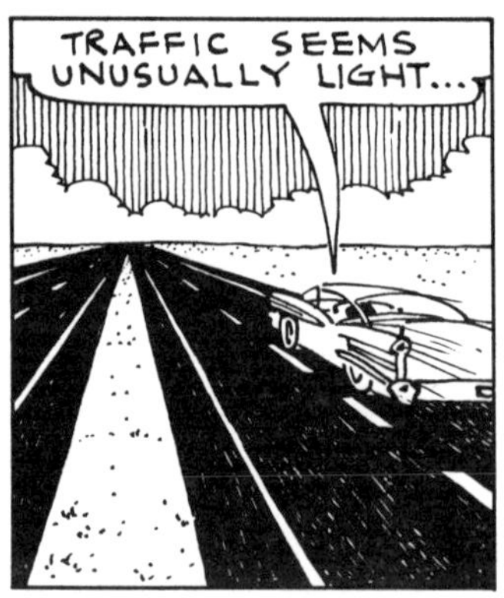
TRAFFIC SEEMS UNUSUALLY LIGHT...
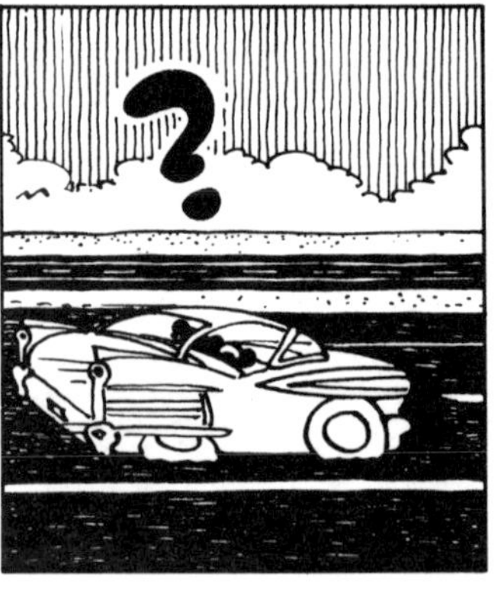
?
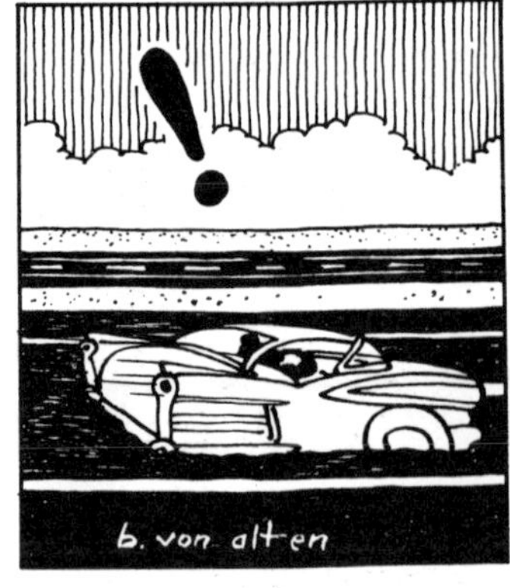
!
b. von alten
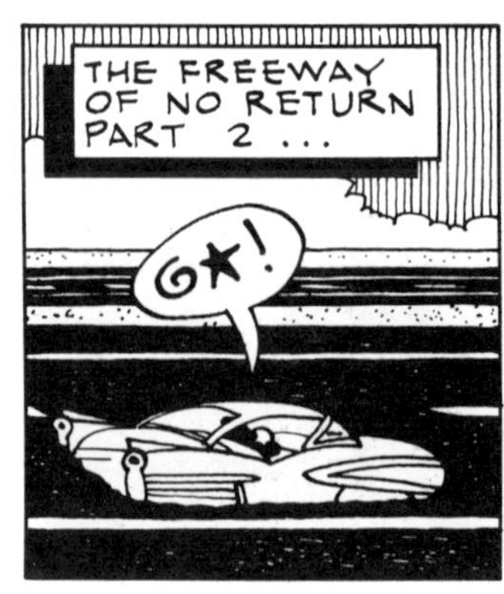
THE FREEWAY OF NO RETURN PART 2 ...
G★!
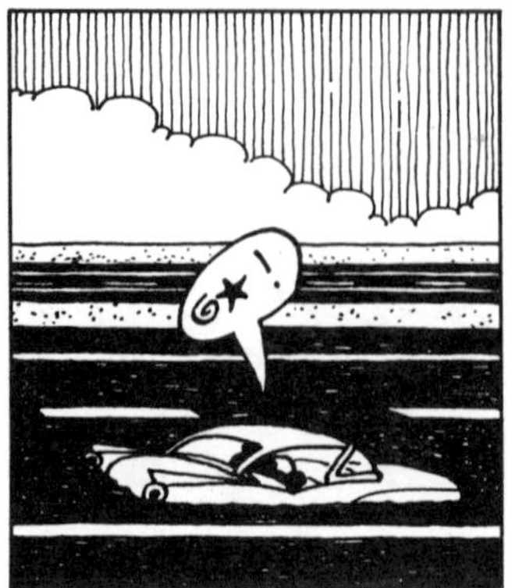
G★!
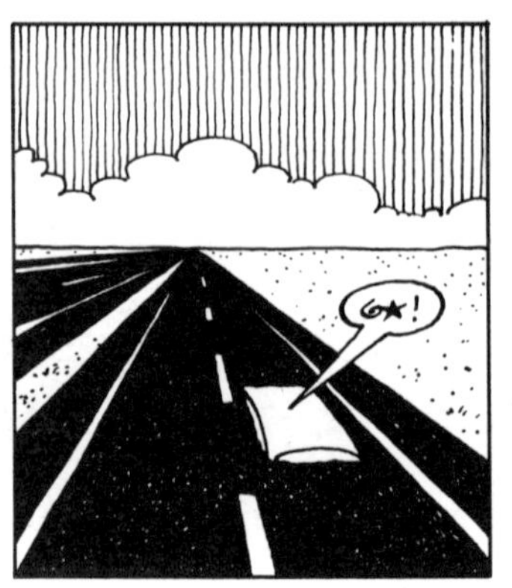
G★!
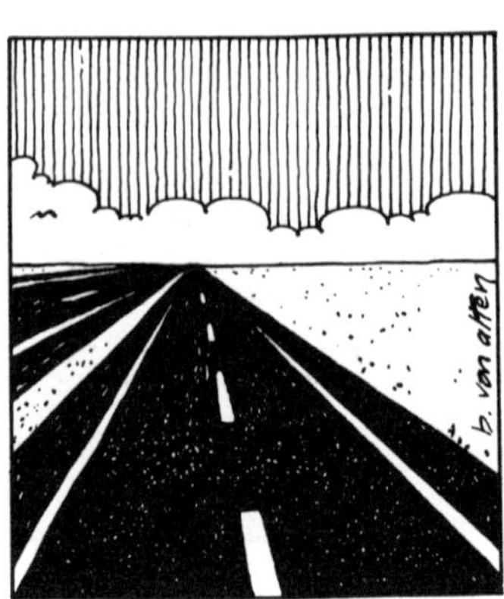
b. von alten